LONDON LIFE IN THE EIGHTEENTH CENTURY

The Industrial Revolution, it has been said, 'was like a storm that passed over London and broke elsewhere'. Whatever happened in other parts, it is clear that in the capital social conditions gradually improved. Between Defoe and Wordsworth, as it were, London progressed from gin and brutality to tea and temperance.

On this period of London's development Dorothy George's exhaustive study is now a standard work, as balanced in its judgements as it is comprehensive in its sources. The observations of such well-known figures as Johnson, Wesley, and Place, of Henry Fielding and his half-brother John, who were so intimately involved with London's poor, are filled out here with evidence from contemporary reports and newspapers, sessions papers and county records, pamphlets and memoirs by foreign travellers.

Certainly no more complete survey has ever been made of the place and the period in which the idea of progress began to become a reality.

Dorothy George was educated at St Leonard's School, St Andrews, and Girton College, Cambridge, where she was later awarded an Honorary Fellowship. She published a number of historical books, including *England in Transition* and *Hogarth to Cruikshank: Social Change in Graphic Satire* as well as working on the British Museum *Catalogue of Political and Personal Satires*. She died in 1971.

M. DOROTHY GEORGE

LONDON LIFE
IN THE EIGHTEENTH
CENTURY

Academy Chicago Publishers

First published in 1984 by
Academy Chicago Publishers
363 West Erie Street
Chicago, Illinois 60610

Second printing, February 2000

Printed and bound in the U.S.A.

Library of Congress Cataloging-in-Publication Data

George, M. Dorothy (Mary Dorothy)
    London life in the eighteenth century / M. Dorothy George.
       p.   cm.
    "First published by Kegan Paul, Trench, Trubner and Co. Ltd 1925.
Second edition published by Penguin Books 1966. Published in 1984 and
2000 by Academy Chicago, Publishers"—T.p. verso.
    Includes bibliographical references and index.
    ISBN 0-89733-147-8
    1. London (England)—Social conditions. 2. Poor—England—
London—History—18th century. 3. Working class—England—London—
History—18th century. I. Title. II. Title: London life in the 18th century.
HN398.L7G4
306'.09421—dc21   99-10241
                                                CIP

CONTENTS

Preface to the second edition 9

Preface to the original edition 13

INTRODUCTION: LONDON *circa* 1700–1815 15

The social history of London shows a marked improvement in conditions after the middle of the century. The development of London has several points of contrast with that of the newer towns; the proportion of manual workers tends to decrease; the ancient City loses importance and prestige. Improvements shown in a decline in the death-rate, an improvement in manners and in the orderliness and safety of London. These improvements due to changes in administration, and the growth of a spirit of humanity and reform which (in England) is closely inter-related with administrative change as well as with improvements in medicine and an increased knowledge of social conditions under the influence of a new spirit of scientific inquiry. Methodism. Education. Reasons for the failure to realize the improvement which took place. The supposed increase of crime and the changed attitude towards the penal code. The growth of discontent. Exceptional position of London in the bad years after 1815. Much evidence against a general deterioration in the conditions of life in spite of the distress which followed the peace.

1 LIFE AND DEATH IN LONDON 35

The Bills of Mortality and the Waste of Life. The theory of depopulation and luxury. Controversy as to whether the population was increasing or decreasing not settled till the Census of 1801. Changes in the Bills, the waste of life disappears at the end of the century. Fall in the death-rate; decline in infant mortality. The decline in births and increase in deaths after 1720 ascribed to gin-drinking. The distilling trade, considered essential to the landed interest, fostered by special privileges. The campaign against gin. The attempt at prohibition in 1736 defeated by the mob. Effects of the Act of 1751. Consequences of the prohibition of distilling from corn during times of dearth. The terrible death-rate among poor children. Measures to protect infant life. The Foundling Hospital. Jonas Hanway and the Parish Infant Poor. Lying-in hospitals and charities. Effect of hospitals on the health of London. Dispensaries. Improvements in medicine. Vaccination. Typhus; the House of Recovery; the Marylebone Infirmary. Other causes of improvement in the health of London. Changes in the diseases of London. The effects of the cotton manufacture.

CONTENTS

2 HOUSING AND THE GROWTH OF LONDON   73

The growth of London *circa* 1560–1815. Early cleavage between East and West London – the contrast marked by the beginning of the eighteenth century. The great parish of Stepney. The development of London influenced by the attempts of Elizabeth and the Stuarts to prevent new buildings. The proclamations against buildings, inmates, and divided tenements. Fear of the increase of poor people. Building by encroachment. Ruinous old houses and ramshackle new ones. Bad bricks. Uncertain titles. Leases for lives and short leases. Legislation: the Building Acts; the Window Tax. The speculative builder. Wars and building. Dangerous districts. Sanitary nuisances. The dwellings of the poor. Tenement houses. Common lodging-houses. Cellars as shops and living places. Sheds and stalls. Garrets. Rents. Custom of living in ready-furnished rooms. The housekeeper. Obstacles to fresh air and exercise. The progress of improvement. Paving and Improvement Acts; their limitations. The lighting of London. Social changes. Housing and sanitary conditions in the eighteen-thirties and forties, bad as they were, had improved since the eighteenth century.

3 LONDON IMMIGRANTS AND EMIGRANTS   116

Migration to London encouraged by the Settlement Laws and necessary to counteract the heavy death-rate. Foreign immigration. Estimates of the proportion of immigrants to native Londoners. The difficulties of newcomers excluded from parish relief; country girls seeking places as servants. Irish immigration of two kinds – seasonal and permanent. Irish colonies in London. Riots against Irish labour. Faction fights between English and Irish. Anti-Irish feeling and the Gordon Riots. The Irish as a police problem; as a sanitary problem; as an industrial problem and a poor law problem. The London Jews; the colony of Sephardic Jews; increasing immigration of the Ashkenazite or German branch as refugees from the Continent. International character of Jewish immigrants. Proposals to restrict immigration. The Jews accused of nefarious traffic. Excluded from industrial occupations and forced to resort to peddling and street-trading. Attempts to provide industrial openings for London Jews. Jew baiting in London. The London populace traditionally hostile to foreigners. Hatred of the French. Kindness to distressed foreigners – the Palatines. Negroes in London. The anomalous position of slaves from the West Indies. The Somersett Case. The settlement of negroes at Sierra Leone. Lascars. The seasonal immigration of country girls to work in market gardens. The movement of population from London. The Army and Navy, the sea-service. Indentured emigration to the colonies and (after 1783) the United States. 'Indented servants' and 'redemptioners'; deceptions practised in London; the position of 'bound servants' in America. State-aided emigration to Georgia. Removal from London under the law of settlement and the vagrancy laws. The lure of London.

4 THE PEOPLE AND THE TRADES OF LONDON   158

Eighteenth-century generalizations on the London populace disregard an almost infinite variety of social grades. Distinctions between artisans and labourers and between trade and trade. London trades. The skill of the London craftsman. Great varieties of industrial organization and of degrees of capitalization. London wages: artisans, textile workers, and labourers. Budgets. Wives expected to contribute to family earnings. Evidence of much easy-going prosperity side by side with much poverty and distress especially among women. The structure of three London trades and its reaction on social conditions: (1) Watchmaking; minute subdivision of the trade, early use of 'engines' or tools. Distress in Clerkenwell. (2) Silk-weaving; organization of the silk trade; the trade peculiarly subject to fluctuation; recruited by child-labour; work done by women and children; misery in Spitalfields, especially 1763–1800. Rioting 1763–73. A period of chequered prosperity 1800–26. Characteristics of Spitalfields weavers; wide variations in skill and social status, but on the whole weavers below the standard of the skilled London artisan in manners and education as in earnings. (3) Shoe-making; subdivisions of the trade. Large and small masters; competition of ready-made shoes from the provinces. Employment of women. Apprenticeship to journeymen. Improvement of the standard of living. London wages after 1815 not subject to heavy reductions as in other places. Changes of the century – absorption of many of the 'chargeable and criminal poor'. Reduction in the number of beggars.

5 PARISH CHILDREN AND POOR APPRENTICES   213

Parish infants, foundlings and illegitimate children at the beginning of the century. Ideals of education and the Charity School movement; the competition for industrial opportunity. Social status under the Poor Law. Varieties of industrial apprenticeship. The distinction drawn between apprenticeship for labour and apprenticeship for education. Parish apprentices generally bound to bad masters. Inherent difficulties in the apprenticeship system. The treatment of poor apprentices. Over-stocking of trades. Grounds on which indentures could be cancelled by the discharge of an apprentice. Appeals to Quarter Sessions. Legislation on behalf of poor apprentices. The Act of 1747 extended and amended in 1792. The Act of 1793. The term of parish apprenticeship reduced by the Acts of 1767 and 1768. Agitation for the protection of Climbing Boys and the Act of 1788. Peel's Act (1802) for apprentices in cotton mills. The act of 1816 for the regulation of parish apprentices. Protection to apprentices by London magistrates. Administrative reforms by London parishes; standing orders under local acts. Disillusionment with the results of apprenticeship, the movement for general education rather than industrial training. Mrs Cappe denounces 'apprenticeship for labour'. Nevertheless the wholesale apprenticeship of London parish children to distant factories takes place; the children probably those for whom individual masters cannot be found; the movement against it characteristic of the new philanthropy. The lot of apprentices in cotton mills compared with that of other parish children. The old philanthropy. The last phase of parish apprenticeship 1816–44. Conclusions.

6 THE UNCERTAINTIES OF LIFE AND TRADE   262

The irregularity of London trades. Social causes of financial ruin. Drinking customs. Apprenticeship as an education for life and work. Out-door apprentices. The manœuvres of masters. The supposed decay of discipline. Lack

CONTENTS

of legitimate amusements. Demoralizing punishments. General attitude towards popular amusements. The English Sunday. Rules of journeymen relating to drinking customs. The principle of 'footing' common to all classes. The house of call. The publican as employer and middleman. The payment of wages in public-houses; attempts to stop the practice. Inland transport dependent on inns and alehouses. The sale of drink in prisons and watch-houses. The publican-constable. Friendly societies and sharing-out clubs. Redundant public-houses and licensing policy. Tea-gardens. The new coffee-shop. Imprisonment for debt; great reduction in the number of prisoners. 'Buying carcasses.' Vicissitudes of London life illustrated in the family history of Francis Place. Fleet Marriages. The State Lottery. Deserted Children. Improving status of the working people. Changes in the character of schemes for poor relief. Improvement in manners seems to out-run the improvement in environment.

NOTES

To the Introduction   313

To Chapter 1   318

To Chapter 2   331

To Chapter 3   347

To Chapter 4   360

To Chapter 5   371

To Chapter 6   382

APPENDIXES

I   VITAL STATISTICS BASED ON THE PARISH REGISTERS AND THE BILLS OF MORTALITY   397

II   INFANT MORTALITY AMONG LONDON PARISH CHILDREN   401

III   THE GROWTH OF LONDON   406

IV   APPRENTICESHIP CASES FROM THE MIDDLESEX SESSIONS RECORDS   415

V   DISPOSAL OF APPRENTICES BY THE PARISHES WITHIN THE BILLS OF MORTALITY   423

VI   WOMEN'S WORK – OCCUPATIONS OF MARRIED COUPLES   425

Bibliography   429

Supplement to the Bibliography, 1964   439

Index   443

PREFACE TO THE
SECOND EDITION

THIS book was first published in 1925 in the History of Civilization series edited by C. K. Ogden, the inventor of basic English. It was at once seized upon as a contribution to the controversy over the early stages of the Industrial Revolution: did they bring exploitation and degradation to the working classes, or a rising standard of living and an improved status? But London was becoming less, not more, industrial as the century went on, and though it had its troubles they were not in general those of Oldham or Manchester. To quote a review by J. L. Hammond: the Industrial Revolution 'was like a storm that passed over London and broke elsewhere'.* In fact, it gave London, like other places, the iron beds and cheap cottons that helped to defeat typhus. Economic historians have now generally (but not universally) agreed that the standard of living rose in the early nineteenth century. But this cannot decide a controversy that depends on a conflict of values, is bedevilled by myth and passion and politics, overshadowed by sinister developments, and remains surprisingly untouched by the universal recognition that only industrialization can raise the standard of life in backward countries. Where *London Life* is directly relevant to the controversy is not in showing that conditions in London improved (as they undoubtedly did), but in examining the domestic or putting out (home work) system, on which many London trades depended, a system seen too often through rose-coloured spectacles and contrasted with the horrors of the factory.

In reconsidering the book after many years' study of the period from other angles, the author is struck by a seeming paradox: the extreme disorderliness of London – the dominance of the mob (Fielding's 'Fourth Estate') – the chaos of local government, and yet, beneath the turbulence, an essential orderliness (always excepting the criminal underworld); an orderliness discoverable even in that climax of

* *New Statesman,* 21 March 1925.

disorder, the Gordon Riots. These exploded only after months of incendiary propaganda and days of virtual encouragement to burn and destroy. In a frenzy of No-Popery the mob burned Lord Mansfield's property, but would not tolerate looting. Law-abiding conduct is not news and we hear little about it. As compared with Paris, London was without a police, but it was admittedly a safer place, both as regards crimes of violence and the dangers of street traffic. A contribution to the safety of London, omitted in the text, was gas lighting: first installed in 1807, almost fifteen miles of rapidly expanding gas mains by 1815.

Turbulence was mitigated by humour and good nature. Grosley, a Frenchman visiting London in 1765 was impressed by

... the great care they take to prevent the frays almost unavoidable amidst the eternal passing and repassing of carriages in the most frequented streets, some of which are exceedingly narrow. If, notwithstanding the great care of the coachmen and carmen to avoid them, there arises some confusion and perplexity, their readiness to turn aside, to retire, to open, and to lend each other a hand ... prevents this confusion from degenerating into one of those bloody frays which so often happen at Paris.

In 1779, an American visitor was astonished by the number of places of 'dissipation and pleasure', but he notes also

How willingly people submit to practice or usages calculated for the common benefit, is evident in large cities. The urbanity in the City of London is extremely remarkable. No coercive laws would obtain so explicit an obedience as is here voluntarily given to customs calculated for convenience. *

In the aftermath of World War II it seems striking evidence of a fundamental orderliness that, despite industrial distress and political unrest, the expected increase of crime did not take place after the Peace of 1815.

To look for origins of the Welfare State is irresistible today. No doubt they can be traced to a Poor Law that (in theory) gave everyone in England (not in Scotland or Ireland) the right to maintenance *somewhere*. But this was qualified (to put it mildly) by the Law of Settlement and the manœuvres of parish officers. A cynic might see the Welfare State in the episode of opening the Foundling Hospital to all poor infants, the cost to be borne by the state. The intentions were excellent,

* H. C. Van Schaack, *Life of Peter Van Schaack*, New York, 1842, pp. 162, 238.

the lavishness unprecedented, the results lamentable. More significant things can, I think, be found. For instance, by 1738 'all the hospitals' were employing a surgical boot-maker to make boots 'for such persons as have deformed feet'. The first school of midwifery for medical students and midwives was started in a very small way in the workhouse infirmary of St James's parish in 1739. More important, because the starting point of a nation-wide development formalized in the National Health system, is the fact that in the best-managed parishes the infirmary, a part of the workhouse, became in practice a subsidiary hospital.*

A few titles have been added to the Bibliography. These are printed separately (page 439), because they were not used for the book.

September, 1964   M. D. G.

* The achievements of the wealthy parish of St Marylebone were remarkable: a dignified building, opened in 1792, accepting patients daily (not weekly as in many hospitals), with a comparatively low death-rate, and making no demand for the deposit against possible burial fees which excluded the poorest from some London hospitals. F. H. W. Sheppard, *Local Government in St Marylebone*, 1958, pp. 176–80.

PREFACE

THIS book is an attempt to give a picture of the conditions of life and work of the poorer classes in London in the eighteenth century – a rash attempt in the face of the developments of a century of transition, of many contradictions and complexities, of the differences between localities and between trade and trade. Much use has been made of quotation in order to give some impression of contemporary points of view. It was a time of rigid class distinction, 'low life' was considered a fit subject for comedy, burlesque or satire only – and 'low life' had a very wide interpretation. Till Lillo's *Barnwell* was played in London in 1731, no writer, Tom Davies says, 'had ventured to descend so low as to introduce the character of a merchant or his apprentice into a tragedy'. Even in satire low life was sometimes thought unsuited to the writer of position. Lord Orrery was shocked that Swift should have written the *Directions to Servants*. 'What intenseness of thought must have been bestowed on the lowest and most slavish scenes of life . . . a man of Swift's exalted genius ought constantly to have soared into higher regions. . . . Let him jest with dignity, and let him be comical upon useful subjects, leaving poor slaves to heat their porridge or drink their small beer in such vessels as they shall think proper.' Lady Mary Wortley Montague complained that the levelling tendencies of the times were reflected in the novels she read so insatiably; 'the heroes and heroines of the age,' she said (with manifest exaggeration), 'are cobblers and kitchen wenches.'

Though fiction, satire and burlesque, ballads and broadsides, do throw light on the lives and manners of the humbler folk, the conditions under which they lived are hard to come by, and are chiefly to be gathered from the incidental information of trials, depositions of witnesses, petitions to Quarter Sessions, reports of coroner's inquests, settlement cases, the publications of charities and the pamphlets of reformers. This is a class of evidence which suffers from the fact that it is concerned largely with calamities and distresses. The same is to a great extent true of Parliamentary reports, where, however, present miseries are often contrasted with past prosperity. Indeed, in such papers, industrial prosperity is often in the past but almost never in the present. Normal conditions are the hardest to discover, and though incidentally, and by implication and allusion, much information is to be gathered from this material as to general conditions and standards, for direct description of the things which were too familiar to the Londoner for comment, the impressions of foreigners are of great value.

The bibliography is a strictly limited one, but I hope that, taken together with the notes, it leaves no room for doubt as to the nature of the material used and the authorities for statements in the text. Whole classes of books which are dealt with in standard bibliographies (notably those of *The Cambridge History of Literature* and *The Cambridge Modern History*) have been omitted.

My thanks are especially due to Miss Alice Clark, for whom the research on which the book is based was originally begun, and to the London School of Economics and Political Science for giving me a research scholarship. I am deeply indebted to Professor Knowles, Dr Eileen Power and Sir William Beveridge for reading the book in manuscript and for many invaluable criticisms and suggestions. I wish also to express my thanks to Mr Thomas for his help in explaining the intricacies of the Guildhall Records, and to the authorities at the Westminster Guildhall for giving me facilities to work from the Middlesex County Records. The editors of the *Economic Journal* have kindly given me permission to reprint an article from the *Journal* for September 1922 – *Some Causes of the Increase of Population in the Eighteenth Century as Illustrated by London*. This has been almost completely rewritten and incorporated in Chapter 1.

M. DOROTHY GEORGE

LONDON *circa* 1700-1815

England, bad as she is, is yet a reforming Nation.
Defoe, *Review*, 26 December 1706

THE later eighteenth century, according to the more modern school of social historians, is regarded as the beginning of a dark age, in which there was a progressive degradation of the standards of life, under the blight of a growing industrialism, while the earlier part of the century is considered a golden age, one of those periods when English working-class prosperity was at its height. The social history of London obstinately and emphatically refuses to adjust itself to this formula. There is a cleavage, certainly, about the middle of the century, but it is improvement, not deterioration, which can be traced about 1750 and becomes marked between 1780 and 1820.

London,[1] it is true, is in a sense exceptional. It underwent a transformation, indeed a revolutionary one, in the course of the century, but the direct results of what is called the industrial revolution were not conspicuous there. Its expansion was not comparable with that of the newer towns of the north, its share of the total population of the country declined, its share of the urban population declined still more. That sense of sudden and unmanageable growth – of invasion by hordes of workers who create new problems – dates for London from the end of the sixteenth century, and never perhaps did London seem so overwhelmingly large as during the following hundred years. In the eighteenth century London was growing more rapidly in bricks and mortar than in population as people left the crowded lanes of the City for the newer parts of the town. The organization of London trades was moreover surprisingly stable, the small workshop and the domestic system which flourished at the beginning of the century held their own to a remarkable extent.

Then again, London was becoming less rather than more industrial. London was a nursing ground for new industries, especially for those

which in their early stages were more or less luxury trades, but as communications improved and the home market grew wider, tended to
migrate in search of cheaper fuel, cheaper labour and cheaper methods.
The process was accompanied by an increase of financial business of all
kinds,[2] and by an enormous development of the port of London, both
fostered by wars and by the use of convoys for merchant shipping.
Wars called into existence whole armies of contractors and clerks, public
bodies and charitable institutions were employing an increasing number of paid officials, and private venture schools multiplied. The result
must have been a greater relative increase in the number of people
employed in distribution (wholesale and retail), in administration and
in education rather than in manual labour. Thus, in the eighteenth
century, London underwent a similar change to that which took
place for the country as a whole during the thirty years or so before
1914.[3]

Then as later, it was true that many clerkly incomes were less than
those of skilled artisans, as were those of the curate and the garreteer,
and schoolmastering, in many cases, was the poorest sort of trade. But
the shifting of occupations must have been an incentive to education,
an important element in the growth of the middle class and in the opportunities of rising in the world.

These changes were accompanied by a lessening of the importance
of the ancient City. Industrial London and residential London continued to grow outside her liberties and beyond her control. Her own
territories were invaded by new financial interests in which the Corporation had no part, and the great City Companies became progressively less important than the newer corporations of the Bank and the
East India Company which had no place in the City structure. The
leading figures in the world of business came to be bankers (who were
no longer goldsmiths) and stockbrokers and commission agents rather
than the Goldsmiths, Drapers and Mercers of the sixteenth and seventeenth centuries. The Corporation lost ground both relatively and
positively – non-freemen were rigidly excluded from retail trade in the
City, but not from wholesale trade and finance. Many merchants and
bankers preferred not to take up the freedom of the City with its fines
for refusing office and its ceremonial which had become antiquated but
not yet historically interesting.[4] The interests of the City thus became

more and more those of the shop-keepers who were the bulk of its resident freemen and common-councillors.

For these and other reasons the administrative changes – the characteristic development of eighteenth-century London – are to be found chiefly in the out-parishes, where the problems of poverty, sanitation and police were greatest and where the simple parish, manorial and county machinery of vestry, court leet and local justices had to adapt itself to an urban population.

The improvement which took place however cannot be entirely accounted for by the special circumstances of London, though these undoubtedly had something to do with it. The contrast between the earlier and later eighteenth century is marked from many directions. The test of the change is in the death-rate, which begins to fall after 1750 and falls more rapidly after 1780. In the latter part of the century it was no longer necessary to receive infants indiscriminately at the Foundling Hospital to prevent their exposure and desertion or their wholesale slaughter in workhouses or by parish nurses. The miseries of poor children and parish apprentices began to receive attention about the middle of the century and their position was progressively improved. The parish poor no longer begged and starved on minute doles.

London had become healthier; the dangers and uncertainties of life had been lessened, partly by a change of manners, greater cleanliness, less drinking, partly by a better police and by the reform of some gross abuses in poor law administration. Crimes of violence were fewer and different in kind, and there had been a great reduction in the number of prisoners for debt. The traditional violence and brutality of the London populace was gradually diminishing. At the end of the century it is no longer a subject of comment by foreign visitors. Baretti noticed a marked improvement between 1750 and 1760;[5] Sir John Fielding in 1776 thought 'the rabble . . . much mended . . . within the last fifty years', though 'still very insolent and abusive . . . sometimes . . . without the least appearance of a cause'.[6]* Francis Place was vividly conscious of a transformation in manners between London as he remembered it in the seventeen-eighties (even then vastly improved since the forties and fifties) and the London of the early nineteenth century:

* See below, p. 50, note.

The progress made in refinement of manners and morals seems to have gone on simultaneously with the improvement in arts, manufactures and commerce. It moved slowly at first, but has been constantly increasing in velocity. Some say we have refined away all our simplicity and have become artificial, hypocritical, and on the whole worse than we were half a century ago. This is a common belief, but it is a false one, we are a much better people than we were then, better instructed, more sincere and kind-hearted, less gross and brutal, and have fewer of the concomitant vices of a less civilized state.[7]

And in 1829 he makes an indignant protest against a *Quarterly* article on the departure within the last thirty years 'of the whole of our community . . . from the simplicity, foresight and frugality of their forefathers':

The people are better dressed, better fed, cleanlier, better educated, in each class respectively, much more frugal, and much happier. Money which would have been spent at the tavern, the brothel, the tea-garden, the skittle-ground, the bull-bait, and in numerous other low-lived and degrading pursuits, is now expended in comfort and conveniences, or saved for some useful purpose. . . .[8]

How had this improvement been possible? Throughout the century Londoners lived in a world in which violence, disorder and brutal punishment (though decreasing) were still part of the normal background of life. Newgate, the gallows, the exploits of felons, figured largely in the press and in the current literature of the day. In spite of the bitter irony of *Jonathan Wild* and the light satire of the *Beggars' Opera*, both are accurate pictures of the manners of the time, and their more lurid incidents are easily surpassed in the record of the Old Bailey. Romilly tells us in his *Memoirs* of the painful impression this state of things made on a sensitive child. The immense vogue of Lillo's play, *Barnwell*, where the apprentice is seduced by a courtesan to rob and then murder his master, and the stories of the apprentices who saw in it a terrifying vision of their own temptations, throw a flood of light on the social atmosphere of London. So do the subjects chosen by Hogarth to impart a moral lesson. An education in brutality was given in the public spectacles at Tyburn and at the pillory, by the constant floggings through the streets, by the methods of press-gangs and crimps. These things were not new in the eighteenth century; how

could a people brought up for so many generations in such surroundings be anything but coarse, violent and brutal? How is the improvement to be accounted for?

First perhaps, by certain definite improvements in administration
and police. One of the chief causes of demoralization was the trading
justice – a London character well known in the days of Elizabeth –
who preyed on the people and exploited their shortcomings. Fielding's
Justice Thrasher (in *Amelia*) is not a caricature, it is a portrait (ironic
but not exaggerated) of a type. His like is to be found in many formal
reports of the Middlesex Sessions to the Lord Chancellor on the
scandalous enormities of justices who were bringing the whole Bench
into discredit. When we remember the manners of the time, the prevalence of 'tippling in alehouses', gambling, swearing, Sabbath-break-
ing, together with laws against these and many other offences, put in
force by informers and punishable with fines, fees accruing to the
magistrates, as they did for commitments and for bailing-out, part of
the business of the trading justice is manifest. Other business came from
the encouragement of petty litigation amongst a people who were by
ancient tradition intensely litigious. The attitude of the better sort of
Middlesex magistrate was in general benevolent, but his activities
seldom went beyond some attention to parish affairs and attendance at
the Sessions which came eight times a year. He left to the trading justice the disagreeable and discredited business of sitting regularly in a
pestilential atmosphere to hear complaints and disputes and to commit,
discharge or bail out offenders.

When the court-justice developed into the police magistrate, and
when, as an intermediate stage (which may be dated from Fielding's
appointment to Bow Street in 1749 as chief magistrate for Westminster
with an official salary), he became disinterested and public-spirited, he
also became a social reformer with expert knowledge and the ear of the
Government. De Veil, Fielding's predecessor at Bow Street, had been
a trading justice whose dissipations demanded a close attention to the
profits of office, though he was more instructed and more capable than
most of his kind. Fielding made his office a public place for the administration of justice instead of a justice-shop for trafficking in fines
and commitments, and set himself to composing instead of inflaming
'the quarrels of beggars and porters'. He realized the terrible state of

the poor and the perversities of the laws with the imaginative sympathy of a great novelist who was also a trained lawyer.

Fielding's magistracy marks a turning-point in the social history of London; it coincides with the first effective measure dealing with the horrors of gin-drinking, due partly at least to himself. Part of his code, it is true, was 'to bring a rogue to the gallows',[9] a maxim which has now a curious ring, but another part was to save the young and reclaimable from the contaminating influence of prison. He was fully conscious of the seething underworld of London, ready to sack and burn, which might at any moment overwhelm the very scanty forces of law and order. 'When a mob of chairmen or servants, or a gang of thieves or sharpers, are almost too big for the civil authority, what,' he asks, 'must be the case in a seditious tumult or general riot.'[10]

The spirit of his magistracy can best be gathered from the *Covent Garden Journal* in which he tried to give the public some of that knowledge of social evils and their causes which he himself learned at Bow Street. For instance,

... several wretches being apprehended the night before by Mr Welch, were brought before Mr Fielding and Mr Errington: when one who was in a dreadful condition from the itch was recommended to the overseers; another, who appeared guilty of no crime but poverty, had money given her to enable her to follow her trade in the market. ...

He used the case of a poor woman, 'mother of three small children, charged with the petty larceny of a cap, value threepence' (whom he discharged against the strict rigour of the law, 'the evidence not being positive') to denounce the law by which those accused of the most trifling thefts, often on very questionable evidence, were committed for trial at the Sessions.[11] He made repeated protests against the public executions at Tyburn: 'we sacrifice the lives of men, not for the reformation but for the diversion of the populace'.

John Fielding, who succeeded him and ruled at Bow Street from 1754 to 1780, developed his brother's policy. He identified the office with social reform, made it more efficient in dealing with street outrages and laid the foundations of a paid and permanent police. He turned his attention especially to the deserted boys and girls from whom the thieves and prostitutes of London were largely recruited. His plan for sending young offenders and vagrants to sea, not as convicts, but properly equipped and 'cured of the various distempers that are the constant companions of poverty and distress' is connected with the foundation of the Marine Society in 1756. His Bow Street experiences led him to propose and carry through in 1758 the establishment of the Orphan Asylum for Deserted Girls.[12] By advertisements and newspaper paragraphs and by his relations with the Secretary of State, he kept Bow Street and his 'Plan of Police' constantly before the public and educated it to accept that un-English thing, a paid police openly dependent on the central government. People, especially apprentices and workmen, came from all parts of London to put their grievances before him.

The Middlesex Bench (who were inclined to be jealous of Bow Street) in 1763 established a number of 'rotation offices' which were the direct precursors of the seven police offices established by the Act of 1792.[13] They were an attempt to eliminate the trading justice – always deeply resented by the Bench as bringing the whole body of magistrates into disrepute – and imitated the methods of the City where two aldermen sat daily in turns at the Guildhall. The rotation office became an accepted feature of London life, and must have curtailed the sphere of the trading justices.[14] These found their occupation almost gone when the Act of 1792 took away judicial business (Bow Street always excepted) from all but seven public offices, each with three paid magistrates and six paid constables – a direct development out of the rotation offices and the Bow Street system. The business of a court-justice, now called a police magistrate, became more a matter of routine and less an almost single-handed struggle against crime and disorder. An immense local improvement followed the establishment in 1798 of the Thames Police Office, due mainly to Colquhoun,[15] another great London magistrate, a friend of Bentham, who drew the Act of 1800 by which it was put on a permanent footing. Police magistrates carried on the tradition of the Fieldings and discouraged litigation. Such laws as there were for the protection of the poorer sort (and there were more than is often supposed)[16] depended in the first instance on a single magistrate or a court of petty sessions – that is, in London after 1792 (outside the City) upon the police magistrates.

In the meantime, the great London parishes had been building up a parochial police and system of local government by means of local Acts.

The vestries, first in Westminster, and then in almost all the metropolitan parishes outside the City, obtained Acts enabling them to levy a watch rate and regulate the watch, then to light and clean the streets, and to 'regulate the poor', by means of watch committees or trusts, boards of all kinds, Governors and Directors and Guardians of the Poor in infinite variety.[17] Paving as a public undertaking began in Westminster (in 1762) under commissioners appointed in the Acts, but the powerful Westminster vestries soon got the business transferred to parochial commissioners and in most of the other parishes paving was a parochial affair from the first. The larger vestries thus acquired something of the powers of a municipal corporation; among their members were justices always ready to do the parish business and thus corresponding to the charter justices of boroughs. With the rapid increase of wealth and population they acquired a large revenue through the rates and were able to borrow on annuities for large undertakings. Local Acts were often elaborate administrative codes and with increasing business vestries developed staffs of paid officers. The Acts aimed at getting rid of the perpetual feasting and jobbery of the uncontrolled vestrymen and parish officers of the early part of the century and in many parishes they did undoubtedly bring a new efficiency and a measure of honesty to parish affairs. Although there was a chaos of authorities there was also a healthy rivalry between district and district and their variety gave opportunities for experiment.

As an administrative system, judged by any abstract standard there was little to be said for the new method, by which the watchmen were by the end of the century 'under the direction of no less than above seventy different trusts, regulated by perhaps double the number of local acts . . . under which these directors, guardians, governors, trustees, or vestries . . . are authorized to act, each attending only to their own particular ward, parish, hamlet or precinct. . . .'[18] This was the condemnation of Colquhoun, in a plea for the unification of the police of London. The devotee of tradition was still more outraged. Ritson, the archaeologist, who was High Bailiff of the Liberty of the Savoy and a believer in the methods of the court leet wrote in 1791:

The private and local acts, everywhere in force and nowhere to be met with are at least as numerous as the public statutes. . . . Every little dirty parish in the environs of London must have a law for itself. The church-wardens or overseers can provide the money, the attorney wants a job, the justice looks forward to the penalties, and the 'gemmen of the westry' like authority, an act of Parliament is accordingly obtained, and being an admirable compound of ignorance and knavery, cannot fail of proving exceedingly beneficial to the community. . . .[19]

But the fact remains that they brought about a vast improvement. Under the old system on which this network of local Acts had supervened, administration still depended chiefly on two types of officer, holding respectively what were known as offices of profit and offices of burden. The former held office for life, usually by purchase, and recouped themselves by fees, fines and perquisites. Such offices were regarded as freehold property which could be sold or mortgaged, their functions were often performed by ill-paid deputies and were for the most part limited to routine duties. The worst consequences of the system were seen in the keepers of prisons and the officers employed by sheriffs and bailiffs. The other type was the unpaid private citizen acting under compulsion for a year as (for instance) the constable, overseer, scavenger, surveyor of the highways or member of an annoyance jury. His object as a rule was either to escape service by paying a fine for exemption or hiring a deputy, or else to turn his office of burden into an office of profit – at least to compensate himself by unlimited feasting at the parish expense. Under local acts a new type of officer appeared in increasing numbers, paid by a salary, liable to dismissal, and strictly forbidden to have any share in parish contracts.[20]

Colquhoun himself pays a tribute to the results of this chaotic system – 'it is only a matter of wonder that the protection afforded is what it really is', and adds in a footnote,

. . . this proves how highly meritorious the conduct of the managers and trustees of this branch of the police of the metropolis must in many instances be. There can indeed be no manner of doubt that great advantages arise from dividing the labour where all the benefits of local knowledge enter into the system.[18]

Under these and other civilizing influences London changed its character. In the eighties it was not the London of Fielding and Hogarth, its dirt and insecurity were no longer worthy of a medieval town, it was less picturesque, but the foreigner could no longer as in

1741 (in the words which Samuel Johnson put into the mouth of Lord Tyrconnel) 'imagine us a people not only without delicacy but without government, a herd of barbarians or a colony of Hottentots'.[21] 'Two of the things which fill the mind of the observer with delight,' said a London guide-book in 1802, 'are the slightness of the restraints of police and the general good order that mutually illustrate each. . . . We venture to assert that no city in proportion to its trade and luxury is more free from danger to those who pass the streets at all hours, or from depredations, open or concealed, on property.'[22] No apologist could have written in such a strain fifty years earlier, and foreigners confirm the assertion: 'none of our cities,' said Silliman, an American, in 1806, 'are safer than London.' Compared with other parts of the town, the City was relatively orderly, but in 1718 the City Marshal remarked:

Now it is the general complaint of the taverns, the coffee-houses, the shop-keepers and others, that their customers are afraid when it is dark to come to their houses and shops for fear that their hats and wigs should be snitched from their heads or their swords taken from their sides, or that they may be blinded, knocked down, cut or stabbed; nay, the coaches cannot secure them, but they are likewise cut and robbed in the public streets, &c. By which means the traffic of the City is much interrupted.[23]

These administrative changes were only one aspect of a general movement for reform. They were closely interrelated with that growth of social compunction which became apparent in the last thirty years of the century, but had been developing from an earlier period. London was not only drained, paved, lighted and policed in a way which was a vast improvement on the earlier part of the century, but the administration of the poor law was improved and relief more liberally given. Through hospitals, dispensaries, workhouse infirmaries and lying-in charities medical aid became more accessible, and by the growth of knowledge far more effective. Industrial disease was receiving attention. Charitable associations of various kinds devoted themselves to reformatory and rescue work, to education and to many other things. Besides the principles of collective effort and personal service, they introduced two new methods – the promotion of reform by legislation and the use of the Press for appeals and propaganda. Gifts and bequests for prisoners for debt had been for centuries a favourite form of charity; The

Society for the Relief of Persons imprisoned for Small Sums succeeded in 1785 in getting an Act to limit the term of imprisonment in certain cases.

This growth of a spirit of humanity – a European movement, which in France drew its inspiration from free thought – is sometimes too exclusively identified with evangelicalism. In England a fundamental element in the new point of view was a greater knowledge of social conditions and a new scientific spirit in dealing with social questions. The Society for Bettering the Condition of the Poor was founded in 1796 to collect and distribute exact information; 'let us . . . make the inquiry into all that concerns the poor and the promotion of their happiness a science,' wrote Thomas Bernard.[24] But in the past fifty years the number of people with a first-hand knowledge of how the poor lived had been increasing. Fielding had said in 1753,

. . . the sufferings of the poor are indeed less observed than their misdeeds; not indeed from any want of compassion, but because they are less known; and this is the reason why they are so often mentioned with abhorrence and so seldom with pity. . . . They starve and freeze and rot among themselves, but they beg, steal and rob among their betters.[25]

Jonas Hanway had discovered by 1762 the necessity of exact statistical information as to the deaths of infants in London workhouses as a basis for measures of reform and for the protection of infant life.

Perhaps the two chief instruments in the diffusion of a new knowledge were the better type of metropolitan magistrate and the dispensary doctors (after 1769) who visited their patients in their homes. Doctors sought for medical experience among the poor, they gained and distributed social as well as professional information. 'I have been too intimately acquainted with the condition and manners of the poor to want facts in support of what I advance . . .' wrote Dr Lettsom in 1775;

. . . those who form their judgement from a superficial observation of a few intoxicated objects who are found in the most frequented places are much mistaken with regard to the body of the laborious poor, who humbly seclude themselves in miserable courts and alleys. . . . When I regard the distresses of the indigent, I rather admire that instances of their misconduct should be so rare.[26]

Changes in local government by which bodies of Directors or Guardians of the Poor supervised and supplemented the work of parish overseers gave both experience and scope to would-be reformers.

Methodism doubtless counted for much both as a civilizing influence among the people and as one of the channels of the growing spirit of humanity and the growing knowledge of the poorer sort. Of the London poor Wesley wrote in 1753:

I found some in their cells underground, others in their garrets, but I found not one of them unemployed who was able to crawl about the room. So wickedly, devilishly false is that common objection, they are poor only because they are idle.[27]

It is sometimes forgotten that a great advance in education dates from the end of the eighteenth century. The Sunday schools, the Lancasterian schools, the National schools are compared with later developments and the period is regarded as a dark age. But there are no absolute standards in such things. Educational reformers have always been concerned to point out defects which indeed have always been obvious enough. At the beginning of the nineteenth century the enthusiasm for education as a remedy for social ills was a great driving force which worked wonders with very small resources. It was complained in 1805 that the belief in education was carried (by political economists and the public) 'to so violent a degree that there can be no time allowed for examination, and the man who should dispute the wisdom of Sunday schools would be considered as unworthy attention'.[28] The spirit of the time was changed since the founders of the charity schools a century earlier had been intent on giving children a carefully limited training which should fit them for 'menial services'. Lancaster's methods have often received less than justice; they curiously anticipate certain modern views on education: at the worst they were a great improvement on the dreary droning of the catechism which was the central part of the charity-school teaching, and they reached a far greater number of children. 'Conceive what a state London must have been in, when there was no provision for school teaching besides the charity schools, which taught the children next to nothing and nothing likely to be useful to them,' said Francis Place in 1835,[29] neglectful, after the manner of reformers, of the achievements of those earlier philanthropists who in their day were almost as much in advance of the more retrograde opinion of the time as were Lancaster and Allen a century later.

The very real improvements that did take place have been obscured for a number of reasons. First, from a habit of reading history backwards – particularly social and economic history – and of interpreting the eighteenth century according to the ideas of the nineteenth or twentieth. Secondly, from the difficulty of distinguishing between the after-effects of the Napoleonic wars and those of industrial change. Thirdly, because an awakening public conscience discovered a number of evils that had long existed and assumed that they were new, while the new outlook regarded as ills to be remedied things which had long been accepted as inevitable. This new spirit of inquiry and reform has left a mass of evidence on social evils embodied in the reports of parliamentary committees which is lacking in an easily accessible form for the earlier periods.

Then, there was in the later part of the eighteenth century, as in most times of social change, a general cry of national deterioration. This is based largely on two ideas, one, the terrible effects of increasing luxury, as seen for instance, in the nabob, or the lamplighter with silk stockings, or the labourer's family consuming tea and sugar. The other is the decline of what Defoe called the Great Law of Subordination, a notion of course much stimulated by the fears of Jacobinism roused by the French Revolution. Though connected with opposite schools of thought, the two ideas merged; the well-dressed lamplighter for instance might be regarded as a symbol of either of the two great causes of degeneration. Contemporary denunciations of luxury and insubordination deserve a rather critical attention, they imply a higher standard of living and some improvement in education. The fine clothes, good food and constant tea-drinking so much complained of after 1750 were incompatible with the wholesale consumption of gin of the earlier part of the century. There was something paradoxical in a complaint by Dr Price in 1773 that 'the circumstances of the lower ranks of the people are altered in every respect for the worse, while tea, wheaten bread and other delicacies are necessaries which were formerly unknown to them'.

The period (roughly) between 1780 and 1820 was thus one when many sections of opinion were agreed that the age was increasingly evil. Social reformers had discovered a terrible state of things. The political reformers were confronted with reaction while the conservative were conscious of a world changing under the influence of revolutionary ideas. The old John-Bullish, Roast-Beef-of-Old-England complacency was gone, the new complacency of the mid-nineteenth century had not begun. Much of the lamentation over the evils of the time is the perennial theme of a golden age in the past, the legend of the good old days to which each generation makes its own contribution. Certain points in the indictment of the age, however, demand a further analysis in relation to the special circumstances of London. These are first, the supposed increase of crime (which contemporaries ascribe [inter alia] to moral deterioration and to the slackening of the penal code, modern writers to increasing misery). Secondly, the growing spirit of 'insubordination' and discontent, which afterwards found expression in the demand for the Great Charter.

The question of moral deterioration and the increase of crime was a burning one after 1815 and was especially investigated by the Committee on the Police of the Metropolis of 1816. Place followed its proceedings with intense interest; he tells us, 'many of the inquiries were suggested by me'. He regrets that earlier committees had not been so searching:

if they had been . . . such scenes would have been depicted as would have shown that both in number and atrocity those crimes and vices greatly exceeded the crimes and vices of the present day. Formerly there were no such societies as these for Suppressing Juvenile Delinquencies and Refuge of the Destitute and for the Improvement of Prison Discipline, neither was there the same disposition to pry into the state of society as has for many years existed. Very few if any of the persons who . . . interest themselves in these matters have any knowledge of the state of society thirty years ago from observation or from any reading on the subject. The information obtained by their inquiries therefore appears extraordinary and new. . . .

It would appear to a cursory reader of these reports . . . that there has been an increase of crimes beyond the relative amount of the population of the metropolis within the last thirty or forty years, and by inference with every other period. That this is not the case is however fully proved by the unqualified testimony of every person examined who was qualified to judge of the state of the metropolis thirty years ago. The circumstances they mention, of gangs of robbers, highwaymen, places of rendezvous, the practice of trading justices, and the state of the police . . . would be ground enough in the absence of all evidence that the commission of crimes must have been relatively more common than now. And when the circumstances are taken in relation with the many then related, respecting the habits of the people, their amusements, the songs, the clubs, the want of schools, and the Lancasterian and National schools, no doubt can remain on the subject.[30]

Place remembered vividly the London of his youth, and he was an indefatigable student of the literature which throws light on the manners of the earlier part of the century – largely of the Newgate Calendar type. As for the Report, the general agreement that crimes were 'much less atrocious than formerly' speaks for itself. Townsend, the famous Bow Street runner, like Sir Nathaniel Conant, thought crimes were fewer:

I am astonished, considering the times. Now, for instance, what was expected [after the peace]? That there would be knocking down and this and that and t'other. . . . With respect to cruelty in robbery, such desperate things as we had formerly, there is not a thing to be compared.

Romilly exposed the often repeated fallacy that an increase in convictions meant an increase in crime.

The conclusion to be drawn from a careful analysis of the Report of 1816, together with the evidence of the Old Bailey Sessions Papers, and much contemporary literature, is that there had been a change in manners and in the nature of crime comparable with, and closely related to, the changed attitude towards the penal code. How great this change had been is hard to realize in face of the opposition met with by Romilly and the other reformers who attempted to mitigate the barbarities of the laws.

In the early part of the century the forces of disorder and crime had the upper hand in London, subject to the extreme ferocity of the law on the comparatively rare occasions when a conviction was secured. The expenses and difficulties of prosecution, the uncertainties of the law, resulted in a dreadful vindictiveness. In 1739 when two men were executed on Kennington Common for a so-called highway robbery – a trifling theft without violence – the prosecutor 'rode at the tail of the cart, jeering them and insulting them all the way'.[31] The brutality of the age and the sense of insecurity were reflected in demands for yet more sanguinary punishments. The writer of a pamphlet called *Hanging not Punishment enough* (1701) points out the increase of highwaymen and housebreakers, 'though the Government has vigorously set itself against them by pardoning very few'. He recommends torture as a deterrent, and also life servitude among the negroes in the plantations, 'first marking them in the face to distinguish them from honest men', as 'a proposal lyable to as few exceptions as any other'. This severity is the more surprising, as he adds,

we need not go far for the reasons of the great numbers and increase of these vermin, for though no times have been without them, yet we may now reasonably believe that after so many thousands of soldiers disbanded, and mariners discharged, many of them are driven upon necessity, and having been used to an idle way of living, care not to work, and many (I fear) cannot if they would.[32]

By the end of the century we are in a different world. If we look back to it we are conscious of its brutalities, but if we attempt to look forward from the then immediate past, we see a revolution in opinion comparable with conversion – with that change of heart which is a phenomenon of individual experience. But the barbarous laws had hardly been modified to suit a more enlightened age which had discovered that they were fit only for a nation of savages.

It is significant of the new spirit which runs through society that there is a growing feeling against cruelty to animals. Of all Hogarth's moralizing designs one feels that the *Four Stages of Cruelty* (1751) had the best chance of success. 'The prints were engraved,' he said,

with the hope of, in some degree, correcting that barbarous treatment of animals, the very sight of which renders the streets of our metropolis so distressing to every feeling mind. If they have had this effect, and checked the progress of cruelty, I am more proud of having been the author than I should be of having painted Raffaele's cartoons.[33]

For ages throwing at cocks on Shrove Tuesday had been an accepted sport for which parents gave their children money. Both the Fieldings set themselves to suppress it,[34] and local paving and improvement Acts made throwing at any 'cock, fowl or bird' a punishable offence.

The supposed increase of crime then, was at least not proven, though changing standards had opened people's eyes to many brutalities which had diminished rather than increased. In 1816 it was not admitted by those whose opinion carries most weight – including Romilly and Place – and the student of eighteenth-century annals of crime can hardly fail to agree with Place that in proportion to the population crimes had diminished.

As for the other count in the indictment of the age, the discontent and spirit of revolution conspicuous between the end of the eighteenth century and the collapse of the Chartist movement in 1848 were doubtless largely due to industrial conditions, but not, in London, to a general worsening of those conditions. On the contrary, they are to be found precisely among those sections of the working classes whose position had improved.[35] Place repeatedly says that the poorest and least skilled labourers in the early nineteenth century were then in the stage of social development of working-men as a whole forty or fifty years before. Mayhew in the eighteen-fifties found that 'between the skilled operative of the West End and the unskilled labourer, the moral and intellectual development is so great that it seems as if we were in a new land and among another race'. It is significant that he found the artisans 'red-hot politicians' (of a Chartist colour) while the labourers had 'no political opinions whatever', though on the whole 'in favour of the maintenance of things as they are'. He found a marked contrast between the radical tailors and the coal-heavers, who were proud of having turned out to a man as special constables on the day of the great Chartist demonstration in 1848. In 1825 the nature of the change in the London artisan had dawned upon the *Edinburgh Review*:

People are aware of these combinations and hear of mischievous tracts widely disseminated, and they compare the careless, vacant, uninquiring clown of fifty years ago, with the busy, restless politician of the present day. They think the change is for the worse, and they impute this change to education.

Conditions in London, in the bad years which followed the peace of 1815, as in the eighteenth century, were exceptional. London to a great extent escaped both the torrent of pauperization which deluged the greater part of agricultural England, and the catastrophic fall in wages which occurred in many places. The workhouse was used as a test of destitution and the more or less permanent organization of paid officials and boards of Directors and Guardians of the poor showed its value.[36] The transition from war to peace undoubtedly brought much misery and unemployment, it was a shrinkage from a period of commercial and industrial expansion under war conditions – a period of chequered and hectic prosperity.[37] But in spite of this, there is much evidence against a general set-back in social conditions in London. Place's evidence is comprehensive and convincing. Foreigners generally comment on the sturdy, well-dressed appearance of working people.[38] Doctors testify to the improvement in health and cleanliness. There was much poverty, but it was being more comprehensively dealt with both by the poor laws and by charities than ever before. The death-rate for London as for the whole country continued to decline. Rickman, who was responsible for the early census returns, wrote to Southey in 1816:

One thing I wish to say as to an opinion which you seem to entertain as to the well-being, or rather ill-being of the poor, that their state has grown worse and worse of late. Now, if one listens to common assertion, everything in grumbling England grows worse and worse; but the fact in question is even a curiosity. Human comfort is to be estimated by human health, and that by the length of human life. . . . Since 1780 life has been prolonged as five to four, and the poor form too large a portion of society to be excluded from this general effect; rather they are the main cause of it; for the upper classes had food and cleanliness abundant before.[39]

It is difficult to follow the social history of London in any detail without being impelled to the conclusion that bad as things were at the end of the great war, they had still been progressively improving, and that people were learning to mitigate the evils of life in a great city; within the limits set by administrative possibilities and deep-seated prejudices something had been achieved. The facts that emerge from this conclusion are the depths of misery, the appalling brutalities of life in earlier periods, for which indeed there is much evidence. But it is not the people whose position is most abject who are most conscious of their miseries – at all events for the most part they suffer in silence. Hardships begin to be talked about when they are no longer taken for granted, and when therefore there is some prospect of relieving them. Irregularity of work and the combination of evils called sweating were of long standing, deeply rooted in the organization of many London trades, yet so little is heard of them till the nineteenth century that they pass as products of modern industrialism. The worst evils of child-labour had already begun to be mitigated when their existence first became generally realized, owing to the sufferings of apprentices in cotton-mills. Cellar dwellings again, often spoken of as a result of the industrial revolution, in London at least date from Tudor times, and were directly encouraged by Tudor and Stuart policy.

This book was begun as a survey of social conditions in London in the eighteenth century. In the process of research it became impossible to escape the conviction of a gradually improving state of things and the century seemed to emerge as a stage in a long, slow process by which life for the mass of the people of London was becoming less nasty, brutish and short, a process of course with many minor fluctuations. A pronounced set-back, for instance, between 1720 and 1750 was almost certainly due to an enormous consumption of very cheap, fiery and adulterated spirits, and there were repeated periods of distress owing to dislocating transitions from peace to war and war to peace, to trade crises and to times of dearth and epidemics. But the new spirit which (rightly or wrongly) regarded the miseries of man as due not to original sin or an inscrutable Providence, but to bad laws and a bad environment, was beginning to be concerned not only to relieve distress but to deal with its causes. As most of our modern social and industrial evils have a longer history than is often supposed, so has the process of improvement and reform. The advance in health, cleanliness, order, sobriety and education which has obviously been going on in London since 1850 can be traced since at least the middle of the eighteenth century.

CHAPTER I

LIFE AND DEATH IN LONDON

Gin, cursed Fiend, with Fury fraught,
Makes human Race a Prey,
It enters by a deadly Draught,
And steals our Life away,

Beer, happy Produce of our Isle
Can sinewy Strength impart,
And wearied with Fatigue and Toil
Can chear each manly Heart.
Rev. James Townley (1751)

THE key to the social history of London is to be found in its changes in population – its growth, and the ratio between births and deaths. It was a key for which contemporaries were for the most part groping; the controversy as to whether the population of the country – and of London – was increasing or decreasing was not finally settled till the census of 1801, followed by that of 1811. Estimates of growth or decline and of the duration of life were largely based on the London Bills of Mortality – the records of burials and baptisms kept by the Company of Parish Clerks. These were obviously unsatisfactory, as only baptisms and burials in parish churches and burying-grounds were registered, and there were many dissenters in London. Moreover, the Bills (the name was extended to the district covered by the returns) stood for the greater London of the seventeenth century; when the plague disappeared the original motive for comprehensive returns disappeared too. Though they included the parishes of Bethnal Green, Bermondsey and Hackney, which at the beginning of the nineteenth century were still partly rural, they did not cover the extensions of London in the west, notably Marylebone and St Pancras. From time to time new parishes appeared in the Bills, but these were subdivisions of parishes which had become more thickly populated and did not extend the area covered by the returns.

The classification of diseases was also thoroughly unscientific and defective, but with all their faults the Bills give a remarkable picture of the fluctuations in the London death-rate and of variations in the causes of death, which though inaccurate, is yet broadly true and is borne out by other evidence. William Heberden the younger, a London doctor of great experience, wrote in 1808:

The Bills of Mortality have often been objected to as erroneous and imperfect . . . and unworthy of credit. This charge is not without foundation, though by no means to be admitted to its full extent. For what they want in accuracy is in a great measure supplied by their magnitude, the large scale upon which they are constructed making their smaller errors inconsiderable. . . . But the surest testimony to their credibility is afforded by the Bills themselves, whose agreement with each other is quite inexplicable upon any other supposition than that of their being drawn from the uniformity of nature and truth.[1]

In the middle of the century there was one fact, which stood out with terrible clearness – making all allowances for defects in the Bills – that the deaths in London greatly exceeded the births, and that this excess represented a drain on the nation. For the greater part of the eighteenth century London is dominated by a sense of the 'waste of life' recorded in the Bills. 'London has grown, and continues still to grow, out of compass, at the expense of, and to the sensible diminution of the other towns and boroughs, at the expense in short of the class of labourers.'[2] And again: 'London will not feel any want of recruits till there are no people in the country.'[3] This was the 'great wen' theory which had existed since the time of Elizabeth.

The waste of life was at its worst between 1720 and 1750; after 1760 it became clear that the burials were decreasing. This lent support to a new theory – that the population of London, like that of the country as a whole, was declining. The theory depended on the hypothesis that the country was being depopulated by the growth of luxury. This was necessary to reconcile the supposed decline of population with the rapidly growing trade returns, the increasing consumption of food and fuel, the building and road-making which was going on. Dr Price was the leader of the pessimists – of the depopulation-cum-luxury school which represented England as a place 'where wealth accumulates and men decay'. The growth of London in bricks and mortar was obvious, but this is how Price explained it in 1779:

The increase of buildings in London has for several years been the subject of general observation. It deserves particular notice that it is derived from the increase of luxury, an evil, which, while it flatters, never fails to destroy. It has been shown from authentic accounts that the decrease of the lower people in London and Middlesex has kept pace with the increase of buildings. The annual deaths alone in the Bills of Mortality have for many years been decreasing, and are now 6,000 per annum less than they were fifty years ago. In particular it is observable with respect to London within the City Walls, that though always filled with houses, the births and burials, and consequently the inhabitants, have decreased one half. The ju t account must be that those who cannot now satisfy themselves without whole houses, or perhaps two or three houses . . . used formerly to be satisfied with lodgings or with parts of houses.[4]

A decrease in the death-rate is taken as a proof of a decline in the population, and a less crowded manner of living is an increase of luxury.

The luxury theory irritated Johnson's sound common sense; when Goldsmith expatiated 'on the common topick that the race of our people was degenerating and that this was owing to luxury', he doubted the fact and denied the cause, 'for Sir, consider to how very small a proportion of our people luxury can reach. . . . Luxury, so far as it reaches the poor, will do good to the race of people; it will strengthen and multiply them'.

The census proved what Price's opponents had maintained, that the population of England had increased during the eighteenth century, slowly at first, and rapidly after 1780, and that of London had done the same, though owing to the more rapid increase of the industrial north, at a slower rate than the country as a whole. The population for the eighteenth century was calculated, not from the Bills of Mortality, but from the parish registers of baptisms, on the assumption that these bore the same relation to the total population that they did in 1801. On this basis it was estimated that the population of London (including five parishes not within the Bills: Marylebone, St Pancras, Paddington, Kensington and Chelsea) was 674,500 in 1700, 676,750 in 1750, as compared with the 900,000 of the census returns of 1801.[5] If the parishes without the Bills are omitted, the slight increase between 1700 and 1750 disappears, and there is actually a decrease of 9,000. While Westminster and the out-parishes had increased, the City and Southwark (apparrently), the oldest and most crowded parts of the metropolis had decreased. As the population had certainly increased between 1700 and 1720[6] the check is greater than appears, and if the calculations had been made from the Bills of Mortality the decline would have seemed still greater.

While there was certainly a decrease in the baptisms it is however by no means clear that this was due to an actual diminution in the population of London. In fact, an estimate based on the number of burials would show an increase. From maps and other evidence it is clear that London continued to expand. 'It is not easy to account for the diminution of christenings between . . . 1740 and 1760,' said Heberden,

but it may be observed that the number of females buried in the same twenty years not being sensibly lessened, the defect seems to have arisen from the smaller proportion among them that bore children. Whatever be the cause of this, the christenings appear, in fact, to have been fewest at a time when the burials were nearly at their highest.[7]

While Price and his followers were wrong in their deductions from the Bills of Mortality, the Bills were certainly confusing and disconcerting. By 1740 it had become evident that burials were increasing and baptisms decreasing, and many calculations were made of the havoc caused by this waste of life. The figures were indeed alarming. The baptisms increased from the beginning of the century till 1724, when they were 19,370, and then decreased till they reached their lowest point, 13,571 in 1742. They continued at a low level till 1760 and then began slowly to increase. The burials reached their highest point just when the baptisms were at their lowest, and were 32,169 in 1741. They did not again during the century come within 4,000 of this maximum, and after 1760 it was evident that they were decreasing. The waste of life recorded in the Bills was at its worst since the days of the plague between 1727 and 1750. From 1728 the ages of those dying were given in the Bills and it became apparent that the great mortality was chiefly among children. The population of London was only kept up by immigrants who had passed the dangerous first years of life and many old people retired outside the Bills to die, yet the percentage of deaths is estimated to have been 1 in 20 in 1750, while a similar calculation for 1740–2 would give a still higher rate.

The changes in the Bills of Mortality during the century were revolutionary. For the first fifty years the burials were to the baptisms roughly as three to two – for the three years from 1740 to 1742 they were more than two to one. From 1750 the average ratio grew steadily less, though in years of special distress, of high prices or bad trade, the burials increased and the baptisms declined. In 1790 for the first time the christenings exceeded the burials. The dearth of 1795 had its inevitable results, but in spite of this, for the five years from 1795 to 1799 the baptisms and burials were almost equal, the average annual excess of the latter being nine. Again the effects of the bad season of 1800 followed by a fever epidemic are seen in an increase of about 5,000 in the burials, and in 1801 there was a marked drop in the baptisms. Nevertheless for the five years from 1800 to 1804 the average number of baptisms exceeded the burials and the excess grew steadily.*

Between 1700 and 1820 the population of London almost doubled (674,000–1,274,000), the number of registered burials did not increase, the number of registered baptisms increased from 16,000 to 28,000.[8] Rickman calculated the London death-rate on the assumption that one-third of the deaths escaped registration in the parish registers, which he used as less ihaccurate than the Bills of Mortality. According to this, the death-rate in 1700 was 1 in 25, in 1750 1 in 21 or 20, from 1797 to 1801 1 in 35, from 1801 to 1811 1 in 38 and in 1821 1 in 40.[9]

The decrease was greatest in the burials of children. For the twenty years from 1730 to 1749 the burials of children under five were, according to the Bills, 74·5 per cent of all the children christened. The proportion steadily decreased and from 1790 to 1809 was 41·3 per cent.†

What is the explanation of this surprising improvement in the health of London? The early part of the eighteenth century between 1700 and 1757 or 1765 is considered to have been one of the chief periods of working-class prosperity in this country. Food prices fell from the level of the seventeenth century, there was a great demand for labour, and wages tended to rise. The standard of living improved. Instead of bread from the coarser cereals, barley, rye and oats, fine wheaten bread, previously a luxury of the well-to-do, became the staple food of the greater part of the country. Between 1700 and 1720 London's share in

* See Appendix I, *B*.   † See Appendix I, *C*.

this prosperity is reflected in the Bills of Mortality. In those years the proportion of burials to baptisms is the lowest during the 85 years from 1680 to 1765, as that between 1740 and 1760 is the highest.[10] How is the set-back after 1720 to be accounted for?

The Bills record the inevitable effects of dearth and fever in the lessening of births and increasing of deaths, but on the whole the period was one of plenty, while the bad years were distributed fairly equally before and after 1720. Fever was perennial in London, and a bad harvest with a rise in the price of bread and a hard winter were inevitably followed by an epidemic. This happened in 1709–10 and again in 1713–14. There were bad harvests in 1727 and 1728 and from 1726 to 1729 the death-rate was very high and the births declined. The dearth of 1740 to 1741 coincided with a very cold winter followed by a very hot summer. The Thames was frozen, there was much distress in London, and a particularly virulent outbreak of fever, which caused much alarm.[11] The dearth, however, was not comparable with the dear years of King William or Queen Anne.[12] Corn rose to 56s. only (it had been 81s. 9d. in 1709–10) but the effects were more disastrous. It was a time of trade depression, shown in a marked drop in the exports, and this added to the unemployment caused by the frost. The effects of these two calamitous years are seen in the terrible excess of burials over baptisms, 15,580 in 1740 and 17,212 in 1741.

The fact that a high death-rate and low birth-rate should have combined between 1720 and 1750 is strange, because during this time London was spreading itself over a wider area and the narrow streets and courts of the City were becoming less crowded as tenements made way for warehouses and counting-houses.[13] The price of corn was very low; in the forty years between 1715 and 1755 there were only three bad seasons, 1727, 1728, and 1740.[14] Meat in London was cheap and plentiful,[15] the markets and stalls were being increasingly well supplied with fruit and vegetables from the neighbouring market gardens. Trade was growing – apart from a set-back after 1739 – and the country was financially prosperous. The sanitary condition of London was of course very bad, but there is no evidence that it was deteriorating – on the contrary, it must have tended to improve with the spreading out of the population. The constant fires and the rebuilding which followed them must have had on a small scale something of the effects of the Great

Fire. The appearance of the plague at Marseilles in 1720 roused a salutary terror in London. As a matter of fact the effects of an improved diet and some sanitary progress are seen in the decline since the seventeenth century in the mortality from scurvy, dysentery and intermittent fever.[16]

The only explanation seems to be that usually given by contemporaries[17] – the orgy of spirit-drinking which was at its worst between 1720 and 1751, due to the very cheap and very intoxicating liquors, which were retailed indiscriminately and in the most brutalizing and demoralizing conditions.

The diminution of births [wrote Corbyn Morris in 1751] set out from the time that the consumption of these liquors by the common people became enormous. . . . As this consumption hath been continually increasing since that time, the amount of the births hath been continually diminishing. . . . Can it be necessary to add to this shocking loss . . . the sickly state of such infants as are born, who with difficulty pass through the first stages of life and live very few of them to years of manhood? . . . Inquire from the several hospitals in this City, whether any increase of patients and of what sort, are daily brought under their care? They will all declare, increasing multitudes of dropsical and consumptive people arising from the effects of spirituous liquors.[18]

A representation to the House of Commons in 1751 on the effects of spirituous liquors estimates the annual loss in London since 1740 by the premature deaths of weakly children under five, and by fewer births as 9,323: 'Other trivial reasons for this great mortality, which in some degree have always subsisted, may possibly require some abatement; but still the real grand destroyer is materially evident.'[19]

Other reasons of course there were – among them the effects of dearth and fever in 1740 and 1741 are apparent, but it is probable that the reason why these were so calamitous in those years, as compared with similar years before and after, was that they were aggravated by the effects of spirit-drinking. Distilling was a new trade in England and one which received special favours from the Government. It produced a revenue and gave farmers a market for cereals at a time when prices were low. It was supposed to be favourable to the balance of trade, though as a matter of fact foreign spirits, even if smuggled, were too dear for general mass consumption. Large vested interests were created, and Lord Hervey (or rather Samuel Johnson) said in 1743:

... that the great fortunes recently made were to him a convincing proof that the trade of distilling was the most profitable of any now exercised in the kingdom except that of being broker to a prime-minister.[20]

The cheapness of British spirits caused a new demand and altered the tastes and habits of the people. Brandy-shops and geneva-shops multiplied in the poorer parts of London. Almost every shop daily resorted to by the poorer classes also embarked upon the selling of spirits. Employers, including the numerous middlemen who worked in cellars and garrets, sold gin to their workpeople. The result was an orgy of spirit-drinking whose effects were seen in the streets of London, in the workhouses, in the growing misery of the poor, in an increase of crimes of violence.

The distilling trade was regarded as the great support of the landed interest. By this trade, said Defoe in 1713 (before its effects had shown themselves),

first, the corn is consum'd, which corn is our own produce, pays rent for our land, employs our people, our cattle, our shipping, etc., and secondly, the importation of foreign spirits is prevented. . . . Nothing is more certain than that the ordinary produce of corn in England is much greater than the numbers of our people or cattle can consume: And this is the reason why, when markets are low abroad and no demands made for corn, that plenty which is other nations' blessing, is our intolerable burthen. . . . The distilling trade is one remedy for this disaster as it helps to carry off the great quantity of corn in such a time of plenty, and it has this particular advantage, that if at any time a scarcity happens, this trade can halt for a year and not be lost entirely as in other trades it often happens to be. . . . But in times of plenty and a moderate price of corn, the distilling of corn is one of the most essential things to support the landed interest that any branch of trade can help us to, and therefore especially to be preserved and tenderly used.[21]

Such considerations could not be disregarded by an eighteenth-century Parliament. Everything was done to promote the production and consumption of spirits. First, the distilling trade was thrown absolutely open. The distillers of London had been incorporated by Charles I and had been given a right of search within a radius of twenty-one miles. The charter was overridden,[22] and to protect distillers from actions brought against them by the Distillers Company, they were also freed from the statutory obligation to serve a seven years' apprenticeship.[23] Anyone was free to distil on giving notice to the Commissioners of Excise and paying the low excise duty, and anyone was free to retail spirits without the justices' licence required from alehouse-keepers, etc.

A yet further privilege was given to distillers and retailers of spirits. By a provision in the Mutiny Act of 1720 all retailers who were also distillers or whose 'principal dealings' were more 'in other goods and merchandize than in brandy and strong waters' and who did not 'suffer tippling in their houses' were exempted from the burdensome obligation to have soldiers quartered upon them which was laid upon innkeepers, keepers of livery stables, victuallers and retailers of strong waters within the Bills of Mortality.

There were two branches of the distilling trade, the malt distillers and the compound distillers. The former, who produced the raw spirit, were few in number, were 'prodigious dealers' and employed 'vast sums' in trade. This branch was, Defoe says, called into existence by the prohibition of French brandy during the wars at the end of the seventeenth century,[24] and was encouraged by the succession of statutes during the reigns of William and Anne by which the trade had been thrown open. The compound distillers or rectifiers, as makers of cordials, etc., had been granted a charter in 1638, but with the development of the malt distillery, their business had completely changed its character. These now catered for the masses, and 'put a quantity of anniseed, juniper berries, or other materials into the malt spirits lowered with water' which they redistilled.[25] The compound distillers abounded in London during the gin-drinking period; they usually retailed the spirits they concocted and, it may be supposed, crudely adulterated, as these were very cheap, fiery and poisonous. This business was undertaken by many 'loose and disorderly persons' and besides other evils the many stills in the crowded parts of London gave rise to frequent and terrible fires (the justices complained in 1730), the less to be wondered at, as according to Defoe they . . . 'carry on their trade as if they were always drunk, keep no books but their slate, and no pen and ink but their chalk and tallies. . . . They are a collection of sinners against the people, for they break almost all the known laws of Government in the Nation'.[24]

The great increase in the consumption of spirits showed itself in the excise returns about 1721 at the same time that its effects begin to be discoverable in the Bills of Mortality. From this year also dates the beginning of the campaign against gin-drinking which at last forced restrictive measures upon the Government. But the dangerous tendencies of spirit-drinking had been seen twenty years earlier. Davenant said of the drinking both of foreign brandy and of strong waters made in England: "'Tis a growing vice among the common people, and may in time prevail as much as opium with the Turks, to which many attribute the scarcity of people in the East.'[26]

In April 1721 the Government was concerned to discover certain 'scandalous clubs and societies of young persons' whose object was blasphemy and the denial of religion, as to which there was much rumour and little evidence. The Westminster justices were ordered to investigate, and to take proceedings against all profaneness, immorality and debauchery. They failed to find the clubs, but took occasion to represent that in their opinion the immorality of the times was due to gaming-houses, play-houses and the great increase of alehouses and spirit-shops.

Nor is there any part of this town wherein the number of alehouses, brandy and geneva shops do not daily increase, though they were so numerous already that in some of the largest parishes every tenth house at least sells one sort or another of those liquors by retail.

This, they 'humbly offer', is

the principall cause of the increase of our poor and of all the vice and debauchery among the inferior sort of people, as well as of the felonies and other disorders committed in and about this town.[27]

From this time onwards the Sessions repeatedly showed its concern with the evils of spirit-drinking. In the same year owing to fear of the plague, a committee of justices was appointed by the Sessions to consider sanitary nuisances under certain heads, one being 'persons retailing brandy, geneva and other distilled liquors'. The committee take notice

... of the great destruction made by brandy and geneva-shops whose owners retail their liquors to the poorer sort of people and do suffer them to sit tippling in their shops, by which practice they are not only rendered incapable of labour . . . (but by their bodys being kept in a continual heat) are thereby more liable to receive infection.[28]

At the same time a representation was made to the Secretary for War pointing out the evils of the exemption from quartering soldiers. Every retailer set up a still, and every inferior trader had been encouraged to sell strong waters, and under these two exceptions almost all spirit-sellers sheltered themselves from taking soldiers. These shops, they say, seem to deserve the least encouragement of any public-houses, as they cause more mischief than all others joined together, and, 'as we are informed by several physitians' are most likely 'to prepare and dispose the bodies of those who usually drink such liquors . . . to receive any infection that may be brought in among us'.

The Government was slow to respond. In 1725 the chairman of the Middlesex Bench in his charge to the Grand Jury said:

. . . the cry of excessive . . . drinking of gin and other pernicious spirits, is become so great, so loud, so importunate, and the growing mischiefs from it so many, so great, so destructive of the lives, families, trades, and businesses of such multitudes, especially of the lower, poorer sort of the people, that I can no longer doubt but it must soon reach the ears of our legislators.[29]

In the following October a committee of justices was appointed to inquire into the increasing number of retailers. Returns were made by the constables of 6,187 houses and shops where spirits were openly retailed in the metropolis excluding the City and the Surrey side of the river.

And although this number is exceeding great . . . (being in some parishes every tenth house, in others every seventh, and in one of the largest, every fifth house) the committee believe it to be very far short of the true number, there being many who sell . . . even in the streets and highways, some on bulks set up for that purpose, and others in wheelbarrows, and many more who sell privately in garrets, sellars, backrooms and other places. . . . The committee observe with deep concern the strong inclination of the inferior sort of people to these destructive liquors, and yet, as if that were not sufficient, all arts are used to tempt and invite them. All chandlers, many tobacconists, and such who sell fruit or herbs in stalls and wheelbarrows sell geneva, and many inferior tradesmen begin now to keep it in their shops for their customers, whereby it is scarce possible for soldiers, seamen, servants, or others of their rank, to go anywhere without being drawn in either by those who sell it or by their acquaintance, whom they meet with in the street, who generally begin by inviting them to a dram. . . . In the hamlet of Bethnal Green above forty weavers sell it. And if we may judge what will happen in other workhouses now erecting, by what has already happened in that of St Giles in the Fields, we have reason to fear that the violent fondness and desire of this liquor, which unaccountably possesses all our poor, may prevent in great measure the good effects proposed by them . . . it appearing by the returns from the Holborn division that notwithstanding all the care that has been taken, Geneva is clandestinely brought in among the poor there, and that they will suffer any punishment . . . rather than live without it, though they cannot avoid seeing its fatal effects by the death of those among them who had drunk most freely of it.

The committee submitted to the consideration of the Sessions 'how far it is in their power . . . to suppress this great nuisance or . . . what application to our superiors may be proper in order to secure a more effectual remedy.'[30]

The Sessions ordered the report to be printed, and in the same month the College of Physicians petitioned Parliament against spirituous liquors as 'rendering not fit for business, poor, a burden to themselves and neighbours and too often a cause of weak, feeble and distempered children. . . .'[31] Nevertheless three more years passed before Parliament paid attention to the crying evil. In 1729 the Grand Jury of Middlesex presented geneva-shops as a nuisance,[32] and at last an Act was passed to check indiscriminate retailing. Retailers were required to take out an excise licence costing £20 and a duty of 2s. a gallon was laid on compound spirits. Although it was openly defied by a concoction called 'parliament brandy' it reduced the sale, and the Act was repealed in 1733 on a complaint from the farmers. Parliament set itself once more 'to consider further methods for encouraging the making and exporting of home-made spirits distilled from the corn of Great Britain' and the first of its resolutions was 'that the Act hath been a discouragement to the distilling of spirits and ought to be repealed'.[33]

The effects of unlimited sale became more appalling than ever. In 1735 the Middlesex Sessions appointed another committee which reported in January 1735–6 much on the lines of the report of 1726, but showing, as do the excise returns, that the evil had spread in the past ten years. The number of retailers – 7,044 (4,939 licensed and 2,105 unlicensed)[34] – the justices consider very far short of the truth, as the returns were made by the constables, about half of whom were retailers themselves. The 'inferior trades' which sold spirits had increased to 'above fourscore . . . particularly all chandlers, many weavers, several tobacconists, shoe-makers, carpenters, barbers, taylors, dyers, labourers and others. . . .' The weavers of Bethnal Green who sold spirits had increased to 'upwards of ninety', besides,

. . . other persons of inferior trades concerned in our manufactures . . . and as they generally employ many journeymen . . . this liquor being always at hand . . . they are easily tempted to drink freely of it, especially as they can drink the whole week upon score, and too often without minding how fast the score runs against them; whereby at the week's end they find themselves without any surplusage to carry home to their families, which must of course starve, or be thrown on the parish. . . . With regard to the female sex, we find the contagion has spread even among them, and that to a degree hardly possible to be conceived. Unhappy mothers habituate themselves to these distilled liquors, whose children are born weak and sickly, and often look shrivel'd and old as though they had numbered many years. Others again daily give it to their children . . . and learn them even before they can go, to taste and approve this certain destroyer.

To the inflaming character of gin the committee ascribed the many crimes of violence, the drinkers being often 'carried to a degree of outrageous passion'. Neglected children 'starved and naked at home . . . either become a burthen to their parishes or . . . are forced to beg whilst they are children, and as they grow up learn to pilfer and steal'.[35]

The Government was moved to a heroic remedy. The Middlesex justices presented a petition to the House of Commons against the excessive use of spirituous liquors; resolutions supporting the petition were carried unanimously, and an Act was passed which was intended to stop the retailing of British spirits. A duty of 20s. a gallon was laid on spirits and retailers were required to take an annual licence costing £50. This step is almost more eloquent of the evils of gin than the reports of the justices. That a land-owning Parliament should attempt to suppress the home consumption of British spirits at a time when corn prices were still low suggests something of the incredible state of things when gin was threatening to destroy the race. Moreover the prohibition of retailing was generally expected to lead to riots, and the Jacobites were ready to take advantage of any discontents. The Bill was opposed on this ground, and on that of the unfairness of destroying a trade which had been deliberately fostered for forty years. The 'regulation will raise great disaffection to the present Government,' said Pulteney, 'and may produce such riots and tumults as may endanger our present establishment, or at least cannot be quelled without spilling . . . blood . . . and putting an end to the liberties of the people'.[36] The loss to the revenue was estimated at £70,000.

The Act could not be enforced. It did at first check the consumption of spirits, but these were sold illicitly, at first secretly, then openly; riots broke out, informers were hunted down and murdered, and the law became a dead letter. In seven years only three £50 licences were taken out, but the quantity of spirits sold progressively increased and reached its maximum of over 8,000,000 gallons in 1743.[37]

The perjuries of informers were . . . so flagrant and common, that the people thought all informations malicious, or at least, thinking themselves oppressed by the law, they looked upon every man that promoted its execution as their enemy, and therefore now began to declare war against informers, many of whom they treated with great cruelty and some they murdered in the streets. By their obstinacy they at last wearied the magistrates, and by their violence they intimidated those who might be inclined to make discoveries, so that the law . . . has been now [1743] for some years totally disused, nor has any man been found willing to engage in a task at once odious as endless, or to punish offences which every day multiplied, and on which the whole body of the common people, a body very formidable when united, was universally engaged.[38]

The Government and the magistrates had been defeated by the mob. The Act had made things worse by making the trade wholly illicit and therefore more disreputable than ever. The Act of 1743 was a reversal of the policy of 1736. Its object and that of subsequent Acts was to suppress the gin-shop as such, to make the sale public, and as far as possible respectable, and to increase the price of spirits. Annual spirit licences costing 20s. were to be granted only to those who had an alehouse licence and distillers were forbidden to retail. The virtual prohibition of 1736 was given up, after a seven years' experience of its consequences, but the change of policy was denounced as a concession to gin. In the words of Sir Charles Hanbury Williams:

> Riot and Slaughter once again
> Shall their career begin;
> And ev'ry parish sucking babe
> Again be nurs'd with gin.

The Act of 1743 reduced the consumption of spirits, but in 1747 there was a set-back. The compound distillers petitioned Parliament to be allowed to retail – urging their financial hardships and their victimization by informers. They were given leave to retail on taking out a £5 licence. Under cover of this Act the old evils came back again and the consumption went up. In 1751 there was a general protest, in which Fielding's *Reasons for the late Increase of Robbers*, Hogarth's *Gin Lane*, and appeals to the evidence of the Bills of Mortality were an effective part. There was a stream of petitions to the House of Commons urging the immediate and absolute necessity of checking the excessive use of spirits – from the Corporation of London and from the authorities of Westminster, from many London parishes, from the Bakers' Company of London, from Bristol, Norwich and Manchester. These petitions pointed out that the common use of cheap spirits was destroying the people, shortening their lives, causing irreligion, idleness and disorder, and if not checked, would destroy the power and trade of the kingdom.[39]

The Act of 1751 really did reduce the excesses of spirit-drinking. It was a turning-point in the social history of London and was so considered when this time was still within living memory.[40] It accepted the principles of the Act of 1743 but enforced them more stringently. The duty on spirits was increased to make them less perniciously cheap. Distillers, chandlers and grocers were expressly forbidden to retail.[41] The sale of spirits at the chandler's shop had been a fruitful source of evil. These shops abounded in London. They provided the poorest classes with their staple food of bread, small beer and cheese – this staple became bread and gin, it was even said, gin only. Market-women and street-sellers went to the chandler's for breakfast when an alehouse was too expensive; provisions were fetched from the chandler's in ha'porths and farthings' worths, coal by the half-peck came from the same source; the link-boy went there for his nightly link, the servant-maid to fetch soap or sand or candles, and was treated to a dram. Hence this denunciation of the chandler in a book on London trades:

The chandler's shop deals in all things necessary for the kitchen in small quantities; he is partly cheesemonger, oilman, grocer, distiller, &c. This last article brings him in the greatest profit, and at the same time renders him the most obnoxious dealer in and about London. In these shops maid-servants and the lower class of women learn the first rudiments of drinking ... and load themselves with diseases, their families with poverty and their posterity with want and infamy. The chandler-man takes no apprentices, and I could wish there were no masters or mistresses.[42]

The measures to check excessive spirit-drinking had been forced upon the Government in the teeth of vested interests by a general protest in which the middle and trading classes had taken a leading part. To appreciate what was implied by the widespread denunciation of gin-drinking one must remember that it was entirely untouched by the spirit of the temperance reformer. Drunkenness was hardly regarded as a vice, the consumption of strong beer was almost regarded as a British virtue. Indeed, Defoe wrote in 1702, 'an honest drunken fellow is a character in a man's praise. . . .' It was considered as one of the evil consequences of gin-drinking that less malt-liquor was consumed.[43] The pendant to Hogarth's *Gin Lane* was *Beer Street*. Sir John Fielding wrote in 1776 (after the worst horrors of the spirit traffic had been checked) of the retailers of spirits 'who are permitted to vend in every part of this kingdom this liquid fire by which men drink their hell beforehand. These shopkeepers are the principal officers of the king of terrors and have conveyed more to the regions of death than the sword or the plague'.[44] The words occur in the uncontroversial pages of a guide-book; they reflect the experiences of a London magistrate with no bias whatever against intoxicating drinks in general.* Indeed, we find him in 1773 summoning a meeting of the Westminster justices and getting them to pass a resolution

... that the combination of the publicans to raise the price of their porter to 4d. per quart is unreasonable and illegal and that the magistrates of West-minster will do everything in their power, both singly and collectively, to prevent so shameful an imposition on the poor, and to bring to justice such as shall attempt to act in such an oppressive manner.[45]

* I find John Fielding repudiated the authorship of this book, ascribed to him in the B.M. Catalogue. He had, however, written in a similar strain in letters to the Press.

It would be hardly possible to exaggerate the cumulatively disastrous effects of the orgy of spirit-drinking between 1720 and 1751. There was a marked improvement after 1751 but the state of things was still appalling and at the end of the century Dr Willan said:

... on comparing my own observations with the Bills of Mortality, I am convinced that considerably more than one-eighth of all the deaths that take place in persons above twenty years old, happen prematurely through excess in spirit-drinking.[46]

These sayings help one to realize what London was like when a smaller population consumed a far greater quantity of spirits – and more poisonous spirits – sold in an incomparably more degrading way. Contemporaries noticed the improvement. In 1757 Burrington wrote:

... the lower people of late years have not drank spirituous liquors so freely as they did before the good regulations and qualifications for selling them. ... The additional excise has raised their price, improvements in the distillery have rendered the home-made distillations as wholesome as the imported. We do not see the hundredth part of poor wretches drunk in the streets since the said qualifications as before.[47]

In times of dearth the distillation of spirits from corn was sometimes prohibited, the price soared and consumption fell correspondingly. The effects of this were an object-lesson in the advantages of restriction. There was a prohibition after the dearth of 1757. In 1759 and 1760 there were many petitions from traders and manufacturers praying for its continuance, and fearing 'fatal consequences' should it be withdrawn.[48] The landed interest on the other hand petitioned that the price of corn had fallen below the cost of production. Parliament agreed that 'the high price of spirits hath greatly contributed to the health, sobriety and industry of the common people', and the duty was increased.[49]

This reduced the home consumption of British spirits to something over two million gallons, where it remained for twenty years, and from 1782 to 1784 fell to one million odd gallons as a result of yet higher duties. By this time the high price of corn had made the distilling trade less vital to the landed interest, but the distillers complained of their burdens (1783–4) and pointed out that owing to an increase of smuggling the revenue had fallen.[50] Duties were lowered in 1785 and 1786 and the consumption crept upwards till 1796 and 1797 when, owing to the dearth of 1795, distilling from corn was prohibited.

It is a curious and important fact [remarks Colquhoun, who was then a police magistrate in the Tower Hamlets] that ... although bread and every necessary of life was considerably higher than during the preceding year, the poor ... were apparently more comfortable, paid their rents more regularly, and were better fed than at any period for some years before. . . . This can only be accounted for by their being denied the indulgence of gin, which became in a great measure inaccessible from its very high price. The effects ... were also evident in their more orderly conduct. Quarrels and assaults were less frequent and they resorted seldomer to the pawnbrokers' shops; and yet during the chief of this period bread was fifteen pence a quartern loaf and meat higher than the preceding year.[51]

Both 1796 and 1797 were good years according to the Bills of Mortality; the favourable returns of 1796 were ascribed to the remarkably mild winter, but the prohibition of distilling probably counted for something. An American visitor to England in 1805 and 1806 commenting on the immense quantities of porter and beer consumed in London, remarks that 'the common people in England drink but little ardent spirits, because its excessive dearness places it almost beyond their reach'. He adds, 'in our country the effects are dreadful, because every man can procure it'.[52]

Distilling was primarily a London trade. In 1783 the corn distillers of London claimed to produce 'upwards of eleven-twelfths of the whole distillery of England'.[50] Gin-drinking too was pre-eminently a London vice. Lord Lansdowne said in 1743, 'the excessive use of gin hath hitherto been pretty much confined to the Cities of London and Westminster'. But as the manufacturing population of the provincial towns increased, their consumption of gin must have increased too. Manchester, Bristol and Norwich joined in the protest of 1751 and Colchester was among the petitioners in 1760. Gin was said to be the drink of the more sedentary trades, weavers particularly, and of women. Labouring men and artisans doing heavy work drank strong beer. Gin-drinking was essentially a disease of poverty. Gin was so cheap, so warming and brought such forgetfulness of cold and misery. It was a passion among beggars and the inmates of workhouses and prisons. It is true that the justices in 1736 said:

... not only the vicious and immoral give in to this practice, but also those who are in other respects sober and regular; not only one person here and there in a family, but whole families, shamefully and constantly indulge themselves in this pernicious practice, fathers and masters, children as well as servants.

But the typical gin-drinkers were the poorest and most wretched of the community, their poverty a cause as well as a result of their craving for gin, and when gin became dearer the reduction in consumption was immediate.

London's share in the total consumption of spirits certainly grew less as the century went on. The fall in consumption in spite of the growth of the population is striking and is borne out by the decline in the number of spirit-retailers in London. In 1736 the justices found a total of 7,044 for the Middlesex part of the metropolis – that is, for the divisions of Westminster, Holborn, Finsbury and the Tower Hamlets. This total does not include the great number of shops that dealt in spirits as well as in other things, or the numerous hawkers and stall-keepers who sold gin. In 1794 Colquhoun gives the total of licensed houses for the whole metropolis as 5,243.[53] Deducting the districts not included in the returns of 1736, the City (825), Southwark and the Surrey parishes (943), and the division of Kensington (258), the total for 1794 is 3,217 – less than half the number in 1736. The returns of 1794 were undoubtedly more complete than the admittedly defective ones of 1736. Yet Colquhoun found that the number in 1794 was excessive and that many publicans were unable to make a living. Moreover, he assumes that the bulk of their business was done in beer.* In 1736, of the 7,044 retailers, 3,853 dealt only in spirits, while the justices concluded from the decay of the brewing trade that the other 3,209 dealt more in spirits than in beer.

A report on the distribution of spirit-retailers just before the Act of 1751[54] gives material for a closer comparison with those of 1794 in the case of three districts:

* In the eighteenth century gin and beer were separate problems. In this chapter gin is considered in its relation to vital statistics. The drinking habits of the people and the abuses connected with the alehouse rather than the gin-shop are described in Chapter 6.

1750		1794	
The City .... licensed 1,050..1,050 (one house in 15)		825 ⎤	(one house in 25)
Westminster ...... licensed 1,300 ⎫ 2,200 (one house in 8)			
unlicensed 900 ⎬		957 ⎬	All licensed
Holborn........... licensed ⎫ 1,350 (one house in about			
and unlicensed ⎭ 5¼)		759 ⎦	

The returns of 1750 were constables' returns and probably incomplete. There must have been unlicensed retailers in the City, indeed they must have abounded in the liberties of the Fleet, the purlieus of Field Lane, Petticoat Lane and Houndsditch. The lowest depth in 1750 was reached in St Giles (included in Holborn) where, out of 2,000 houses, 506 were gin-shops, 'besides about 82 twopenny houses of the greatest infamy [common lodging-houses] where gin was the principal liquor drunk'. Yet by 1794 the population of Holborn had much increased, as the division included the two parishes of Marylebone and St Pancras, whose rapid development dates from about 1750.

The tragic episode in the history of London – the great gin-drinking period – and the history of the distilling trade go far to show why cheap and plentiful corn did not bring prosperity to the people. Imagination pales before the horrors of the time in the back streets and alleys of London. Hogarth's *Gin Lane* is a historic document whose essential truth is confirmed in numberless details incidentally recorded in the Old Bailey *Sessions Papers*. The scene is in St Giles where in 1750 every fourth house at least was a gin-shop. Its eighty-two 'twopenny houses' were also brothels of the lowest class and places for receiving stolen goods. Many of the crimes of the time bear all the marks of a gin-inflamed insanity. There is the case of Judith Dufour who fetched her two-year-old child from the workhouse, where it had just been 'new-clothed', for the afternoon. She strangled it and left it in a ditch in Bethnal Green in order to sell its clothes. The money (one and fourpence) was spent on gin and was divided with a woman, who (she said) instigated the crime. She worked all the following night at a silk-throwster's and confessed the deed to a fellow-workwoman. This poor creature was, her mother said, 'never in her right mind but always roving'.[55]

The children of gin-drinking mothers were entrusted to workhouse women who were as Hanway said, 'indigent, filthy and decrepit'.[56] 'What must become of an infant,' Fielding asks, 'who is conceived in gin, with the poisonous distillations of which it is nourished, both in the womb and at the breast?'[57] The number of births was inevitably reduced by prostitution and disease. The number of burials was almost certainly increased by a large number of children who died unchristened, and therefore do not appear among the baptisms. So the difference in the ratio of burials and baptisms was accounted for. In Paris children were christened directly they were born and sent within a day or two to the country to be nursed, so that their deaths did not appear among the Paris returns.[58]

The measures to check excessive spirit-drinking had been carried through in the teeth of vested interests. The reform which after this had probably the most direct effect upon the London death-rate was that which aimed at reducing the mortality among London parish children. If, in the worst years, according to the Bills, over 74 per cent of the children born in London died before they were five, parish children, that is, children in workhouses, or put out to nurse by the parish, died in still greater numbers. 'The parish infant poor's mortality,' said Hanway, 'may be called 80 or 90, or if you please, upon those received under twelve months old, 99 per cent.'[59] The impulse to social reform in London was largely the desire to lessen the terrible waste of life.

The problem of deserted children – children exposed in the streets, orphans, and the children of poor parents – had long been an urgent one in London. Christ's Hospital in its origin had been an attempt to provide for them. Sir Thomas Rowe's short-lived 'Colledg of Infants' established in 1686 under the patronage of the Middlesex Sessions was an attempt to make a better provision for parish children than boarding them out with nurses.[60] The parish workhouse movement in London which began about 1723 aimed at the same thing, but workhouses proved almost completely fatal to infants. All the horrors connected with the treatment of infants by nurses and in workhouses naturally became worse under the influence of gin.

The Foundling Hospital aimed at stopping the exposure, desertion and murder of infants. Thomas Coram the sea-captain, appalled at the sight of children exposed and dead in the streets, worked for seventeen years to establish a hospital.[61] At last in 1739 he got the support of a number of ladies of rank who signed a memorial to the Government:

> No expedient has yet been found out for preventing the murder of poor miserable infants at their birth, or suppressing the inhuman custom of exposing newly-born infants to perish in the streets; or the putting of such unhappy foundlings to wicked and barbarous nurses, who undertake to bring them up for a small and trifling sum of money, do often suffer them to starve for want of due sustenance or care, or if permitted to live either turn them into the streets to beg or steal, or hire them out to loose persons by whom they are trained up in that infamous way of living and sometimes are blinded or maimed and distorted in their limbs in order to move pity or compassion, and thereby become fitter instruments of gain to those vile merciless wretches.

Subscriptions poured in, the charter was granted in 1739, the first children were received (in houses in Hatton Garden taken temporarily), the Earl of Salisbury's estate lying north of Great Ormond Street and west of Gray's Inn Lane was bought. In 1742 the foundation-stone of the present building was laid in Lamb's Conduit Fields and one wing was inhabited in 1745. Till 1756 the number of children admitted was small and by the standards of the time the death-rate was low. Out of the 1,384 children received in those fifteen years, it was 'very remarkable', Hanway tells us, that 'only 724 . . . died in all this time'.[62] The effect of the Foundling Hospital was to reduce the burials of children within the Bills, as the foundlings were buried in the parish of St Pancras.

The financial difficulties of the Hospital, the great demand for places and the terrible records of the deaths of children in the Bills of Mortality, led the Governors to appeal to Parliament for help. This was given on condition that all children brought to the Hospital should be taken in. From June 1756 to Ladyday 1760 the Hospital opened its doors to all who brought children, the cost being borne by the Treasury. This was an attempt to provide an alternative for the parish nurse, the parish workhouse and the deserted child, owing to the notorious shortcomings of parish officers.

> It was hardly thought [said Hanway (a Governor of the Hospital)] that any more children would be sent . . . than such as had usually been exposed in streets and at people's doors . . . or died in parish workhouses where their mothers had deserted them.[63]

But the gates were besieged. Children were brought in a dying state and even stripped of their clothes, so that they might be buried at the expense of the Hospital. Many were sent from the country, and many died on the way. Infants were entrusted to carriers, wagoners and even to vagrants. Disreputable people trafficked in the conveying of children to London. Many parish officers both in London and the country sent children to the Hospital, sometimes openly, sometimes secretly. Sometimes legitimate children born in workhouses were forcibly taken from their mothers; sometimes the fathers of children took them from their mothers and sent them to the Hospital. Sometimes mothers sent their children there in order to be employed by the Governors as paid nurses to other foundlings.

The idea had been by the Foundling Hospital and subsidiary branches in the country, to supersede the poor law in so far as the care of infants was concerned. 'So far as appears,' wrote Hanway in 1759, 'the design of the Legislature is to form a new poor's law, and recommend it to be executed by men of fortune and condition. . . .'[64] But the plan of wholesale reception could not survive the abuses it gave rise to. As the number of admissions increased so the death-rate rose. The site of the Hospital, it was said, was converted into a burying-ground, and untold numbers sent from the country died on the way. There was great difficulty in providing satisfactory nurses for so many children and at that time infants brought up by hand had a poor chance of life. During the three years and ten months of wholesale admission 14,934 children were taken in of whom only 4,400 lived to be apprenticed. In February 1760 the House of Commons decided that indiscriminate reception should cease. Parliament continued to make grants for the support of the children already admitted, but the Hospital gradually reverted to a private charity and its character changed.[65] It ceased to be, properly speaking, a foundling hospital, as from 1763 children were admitted only on a statement of the particular circumstances of each case.[66]

The death-rate of the foundlings reflects the changes in the administration of the Hospital as well as in the health of London and the general treatment of children. From 1742 to 1756 a rate of over 50 per cent was regarded by Hanway as something of an achievement. Of those received during the period of wholesale admission less than a third survived to be apprenticed. After 1760 the deaths were reduced to one in four, later in the century they were one in six and by 1800 were below that rate.[67]

Hanway's experiences as a Governor convinced him that the Foundling Hospital could not provide a satisfactory alternative to the parish care of children. He therefore evolved a plan for forcing the parish officers to do their duty. First, between 1757 and 1763, he visited every workhouse in London and collected and published facts and figures as to the death-rate among infants. These were 'so melancholy that they were generally disbelieved'. His object was to bring shame and a wholesome rivalry to bear upon parish officers by pillorying some parishes and praising and encouraging those whose records were least bad. He discovered the difficulty of getting precise figures, 'some officers not chusing to say, "all our children have died".' He therefore in 1762 obtained an Act obliging all the parishes within the Bills to keep a register of infants giving minute particulars as to their reception, death or discharge, making returns to the Company of Parish Clerks (as in the case of baptisms and burials) who were to compile a yearly abstract.

In December 1763 Hanway wrote an open letter (published in the magazines and newspapers) to the vestries and parish officers within the Bills.

It is very obvious that this annual register is meant to strike alarm on the breast of those on whose humanity and circumspection the lives of these poor babes depends and not simply to inform us that such a number of them died. ... This Register is a favourite child of mine, I mean to watch the progress of it, and as far as may be in my power, to do you justice, as well as the poor infants. ... I have already the pleasure to see the Register productive of great good in some particular parishes. ...

Hanway's efforts did not slacken. He reinforced his visits to workhouses by publishing books and writing to the newspapers. Taking the returns for the first complete year, 1763, he found that in eleven parishes 291 children had been received exclusive of those discharged with their mothers within the year. Of these 16 had been discharged in 1764 and 1765, leaving 275, of whom 256 were dead by the end of 1765. These parishes he selects as examples of the best and the worst. He concludes that 'we pay very dearly in lives by not taking proper measures to counteract the effects of living in such vast crowds'.[68] The next step was to use the material provided by the registers which showed the appalling mortality among children in London workhouses, while the rate among children sent to the country to be nursed was lower. Hanway's biographer, who knew him personally, describes him as

... going from one workhouse to another in the morning, and from one Member of Parliament to another in the afternoon, for day after day, and year after year, with steady and unwearied patience, enduring every rebuff, answering every objection, and accommodating himself to every humour for the furtherance of this beneficial design almost without assistance.[69]

A parliamentary committee was appointed in December 1766 to inquire into the state of Parish Poor Infants. It examined the registers kept under the Act of 1762, and its recommendations were embodied in the important Act of 1767. This made compulsory the principles adopted by the Foundling Hospital, and already practised by certain wealthy and enlightened parishes – notably that of St James Westminster which boarded out its children with carefully selected cottagers on Wimbledon Common.[70] All parish children under six were to be sent out of London to be nursed – those under two at least five miles from the Cities of London and Westminster, those under six at least three miles. Nurses were to be paid at least 2s. 6d. a week, and for children over six at least 2s. They were to have a reward of 10s. for rearing children sent to them under nine months old.

The effect of the Act was immediate. It is said that 'the poor called it the Act for keeping children alive'.[69] Howlett estimated that the London burials were reduced by 2,240 in the first year, and that allowing for the children who returned to London and died there, the annual average reduction in the London burials was 2,100.[71] This of course was not pure gain, as some of the children must have died in the villages to which they were sent. In 1778 a parliamentary committee inquired into the state of the infant poor and the working of the Act of 1767, and found that it had produced 'very salutary effects'. They made returns (from a few parishes only) which show a great reduction in mortality from the earlier figures published by Hanway, and also show that a greater proportion of children had been reclaimed by their parents.* The figures probably reflect not only the improvement directly due to the Act, and to administrative changes made by several parishes under local Acts, but also the reduction in the consumption of gin.

The Act is a very important landmark; it also improved the position

* See Appendix II.

of parish apprentices, and its chief significance lies in the fact that for the first time legislation aimed at checking, not extravagance, but 'undue parsimony' in parish officers. It was however necessarily limited in its scope and a further cause of the decline in the burials which caused so much alarm after 1770 was the improvement in medicine and midwifery which began about the middle of the century and was accompanied by, and partly due to, an extension of medical practice among the poor. The chief factors in this extension were the lying-in charities and the dispensaries.

The impulse to lying-in charities seems to have been partly the desire of teachers of midwifery for clinical practice for their pupils, partly the alarming disproportion between births and burials before 1750. In 1739 a lying-in infirmary on a very small scale was started by Sir Richard Manningham as a school of midwifery both for medical students and midwives.[72] It was in the infirmary belonging to the workhouse of St James Westminster. In 1741 Smellie began to teach midwifery in London, and to give instruction to his pupils he established a scheme for attending poor women gratuitously in their homes, and made it a condition that all who attended his practical courses should contribute 6s. to a fund for the support of the women. He was the founder of scientific midwifery in England, raised the status of practitioners and trained over 900 pupils, exclusive of his women students. The impulse which he gave to midwifery helped to establish a number of lying-in hospitals in London.[73] In 1747 the Middlesex Hospital made arrangements for receiving maternity patients and appointed a physician accoucheur; in 1749 the Lying-in Hospital for married women, and in 1750 the City of London Lying-in Hospital were founded. Queen Charlotte's Hospital for unmarried as well as married women was opened in 1752, the Royal Maternity Hospital in 1757, the Westminster Lying-in Hospital in 1765. The Lying-in Charity for delivering poor married women at their own homes founded in 1757 was the first of a number of similar institutions. This charity gave a free training to midwives, who were not allowed to practise till they had obtained a certificate of proficiency from the physician of the charity. They were then pledged to work for it at low fees for two years in return for their training. The matrons of lying-in hospitals had to be skilled midwives.

Before the founding of these institutions the only resource for the poor woman had been the workhouse – which was used as a lying-in infirmary – or the attentions of those who often combined 'the nursing of lying-in women' with the hawking of fish or vegetables or with other less reputable occupations. 'In the nurture and management of infants as well as in the treatment of lying-in women,' wrote Dr Lettsom in 1774, 'the reformation hath equalled that of the smallpox, by these two circumstances alone incredible numbers have been rescued from the grave.'[74]

Within the space of a few years many lying-in hospitals have been established; in the lying-in charity alone near 5,000 women are delivered annually in their own houses, by persons well instructed ... whereby not only many infants, but likewise many women are saved.[75]

The records of the Lying-in Hospital certainly show a progressive reduction in the mortality of mothers and children. For the first ten years from 1749 the deaths among women averaged 1 in 42, among children, 1 in 15. By 1799–1800 the deaths had been reduced to 1 in 913 among women and 1 in 115 among children.[76]

A great improvement in the management of young children followed Dr Cadogan's book, *An Essay on the Nursing and Management of Children* (1750), which went through twenty editions in nine years. The Foundling Hospital adopted its principles and in 1754 made him their physician, so that his instructions, which included loose clothing and a simple diet, must have been widely diffused by means of the nurses to whom the foundlings were entrusted. Dr Heberden, commenting in 1808 on the decrease in the burials of children under five in the Bills of Mortality, remarks, 'if we reflect on the swathing and diet, the confinement and dirt, in which the children of the poor used till lately to be brought up, we shall cease to be surprised at this effect'.[77]

Besides the lying-in hospitals, other hospitals were added to the ancient foundations of St Bartholomew's, St Thomas's and Bedlam: the Westminster Hospital in 1719, Guy's in 1723, St George's in 1734, the London in 1740, the Middlesex in 1745, the Lock Hospital in 1746, the two smallpox hospitals (one for inoculation) in the same year, St Luke's Hospital for lunatics in 1751. Their establishment happens to coincide with that part of the century when the death-rate was at its highest, so that no immediate improvement in the health of London can be ascribed to them. And this perhaps is not surprising, as ventilation and cleanliness were reforms of the latter part of the century; hospitals were frequently ravaged by typhus which was known indiscriminately as jail or hospital fever, not to be wondered at when their wooden beds were infested with vermin.[78] Dr Percival wrote in 1771, 'it is a melancholy consideration that these charitable institutions, which are intended for the health and preservation of mankind, may too often be ranked amongst the causes of sickness and mortality'.[79] Another great hindrance to their usefulness was the deposit or security demanded in some hospitals to indemnify them for burial charges, so that, except in cases of accident, the poorest and most friendless were excluded. There were also ward fees to nurses. But some of the hospitals were run on more generous lines – the London, and the Westminster (by 1788 at least) made no charges,[80] and from the beginning it had been the principle of the Lock Hospital that no 'perishing wretch' should be refused admission. But as schools of medicine and surgery and places of clinical practice they must have been important factors in the improvement of medical science. There is evidence of a decline in their death-rate, but it was slow and there is nothing approaching the enormous saving of life due to the improvements in midwifery. In 1685 (according to Perry) deaths at St Thomas's and St Bartholomew's were 1 in 7; in 1689 at St Thomas's they were 1 in 10; in 1741 they were still 1 in 10·9; from 1773 to 1783 1 in 14; in the latter year there were improvements in cleanliness and ventilation and for the next ten years deaths were 1 in 15. From 1803 to 1813 they were 1 in 16. At St George's in 1734 deaths were 1 in 8; from 1823 to 1827 they were 1 in 9. Rebuilding which had long been urgent was then going on.[81]

The dispensary movement began in 1769. The principle of the dispensary was the establishment of a centre at which the poor might attend for advice and free medicine, while those who could not attend were visited in their homes.[82] Creighton has pointed out that medical practice in the eighteenth century lay chiefly among the richer classes, and that physicians knew little of the state of health in cellars and tenement houses. The dispensary doctors knew a great deal, and some of them published the result of their experiences.[83] Their activities had a double effect, resulting in a cumulative improvement in the health of London: the poor learned something of the rudiments of hygiene, the doctors learned to diagnose the diseases of poverty and dirt; the richer classes began to hear of the conditions under which the poor lived. As a result a new current of opinion was formed, small at first, which began to run counter to the generally accepted theory that the London poor were brutal and depraved and that their distresses were due to vice, or at the best, improvidence.

The first dispensary was founded in 1769 by Dr Armstrong in Red Lion Square 'for the Relief of the Infant Poor'.[84] After improving the lot of the poor-law children, the next step was to provide help for 'the infants of the industrious Poor'. At this time very little attention had been paid to juvenile ailments. A report of this dispensary in 1794 says:

When children are ill it is but too common an opinion, however absurd, especially among the lower class, that a physician cannot be of any use to them from their not being able to describe their complaint. Thus every old woman thinks herself as competent to prescribe as a physician.

The best known of the dispensaries was the General Dispensary founded in 1770 and usually, but incorrectly, said to be the first. Dr Lettsom claimed in 1775 that it had contributed not a little to the decrease in burials since 1770. He says that in the two great London hospitals, St Bartholomew's and St Thomas's, about 600 patients, or 1 in 13 of all admitted, died annually, while in the dispensary the deaths were not 1 in 33. He also says that by the instructions of the physicians many lives must have been saved in every part of London that would otherwise have been sacrificed to ignorance and quackery. He writes:

In the space of a very few years I have observed a total revolution in the conduct of the common people respecting their diseased friends. They have learned that most diseases are mitigated by a free admission of air, by cleanliness and by promoting instead of restraining the indulgence and care of the sick. Such instruction was new to the poor, though important to their preservation, and when we consider how late they have acquired this information, we must lament that so many centuries have elapsed before an institution like the General Dispensary became the object of public attention.[85]

Dispensaries spread rapidly in London and from London to the provinces.[86] Many dispensaries undertook inoculation and, after 1798, vaccination, while institutions for free vaccination multiplied. There was, however, a reluctance among the poorer classes to submit to vaccination, and also, Dr Lettsom says, a fatalistic attitude towards smallpox. Pictet gives a pleasant picture in 1801 of the methods of Mr Ring, a London surgeon who vaccinated gratuitously the inhabitants of whole streets at a time in poor districts. 'I do not seek them out,' said Ring, 'I do not force them at all. I discover some gossip of the street with children who will agree to try it. She does not fail to spread the result and immediately I have all the patients I can wish.' Pictet went with Ring on one of his rounds and witnessed 'the deep gratitude of mothers who looked upon him as the saviour of their children'.[87]

Dispensaries led to measures for the cure and prevention of typhus, and at last, after a virulent outbreak in 1800 and 1801, steps were taken for the isolation of fever cases.[88] The London House of Recovery in Gray's Inn Road, established by the Institution for the Cure and Prevention of Contagious Fever, was opened in February 1802. Before this time there had been no possibility of isolating poor patients. Typhus persisted in workhouses and in the hospitals, where those suffering from it were not separated from the other patients. When a fever patient was taken to the workhouse, he went in the first hackney coach or chair that could be found. Courts and alleys where cases had occurred continued to be centres of infection.

When the fever has depopulated a building by death and terror, poverty and ignorance bring new inhabitants who sicken and die or linger and relapse, and after being carried to the workhouse or the grave, leave the same pestilential apartment to their ill-fated successors. From these pest-houses concentrated contagion pours into the adjacent courts and alleys ... it is disseminated through the neighbourhood by the frequent intercourse of the needy, who repeat ... their visits in endeavours to supply each daily want, who are frequently reduced to beg, borrow, or pawn one article to enable them to buy another.... Through a medium of pawnbrokers, old-clothes men, rag-shops, and by contact in a variety of ways, the poison is communicated where least suspected.[89]

The 'fever' which was perennial in London with occasional epidemics, seems first to have been identified with jail fever by Dr John Hunter in 1779. He found it to be the result of poverty, overcrowding and dirt.[90] The terrible epidemic of 1740–1 had been regarded as a mysterious visitation in some way connected with the dearth it followed.[11] Dispensary doctors soon became familiar with it and some lost their lives from it. When the House of Recovery was opened a committee was appointed to organize the cleansing of infected houses by whitewashing with hot lime,[91] and printed instructions were circulated. Fever cases were admitted immediately without waiting for the subscriber's letter and the approval of the weekly board as was general in other hospitals.[92] To avoid infecting hackney coaches patients were carried in a litter with a detachable linen lining (this was mobbed when it first appeared).

The committee soon discovered that there were places where the infection had continued for many years, and they offered to whitewash and cleanse those parts of London which were particularly subject to fever.[93] The effects in the parish of St Clement Danes were so marked that the Vestry voted twenty guineas to the Institution and recommended their successors to make a liberal annual donation.[94] The House of Recovery was supported by the London parishes, though at first there was said to be reluctance in some workhouses to send their fever patients there. Some parishes subscribed to the Institution, others paid two guineas a week with each patient.[95] In May 1804 the Institution was given a Treasury grant of £3,000 on condition of raising an additional sum by subscription, and with this it was able to buy one of the smallpox hospitals in Pancras Road – a large building in which part was set aside for scarlet fever.

The result of these measures was seen in a sudden drop in the number of fever cases, due partly of course to the subsiding of the epidemic of 1800–1, partly to a period of war-prosperity in London.[96] While the annual average mortality from fever in the eighteenth century had been 3,188, the deaths for 1802 were 2,201, and by 1815 had been reduced to 1,033. The number of fever patients at the Carey Street Dispensary, which had previously averaged 250 a year, was only 4 in 1804. There had also been a great reduction in the mortality of the disease; one in four of those attacked is said to have died before the House of Recovery was opened; during its first nine years 785 patients were admitted, 696 of whom had been cured, a mortality of less than 1 in 9, though some were 'sinking under the fatal effects of dram-drinking'.[97] In 1810 Dr Lettsom regarded typhus as 'almost extinct' in London,[98] and the experiences of the doctors of the House of Recovery taught them the possibility of stamping out the disease by sanitary reform. They received certificates of health from the infected districts where they carried out measures of disinfection.[99] Though no fundamental reforms were attempted till after the cholera epidemics many years later, the comprehensive measures urged by Dr Stanger, one of the doctors of the Institution, are a remarkable anticipation of future policy. These included the widening of lanes and alleys, the proportioning of the space to the number of persons in manufactories, workhouses, prisons, hospitals and public charities – to be enforced by inspection. He suggested that the inhabiting of cellars should be regulated if not forbidden, that there should be public baths and an abundant water supply and that the labouring classes should be exempted from the window tax. As these measures could not be effected without interfering with private property and domestic economy, he urged that they should be enforced by legislation and some years later Dr Bateman made similar proposals.[99]

The methods of the House of Recovery had been anticipated by the workhouse infirmary of Marylebone. While many London workhouses were crowded, ramshackle, insanitary places, perennially ravaged by fever, standards of order and cleanliness and even sanitation were being evolved in the richer and better managed parishes, and Marylebone was fortunate in its physician, Dr Rowley, who was an advocate of the newer methods of treating fevers by bathing, fresh air and scrupulous cleanliness instead of by what he calls 'the inflammatory practice'. In 1793 Rowley said that he prescribed at the Infirmary for about 400 patients weekly and he estimated the annual practice there at '14,000 prescriptions'. In 1804 he described the Infirmary as 'an hospital as extensive in seeing numerous patients as any in London or perhaps in Europe, especially in admitting putrid fevers'. He then, after nearly twenty years' practice there, claimed that for years they had 'not lost five or six in a hundred in the most malignant putrid fevers, scarlet fever, confluent smallpox and other putrid affections', while by the old-fashioned methods the death-rate was from 60 to 80 per cent.[100]

Even in the eighteenth century workhouse infirmaries in London were beginning to count as supplementary hospitals; they could not, like other hospitals, refuse to receive patients suffering from certain diseases and therefore they were peculiarly liable to be ravaged by infection, unless like Marylebone they could make arrangements for isolation. The credit for the first maternity institution in the country (1739) belongs to the parish infirmary of St James Westminster.

Other medical charities were founded in the eighteenth century, too many to enumerate here. One may be just mentioned, as illustrating the growing realization of social needs, the Samaritan Society, founded in 1791 by some of the Governors of the London Hospital for the after-care of patients who on discharge were unfit for work, or unable to find it. Patients were provided with clothes, with journey-money, sometimes sent for a visit to Bath or to the sea.[101]

The causes of improvement which have been considered were chiefly due to conscious effort – and in the first instance largely to a realization of the horrors implied in the returns of the Bills of Mortality. There were of course many others. Contemporaries laid stress on the less crowded manner of living, the great improvement in the streets of London after the succession of Paving Acts beginning in 1762, the removing of the signs and obstructions that impeded the circulation of air, the greater attention of scavengers and the influence of improved agriculture in creating a demand for the filth of the streets as manure. The better drainage of London and the increased supply of water and fuel were much remarked on.[102] The increasing consumption of tea and sugar was, in spite of moralists, sometimes admitted to be beneficial.[103]

The record of the causes of death in the Bills of Mortality,* unscientific though it was, reflects the social history of the period. Intermittent fever was prevalent and fatal in London between 1661 and 1665; for some years after the Great Fire it was very rare, but was epidemic from 1677 to 1685 and fairly common in the early part of the eighteenth century. With improvements in the paving and draining of London it was greatly reduced, and Dr Blane found that it occurred chiefly among labourers from marshy districts, especially Kent and Essex. Scurvy declined at the end of the seventeenth century, and during the eighteenth vanished as a cause of death.[104] This is ascribed to the changes which had provided winter fodder for cattle, and so prevented the necessity of salting meat for the winter, and to the plentiful supply of fresh vegetables. The annual average of deaths from fever or typhus decreased after 1770. Deaths from rickets declined steadily, this was

* See Appendix I, *D* and *E*.

attributed to 'more maternal attention to the suckling and rearing of children'.[105] The disuse of the old system of tight swaddling clothes probably saved many lives.

The diseases of infants recorded as 'convulsions and chrysoms' were at their worst between 1728 and 1757.

In and about London [wrote a controversialist on the population question in 1757] a prodigious number of children are cruelly murdered by those infernals called nurses. These infernal monsters throw a spoonful of gin, spirits of wine or Hungary water down a child's throat, which instantly strangles the babe. When the searchers come to inspect the body, and inquire what distemper caused the death, it is answered, 'convulsions'. This occasions the articles of convulsions in the Bills so much to exceed all others.[106]

Between 1718 and 1751 the deaths from dropsy were, it was said in 1801, 'one-tenth greater than at any period before or since'.[107] Deaths recorded under the heads of 'apoplexy, palsy and suddenly' gradually and constantly increased and about doubled in the course of the century (the increase must be discounted to the extent of the growth of the population). Dr Black thought this increase in paralytic diseases due to the mechanical arts where lead or quicksilver was employed.[108] After 1770 smallpox increased in London, it is said because inoculation, though a protection to the inoculated, spread the disease owing to ineffective isolation.[109] After the introduction of vaccination it rapidly decreased.

The improvement is the more surprising as it happened in spite of the general rise in prices and during a period when bad seasons were frequent. Between 1763 and 1773 there was a check in the development of foreign trade, high prices were acutely felt, and there was much distress in London. The trade crisis of 1792–3 was followed by a time of yet higher prices. Drink, ignorance and dirt were positive checks on the population of London whose effects progressively diminished. The results of these changes were cumulative, they imply a corresponding improvement in manners and morals which in its turn reacted on the health of the people. The extent of the improvement has been obscured, first by eighteenth-century observers and moralists who maintained that manners and morals were progressively deteriorating and imaginatively assumed that a state of unspoiled simplicity had prevailed in the early part of the century. This attitude though unhistorical, is evidence of a growing sense of public decency and of a growing knowledge of social conditions. Petty had summarily classified the poor as 'the vile and brutish part of mankind'. Colquhoun and the writers of his day who were most conscious of the shortcomings of the poor did not ascribe them to original sin but to defects in the laws and the police.

Later writers find a mass of evidence that at the end of the eighteenth and in the early nineteenth century the state of things was appalling and sometimes fail to realize that before this time worse conditions were accepted as inevitable. Everything is relative. As the lights of London seemed amazingly brilliant at the end of the eighteenth century, and, after gas had replaced the old oil-lamps, these same lights appeared in retrospect so incredibly dim, so, at the beginning of the nineteenth century, did London seem clean and healthy compared with the unforgotten past. Mr and Mrs Webb thus visualize in 1922 the London which contemporaries regarded so differently:

To any Englishman of the present day . . . transported to the London or Birmingham of . . . a century ago, the most striking feature would be the 'general nastiness' of the ground he trod upon, defiled with an almost incredible accumulation of every kind of filth . . . the dense swarms of pallid, undersized and wretchedly clad wage-earners, who constituted all but a tiny minority of the population, might have been noticed . . . to be perpetually suffering from ill-health, and to be in fact, practically all either sickening for, or recovering from, attacks of what we should now call enteric or typhus.[110]

Yet the most experienced London doctors of the time were deeply impressed with the disappearance or decline of the diseases of dirt and 'sordid living' that had formerly ravaged London.

Anyone who will be at the pains to compare the conditions of London and all the great towns of England during the seventeenth century with their actual state [said Heberden in 1807], and note the corresponding changes which have taken place in diseases, can hardly fail to consider cleanliness and ventilation as the principal agents in producing this reform. And to this may be added . . . the increased use of fresh provisions and the introduction of a variety of vegetables among the ranks of our people. The same spirit of improvement which has constructed our sewers and widened our streets and removed the nuisances with which they abounded, and dispersed the inhabitants over a wider surface and taught them to love airy apartments and frequent changes of linen, has spread itself into the country where it has drained the marshes, cultivated the wastes, enclosed the commons. . . . Few have adverted with the attention it deserves to the prodigious mortality occasioned formerly by annual returns of epidemical fevers, of bowel complaints and other consequences of poor and sordid living to which we are entire strangers.[111]

Dr Blane (of St Thomas's Hospital) and Dr Bateman (of the Fever Hospital or House of Recovery) were equally impressed with the improvement and ascribed it to the same causes. After an epidemic of typhus in 1817–18 had followed the comparative immunity since 1801, Dr Marshall gave the following evidence on the diseases of London to a parliamentary committee:

At one time in this country we had well-marked aguish and asthenic or inflammatory complaints: Now we have few instances, at least in London, of pure agues, and our inflammatory complaints degenerate into asthenic congestions or defluctions. We have had a change from nervous to bilious ailments, and this not founded on the caprice of medical systems, but in the nature of the complaints themselves. In Sydenham's time . . . it was computed that sixty-six thousand out of the hundred thousand died in London of fevers. This large proportion of fevers is now supplanted by other diseases; and even our fevers are not of the same complexion they were in those days, for we are strangers to the symptoms in them denoting their former pestilential or malignant quality. But certainly, if any causes could have contributed to the immunity we enjoy from the plague and bad fevers, they are to be found in the greater cleanliness and less crowded state of the inhabitants, with the widening of the streets, and the better and more general construction of common sewers and drains, to which may be added the profusion of water now distributed through the metropolis.[112]

Thus the doctors. We can also compare with the impressions ascribed to the modern Englishman transported to the London of the eighteen-twenties, those of a tireless investigator of social conditions who remembered the London of the seventeen-eighties, a London even then vastly improved since 1750. Francis Place, after commenting on the improvement in health shown in the fall in the death-rate between 1700 and 1821, remarks on the visible improvement in the appearance of the people within his own memory. 'There are no such groups of half-starved, miserable, scald-headed children with rickety limbs and bandy legs as there were in the days of my youth,' he writes in 1824, 'neither is there anything like the same mortality amongst them.'[113] And again after a tour of inspection through the poorest parts of London, from the Tower to Limehouse by the water-side, and back by Ratcliffe Highway and Rosemary Lane:

I carefully observed the children and can safely say they are equal in every respect and in many respects superior to the children of tradesmen in much more wealthy districts . . . within my memory. Although it was Friday, the children were clean and healthy. The children of tradesmen . . . keeping good houses in the Strand for instance . . . all of them when I was a boy had lice in their hair. The children I examined today do not seem to be at all troubled with these vermin. In many of the narrow alleys there were numbers of very poor children, but even these were cleanly compared with former times, for among these, the most miserable part of the community, there were evident gradations, matching the poverty and habits of the parents. Few were so wretchedly clothed or so filthy as numbers used to be. Many carried with them some mark of the wish of their poor parents to do their best for them, a clean rag of a shirt, or a frock, or some such thing was common among them. Multitudes now wear shoes and stockings . . . who within my recollection never wore any. . . . I did not see one child with a *scald head*, nor one with bandy legs called cheese-cutters, that is with the shin-bone bowed out. The number of children who had 'cheese-cutters' was formerly so great that if an estimate were now made it would not be believed.

Much of the improvement he ascribes to the cheapness of cotton for garments and bed-hangings and the ease with which they could be washed. He found out the prices of these things in the shops of East London: stays, 3s. 6d. and 2s. 6d. a pair, printed cotton from 4d. to 2s. a yard, white cotton stockings from 11d. upwards; rugs, counterpanes and blankets were correspondingly cheap. 'These prices,' he says, 'show the facility with which the working people who have any means at all may provide themselves.'[113] He remembered the time when

. . . the wives of journeymen, tradesmen and shopkeepers either wore leather stays, or what were called full-boned stays. . . . These were never washed although worn day by day for years. The wives and grown daughters of tradesmen, and gentlemen even, wore petticoats of camblet, lined with dyed linen, stuffed with wool and horsehair and quilted, these were also worn day by day till they were rotten.

A great change was produced by improvement in the manufacture of cotton goods.

These were found to be less expensive and as it was necessary to wash them, cleanliness followed almost as a matter of course. . . . This very material change was not confined to the better sort of the people as they were called . . . it descended, although rather slowly, to the very meanest of the people, all of whom so far as respects females, wear washing clothes. Cleanliness in matters of dress was necessarily accompanied by cleanliness in other particulars, and this again by the desire to possess more conveniences, and better utensils, and thus again the houses of tradesmen and the rooms of working people came to be kept in better condition, to be better furnished and in all respects neater than formerly. Part of the money formerly spent at the alehouse was applied for these commendable purposes, and yet they were condemned as luxuries, by moralists and religionists and magistrates.[114]

He summarizes the causes of the decline in the London death-rate between 1700 and 1821.

Much of this is attributable to the increased salubrity of the Metropolis, much to the increase of surgical or medical knowledge, much also to the change that has taken place not only in London, but all over the country, in the habits of the working classes, who are infinitely more moral and more sober, more cleanly in their persons and their dwellings, than they were formerly, particularly the women, partly from the success of the cotton manufacture . . . partly from increased knowledge of domestic concerns and general management of children. Notwithstanding the vice, the misery and disease which still abounds in London, its general prevalence has been greatly diminished.[115]

CHAPTER 2

HOUSING AND THE GROWTH
OF LONDON

London, the Metropolis of Great Britain, has been complained of for ages past as a kind of monster, with a head enormously large, and out of all proportion to its body. And yet, at the juncture when this complaint was first made (about 200 years ago) the buildings of London hardly advanced beyond the City bounds. . . . If therefore the increase of buildings, begun at such an early period, was looked upon to be no better than a wen or excrescence upon the body-politic, what must we think of those number-less streets and squares which have been added since!

Tucker, *Four Letters to the Earl of Shelburne*, 2nd edition, 1783, p. 44.

IN the seventeenth and eighteenth centuries the records of population and of the number of houses – such as they are – show London expanding irregularly from its centre, the City within the Walls, in a succession of waves. The earliest and most central extensions first ceased to expand, having spent their force and filled up the space available, and then the districts which they cover tended to grow less rather than more thickly populated.* In the reign of Elizabeth the suburbs of London grew in a long line. On the west, noblemen's houses fringed the Thames along the Strand from Temple Bar to Charing Cross and the north side of the Strand was also built upon. On the east a growing seafaring and industrial population was strung out along the river from the Tower to Ratcliffe. Houses had begun to fill the space immediately north and east of the City and to spread along the roads of Shoreditch and Whitechapel. They extended from Smithfield to St John's Clerkenwell and along Holborn towards St Giles. There was also a great increase of population, largely of artisans, in Southwark.[1]

Already in the sixteenth century the distinction had begun to show itself between the industrial districts east of the City and south of the Thames, and a district of wealth and leisure stretching towards West-minster and the Court. This rich district, however, had its poor, who were the poorer for having no industries to depend on. By Elizabeth's

* See Appendix III *B*.

reign there was a very poor population clustered round the Abbey of Westminster, 'for the most part without trade or mystery . . . many of them wholly given to vice and idleness'.[2]

This citie of Westminster [said Norden in 1593] is knowne to have no generall trade whereby releefe might be administred unto the common sort, as by marchandise, clothing or such like . . . had they not therefore some other meanes, the common sorte could not be susteined. The first and principall meanes . . . is hir Majesties residence at Whitehall or St. Jeames, whence if hir Grace be long absent, the poore people forthwith complaine of penurie and want, of a hard and miserable world.[3]

According to Petty, in 1662, London grew westward to escape the 'fumes, steams and stinks of the whole easterly pyle', the prevailing wind being from the west, 'the pallaces of the greatest men' and the dwellings of those who depended upon them moved towards Westminster, and the old great houses of the City, became, he says, halls for companies or were turned into tenements.[4] The process was much hastened by the Fire.[5]

In the seventeenth century houses surrounded Soho and Leicester Fields; much of the parishes of St Giles in the Fields and Clerkenwell was built upon. Covent Garden (the convent garden) was built over and became a separate parish, though it was an enclave in St Martin's – now no longer in the Fields. The Seven Dials were built and streets spread out beyond the Haymarket and St James's Church to St James's Street. There was much unobtrusive building in the eastern parishes; Great Russell Street was built about 1670 and for more than a century looked northward over open country.

In the first half of the eighteenth century Cavendish Square, Hanover Square, Grosvenor Square and New Bond Street with the adjacent streets were built, while the eastern parishes and Clerkenwell continued to fill up their empty spaces. The fashionable world was moving westwards from Covent Garden, Soho and St Giles and many houses there were turned into tenements. In the second half of the century there was a new kind of building development. Hitherto London had crept outwards gradually (it seemed to contemporaries an amazingly rapid progress) along the lines of existing roads or country lanes. Roads were now made which opened up new tracts of country for building purposes.

Among these were the roads from Westminster and Blackfriars Bridges which opened up parts of Lambeth and St George's Fields. Still more important was the New Road from Paddington to Islington. This was made across fields in 1756-7 and different sections of it are now known as the Marylebone Road, Euston Road and Pentonville Road. After 1750 Marylebone grew rapidly, and various building estates were developed in the parish of St Pancras opened up by the New Road. Speculative builders built on St George's Fields.

During this second half of the century roads and improvement Acts for opening thoroughfares and clearing away dilapidated and obstructive buildings and the great increase of warehouses in the City and the bordering parishes on the north and east reduced the population of the central parts of London, a process which was hastened towards the end of the century by the migration of families from the City to the newer parts of London, especially Marylebone and St Pancras. The building of the London Docks cleared away a number of small and insanitary dwellings.

The dominant fact in the development of London from the time of Elizabeth has been the cleavage between the East and West, accentuated by the position of the City between the two. Many factors have combined to produce this, and the process once started has been cumulative: as poor people flocked into a district the well-to-do withdrew.[6] While West London was developed largely by the laying out of streets and squares on long leases, regulated by private and local Acts, East London grew obscurely, its development apparently influenced by the customs (confirmed by statute) of the great liberty of the manors of Stepney and Hackney, by which the copy-holders were empowered to grant leases of thirty-one years without fine to the lord of the manor, under penalty of forfeiture of the copy-hold if a longer lease was granted.[7]

Stow complains that forty years before he wrote there were no houses from St Katherine's eastwards along the river, while in 1598 there was 'a continual street or filthy strait passage with alleys of small tenements or cottages built, inhabited by sailors' victuallers, almost to Ratcliffe. . . .' The road from Aldgate to Whitechapel Church had likewise been built along and the adjoining common field was also 'pestered with cottages and alleys'.

But this common field I say being some time the beauty of this City on that part, is so encroached upon with building of filthy cottages, and with the other purprestures [encroachments], enclosures and laystalls (notwithstanding all proclamations and acts of parliament to the contrary) that in some places it scarce remaineth a sufficient highway for the meeting of carriages and drovers of cattle.

In the same way from St Mary Spittle to Shoreditch there was 'a continuous building of small and base tenements for the most part lately erected'. From Shoreditch buildings extended 'a good flight shot' towards Kingsland, Newington and Tottenham. Southwark was undergoing similar developments.

The character of the inhabitants of the nineteen parishes and hamlets included in the easterly district of the Tower Hamlets (the hamlets being 'as numerous as most parishes in England') is thus described by the justices in 1684: '... the people for the most part consist of weavers and other manufacturers and of seamen and such who relate to shipping and are generally very factious and poore'.[8] The contrast between the two Londons was commented on by Archenholtz about 1780:

... the east end, especially along the shores of the Thames, consists of old houses, the streets there are narrow, dark and ill-paved; inhabited by sailors and other workmen who are employed in the construction of ships and by a great part of the Jews. The contrast between this and the West end is astonishing: the houses here are mostly new and elegant; the squares are superb, the streets straight and open. ... If all London were as well built, there would be nothing in the world to compare with it.[9]

The contrast was already marked by the very beginning of the eighteenth century. A survey of the great parish of Stepney and its hamlets in 1703 shows how these had developed.* There was much pasture or arable and garden ground but the hamlets were in different stages of development into closely packed urban communities, networks of lanes, courts and alleys.[10] Spitalfields was already almost completely built over.[11] Bethnal Green was mostly open land, and in the middle of the hamlet there were buildings on each side of Dog Row, suggesting an agricultural community. But at its western side, and merging with

* See Appendix III. *B* for the formation of parishes out of the hamlets of Stepney.

Spitalfields there was a district densely built upon and evidently industrial. The same manner of building is seen in Ratcliffe, Limehouse and Wapping-Stepney (afterwards the parish of St George's in the East). Shadwell had already become a separate parish. Mile End New Town was already beginning to be built over. In Mile End Old Town and Poplar the buildings are comparatively few, but even in Stow's time buildings were almost contiguous from Ratcliffe to Poplar, 'shipwrights . . . and other marine men' having built 'many large and strong houses for themselves and smaller for sayiers'. The poverty of Bethnal Green especially, owing to its population of journeymen weavers, is repeatedly a subject of complaint in the eighteenth century.[12] Over the open spaces wandered 'common sewers' which flowed through or past these crowded communities; in Limehouse one flowed down the middle of one of the principal thoroughfares, Nightingale Lane, off which were courts and alleys.[10]

According to the surveys, there are no large houses, except Bishop's Hall, or Bishop Bonner's House in Bethnal Green, a landmark in the fields, long fallen from its ancient glory as a country house of the Bishops of London when the See owned the manors of Stepney and Hackney. The days when wealthy citizens had country houses in the district were already legendary by 1735, when we are told that there were remains of houses scattered about which survived from those times. The house for instance of one John Kirbie who died in 1578 having built 'a fair house upon Bethnal-green' was supposed to be that known as the Blind Beggar's House.[13] The rapid growth of the district appears from the parish registers of Stepney and its daughter parishes: according to these (which tend to underrate the growth of population) the population of the area covered by the original parish trebled between 1590 and 1630 and multiplied thirteen times in the two hundred years before 1795.[14]

In the eighteenth century the metropolis was made up of a number of self-contained communities to a far greater extent than it is now. This was due partly to the difficulty of getting from one part of the town to the other, partly to the more rigid lines between classes, trades and occupations, partly to the dangerous character of many districts to those who were at all well dressed, partly to the intense individualism of local government.[15] By the end of the century the peculiarities of classes and localities had already lessened. In 1792 Boswell and Windham, advised nearly ten years before by Johnson to explore 'the wonderful extent and variety of London' with its different modes of life 'such ... as very few could even imagine', made a tour of discovery to Wapping, 'but', says Boswell, 'whether from that uniformity which has in modern times, in a great degree, spread through every part of the Metropolis, or from our want of sufficient exertion, we were disappointed.'

The poorest parts of eighteenth-century London – the dilapidated courts and alleys, the crumbling tenements and the dangerous districts – were chiefly in the belt which had grown up round the City between the reign of Elizabeth and the end of the seventeenth century. That is, they had for the most part been built during the period of restrictions on new buildings, on the dividing of houses and on the taking of 'inmates' or lodgers. When London began to expand beyond the ancient limits of the City, the growth was regarded with horror. For about a hundred years attempts were made to restrain building on new foundations. This policy was completely ineffective in checking the growth of London, but it did affect the process of expansion.

It was feared that such numbers of people would give rise to disorders of all kinds, that the danger of plague would be increased and that provisions would be dearer. The new buildings were resented by the City and feared by the queen who dreaded masterless men and the conspiracies of foreigners. 'There was great confluence hither out of the counties,' says Strype,

... of such persons as were of the poorer sorts of trades and occupations ... they took abundance of apprentices and kept them not their full time according to law. ... The preservation of the people in health seeming impossible to continue where such great numbers were brought to dwell in small rooms, whereof a great part were very poor and such as must live by begging or worse means, and they heaped up together and in a way smothered with many families of children and servants in the house. And the plague ... when it might happen in the City would (by a contiguity of buildings) spread ... and so a danger to the Queen's own life and the spreading of a mortality over the whole nation.[16]

Hence the first proclamation against new buildings and inmates in 1580 defined a policy which was fitfully followed for about a century.

The growing industrial population had to go somewhere. It was excluded for the most part from the City liberties because these new-comers, native and foreign, were not freemen and were therefore forbidden to exercise their trades there. It settled on the north and east of London and in Southwark. Tudor and Stuart proclamations against new buildings tended to drive it into those places where the authorities of City or county could be virtually defied. To this probably is due the crowding at an early date with a poor population of the precinct of St Katherine's by the Tower,[17] of the liberty of East Smithfield, of parts of Southwark, and of places in the great liberty of the manors of Stepney and Hackney belonging to the Wentworth family. The early growth of east London was of course also due to the demands of the water-borne trades and the necessity of riverside victualling houses for seafaring people.

In short, proclamations could not stop the

... strong propensive in the people for building new houses, such flocking there was notwithstanding to the City continually and such numbers of people (and they for the most part idle vagrant persons) ... filling the houses with inmates.[16]

It was, however, natural that houses built under the blight of a possible order that they should be razed to the ground for infringing the proclamation should be wretched places, as far as possible out of sight in courts and alleys. Such places could hardly have a secure title. East London as Stow describes it at the end of the sixteenth century began its building development by an extension of 'small and base tenements' often encroachments on the highway or the common field, set up under the ban of the authorities to provide shelter for increasing numbers of artisans and poor people.

The effect of the proclamations upon existing houses was to set their owners upon patching up tumble-down buildings, adding to them and digging cellars under them. These attempts to get round the letter of the proclamations were repeatedly denounced.[18] In 1625 it was forbidden to

... support or strengthen any buildings so ruinous and old as are unfit to be continued, by digging of cellars and bringing up newe back walls, by erecting new chimneys and staircases, by placing pieces of timber, by setting on new roofs or rafters and thrusting out of dormers, knitting and fastening to gether the said new additions unto the old timber by barres and crampes of iron, and other like devices. . . .

On the other hand, in 1607 the building upon the inner court or yard of an existing house had been expressly sanctioned.

The measures against new buildings, both in practice and intention, were directed against dwellings for the poor. The Elizabethan statute against new buildings, inmates and divided houses (1593) exempted houses 'fit for inhabitants of the better sort' though there was a clause allowing mariners, sailors and shipwrights to build near Thames side – victualling houses excepted. The Act aimed at houses 'fit only to receive poor people and vagrants', says an apologist for new buildings in Charles II's reign,

. . . for it would be very strange, if noblemen and gentlemen might not build houses for their habitations which are ornaments to the place as the Square in St James Fields . . . and other places built by virtue of his majesty's letters patent and the express contrivance of his officers.[19]

To the Stuarts the building proclamations were one of many similar ways of making money with a characteristic element of paternalism. The well-to-do paid for the privilege of building. For instance in 1634 Lord Maynard compounded for some twenty houses built in Tuttle (Tothill) Street by a fine of £500.[20] Courtiers obtained licenses to build and were active in proceedings against the less privileged who ignored the proclamations. Those who could not afford a fine, and whose houses could be regarded as nuisances ran the risk of having their new buildings razed to the ground, while they themselves were sometimes imprisoned by a decree of the Star Chamber.

Mixed and incompatible motives ran riot in the proclamations of James I. He aimed at stopping the growth of London, at raising money for the Crown from the builders of houses, at rewarding his courtiers, at persuading his subjects that his object was not pecuniary profit, at turning London from sticks into bricks by encouraging building in brick and clearing away the many wooden sheds and hovels thatched with reeds.[21] Yet brick was still only possible for the comparatively well-to-do. Exceptions were made permitting wood for houses occupied by a 'retayling shopkeeper' or situated in 'obscure or mean lanes and alleys'.[22]

If proclamations could not prevent building, still less could they prevent the subdividing of houses and the taking of lodgers. Stables and warehouses were turned into tenements. In the parish of St Lawrence Pountney about 1583 a brew-house was divided into thirty-six tenements and some fifty years later two of the thirty-six were again subdivided, most of the occupants being (in 1637) dependent on the parish. The Company of Free Masons in James I's reign divided their common hall into five tenements, inhabited by poor people.[23]

In spite of the ineffectiveness of proclamations against new buildings and the chicanery and oppression to which they gave rise in practice, the principle of stopping the monstrous growth of London was generally approved. Cromwell endorsed the policy of the Stuarts by an Act of 1656 forbidding new buildings with less than four acres of land within ten miles of London and imposing a fine of a year's rent on all houses built since 1620. In 1678 there was a proposal in Parliament to raise money by a similar fine on all houses (other than those rebuilt after the Fire) built since Oliver's Act. At this time the restrictions on building on new foundations though widely disregarded were still considered enforceable in law. In 1673 Lady Wentworth obtained a patent from the king enabling her to build or grant building leases for houses on West Heath on the road to Stratford Bow, and within the hamlet of Bethnal Green, suitable for 'mariners and manufacturers' notwithstanding the building restrictions.[24] This, however, was probably to secure a good title and to escape litigation; the days when houses could be razed to the ground by Star Chamber decree were over.

The dominating fear after the Restoration was the increase of poor people in London, especially in the newly built parts of Westminster, and a shortage of labour and decay of rents in the country. 'At this end of the town,' said Sir John Duncombe in the House of Commons in 1675, 'whole fields go into new buildings and are turned into alehouses filled with necessitous people.' He proposed to restrict the building of houses to those in which each storey was at least twelve feet high with four rooms on a floor.[25] 'Nothing decays rents in the country like new buildings in London,' said Mr Solicitor Winnington in 1678, urging a tax on new buildings.

Labourers in the country at sixpence and eightpence a day come here and turn coachmen and footmen and get a little house and live lazily, and in the country the farmer is constrained to pay sixteen or eighteen pence a day and therefore can pay less rent.[26]

There were later proposals to restrict buildings and even in 1709 a Bill was brought in to restrain the building of houses on new foundations in London and Westminster; it called forth a number of petitions from those interested in various building schemes and was dropped.[27]

It seems probable that the peculiar squalor and infamy of some of the courts and alleys built in the seventeenth century is partly due to the building policy begun by Elizabeth and carried on by the Stuarts and Cromwell. Buildings of a sort were put up in yards behind thoroughfares and in the courts of existing houses and by encroachments on waste land. The object must have been to escape notice and build in such a way that demolition would be no great loss. Overcrowding and poverty continued the process long after the restrictions had been given up. The results in the older parts of Westminster were described in 1839 when the evils recorded had been of long standing, and had indeed in the very place described diminished since the eighteenth century.

Another of the peculiarities which this district presents is the number of middlemen it contains; these generally possess themselves of a house or houses with gardens . . . here they erect, in open defiance of all building or sewers acts, a number of tenements of the most wretched description and to which the only access is by a passage through one of the front houses; in process of time these become lanes or courts or alleys or buildings or yards. These tenements are divided into separate rooms and let weekly by the middleman. . . . These places are most of them very old and very slightly built, frequently with boards held together by iron hoops, are so utterly destitute of every convenience that the heretofore pleasant gardens of Tothill are most terrible nuisances.[28]

It had long been the custom to build in courts and alleys at right angles more or less with the few thoroughfares. Some of these courts were pleasant dignified places with the free-stone pavements so much admired by Strype and were sometimes closed at night with a gate. There were however, in densely populated districts, courts within courts and alleys behind alleys forming perfect labyrinths and suggesting by their ground plan that closes and yards had been progressively and in a haphazard way covered with buildings. Such buildings were often mere encroachments. Even the thoroughfares were encroached upon. A temporary stall or shed would imperceptibly grow into a permanent building. The common fields existing in many of the parishes round London dwindled or disappeared, not by enclosure Acts. Holinshed records that the common at Mile End

... was sometimes, yea, in the memory of men yet living, a large mile long (from Whitechapell to Stepenheth [Stepney] church), and therefore called Mile End Greene; but now at this present, by greedie (and as seemeth to me, unlawfull) inclosures and building of houses, notwithstanding hir Maiestie's proclamation to the contrarie, it remaineth (1587) scarse halfe a mile in length.[29]

Two things are conspicuous in the London of the eighteenth century. One, the number of old ruinous houses which frequently collapsed. In different stages of decay they were patched together and let as tenement houses, common lodging-houses or brothels, or were left empty and derelict, inhabited 'only by such as paid no rent', vagrants, beggars, runaway apprentices. At midnight, according to the writer of *Low-life* (1764), 'houses which are left open and are running to ruin are filled with beggars, some of whom are asleep, while others are pulling down the timber and packing it up to sell to washer-women and clear starchers'.[30] To Samuel Johnson in 1738 London was a place where 'falling houses thunder on your head'. When a messenger ran into a City tavern with an urgent piece of news, the instant supposition (in 1718) was that he had come to warn the inmates that the house was falling.[31] By the end of the century there had been some improvement, but in 1796 the *Annual Register* records the collapse of two houses in Houghton Street, Clare Market, sixteen people being buried in the ruins.

The collapse of new or half-built houses is frequently commented on in eighteenth-century newspapers. It was usually ascribed to defective bricks.

Let any person attend to the continual accounts given in the papers of the number of half-built houses that tumble down before they can be finished [said the *London Chronicle* in 1764], and he will tremble for those who are to inhabit the many piles of new buildings that are daily rising in this metropolis. When we consider the practice among some of the brickmakers about this town, we shall not wonder at the consequence, though we must shudder

at the evil. The encrease of building has encreased the demand and consequently the price of bricks. The demand for bricks has raised the price of
brick earth so greatly that the makers are tempted to mix the slop of the
streets, ashes, scavenger's dirt and everything that will make the brick earth
or clay go as far as possible.[32]

Exactly the same complaints had been made twenty years before. To
remedy the evils an Act had been passed giving the Company of Tilers
and Brickmakers power to search for defective bricks and impose fines
on those not of the standard size and not made by the approved
methods. This made things worse than ever. The members of the
Company evaded the Act or perverted it in their own interest and after
a heated controversy a new Act was passed giving equal powers of
inspection to the Company and to the justices in Sessions.[33] This also
was a failure and the attempt to regulate the making of bricks was given
up.[34]

Ruinous old houses and ramshackle new ones were often the result of
uncertainty of title and short leases. Furtive building and the appropria-
tion of scraps of land, the purprestures and concealments so common
in the seventeenth century, naturally produced bad titles. When building or re-building schemes on a large scale were undertaken, a private
Act was generally necessary to enable long leases to be granted and to
provide for uncertain or litigated titles.

It often happens [said Noorthouck] that when houses in obscure parts of
London belong to indigent or avaritious persons, when clear titles cannot be
made out for them, or while such titles are in the course of tedious litigation,
they are suffered to stand in a ruinous condition, to the great hazard of those
who are tempted by trifling rents to risk their lives in them.[35]

Much property in London was church or other corporate property;
corporate owners and those with life interests in estates were apt to
regard only their own immediate profit. Thus Killegrew, Master of the
Savoy from 1663 to 1700, had by his patent the right of granting leases
for three lives. He did this by taking heavy fines and reserving a nominal
quit rent. The result was that the rents became 'concealed' – many
people lived in the Savoy rent free, 'nobody appearing to make any
demand from them'.[36] As their title was not good however, they were
liable to be dislodged by force or stratagem. Lodgers or servants would

turn the occupier's goods into the street and bar the door against him. Sometimes an entry would be forced from outside and the invader would entrench himself against attempts to dislodge him. People who had thus jumped a claim would bequeath or dispose of the tenements thus acquired. In this way certain shops in the Strand changed hands for many years, 'according to Savoy law'.[37]

In the Clink liberty in Southwark belonging to the Bishopric of Winchester at the end of the century most of the houses were held on leases for lives 'most of them subject to renewal under particular covenants, others very doubtful'.[38] This uncertainty had kept the place a ruinous and filthy slum. In Charles I's reign it was already crowded with poor tenements.[23] By two statutes of Elizabeth leases of church lands were limited to twenty-one years or three lives,[39] a speculative tenure obviously unsuitable for building leases, and one which was apt to lead to 'concealed rents'.

On the extensive Crown lands leases of more than fifty years were forbidden by the Civil List Act of Queen Anne. It was customary to take at least seven-eighths of the value in fines and only one-eighth in rent, lessees were allowed to renew as often as they pleased and in such a haphazard way that any general scheme of improvement was out of the question. Entire streets belonged to the Crown and 'considerable districts most advantageously situated' which in 1797 were 'covered with buildings of little value, the access to them in many places inconvenient and the streets or lanes narrow and irregular'.[40]

Grosley describes the result of what he conceived to be the leasehold system in 1765.

All the houses in London excepting a few in the heart of the City belong to undertakers, who build upon ground of which a lease is taken for 40, 60 or 99 years. . . . The agreement made, the solidity of the building is measured by the duration of the lease, as the shoe by the foot. . . . Those which are let for a shorter term, have if I may be allowed the expression, only the soul of a house. . . . It is true the outside appears to be of brick, but the wall consists only of a single row of bricks, these being made of the first earth that comes to hand, and only just warmed at the fire. . . . In the new quarters of London, brick is often made upon the spot where the buildings themselves are erected and the workmen make use of the earth which they find in digging the foundations. With this earth they mix the ashes gathered in London by the dustmen

... inside of these buildings is as much neglected as the outside; small pieces of deal supply the place of beams, all the wainscoting is of deal and the thinnest that can be found. ...

It is true that there were building Acts to regulate the building of London houses. These started with the two Acts for rebuilding the City after the Fire. The succession of Acts from 1667 to 1772 aimed primarily at reducing the risk of fire by regulations for party walls. The Act of 1774 which remained in force for seventy years was an outcome chiefly of the improvement schemes and re-paving Acts which began with the Westminster paving Act of 1762. Building was to accommodate itself to the strict alignment of the streets and the removal of all projections aimed at by the paving commissioners. Party walls were regulated with greater strictness, seven classes of buildings only were sanctioned and district surveyors of buildings were appointed. Old houses, rookeries, and probably courts and alleys did not come within the range of the surveyors. The question as to whether or not houses were habitable from a sanitary point of view was not within the scope of the Act, which was conceived from the point of view of the street rather than of the occupier.

The window tax on the other hand did affect most classes of London houses, and had the disastrous consequence of inducing people to block up windows and reduce the admission of light and air to a minimum. It was first imposed in 1696, was repeatedly stiffened up and was not repealed till 1851.[41] Houses not rated to church and poor on account of poverty were exempted, but this would not as a rule apply to London tenement houses, it being a constant preoccupation of London parish officers to prevent the landlords of such houses from evading the payment of rates. When the duty was increased in 1710 it became 'a universal practice to stop up lights'.[42] How increasingly general the practice became may be gathered from the fact that in 1766 when the tax was extended to houses with seven windows and upwards, the number of houses in England and Wales having exactly seven windows was reduced by nearly two-thirds. In 1798 it was extended to houses with six windows, but in spite of this and in spite of the increase of building and population, the number of chargeable houses was less in 1800 than it had been in 1781, 1759 or 1750.[43]

Thus the law had done little to improve housing conditions and something to worsen them. The speculative builder and the investor in house property added their share to the chaotic development of London; they sprang into existence with the beginning of the rapid increase of population in the later sixteenth century.[44] All classes tried to snatch a profit from the demand for houses. The working carpenter or bricklayer ran up, repaired or divided houses. The occupant of a tenement, himself dependent on the parish, would divide and sublet it or take in an inmate or undersitter. The well-to-do citizen or small speculator built rows of tenements, places which came to be known as (for instance) Brown's or Robinson's Rents.[10] The parish of St Margaret Lothbury complained in 1637 that Raphe Harrison, Draper, was

... possest of divers small tenements, five in number all in on gallroy called the Dark Entrey ... being so noisome and unhealthfull a place as few the like in London, some ... having beene devided of late years and the rents of them much raised by the said Raphe Harrison all ... being inhabited by poore and needy people which are a ... continuall burden and chardge to the said parish. ...

In All Hallows in the Wall 'Mr Sales, being a gentleman and living forth of towne, hath a little alley of small roomes conteyninge ten or twelve small dwellinges in it, which he hath putt poore people in. ...' Mr Sales however 'denyes to pay anythinge to the poore'.[23]

Under the early Stuarts the projector and the patentee made a profit out of licences to build. After the Restoration owners of large houses on the outskirts of London discovered the profits to be made by building on their grounds. Evelyn in 1684 deplored Lady Berkeley's decision to curtail the garden of Berkeley (afterwards Devonshire) House, and let land for building two streets (Berkeley Street and Stratton Street). He admitted there was 'some excuse' for her in the fate of the neighbouring Clarendon House 'all demolished and designed for piazzas and buildings', and the high price offered, 'advancing near £1,000 in mere ground rents, to such a mad intemperance was the age come of building about a City by far too disproportionate to the nation. ...'[45]

According to Roger North, speculative building on a large scale began with Dr Barbone after the Great Fire which gave him his opportunity.

He was the inventor of this new method of building by casting of ground into streets and small houses and to augment their number with as little front as possible and selling the ground to workmen by so much per foot front, and what he could not sell build himself. This has made ground rents high for the sake of mortgaging, and others, following his steps, have refined and improved upon it, and made a superfoetation of houses round London.

Much of Barbone's building was well planned and carried out. He developed the Essex and Buckingham estates in the Strand, built the much-admired Six Clerks Office in New Square, Lincoln's Inn, rebuilt part of the Temple and built on Soho and Red Lion Fields. But he deliberately over-traded his stock, could not pay his bricklayers and forced his creditors to take houses instead of money and died in debt.[46] It was a commonplace in the eighteenth century that those who embarked on large building schemes often ruined themselves. The building of the Adelphi by the Adams brothers was a financial failure.

The frequent wars increased the risk of building undertakings. Each war is said to have checked building operations in London; builders' labourers joined the army or navy and materials became dearer, while peace brought a renewed outburst of building.[47] During the latter part of the American War it was said that the speculative builders were for the most part ruined and that 'the road over St George's Fields to the obelisk presented for years a melancholy sight of half-finished shells of houses . . . crumbling to ruin. . . .'[48] After the war building went on apace. The Foundling Hospital began to develop its estate after 1789, Sloane Street, Sloane Square and the adjacent streets were laid out by Lord Cadogan and others. Somers Town began to be built in 1786, Camden Town in 1791, but with the outbreak of war in 1793 there was another check.[49]

As Somers Town, though starting as a middle-class settlement, rapidly developed into a slum, the early stages of its growth are of interest. These have been described by Malcolm the topographer.[50] It was planned as a pentagon with a number of streets by Mr Jacob Leroux, the principal leaseholder under Lord Somers. A chapel was opened, and 'everything seemed to proceed prosperously when some unforeseen cause occurred which checked the fervour of building and many carcasses of houses were sold for less than the cost of the materials'. However, an influx of French refugees restored a measure of prosperity and in 1802 it contained some thousand French inhabitants. Building had then been at a standstill about six years, but a new boom set in. The inflation of the currency raised prices and 'paltry erections' which had been sold for £150 were let for thirty to forty guineas yearly;

. . . hence every person who could obtain the means became builders; carpenters, retired publicans, persons working in leather, haymakers and even the keepers of private houses for the reception of lunatics, each contrived to raise his house or houses and every street was lengthened in its turn.

In the meantime the development of the Foundling and Bedford estates had gone on, hindered but not stopped by the war. The Somers Town boom induced the owners of neighbouring land to develop their property. The Skinners' Company let land on the south of the New Road on building leases; Burton Crescent, Judd Street and other streets were built and filled up the gap between Somers Town and the Bedford and Foundling estates. 'And thus,' wrote Malcolm in 1813, 'we have lived to see Somers Town completely annexed to London.' The latter part of the great war reversed the tradition as to building in war-time and was a period of great building activity. The docks were built; Waterloo, Vauxhall and Southwark Bridges were all begun during the later years of the war. In 1813 the Act for building Regent Street was passed, and the slums of St James Market were swept away by its construction.

At the other end of the scale from the 'eminent builders' who undertook the development of whole estates (usually on ninety-nine year leases) were the small men in the building trade or the little speculators in house property who ran up houses or patched up old ones and let them out in tenements. In 1743 there was a petition against the Bill to make the hamlet of Bethnal Green into a parish from the owners of the cheap tenements of which the place chiefly consisted for fear lest the rates should be increased. It runs:

. . . several of the petitioners who are artificers in building have very lately taken long leases of a great number of houses within the said hamlet . . . and have laid out very large sums of money in order to make the same tenantable. . . .[51]

By far the greater part of the houses, they say, were let at £10 a year and under,

> ... mostly lett out by the owners ... in two or three distinct parts or tenements, by reason of the poverty of the inhabitants ... the chief part of the parochial taxes for such houses is now paid and allowed by the landlords thereof, otherwise few tenants could be found to inhabit therein, which is a sensible hardship to such landlords. ...

The other side of the story appears from a petition twenty years later for a local Act for the parish, to include among other things power to rate the landlords instead of the tenants of tenement houses because 'many hundred houses ... are taken on lease by a few people who chiefly let them out in lodgings ... to journeymen weavers and others, which divided houses do not pay anything towards the poor rates'.[52] From the seventeenth century onwards there are frequent incidental references to bricklayers and carpenters as landlords of tenement houses.[53]

The ease with which the small house could be run up appears from an account in 1834 of the way in which journeymen earning twenty or thirty shillings a week had been able to invest money in building cottages. The method was probably an old one and has points of similarity with Barbone's system.

> A builder makes up the carcass, the house being just tiled in. He then lets them for an additional ground rent to mechanics, chiefly carpenters, bricklayers and plasterers. He will give them a hundred of deals and a proportionate quantity of lime to begin with. The carpenter then agrees with the bricklayer and plasterer, that each shall do the work of the other, and with their reciprocal labour and their savings they finish the house.

Sixteen or twenty small houses had been built in Henry Street, Lambeth, in this way.[54]

That large profits could be made in running up wretchedly built houses is shown by the exploits of the notorious Hedger of the Dog and Duck in St George's Fields. From about 1789 he rented a large tract of land in the Fields on a twenty-one years' lease from the Bridge House Estate under a penalty of £500 for building. As soon as he had secured the lease, he paid the penalty, and, in spite of the protest of the commoners, ran up a number of small houses that barely stood till the end of his lease. They were pulled down in 1811 for the rebuilding of Bethlehem Hospital.[55]

When we come to consider the parts of London in which the poor lived the most striking thing perhaps is that these were in many cases also dangerous districts. They were chiefly to be found in the labyrinthine courts and alleys of the sixteenth, seventeenth and early eighteenth centuries.

Whoever considers the Cities of London and Westminster with the late vast increases of their suburbs [wrote Fielding in 1751] the great irregularity of their buildings, the immense number of lanes, alleys, courts and bye-places, must think that had they been intended for the very purpose of concealment, they could not have been better contrived. Upon such a view the whole appears as a vast wood or forest in which the thief may harbour with as great security as wild beasts do in the deserts of Arabia and Africa.[56]

The localization of such places depended partly on the chaos of police and local government. The activities of constable and watchman were for the most part limited to his own parish, precinct or liberty, and where the authorities of City and county marched there was every opportunity for the development of little Alsatias.

One of the worst of these districts, and one of the best-situated to be a refuge for evil-doers, was the network of lanes and alleys round Chick Lane and Field Lane communicating with Turnmill Street and Cow Cross. In a small space authority was divided between the City and Middlesex and between the parishes of St Sepulchre's, Clerkenwell, St Andrew Holborn and the Liberty of Saffron Hill. The way in which the possibilities of the place (known as Jack Ketche's Warren) were exploited appears in the account of a night search towards the end of the Gordon Riots:

One of our detachments visited Chick Lane, Field Lane, Black Boy Alley and some other such places. . . . These places constitute a separate town or district calculated for the reception of the darkest and most dangerous enemies to society. . . . The houses are divided from top to bottom, and into many apartments, some having two, others three, others four doors, opening into different alleys. To such a height is our neglect of police arrived, the owners of these houses make no secret of their being let for the entertainment of thieves.[57]

A curious fact about these places is that their bad character began so early and persisted so long.

The Turnmill (or Turnbull) Street and Cow Cross district had long been notorious. Falstaff says that Justice Shallow 'hath done nothing but prate to me of the wildness of his youth and the feats he hath done about Turnbull Street'. Nash, in *Pierce Penniless* (1595), enumerates the places with an evil reputation: Shoreditch, the Spittle, Southwark, Westminster and Turnmill Street. Later, *The Merry Man's Resolution* gives a similar list for pre-Restoration London: St Giles in the Fields, Turnbal Street, White Crosse Street, Golden Lane, and every street between Golden Lane and Smithfield. Saffron Hill, a den of iniquity in the time of Dickens, was notorious for its brothels in the reign of James I.[58]

In the eighteenth century such districts made a network over the older parts of London. There were the courts off Holborn and Gray's Inn Lane, the rookeries of St Giles and some dreadful places off Great Queen Street and Long Acre.[59] There was a rookery between St Martin's Lane, Bedford Street and Chandos Street, known in Ben Jonson's time as the Bermudas and later as the Caribbee Islands, noted for its cook-shops, and round St Martin's Church and the King's Mews there were many dangerous byways. The older parts of Westminster, notably Petty France, Thieving Lane and the Sanctuaries had long been ill-inhabited; Orchard Street, Peter Street and Pye Street, pleasant places in the days of Elizabeth, had acquired an evil reputation. Many courts and lanes round the Haymarket and St James's Market were unsafe.

Going eastward, many courts off the Strand bore an infamous character. Covent Garden acquired its bad reputation as soon as it ceased to be a fashionable district – when the quality moved westwards, or was this migration hastened by the character of the place, for which its theatres, gaming-houses and night cellars were largely responsible? It could not have been a pleasant spot to live in. The shopkeepers and traders in 1730 appealed to the Westminster Sessions:

Several people of the most notorious characters and infamously wicked lives and conversation have of late . . . years taken up their abode in the parish. . . . There are several streets and courts such as Russell Street, Drury Lane, Crown Court and King's Court and divers places within the said parish and more particularly in the neighbourhood of Drury Lane infested with these vile people. . . . There are frequent outcries in the night, fighting, robberies and all sorts of debaucheries committed by them all night long to the great inquietude of his majesty's subjects. . . .[60]

Eight years before it was complained that when any house in or near either of the playhouses was vacant professional gamesters and sharpers took them 'over honest tradesmen's heads' and turned them into 'thieving shops for the reception of highwaymen, bullies, common assassins, and affidavit-men', so that the parts of the town frequented by them were 'dangerously infested with robbers and thieves and the streets as dangerous in the night as they are in Padua'.[61] Gay's warning was written earlier still – in 1717:

> O may thy virtue guard thee thro' the roads
> Of Drury's mazy courts and dark abodes!
> The harlot's guileful paths who nightly stand
> Where Catherine Street descends into the Strand.

Clare Market, the Back of St Clement's and Butcher Row were dark, tumble-down places, the last occupied by butchers and their slaughter-houses. St Clement's Lane contained beggars' lodging-houses.[62] After 1697 Whitefriars ceased to be a declared Alsatia but its lanes were thoroughfares to the laystalls on the riverside and it was ill-inhabited. The precinct of Blackfriars was improved by the building of Black-friars Bridge: previously it had been a haunt of thieves and prostitutes.[63] There were many narrow disreputable courts opening off Fleet Market and Shoe Lane (noted for spunging-houses) and there were the purlieus of the Fleet Prison. The City had other bad spots, but, helped by the poor-law policy of its tiny parishes, they were shrinking as the needs of commerce and finance for warehouses and offices became more insistent. Just outside the City wall on the east and within the City liberties, there had been a deplorable district, but the improvement scheme of 1760 had worked wonders there by 1775.[64] The neighbourhood of Goodman's Fields with its theatres acquired something of the reputa-tion of Covent Garden.[65] East Smithfield, Houndsditch, parts of Shore-ditch and Whitechapel, Rosemary Lane (Rag Fair), Petticoat Lane, Ratcliffe Highway were dangerous neighbourhoods. In this eastern dis-trict as in Southwark, many courts and alleys are described by Maitland as mean, nasty, ordinary or even beggarly, even by the standards of 1756. The riverside districts from St Katherine's to Limehouse were honeycombed with places of bad character. Across the river Kent Street, the Mint and the Clink liberty were particularly bad spots in a squalid district.

These places took up so much of the central parts of London and of the busy shipping and industrial quarters on both sides of the river where porters, market sellers, labourers and artisans of necessity lived that the workers were forced to live among disreputable and filthy surroundings. These unfortunate places often owed part of their bad character to sanitary nuisances and nauseous trades. The Field Lane district was intersected by the filthy channel of the Fleet ditch (called in 1722 'a nauceious and abominable sink of nastiness'), into which the tripe dressers, sausage makers and catgut spinners, who shared the Lane with professional thieves, flung their offal. Whitechapel and Aldgate had their slaughter-houses and hog-yards. On both sides of the river-banks laystalls and 'common shores' abounded. On the Surrey side the ditches of Jacob's Island in Bermondsey, whose memory has been pre-served by Dickens, were the survivals of far more extensive and more filthy tide-ditches. In 1722 an anonymous writer, perhaps Defoe, calls them 'those most loathesome and byplaces'. They then intersected the river hinterland from Lambeth to Rotherhithe, and ran inland towards St George's Fields, 'running through Bandy Leg Walk and the back of the Old Bear Garden up to the Mint'.[66]

At the beginning of the nineteenth century the poor quarters of London are indicated by the places where typhus cases were to be expected. These were 'Shadwell, Whitechapel, Bethnal Green ... Shore-ditch, St Luke's, about Old Street and Golden Lane and Cow Cross and Saffron Hill. Near Smithfield and also St Giles, the neighbour-hood of Clare Market and Drury Lane and the parish of St Clements and also very much in . . . St George's, Southwark, Kent Street and the Borough'. After a period of comparative immunity from 1801 to 1816 an epidemic broke out in 1817–18 which reached, besides the districts enumerated, Somers Town and other parts of the parish of St Pancras, and Newington, Walworth, Hackney and Hampstead.[67]

Among working-class people it was common for a family to live in a single room. A house would be occupied by people of different degrees of prosperity and even of different social grades. The very poor, that is, casual labourers, street sellers and the like, silk winders, char-women and those who kept a mangle, as a rule lived in cellars or else in garrets. In a plea for the Lying-in Hospital Maitland says,

... poor women, in a state of child bearing ... are of all objects the most miserable. They are quite unfit for labour ... and consequently deprived of the means of supporting themselves in their great day of affliction. Their lodgings are generally in extreme cold garrets open to every wind that blows, or in damp uncomfortable cellars underground, subject to floods from excessive rains. . . .[68]

The manner of life and housing of the poorest classes in London at the end of the eighteenth century is thus described by Dr Willan:

It will scarcely appear credible, though it is precisely true, that persons of the lowest class do not put clean sheets on their beds three times a year; that even where no sheets are used they never wash or scour their blankets or coverlets, nor renew them until they are no longer tenable; that curtains, if unfortunately there should be any, are never cleansed but suffered to con-tinue in the same state till they fall to pieces; lastly, that from three to eight individuals of different ages often sleep in the same bed; there being in general but one room and one bed for each family. . . . The room occupied is either a deep cellar, almost inaccessible to the light, and admitting of no change of air; or a garret with a low roof and small windows, the passage to which is close, kept dark, and filled not only with bad air, but with putrid excremental effluvia from a vault at the bottom of the staircase. Washing of linen, or some other disagreeable business, is carried on, while infants are left dozing and children more advanced kept at play whole days on the tainted bed: some unsavoury victuals are from time to time cooked: in many instances idleness, in others the cumbrous furniture or utensils of trade, with which the apart-ments are clogged, prevent the salutary operation of the broom and white-washing brush and favour the accumulation of a heterogeneous filth.
    The above account is not exaggerated: for the truth of it I appeal to the medical practitioners whose situation or humanity has led them to be acquainted with the wretched inhabitants of some streets in St Giles parish, of the courts and alleys adjoining to Liquor Pond Street, Hog Island, Turn-mill Street, Old Street, Whitecross Street, Grub Street, Golden Lane, the two Brook Lanes, Rosemary Lane, Petticoat Lane, Lower East Smithfield,

some parts of Upper Westminster, and several streets of Rotherhithe, etc. . . .

The inhabitants of the second floor, in houses occupied by the poor, are usually better accommodated, and therefore experience during sickness of any kind the best effect from public and private charities. But persons thus situated suffer from contiguity and from their friendly attentions to those above them or to the tenants of the cellars. . . .[69]

Another doctor's description adds further details:

In a large proportion of the dwellings of the poor a house contains as many families as rooms: on the ground floor resides almost universally the master of the house with his family, which, if pretty numerous, sometimes occupies the whole of that floor, if not, the back room is occupied by another family. This apartment is in many instances of a size scarcely more than sufficient to admit of a bed, with space for a person to pass it, and so much as is necessary for a fireplace. The rooms which are in the front part of the house are usually larger but they are often occupied by families more than proportionally numerous.

But although the accommodations in the middle and upper part of the house are extremely uncomfortable, they are in every respect preferable to those in the lowest apartment or cellar, where darkness, dirt and stagnant air combine to augment all the evils resulting from such a situation. . . . Many of the windows cannot be opened without admitting air apparently more noxious, certainly not less offensive, than that already contained in the room; in other instances the sashes have frequently been rendered by age or accident immovable; wood or paper has been substituted for broken panes of glass; every crevice is so carefully stuffed by woollen rags or some other filthy substance, that as a means of admitting fresh air the windows are often totally useless.[70]

The difference of social grade between those occupying rooms in the same tenement has been indicated in a lighter vein by Grose, who gives what he calls a table of precedency:

First then in order of all those who occupy only parts of houses stand the tenants of stalls, sheds and cellars, from which we take our flight to the top of the house in order to arrange in the next class the residents in garrets; from thence we gradually descend to the second and first floor, the dignity of each being in the inverse ratio of its altitude, it being always remembered that those dwelling in the fore part of the house take the *pas* of the inhabitants of the back rooms, and the ground floor, if not a shop and warehouse, ranks with the second story. Situations of houses I conceive to rank in the following order, passages, yards, alleys, courts, lanes, streets, rows, places and squares.[71]

Lowest in the social scale came common lodging-houses, omitted in this list. They multiplied in the eighteenth century, and were partly due to the number of ruinous, derelict houses to which the title was often doubtful, a cause of many evils.[60] One of the earliest references to them was in 1721, when fear of the plague which was raging at Marseilles roused the authorities to denounce many sanitary horrors of long standing. 'It is now become a common practice,' said the Middlesex justices,

in the extreme parts of the town, to receive into their houses persons un-known, without distinction of sex or age on their paying one penny or more per night for lying in such houses without beds or covering, and . . . it is frequent in such houses for fifteen or twenty or more to lie in a small room.[72]

Saunders Welch wrote in 1753:

There have [sic] within a few years arisen in the outskirts of this town a kind of traffic in old ruinous houses which the occupiers fill up with straw and flock beds, which they nightly let out for twopence for a single person or threepence for a couple. . . . Four or five beds are often in one room, and what with the nastiness of these wretches and their numbers such an incon-ceivable stench has arose from them that I have been hardly able to bear it the little time that my duty required my stay. Spirituous liquors afford means of intoxication . . . and the houses are open all night to entertain rogues and receive plunder. Great numbers of desperate fellows have been taken out of these places and executed. One woman occupied in the parish of St Giles near twenty of these places. Black Boy Alley abounds with them and they were the shelter of that dreadful gang who about nine years ago robbed and wounded people at noonday. . . . Shoreditch has also numbers of them. Suppose the number of these houses to be only two hundred, and compute only twenty persons to a house. . . . What evils are the public not liable to from such a villainous mixture as this?[73]

Perhaps the woman who had twenty common lodging-houses in St Giles was Mrs Farrel whose death was recorded by the *Annual Register* in 1765. She, 'by letting out two-penny lodgings amassed upwards of £6,000'. As these houses were largely inhabited by the Irish,* the landladies seem also to have frequently been Irish.

* See Chapter 3.

Common lodging-houses were by no means the cheapest form of shelter; the cellar or the garret at a shilling or eighteenpence a week housed a family – among the Irish more than a family. The cellar dwelling in London, was, as we have seen, called into existence or at least encouraged by the proclamations against new buildings. The proclamation of 1607 forbade cellars made in the past five years to be used 'for lodgings or tipling or victualling houses'. At the time when parish authorities, fearing the burden of the poor, were doing their best to enforce the regulations against inmates, only respectable householders licensed by the constable were allowed to harbour them and these found it to their interest to let their cellars to poor people.[74] Consequently cellar dwellings became general. In the seventeenth century (as in the eighteenth) the poorer artisans and traders had shops and dwellings in the cellars of houses they never entered. These cellars were entered by steps from the street down a well which was supposed to be closed at nightfall by a flap for the safety of passers-by, but open cellars were one of the many dangers of the streets after dark.[75] The cellar became the natural resort of the small dealer or artisan whose business made it necessary that his customers should have easy access to him from the street. Hence the greengrocer and the cobbler are often to be found in cellars while the mechanic who worked for a shopkeeper went by the generic name of garret-master or chamber-master.

Milk cellars were common, in fact the cellar seems to have been the usual base for the retailer of milk. Milk walks, like newspaper walks, were bought and sold. The stock-in-trade of the business was of the scantiest. The milk-carrier fetched the milk from one of the cow-keepers round London in the early morning and cried it through the street or streets included in the milk walk. The milk score was chalked upon the door-post of the customer and the pails and wooden tallies – the books of the business – were kept in the cellar occupied by the proprietor of the walk and his or her family, including perhaps a weekly servant or a parish apprentice girl to carry the pails.[76] It was no wonder that milk from the cow – from one of the cow-keepers in the parks or from the 'Lactarium' in St George's Fields – was one of the minor luxuries of Londoners.[77]

Cellars which were also business premises of a sort, where the tenant would often occupy the front and back cellar, would naturally have higher rents than those that were mere wretched underground sleeping-places such as those occupied by the Irish in St Giles. Monmouth Street, the mart for old clothes, was a great place for cellars. A boy who lived there in 1786 said that he paid a rent of £9 a year:

I am a shoemaker, I keep a kitchen in Monmouth Street [*i.e.* I am a cobbler or translator, I live in a cellar], . . . I have no father or mother, I mend shoes and hang them up at the door, . . . I do not know the landlady's name, she sells gowns and things, I pay my money every Monday.[78]

Night cellars were notorious, places where shelter was given to the prowlers of the night and drink sold to thieves and others. 'I keep a public cellar' seems to mean I offer a night's shelter and by the sale of drams make up for the absence of beds.

Grose classes sheds and stalls with cellars. As dwelling-places these were more characteristic of the seventeenth than of the eighteenth century and Improvement Acts waged war upon them. Stalls which were both working- and sleeping-places were of course a little more commodious than the bulks or stalls where there was room only for one person to sit and (for instance) mend shoes; the latter were closed at night and were often used as sleeping-places by vagrants. The larger sort of stall is thus described by a woman who lived in one so late as 1790 and took in mending to do. 'I live in South Street, St George's, Hanover Square, it is a stall I keep. . . . It has only one floor, there is a bed in it, it is all the dwelling-place I have; it has a door and a window.'[79] In the hard winter of 1768 a cobbler was frozen to death in the stall in which he both worked and slept.[80]

The shed-dwelling was probably most common in the outskirts of the town. One Alexander Mitchell living at Clapton in 1794 had a 'house' consisting of one room built as a shed, 'in that room', he said, 'is my bed and shop'. It was robbed by a thief who got in by removing tiles from the roof.[81] The place in Star Court, Westminster, where one Ann Barrington lodged must have been less eligible than a shed. In defending herself against a charge of theft, she said, 'I lodge by myself. I have no fastenings to the door, it is sixpence a week, and under the straw and hay which I had to lay on these things were found'.[82] That was the sort of place in which the ballad singer or match seller appears to have lived. Margaret King, who explained 'I was out all day at hard labour. . . . I had been begging all that day', paid ninepence a week for 'lodging . . . in a sort of room where there was a sort of bed', which she shared with a woman who carried about chips to sell and paid sixpence a week for lodging.[83]

The garret, the traditional lodging of the bookseller's hack, or garreteer, marks a step upwards in the social scale, though garrets were often mere shelters under the tiles. John Elliott, the young apothecary who made a sensation by firing pistols at Alderman Boydell's niece, lodged in a small garret at two guineas a year. It had no fireplace or window, only a skylight. He slept on a mattress on a sliding board.[84] The garret where the milkmaid duns Hogarth's distressed poet was comparatively a pleasant place.

A large proportion of the poorer classes in London lived in ready-furnished rooms, paying a weekly rent. The custom was by no means confined to the poorer sort; there were furnished lodgings for all classes and the letting of lodgings was a great industry,[85] besides being, as Adam Smith pointed out, a by-industry of London shopkeepers. The surprising thing is that so many working people should have lived in furnished rooms. Most of the poorer parishes in London in their application for local Acts to regulate their poor lay stress on the difficulty in collecting rates owing to the number of houses let out in 'ready-furnished tenements' and the temporary nature of the tenancies. For instance in 1772 the parish of St Botolph Aldgate gave evidence that there were 555 houses in the parish let at under £10 a year (chiefly in tenements) and (according to another witness) 500 were let as tenements ready-furnished.[86] There is an enormous number of cases in the Old Bailey *Sessions Papers* in which the weekly tenant of a furnished room is prosecuted for pawning the furniture.

The standard rent of a London artisan before the great rise in prices after 1795 seems to have been 2s. 6d. a week. The rent of a furnished room in a poor district appears to have varied from 2s. to 3s. 6d. (cellars and garrets were often cheaper) with a tendency to rise as the century went on. The budget of an unmarried clerk in a public office at £50 a year, according to a pamphlet of 1767 to show the pressure of high prices on those with fixed incomes 'in a middling station', includes a rent of 2s. 6d. a week. For this he gets a furnished room 'two pair of stairs forwards in Grub Street, Golden Lane, Moor Lane, Fee Lane,

Rag Fair or the Mint' to which 'dirtiest and meanest parts of the town' the writer has sent him 'to seek a cheap lodging'. The room contains,

as per inventory duplicated and exchanged, a half-tester bedstead, with brown linsey woolsey furniture, a bed and bolster, half flocks, half feathers ... a small wainscot table, two old chairs with cane bottoms, a small looking glass six inches by four in a deal frame painted red and black, a red linsey woolsey window curtain, an old iron stove, poker, shovel, tongs and fender, an iron candlestick mounted with brass, a tin extinguisher, a quart bottle of water, a tin pint pot, a vial for vinegar and a stone white tea cup for salt. Also two large prints cut in wood and coloured, framed with deal but not glazed, viz. (1) Hogarth's *Gate of Calais* ... (2) *Queen Esther and Queen Ahasuerus*. ...[87]

From the many cases in which the furniture of a room was pawned by the tenants, such rooms contained little but necessaries. Colquhoun ascribed the frequenting of alehouses to the custom among 'the improvident poor' of living in 'a miserable half-furnished lodging from week to week'.[88]

There were people who took in only single men as lodgers. About 1795 Elizabeth Brady of Cursitor Street had a bill in her window, 'lodgings to let for single men'. A man asked to see the room: 'I told him 5s. a week, says I, "Young man, what is your trade? I am afraid it is too much for you"; says he, "I am a painter and glazier"; says I, "If you had another young man to partake of half the bed with you it would make it better".'[89] Owing to the custom for shopkeepers and respectable widows to take in lodgers, the unmarried journeyman of steady habits could probably find a room where he would have some of the comforts and decencies of life. Benjamin Franklin, in 1725, when a journeyman printer in London, lodged with a widow in Duke Street, a clergyman's daughter, paying at first 3s. 6d. a week, which his landlady afterwards reduced to 1s. 6d. rather than lose a good tenant.[90] For the same money the man with children would have to put up with worse quarters, probably a room in a house where every room from the cellar to the garret had its family. When the journeyman had money or credit and enterprise enough to take unfurnished rooms or enough rooms to be able himself to take a lodger, or even to become a 'housekeeper', he would of course be able to live either more cheaply or more comfortably.

Colquhoun complained that 'numerous families of labourers lodge with their wives and children in common alehouses in the metropolis and probably in most of the large cities and towns in different parts of the kingdom'.[91] Rooms were taken in alehouses as in tenement houses and at similar rents, chiefly one would gather by men in the building and other trades who had to move from place to place. We hear of the keeper of a public-house in Parker Street, Drury Lane, who had a garret where anyone could have a night's lodging, and presumably there were many similar places, verging on the common lodging-house.[92] There were numerous hangers-on of doubtful character at the inns which were the headquarters of coaches, wagons and carriers and some of them appear to have slept in the galleries of inn yards. One of these men charged with highway robbery in 1785 had 'lodged in the gallery of the White Bear for six years . . . there is all manner of people lays there'.[93]

The impression given by accounts of housing conditions in London is of a floating population living largely as weekly tenants in furnished rooms. This is in keeping with the general uncertainty of life and trade characteristic of the period and with the perpetual flow and ebb to and from the metropolis. There were, Colquhoun estimates, at the end of the century,

. . . above twenty thousand miserable individuals of various classes, who rise up every morning without knowing how . . . they are to be supported during the passing day, or where in many instances they are to lodge on the succeeding night.[94]

Some of these were doubtless the frequenters of common lodging-houses, alehouse garrets and night cellars; others those who slept in the streets, in brickfields, in markets or in half-built houses. Empty and ruinous houses, bulks and glass houses, the resort of the homeless in the time of Savage, seem to have been no longer generally available; Improvement Acts and hoardings had cut off many shelters for the night.

The permanent element among the inhabitants of London was represented by the 'housekeeper', whose superior status as compared with the fluctuating mass of lodgers seems to have depended partly on his comparative rarity, partly on tradition – he was supposed to be the man who paid scot and bore lot, while the presentments of annoyance juries kept up the memory of the old regulations against inmates.[95] The crowded manner of living in London was also due in part to social custom and tradition as well as to economic causes. The shopkeeper or the well-to-do artisan who was in the proud position of a housekeeper lived in one or two rooms and let the rest as a matter of course. Servants and apprentices slept in the kitchen, the shop or the garret as a matter of course. The pupils in expensive boarding-schools slept two in a bed.[96] The cramped way of life of the comfortably-off classes is illustrated by the popularity of beds concealed in various articles of furniture. London cabinet-makers made beds which masqueraded in the daytime as tables, toilet-tables, bureaus, cupboards and bookcases.[97] All classes lived so much at coffee-houses, alehouses or clubs that house-room was a secondary consideration. 'A man might live in a garret at eighteen-pence a week,' as Johnson was told before he came to London in 1737, 'few people would inquire where he lodged and if they did it was easy to say, "Sir, I am to be found at such a place".' The necessary 'good address' was provided by the coffee-house or tavern.

In this, as in other things, the eighteenth century was a stage in the transition from medieval conditions. Space and air first became a luxury of the rich and the demand for it gradually spread from class to class. There was a perpetual contest between the pressure of population on house-room and the growth of London in bricks and mortar, but it is clear that in the eighteenth century bricks and mortar were gaining ground, largely owing to that growing desire for a more spacious way of life which was stigmatized as luxury. There was, however, a counter-current from the ever-increasing flow of Irish immigrants who found their way to the most crowded and unhealthy parts of the town and helped to spread the disease that was always rife there.*

Although, for want of statistics, generalizations on housing conditions are rash, yet certain conclusions may be drawn from the mass of miscellaneous and incidental information which is available. In the first place overcrowding was general. Among its causes (besides the perennial one of poverty) was the necessity for workers to live near their place of work, owing to the absence of any means of cheap transport and the unpleasantness and danger of walking through the streets, much more the outskirts, of London after nightfall.

* See Chapter 3.

The custom of living at a distance from the place of work was introduced by the City merchants, who found the narrow, damp, dark lanes of the City an unpleasant contrast with the streets and squares of west London. The practice first appears to have become noticeable after the Seven Years' War when it was stigmatized as a new-fangled luxury[98] and was far from universal in the early nineteenth century. Archenholtz, writing about 1780, says,

... there has been within the space of twenty years truly a migration from the east end of London to the west, thousands passing from that part of the City, where new buildings are no longer carried on, to this end, where fertile fields and the most agreeable gardens are daily metamorphosed into houses and streets.[99]

In 1801 the recent increase of houses is ascribed to a change of manners according to which merchants 'make a part of their well-being consist in living in a different quarter of the town from that in which they work'. The custom caused much surprise among foreign observers, and it was remarked that it was one only possible to the English with their passion for exercise in the open air. It was long before the practice was extended to the poorer sections of the community.

Secondly, the standard dwelling of the artisan, even in a 'genteel trade', seems to have been a single room – and in very many cases a furnished room – while in many trades this was workshop as well as living and sleeping-place. Differences of social grade among the workers were marked by the part of the house occupied, by the respectability or otherwise of the street or court, and by the distinction between the lodger, 'the room-keeper' (who might take in other lodgers) and the 'housekeeper', rather than by the occupation of a greater number of rooms. The causes of this crowded state of living may be supposed to have been social custom and want of house-room acting and reacting on one another in a vicious circle. The evidence of budgets is that about one-eighth part of earnings went on rent.* As these are not authenticated accounts, but statements to show the inadequacy of wages, the proportion is probably over- rather than under-rated. The prevalence of living in ready-furnished lodgings may be ascribed to that improvidence which was an outcome of the social conditions of the time, to the number of people who made or eked out a living from letting furnished

* See Chapter 4.

rooms, and to the constant migration (partly seasonal) of labourers and artisans to London – cause and effect being inextricably inter-mixed.

Although eighteenth-century London was incredibly dirtier, more dilapidated and more closely-built than it afterwards became, was there no compensation in its greater compactness, the absence of straggling suburbs, the ease with which people could take country walks? This is at least doubtful. The roads round London were neither very attractive nor very safe. The land adjoining them was watered with drains and thickly sprinkled with laystalls and refuse heaps. Hogs were kept in large numbers on the outskirts and fed on the garbage of the town.[99] A chain of smoking brick-kilns surrounded a great part of London and in the brickfields vagrants lived and slept, cooking their food at the kilns. It is true that there was an improvement as the century went on. In 1706 it was said of the highways,

... tho' they are mended every summer, yet everybody knows that for a mile or two about this City, the same and the ditches hard by are commonly so full of nastiness and stinking dirt, that oftentimes many persons who have occasion to go in or come out of town, are forced to stop their noses to avoid the ill-smell occasioned by it. . . .[100]

In 1751 Corbyn Morris remarks that the roads round London had greatly improved of late.[101] But footpads and vagrants made the roads and fields round London unsafe, except on Sundays, when numbers gave safety and the people streamed in crowds to the various tea-gardens and pleasure resorts near the town.

Graziers, cow-keepers, hog-keepers, brickmakers, scavengers, night-men, nursery- and market-gardeners monopolized most of the land round London. There were certain fields more or less given up to sports, such as the Long Fields (or Field of Forty Footsteps), east of Totten-ham Court Road, behind Montague House, but the sports attracted the roughest of the community – they were dog-fighting, badger-baiting, bull-baiting and the like.[102] Tothill Fields, in Westminster, or 'Tuttle Downs', was used as a dumping ground for filth, and swine prowled about on it. At the beginning of the nineteenth century it is described as the 'campus martius of blackguardism',[103] and was almost, if not quite, the last place in London where bull-baiting was regularly carried on.[104] It had then much the reputation that Moorfields and Lincoln's Inn Fields had at the beginning of the century.

Hanway wrote of London in 1767, 'we have taken pains to render its environs displeasing both to sight and smell. The chain of brick-kilns that surrounds us, like the scars of the smallpox, makes us lament the ravages of beauty and the diminution of infant aliment'. The 'city bard' (in 1773) deplores the absence of 'pastoral images' round London:

> Where'er around I cast my wand'ring eyes,
> Long burning rows of fetid bricks arise,
> And nauseous dunghills swell in mould'ring heaps,
> While the fat sow beneath their covert sleeps.
> I spy no verdant glade, no gushing rill,
> No fountain gushing from the rocky hill,
> But stagnant pools adorn our dusty plains,
> Where half-starv'd cows wash down their meal of grains.
>
> Since then no images adorn the plain,
> But what are found as well in Gray's Inn Lane,
> Since dust and noise inspire no thought serene,
> And three-horse stages little mend the scene,
> I'll stray no more to seek the vagrant muse,
> But ev'n go write at home and save my shoes.[105]

About 1770, when Dr Lettsom was applying the fresh-air treatment to typhus, he found it necessary to recommend his patients to loiter on the bridges across the Thames,[106] then much frequented by Londoners anxious for fresh air.[107] In 1800, Dr Ferriar in his *Advice to the Poor* says, 'it should be unnecessary to remind you that much sickness is occasioned among you by passing your evenings at alehouses, or in strolling about the streets or in the fields adjoining the town. . . .'[108] Later, when official attention was first directed (by the Commissioners under the new poor law after 1834) to bad housing and insanitary conditions as a cause of sickness and poverty, the state of fields and open spaces in the outskirts of London attracted special notice. Open stagnant pools and undrained marsh land (much of Bethnal Green as well as of rural Stanmore was still in this state) were a cause of fevers. So was the water which remained on brickfields after brick-making.

Lamb's Fields and Hare Street Fields in Bethnal Green and the pond on Camberwell Green were instanced as terrible nuisances.[109]

When did improvement in the state of London begin? James I prided himself on the changes in his reign, which include the New River water-supply and the new-paving of the Strand.[110] He waged war on timber-fronted houses and reed-thatched hovels and these things may perhaps be set against the overcrowding and cellar-dwellings encouraged by the proclamations. The Great Fire of course produced a vast improvement and marks the first stage in the thinning out of the densely-inhabited medieval city. Of the 13,000 houses said to have been destroyed, only about 9,000 were rebuilt. The Thames was embanked from the Fleet to London Bridge; thoroughfares were opened and standardized brick houses replaced both the old buildings of timber, lath and plaster and the wooden sheds of the poor.[5] The clearing away of insanitary places under Improvement Acts began in the eighteenth century. First, the inhabitants of squares applied for powers to enable them to 'enclose, adorn and beautify' them in order to prevent their continuing to be a dumping ground for filth and a camping ground for vagrants – the inevitable fate of open spaces in the metropolis. Ralph wrote of Lincoln's Inn Fields just before its enclosure, 'no place can be more contemptible and forbidding; . . . it serves only as a nursery of beggars and thieves and is a daily reflection on those who suffer it to lie in its abandoned condition'.[111] The City covered in the filthy open drain of the Fleet from Fleet Bridge to Holborn Bridge and built Fleet Market (opened in 1737) on the site thus gained. Improvements in Westminster began with the building of Westminster Bridge (1737–50); many wretched and dilapidated houses were cleared away and thoroughfares were opened. Blackfriars Bridge produced similar improvements in the precinct of Blackfriars.[63] In 1760 the City embarked on an extensive improvement scheme for opening and widening thoroughfares, carried out (very slowly) by the Committee of the City Lands.

A new era began with the first Westminster Paving Act of 1762. Before this all the eighteenth-century Acts for the metropolis relating to street paving had merely been attempts to enforce the old personal obligation of each householder to pave and keep in repair the street in front of his own door.[112] The appointment of commissioners to pave and repair the streets was only a part of the changes under the new scheme. The dangerous kennel in the middle of the road was replaced by gutters on each side, and in the principal streets the old round pebbles gave way to flat Purbeck stone. The Acts provided for the scavenging of the streets and removal of household rubbish as well as for the removal of encroachments on the streets, of the bulks or stalls, the show-boards, the projecting balconies, the dangerous unfenced open cellars, and the unprotected coal-shoots. The many signs which had extended completely across narrow streets to the obstruction of light and air were taken down and the water which in rainy weather spouted freely from the gutters on the house tops, was confined to pipes. As one Act followed another in quick succession, a new code of street behaviour was laid down, and some restraint was put on the manifold operations of industrial and domestic life which had taken place in the roadway.[113] The Paving Commissioners found themselves obliged to undertake, or require the Commissioners of Sewers to undertake, the construction and deepening of sewers and drains.[114]

The change both in appearance and sanitation was immense. The Westminster paving enterprise was described in 1787 as 'an undertaking which has introduced a degree of elegance and symmetry into the streets of the metropolis, that is the admiration of all Europe and far exceeds anything of the kind in the modern world'.[115]

Many parts of the City especially are made more open by pulling down houses [wrote Wales, a master at Christ's Hospital, in 1781] and all the streets are more airy and wholesome by removing the signs. . . . The streets are also better and more regularly cleansed; and by the addition of several new works, water is become much more plentiful than it was heretofore; and this has been a great means of contribution not only to greater cleanliness in our houses, but also towards purifying the air by washing the filth out of the kennels and common shoars. . . .[116]

Paving Acts on the new model were effective, while earlier ones were unenforceable, because they provided for a staff of paid officials and because infringements of the Acts were made punishable in a summary way before the magistrates. The old methods of presentment and indictment were slow, expensive and uncertain, and where street nuisances were concerned, very seldom carried through. The presentments of annoyance juries to courts leet were futile and the fines they imposed notoriously difficult to levy. If the streets before the new Paving Act had suggested a colony of Hottentots, this was partly because it was difficult to restrain the nightmen and scavengers from emptying their carts in the streets instead of in the places allotted by the justices, while the accumulated filth of the eighteenth-century house was in many cases simply thrown from the doors or windows.[117]

The lighting of London under local Acts was an immense improvement with an obvious reaction on the dangerous districts. At the beginning of the century the lighting of London depended on an Act of William and Mary which provided for street lighting from Michaelmas to Lady Day only, and then only from dark till midnight. Those inhabitants who did not contribute to certain public lights were to hang out lights of their own. Such as it was, the statute was unenforceable. Saunders Welch tells us in 1754 that it remained 'unexecuted'.[118] In 1745 the Westminster Sessions had tried to enforce it as, they said, 'its due execution would greatly contribute to the preventing of murders, burglaries, street robberies, fires, misdemeanors and debauchery'.[119]

The City made its own regulations by an Act of Common Council of 1716. According to this, householders were to hang out lights in the six winter months from 6 to 11 p.m. on 'dark nights' by the calendar, namely, on eighteen nights in each moon. As a result the lighting of the City, Maitland says, was perhaps worse than that of any other great city till 1736, when an Act was passed, giving powers to rate the inhabitants in order to hang out lamps throughout the year.[120] Outside the City the first parish in the Bills of Mortality to get a similar Act was Christchurch Spitalfields, which got a Watching and Lighting Act in 1738. After this several parishes obtained combined Lighting and Watching Acts. When Paving Acts on the new model became general it was usual to give paving and lighting powers to the same body of trustees or commissioners. Turnpike trustees obtained powers for lighting and watching highways into London. The result was that the lighting of London as well as the surface of the streets became the admiration of foreigners. It is said that when the Prince of Monaco came to London at the invitation of George III he arrived in the evening and imagined the street lamps to be a magnificent illumination in his honour. Archenholtz tells the story and describes the lighting of the streets as it was about 1780:

As the English are prodigal of their money and attention in order to give everything that relates to the public an air of grandeur and magnificence, we might naturally expect to find London well lighted, and accordingly nothing can be more superb. The lamps, which have two or four branches, are enclosed in crystal globes and fixed on posts at a little distance from each other. They are lighted at sunset in winter as well as in summer whether the moon shines or not. In Oxford Road alone there are more lamps than in all the city of Paris. Even the great roads for seven or eight miles round are crowded with them which makes the effect exceedingly grand. . . .[121]

As an example of how the point of view changes, a retrospective account of these same lamps, made after gas had become general, is illuminating:

Forty years ago the lighting of the streets was effected by what were called 'parish lamps'. The lamp consisted of a small tin vessel, half filled with the worst train oil, that the parochial authorities, for the most part the chosen of the select vestries, could purchase at the lowest price to themselves and the highest charge to the rate payers. In this fluid fish-blubber was a piece of cotton twist which formed the wick. A set of greasy fellows redolent of Greenland Dock were employed to trim and light these lamps, which they accomplished by the apparatus of a formidable pair of scissors, a flaming flambeau of pitched rope and a rickety ladder, to the annoyance and danger of all passers-by. The oil vessel and wick were enclosed in a case of semi-opaque glass . . . which obscured even the little light it encircled.[122]

It is characteristic of contemporary fluctuations of opinion and of the rapid material changes that were taking place that the outburst of joy and pride that hailed the Paving Acts was short-lived. This had depended upon a comparison between the old state of things and the new, but the old horrors were soon forgotten, and the standard of order and decency continued to rise. The pride was based on real achievements, which had an undoubted effect on the health of the town, and in which London was a pioneer among large cities. The foot-pavements, the lamps, the water-supply, the fire-plugs, the new sewers, defective enough by later standards, were admired by all:

Almost every house has a glass lamp with two wicks. . . . Beneath the pavements are vast subterraneous sewers arched over to convey away the waste water which in other cities is so noisome above ground, and at a less depth are buried wooden pipes that supply every house plentifully with water,

conducted by leaden pipes into kitchens or cellars, three times a week for
the trifling expence of three shillings per quarter. . . . The intelligent foreigner
cannot fail to take notice of these useful particulars which are almost peculiar
to London.[123]

There were many things that Paving and Improvement Acts did not
do. It is clear from the tenor of the Acts and from the descriptions of
the rookeries of London that there were courts and alleys outside the
range of paving commissioners and their surveyors. Nothing but rebuilding could have reclaimed such places. But a good deal of demolish-
ing and opening of thoroughfares was provided for in the Acts and
some dreadful places disappeared. They did not deal with the slaughtering of animals in markets and in private slaughter-houses (under the
same roof as dwelling-houses) in thickly-populated districts. They did
not touch the terrible abuse of overcrowded graveyards and the 'poor's
holes' or open pits for pauper coffins.[124] But they made London cleaner
and drier and transformed its aspect and they were a rudimentary education to Londoners in some of the decencies of life.

Appalling as was the state of things revealed by the nineteenth-
century reports (1840-5) on the sanitary state of towns it can hardly be
doubted that the state of London was far worse in the eighteenth century. It is true that as rookeries were pulled down their wretched inhabitants went to new slums such as Somers Town, Agar Town, the
newer parts of Bethnal Green, Lambeth and Walworth, but these were
at least built rather in streets than in labyrinths of courts and passages.
Francis Place had no doubt that the new districts were better than the
old rookeries. He writes in November 1832:

To Walworth on business, and this being a damp, drizzling, rainy, disagreeable day, I resolved to make a tour among the habitations of the poor
and see how they looked. . . . The space between the Walworth Road and the
Kent Road is nearly filled with streets of very small houses, many of four
rooms – others of six, eight or more, houses let at from £16 to £35 a year.
Many of these streets are unpaved, having gravelled footpaths, . . . some are
paved. The houses are in all sorts of conditions – some new, some in a bad,
some in a very bad state. But the streets are none of them narrow, and as they
are inhabited by poorer and poorer people and are smaller and lower, they
are proportionally wider. . . . Some of them are of considerable width – as
much I think as thirty feet, and one or two, the houses in which are only one

or two stories high, must be forty feet wide. Many of these streets are inhabited by very poor people – but neither the streets nor the houses are by any means so dirty as were the narrow streets and lanes which have been destroyed to make way for modern improvements – nor do they stink as such places used to do.[125]

Among the causes of improvement were those subtle social changes which are so difficult to trace. In 1824 Place instanced the improvement in the houses, even the older houses, of the poor as one of the clearest proofs of their advance in cleanliness:

There is a street at Lambeth still paved with pebbles and without any flagstone footpaths, in which the houses are small and old and then as now inhabited principally by fishermen and other poor people. These people are by no means so well off as they were thirty or forty years ago. Fishing in the river is by no means so good a trade as it was even ten years ago. Thirty years ago, perhaps I may say with truth, twenty years ago, all these houses had casement windows, none of them had sash windows. The window frames and door posts were perfectly black with soot and dirt, the rooms were neither painted nor whitewashed for many years together; patches of paper or a rag . . . kept out the cold where the glass was broken. No such thing as a curtain, unless it was a piece of old garment, was to be seen at any window. Now these same houses have nearly all of them sash windows, the frames of which are painted white and kept white and scarcely a window is to be seen without a white curtain. Formerly the women young and old were seen emptying their pails or pans at the doors, or washing on stools in the street, in the summer time without gowns on their backs or handkerchiefs on their necks, their leather stays half laced and as black as the door posts, their black coarse worsted stockings and striped linsey-woolsey petticoats 'standing alone with dirt'. No such things are seen now. Compared with themselves at the two periods, even these people are gentlefolks.[126]

Chadwick confirms Place's evidence. In 1828, discussing the increased duration of life since the eighteenth century, he ascribes it to

. . . considerable improvements . . . in the domestic habits of artisans; they are more cleanly and regular, their houses are better constructed, they have acquired some notions that fresh air is conducive to health, and the streets where they reside are less filthy and pestilential than formerly.[127]

On reading the descriptions of the state of London in the eighteen-forties it is hard to realize that things could ever have been worse. Yet there is much evidence that they had. In the eighteenth century, as in the nineteenth, the worst and filthiest streets, courts and houses had been those inhabited by the Irish. The Irish quarter of St Giles was gradually demolished and rebuilt with the effect, it is said, of increasing the overcrowding in the parts which remained. In 1848 the overcrowding of Church Street was extreme, owing to the Irish famine and to the building of New Oxford Street and the demolitions it caused. A house-to-house investigation by the Statistical Society nevertheless reveals a state of things which does not equal in horror the glimpses we get of St Giles in the eighteenth and early nineteenth century. Among the most overcrowded houses was one in which each adult paid threepence a night, while a man, his wife and children occupying a bed for a week paid 3s. In this house eleven persons slept in the cellar in three beds – adults paying threepence a night as in the other rooms. This was the only house visited in which there were beds in the cellar.[128] But in the reports of 1816–17 we read of forty in a cellar, and of cellars and rooms being shared with pigs and asses.*

Parts of the old Rookery thus survived – an object-lesson in horrors that had once been far more general. In the eighteenth century, at least from the building of Westminster Bridge, many courts, alleys and crumbling houses inhabited by thieves and beggars had succumbed to Improvement Acts and gradual rebuilding. Place writes in 1826 that much had been done within his memory

. . . in the destruction of several of the most dirty, wretched and miscreant neighbourhoods. In a few years from this time it will hardly be believed that an immense number of houses were built in narrow courts and close lanes, each house being at least three stories and many of them four stories above the ground floor. That in these courts and lanes the dirt and filth used to accumulate in heaps and was but seldom removed, that many of these tall houses had two, three and sometimes four rooms on a floor, and that from the garrets to the cellars a family lived or starved in each room. Circulation of air was out of the question, the putrid effluvia was always stagnant in these places, and had not London been in other respects a healthy place, the plague must still have continued among us.[129]

All the causes of ill-health arising from bad sanitary conditions enumerated in 1838 by the medical officers of the London parishes[109]

* See the account of the Irish in St Giles in Chapter 3.

existed in the eighteenth century and almost certainly in a more extreme form. They are divided into two classes, the first being causes for which the sufferers could not be considered in any way responsible:

1. Imperfection or want of sewers and drains.
2. Uncovered and stagnant drains or ditches.
3. Open stagnant pools.
4. Undrained marsh land.
5. Accumulation of refuse in streets, courts, etc.
6. Exhalations of cesspools and
7. Slaughter-houses.
8. Burial-grounds.[124]

The second class consists of causes arising from social conditions:

1. The state of the lodging-houses of mendicants and vagrants and of a certain class of the Irish poor.
2. Overcrowding.
3. Gross want of cleanliness.
4. Intemperance.
5. The habit of lodging in previously deserted houses, cellars, etc.
6. Keeping hogs in dwelling-houses.
7. Indisposition to be removed to the hospitals when infected.
8. Neglect of vaccination.

In most of these things there had been a gradually cumulative improvement, at all events since the middle of the eighteenth century, with occasional interruptions from an epidemic, an influx of Irish immigrants or the local reactions of demolitions or ill-conceived drainage schemes. The measure of improvement is the change in the death-rate and in the diseases of London. Improvement in housing however, was for the most part a by-product of other changes. No provision was made by central or local authorities for housing the people dislodged from the demolished rookeries. Here and there appeals were made by individuals who urged a housing policy in the interests of health and decency.* But in practice housing was one of the last reforms to

* See for instance in Chapter 1 the proposals of Dr Stanger and Dr Bateman.

receive the attention of philanthropists or public bodies. The point of view of the Improvement Acts of our period was that of removing nuisances of all kinds, including dilapidated hovels and their inhabitants. Civic pride had its share in expensive rebuilding schemes, but hardly humanity.

CHAPTER 3

LONDON IMMIGRANTS AND EMIGRANTS

When a man is tired of London he is tired of Life.
Johnson (1777)

THE framework of English society was in the eighteenth century still largely based on the ideal of a population which moved about as little as possible. The poor laws and the vagrancy laws provided for sending the wanderer back to his place of settlement. Corporate towns aimed at excluding newcomers from exercising trades or handicrafts. It became the object, however, of parish officers to keep down the number of inhabitants with settlements, cottages were pulled down and marriages discouraged, children were apprenticed in some other parish. Thus the result of the settlement laws was not to check movement but to encourage it. People dislodged in the country went to towns, especially to London and the growing industrial districts; it was impossible for large urban parishes to protect themselves after the manner of country villages. This was soon realized in London and a proposal was made to stop immigration by the old policy of forbidding new buildings. This was a subject of debate in Parliament in 1675: 'We are undone in the country without buildings; the relief of the poor ruins the nation. By a late Act they are hunted like foxes out of parishes, and whither must they go but where there are buildings?' . . . 'The Act for settlement of the poor does indeed thrust all people out of the country to London. This Bill remedies the matter.'[1]

London needed a large supply of immigrants to make up the ravages of her heavy death-rate. There was also a constant emigration that had to be counterbalanced; London was said to be the best recruiting ground in the kingdom for the army and the plantations owing to the many country people who came to seek employment which they failed to find.[2] The successful citizen retired to his villa in the suburbs or bought

an estate in the country. Many parish children were bound apprentices
to masters outside London or to the sea service. There was a constant
flow outwards as well as inwards. The high death-rate among London
children meant a low physique among the survivors and country people
were necessary for heavy manual labour, while the better education in
Scotland and the north of England made boys from the north in request
for shops and offices.[3] There was a conviction that the London poor
were vicious and dishonest and consequently there was a great demand
for domestic servants – then a far larger proportion of the community
than they afterwards became – from the country. London was naturally
the favourite place of resort for the beggars and vagrants who were so
largely a product of the vagrancy and settlement laws.

If any person is born with any defect or deformity [it was said about 1730] or
maimed by fire or other casualty, or any inveterate distemper which renders
them miserable objects, their way is open to London, where they have free
liberty of showing their nauseous sights to terrify people, and force them to
give money to get rid of them; and these vagrants have for many years past
been moved out of several parts of these kingdoms and taken their stations
in this metropolis, to the interruption of conversation and business.[4]

London attracted the best and the worst, the enterprising and the
parasitic classes, and the tendency of the poor laws was to reduce the
seeker for work to the tramping vagrant.

In so large and constant a supply of country people, there must unavoidably
be a number of men and women who cannot get speedy employment or are
seduced by artful practices into evil courses of life; there certainly ought to be
some better provision made than that of sending them back to their parishes
... with a pass. ... When both law and justice have thus given a sanction to
begging it is very natural for a poor man or woman to take up the trade of a
strolling beggar who would not otherwise have done it.[2]

Besides the internal reasons for migration to the metropolis, London
then to some extent took the place now taken by the United States as
the obvious resort of those driven out of their own countries by
economic or political pressure. Apart from the French Huguenots who
settled in Spitalfields and Soho at the end of the seventeenth century,
this applies more particularly to the Irish and to the Polish Jews who
found their way in large numbers to London. Though there was

emigration to the American plantations from Ireland and Germany, Scotland and England, distressed and adventurous races and classes also came to London.

What proportion immigrants, British and foreign, bore to native Londoners can be only a matter of conjecture. Burrington, whose main contention – that the population of London was not declining – was accurate, puts the proportion very high. 'Ireland,' he writes in 1757,

... greatly assists in filling up the capital ... foreigners from all protestant countries and too many papists come to London continually, ... not above one in twenty of shop and alehouse keepers, journeymen and labourers, living in the Bills of Mortality, were either born or served their apprenticeships in town. ... It is very probable that two-thirds of the grown persons at any time in London come from distant parts.[5]

It was often asserted that those who did well in London were not as a rule London-bred. A Blackwell Hall factor gave evidence in 1816 of the well-known fact that tradesmen and merchants preferred country people as porters, warehousemen and clerks. He thought that a large proportion of London householders had come from the country, mostly without property and had risen generally from clerks, often from inferior positions, while a majority of the principals of trading and commercial houses in the City he believed had been country people.[6]

The only attempt at a serious investigation seems to have been that of Dr Bland who kept a record of cases at the Westminster General Dispensary from 1774 to 1781 to discover the proportion between native Londoners and others. He found that among 3,236 married people the proportion was as follows:

824 or one-fourth, were born in London.
1,870, or four-sevenths, were born in the different counties of England and Wales.
209, or one in fifteen, were born in Scotland.
280, or one in eleven, were born in Ireland.
53, or one in sixty, were foreigners.

Among these males and females were in the following proportions:

Men	Women	
329	495	were born in London.
952	917	were born in England and Wales.
135	74	were born in Scotland.
162	119	were born in Ireland.
40	13	were foreigners.[7]

Westminster was not a specially Irish district and a similar investigation in St Giles, Whitechapel or Marylebone would probably have shown a higher percentage of Irish.

Many of these immigrants eventually obtained settlements in London parishes, but many did not, and the casual or unskilled labourer who was most likely to need relief was also the least likely to be able to gain a settlement. And in any case, when they first came to London, poor and friendless, they had no possible claim to parish help. To apply for it would result in their being sent back to their own parishes. The dangers to the countryman who came to London seeking work are illustrated by the case of poor Matthew Lee of Croft in Lincolnshire where he had been apprenticed to a shoe-maker 'and served his time to the approbation of his master'. When he came out of his time he went to London, 'but being used to coarse country work, unskill'd in the method of working in London and but a slow hand withal', he found it impossible to live by his trade and got work as a drawer or waiter at inns. He was lured away from the Three Tuns in Newgate Street by an offer of 'great wages' in the service of an acquaintance. No money was forthcoming, but he was given a pistol and forced with threats to be a footpad. His hard case did not save him after he had been taken 'with the watch upon him' and at the age of nineteen he was executed at Tyburn.[8]

There was one numerous class whose position was especially difficult and dangerous. These were the girls who came from the country to find places as domestic servants. Colquhoun estimated in 1800 that there were seldom less than 10,000 domestic servants of both sexes out of a place in London.[9] John Fielding in 1753 speaks of the 'amazing number' of women servants wanting places, though there was always a shortage of maids of all work.

The body of servants ... that are chiefly unemployed ... are those of a higher nature such as chambermaids, etc., whose number far exceeds the places they stand candidates for, and as the chief of these come from the country, they are obliged when out of place to go into lodgings and there to subsist on their little savings, till they get places agreeable to their inclinations ... and this is one of the grand sources which furnish this town with prostitutes.[10]

But besides the danger of unemployment, the journey and arrival in town were full of danger to the country girl. The writer of a London guide-book (1776) gives

... a word of advice to such young women as may arrive strangers in town. ... Immediately on their arrival ... and sometimes sooner, even upon the road to it, there are miscreants of both sexes on the watch to seduce the fresh country maiden, with infinite protestations of friendship, service, love and pity, to prostitution. ... For this reason, the very carriages which convey them are hunted and examined; the inns where they alight are beset by these infernal hirelings who ... put on the demure shew of modesty and sanctity for their deception. If she applies to an office of intelligence, 'tis odds but she falls into the hands of some procuress. ...[11]

It was the custom of mistresses to meet the wagons which brought country girls to London in order to find and engage servants.[12] It is clear that this must have given great opportunities for what were called 'the delusive snares ... laid daily by the agents of Hell for the ruin of innocence'.[11] The first scene in Hogarth's *Harlot's Progress* was one frequently played in real life.

Irish immigration was of great industrial importance and profoundly affected social conditions in London. The original Irish colony, dating from the early seventeenth century, was in the parish of St Giles in the Fields, but as time went on settlements were made all over the metropolis, outside the City. The Irish in London were for the most part unskilled labourers. They were builders' labourers, chairmen, porters, coal-heavers, milk-sellers and street hawkers, and they were publicans and lodging-house keepers, apparently chiefly catering for their own countrymen. There were also Irish weavers in London; there was a close connexion between the silk trades of London and Dublin, and linen weavers came over from Ireland and took to silk weaving. The wives of the Irish labourers who lived near the markets often carried loads of fruit, vegetables, etc., through the streets. There was a seasonal immigration of Irish labour for the hay harvest round London, from which doubtless the permanent colonies were partly recruited. The Irish thus supplied a considerable part of the casual and unskilled labour of the metropolis and there were many among its professional beggars.

The population of the Irish colonies in London was partly permanent, partly fluctuating. The cow-keepers round London cultivated hay intensively and employed large numbers of Irish for the harvest. Many of these arrived in London before the time of the harvest with their wives and children, having begged their way to town. In 1815 it was said that far more came than could be employed, and in June it was estimated that by reason of this annual influx there were then 5,000 more Irish in London than there had been five weeks before.[13] Some of these annual immigrants worked as bricklayers' labourers. Many it was supposed came over as professional beggars, though all would say they were looking for work. Many were of the poorest class of cottars from Galway, Roscommon and Mayo who came to earn money during the summer in order to be able to pay their rents and subsist during the winter. Some stayed in London for years sending money periodically to Ireland.[14] This annual immigration undoubtedly increased with the agricultural distress in Ireland which followed the peace. But it had been going on at all events since the early eighteenth century and was a great burden on the poor rates of Liverpool and Chester as well as of the London parishes.

There were many different types of Irish in London. St Giles was a centre for beggars and thieves and the headquarters of street sellers and costermongers and it had a reputation in Ireland for being generous in the matter of poor relief; the Rookery was a thieves' quarter. Therefore it attracted the least desirable type of Irish and those who went there could hardly escape demoralization.[15] The adjoining district of Saffron Hill had much the same character. But to other parts of the town, the Irish went for work. There were coal-heavers and ballast-men in Wapping and Shadwell. Their work was terribly irregular and heavy drinking was forced upon them by the middle-men in the trade. Though these labourers were described in 1816 as 'dissolute and depraved' the same witness gave it as his opinion that 'the lower classes of the Irish do not generally employ their children in begging'.[16]

Wherever building went on, there colonies of Irish bricklayers' labourers sprang up. After 1798 such a colony developed at Lisson Grove and the Gravel Pits where the parishes of Marylebone and Paddington joined. The land belonged to the Bishop of London and was then in a more or less derelict state as undeveloped building ground. Little huts were set up for which a small ground-rent was paid. They were liable to be moved at six months' notice and were then taken down and put up again on some other part of the land. Irish labourers, many of whom were then employed on the Paddington Canal, were attracted to the place as potatoes could be planted round the huts.[17] Charles Knight describes the place as it was in 1812:

The extensive waste which Tyburnia now covers was occupied with the most wretched huts, filled with squatters of the lowest of the community, whose habitual amusement on a Sunday morning was that of dog fights. Paddington had then an evil reputation. To walk in the fields there through which the canal flowed was not very pleasant and certainly not safe.[18]

Such a colony was in the nature of things temporary. There were Irish settlements in Whitechapel, Poplar and Southwark, but these in the middle of poor districts were inconspicuous. A self-contained Irish colony in Marylebone, Calmel or Callmel Buildings, a court off Orchard Street close to Portman Square, attracted the attention of generations of social reformers. In 1799 the renewal of the licence of the Wheatsheaf in Calmel Buildings was refused 'on account of the many irregularities committed in the said house by gamblers and other persons of the most abandoned characters'.[19] The general disorder and sanitary condition of the court were such that a society was formed, the Calmel Society, to deal with a nuisance that the Marylebone vestry could not cope with and to provide some education for the neglected children there. It found 'such a scene of filth and wretchedness as cannot be conceived ... the children employed there in begging and thieving' that it was led to extend its activities to other districts and by 1815 had developed into a society for 'the relief of the lower-class Irish in London'. The secretary, Montagu Burgoyne, told the Mendicity Committee that he had heard that 700 Irish lived in twenty-four small houses. He found the number more than this – there were often three or four families in a room – and since his investigation the number was said to have increased. (There were also a hundred or so pigs in the court.[20]) The place was never cleansed, people were afraid to enter it for fear of infection, and repeated applications to the vestry had been ineffectual. 'I have been into every room myself,' said Burgoyne, '. . . neither in town nor in the country have I ever met with so many poor among whom there was so much distress, so much profligacy and so much ignorance.' He was asked why the proportion of children was so small (among the Irish in London known to him from a house-to-house visitation there were 6,876 grown people and 7,288 children), he answered, 'from the great want of care taken of them in infancy . . . and not only many die, but a great proportion of those who live are crippled and crooked and very unhealthy'.[13] The Calmel Society distributed a certain amount of relief and sent from three to four hundred children to Catholic schools, but it failed to deal with the filth and misery in Calmel Buildings.[21]

Simond, who visited England in 1810–11, has recorded his impressions of the place.

We have in our neighbourhood [he writes] one of those no-thoroughfare lanes or courts. . . . This one is inhabited by a colony of Irish labourers who fill every cellar and every garret . . . very poor, very uncleanly and very turbulent. They give each other pitched battles, every Saturday night particularly, when heroes and heroines shew their prowess at fisticuffs and roll together in the kennel, precisely as at Paris in the Faubourg St Marceau. We should never have known there were such wretches as this in London if we had not happened to reside in Orchard Street, Portman Square, which by the way, is one of the finest parts of the town. The uproar continued all last night from Saturday to Sunday . . . and it was impossible to sleep. . . . A watchman called for assistance with his rattle. One or more of his brethren assembled and I overheard from the window one of them say, 'If I go in, I know I shall have a shower of brickbats'. To which another answered very considerately, 'let them murder each other if they please'.

In the eighteenth century information as to the Irish is chiefly incidental. They appear in accounts of trade disputes and street fights, in the records of the Old Bailey and of the Middlesex Sessions. As elements in the problem of vagrancy and sanitation they were hardly discussed before the Parliamentary reports of the early nineteenth century; but there can be little doubt that the characteristics of the London-Irish had been much the same for a hundred years, probably for two, though their numbers progressively increased under the stimulus of building activities and a more liberal distribution of poor relief in London and the pressure of population upon the land in Ireland. Irish vagrants had been a cause of alarm in the sixteenth[22] and seventeenth centuries: 'Whereas this realm hath of late been pestered with a great number of Irish beggars, who live here idly and dangerously, and are of ill-example to the natives of this kingdom,' ran a proclamation of 1629.[23] At this time the Irish seem already to have turned to the occupation of street hawking; Dekker wrote in 1607, 'as Frenchmen love to be bold, Flemings to be drunken . . . and Irish to be costermongers'.[24]

Riots against Irish harvest labour were common in the eighteenth century.[25] Jealousy of Irish labour seems to show itself in an order of the Tin Plate Workers Company in 1724 that all the unskilled Irishmen (were these tinkers?) should be prosecuted for working.[26] There was a violent outburst against the Irish in Spitalfields in July 1736. Irish weavers and builders' labourers were accused of working at under rates. Sir Robert Walpole wrote,

. . . this complaint against the Irish . . . is founded upon greater numbers than ordinary . . . of Irish being here, and not only working at hay and corn harvest, but letting themselves out to all sorts of ordinary labour considerably cheaper than the English labourers have, and numbers of them being employed by the weavers upon like terms. . . . They are building a new church at Spitalfields where, I am told, the master workmen discharged at once a great number of all sorts of labourers and took in . . . Irishmen who served for above one-third less per day.[27]

According to another account some Irish weavers who were employed as bricklayers' labourers 'offered to work at half the price of the English, this bred the first disgust'. On two successive days there was a pitched battle. The English cried 'down with the Irishmen', broke the windows of the houses where they lodged and 'almost demolished' two Irish public-houses. The Riot Act was read without effect, the Tower Hamlets Militia was called out, but the mob was not dispersed till companies of Guards from the Tower appeared. A report had arisen that numbers of Irishmen had recently arrived in London to supplant English workmen by working at low rates. The strength of the anti-Irish feeling is shown by the fact that a few days later 'mobs arose in Southwark, Lambeth, and Tyburn Road and took upon them to interrogate people whether they were for the English or the Irish, but committed no violence'.[28]

Faction fights between English and Irish seem to have been common. In 1740 there was a general onslaught by a body of Irish upon the butchers of Clare Market. It seems that it was the custom to burn a 'Taffy' in effigy on St David's day, and some rash butchers' boys had ventured to burn a 'Paddy' on St Patrick's day. The Irish were said to be a great body of men of whom over twenty were armed with cutlasses and thirty or forty more with sticks and bludgeons. When three ring-leaders were taken before Colonel de Veil, a 'prodigious mob', it is said, surrounded his office and many persons armed with pistols and cutlasses assembled in Covent Garden.[29] In 1763 there was a pitched battle (one of the many disturbances of a Westminster election) between a party of sailors and a number of Irish chairmen in Covent Garden. A chairman offered to fight the best sailor present and was beaten. This was followed by a general mêlée in which the sailors demolished every chair they could find.[30] It was an understood thing that the outcome of a street dispute should be a fight for which the by-standers formed a ring, but when one of the combatants was an Irishman, his fellow-countrymen would join in and a general battle was apt to follow.[31]

Though the excesses of the Gordon Riots are to be explained by the effects of drink and a swamping of the forces of order by the inhabitants of the dangerous districts in London who were always ready for pillage, a strong anti-Catholic spirit undoubtedly played its part. Was this partly due to that prejudice against the Irish of which there are so many indications? Defoe, it is true, said that he believed there were 'ten thousand stout fellows that would spend the last drop of their blood against Popery that do not know whether it be a man or a horse',[32] but by 1780 the sectarian feuds of the early part of the century had subsided. Irish public-houses seem to have been demolished in much the spirit of the riot of 1736. For instance, one Susannah Clark was tried in connexion with the destruction of a public-house in Golden Lane kept by a certain Murphy. Evidence was given that she had said:

... it was a Roman Catholick's house and there was nothing but Roman Catholicks in it and it must be pulled down and down it should come ... there had been an Irish wake in the houses, they were Irish Roman Catholicks and the house must come down.[33]

The Irish in London were a police problem, a sanitary problem, a poor-law problem and an industrial problem. It was the first aspect of the question which first attracted the attention of the authorities. Saunders Welch, the London magistrate, in 1753 divided the Irish immigrants into two classes:

The Irish imported into this kingdom of the lower class [he wrote] are those who annually come to harvest work and when that is over return with the savings of their labour to their own country. These are useful, faithful, good servants to the farmer and as they are of great use to the kingdom, deserve protection and encouragement. The others are a set of fellows made desperate by their crimes, and whose stay in Ireland being no longer safe, come to London to perpetrate their outrages, and it may be justly asserted that most of the robberies, and the murders consequent upon them, have been committed by these outcasts from Ireland. . . . That London is the asylum of these rogues and vagabonds as well Irish as English who are driven by their rogueries to seek shelter and concealment is a truth beyond dispute. . . .

He considered that the two great causes of the supply of rogues to London were 'the unlimited wandering of the poor of our own king-dom and the uncontrouled importation of Irish vagabonds'.[34] Except for the two Fieldings, there could be no better authority on the under-world of London than Saunders Welch, and the Fieldings were of much the same opinion. Henry Fielding is reported to have said that the greater number of those committed at Bow Street were Irish[35] (this of course would include a number of trivial assault cases). Sir John Fielding in a letter to the Secretary of State (on the subject of Jews) raised the question of Irish immigration. 'If some restraint could be laid on the importation of the abandoned Irish,' he wrote in 1771, 'it would be another means of preventing many robberies in this country. There are certainly a much greater number both of Jews and Irish than can possibly gain subsistence by honest means.'[36]

The evidence of the Old Bailey *Sessions Papers* supports this theory; it appears that Irishmen deserting from the Irish Brigade came to London from the Continent as well as from Ireland to live by plunder.[37] Things seem to have been at their worst in the forties and fifties and towards the end of the century the criminal element among the Irish seems certainly to have diminished. Crime changed its character with the improvements in street lighting and police, and foot-pads (among whom the Irish had been conspicuous) and highwaymen gave way to burglars. One of the reasons for crime among the London-Irish was certainly the character of the common lodging-houses in St Giles and Bloomsbury where beds were let at twopence a night and gin sold at a penny a quartern, whose inhabitants, Fielding says, were chiefly Irish.

He describes these places in 1751, his authority being Saunders Welch and his own experience.

If one considers the destruction of all morality, decency and modesty, the swearing, whoredom and drunkenness which is eternally carrying on in these houses on the one hand, and the excessive poverty and misery of most of the inhabitants on the other, it seems doubtful whether they are most the objects of detestation or compassion: for such is the poverty of these wretches, that, upon searching all the above number the money found upon all of them ... did not amount to one shilling, and I have been credibly informed that a single loaf hath supplied a whole family with their provisions for a week. Lastly, if any of these creatures fall sick (and it is almost a miracle that stench, vermin, and want should ever suffer them to be well) they are turned out into the street by their merciless host or hostess, where, unless some parish officer of extraordinary charity relieves them, they are miserably sure to perish, with the addition of cold and hunger to their disease. This picture, which is taken from the life, will appear strange to many, for the evil here described is, I am confident, very little known, especially to those of the better sort. Indeed, this is the only excuse, I believe the only reason, that it hath been so long tolerated: for when we consider the number of these wretches, which in the outskirts of the town amounts to many thousands, it is a nuisance which will appear to be big with every moral and political mischief.[38]

All the problems connected with the Irish in London merge into one, dependent on their poverty, ignorance and low standard of living, for which conditions in Ireland were mainly responsible. As Robert Bell wrote in 1804, 'the turbulent and barbarous habits of the lower orders of the people of Ireland, their abject poverty, and their sufferings have long been a subject of unavailing complaint'.[39] Add to this their traditional attitude towards the forces of law and order. Bell says, 'If a man in any public place was charged with a felony, the spectators would frequently assist him in making his escape' (while the London populace was always ready to chase a thief or foot-pad) and imagine such people in the surroundings of eighteenth-century London. Nevertheless they improved.

The Irish came to London from cabins where they had lived among cows, pigs and hens. Arthur Young describes the hovels of the peasants and even of the comparatively well-to-do farmer or dairyman.

The furniture of the cabbins is as bad as the architecture, in very many consisting only of a pot for boiling their potatoes, a bit of a table and one or two broken stools; beds are not found universally, the family lying on straw, equally partook of by cows, calves and pigs, though the luxury of sties is coming in in Ireland.

He compares the Irish with the English peasant to the latter's disadvantage: 'In England a man's cottage will be filled with superfluities before he possesses a cow ... a hog is a much more valuable piece of goods than a set of tea things.'[40] But in a crowded London tenement a set of tea things would have been more suitable than a hog. Far lower depths of misery were reached than among the people described by Arthur Young, with whom potatoes and milk were plentiful; sheer starvation sent some of the cottier tenants to England for the hay harvest.

'The Irish are a description of people,' said the beadle of St Giles in 1817,

... that if they are in labour and they come home on the Saturday night with their wages, those wages are spent on the Saturday night or the Sunday morning and then they shuffle on the rest of the week with their herrings or potatoes. ... Then on the Sunday morning there is nothing but fighting. ...

Another witness said, 'early on the Sunday morning you will see Irishmen quite drunk and fighting with their shelalas ... at times three or four hundred ... will collect together'.[41] The beadle, though he said that in the slums of the parish the boys were brought up as thieves and the girls as prostitutes, when asked if the manners of the lower Irish had not considerably improved from what they were some years ago, answered that they had and that there was a school in the parish which had much benefited the children.[42] In the eighteenth century, as in the early nineteenth many of the most wretched of the London poor were Irish. Place, commenting on a description of the 'dissolute manners' of the Irish in St Giles in 1816, says,

... this account is no doubt correct, and is a fair picture of the manners of a much larger proportion of the people half a century ago. Such people ... are now only to be found in a few places, such as the back settlement of St Giles, some places in the parish of St Luke and Ratcliffe Highway, and almost wholly among the Irish. The poorest and most dissolute people in Spitalfields are several grades above the mere Irish.[43]

The Irish in St Giles were probably less wretched than they had been in Fielding's time because they no longer depended upon the chance benevolence of some parish officer of 'extraordinary charity'. It was stated in 1815 by an overseer of the previous year that of £32,000 a year raised in the parish, £20,000 went to the 'lower Irish',[44] and in 1817 it was estimated that nineteen in twenty persons receiving relief were Irish, the other twentieth including English, Welsh and Scots.[45] This distribution of poor relief however, had undoubtedly increased the number of Irish claimants for it.[46]

From a sanitary point of view there were three Irish customs which were peculiarly unfortunate. First that of sharing their rooms with pigs and other animals. The Rookery or the Irish quarter of St Giles was described in 1816 by the surgeon of the Great Russell Street Dispensary. The streets, neglected by the parish scavengers, were 'exceedingly noisome', human beings, hogs, asses and dogs were

... associated in the same habitation ... and great heaps of dirt may be found piled in the streets. ... Some of the lower habitations have neither windows nor chimneys nor floors, and are so dark that I can scarcely see at mid-day without a candle.

Many of the houses were common lodging-houses, where, as in the time of Fielding, drams were sold. Forty people would, it was said, frequently occupy one cellar.[47]

Another Irish custom was for the tenant of a single room to take in other lodgers as sub-tenants either permanently or for the night. Indeed there were people to whom this form of room-letting or rather space-letting was a sole means of livelihood. In Calmel Buildings in 1837 were to be found

... instances of single rooms, sublet in portions to three or four different families and even these portions were again sublet. The occupant of a bed ... say a labourer would take as a lodger, as a tenant of half his bed, another labourer at a weekly rent.[48]

Thus the operations of the Irish middle-man who leased and sublet land in agricultural Ireland were reproduced in a London slum from the same causes of poverty and overcrowding.

A third unfortunate custom was that of the Irish wake. The corpse, no matter what had been the cause of death, was laid out upon the only bed and burial was delayed, often for very many days, till money had been collected from the neighbours for the wake, which was open to all comers as long as there was anything to drink or smoke. A terrible case which occurred in Saffron Hill was described in 1817. A certain Mrs Sullivan, whose daughter had died in the workhouse, had prevailed upon the parish authorities to let her have the girl's body 'to bury her decently'. She raised three successive subscriptions for the burial. All were spent in drink, and burial was so long delayed that 'a fever got into the house and there were six buried and eighteen or twenty ill'. In the end the parish was obliged to bury the girl. This was an extreme case. Mother and daughter were paupers and the mother had lived on the prostitution of the daughter.[49] But wakes generally led to fights and often to illness and death. 'Thus fevers and other diseases are fearfully propagated,' wrote Chadwick in 1843.[50]

The Irish were thus a disturbing element in London life. Their low standard of life and their increasing numbers lowered the wages of casual and unskilled labour. There were many reasons for the prevalence of typhus, but the courts where they lived were known to be breeding-places of the disease.[51] In the early nineteenth century however, the Irish, who had certainly become more numerous, figure less prominently in criminal trials than in the middle of the eighteenth, though even in 1815 it was said, 'we hardly ever hear of a riot or a murder or a burglary in which several persons are concerned, in which some of these poor creatures are not implicated'.[52] Of the Irish in Marylebone it was said in 1828 that 'there was not much crime among them, though there was a great deal of disorder, . . . dreadful affrays where they half murder each other'.[53] A corresponding change seems to have taken place in the morals of the women. Adam Smith had said that the greater part of London prostitutes were supposed to be 'from the lowest rank of the people in Ireland' and the records of the Old Bailey and of the Middle-sex Sessions show that many Irish women were of this unfortunate profession. In the middle of the nineteenth century Mayhew found the Irish street seller conspicuously more moral than Englishwomen of the same occupation, but said that when Irishwomen did fall into evil ways they were the most 'savagely wicked' of any.

While Irish ruffianism in London decreased, the number of 'industrious Irish' increased. In the middle of the eighteenth century it was held (by the employing classes) that these were an economic necessity, but after 1815 at least they were an economic danger. Till 1819 the law gave the Irish an advantage over the English poor in allowing them to apply for poor relief without fear of being sent back to their parishes.[54] They had a special gift for relating stories of distress, 'you never can believe one word they say', said Burgoyne, 'they have so much ingenuity and so much imagination. . . .' The pressure of the Irish poor threatened to break down the poor-law machinery in some of the London parishes as well as in Liverpool and Manchester, and made the administration of the vagrancy laws more defective than ever. Peace brought poverty and unemployment to England, and in Ireland, without a poor law, distress reached such a point that emigration to England was forced upon the people. The effects of this immigration in London is illustrated by the experiences of the Mendicity Society which offered work at stone-breaking to the poorest able-bodied men who came to their office at which they earned from a shilling to eighteenpence a day. The Irish, however, undertook the work at a rate which gave them only sixpence or eightpence a day.

The most destitute of the English would not work for those wages, yet the Irish did it cheerfully and regretted when they could not have the work to do. . . . The news of their being thus employed reached Ireland, the natives came over in large numbers, men, women and children, and sat themselves down in the street near the office – their numbers caused great alarm.[55]

The Irish had other qualities besides a low standard of living which gave them an advantage in the London labour market. They had greater physical strength than Londoners, and some of them (those of St Giles always excepted) were perhaps thriftier than the English of a corresponding class. Mayhew found that this was the case in the nineteenth century, and it was probably equally true in the eighteenth.[56] It might be expected from their peasant origin and their habit of saving money for the rent of their land and cabin in Ireland. Two characteristically Irish occupations, that of the chairman and the milk-seller (milk walks were bought and sold by the milk-sellers) both needed some small amount of capital as well as physical strength.

Many of the Jews, like many of the Irish, came to England, not because there was a demand for their labour or even a possibility of earning a living, but to escape starvation and obtain charity. During the Protectorate and in the reign of Charles II a body of Spanish and

Portuguese Jews had settled in London. These, the Jews of the Sephardim, were for the most part rich and respected. The beginning of the Ashkenazim settlement in London consisting of Jews using the German ritual dates from the end of the seventeenth century. The first Synagogue of the Ashkenazi was established in Duke's Place, Aldgate, in 1722, and after this London began to be looked upon as a place of refuge for distressed Jews from the Continent. All European disturbances in which the Jews were sufferers stimulated the migration to England. There were persecutions in Bohemia in 1744. The war that ended with the partition of Poland in 1772 brought a fresh influx. During the siege of Gibraltar in 1781 several shiploads of Moroccan Jews who had settled there managed to escape to England. These immigrants were for the most part poor, and came to England relying on the charity of the Jews of the Sephardim, to whom they were far from welcome, and from about the middle of the century the burden became increasingly heavy.[57]

The outburst of anti-Jewish feeling which led to the immediate repeal of the Jewish Naturalization Act of 1753, though largely the result of violent and unreasoning prejudice, fostered by certain City interests, had some economic excuse. It was maintained that it

... would deluge the kingdom with brokers, usurers and beggars ... that the rich Jews would purchase lands ... and influence the Church of Christ ... that the lower class of that nation would interfere with the industrious natives who earn their livelihood by their labour, and by dint of the most parsimonious frugality, to which the English were strangers, work at an under price, so as not only to share, but even in a manner exclude them from all employment. ...[58]

The fear that Jewish labour would undercut English workmen was not justified in the eighteenth century. It was the misfortune of the Jews that they were virtually excluded from industrial employment by the impossibility of their apprenticeship to a Christian master.

The history of the poorer London Jews in the earlier eighteenth century is obscure; the Jewish Synagogue accepted responsibility for them, and it was apparently not till after 1770 that it was realized that Jewish immigration constituted a social problem. For this reason the life history of certain Jews which has survived because they formed part of a gang of thieves is of great interest as showing their curiously international character. Joseph Isaacs (otherwise called McCoy) was born about 1724 of Dutch-Jewish parents in Duke's Place, and went to a Jewish school in Houndsditch. He also lived as a child with his mother in Amsterdam and worked for his father in London for nine years at pencil-making. At this he could earn it was said about 16s. or 17s. a week, and 'at vending such goods' three guineas a week. He spent part of his time in Holland, France and Germany and used to travel to Frankfort hawking knives, buckles, razors and the like. He could read Hebrew and understood French, Spanish and Italian (and presumably Dutch and German). At the time of his execution in 1744 his parents and other relations were in Poland.

Jacob Cordosa, who was executed at the same time, had been born in Amsterdam and worked as a snuff-maker in London, frequently travelling to Holland. About three years before his death the 'vestry' of the Synagogue in London, 'hearing there were many robberies committed by the Jews, sent several of them to Holland'. One of these was Cordosa, who was given two guineas and told that if he returned within two years he should be arrested. Cordosa explained, ''tis a custom among the Jews, if a man goes abroad ... for ... two or three years according to the agreement, if he returns within that time he is liable to be arrested'. He received the two guineas and 'a person passed his word (according to the custom) that he should go abroad'. However, he used to visit London five or six times a year and buy hardware and pewter and take it to Holland. He always travelled, he said, 'by the King's packet boat, because he went for nothing, only giving a shilling or two to the clerk for making out a pass'.[59]

The immigration of poor Jews to England was a serious burden to the established Jewish colony in London. In 1753 the Great Synagogue tried to check the flow by refusing relief to those who left their country without due cause. This proved to be impossible.[57] In 1771 attention was drawn to the Jews by a murder and robbery in the King's Road, Chelsea, committed by a gang of Jews. It was found that immigration was increasing and that the packets from Holland were full of Jews. Sir John Fielding asked the Elders of the Synagogue what was the cause of this and they answered that it was 'partly on account of the late disturbance in Poland, partly to share charities distributed in this kingdom from their chest at the Synagogue'. 'They travel to Helvoetsluys,' wrote Fielding, 'there plead poverty and get passes by our agent there, by which means they get their passage free.' The Elders were anxious for some restriction on the influx to England. This it was suggested might be done by requiring them to produce a certificate passed by the Home Office that their presence in England was required by some business. In any case, the Elders wished, and Fielding supported their wish in the interest of order in London, 'that some restraint could be laid on this importation consistent with the wisdom and policy of good government'. The Elders complained that their charity chest was almost bankrupt, and Fielding pointed out that the Jews in England, like the Irish, far exceeded the number that could subsist honestly.

As a result orders were given that no Jews were to come to England on board the king's packet boats unless they paid the usual freight or were furnished with a passport by a British minister abroad. The Elders were certain that all who came over by the poor pass were vagabonds, not able to earn a living, and it was thought necessary 'to prevent the too frequent importation of vagrant and vagabond Jews, who cannot be considered either as useful or beneficial to society'.[60] The Elders of the Great Synagogue expressed their gratitude for this order, but it does not seem to have seriously checked immigration, and the Jews of the Ashkenazim continued to increase, though under the Alien Act of 1792 poor Jews were frequently expelled as undesirable. Lacombe, a Swiss visitor to London, wrote in 1777, '*ce peuple, disperse et errant sur le globe, par la stupidité et l'ignorance atroce des gouvernements arbitraires, tourmente cette nation antique et revérée*'.[61]

In 1734 the Jews in England were estimated at 6,000, in 1753 at 5,000.[62] According to Colquhoun there were in 1800 from 15,000 to 20,000 Jews in London, and perhaps 5,000 or 6,000 more distributed among the provincial and seaport towns. Of these from 12,000 to 15,000 were of the German-Dutch Synagogue which included Polish, Russian and Turkish Jews. These, he said, were completely uneducated and mostly very poor. They lived chiefly by their wits and had established 'a system of mischievous intercourse all over the country, the better to carry on their fraudulent designs in the circulation of base money, and the sale of stolen goods'. He pointed out that this fraudulent traffic was the result of their exclusion from industry and their desperate poverty. They were entirely dependent on Jewish charitable funds for poor relief, and these were quite inadequate. Relief was therefore given them in the form of small loans at interest, with which to set up some kind of hawking business; the loans had to be repaid in weekly or monthly instalments on pain of forfeiting all claim to assistance. This multiplied the number of Jewish pedlars to a point at which it was impossible for them all to gain a living, and they were driven to tricks and frauds and the receiving of stolen goods. 'Educated in idleness from their earliest infancy,' says Colquhoun,

... they acquire every debauched and vicious principle which can fit them for the most complicated arts of fraud and deception ... from the orange boy and the retailer of seals, razors, glass and other wares in the public streets, to the shopkeeper, dealer in wearing apparel or in silver and gold, the same principles of conduct too generally prevail.

This state of things however he thought was 'perhaps ... generated in a greater degree by their peculiar situation in respect to society than by any actual disposition on their part to pursue these nefarious practices'.[63]

This challenging indictment was taken up by a Jew called Van Hoven, who wrote a letter to Colquhoun afterwards published (1802) in a pamphlet called *Letters on the present State of the Jewish Poor in the Metropolis*. He did not deny Colquhoun's allegations, but pointed out how distressing was the position of the poor Jew. The Jews maintained their own poor, who were excluded from Christian hospitals and workhouses.

Until these last fifty years this was no great evil, their numbers being small, and the rich always within reach of the poor, whose wants were thus (although in a desultory way) relieved by the vestries and the opulent individuals. The case however is very different at present; they have greatly multiplied both by propagation and importation, but property has not kept pace with this increase ... the bulk of the nation ... have no regular trade whereby to earn a maintenance. The few they follow, such as dealing in old clothes, &c., are daily becoming less productive, and at present they know no other. . . .[64] There is no circumstance in life more distressing to a Jewish parent (of whatever rank ... in society) than how to put his son forward in life in some honest industrial occupation. The restraints and observances of the Jewish ritual are such an insuperable difficulty in the initiation of the Jewish lad into any craft or trade, as makes it almost impossible for him to be bound to a master who is not of the same persuasion. . . . It is clear how deplorably this affects the poor who from this cause are totally deprived of the possibility of acquiring a trade or of being employed at day-work more than four days and a half, unless extra on Sundays.

Considering the nature and extent of crime in London, the so-called German Jews can hardly be considered as exceptionally and racially dishonest. The chief characteristics of the Jewish immigrants from Eastern Europe at the end of the nineteenth century were found to be 'dirt, overcrowding, industry and sobriety', while in certain streets of the East End where Londoners were displaced by immigrants, a decently behaved set of people replaced a population of roughs and criminals.[65] Probably something of the same sort could be said of the Jewish settlements in Petticoat Lane and its purlieus in the eighteenth century. There was this essential difference, however; the earlier immigrant found his only source of livelihood in peddling and street-trading which was almost necessarily less than honest because the legitimate returns were too small to exist upon. The Jews came from the ghettoes of Eastern Europe and found themselves in a part of London where usury and dealing in second-hand (and stolen) goods had long been carried on. Houndsditch did not owe its bad reputation to Jews: 'A Houndsditch man, Sir. One of the Devil's neere kinsmen, a broker,' wrote Ben Jonson in 1598.

But the Jews had special facilities for disposing of stolen property which made them effective competitors with the English fences who had long carried on a nefarious traffic. They also specialized in offering fraudulent bail, hence the term 'Jew Bail'. In this, as in manners and appearance, they were entirely distinct from the Jews of the Sephardim, whose colony in London dates from Cromwell and the Restoration. 'We are astonished at the difference between the Portuguese and the German Jews established in this island,' says Archenholtz,

... dress, language, manners, cleanliness, politeness, everything distinguishes them, much to the advantage of the former. .... All the children of Israel who are obliged to quit Germany and Holland, take refuge in England, where they live by cheating and nocturnal rapine; and if they do not themselves steal, they aid the thief in concealing and disposing of stolen goods. Thus they are so much abhorred by the English that the honesty of the Portuguese Jews cannot obliterate the unfavourable impression which this host of banditti has made on them.[66]

The outcome of the correspondence between Colquhoun and Van Hoven was a comprehensive scheme for dealing with the whole Jewish problem – poor relief, lack of industrial education and undesirable immigrants – drawn up by Colquhoun from notes by Van Hoven and approved by Abraham Goldsmid. It was embodied in a private Bill which was opposed from all quarters and dropped: the Sephardim objected to amalgamation with the much poorer Ashkenazim, the Ashkenazim feared a levy on their resources, the London parishes protested against the proposal to allocate to the scheme half the poor rate assessed on Jews.[67] Its only result was the Jews' Hospital at Mile End founded in 1806 'for the aged poor and the education and employment of youth'. Here the boys were taught shoe-making and basket-work and in course of time a mahogany-chair manufactory was started, but in 1840 the lack of industrial openings for the London Jews still existed. The Hand Loom Commissioners found in all Jewish educational institutions a desire to bring up the children to some trade so that they should not be forced into street-trading, and thought that the Jews' Hospital would in the course of a generation remove the difficulty by providing a sufficient body of Jewish master-tradesmen to whom boys could be apprenticed.[68]

All foreigners in London who had an outlandish look were liable to be roughly treated, or at least abused, by the mob. The Jews were very unpopular (Moritz says more so than in Germany), Jew-baiting became a sport, like cock-throwing, or bull-baiting or pelting some poor wretch in the pillory. Place ascribes the special ill-treatment of Jews to the robbery and murder in Chelsea (which drew upon them the attention of Sir John Fielding in 1771) for which four Jews were hung.

Every Jew was in public opinion implicated, and the prejudice, ill will and brutal conduct this brought upon the Jews, even after they had been detected and punished for it, did not cease for many years. 'Go to Chelsea' was a common exclamation when a Jew was seen in the streets and was often the signal of assault. I have seen many Jews hooted, hunted, cuffed, pulled by the beard, spit upon, and so barbarously assaulted in the streets, without any protection from the passers-by or the police, as seems when compared with present times, almost impossible to have existed at any time. Dogs could not be used in the streets in the manner many Jews were treated. One circumstance among others put an end to the ill-usage of the Jews. . . . About the

year 1787 Daniel Mendoza, a Jew, became a celebrated boxer and set up a
school to teach the art of boxing as a science, the art soon spread among the
young Jews and they became generally expert at it. The consequence was in a
very few years seen and felt too. It was no longer safe to insult a Jew unless
he was an old man and alone. . . . But even if the Jews were unable to defend
themselves, the few who would [now] be disposed to insult them merely
because they are Jews, would be in danger of chastizement from the passers-
by and of punishment from the police.[69]

Moreover, Jewish proficiency in the ring gained the sympathies of the
mob and much of their unpopularity disappeared. Jewish pugilists introduced a new school of boxing, relying more on science and less on
brute strength, whose heroes were Mendoza, Dutch Sam, and Young
Dutch Sam.

There were many foreign artisans in London, especially in Soho and
St Martin's, besides the French colony in Spitalfields, which became
more or less absorbed in the English community. Lacombe, writing in
1777, says,

. . . depuis douze années la quantité d'ouvriers étrangers établis à Londres a
produit une efflorescence utile au commerce, malgré le peu d'encouragement qu'ils
reçoivent de la nation et des riches entrepreneurs, mais la misère et la despotisme
Allemande et Française peuplera toujours cette Babilone, le seul refuge des
infortunés.[70]

The labourers employed by the sugar refiners, a rapidly-increasing
industry of East London, were chiefly German with some Dutch and
Irish.[71]

London was said to swarm with foreign refugees, criminals, bankrupts and adventurers, 'canaille chassé de leur pays'. The London populace still continued its traditional hostility to foreigners, who were
generally classed indiscriminately as French, but Baretti noticed a
distinct improvement in the ten years between 1750 and 1760 and towards the end of the century foreign visitors no longer comment on it.
After the Peace of 1815 it seems to have disappeared.[72] Grosley, a
Frenchman who came to London in 1765, analyses the causes of the
hatred, as he calls it, which he himself encountered: 'My French air,
notwithstanding the simplicity of my dress, drew upon me at the corner
of every street a volley of abusive litanies in the midst of which I slipt

on, returning thanks to God that I did not understand English.' He ascribed it to the Huguenots who had abused France and the French Court, while some

... reduced to beggary had ... exhausted ... the charity of the English. London is still a place of refuge for bankrupts ... for criminals. ... Can such people as these give an advantageous idea of their country? ... A crowd of adventurers and sharpers helps to complete what these fugitives began.

The frequent wars, he says, increased the feeling of hostility, while the French were perpetually held up to ridicule on the stage as 'coxcombs and ludicrous marquisses'. The fear that the French with a lower standard of living would come over to England and work at a cheaper rate than the English perhaps lay at the root of this feeling. The proposal to naturalize foreign protestants in 1753 was as unpopular as that to naturalize Jews, the cry being 'no Jews, no wooden shoes', that is, no Frenchmen.[73]

Distressed foreigners, however, were kindly treated in London. When 800 poor Palatines were landed destitute in London in 1764 by those who had undertaken to ship them as emigrants to America, they were supported for five months and then sent to South Carolina where land was granted to them by the King. This impressed Archenholtz as a triumph of improvized organization and of the marvellous effects of a single letter to a newspaper. The poor people on being landed were taken to Goodman's Fields where they lay without food or shelter for a day or two, their presence unknown in the City and in West London. A German pastor wrote a letter to the Press appealing for help, a committee was at once formed, subscriptions poured in, organizers were chosen, physicians, apothecaries, nurses and interpreters were appointed and the people lived in tents (provided by the Ordnance Office) till they could be sent to their destination, when the committee chartered ships, stipulating for adequate rations, and providing a doctor for each ship.[74] The story calls to mind the Belgian refugee committees of 1914.

Negroes in London were immigrants of a class apart, and their position must have been strangely friendless and anomalous. They did not live in colonies with their countrymen; some who had been brought to England had run away from or been deserted by their masters, others had come from the West Indies as stowaways or refugees to seek free-dom in England, often to find starvation. Their great number in the eighteenth century has been little commented on. In the famous Somer-sett case (1771–2) it was stated that there were then, according to the most exact estimate that could be made, about 14,000 slaves in the country, and Lord Mansfield accepted the number as between 14,000 and 15,000; a large proportion of these must have been in London, where they seem to have lived chiefly in the eastern and riverside parishes.[75] From time to time Negroes appeared at the Old Bailey charged with petty thefts, and in 1780 one was tried as a Gordon rioter. Sir John Fielding protested against the practice of bringing these poor creatures over from the West Indies:

The immense confusion that has arose in the families of merchants and other gentlemen who have estates in the West Indies from the great numbers of Negro slaves they have brought into this kingdom . . . deserves the most serious attention. Many of these gentlemen have either at a vast expense caused some of their blacks to be instructed in the necessary qualifications of a domestic servant or else have purchased them after they have been in-structed; they then bring them to England as cheap servants having no right to wages; they no sooner arrive here than they put themselves on a footing with other servants, become intoxicated with liberty, grow refractory, and either by persuasion of others or from their own inclinations, begin to expect wages according to their own opinion of their merits; and as there are already a great number of black men and women who have made themselves so troublesome and dangerous to the families who brought them over as to get themselves discharged, these enter into societies and make it their business to corrupt and dissatisfy the mind of every black servant that comes to England; first, by getting them christened or married, which, they inform them, makes them free. . . . Though it has been decided otherwise by the judges. However it so far answers their purpose that it gets the mob on their side, and makes it not only difficult but dangerous . . . to recover possession of them, when once they are spirited away; and indeed, it is the less evil of the two to let them go about their business, for there is great reason to fear that those blacks who have been sent back to the Plantations . . . have been the occasion of those . . . recent insurrections in the . . . West Indies. It is a species of inhumanity to the blacks themselves, to bring them to a free country.[76]

General sympathy was with the Negroes. Before 1772 the uncertainty as to their legal position must have made it very difficult for them to get work after they had left, or been deserted by, their original masters,[77] and the decision in Somersett's case that 'as soon as any slave sets his foot upon English territory he becomes free' increased the number thrown on their own resources. Something of the earlier position of the poor blacks in London appears from appeals made to the Middlesex Sessions. In 1690 Katherine Auker, a black, petitioned to be discharged from her master as he was in Barbados. She said that she had been brought to England about six years before by Robert Rich, a planter from Barbados. She was baptized at St Katherine's by the Tower and after that her master and mistress 'tortured her and turned her out; her said master refusing to give her a discharge, she could not be entertained in service elsewhere'. Her master had caused her to be arrested and imprisoned in the Poultry Compter. The Court ordered that she should be free to serve anyone till her master returned.[78]

More fundamental issues were raised by the case of John Caesar, whose wife petitioned the Sessions in 1717. Her husband, she said, had served Benjamin and John Wood, who were printers and embossers in Whitechapel, as a slave without wages for fourteen years. They had very much abused the said John with very hard usage and for the greatest part of the time had imprisoned him in their dwelling-house. Seven years ago he had been baptized, nevertheless he was still detained as a slave, though, 'as the petitioner is advised, slavery is inconsistent with the laws of this realm'. She herself was very poor and destitute and likely to become chargeable to the parish unless her husband was released from his slavery and confinement and so enabled to provide for himself and the petitioner. The Court recommended the master to come to some reasonable agreement with regard to wages, and as the recommendation was not acted upon, in the next Sessions certain justices were ordered to consider what wages ought to be allowed to Caesar.[79]

Difficulties of this kind seem sometimes to have induced the owners of slaves to enter into indentures with them and so secure a property in their labour by a contract recognized in English courts and not open to doubtful constructions. This at all events seems to be the explanation of certain advertisements for runaway negroes, one of which may be quoted:

Run away on Wednesday, the 28th ult., and stole money and goods from his master, John Lamb, Esq., an indentured black servant man about twenty-four years of age named William, of a brown or tawney complexion; had on when he went off, a parson's grey coat, blue breeches, white Bath flannel waistcoat, yellow gilt shoe buckles, and a beaver hat with a white lining.

Whoever apprehends him and brings him to his master at the Rookery House in Lewisham, Kent, shall have ten guineas reward and ten more on conviction in court of any persons harbouring or concealing him either on board ship or on shore.

N.B. He is also the property of his master, and has a burnt mark L.E., on one of his shoulders (1770).

On the other hand we hear of 'a black' as an apprentice boy and apparently as free as other apprentices which is perhaps not saying much. Anthony Emmannuell had been bound in 1723 to one Samuel Johnson, with the consent of his then mistress. Two years later his master petitioned for his discharge as notwithstanding his kindness the apprentice ran away, embezzled money and remained incorrigible in spite of having been put in the House of Correction.[80] There were doubtless many Negroes who were either legally or virtually free, and lived uneventfully as domestic servants; there is the famous case of Dr Johnson's faithful Francis Barber. There seems to have been little prejudice against them on account of their race and colour. There was Ignatius Sancho, born on a slave ship, the butler of the Duke of Montague, afterwards a grocer, who was a well-known London character, his portrait painted by Gainsborough and engraved by Bartolozzi, whose letters (in rather painful imitation of the manner of Sterne) were published after his death. In the earlier part of the century little black boys as pages or playthings were favourite appendages of fashionable ladies or ladies of easy virtue.

Nevertheless there were many derelict unfortunate Negroes in London, and their number was increased by the peace of 1783 when the Negroes who had served with the British forces in America were sent, some to Nova Scotia, some to the Bahamas, some to London, where they quickly fell into distress. Negroes became conspicuous among London beggars and were known as St Giles black birds. Granville Sharp, to whose efforts the Somersett trial was due, was regarded by them as their protector, and he found himself with some 400 black pensioners.[81] The urgency of removing them from London became apparent and a Committee for Relieving the Black Poor was formed with Jonas Hanway as its chairman. A scheme was formed in 1786 for establishing a colony of free Africans and other settlers on the west coast of Africa, and the Government undertook to pay up to £14 a head for their transportation. Applications were invited from those who were 'desirous of profiting by this opportunity of settling in one of the most fertile and pleasant countries in the known world'. Some 700 blacks offered themselves (of whom 441 embarked) and about sixty whites, chiefly London prostitutes, were sent with them, removal to the colonies being a favourite project of the age for reforming and providing for these poor women. This first settlement (1787) at Sierra Leone was an ill-fated one, the climate was not all that had been supposed, and the emigrants were not of the stuff to make successful pioneers.[82]

Other Negroes went to the West Indies where they worked as free labourers, but 'blacks' continued to be conspicuous among London beggars, and in 1814 a Parliamentary Committee reported that there were many Negroes in London whose condition deserved the attention of the House of Commons.[83]

The lascars, who apparently began to be conspicuous in London about 1783, were in many ways in a more unfortunate position than the Negroes. They were brought over in the East India Company's ships; on arriving in the Thames they were discharged and left in London for some months before they were shipped for a return voyage. Ignorant of English and of the ways of English people, they were exploited by each other and by the worst products of the riverside slums of Wapping and Shadwell and Poplar. Some of them made their way as beggars to the west of London and found shelter in the common lodging-houses of St Giles. A pamphlet of 1784 protesting against the beggars of Westminster and those who gave way to their importunities, makes an exception in favour of the 'vagrant blacks':

Do not deem me so uncharitable as to conclude I wish to steel your heart against the feeble but interesting efforts of those poor sons of misery, who, strangers to the climate, to the manners, and to the people of this country, have traversed the town naked, pennyless and almost starving in search of subsistence. Their situation is as singular as it is deplorable; they have been brought into this country as the friendly assistants of natives. . . . While the dispute lasted as to who should maintain them they have been left a prey to melancholy and distress. The dispute, you know, has been between the husband of the ships and the Directors of the East India Company.[84]

This particular dispute, which left the lascars so completely destitute, was presumably short-lived, but their position remained deplorable, though it was not till 1814 that their miseries attracted public attention. It was only then that Wilberforce, with all his interest in distressed blacks and in openings for missionary effort, became conscious of the existence of the lascars in London, though he says, 'there had been much private enquiry and long and numerous discussions before I was apprised of it'.[85] From about 1812 there seem to have been attempts to convert the lascars to Christianity, and to teach them English. The missionary attitude towards them was that they were utterly depraved.

They are practically and abominably wicked. They are a prey to each other and to the rapacious poor, as well as the most abandoned of our fellow-countrywomen. They have none or scarcely any who will associate with them but prostitutes and no house that will receive them except the public-house and the apartments of the abandoned. They are strangers in a strange land and demand our hospitality.[86]

In 1814 and previously the number coming annually to England was about 2,500 and it was expected that for the future the total would be doubled. In 1810 it was estimated that about 130 died yearly.[87] The East India Company quartered them in barracks in the Ratcliffe Highway paying, in 1814, ten shillings a week for their board and lodging to a contractor.[85] In 1814 an Act was passed compelling the Company to provide food, clothing and other necessary accommodation for Asiatic sailors[88] and a Parliamentary Committee was appointed to consider the Act and report what further regulations were necessary. The Committee made a surprise visit to the barracks where the lascars were housed. They reported that at certain times of the year these received from 1,000 to 1,100 men, which meant great overcrowding. But even when not overcrowded they were very dirty, there was no bedding or furniture, no fireplaces, and the men had only a blanket apiece. There was no accommodation for the sick. On the other hand, it was said that if beds were provided, the lascars sold them, and that there were stoves in winter. The buildings for Chinese sailors were also inspected, at a time when there were few in London, though on the arrival of the China ships there were a great many. These places were much more clean and airy than the barracks of the lascars.[83] This seems to have been the first attempt of the Government to exercise any sort of control over housing conditions, and the cellars of St Giles were probably far worse than the barracks of the lascars. The lascars, however, were an imperial obligation and the Government's relations with the East India Company gave it a basis for action. At this time lascars were prominent among the professional beggars of St Giles and seem to have been successful. One who had frequently been taken to the St Giles watch-house for begging, at other times was accustomed to go there to charge people with robbing him of 'a great deal of money'; he lodged at a public-house and was said to spend 5os. a week on his board.[89]

Besides the unending flow and ebb to and from London, there were thus two main tides of seasonal immigration. That of the Irish travelling on foot, often in family parties, from Liverpool, Chester and Bristol, and finding shelter chiefly in St Giles and Marylebone. These arrived before the hay harvest began and filled the streets of London with beggars. Secondly, that of the lascars, who were deposited in the eastern riverside districts from the East India Company's ships to live for some months in more or less enforced idleness, some of them drifting to the common lodging-houses of St Giles.

There was another seasonal migration to London, that of the women who came on foot chiefly from Shropshire and North Wales to work in the market-gardens round London and returned in the autumn. They were employed in picking fruit, gathering peas (hence the old name of codder[90]), weeding, haymaking and especially in carrying loads of fruit to Covent Garden. Their earnings at the end of the century were only five or seven shillings a week as compared with ten or twelve paid to men for the same work. But they slept in barns and outhouses and lived chiefly on garden produce allowed them by their employers, so that they returned to their homes with a little fund for the winter. They would carry a heavy load of fruit from Ealing or Brentford to Covent Garden, about nine miles, and would sometimes make the double journey twice a day.[91] Londoners admired their gay, healthy appearance and neat clothes. There was a corresponding exodus from London of men and women who spent the winter in the workhouse and went out in the summer for tramping or harvesting,[92] but it is difficult to see how these could compete with the Irish and the sturdy country people who worked so hard for such small pay.

This constant flow to London tended to make it always overcrowded. The outlets for an ever-redundant population (in spite of a general shortage of many kinds of labour) were the Army and the Navy (enlistment under the pressure of starvation being reinforced by the press-gang and the crimp as well as the penal system); indentured emigration to the colonies, and removal under the poor law and the Vagrant Act. Press-gangs directed their energies not only against seamen, but against those whom their officers chose to consider idle fellows, the attempt on Tom Jones being a case in point; 'neither law nor conscience forbid this project', said Lady Bellaston, 'for the fellow, I promise you, however well drest, is but a vagabond, and as proper as any fellow in the streets to be pressed into the service'. Magistrates encouraged the application of this principle. In 1776, for instance, the Lord Mayor refused to back the press warrants for the impressment of men in the City but ordered the City Marshals to go in force to search the public-houses and take into custody all 'loose and disorderly men' and bring them before him. Those who, like Goldsmith's private centinel, could not give a satisfactory account of themselves, were sent by the Lord Mayor on board the tender for service in the Navy. 'By this judicious step,' says a contemporary annalist, 'many idle persons were obtained, and the more industrious escaped being illegally forced from their friends and families.' The magistrates of Westminster took similar steps, great numbers, it is said, were obtained in this way, 'the principal part of whom were persons who had not any visible method of livelihood'.[93]

A less questionable method of recruitment was that of the Marine Society founded in 1756 to supply men and boys for the Navy, and to save boys from a life of vagrancy and crime. Landsmen who joined voluntarily were clothed and given bedding and a complete sea kit. After three years of war the Society gave up providing for men in order to devote all its funds to the boys, as it was found that there were comparatively few men in the London streets in such a ragged and vagabond condition, an interesting sidelight on the reactions of war.[94]

In peace-time the Navy was no longer available for derelict landsmen and vagrant boys, but these could sometimes get a berth on a merchant-man, a Greenland ship, a coasting vessel, or a fishing smack. The second and permanent establishment of the Marine Society in 1769 was again the result of an appeal from Sir John Fielding for help for dis-tressed friendless boys. This he called 'a Preventive Plan of Police' – 'from this black fountain it is that the late gangs of housebreakers, street robbers and foot-pads have been supplied'. Within two months £2,000 was received from subscriptions and 'near three hundred friend-less boys and distressed boys who flocked from brickfields, bulks, coal-wharfs, glass-houses and other places of shelter' were fitted out and apprenticed to masters of ships.[95] It was not, however, always easy to find masters for the boys in peace-time.[96]

There remained indentured emigration to the plantations, and, after the War of Independence, to the United States. Those who wished to emigrate, but could not afford to pay for a passage, entered into a con-tract with the master of a vessel to allow themselves to be sold for a term of years in return for their passage. Except that the term of servi-tude was shorter, being generally four years as compared with seven or fourteen, the position of these indentured servants was much the same as that of transported felons. After the Restoration kidnapping for the plantations was common in London, and young people especially were spirited away by people called spiriters,[97] but by the Revolution the practice seems to have been checked (in spite of the very small penalties imposed on spiriters in the few cases when the offence could be proved).[98] The spiriter was superseded by the 'office-keeper' who en-rolled emigrants and used many arts to induce them to enter into indentures. Ned Ward describes such an office in 1699, the staff, 'three or four blades, well drest but with hawkes countenances', the emigrants:

Half a dozen ragamuffinly fellows, shewing poverty in their rags and des-pair in their faces, mixed with a parcel of young wild striplings like run-away prentices. . . . That house . . . which they are entering is an Office where servants for the plantations bind themselves to be miserable as long as they live. . . . Those fine fellows who look like footmen upon a holiday crept into cast sutes of their masters . . . are kidnappers who walk the Change in order to seduce people who want services and young fools crost in love and under an uneasiness of mind to go beyond seas, getting so much a head of masters and ships and merchants who go over for every wretch they trepan into this misery. Those young rakes and tatter-demalions you see so lovingly handled are drawn by their fair promises to sell themselves into slavery.[99]

It is clear that all sorts of villainies were practised. For instance, the captain of a ship trading to Jamaica would visit the Clerkenwell House of Correction, ply with drink the girls who had been imprisoned as disorderly and invite them to go to the West Indies.[100] But, as an alternative to destitution in London, there was something to be said for the system apart from its abuses and deceptions. In any case, the passage, paid for or otherwise, except for the cabin passenger, must have been a thing of horror, but the nature of the contract made it to the captain's interest that emigrants should be as healthy as possible on arrival. According to Defoe, both indentured labourers and transported felons[101] did well in Maryland and Virginia. He returns again and again to the subject, both in *Moll Flanders* and in *Colonel Jack*, though it is difficult to know whether he writes as the realist, recording facts of colonial life, or as the moralist, encouraging those in straits in London to start again in the new world. Colonel Jack is kidnapped and sold as a servant, Moll Flanders goes as a felon. Her story shows, what is clear from other sources, that transportation to the convict with money had few terrors – he or she travelled as a cabin passenger and bought freedom on arrival. In *Colonel Jack* a felon is told by his purchaser that 'he ought to look on it to be no more than being put out apprentice to an honest trade, in which, when he came out of his time, he might be able to set up for himself and live honestly'. In Virginia, Moll Flanders is told that most of the inhabitants had come there in 'very indifferent circumstances', being either felons or servants sold by masters of ships between whom no difference was made, both working together in the fields. When their time was out, both in Maryland and Virginia, they were allotted land and given tools and necessaries on credit.

From this little beginning [Defoe says] have some of the most considerable planters . . . raised themselves to estates of 40 or 50,000 pound. In a word, every desperate forlorn creature, the most despicable ruin'd man in the world, has here a fair opportunity put into his hands to begin the world again.

There can be little doubt that there was a steady flow of this kind of emigration from London, increasing in bad times: there was much de-

mand for the labour in certain colonies,[102] much profit to be made out
of the traffic by agents and masters of ships, a constant supply of those
out of work, in debt or in difficulties of one sort or another. These were
ready to accept a free passage, notwithstanding its obligations, which
indeed were much misrepresented by specious agents. Advertisements
were posted up in London (and in seaport towns) asserting the great
opportunities for advancement in life and referring inquirers to agents
who represented 'the advantages to be obtained in America in colours
so alluring that it is almost impossible to resist them'.[103]

There were three kinds of 'bound servants' who went from England:
convicts, 'indented servants', and (by 1770 at least) 'redemptioners' or
'free willers'. By 1770 Maryland was the only colony which still
regularly accepted convicts, as in spite of the sentiment against them,
their labour was much valued.[104] Indented servants agreed to serve the
master of the ship or his assigns for a term of years according to a
written contract made before departure, which occasionally specified a
certain kind of labour. Redemptioners were promised a certain number
of days after arrival in which to find a master for themselves who would
advance their passage money, and so redeem them, failing which the
master of the ship was to dispose of them for a term of years. The poor
emigrants did not know that there was virtually no chance of finding a
master on these terms on arrival, and as a matter of fact it is said that
they were seldom allowed to set foot on shore till they had discharged
their passage, in 1770 rated at about £9, which it was almost impossible
for them to raise. The position of the redemptioner and the indented
servant was thus the same except that the former had not whatever
slight protection there might be in the conditions of the indenture,[105]
and except – essential difference – the deception which had been practised on him. 'The situation of the free-willer,' said Eddis in 1770, 'is
in almost every instance more to be lamented than either that of the
convict or the indented servant; being attended with circumstances of
greater deception and cruelty.'

These 'bound servants' went mainly to three colonies, Virginia,
Maryland and Pennsylvania; those going to the last were largely
German, Swiss, and Irish; the greater number of English emigrants
went to Maryland. It is said that white servitude was at its height in
Maryland in the middle of the eighteenth century, and from that time to

the Revolution gradually decreased.[106] However, it was in the seventies
that this kind of emigration attracted most attention in England. In
1773, a year of distress and bad trade, there was a scare of excessive
emigration and depopulation, especially in Scotland and Ireland, and
the Government required returns to be made through the customs
officers of persons leaving the country, so that for 1774 and part of 1775
we have something approaching emigration statistics for English
ports.[107] They are incomplete, but those for the port of London (except
that convicts are not included) apparently are complete. In 1774 the
numbers of indented servants and redemptioners sailing from London
are 1,124 for Maryland, 548 for Virginia, 456 for Philadelphia, 35 for
Georgia, 23 for Carolina and 8 for Jamaica, which probably is fairly
representative of the usual proportions.[108] In 1773 the numbers would
almost certainly have been higher.

These lists have a poignant interest, they give names, ages, occupations and former place of residence. People of most ages from fifteen
to fifty appear on them, those in the twenties predominating; most
handicraft trades are represented (with a predominance of weavers
reflecting the distress in Spitalfields) and there is a sprinkling of clerks
and book-keepers, of schoolmasters and surgeons, besides labourers
and servants. The women are comparatively few, there are almost no
family parties, and married couples are rare. The usual term of servitude
is four years, sometimes five, six or seven, in a few cases two. Londoners are numerous, but people come from all parts of the country
including Scotland and Ireland and there is at least one party of Ger-
mans. Little difference in social status appears between indented servants and redemptioners; if there is a distinction it appears to be in
favour of the former, who have perhaps fewer young people described
as servants.

We get a gleam of light on the hopes and tragedies so mysteriously
summarized in these lists in the case of the brig *Nancy* which sailed for
Baltimore in June 1775 with a freight of ninety-nine redemptioners. On
the list is Elizabeth 'Brittleband', described as a servant aged twenty-
one. This was a girl of seventeen who was decoyed from her mother's
house to an office where she was virtually kidnapped and sent on board
the *Nancy*. Owing to her mother's extraordinary persistence and
courage (too late to save the girl) the office-keepers – a man and wife –

and their clerk were brought to trial 'for conspiring to send into foreign countries one Elizabeth Brickleband'. The trial throws light on the infamous character of the people implicated, who kept a 'lock-up house' (a spunging-house presumably) and admitted that they had received £9 7s. 6d. for obtaining 'near an hundred people'. An attempt was made to buy off the courageous prosecutrix for £500, on the plea that they would all be hanged. However, the offence was technically a misdemeanour only and the sentence was a light one.[109]

What was the fate of these servants in America? Conflicting accounts are given, and doubtless conditions varied in individual cases from consideration and kindness to great brutality. American writers lay stress on the fact that there were laws to protect the servant against gross ill-treatment, and that these were not a dead letter.[110] However, the servants were bought and sold freely during their term of servitude; in Maryland and Virginia they worked in the tobacco plantations together with convicts and Negroes. In Maryland, according to Eddis, who as a surveyor of customs at Annapolis had every opportunity of judging, indented servants, whose term was usually four years, were considered less profitable than convicts who served for seven or more, and, he says, 'there are but few instances where they experience better treatment';[111] while Negroes,

being a property for life are therefore almost in every instance under more comfortable circumstances than the miserable European, over whom the inflexible planter exercises an inflexible severity. They are strained to the uttermost to perform their allotted labour, and from a prepossession in many cases too justly founded, they are supposed to be receiving only the just reward . . . for repeated offences. There are doubtless many exceptions, yet generally speaking they groan beneath a worse than Egyptian bondage.[103]

The American purchasers regarded their servants as ne'er-do-wells and fugitives from justice; they were ignorant of the deceptions practised in England, and thought it incredible that any reputable person should leave England on such terms. As a matter of fact many servants represented themselves as knowing trades of which they were ignorant, had no intention of performing their contracts, and, like escaped convicts, became professional runaways. Many servants when their term expired swelled the ranks of the 'white trash'. Many undoubtedly did well, and the large proportion of servants to the inhabitants in Maryland shows that freedmen must have formed a considerable part of the population.[112]

Such as they were, they were entrusted with much of the education of Maryland.

At least two-thirds of the little education we receive [it was said in 1773] are derived from instructors who are either indented servants or transported felons; not a ship arrives either with redemptioners or convicts, in which schoolmasters are not as regularly advertised for sale as weavers, tailors or any other trade, with little difference than I can hear of, excepting perhaps that the former do not usually fetch so good a price as the latter.[113]

The status of the schoolmaster was often so very low that this is hardly to be wondered at. It is related, however, that about 1776 one Palfrenan was bought at Williamsburg by a Colonel Preston as a tutor for his family, who was a poet and scholar, a friend and correspondent of Dr Johnson and the learned Mrs Carter.[114]

The war (1776–83) stopped this emigration. It went on afterwards but was discouraged in England and certainly diminished. It continued, however, from Ireland and Germany. The traffic from Ireland to Pennsylvania was carried on under terrible conditions by ship captains known as White Guinea Men, but by 1796 Hibernian and German societies had been formed in America to protect indentured servants.[115] White servitude did not come to an end in Maryland till 1819, and in Pennsylvania it continued even later.[116]

The American historian of white servitude in Maryland considers that 'by drawing off the superfluous population of Europe, it did more to lessen pauperism and crime than all the laws on the Statute Books'. It was certainly an economic advantage to America, probably to the peasants of Germany, Switzerland and Ireland, and it was a safety-valve for London. But it is a nice question in the eighteenth century whether the net result of the laws on the statute books was to encourage or discourage pauperism and crime. In England undoubtedly the laws relating to imprisonment for debt encouraged both and also emigration, which was complained of as a drain on the population of the country. This form of emigration, possible without expense or premeditation, founded on false hopes, promoted by the wiles of office-keepers, must have been a temptation to those in temporary difficulties as well as a real resource to the unfortunate. The practice goes some way to explain how 'absconding' among fathers of families, one of the great causes of poverty and crime, came to be so general.

As to the harshness of the conditions, the term of servitude by sale could not have seemed so outrageous to those who were accustomed to the obligations of apprenticeship as it now appears. Blackstone defends the master's right to the perpetual service of the Negro slave brought to England, which, he says, in spite of the liberty he may acquire 'will remain exactly in the same state of subjection for life, which every apprentice submits to for the space of seven years and sometimes for a longer term'.[77]

There were also two well-known attempts at philanthropic and state-aided emigration as a means of relief to those in distress in England, especially in London. One was the settlement of free Negroes and London prostitutes at Sierra Leone, which as we have seen, did not prosper. The other was the founding of Georgia by General Oglethorpe and his board of trustees in 1732. Oglethorpe was moved to this undertaking by his experiences in London debtors' prisons in 1729 when a Parliamentary Committee discovered the horrible barbarities committed by keepers and jailers who had bought their offices, especially by Bambridge in the Fleet. He thought that there were many who had failed in England and become a burden to the country who might do well in the new world:

Let us cast our eyes on the multitude of unfortunate people in the kingdom of reputable families and of liberal or at least easy education: some undone by guardians, some by lawsuits, some by the accidents of commerce, some by stocks and bubbles and some by suretyship. . . . What various misfortunes may reduce the rich and industrious to the danger of a prison and a moral certainty of starving! These are the people who may relieve themselves and strengthen Georgia by resorting thither, and Great Britain by their departure.[117]

Unfortunately, many of them proved not of the kind to strengthen Georgia, and in 1734 the trustees decided that embarkations should consist chiefly of Highlanders from Scotland and of German Protestants (who from the first had been intended colonists), 'as many of the poor who had been useless in England were inclined to be useless likewise in Georgia'.[118] Among the earliest settlers were two ship-loads of

Jews sent out by the Jewish community in London. The first, about twenty families of Portuguese Jews who were independent; the second, about twelve families of German Jews, dependent on charity, whom Oglethorpe allowed to stay in the colony, in spite of protests from the trustees.[119] The emigrants sent by the trustees went with their wives and children, and under much more favourable conditions than the indented servants; as Oglethorpe said, 'the unfortunate will not be obliged to bind themselves to a long service to pay for their passage, for they may be carried gratis into a land of liberty and plenty'.[120] The colony, however, from its early days also had indented servants. In 1742, one of the hindrances to progress had been the 'great misfortune... upon many persons, who brought over persons indented to serve them, who, being picked up in the streets of London, their masters found them unfit for labour'.[121]

The effects of the settlement laws on the population of London are rather complicated, and conclusions must be to some extent hypothetical. There can be little doubt that they encouraged the flow to London from the country and tended to increase the population of the large out-parishes, but not of the tiny City parishes. In these it was possible for beadles and overseers to keep up that constant scrutiny over newcomers in order to remove those 'likely to become chargeable', which was the ideal of parish officers. In the larger parishes such a policy was out of the question, and after the early part of the century does not seem to have been attempted. But measures were taken to restrict the obtaining of settlements, both by general legislation whose intention was to make labour more mobile by lessening the motive for a precautionary removal, and by local Acts obtained by the metropolitan parishes to protect themselves from a heavy burden. It therefore became more and more possible for people to live for years in a parish without obtaining a settlement there, and when through illness or old age they were compelled to ask for relief, they were removed to their supposed place of settlement. (The London parishes however, became progressively more generous in the matter of casual relief and would often give temporary assistance rather than obtain a removal order.) For this reason, while the movement of population in general was, it was said, from the country parish to the county town and thence to London (also of course to the manufacturing districts) the course of removals under the settlement laws was 'generally from cities or market towns to rural parishes, most of the poor people so removed are sent from places where they might be employed to . . . places which they left for want of employment or maintenance'.[122] Although there were endless cases of hardship and cruelty in removals, perhaps the tendency to remove those who had become permanently dependent on poor relief from London to the country had something to be said for it, though in many cases the poorhouse of a country parish was a far more insanitary and wretched place than the London workhouse.[123]

Playfair in his annotated edition (1805) of the *Wealth of Nations*, commenting on the remark that 'there is scarce a poor man in England of forty years of age . . . who has not in some part of his life felt himself most cruelly oppressed by this ill-contrived law of settlement', says,

one of the effects is the forced peopling of large towns, where, though a settlement may not be easily obtained, labouring people are allowed to reside till they become burthensome, which is not, as it ought to be, the case in every part of the country.

When (after 1815) the effects of the change in poor law policy of 1795–6 were fully felt, this state of things was to some extent reversed. Villagers were afraid of losing their settlement if they moved, they preferred the certainty of maintenance to the uncertainty of work, migration to the towns was hindered and between 1811 and 1831 there was a great increase in the agricultural population just at the time when agricultural employment was decreasing. On the other hand the Irish poured into London and other industrial towns.

The vagrancy laws encouraged a perpetual travelling and their effect was probably rather to bring people to London than to remove them from it. In theory they were separate from the poor laws, or rather they were the penal side of the poor laws, but in practice the two branches were inextricably mixed. Under the poor laws, a poor person had to be removed to his place of settlement under a removal order signed by two justices, and was supposed to be delivered to the parish officers there by an overseer of the removing parish which bore the cost, often very considerable. It was therefore a constant practice when the settlement was a distant one to remove by means of a vagrant pass. By this in theory a person who had committed some act of vagrancy, such as 'wandering and begging' or 'sleeping abroad in the open air', after being duly punished by whipping or imprisonment in a house of correction or both, was 'passed', that is, conveyed in a cart from constable to constable till he reached his parish, the expense being borne by the counties through which he passed. The vagrancy laws were so severe that they defeated their own ends and punishments were seldom inflicted except in exceptional circumstances. Still less of course could they be given to people who were not vagrants at all. A practice grew up of giving what were called walking or begging passes, used as a licence to beg, with which the bearer made his own way to his (alleged) place of settlement. The result was that in many cases no distinction was made between the vagrant and the poor person who was passed instead of removed to save the pocket of the removing parish. The latter was encouraged to become a beggar or subjected to the degradation of the pass-cart; the real vagrant, to whom a pass was a much desired object and the pass-cart a sought-after means of free travel, was encouraged.[124]

In 1757 the Middlesex justices in the interests of economy decided to contract for the passing of vagrants with a man who undertook to collect or receive them and take them to the county border. There is no reason to suppose that this made the lot of the vagrants any worse than before, as the constables who had been appointed to do the work had farmed it out and made a trade of it.[125] The number of vagrants progressively increased and in course of time the contractor or pass-master as he was called built a brick barracks or receiving-house at Enfield and another at Islington which were, as might be imagined, wretched places. They had, however, few terrors for the able-bodied vagrant. At the end of their English season the Irish in particular frequently applied to be shipped back to Ireland as vagrants, either concealing their money or sending it over by a friend in order to escape paying for a passage. Their sojourn in a receiving-house, a bare shelter, because the inmates cut up and appropriated the rugs, is thus described by the pass-master for Middlesex,

... my wife perhaps goes out and buys them herrings and potatoes out of the county allowance of 6d. a day for food and some of them perhaps are fond of smoking, and they throw their money together and live very comfortably. I took a man and his wife and five children away yesterday, I told that man, you have never earned so much in your own country as 3s. 6d. a day for yourself and all your family, and rent found and cups and saucers.[126]

These voluntary travellers were, it was complained, almost the only people who arrived at their destination under a vagrant pass.[127] Vagrants who were being deported from London against their will easily escaped and returned. Many Irish convicted of begging were sent to Ireland as vagrants but for the most part escaped being shipped. It was easy enough to get away even in the first Middlesex stage of the journey; 'no one in the world could prevent that', said the pass-master, 'in the dark, in the winter, they would get away unless I stood over them with a drawn sword. . . . There is not one in ten that is shipped though the pass expresses they are to be put on board ship for Ireland'.[126]

On the whole, the internal drift to London was voluntary, the movement from it under compulsion – the compulsion of the poor laws and of the pressure of debts or starvation. For though the war on cottages counted for much, the lure of London probably counted for more. Arthur Young wrote in 1771:

Young men and women in the country fix their eye on London as the last stage of their hope; they enter into service in the country for little else but to raise money enough to go to London, which was no such easy matter when a stage coach was four or five days creeping an hundred miles; and the fare and the expenses ran high. But now! a country fellow one hundred miles from London jumps on to a coach-box in the morning, and for eight or ten shillings gets to town by night, which makes a material difference; besides rendering the going up and down so easy that the numbers who have seen London are increased tenfold and of course ten times the boasts are sounded in the ears of country fools, to induce them to quit their healthy clean fields for a region of dirt, stink and noise. And the number of young women that fly thither is almost incredible.[128]

CHAPTER 4

THE PEOPLE AND THE TRADES
OF LONDON

Where finds Philosophy her eagle eye,
With which she gazes at yon burning disk
Undazzled, and detects and counts his spots?
In London. Where her implements exact,
With which she calculates, computes and scans
All distance, motion, magnitude, and now
Measures an atom, and now girds a world?
In London. Where has commerce such a mart,
So rich, so throng'd, so drain'd and so supplied,
As London, opulent, enlarged, and still
Increasing London?

Cowper

EIGHTEENTH-CENTURY London inevitably suggests the brilliant society which made up the world of politics and fashion. This small world of statesmen and politicians and placemen, of wits and rakes and fops, was so self-sufficient, so conscious that it was the only world that counted, that it imposes its point of view on us. The social life of the eighteenth century lives for us chiefly in the letters and memoirs of these people, their houses, their portraits, their furniture. The chief relics of eighteenth-century London – St James's Street, St James's Square, parts of Mayfair – are dominated by famous names and peopled by the ghosts of Pitt and Burke and Fox, Selwyn and Lord March. This world and the closely-connected world of literature and art, of Reynolds and Johnson, Goldsmith and Garrick, seem to fill the whole stage. We know little of the artisans and labourers, the shopkeepers and clerks and street sellers, who made up the mass of the population. The houses they lived in have been swept away or transformed out of recognition. The people live for us chiefly in the pictures of Hogarth – *Southwark Fair*, the *March to Finchley*, the crowd at Tyburn. We are apt to see them through the eyes of that other world as the Mob, the Fourth Estate as Fielding called it.

London then seemed the all-devouring monster which drained the countryside of a laborious and innocent peasantry. It was a commonplace that the London workman was idle, profligate and drunken. Shebbeare, writing in the middle of the century says: 'In London amongst the lower class all is anarchy, drunkenness and thievery, in the country, good order, sobriety, and honesty, unless in manufacturing towns, where the resemblance to London is more conspicuous.'[1] Baretti, travelling from London to Plymouth in 1760, says, 'the further I went from London, the more tractable appeared the low people ...',[2] and a German pastor, who had ministered to a German congregation in London for twenty years, wrote in the eighties, 'the farther off from London, the more in general the air as well as the manners grow purer. The people appear more civil and tractable, more sociable and frugal and more given to cleanliness'.[3] In 1773 Mortimer wrote of 'the sober and industrious labouring poor in the manufacturing towns at a great distance from the capital', adding, 'workmen of every species in and near the capital being justly reputed idle, profligate and debauched, these are excepted'.[4]

These are generalizations. Who are the workmen of every species? Grosley, who came to London in 1765, is a little more precise. 'Among the people of London,' he says, 'we should properly distinguish the porters, sailors, chairmen, and the day labourers who work in the streets not only from persons of condition, most of whom walk a-foot, but even from the lowest class of shopkeepers. The former are as insolent a rabble as can be met with in countries without law or police ... the obliging readiness of the citizens and shopkeepers even of the inferior sort, sufficiently indemnify and console us for the insolence of the mob. ...'[5] The distinction drawn is – broadly – between the unskilled labourer and the skilled artisan who belongs more to the shopkeeping class than to that of 'the mob', who were essentially the chairmen, porters and labourers together with actual roughs.

To learn something of the social life of these people, who were classed (misleadingly) as the workmen, or the poor, or the low people or the mob, involves some examination of the structure and nature of London trades. It was an age of minute social distinctions. Lines were drawn between the artisan and the labourer, the master and the journeyman, as they were drawn between the lodger and the housekeeper. They were however drawn with difficulty. In many trades a journeyman took work by the piece and employed other journeymen and apprentices, thus verging into the small master. There were other trades in which the skill and the capital required were so small that it was said that every man was his own master, though the earnings of such a master might be below those of an unskilled labourer. Apprenticeship tended to make trades hereditary – trades had their own customs, their own localities, often a distinctive dress and much corporate spirit (shown for instance in the customary obligation to attend the funeral of a fellow-workman).

Defoe (in 1705) describes a class of 'topping workmen':

> How well some of them do live who are good husbands and regard their families, who only by their handy labour as journeymen can earn from fifteen shillings to fifty shillings per week wages as thousands of artisans in England can. . . . 'Tis plain the dearness of wages forms our people into more classes than other nations can show. These men live better in England than the masters and employers in foreign countries can, and you have a class of your topping workmen in England, who, being only journeymen under manufacturers, are yet very substantial fellows, maintain their families very well. . . .[6]

Below the journeymen or artisans in skilled trades came the unskilled labourers, and a mass of street sellers (often the women-folk of the labourers) and casual workers. The distinction between the labourer and the artisan was ancient, and deeply rooted in tradition: 'I think,' wrote Edward VI, 'this country can bear . . . no artificer worth above 100 marc; no labourer much more than he spendeth.'[7] The distinction, however, was becoming blurred by the existence of trades which employed workmen under a skilled foreman instead of journeymen who had served an apprenticeship. Among the most important of these trades were the brewers, the distillers, the vinegar-makers, makers of colours, of blue, of varnish, of glue, of printers' ink, the tobacconists and snuff-makers, the sugar refiners and soap-boilers. These were highly capitalized undertakings, apprentices to which paid a large fee with a view to a partnership or to starting in business for themselves, or in some cases to becoming foremen or book-keepers. Workers in these trades were considered as labourers but their wages were often as high as those of journeymen in the less well-paid trades, they learnt the business by constantly working at it, and their position was probably more stable than that of many artisans. It is to be noted that the practice of employing such workmen was almost confined to trades which (on a large scale) were comparatively new. The older trades of a similar character – the tallow-chandlers and the wax-chandlers, the fell-mongers and the tanners – employed journeymen, often at labourers' wages.[8]

The skilled artisan who works at home and either makes goods to the order of his master or sells to the trade verges into the shopkeeping class. On the other hand, the lowest type of shopkeeper, the chandler, the dealer in old iron (both considered disreputable), the tripe-shop, the milk-retailor (often a street-seller rather than a shopkeeper), the keeper of a cook-shop or a green-cellar, belong rather to the class of unskilled and casual labour. The stock-in-trade of a green-cellar, for instance, might be 'no more than a gallon of sand, two or three birch-brooms and a bunch of turnips'. The market-woman on the other hand was often a person of considerable possessions. The chimney-sweeper, though often ranked among beggars and thieves, served an apprentice-ship, and was in his way a master, and (towards the end of the century at all events) sometimes undertook the business of a nightman, employ-ing a number of men and carts.

The watermen and lightermen, by virtue of their fellowship and their apprenticeship and often the ownership of a boat, belonged to the class of skilled labour. Carmen (reputed an ill-mannered set) ranked rather with chairmen and workers at livery stables. Porters were of various kinds from the City Tackle House Porters to the casual street porter. Coal-heavers, laystall-men, scavengers, drovers, miscellaneous 'workers by the water-side', stokers in glass-houses (Defoe's 'black wretches') belonged to the class of labourers. Artisans in the building trades and paviours had their appropriate labourers, smiths (except in the lighter branches) had their hammermen to do the heavier part of the work at labourers' pay. Among women the lowest grade of workers seems to have been the cinder-sifters who worked at Tottenham Court[9] and probably in all the outskirts of the town. Women also 'attended dust-carts'. The street rag-pickers or bunters, the ballad-sellers and match-sellers belonged rather to the class of beggars. Among street sellers the hawker of fish seems to have been regarded as of inferior rank – perhaps from the associations of Billingsgate; Mrs Charke, Colley Cibber's daughter, describes how she made and hawked sausages, but denies with some indignation a report that she had sold flounders.

Then there were the people who performed or traded at the many fairs round London in the six summer months, who described their occupation as 'keeping the fairs and statutes'.[10] The London tea-gardens and places of amusement which were opened in the summer only needed a supply of musicians, waiters, and helpers, whose occupation was casual in the extreme, though well-known singers and musicians were sometimes engaged, and actors of repute were not above appearing in such places when the patent-theatres were closed. There was in London an enormous number of domestic servants of all grades and both sexes, a large proportion of whom was always 'out of a place' and adding to the floating population in 'ready-furnished lodgings'. The riverside parishes, more especially Wapping, were inhabited by a fluctuating population of seafaring men, mostly lodging in alehouses and preyed upon by a number of parasites of both sexes.

London trades were (and are) so numerous that it is difficult to find one not represented there. Speaking generally however, in the eighteenth century they fall into three classes. First, trades dependent on the fact that London was the chief port of the country and the headquarters of the important coasting-trade as well as the centre of the inland distributing trade, especially before canals opened up cross-country traffic. Hence the many trades connected with ship-building and boat-building, the cooperages, breweries, distilleries and sugar-refineries and other large businesses producing for export as well as the home market, together with the great warehouse and entrepôt trade. Secondly, London produced high-class goods reputed to be brought to a greater degree of perfection than elsewhere in England, clocks and watches, cutlery (especially surgical instruments), optical and mathematical instruments, plate, jewellery, furniture, saddlery and coach-building. This group merges into the third, namely, the trades that supplied the wants of a large, luxury-loving population – coffee-houses, chocolate-makers, peruke-makers and barbers, shoe-makers and tailors, mantua-makers and milliners were surprisingly numerous, and the various branches of the building trade naturally figure largely.

It was a great age for decorative craftsmanship, more especially in the first sixty or seventy years of the century. The plumber, for instance, ignorant of the mysteries of hot-water engineering, was often a caster of lead statues and of decorated lead cisterns. The plasterer was sometimes also a stucco-worker, though much stucco-work was done by Italians. House-carving, like ship-carving, was a recognized trade, though in the forties it was admitted to be in its decadence, that is presumably, to have declined since the great days of the Grinling Gibbons school:

The carving now used is but the outlines of the art, it consists only in some unmeaning scroll, or a bad representation of some fruit or flowers. The gentry, because it is the mode, will have some sort of carving, but are no judges of the execution of the work: they bargain with the master-builder or architect for something of the kind; he, to make the most of it, employs such hands as can give him a slight flourish for his money, no matter how it is done, therefore it is not necessary to spend much time or money to acquire this superficial kind of carving.[11]

There was more scope for the chair-carver, a separate trade and a thriving one,[12] and for the coach-carver, who had to be 'pretty expert in representing naked boys, festoons of fruit, flowers and other ornaments', but 'had no occasion for perspective'. The smith's trade had many branches, among which the lock-smith, the grate-and-stove-smith and the gate- and palisade-smith stand out for the beauty of many of their productions. It was that golden age when the artist was a craftsman, and the craftsman an artist. Coach-painting and sign-painting were both trades and arts. It was the custom to apprentice budding artists to sign- or coach-painters, and it was complained that the coach-painter was badly exploited by the coach-builder:

That fraternity, not content with a moderate profit, upon a part they are unable to execute themselves, make a common practice of doubling and trebling the charge to their employers, and at the same time continue by all possible means to reduce and undervalue the productions of these ingenious people who, exclusive of their labour, furnish oil, gold, and colours. . . .[13]

The sign-painter was in a better position. For the sign of Shakespeare which hung in Little Russell Street, Drury Lane, the artist (said to be Clarkson) is reputed to have been paid £500, a sum which seems incredible compared with the prices paid to Reynolds and Gainsborough, though it certainly included the cost of gilding, carving and ornamental ironwork. The more ordinary sign-painters of commerce had their headquarters in Hoop Alley, Shoe Lane, where (till their trade declined after the regulations against projecting signs) they kept large stocks of signs both carved and painted, gilt grapes and sugar-loaves, lasts and teapots in the round, as well as the still familiar red lions and white harts.[14]

The London artisan was admitted to be a most excellent workman; Leblanc, a Frenchman by no means prejudiced in favour of England, gives him a magnificent testimonial: he is never content to work below his own standard of good workmanship (in this he differs from the Frenchman) and 'the vilest workman thinks nobly of his trade'. On the other hand (according to Leblanc) his notion of beauty is limited to accuracy, elegance escapes him; his invention in the mechanic arts is admirable (this is before 1745) but he is deficient in the arts of taste. The conclusion drawn is that perhaps a too scrupulous accuracy chills genius.[15] Grosley, some twenty years later, writes, 'the perfection of handicraft and the love of liberty in the lowest class of artificers, contribute equally to render English manufactures very dear'. The 'dissoluteness', so much complained of did not necessarily mean idleness: Place describes the foreman he employed in 1799 as 'a journey-man of the old blackguard school, who ... had given in to all sorts of dissipation. ...' He adds, 'he was one of the most diligent men living, and when business was brisk, frequently came to his work at four o'clock in the morning and sometimes earlier'.

In London in the eighteenth century almost every variety of industrial organization is to be found, corresponding with widely different stages of development, and these different stages often existed in the same trade. For instance, in 1758 and earlier, there was at least one capitalist who owned six fishing vessels worth £600 apiece with crews of eight or nine men, and was also an importer of fish, a Billingsgate salesman and a retailer on a large scale. He claimed to import 12,000 kits of pickled salmon from Scotland in a year besides great quantities of fresh salmon and from 1,500 to 2,000 salmon trout from Berwick in a week. For six months in the year he employed, he said, from 1,300 to 1,500 men.[16] At the same time the typical Thames fisherman who lived at Barking or Bankside, Lambeth or Hammersmith, if he owned a boat and nets (these cost £50 or £60 in the middle of the century) carried on his business with an apprentice and a partner. The boat was usually mortgaged at 10 per cent, one-third of the catch was the share of the owner of the boat, the rest was divided equally between the two partners. The fish was sold for them by the Billingsgate salesmen, who charged from 3 per cent to 10 per cent. The fishmongers took the better and larger fish, the 'basket people' or the Billingsgate hawkers took the rest. The fishermen's was a very poor trade, 'being exposed to the weather by night as well as by day', they were 'glad for the most part to take apprentices without money' and they were 'apt to take to the sea-service'.[17] The fisherman's apprentice in the nineteenth century was required to sleep in his master's boat to prevent its being stolen,[18] a custom apparently dating at least from the days of Pepys.

The cabinet-maker might be the owner of a shop 'so richly set out that it looked like a palace', as well as an exporter of furniture and possibly an importer through the East India Company of Chinese lacquered furniture made for the western market from European patterns, or he might have no other capital but a chest of tools, in which case he worked for the shopkeeping masters or the upholsterers, who dealt in house furnishings of all kinds. While there were different grades within the same trade, depending on the position of the master and the fee which his reputation and the size of his business enabled him to ask, each trade had a status of its own, trades ranging from the 'genteel' through the 'dirty genteels' and the 'genteelish' to the 'ordinary', the 'mean' and even the 'mean, nasty and stinking', a grading that depended partly on earnings, wages and capitalization, partly on custom, and the relative cleanliness of the work or the artistic talent required. Speaking generally, and subject to many exceptions, an apprentice fee of £5 or less meant a poor or disagreeable occupation, resorted to by parish children and the children of 'the labouring poor'. But a strong well-grown boy of fifteen or so who had been given some education or had picked up the preliminaries of a trade might sometimes be apprenticed advantageously for a low fee. Artisans would often pay £10 or £15 and upwards, or bind their children to themselves. A fee of from £15 to £20 was usually paid for clergymen's children apprenticed by the charity known as the Feast of the Sons of the Clergy.[19] Apart from the many apprenticeships which came to an untimely end, it by no means followed that a boy would find an opening in the trade to which he had been bound. For instance, we are told in 1761 that most apprentices to colourmen turned journeymen house-painters (a badly over-stocked trade) as master colourmen employed labourers only, with perhaps a journeyman to serve in the shop. Calenderers' apprentices were said to make the best porters, as they were accustomed 'to be continually carrying backwards and forwards heavy weights'.[20]

In the complicated medley of London trades the question of wages is a vast one. They were to some extent customary and traditional and though there was a trend upwards, they varied comparatively little till after 1793 when advances were rapid. From about 1760 onwards we hear progressively more of strikes and combinations for higher wages, and these have a direct relation to the cost of living.[21] During the long war period (1793–1815) strikes were common and for the most part successful.[22] As a rule wages reached their highest point about 1810 or 1811. In 1816 there were slight reductions in many trades.[23] They were, however, surprisingly slight and Francis Place says in 1834 that in most skilled London trades wages had not fallen since the highest war level.[24]

Before 1765, speaking very broadly, labourers' wages varied from 9s. to 12s. a week, 10s. being perhaps the usual rate. The 'common wages of a journeyman' in the less well-paid trades were then from 12s. to 14s. or 15s. In the seventies they seem to have been from 15s. upwards.[8] In 1775 the masons complained to Parliament that their wages had been settled nearly seventy years before and were only 15s. a week, out of which the upkeep of their tools cost them about a shilling, while the present wages of the labourers in the masons' business, who served no apprenticeship and had no expenses for tools, were from 12s. to 14s.[25] In 1777 the journeymen saddlers complained to Quarter Sessions that their wages were lower than in 'almost every other handycraft trade', being only from 12s. to 15s. a week (these were chiefly piecework earnings). The petitioners

... cannot help lamenting that after their friends have been at a considerable charge in apprentice fees and other expenses to bring them up in (what is generally called) a genteel business, that the price of their labour should not be sufficient to afford them a comfortable subsistence.[26]

In 1786 their wages are given as from 14s. to 16s. a week, while apprentice fees ranged from £30 to £100 – a strange state of things. In 1811 they again complained – this time to the master-saddlers, that their wages were much lower than in any other London handicraft trade, while apprentice fees were from £40 to £100; their earnings, they said, did not average more than 25s. a week, and they asked that there should be a minimum rate of 27s.[27]

The printers may be taken as typical of the better paid London journeymen. In Johnson's opinion they were particularly fortunate. 'When you consider,' he said to Strachan's apprentice boy, 'with how little mental power and corporeal labour a printer can get a guinea a week, it is a very desirable occupation for you.' Place in 1818 collected detailed information on earnings from 1777. Earnings of compositors were 4d. an hour or 24s. a week of six twelve-hour days in 1777. They rose in 1785 (according to another informant in 1796) to $4\frac{1}{2}$d. or 27s., in 1800 to 5d. or 36s., and to 6d. or 48s. in 1805. Men on newspaper work had a shilling a day above these rates.[28] In 1816 there was a reduction of $\frac{3}{4}$d. an hour or 1s. 6d. in the pound, but work from MS. was not reduced, thus equalizing earnings and removing a grievance of long standing.[29] There must have been considerable variations round this average according to the skill of the compositor. In 1747 weekly earnings were said to be up to a guinea,[30] in 1761 from 14s. to a guinea, and in 1787 from 18s. to 26s. In 1791 John Walter complained to the City Chamberlain of an apprentice of three years' standing who (amongst other delinquencies) had only earned 7s. in the last week when he was capable of earning £2 7s. od.,[31] but such high earnings for a boy seem hardly credible.

Skilled and rapid workmen on piecework could in many trades in the eighteenth century earn from £1 to £3 or £4 – for instance, the jeweller, the maker of optical instruments, or the chair-carver. The earnings of such workmen were often increased by those of an apprentice. The earnings of workers in the textile trades were in general below those of other artisans. The silk-weavers as a class were among the poorest of London workpeople. There was a sailcloth industry in the Tower Hamlets in the hands of a few large masters, who employed both spinners and weavers, their workpeople being 'of both sexes from the age of seven to seventy'.[32] The spinning was done in a long building on the same system as rope-making and both men and women were employed. In 1771 the sailcloth-weavers petitioned the Middlesex Sessions to consider their hard case, and 'to interpose and give them such relief as the laws now in being will admit'; they could only earn at the present rates 9s. a week on 'a number one duck canvas', other works being in proportion, whereas over twenty-three years before the price of a number one was 9s. 6d. and the money 'easier earned than it would be now at 12s. on account of the additional labour which is required to compleat a piece of work such as the London manufacturers produce'. The Sessions heard both masters and men, but dismissed the petition and ordered the weavers to work at 'the accustomed rates till other rates . . . shall be duly authorized'.[33]

Framework-knitting or stocking-weaving, though better paid in London than in the provinces, was badly paid, and was one of those trades which were steadily leaving London:

It is abundantly profitable to the master [it was said in 1747] but not so much so to the journeymen, for few of them earn above 9s. or 10s. a week, they are paid so much for a pair of stockings, and if they have not a loom of their own, allow the master 2s. a week for the use of his.[34]

In 1761, on the best silk or cotton stockings from 12s. to 18s. could be earned, less 1s. 6d. for the use of the frame, and on coarse worsted stockings not more than 9s. or 10s. 'with the closest application'. A London employer stated to a Parliamentary Committee in 1778 that wages were too low and frame rents too high, but that he did not lower the rents because he could not get the other masters to agree.[35] Women in London do not seem to have worked at the frame as they did elsewhere, but were employed in winding and doubling the silk and in seaming and trimming the stockings.

Labourers' wages, like those of the artisan, rose at first gradually and more rapidly in the long war. In trades like the building trades, where the skilled tradesman had his appropriate labourer, the wages of the latter were generally two-thirds of those of the former. The earnings of the coal-heavers or coal-whippers on the Thames were very high but very irregular, and subject to heavy deductions from the middle-men who employed them. They were said to be up to 10s. a day before the war, while in the war men were occasionally able to earn from £1 to

27s. in a long day.[36] In 1816 an ordinary labourer's wages were given as 3s. a day or from 18s. to 25s. a week in Shadwell, in St George's, Hanover Square, from 15s. to 16s. a week and in summer something more.[37]

To the difficult question of the spending power of wages there can be no definite answer, but some light is thrown by budgets presented to Quarter Sessions in 1779 by the journeymen saddlers as evidence that their wages were too low. They are estimates of the expenses of a London 'working man and his family consisting of a wife and three children'.

The man being obliged to work from home early every morning, breakfast for his wife and children every day for six days at 1s. per day	£0	6	0
Breakfast and dinner for the man and supper for the whole family at 1s. per day	0	6	0
Lodgings, coals, candles, soap and other necessaries cannot amount to less than	0	5	0
Sunday's breakfast, dinner, and supper for the whole family	0	2	0
	£0	19	0

The saddlers also drew up an alternative estimate:

12 pounds of coarse beef at 3½d. per pound	£0	3	6
2¼ ounces of tea at 4½d. per ounce	0	0	11¼
1 pound of lump sugar at 7d. per pound	0	0	7
2 „ of coarse sugar at 5d. per pound	0	0	10
Salt, pepper, etc.	0	0	2¼
3 pounds of salt butter at 8d. per pound	0	2	0
2 bushels and a half of coals at 14d. per bushel	0	3	1
Soap, blue, starch, etc.	0	1	0
Lodging	0	2	6
Bread	0	4	11
Cheese	0	1	0
	£1	0	6½[26]

Neither of these estimates is very convincing; in the second beer and milk are both absent. They look like the joint production of a number of unmarried journeymen intent on impressing the justices favourably, but they show something of the standard of living. The fare of an unmarried clerk at a salary of £50 a year, described as 'even worse' than that of a day labourer, is thus budgeted for in 1767, a year of dearth and high prices:

Breakfast

Bread and cheese and small beer from the chandler's shop	£0	0	2

Dinner

Chuck beef or scrag of mutton or sheep's trotters or pig's ear soused; cabbage or potatoes or parsnips, bread, and small beer with half a pint of porter	0	0	7

Supper

Bread and cheese with radishes or cucumbers or onions	0	0	3
Small beer and half a pint of porter	0	0	1½
	£0	1	1½
Per week	£0	7	10½
An additional repast on Sunday	0	0	4
	£0	8	2½

The clerk was provided with coal and candles from Michaelmas to Ladyday only, at a cost of 1s. 6½d. a week: 26 bushels of coals at 1s. 3d., 13 pounds of candles (fourteens) at 7d. Soap, blacking, pepper, vinegar and salt cost him 10s. a year; washing, 10d. a week, 'shaving and combing a wig twice', 6d. Clothes were a heavy item, though he was 'cloathed . . . in the plainest and coarsest manner'. He paid half a crown a week for a furnished room.[38]

The 'expences of a journeyman taylor' in 1752 (when prices were lower than in 1767 or 1779) show something of the manner of living in an occupation distinctly less genteel than that of the saddler or clerk:

For breakfast more than the master's allowance [of 1½d.]	£0	0	0½
For meat, drink, and bread for dinner	0	0	6
On the shop-board in the afternoon a pint of beer	0	0	1½
Bread, cheese, and beer for supper	0	0	3
One day's expenses	£0	0	11
Sunday's expense	0	1	0
The other five days' expense	0	4	7
Lodging for a week	0	1	0
Washing for a week	0	0	8
Shaving for a week	0	0	4
	£0	8	6[39]

The wife was expected to contribute to the family income.* The wife of a day labourer usually hawked fruit or fish or carried loads through

* See Appendix VI.

the streets from the markets – these were especially the occupations of Irish women who were as a rule unable to sew or even go out charing, washing or 'nurse-keeping' as English labourers' wives often did. The journeyman's wife in trades where women were not employed often had a small shop or took in washing or needlework. A shopkeeper's wife generally served in the shop or superintended it unless she had a separate business of her own;[40] if she had been a widow she frequently continued in nominal or actual charge of her first husband's business. Marriage was a business partnership – the wife's portion was often the means of setting her husband up as a master. It was only the well-to-do shopkeeper's wife whose dowry had been a large one who was considered entitled to be relieved from the obligation of work in house or shop. 'Consider my dear girls,' runs *A Present for a Servant Maid* (1743), 'that you have no portions, and endeavour to supply the deficiencies of fortune by mind. You cannot expect to marry in such a manner as neither of you shall have occasion to work, and none but a fool will take a wife whose bread must be earned solely by his labour and who will contribute nothing towards it herself.'

Nevertheless there is a surprising unanimity among foreigners as to the freedom of married women in England from the obligation to work. 'Among the common people the husbands seldom make their wives work,' says Muralt.[41] According to de Saussure, English women were lazy and 'even women of the lower class do little needlework'.[42] Zetzner, a merchant's clerk of Strasburg, who came to London in 1700, was filled with admiration of the women whom he calls 'perfect creatures', though he admits that they were addicted to drink, gaming and idleness.

Their husbands [he says] love them to such a point that they do not give them the least domestic work to do. They do not even permit them to suckle their own children. . . . Their dress is more than luxurious and one sees the wives of tailors and shoemakers wearing clothes embroidered in gold or silver and adorned with gold watches. Hence the old proverb, if there was a bridge over the channel, most of the women of Europe would hasten to England.[43]

How are these sayings to be reconciled with the undoubted facts of business and domestic life revealed by the *Sessions Papers*? In the first place one may conclude that the wives of shopkeepers on the Continent did much heavier and more exacting work than those of a corresponding class in and near London. London and its neighbourhood had reached a stage of industrial development where spinning, weaving, baking, brewing and candle-making were no longer done by housewives. In London too, even cooking was not a necessary part of domestic economy; the coffee-house, the tavern, the cook-shop (of many grades), the alehouse, the chandler's shop, the itinerant pieman, the stall, provided food and drink for various classes of the community. The baker cooked many Sunday dinners, from the pie or pudding to the dubious piece of meat thrust through with a skewer. The poorer sort, too, bought their clothes from the many dealers in old clothes of Monmouth Street and Rag Fair.

Secondly, these foreigners are dazzled by the easy-going prosperity of the trading classes and confused by the comparative absence of class distinction in dress. 'The common people' and 'the lower class', vague terms at best, had then a different implication in England and on the Continent, and as a matter of fact the visitors paid comparatively little attention to the humbler folk. It is indeed true that among Londoners we have to go very far down the social scale to find the woman who did not employ some other woman or child to help her in washing and scouring or in the 'minding' of children. It is true that Polly when she married Macheath said she proposed 'like other women' to live upon the industry of her husband, but against this aspiration may be set the very active part taken by Mrs Peachum in the maintenance of her family. When we reach the level of the 'labouring poor' it can almost be said that there is no work too heavy or disagreeable to be done by women, provided it is also ill-paid. A description of the itinerant trades of London in 1804 remarks of the sale of cats' and dogs' meat 'although this is the most disagreeable and offensive commodity cried for sale in London the occupation seems to be engrossed by women'.[44] We even find a woman apprenticed to a butcher in Carnaby Market, who, when out of her time, 'lived by killing of beasts in which . . . she was very expert'.[45] There were many women butchers in the London markets, but whether they usually did the slaughtering part of the business does not appear.

There is a good deal of evidence – apart from the many complaints of excessive luxury – of a comfortable easy-going life among working people – side by side with much poverty and distress and great irregularity of work. It was the century of the Roast Beef of Old England. Voltaire, on his first day in England (1726), fresh from the wooden shoes of France, took the servant-girls, apprentices and journeymen decked out in their best,* some riding hired horses, for 'people of fashion' and admired 'the skill with which the young women managed their horses and was greatly struck with the freshness and beauty of their complexions, the neatness of their dress and the graceful vivacity of their movements'.[46] Labouring men, as well as artisans, frequently possessed silver watches and silver shoe buckles.[47] in 1767 a working mason and his wife who lodged in Plumbtree Court, Shoe Lane, were robbed, among other things, of a silk coat, silk waistcoat, five neck-cloths, a gold-laced hat, a silk bonnet, a silk gown, a tortoiseshell snuff-box and two gold rings. This was done, he said, 'while I went over the way to the King's Arms to dinner. I staid an hour, my usual time'.[48]

The other side of the picture is dark. Saunders Welch the magistrate told Johnson that more than twenty people in London died weekly of starvation – not directly, but indirectly. Light is thrown on the obscure tragedies of London by a case in 1763 which shocked a community which (justifiably) regarded itself as humane. A prospective purchaser was being shown over an empty house in Stonecutter Street when in two of the rooms three dead women were found, terribly emaciated, and almost completely naked; in the garret were two women and a girl of about sixteen, two of whom seemed on the verge of starvation, the other (named Pattent) in better case. One of the three living women had taken shelter on the ground floor only a day or two before and had been invited to the garret by Pattent. Two of the dead women had sheltered there for some months at least; they were both basket-women who carried loads in Fleet Market, and were both known only as 'Bet'. Pattent, when out of a place, went to seek work in the Market and was told by the two Bets of this empty house. She then went to work for a former mistress who kept a cook-shop in King Street, Westminster, for her food only and slept in the house at night. The girl, Elizabeth Surman, was the daughter of a jeweller in Bell Alley, Coleman Street, her

* At Greenwich Fair.

parents died when she was six; a neighbour who took charge of her, four years later. The child was told she could get work in Spitalfields; she first wound quills for a woman who shortly after left London, and was then hired in Spitalfields Market to wind silk, but discharged in a week. She was again hired in the market, this time by a woman who took in washing and nurse-children, who kept her for six years and then discharged her when she was taken ill. She appealed to the church-warden of her father's parish, who refused her all help and did not even tell her that she had gained a settlement in the parish where she had worked for six years. She slept in the streets till she was told of the empty house, where after lying ill for a week with ague and without food of any kind, she was helped by Pattent, and when she was better went out to beg. She had recently been for a week in the workhouse of St Andrews, Holborn, had returned to the house ill, and was again looked after by Pattent. Pattent, who was out in the daytime at her unpaid work, and attending to the girl at night, knew nothing of the death of the two basket-women, but they had been ill, and a few days before she had pawned her apron for sixpence and taken them some food. No one seems to have known anything of the third dead woman; their clothes had perhaps been taken by someone who had come into the house. This was the story elicited by the coroner's inquest. According to the Poor Law such things should have been impossible, but when one empty house sheltered five starving people, it is to be feared they were not exceptional. Indeed, in the following month another woman was found starved to death in a house in the same district.[49]

It is significant that all the victims should have been women; there can be little doubt that the hardships of the age bore with especial weight upon them. Social conditions tended to produce a high propor-tion of widows, deserted wives,[50] and unmarried mothers, while women's occupations were over-stocked, ill-paid and irregular.

Earnings were of course profoundly influenced by the custom of different trades. The type of industrial organization most common in London was that which is generally called the domestic, in which work was given out to be done in the homes of the workers. This putting-out system (it includes cases where the worker hires a seat or standing in another man's workshop or loom-shop) prevailed in various forms, work being undertaken for a shopkeeper or trading master, by a person known, according to the custom of the trade, as a chamber-master, garret-master, piece-master or journeyman.

This is a system which leads to sweating, and it undoubtedly did so in the eighteenth century in many trades, and more particularly in the women's trades, such as silk-winding, slop-work and other branches of needlework – stitching of stays and quilting for instance. The apprenticeship system in certain occupations was simply an exploitation of juvenile labour. Where the trade was exclusive, highly skilled, or depended on artistic talent, the working tradesmen as a rule held their own, and could sometimes make large earnings. The domestic system leads also to irregularity of work; first, because the employer, having little fixed capital, can stop or reduce work on any check to the trade; secondly, on account of delays in obtaining materials and the preference of the worker for times of leisure compensated by times of excessive labour. To quote a pamphlet of 1722:

The weavers, taylors, shoemakers and most other mechanical trades within the weekly bills, now lose two days in every six throughout the year, the greatest part whereof is lost thro' an idle or some other vicious inclination; some part . . . is lost for want of work. A great part of their time is spent in fetching their materials, or carrying home their work, or in seeking after their money, or in spending too much time in providing their food.[51]

Various forms of the putting-out system were used in the three great London trades of watchmaking, silk-weaving and shoe-making.

The London watchmaking trade was minutely subdivided; the making of a watch was chosen as early as 1701 to illustrate the advantages of division of labour.[52] By the end of the seventeenth century tools had been invented which had reduced and simplified the necessary handwork; Derham (1696) speaks of 'the inventions of cutting engines, fusy engines, etc', as 'contrivances of this last age'.[53] By 1747 the use of such tools or 'engines', combined with division of labour, was regarded as having transformed the art of watchmaking. In the course of the century the working part of the trade located itself in Clerkenwell and the neighbouring parish of St Luke's. The watchmakers and clockmakers of repute, who supervised the workmanship and put their names on the cases, though they sometimes had shops in Clerkenwell, notably in Red Lion Street, were to be found in the chief streets for shops, such as Cornhill, Cheapside or the Strand. English watches had a great reputation on the Continent; in 1698 the exportation of empty cases or dials, with a maker's name on them, was forbidden by statute; while in 1703 complaints were made to the Clockmakers' Company that the names of Tompion, Windmills and Quare (famous London makers) had been set on watches made in Amsterdam, which were then sold as English. In 1747 they were said to have been recently brought to the highest perfection and to be exported to every part of the known world. In 1798 an English maker who had had an establishment in Paris for thirty years said he was always obliged to send to London for works connected with jewelling. At this time the watchmaking artisans in St Luke's Without Cripplegate were estimated at 1,000 and those in Clerkenwell at 7,000. Before the building of Pentonville it had been supposed that half the population of the parish was dependent on watchmaking. The watches made in Clerkenwell before the ruinous clock and watch duty of 1797 (repealed in 1798) were estimated at about 120,000 a year, about 70,000 being for export and 50,000 for the home trade. There were London makers who supplied the country trade, putting the name of their customers, the provincial retailers, on the case. One of these, Bayley of Red Lion Street, said that in 1795 and 1796 he made from 3,000 to 4,000 watches a year, employing over a hundred workmen.[54]

The parts of the watch were made by different artisans, for the most part in the garrets of Clerkenwell. The methods of the trade are thus described in 1747 when the use of 'engines' had

... reduced the expense of workmanship to a trifle in comparison with what it was before and brought the work to such an exactness that no hand can imitate it. The movement-maker forges his wheels and turns them to the just dimensions, sends them to the cutter and has them cut at a trifling expense. He has nothing to do when he takes them from the cutter but to finish them and turn the corners of the teeth. The pinions made of steel are drawn at the mill so that the watchmaker has only to file down the points and fix them to the proper wheels. The springs are made by a tradesman who does nothing else, and the chains by another. These last are frequently made by women. . . . There are workmen who make nothing else but the caps and studs for watches. . . . After the watchmaker has got home all the . . . parts of which it consists, he gives the whole to the finisher, having first had the brass wheels gilded by the gilder, and adjusts it to the proper time. The watchmaker puts his name on the plate and is esteemed the maker, though he has not made in his shop the smallest wheel belonging to it. It is supposed, however, that he can make all the movements, and apprentices are still learned to cut them by hand. He must be a judge of the goodness of the work at first sight, and put his name to nothing but what will stand the severest trial, for the price of the watch depends upon the reputation of the maker only.[55]

This account leaves out many of the different branches of watch-making. It says nothing of the dial-plate enamellers, the casemakers, with their engravers, jewellers, chasers and enamellers. Movement-making and motion-making, according to an account of 1761, were often subdivided. Watch-springing and lining (work done on the case of a watch) was a separate trade, and was often done by women. Watch-hand-making and key-making were separate trades and the tendency to more and more subdivision was probably progressive; in 1817 it was said there were 102 separate branches. The workmen were sometimes considered as journeymen employed by the watchmakers – one man would make for a number of masters – or as chamber-masters, making parts and offering them for sale. All of them took apprentices at fees varying from £5 upwards, except the finisher and motion- and move-ment-makers, who asked higher fees.[56] The maker himself, who asked a fee (1761) of from £10 to £50, might be either a shopkeeper or a chamber-master working for the shops, in which case the name of the shop would be put on the dial – sometimes the name of a jeweller, a toyman or even a pawnbroker, who knew nothing of watchmaking. Thus, at least by the middle of the eighteenth century, of the many watchmaking artisans, only the watchmaker and finisher could be considered complete craftsmen, while some branches of the trade in-volved only a simple repetition process done by its appropriate tool or 'engine'. It was from the watchmaking artisans however, that the makers of textile machinery were said (at the end of the century) to be chiefly recruited.[54] In the person of the eminent watchmaker, the inventor and the man of science, the craftsman and the shopkeeper met. Such men as Tompion and Harrison ranked with the famous optical instrument-makers, such as Graham,[15] Dollond and Ramsden , men with a European reputation who made London renowned for its scientific craftsmanship.

The apprentices, as they advanced in their term, were expected to earn an increasing weekly sum for their masters. In Coventry, after about 1773, it became the custom to take numbers of outdoor apprentices who worked in factories and overstocked and degraded the trade. In London, however, there seems to have been great moderation in taking apprentices. In 1798 the trade was in a terrible state of distress, partly at least due to the ill-judged clock and watch duty of 1797. A society was formed to relieve the artisans and help them to redeem the tools they had pawned. They visited 1,101 distressed artisans in Clerkenwell and found among these 886 wives, 1,945 children and 301 apprentices – a very small proportion, though probably many of the children worked. These people's gross weekly earnings before the tax had been £1,511; £416 since. Tools, working-room and light of course came out of this. Between them they had pawned things to the value of £1,503. Weekly earnings in 1786 in the various subordinate branches were estimated at from 12s. to 30s. a week, those of a watchmaker or finisher working as a chamber-master at three guineas.[54]

Though some branches of the watchmaking trade were certainly not highly paid, wholesale distress among the London watchmaking artisans was new,[57] but cries of starvation from Spitalfields were recurrent. The Spitalfields weaver is often taken as the type of the highly-intelligent and skilled craftsman who flourished under the domestic system. Some examination of the conditions of his life, which were dependent on the structure of his trade, will throw light on the system as well as on a large section of the working classes of London.

The London silk trade as an important textile industry dates from the immigration of Huguenots after the Revocation of the Edict of Nantes in 1685. Long before that however, there had been a silk industry in London, and in 1675 it was asserted that there were 'an hundred thousand people small and great' dependent on the London trade.[58] This is doubtless an exaggeration, but Defoe in 1705 credits the still more incredible estimate of 50,000 ribbon-weavers in London about the year 1679.[59] At all events there were in the later seventeenth century many silk-weavers in the eastern outskirts of London, chiefly employed in making ribbons for which the fashions of the time created a great demand. The French taught these weavers to make broad silks of a workmanship which was new in England, notably lustrings and alamodes. The silk trade expanded rapidly, and Massie calls William III its 'royal founder' because he secured a regular importation of Italian raw and thrown-silk.[60] A second stage of expansion was ascribed to the reduction in 1750 of the duties on China raw silk to the level of those on silks from Italy.[61]

In the later seventeenth century the silk-weavers were spreading from Shoreditch and Whitechapel to the hamlets of Stepney, and there were still silk-weavers in Southwark as there were in the reign of Elizabeth. They spread first to Spitalfields where the Huguenot colony settled, and in the eighteenth century journeymen became very numerous in Bethnal Green and Mile End New Town. The whole silk-weaving district was known as Spitalfields, the name of the hamlet of Stepney which became the parish of Christchurch. The masters remained in Spitalfields itself, in Spital Square (in the Liberty of Norton Folgate) and in the City. There were many branches of the silk trade. First, there was the silk importer or silk merchant, then the silk man, who bought and sold raw silk and sometimes imported it. He might be considered, we are told in 1747, as warehouse-keeper and retailer or as merchant. Then came the throwster who twisted or threw the raw silk for the weaver by various processes corresponding to the roving and spinning of cotton. The thrown-silk was then dyed, silk dyeing being a considerable London industry. It was then bought by the master-weaver, given out by him to the journeymen weavers and the finished piece was sold to the mercer, to whom (in 1765) it was customary to give twelve months' credit. The mercers sometimes employed working weavers to make pieces from their patterns which were often taken from imported French silks, thus acting as master-weavers. Patterns were also supplied to the masters by the professional pattern-drawers of Spitalfields.

The master-weavers occasionally opened warehouses at the west end of the town to sell their silks direct to the quality without the intervention of the mercer.[62] The London weaver was not dependent on the native throwster as much ready-thrown or organzined silk was imported from Italy. This seems to have been the normal organization of the trade about 1760 but doubtless there were many variations.[63] The small master and the large master existed side by side, though there was a progressive tendency to greater capitalization.[64] Even in 1823 there were small men employing from ten to forty looms, some of whom had been journeymen themselves. The working weaver owned or hired his own loom. In the earlier part of the century there were two intermediate sets of dealers between the weaver and the mercer who seem to have dropped out as the trade became more capitalized. These were the macklers, who sold weavers' goods to shopkeepers and sometimes wove themselves, but appear to have been used only by small working weavers or else for the disposal of damaged lengths of silk. There were also piece-brokers who bought sometimes of the macklers, sometimes of the weavers.[65]

Silk-weaving, as it was carried on at Spitalfields, was subject to most of the known causes of trade fluctuation to an extreme degree. Its raw material came from abroad and the supply was sometimes interrupted.[66] Though heavily protected, the trade maintained that it could not hold its own against French competition, and smuggling was a constant grievance; the complete prohibition of foreign silk fabrics (1765–1826) did not bring prosperity to the weavers. The trade was subject to periods of over-expansion and subsequent depression, to sudden changes of fashion, to disastrous interruptions from court mourning; it was also seasonal, and the small master was often unable to withstand even seasonal fluctuations: 'Many manufacturers,' it was said in 1706,

and especially London weavers and other workmen who keep several men at work, are sometimes much streightened for money, either to pay their men's wages or to find goods to employ them, especially at a dead time of year, or when money is scarce to be had, and thereupon, being forced to pawn some of their goods for what pawnbrokers are pleased to lend on them, they do not only impoverish themselves, and turn away their men, who, for want of work, do with their families become a burthen to the public, but it also discourages the said manufactures. . . .[67]

It was fatally easy for the master to 'put down looms' or reduce the quantity of work on any check to the trade, and Spitalfields was peculiarly sensitive to any fluctuation of demand, more so, it was said, than the more highly capitalized clothing trade, where the clothier undertook all the processes of manufacture from the buying of raw wool to selling the cloth through the Blackwell Hall factors:

The clothier in the country goes on as long as he can get credit for a bag of wooll to work on or a peny to pay his workmen . . . but in Spitalfields the case alters, there the manufacturers, I mean the masters, are near the market, they do not put the wooll [or silk] to spinning, but buy it in the yarn: As soon as the market stops they stop. If they cannot sell their work they immediately knock off the looms and the journeymen as immediately starve, and want work.[68]

The history of Spitalfields in the eighteenth century is a repeated illustration of this process. 'I have known instances,' said Hale, the master-weaver, in 1806, 'wherein trade in general has experienced a temporary depression. . . . Many manufacturers have discharged fifty to a hundred men each and put as many more upon half work; in a little time after the distress has been beyond description. . . .'[69]

The fluctuations were the more disastrous as the trade tended to be overstocked with workers except in times of exceptional prosperity. It had a number of branches, some highly skilled, others 'slight and easy'. The weaving of plain silks required 'little ingenuity', the weaving of ribbons and handkerchiefs less still. Even in its higher branches weaving was one of the worst paid of London trades. 'The wages of weavers in general are but poor,' said *The Parents' Director* in 1761, a time of great prosperity in the silk trade, 'the best hands among the journeymen being seldom able to get above 15s. a week', and again, of brocade-weaving, 'though this art requires great ingenuity, a journeyman cannot earn above 12s. or 15s. a week'.[70] Doubtless the skilled weaver with apprentices who employed other journeymen might do well in good times, and even very well on 'new works', for which there was a sudden demand, but these opportunities were only for the few, and were apt to lead to reactions of under-employment. The trade suffered from the ease with which women and children could be employed, and from the drifting to London of country weavers and Irish weavers, attracted by hopes of higher pay. 'How many country weavers come daily to town, and turn their hands to different kinds of work than that they are brought up to,' wrote a controversialist in 1719.[71] In 1736 there were riots in Spitalfields against Irish weavers who were supposed to be working 'at an under rate',* and a hundred years later Irish labour was a serious grievance. A skilled weaver of Huguenot descent complained in 1838: 'There are many Irish weavers in Spitalfields, and although the wages of weavers are higher in their country, as I understand, through

* See Chapter 3.

their trades unions, yet they come here and work among us at a lower rate than they were willing to do at home, and injure both themselves and us.'[72]

The outburst of rioting in London in 1719 against the wearers of printed calicoes was the result of a time of depression, severely felt by the weavers, whose numbers had been rapidly increased. The controversialists speak of 'the unreasonable and unlimited increase of weavers in London when hands are so much wanted in other handycraft trades'.[73] This 'makes it impossible for them to have work all the year round and when they are idle they form themselves into clubs and from thence into riotous and tumultuous assembleies. . . .'[74] Again, 'the grand cause of the weavers wanting work is the covetousness of the masters and mistresses in taking so many apprentices for the sake of the money they have with them'.[75] A silk-weaver's answer to this last accusation throws much light on the way the trade was recruited, and shows that the causes of distress discovered by the Hand-loom Commissioners in 1840 were deeply rooted in the early organization of the Spitalfields trade. 'In the first place,' he says,

few masters take apprentices, and when they do, seldom more than one, and perhaps a son or near relation. Secondly, as to the journeymen, the essence of the charge is false . . . for where there is one that has money with an apprentice there are fifty that have none at all, and the most they have, when they can get it, is not above £5 or £6, and the reason of this proves itself. For in the first place they commonly take such poor boys apprentices as have been first brought up to the trade, for you must know that every workman has a boy to attend to him, to help him pick his silk clean, to fill his quills, and in a flowered work to draw up the figure. Some of these things these boys are able to do at the age of six or seven, for which they receive 2s., 3s., 4s., and 4s. 6d. a week, which is a great help to their poor fathers and mothers. This they continue till fourteen, at which time they seek for a master and masters also seek for such boys. Secondly, it is of much more advantage to a master to take such a boy without money, than a stranger with money, and the parents of such boys being very poor, 'tis ridiculous to say they are taken for the sake of the money.[75]

In other words, they were taken for the sake of cheap labour. In 1769, according to the *Public Advertiser*, it was 'a certain fact that there are several weavers in Spitalfields who have from ten to twenty apprentices each.' 'How,' it is asked, 'are all these to find employment when their time is expired?'[76]

The London silk trade employed a number of women and children. These fall into three groups, first, women weavers; secondly, women and children who worked for the weavers; and thirdly, those who were employed by the throwsters (this leaves out of account those dependent on the silk-dyeing and framework-knitting trades who were probably not numerous). Throughout the century we hear of women weavers in Spitalfields, for instance, Sarah Brown, executed in 1718 for murder and theft, said that she was 'born in Spittlefields and learned the weaving trade, weaving stuffs, and might by it have got a pretty livelihood'. In the sixties, women seem often to have been ribbon-weavers, both engine-loom and single-hand, and the *Parents' Director* of 1761 instances the trade as a suitable one for girls. In 1769, a time of price-cutting, unemployment and rioting, there was an attempt to exclude women from the better-paid branches except in war-time. *The Book of Prices* or piece rates for weaving agreed to by masters and men in 1769 lays down the following conditions:

No woman or girl to be employed in making any kind of work except such works as are herein fixed and settled at 5½d. per ell or . . . per yard or under for the making and those not to exceed half an ell in width. . . . And no woman or girl is to be employed in making any sort of handkerchief of above the usual or settled price of 4s. 6d. per dozen for the making thereof PROVIDED always . . . that in case it shall hereafter happen that the Kingdom of Great Britain shall engage in war . . . that then every manufacturer shall be at liberty to employ women or girls in the making of any sort of works as they shall think most fit and convenient without any restraint whatsoever. . . .[77]

By the end of the century the attempt to restrict women weavers seems to have been given up. In the expansion of the trade that began about 1798 or 1800 after a prolonged period of depression, enough women could not be found to wind the silk, as so many had taken to weaving. Some of the masters suggested that the difficulty could be overcome by preventing from weaving those who had not served a regular apprenticeship and so 'obliging those who were now weavers to take to their former employment of winding the silk. This project *at first* pleased the weavers, but on mature consideration they found . . . their own children in comparison with others would be the greatest sufferers. . . .'[78] The outcome was that winding machines were introduced which the journeymen could not afford to buy and winding was done on the masters' premises.[79] It became the usual thing for a weaver to marry a weaveress, and for their children to learn to weave.

The second group of women in the silk trade, those who wound silk for the weavers, thus belongs almost entirely to the eighteenth century when a large part of the wives and daughters of the weavers were so employed. When the weaver had no member of his own family at hand, he would hire a winder in Spitalfields Market at so much a week. John Norbury, for instance, in 1760 said: 'I am a weaver, . . . I hired the prisoner out of Spittlefields Market at 3s. per week . . . to work in my house at winding of silk.'[80] Silk-winders or windsters easily became weavers. Sarah Whiteman, accused in 1760 of stealing a silver quart mug from a public-house, was described by her employer as 'an honest poor industrious woman, she sometimes winds silk, and sometimes works in the loom with me'. 'I am a windster by trade, a weaver by rights, only I have no work to do,' said the wife of a market porter in 1784.[81] While weavers employed windsters, the windsters employed yet other women to help them wind. The most skilled windster, called a four-swift-engine-windster, was one who could work with an 'engine' that wound four spindles at once; a woman employed in 'the shop' of such a windster said: 'I had a shilling a week allowed me from the parish . . . I was almost naked, the church-wardens would not give me any more money, but took me into the house.'[82]

Quite young children worked at filling quills for the weaver's shuttle: one child could keep several men supplied. Little parish apprentice girls were sometimes taken into weavers' families to wind quills.[83] The brocade-weaver employed older boys as draw-boys to draw the threads in the loom by which the pattern was produced. This was terribly exhausting work. In the Napoleonic War a shortage of boys led to the introduction of the 'wooden draw-boy', apparently a rudimentary form of Jacquard loom. The boys were then paid from 6s. to 8s. a week, but a weaver expressed his preference in 1823 for 'a hardy boy that has legs as well as hands over a wooden machine that has only legs and no hands'. The drawback to a human boy was that 'it was often found that a boy cannot go on if he has worked five or six hours . . . sometimes he was taken ill . . . and a weaver was obliged to lose half a day or a whole day'.[84]

The third group of women and children worked for the silk-throwsters. These again fell into two divisions: those who attended to the throwing mill on the throwster's premises, and those to whom work was given out to be done at home. These people were the poorest of the poor; in fact one of the chief grounds on which the throwsters appealed for favours for their trade was that they employed many hundreds of poor people, chiefly women and children from about the age of seven.[85] The throwing mill in its early form was a kind of wooden cage or turret turned by a handle connected with a cog-wheel. A number of bobbins on which silk had been wound were attached to the mill whose turning gave a twist to the silk and transferred it from the bobbins to the arms of 'windles or reels' where it was wound in skeins. The mills used in London were made by the loom-makers who could set up in business with £50, while the capital needed by the throwster was chiefly used for silk, so that the machinery and premises of a throwster employing 'hands' by the hundred must have been of a rudimentary kind.[86] Thomas Pearson, a silk-throwster of Goodman's Fields, said in 1755 that he employed about 800 people, some of whom worked on his mill which had 160 bobbins, and some at home.[87] Far the greater number apparently worked at home, as it was said that one person was enough to attend a mill with 200 bobbins 'to put new bobbins or spools in lieu of those discharged of their silk and to tie the ends when they break'. The work done at home seems to have been winding the silk on the bobbins ready for the mill and 'doubling' it when it had been thrown once.

From about 1732 silk-winding was a common occupation in London workhouses where it superseded the less profitable spinning of mop-yarn.[88] It hardly seems possible that this can have lowered the wages of silk-winders or degraded the occupation which was evidently in the lowest grade of casual unskilled work. As the silk was constantly being 'embezzled' there is a good deal of incidental information in the *Sessions Papers*. One poor woman who was a lodger in a tenement would take in winding or doubling and employ others still poorer, who often divided their time between winding and 'selling things about the streets'.

After the middle of the century many silk mills were set up in the country and less is heard of winding for the throwsters as a London occupation. Silk-throwing gradually became a factory industry where water power was available and disappeared from London sheds and garrets. The organzine silk which was necessary for the warp could not be thrown in England till Lombe's mill was established in Derby in 1719. His patent expired in 1732, but the great increase of large silk mills in England is said to date from 1750 when the duty on raw China and India silk was reduced: 'this was the means of setting up a number of mills in imitation of those originally built for Sir Thomas Lombe'.[89] Mills were built in the fifties in Congleton, Macclesfield, Leek and elsewhere and London throwsters sent their silk to the provinces to be worked. One Sherrard stated in 1765 that before 1762 he employed 1,500 people at a time, 500 in London, 200 in Gloucestershire, 400 in Dorsetshire, 400 in Cheshire, but had been reduced to 100 in London.[89] By 1823 the memory of silk-throwing as a London industry had almost disappeared; there were then supposed to be about a hundred people employed in it, according to a silk broker who thought it had never been a London trade.

Thus by the beginning of the nineteenth century silk-winding for the weavers and the throwsters as domestic and largely casual occupations in London had disappeared, and women wove as freely as men. The winders and warpers who used to work for the journeymen were replaced by others working in the warehouses of the master-weavers. The great event in the trade had been the Spitalfields Act of 1773 by which combinations were forbidden, prices for weaving were fixed by an order of Quarter Sessions and the weavers were forbidden to have more than two apprentices at a time.[90] This put an end to a ten-years' period of intermittent rioting and loom-cutting in Spitalfields, the result of much misery and unemployment during a period of depression following one of expansion during the Seven Years' War, in which the English had temporarily captured the French foreign trade.[91] The Act brought peace to Spitalfields but not prosperity. Till the end of the century there are repeated and harrowing accounts of misery and starvation amongst the weavers. There was nothing new in this; at the end of the seventeenth century the weavers employed by the Lustring Company said that the opposition of some of the masters to the

Company was 'because they cannot oppress their poor workmen as they used, when they might have the choice of a hundred weavers at their doors every day, the manufacture being a continual refuge for the indigent and distressed'.[92]

The history of the parishes of Christchurch and Bethnal Green in the eighteenth century is one of a continual struggle with poverty and debt, their workhouses repeatedly swamped with destitute weavers. Indeed, there were protests in 1743 against raising the hamlet of Bethnal Green to a parish, on the ground that a church and clergyman were luxuries that the place could not afford:

The inhabitants . . . consist chiefly of journeymen weavers and other inferior artificers belonging to the weaving trade, who by hard labour and industry can scarcely in the most frugal way of life support themselves, and as . . . they are extremely numerous, so a great part of the community consist likewise of bakers, butchers, victuallers, chandlers and such like trades who . . . maintain themselves . . . in supplying such journeymen weavers with the necessaries of life, and . . . by far the greater number of the houses are lett at £10 per annum and under by reason of the poverty of the inhabitants. . . .[93]

In 1763 the parish complained of the heavy burden of the poor owing to the great number of journeymen weavers who took apprentices,[94] and from this time onwards there were repeated appeals to Parliament setting forth the misery of Spitalfields. In 1785 the 'working weavers of Spitalfields' in a protest against the Irish Propositions said that their trade had been 'in a very declining condition for several years . . . for want of employment poverty and distress are deluging like a torrent the whole trade'.[95] The trade crisis of 1792–3 was severely felt there; a dispensary doctor thus described the state of the weavers:

It is not in the power of language to describe their long and continued miseries not brought on by idleness, intemperance or a dissolute course of life, but human wretchedness, absolutely produced by want of employment . . . whole families without fire, without raiment, without food. . . .[96]

Four years later things were much the same: 'The poverty and distress of these people at this time (February 1797) are inconceivable,' said Middleton; 'very generally a family in every room with very little bedding, furniture or clothes. The few rags on their backs comprise the principal part of their property.' He writes later, 'in 1805 and 1806 these people were generally employed, and that has relieved them of much of their distress'.[97] But in 1808, according to William Hale, three-fourths of the poor of Spitalfields were unemployed.[98] Great distress was caused by the Milan Decrees which held up the supply of raw silk in 1812, and in 1816–17 there was again a period of acute depression; according to a master-weaver, the manufacturers were living on their capital. 'My opinion,' he said in 1817, 'had been ever since the Peace, that the silk trade would leave Spitalfields, that it would leave London entirely.'[99]

While it was agreed that before 1798 or 1800 the silk trade was depressed (owing it is said to the preference for cottons[100] and the fashion for muslins), the period from 1800 to 1826 was, in the bad years that followed the repeal of the prohibition of foreign silk fabrics, referred to as the golden age of the trade. The less skilled branches had been leaving London at least since 1765.[89] This was a double-edged benefit, producing much temporary distress, but it probably raised the standard of the Spitalfields trade. Although apprenticeship was not a necessary introduction to weaving, the restriction of the number of apprentices by the Spitalfields Act must have prevented much misery[101] and helped to eliminate the half-skilled worker. In spite of fluctuation, from 1800 to 1826 the trade was expanding, and between 1816 and 1826 absorbed many cotton-weavers and many weavers from Ireland without (it is alleged) becoming over-stocked.[102]

The introduction of machinery had little to do with the vicissitudes of the Spitalfields weavers before 1840 (except in so far as the power loom was responsible for the cotton-weavers and Irish weavers who sought work in London). Indeed it was supposed in 1832 that the power loom was not applicable to broad silk.[103] For rioting in Spitalfields against machinery we have to go back to 1675. The Dutch engine-loom which wove several breadths of ribbons or tapes at the same time had been prohibited by Charles I,[104] and in 1675 was described by the Attorney-General as an instrument 'used above these sixty years'.[105] On four successive days in 1675 there were riots in St Leonard's Shoreditch, Whitechapel and Stepney, in which 'engine-looms' or 'wooden machines' were broken and then burnt in the highway,[106] because with these looms 'one man can do as much . . . as near twenty without them'. The riots extended to Stratford Bow (where there were said to be 1,500 rioters), Essex, Kent and Southwark.[105] In

1768 single-hand and engine-loom weavers attacked each other, but the grievance was 'working at an under rate' and seems to have had nothing to do with the use of the long-established engine-loom.[107]

What sort of people were the working weavers of Spitalfields? There were undoubtedly some who were not only highly skilled but among the most intellectual of London workmen. Simpson the mathematician and Dollond the optician had been silk-weavers. A Mr Charles, a solicitor of Spital Square, enumerated in 1838 the clubs that had formerly existed among them – a floricultural society, a historical society, a musical society and many others – all had disappeared. He also said that many of the former masters had been reduced to journeymen.[108] Everything we know of Spitalfields suggests that these had been the recreations of a small minority. It was then only thirteen years since the trade had been at its highest point of prosperity and the intellectual movements of London artisans in the first quarter of the nineteenth century had not found a congenial soil among the weavers.[109] The circumstances of the trade encouraged extremes. The irregular nature of the work was either a great stimulus to thrift and prudence or exactly the opposite. In 1835 it was said to be one of the greatest misfortunes of the Bethnal Green weavers that they were paid only on the completion of their work, after perhaps five or six weeks, getting trifling advances in the meantime, 'consequently the pawnbroker's shop is frequently resorted to . . . this . . . induces general habits of improvidence'.[110] The weaver might be a highly-skilled craftsman, or he might be incapable of any other work than of throwing the shuttle, having to pay someone to 'turn on' the warp to the beam of his loom, and also to 'twist in' the threads when a new length of warp was necessary. 'There never was a time in my recollection,' said Bresson (in 1838), the grandson of a Huguenot immigrant and a skilled journeyman velvet-weaver, 'when some in the weaving trade could not earn very large sums and others next to nothing.'[72] It is inevitable that in accounts of better days and the glories of the past, stress should be laid on the good earnings.

But irregularity of work and low wages were the natural result of the structure of the trade; weaving was a resource of those who found themselves without a livelihood and ignorant of a trade as well as of those who came to it from other occupations. 'Whenever the trade is brisk men come to it from other employments,' said a Spitalfields weaver in 1838, 'and such as have ability gradually get to the other branches of weaving, and thus the number of weavers is left too great.' The trade was perforce hereditary: 'Weavers bring up their families to be weavers from a desire to get something from their labour as soon as possible and also from an inability to put them into other trades and pay a premium.'[111] These things were at least equally true in the eighteenth century. 'There are now many hands in the weaving trade who were not brought up to it,' said a master-weaver in 1766.[112] We find boys of fifteen who are weavers, and weavers shifting to street-selling and back again to weaving. Poor Thomas Bonney executed in 1744 for robbery on the highway was a weaver, born in Whitechapel and given no education as his parents were very poor: 'his father, being a weaver, taught him how to be useful to him in his trade, and he orked about three years for him and then set up for himself, and arned generally about ten or twelve shillings a week. Business being a little dull, he entered a man-of-war', he returned, worked again at his trade and married. 'When his wife lay-in he happened to be out of work and had not a penny to help,' so went out robbing. All this before he was twenty-one.[113]

Another weaver who had the same melancholy end was Richard Quayle, born in Cork in 1708 and apprenticed to a weaver,

. . . that trade failing in Ireland, he came to London where his parents were . . . and worked at his trade at times. When his business was dead he sold butter, eggs, roots, greens, or any small things he was capable of. He married . . . had children, but having little to do and being brought into great straits by the hard weather last year . . . he took to bad company. . . .

He was a foot-pad, seized 'after the fact' by the mob.[114]

By all the canons, many of the weavers did not rank as skilled artisans, they had picked up the trade without apprenticeship, they did not own their own tools but hired a loom and paid for a loom-standing or worked for another journeyman; they were sometimes capable of throwing a shuttle only, and their wages were far below the standard of a skilled trade. At the other end of the scale were highly-skilled and intelligent craftsmen, housekeepers, owning several looms. The weaving of fine velvets, Bresson said, required a skill that not one workman in a hundred attained to. The greater part of the weavers came between these two extremes. To quote the Hand-loom Commissioners of 1840, there was

... the greatest possible diversity from a highly respectable class of workmen, down to a sort of men who are a disgrace to the trade and would never be employed if it were not that occasionally there is an extraordinary demand and the manufacturers are then eager to avail themselves of every man who will throw a shuttle.

Before the Jacquard loom came to Spitalfields, Bresson says, 'there were weavers among us able to earn (under peculiar circumstances) a guinea a day'. But on the whole there is much evidence that allowing for expenses and slack times few weavers could earn more than an average of 15s. a week and some very much less. This was the state of things in 1838 as it was in 1761. In 1823 (when times were good) average earnings were said to be 15s. or 20s. a week. Weaving prices rose in 1795, in 1800 and again in 1805 under the Spitalfields Act, and they did not fall till after 1825, though it was said that earnings were reduced. By 1832 prices, that is piece rates, in some branches were the same as they had been in the book of 1769, in some they were lower.[115] But the rise in weaving prices under the Act was not comparable with that in other trades during the same period.[22]

It seems probable that the societies enumerated by the Spital Square solicitor had been chiefly supported by small masters or those journeymen who took jobs of work and employed other journeymen and had thus almost the status of masters. The sports of the journeymen weavers were traditionally boisterous, to put it rather mildly. The weavers' breed of splasher spaniels described by Mr Church is more consistent with what we know of Spitalfields. They were doubtless used for duck-hunting, a favourite sport of London journeymen in the ducking-ponds kept at tea-gardens and public-houses in the suburbs. Bullock-hunting (or bull-hanking) flourished in Bethnal Green. The rector thus describes his parish in 1816:

It consists of a population of about 40,000, generally the lowest description of people, the overflowing population of Spitalfields have settled in that parish. ... Every Sunday morning, during the time of divine service, several hundred persons assemble in a field adjoining the churchyard, where they fight dogs, hunt ducks, gamble, enter into subscriptions to fee drovers for a bullock. . . . 'This on the Sunday?' At all times, chiefly on Sunday, Monday, and sometimes Tuesday; Monday is the principal day; one or two thousand men and boys will on these occasions leave their looms and join in the pursuit, pockets are frequently picked, persons are tossed and torn. . . .[116]

Samuel Wilderspin, who started an infant school in Spitalfields in 1820, gave an account (in 1835) of the neighbourhood at that time:

Those who know that district know it to be as bad as perhaps any in London. When I commenced there I was pelted by the people with various kinds of filth and they used to call after me, 'there goes the Baby Professor' . . . afterwards they turned round and treated me with the greatest kindness . . . the parents improved both in manners and habits. At the time we commenced there it was a regular plan to go to Smithfield and steal an ox, and drive it into that neighbourhood, and make it mad by putting peas in its ears and so on, and then when they had finished their sport they would lead it into some field, and there leave it, but before we left that was entirely done away with.[117]

The prevalence of child labour from about the age of six was naturally an obstacle to education, though the schools set up in Spitalfields in the early nineteenth century had improved things. Mr Hickson, one of the Hand-loom Commissioners, describes (in 1838) the market in Bethnal Green Road, where children were hired as weekly servants by the weavers, the boys for the loom or silk-winding, the girls as little maids of all work.[118] Very few of these children had been given any education at all. In the eighteenth century women and girls were hired by the week in Spitalfields Market – children too (as we know from the case of Elizabeth Surman, hired about 1757 as a little domestic drudge), though these were also obtained by the cheaper process of taking a little parish apprentice.[83] Bresson gave a very interesting account to Mr Hickson of social conditions in Spitalfields. Asked as to the state of education among the weavers, he answered:

We have never wanted for men of superior intellectual qualifications when it was thought desirable to go up to ministers or to give evidence before a committee of the House of Commons, but as a body I cannot say the Spitalfields weavers are an educated class. Perhaps the majority are not able to read and write, certainly this is the case with a very large portion of them.

The sanitary state of Spitalfields was, he said, very bad: 'this arises in a great measure from the dirt and filth of some of the close neighbour-hoods inhabited by the Irish'. Hickson's account of Bresson's own house is interesting. Besides being a skilled velvet-weaver, he was some-thing of a capitalist, as he owned about 200 looms, the value of each about £1, which he let out at from 3½d. to 4d. a week. The proceeds varied according to the state of trade, but were often £50 a year and had been £75. His son and son's wife, both weavers, shared his house, which consisted of three very small rooms and a fourth barely large enough for the six looms it contained. It had neither cesspool nor sewer and could have been built from the ground for £80. For this, he paid £16 a year and £2 5s. for a strip of flower-garden in front of ninety feet by twenty.[72]

Bresson represents the highest class of weaver. At the other end of the scale was the improvident weaver who rented a loom. It was cus-tomary in the eighteenth century for weavers to sleep in the garret or loom-shop of another weaver's house, and in 1817 it was one of the difficulties of the Society for preventing Contagious Fever in their campaign of whitewashing infected places 'that among the weavers of Spitalfields a man has a loom in his room and sleeps in it with all his family'.[119] 'It frequently occurs,' the parish officers of Mile End New Town complained to the Poor Law Commissioners,

that a person will occupy one room at a rent of perhaps 1s. 9d. or 2s. per week, and who are on the least stagnation of the silk trade thrown on the parish for relief . . . although their master may be a man of the most abject poverty and have never paid one farthing rent for the room he occupies, yet he is (perhaps by the management of the officers of some other parish) enabled by a resi-dence of forty days to entail a heavy and lasting burthen on the parish. . . .[120]

Whatever the distress in Spitalfields may have been in the thirties and forties of the nineteenth century, there is nothing in the reports of the Hand-loom Commissioners to suggest a state of things approaching the starvation and misery of which we hear repeatedly between 1763 and 1800. Before 1763 the silk trade was apparently more prosperous and certainly less vocal. In that period, too, less attention was given to the sufferings of 'the industrious poor'. But in 1719, a year of crisis, silk-weaving is said to be 'in a starving condition',[121] and evidence of the wretched plight of individual weavers throughout the century is scattered through the *Sessions Papers*. Something of the despairing bitterness of the weavers in 1765 is reflected in *A Letter from a Spitalfields Weaver to a noble Duke* [Bedford?], asserted to have said that 'was you a Spitalfields Weaver you could live upon tenpence a day'. The writer suggests, in the spirit of Swift, a market for the sale of children,

which would make men as fond of their wives during the time of their pregnancy as they now are of their rabbits when big . . . nor offer to beat or kick them (as is too frequent a practice) for fear of a miscarriage. . . . Some persons of a despairing spirit may perhaps be concerned about the immense number of poor people who are aged, diseased or maimed; but let them not have the least pain upon that head, because it is well known that they are every day dying and rotting by cold and famine, filth and vermin, as fast as can reasonably be expected, and as to the young labourers, they are now in almost as hopeful a condition. They cannot get work and consequently pine away for want of nourishment to a degree that, if they are accidentally hired to common labour, they have not strength to perform it, and thus the country and themselves are happily delivered from the evils to come.

Though the prosperity was chequered, the period from 1800 to 1826 evidently raised the status of the Spitalfields weaver, and those are the good years to which they afterwards looked back with such regret. The gradual migration of silk-throwing from London removed a number of workers dependent on the varying fortunes of the silk industry, who even in good times were on the verge of starvation. At its best, weaving in Spitalfields was an unhealthy occupation; work at the hand-loom was both sedentary and physically trying; the constant pressing of the bar of the loom against the stomach was a cause of ill-health. The work was done in small, crowded rooms in horribly insanitary dwellings, and the air was carefully excluded by paper pasted over the cracks of the windows, to prevent the silk from losing weight and so making the weaver liable to deductions from his earnings.[122] Children began to work very young, and the trade was hereditary, subject to new blood from the less successful of other occupations. It was no wonder that the weavers were a diminutive race.

Francis Place considered that in manners and education the Spitalfields weavers were in a class below that of other London artisans, but above that of common labourers. (The eighteenth century classed them as 'inferior artificers'.) He says:

In 1826 when the silk business was before the House of Lords, the weavers came to Palace Yard in great numbers. . . . I went among them and found them as compared with other trades, a physically degraded people. There were no tall men among them. Their manners are coarser than that of any other tradesmen.[123]

Again in 1824, at a time looked back upon as prosperous, he wrote:

Last session I took some pains to ascertain the real situation of these people. I went among them several times, and can safely assert that in intelligence, in size, in strength, in form, in manners, in cleanliness, they are below every other trade in the metropolis; they are in some respects nearly in the state other tradesmen were in forty years ago.[124]

Place regarded the weavers with a jaundiced eye: they clung to the Spitalfields Acts, which he as a *laissez-faire* radical wished repealed. But he was a scrupulous and accurate observer and there is no room to doubt the truth of his estimate with regard to the majority of the weavers, though he ignores the small class of the élite, who loom so large in retrospective descriptions.

In Place's opinion, the causes of this inferiority were, 'first the peculiar laws which relate to them and make them a separate people, and next, the nature of their business'. The first we may discount. It may not be true, as a modern writer says, that the Spitalfields Acts made the weavers an aristocracy of labour, but they tended to protect them from some of the disadvantages of their trade. They helped to drive silk-weaving from London, but then it would probably have left London in any case, as stuff-weaving did early in the eighteenth century, and framework-knitting rather later. The process of migration had begun before 1773; handkerchiefs and gauzes were leaving London for Scotland in 1765. As to the nature of the trade, the fatal characteristic to Place was the employment of women and children.

It is the ease with which women and children can be set to work, that keeps these weavers in poverty and rags and filth and ignorance. There are certain employments which to a small extent married women might follow, but in these cases in which the woman and her children can generally find employment in her husband's business, the very worst consequences must follow.

In a trade, say that of a mill-wright, the man alone can work at . . . his wages must be sufficient to keep himself, his wife and a couple of children, and it is so. . . . Trace this through all the trades of the metropolis, and you will find it holds good. . . . If a man, in the ordinary run of his trade, has a wife and two children, who can, and by the custom of the trade do, work with him, they will altogether earn no more than he alone would earn if only men were employed. This is the case with these debased Spitalfields weavers . . . and . . . the earnings of a single man is far below that of a single man in other trades.[124]

The Spitalfields weavers, even in their turbulent days, were regarded as objects of compassion, but the journeymen shoe-makers seem to have been considered as black sheep among London artisans, a very different point of view from the popular one of the seventeenth century towards the 'gentle craft'. Here again the gradations of the trade were many, and it was also subdivided into men's shoe-makers and women's shoe-makers, and these again were subdivided; the making of the peculiar type of shoe worn by the London chairmen was a separate business,[125] so was that of the 'child's pump-maker'. It is interesting to find that by 1738 there was at least one master who worked 'only for such persons as have distorted feet', and that he was employed by all the hospitals.

By 1738 (and probably long before) the methods of the London trade were substantially the same as they still remain in an old-fashioned 'bespoke' business: indeed the distinction between 'bespoke' and ready-made or 'sale-shoes' already existed. The customer was measured, the clicker cut out the upper leathers, which were given to the closer to be closed, and then to the 'maker' for the sole and heel to be put on.[126] Last-making was a separate business, and a poor one, the last-maker also making wooden heels. In this way the London shop-keeper carried on his business, also selling ready-made shoes, but there was another class of shoe-maker, working alone or with an apprentice, in a garret, cellar or stall, using pieces of leather cut out for him by the currier or the leather-cutter. There was thus a division in the trade between these small masters, and the large shop-keeping masters, not because they were trade rivals, but because the ease with which a man could set up for himself reduced the number of journeymen and led to increased wages.

The large masters, acting through the Cordwainers' Company, attempted to squeeze out of existence the garret-masters, as they were called, by prosecuting curriers under an Act of James I, 'for executing the trade of a shoe-maker by cutting leather'. They followed this up by bringing forward a Bill in 1738 intended to prevent all but the shoe-makers from cutting leather.[126]

It is plain that the drift of the rich shoe-makers is to engross the business of shoe-making in the hands of a few [runs the *Case of the Middling and Poorer Sort of Master Shoemakers*] to the prejudice not only of the publick, but of thousands of their own trade, who will, in all likelihood, be under the necessity of leaving their families to their respective parishes, to travel foreign countries for bread, to the great detriment of the British nation.

The large masters failed to carry their point and both large and small masters existed side by side. The latter in many cases were not masters of the whole of their trade, and their business was a poor one, recruited by parish apprentices and poor children. The organization of the London trade is thus described by Collyer in 1761:

The master shoe-makers in London keep shop and employ many workmen and workwomen. Some of them export great quantities to our Plantations, both of shoes and boots, made in London and of those they contract for in the country. The principal business of these shopkeepers and of their journeymen and apprentices is cutting out shoes, delivering them to the makers, receiving them when finished, fitting them on the feet of their customers, and keeping their books: but it is usual and very necessary for an apprentice before he is out of his time to spend a month or six weeks in learning to make a shoe. These shopkeepers take from £10 or £20 with an apprentice, who, when out of his time, may have from £15 or £20 and his board by being a clicker, for by this name they call their journeymen who work in their shops; or, with £100 he may set up a small shop. But some of them employ several thousand pounds in the trade, and from small beginnings raise great fortunes. The men who really make the shoes are considered as journeymen, though they take apprentices. . . . The journeymen and the women who bind the shoes and sew the quarters together when they are made of silk, velvet, callimanco, etc., get but small wages. These journeymen take about £5 with an apprentice, who when out of his time may get about 9s. or 10s. a week, or if he have a little money and some acquaintance, he may set up as a chamber-master and work for his customers.

As such a man had never learned to cut out shoes, want of skill as well as want of capital drove him to buy from the leather-cutters, whose journeymen were said to be decayed shoe-makers. This was a trade said in 1747 to have recently sprung up owing to the great number of small makers.[127] Some of these small men gave evidence in 1738 as to the ease with which a garret-master could set up. One said that he 'began his trade with half a crown, and with so small a sum a poor man may have materials sufficient to make a pair of shoes and maintain his family'. Another said that if he had had to buy leather in the market (that is, in the hide) he could not with less than £20 have carried on his business, 'but buying of the currier, he can begin with 5s. and within two days make 10s. of it. . . .' Those who bought leather in the hide were asserted to be less than a tenth part of the masters. In 1738 there were six or seven hundred masters on the books of the Cord-wainers' Company, and, according to the small masters, there were 30,000 shoe-makers in London not counting cobblers (probably a wild exaggeration).

The large masters also gave evidence to the Parliamentary Committee of 1738: one said he was a shoe-maker and clog-maker, working in every branch of the trade except boots and children's first shoes; he had set up with £20, but then employed 162 persons 'from eight years to seventy'. At this time leather and wages had gone up, though it was admitted that there were 'a greater number of hands than formerly', and the best shoes were sold at the advanced price of 10s. a pair; advanced, because costs were higher, and 'gentlemen more curious in their work'. A master of forty years' standing complained that he paid 2s. 3d. for work formerly done for 14d.; the journeymen 'will stand still sooner than reduce their wages, and some of them can earn 19s. a week'. According to another of the rich masters,

. . . there are a great number of shoe-makers who work in garrets, and some of them good workmen, who, if they were not employed as masters, must then work journey-work, and could get more money in that way than by working for the curriers, some of them being able to earn 15s., some 18s. a week.[126]

These maximum earnings one may be sure were possible only for the man who was helped by at least one apprentice and perhaps a wife. Both women and children worked at shoe-closing and shoe-binding in the eighteenth century. The competition of the large masters and of cheap ready-made shoes was probably too much for the small self-employing workmen, who seem later in the century to have been chiefly cobblers and translators. As early as 1751 it was said that the shoes sold in London were chiefly made in the country where labour was cheaper.[128] In 1738 the London merchant bought offal leather to send to Scotland, where it was made up by 'the poorer sort of shoe-makers' to be exported to the Plantations, and he also bought leather to send to Northampton. Keeping a 'Yorkshire shoe warehouse' was a common London occupation, and we are told in 1764 that after midnight on Saturdays,

the shoe-makers' shops in Old Turnstile, Holborn and Cow Lane . . . and the Yorkshire and other country shoe-houses in almost every publick street in London are filled with noisy and difficult customers, especially the night-men, penny-post-men and slaughter-house-men, who have just received their week's wages.[129]

In 1761 the shoe-making trade in London was said to be over-stocked.

There were trade clubs among the shoe-makers, at all events in the latter part of the century, and wages rose repeatedly in the Great War. The London masters said that about 1809 they began cutting out boots and shoes and sending them to Northampton to be made at little more than half the London price.[130] About 1816 wages were reduced, except in twelve West End shops, where they were kept up to secure the best workmen.[131] The employer's attitude towards his men was thus expressed in 1838 to one of the Hand-loom Commissioners: asked how many hours they worked he answered:

No man on earth can tell that; they begin in the morning when they like, but if any mortal thing happens, up they are from their stools and after it. . . . They will work sometimes till 11 and 12 o'clock. . . . I never knew a dozen steady men among them in my life. . . . Their families are in a filthy, abominable state, all in dirt and wretched. Many of them, instead of having lawful married wives, keep women whom they call tacks. . . . A man will send out his coat from the tap-room to pawn, or even his shoes, in order to get money to keep up the fuddle. . . .[130]

They would strike, he said, if they were asked to work on the master's premises. Allowing for bias and exaggeration, it is clear that the shoe-makers were not among the most respectable of London workmen, and that the reason lay in the organization of their trade. Place, always anxious to defend the artisan against inaccurate and prejudiced assertions, wrote in 1824:

> The nominal wages of boot and shoe-makers, except for the very commonest kinds of work, are high, particularly those at the west end of the town. But the wages earned are not higher than those earned by other tradesmen. It is all piecework, almost all the men work at their own lodgings, and have generally to wait between job and job. When a boot is cut out, it is sent to the closer, and when partly closed is returned to the maker, and it is then sent again to the closer to be completed. Many of the wives of the snobs [shoe-makers not belonging to a trade club] are closers, and it is quite common for two or three men and a woman to work in the same room. The work is dirty, and as it generally happens that one or more of the parties is waiting for a job, he, being idle, gets to drinking, and the others drink too. By the time he gets a job, he is not in a state to begin it, and by that time another is perhaps without a job, and thus it is that the snobs are less respectable than most other tradesmen. It is a singularly great evil [Place speaks from personal experience] for a man to have to work in the room he lives in with his wife, and if she works with him, too, the evil is greatly increased.[132]

Saint Monday was traditionally observed by the London shoe-makers, partly from choice, partly from necessity, but the jovial independence of the journeymen which had made them favourites of the ballad-makers, was less appreciated in the nineteenth century:

> Tho Munday Sundaye's fellow be
>   When Tuesday comes to work fall we
> And fall to work most merrily
>   For money to serue our need.[133]

In spite of Place, wages do not seem to have been high. In 1824 a boot-closer fully employed could earn £3 a week, but the work was done by himself, his wife, his son and an apprentice. At the same time a 'maker' employed by the same master earned only from 13s. 10d. to 18s.[131] The putting-out system, and the custom among the journeymen, who did only a part of the work on the shoe or boot, of taking apprentices, degraded the trade. The journeyman could take as many poor apprentices as he could feed, clothe and house, probably indeed far more. A shoe-maker described the system to Mayhew, unchanged since the eighteenth century, except that the parish had become more liberal. He had been one of seven apprentices, two bound by the parish, five by the Refuge for the Destitute. The latter gave £5, three suits of clothes and a kit of tools with each boy; the parish, £5 and two suits.

My master was a journeyman, and by having all us boys he was able to get up work very cheap, though he received good wages for it. We boys had no allowance in money, only board and lodging and clothing. He was severe in the way of flogging. I ran away six times myself, but was forced to go back again as I had no friend in the world. . . . Of the seven only one served his time out. . . . Of us seven boys (at the wages our employer got) one could earn 19s., another 15s., another 12s., another 10s., and the rest not less than 8s. each, for all worked sixteen hours a day.[134]

Nevertheless, shoe-makers like weavers have a reputation (or had, when education was less general) for being among the most intellectual of working-men, and of having produced a large number of distinguished people in different walks of life. Extremes meet, and the opportunities for conviviality which proved disastrous to some of them, were for others opportunities for thinking and discussing, writing and reading and ballad-making.

> Crispin's sons
> Have from uncounted time, with ale and buns
> Cherished the gift of song, which sorrow quells,
> And working single in their low-built cells
> Oft cheat the tedium of a winter's night
> With anthems.[135]

As for the illustrious shoe-makers who live in history, their number is doubtless partly to be accounted for by the great number of men in the trade (they are also numerous, and probably for the same reason, in lists of inmates of workhouses), partly by the traditions and methods of their craft, which encouraged some of them to be active political and social reformers and local preachers and teachers.[136] But it can hardly be counted to the credit of the gentle craft that Sir Cloudesley Shovel worked for a village shoe-maker before he ran away to sea as a boy, or that Gifford, the first editor of the *Quarterly*, passed an unhappy youth apprenticed against his will to a shoe-maker.

These three trades, watchmaking, silk-weaving and shoe-making, show something of the general characteristics of London occupations. In all, the large master existed side by side with the small working master. The putting-out system was common to all of them, so was apprenticeship to journeymen working on piecework. In none is there any revolutionary change of method over a long period; in fact, their general structure is extraordinarily stable, though all were undergoing slight and gradual modification. In watchmaking and (after 1773) in silk-weaving, the London trades were free from the abuse rampant at Coventry at the end of the eighteenth century, where numbers of colt-apprentices were taken as a form of indentured cheap labour. All of them were being increasingly threatened by the competition of lower wages and cheaper methods in the provinces and the chief safeguard against this was the admittedly high quality of London workmanship, which was probably also a barrier against the reckless multiplying of apprentices. All three had a much-cherished independence as to hours and place of working and in two of them there was (in certain branches) scope for the artistic skill of the craftsman.

Except watch-gilding, a dangerous operation (and one often done by women), none of them is among the trades considered by eighteenth-century standards as especially unhealthy. Though these standards were not high, many trades were recognized as dangerous, others as 'slavish' or 'fit only for sturdy lads'. How dangerous to health many trades must have been is clear when we remember that work was done for the most part either in close confined places (often in cellars), or entirely exposed to the weather. It was sometimes done over charcoal fires and the motive force was largely supplied by human muscles. The workman was usually in direct personal contact with the dangerous substances he handled, and though personal cleanliness was recognized as some protection against the poisonous properties of (for instance) lead, the habits and resources of the time made cleanliness a counsel of perfection for journeymen and apprentices. Moreover, these often slept in workshops among the materials of their trade.

The physical strain of labour before the days of machinery is often forgotten; already in 1797 it was noted that Sheffield no longer abounded 'in cripples and weak, deformed people', as it had when iron and steel were forged without the use of power.[137] In London such trades as those of the anvil- and anchor-smiths must have put an enormous strain on human endurance. Planing and sawing timber by hand was heavy work, and Adam Smith remarked that a London carpenter was not supposed to last in his utmost vigour above eight years. In a pair of sawyers, one man was always the top-sawyer; he had the harder work, but escaped the blinding shower of sawdust that affected the eyes of the under-sawyer. Hernia was very prevalent; so late as 1842 it was estimated that a tenth part of the labouring population was suffering from it,[138] but in the eighteenth century the proportion must have been higher; apprentices complain that they are 'bursten', owing to the heavy work they have been made to do.

In 1747[139] we hear of works for making red and white lead in Whitechapel and other places round London where the work was done by engines, horses and labourers, 'who are sure in a few years to become paralytic by the mercurial fumes of the lead'. A plumber's business was then carried on by working in molten lead and plumbers suffered much from paralysis. The glaziers' business also involved the melting of lead, and they were said to be more subject to the palsy than any other trade except the gilders and the plumbers. A glazier's apprentice complained in 1787 of having no proper bed, but being forced to sleep where the lead was melted.[140] Painters, of course, suffered from lead-poisoning; in 1838 it was stated on the authority of a charity administered at Painters' Hall, that there had been a marked improvement in the health of painters owing to greater cleanliness.[141] Lead-poisoning, however, was receiving considerable attention from the doctors,[142] and in 1792 a dispensary (the Universal Medical Institute) was founded in the Tower Hamlets to provide cold, warm and vapour baths as well as medical help for makers of white lead, painters, plumbers, and others subject to the effects of lead.[143]

The London pewterers and letter-founders suffered from the fumes of the metals they worked with; refiners of silver and gold became paralytic from the use of mercury and looking-glass makers were affected in a similar way. Workmen, Ramazzini says, speaking of Italy, 'cannot possibly avoid receiving poisonous steams at the mouth and . . . quickly become asthmatic, paralytic and liable to vertigoes and their aspect becomes cadaverous and ghostly. . . .' He describes how coppersmiths were affected by particles of copper which entered their lungs and stained their hair and beards green; braziers became deaf, and gibbous from the crooked position in which they sat; potters became 'paralytic, lethargic, splenetic, cachetic and toothless'. His book, translated into English by Dr James of Fever Powder fame, was the standard eighteenth-century work on industrial disease.[144]

The work of the London confectioner was 'very slavish and unwholesome . . . not only fatiguing, but performed in close places, and much of it by ovens and over charcoal fires'. Chocolate-making was the same, and the trade of a baker was intolerably exhausting. Glass-blowing was 'slavish, hazardous and pernicious to health'. The London sailcloth-weavers complained that the charcoal fires used in their business were very unhealthy.[33] Felt-making or hat-making was 'very slavish work, being continually obliged to be stooping over the steam of a great kettle'. This was the felting process; at a later stage, after the dyeing, 'a vast quantity of dust, very prejudicial to the workmen', was given off, but in 1800 recent improvements in France were said to have remedied this.[145] Ramazzini instances a number of trades so 'nauseous' as to be unhealthy; among these were tanning, the making of catgut and of tallow-candles – hence perhaps the beer-money given to the London journeymen on melting days. Tailors were traditionally sickly – 'societies of taylors and shoe-makers on festival days', says Ramazzini, 'make a crooked, hump-backed, lame figure'. These trades however were refuges for some of the many deformed people of the age.

The list could be much extended. At the end of the century Willan enumerates some of the London workers whose occupations were injurious to their lungs:

Hairdressers, bakers, masons, bricklayers' labourers, laboratory men, coal-heavers and chimney-sweepers are liable to be affected with obstinate pulmonic diseases . . . also . . . the dressers of flax and feathers, and the workmen in the warehouses of leather-sellers. . . . The workmen employed by sugar-bakers are exposed to strong heat and often drink immoderately. They are liable to . . . pulmonic disorders and to rheumatism. By persevering in the work for a long time they become sallow, emaciated and dropsical, and die at an early period of life.[146]

The violence of industrial disease was not due only to the methods of work, but to its irregularity, slack periods alternating with bursts of intense, unremitting labour. Another London doctor gives an account of the health of the London population:

The working part of the manufacturers and labourers of all denominations [he describes as] working hard and being dexterous in their operations, and of course earning large sums . . . which they spend in drinking, exposing themselves at the same time to the inclemency of the weather; always idle when they have any money left, so that their life is spent between labour and attention above their powers, and perfect idleness and drunkenness. Their women also, passing from affluence to distress almost every week, are forced, though soberly inclined, to lead very disorderly lives. Pulmonary diseases are more common and particularly fatal in this class, as well as all other diseases.[147]

This description applied more fully to the labourer than to the artisan, and especially to such occupations as brick-making and coal-heaving, which were seasonal and very irregular from no fault of the workman, very exhausting, with high occasional earnings. But drunkenness was a prevailing vice among all classes, and irregularity of work was general.

Hours in most London trades were long, but as the greater part of the work was piecework, done at the journeyman's own time, there was comparatively little disputing over them. When the men worked by the day, or when there was a fair proportion of weekly or daily men besides out-workers, we find them trying to get hours reduced. The tailors, whose wages and hours were regulated after 1721 by an Act to prevent combinations, worked at first from 6 to 8, one hour being allowed for dinner. During periods of court-mourning they were to work at night as well as all day for double wages. In January 1764, the journeymen, who were strongly organized,[148] appealed to the Sessions under the Act and got an increase of wages and a reduction of one hour in the winter half-year. In the following May, they again appealed for a reduction of summer hours to the winter level:

The petitioners are content with the wages thereby settled, but . . . their sedentary course of life and constant attention to their business for such a length of time as from six o'clock in the morning till eight o'clock at night greatly impairs their health and constitution and prejudices their sight and faculties. . . .

The reduction was agreed to by counsel on behalf of the master-tailors and was accordingly ordered by the Sessions, who declared themselves 'convinced of the truth' of the petitioners' allegations.[149] Not all the masters, however, accepted the award, with the result that there was a strike of tailors in July.[150] By an Act of 1768 to amend that of 1721 wages were again raised and the hours of the award of 1764 were accepted, while in a time of general mourning wages were to be doubled without any extension of hours, overtime being paid for at 6d. an hour instead of the usual 3d.

The hours of the bookbinders were shortened still more. In 1747 the recognized hours of the trade were from 6 to 9. In 1785 the journeymen were trying to get them reduced from 6 to 8 to 6 to 7; they eventually got the hour, though the effort involved them in an indictment for conspiracy. In 1794, this time by agreement with the masters, another hour was taken off – a total reduction of three hours in half a century.[151]

In the middle of the century (1747) in handicraft trades, hours of from 6 a.m. to 8 p.m. were common; in many trades they were from 6 to 9 and in one or two from 5 to 9. These times represented the normal day during which the apprentice was required to work, and in which the journeyman on piecework could make the standard earnings of his trade. The building trades for the most part worked from 6 to 6 or during daylight. Ship-building artisans worked according to tides. Rope-making hours were irregular; to quote a rope-maker of Sun Tavern Fields in 1742: 'We cannot make ropes when the sun shines . . . we begin at 8 o'clock at night and work till 8 in the morning, and sometimes we work all day if we can hold it.'[152]

Shopkeeping hours were said in 1747 (in the City) to be in general from 7 to 8, but hours grew later as the century advanced. Robert Owen, when an assistant in a London haberdasher's (1786) had to be in the shop by 8; in the busy season it was crowded with customers till 10 or 10.30 at night, after which the place had to be put in order, and this was often not finished till two in the morning.[153] 'An old quaker' has left it on record

. . . that he served his apprenticeship to a grocer in Cheapside between 1786 and 1793, that the shop was opened at 7 a.m. and closed at 10 p.m., that his ablutions were limited to his countenance, and that he never went out except to meeting on First Days, adding that he had no sense of being hardly dealt with, for it was the custom of the time and he was as his fellows.[154]

There was no limit at all for some of the wretched apprentice girls who did tambour work – not even that of human endurance,* and the same can be said presumably for the women who earned 5d. a day in 1813 by making soldiers' coats,[155] and in general for those who took in work from a shop or from some middle-man or woman to do at starvation rates in their own rooms. Among the longest hours of out-workers were those of the wretched women who went out to wash by the day. We find them arriving at their employer's house overnight in order to work all night and all next day. 'Women who go out a-washing for their livelihood,' according to *Low Life*, had to be at work by one in the morning, but as a matter of fact they often went earlier. Ann Nichols, who washed and scoured for a master-builder at Hackney in 1753, arrived about 12 at night – 'that is what we call a day and a half's work', her master said.[156] In 1765 a woman who went monthly to the house of an attorney, said (in connexion with a robbery): 'I went that night a little before dark, time enough to have filled my tubs and copper.'[157] In the early nineteenth century things were a little better. J. T. Smith says:

Perhaps there is not a class of people who work harder than those washer-women who go out to assist servants in what is called a heavy wash; they may be seen in the winter-time, shivering at the doors at three and four in the morning, and are seldom dismissed before ten at night.

For this they were paid half a crown.[158]

Recognized holidays were few. Place says that while he was an apprentice he worked at least twelve consecutive hours six days a week with three holidays only – at Easter, Whitsuntide and Christmas.[159] However, it was customary for the London journeymen to take a holiday on hanging-days at Tyburn, and these came eight times a year. 'It was common through the whole metropolis,' says Angelo, 'for master-coach-makers, frame-makers, tailors, shoe-makers, and others who had engaged to complete orders within a given time, to bear in mind to observe to their customers "that will be a hanging-day and my men will not be at work".'[160]

Le peuple Anglais, naturellement paresseux, ivrogne et brute [said a French visitor to London in 1777] *est distrait, tantôt par une pendaison, tantôt par une*

* See Chapter 5.

élection, par des fêtes, et par d'abominables combats de bœufs avec des chiens en plein rue, et chaque jour on-y-perd bras, jambes et la vie.[161]

On the whole, then, terribly long hours seem to have been the rule, tempered by much irregularity, partly involuntary, partly customary, partly the inevitable reaction from over-pressure.

I know not how to describe [wrote Place] the sickening aversion which at times steals over the working man, and utterly disables him for a longer or shorter period from following his usual occupation, and compels him to indulge in *idleness*. I have felt it, resisted it to the utmost of my power, but have been so completely subdued by it, that, in spite of very pressing circumstances, I have been obliged to submit and run away from my work. This is the case with every workman I have ever known; and in proportion as a man's case is hopeless will such fits occur and be of longer duration. The best informed amongst the workmen will occasionally solace themselves with liquor, the uninformed will almost always recur to the same means to provide the excitement which must be procured.[162]

There is thus some evidence, where tests are possible, of an improvement in the conditions of labour – the reduction of hours in certain trades. In many occupations, the prevalence of out-work and of apprenticeship to journeymen made it not the men's interest to reduce the recognized hours of the trade. Apprentices could and did complain (though often to little purpose) of having to work after the customary time.[163]

In the skilled London trades wages rose after 1793 in a proportion, which, in spite of the fall in the value of money and of very high bread prices in certain years, still allowed for an improved standard of living, which was both a cause and a consequence of the increased sobriety which accompanied it. Place considered that one cause of the improvement of the working-people of London by the early nineteenth century was to be found in the higher wages due to trade clubs and successful strikes during the war:

The consequence . . . has been a main cause of the increase of knowledge, of the sobriety, of the comfort, of better manners and better conduct than previously existed among workmen; of an end being put to riotous proceedings, public indecencies and gross conduct of all sorts, the extent of which is thoroughly known to none but those who can remember the state of the journeymen tradesmen thirty or forty years ago.[164]

The difference between the position of London journeymen and workmen in the provinces had puzzled the trade union or trade club deputies sent from manufacturing towns and they had asked Place to explain it. Why had the former been able to prevent a reduction in their wages from the war-time level, while the others had not? Place attributed the London artisan's advantage to the seasonal nature of London trades and a shortage of labour in brisk times.

If then the masters were to strike against the men in the slack time, the men would strike against the masters in the brisk time, and the inconvenience, vexation and loss would greatly over-balance any good to the masters, even if they succeeded, which it is pretty certain they would not, in reducing the wages of their journeymen. Very few attempts have therefore been made in London to reduce their wages, and the few which have been made have not been pushed to extremities.[165]

Place is speaking only of 'the journeymen tradesmen and considerable bodies of workmen in London'. The vital question, and one to which there can be no certain answer, is the relative numbers of the skilled artisans, labourers, casual workers, street sellers, and of the mass of beggars, thieves and prostitutes. Accounts of the working-classes in the early nineteenth century were apt to confuse these indiscriminately, a middle-class point of view which exasperated Place.

If the character and conduct of the working-people are to be taken from reviews, magazines, pamphlets, newspapers, reports of the two Houses of Parliament and the Factory Commissioners, we shall find them all jumbled together as the 'lower orders', the most skilled and the most prudent workmen, with the most ignorant and imprudent labourers and paupers, though the difference is great indeed, and indeed in many cases will scarce admit of comparison.[166]

Such a confusion is to be found in an extreme form in Engels's *Condition of the Working Classes in England in 1844*, a collection of authentic and terrible facts carefully selected from the material Place criticizes. It is implicit in Disraeli's 'two nations'. Such books obscure the real question: how did the different grades of workers vary in relation to each other and to the residuum of non-workers? Changes in administration prevent the poor law figures from throwing much light on the problem. In so far as London is concerned the high wages Place speaks of were not confined, as one might suspect, to the exclusive trades, such as the hatters and mill-wrights. The very numerous tailors who were especially well organized and whom Place particularly instances were not exclusive at all. The trade could be entered without a formal apprenticeship and parish boys were often bound to tailors. The barrier against invasion by the semi-skilled seems to have been the 'Log' fixed by the London trade clubs as the amount of work required of each man in a working day. A lad of 17 who had picked up his trade in the country without a formal apprenticeship on coming to London in 1810 was at once admitted to work on inscribing his name at a house of call.

It required my utmost efforts [he writes] to get through the allotted amount of a day's work within the appointed time – for the time as well as the amount of work was strictly regulated. This daily task was considerably too much for any but a clever and very quick hand, but then, as it was fixed by the work-men themselves, there was neither room for complaining of the masters, nor any good end to be answered by grumbling to the men. . . . Yet as it showed the equitable principles upon which our trade unions were founded – in providing that the largest possible amount of labour should be given in exchange for the good wages demanded – it was generally approved of, even by such, as, like myself, were not fully equal to the labour it involved.[167]

The tailors' high wages, however, were always accompanied by much seasonal unemployment or under-employment. 'Cucumbers two a penny, tailors twice as many', was a Covent Garden saying.

If Place is accurate, real wages in skilled London trades must have risen with the fall in prices after the Peace. This was not the case among the poorest London workpeople, the weavers and the unskilled labourers, but even among these there is some evidence against a fall in wages resulting in a deterioration of the standard of life. In 1826 Place wrote, after a tour of inspection in the poorest parts of London, Rag Fair, Petticoat Lane and Spitalfields in 'this time of much distress. . . . Everywhere improvement has been going on and is still going on. Real wages have not increased, but frugality, sobriety and better manage-ment and self-respect have greatly increased'.[168]

Silk-weaving from an early stage in its history had been 'a continual refuge for the indigent and distressed'. This and other textile trades had probably played a considerable part in 'setting the poor on work', as indeed the employers frequently claimed. There can be little doubt that the industrial expansion of the eighteenth century absorbed much of that terrible residuum of beggars and vagrants which had been so great a problem in the sixteenth, seventeenth and early eighteenth centuries. Sir Josiah Child stated as obvious facts on which all men were agreed:

1. That our poor in England have always been in a most sad and wretched condition, some famished for want of bread, others starved with cold and nakedness, and many whole families in all the out-parts of cities and great towns, commonly remain in a languishing, nasty and useless condition, uncomfortable to themselves and unprofitable to the kingdom. . . .

2. That the children of the poor bred up in beggary and laziness, do by that means become not only of unhealthy bodies, and more than ordinarily subject to many loathsome diseases, whereof very many die in their tender age, and if any of them do arrive to years of strength, they are, by their idle habits . . . rendered for ever after indisposed to labour, and serve only to stock the kingdom with thieves and beggars.[169]

Simond, who visited England in 1810–11, writes: 'vices and poverty are less apparent than in any other country I know, not excepting the United States'. The reduction of the mass of the submerged and unemployable must have followed from the growth of trade, the check to the consumption of gin, the improvement in health and administrative changes in the management of parish children. The parish nurses, who were said to hire out to beggars the infants in their charge, were superseded. The workhouses received deserted children irrespective of their settlement, and parishes became less rigid in refusing relief to the unsettled poor. The practice of exposing infants in the street or leaving them on the door-steps of well-to-do people, very general in the earlier part of the century, declined; '*dropping* of children is but little known at present', said Malcolm in 1808.[170] The complaints as to crowds of beggars in the streets gradually diminish, and it is clear from the Mendicity Report of 1815, much as it is concerned with the appalling problems of vagrancy and the stream of destitute Irish daily arriving in London, that there were fewer than there had been thirty years before. This, Sir Nathaniel Conant, a Bow Street magistrate of thirty-three years' standing, ascribed to 'a certain liberality in parish officers, which did not exist formerly, and to the facility which the poor have by means of the police magistrates, to get relief from parish officers'. 'You walk through the streets without seeing beggars in crowds; you see only those that either with fear or trembling whisper to you as you pass of their distresses, those with an absolutely impotent appearance upon them.'[171]

The improvement noticeable in 1815 was rapid in the next ten years. Place writes in 1825:

There is not now one beggar where there were ten or even twice ten. We are no longer tormented by regular vagabonds who make themselves loathe-some objects in the streets. Those who were not old enough some twelve years ago ... to have noticed the beggars in the streets can scarcely believe it possible that they should have existed in such large numbers and can form no conception whatever of the horribly disgusting state in which they were. The countenances of many of them distorted from disease or diseased on purpose to produce pity, the sores ... produced in the same way ... the horrible contortions and distortions with which our streets abounded.[172]

CHAPTER 5

PARISH CHILDREN AND POOR APPRENTICES

When my mother died I was very young,
And my father sold me while yet my tongue
Could scarcely cry ''weep, 'weep, 'weep, 'weep !'
So your chimneys I sweep and in soot I sleep.

Blake

ONE of the worst results of the social conditions of London in the early eighteenth century was the large number of deserted children either entirely abandoned to the streets as vagrants or thrown on the tender mercies of the parish – some as foundlings, exposed in the streets, others as illegitimate children handed over to the parish officers for a lump sum or for whom a weekly payment was made under an affiliation order. Then there were the children of the 'settled poor' who were given poor relief and one of the regular categories of parish pensioners was 'parents overburdened with children'.

The foundlings and the illegitimate children were in a special sense the children of the parish – foundlings being generally given the name of the parish in which they were found. Thus in 1679 St Clement Danes had on its parish books eighty-nine children, sixteen of whom were Clements, 'children laid in the streets'; by 1686 a hundred and ten more children had been added to the roll, fifty-one of whom were Clements. The Middlesex justices, who in 1686 investigated the way in which the parish had disposed of its children, found that of the supposed sixty-seven foundlings called Clement only sixteen were – that is presumably, were said to be – still in being, while out of the total of one hundred and ninety-nine received by the parish officers in the past seven years ninety were left. The others were either 'lost and dead . . . or never were'. The justices thought that fictitious children had been recorded in the books to justify much parish spending – £1,943 9s. 0d. to nurses, £109 8s. 0d. on apprentice fees (fifty-five had been apprenticed), and £645 on 'extraordinary charges' for which we may safely read 'parish feasts'.[1] Whether these suspicions were justified we cannot tell, but worse things in relation to parish children were commonly laid to the charge of parish officers. At all events the proportion of surviving children is high compared with the later rate among workhouse children, and with the later record among the nurse-children of St Clements itself.[2]

The law by which the settlement of illegitimate children was that of the parish in which they were born, irrespective of the parents' settlement, and the general presumption that an illegitimate child would sooner or later be a burden to his parish, made parish officers keep a watchful eye on all non-residents who were expected to lie-in. Even apparently well-to-do and respectable visitors to a place where visitors were as frequent as Bath, did not lightly escape, if we may credit Defoe.[3] Failing satisfactory assurances, the woman was either hustled out of the parish (and if a poor woman often in circumstances of the greatest barbarity) or security was demanded that the child should not become a burden upon the parish.[4] Often, instead of a security against future contingencies, a lump sum was paid, and in this case the general rule seems to have been that the child was completely handed over to the parish officers, and the money was held to free the parents from all future claims. The 'Form of a Release from the Overseers of the Poor to one that had given £10 to be free from keeping a bastard child' given in a handbook of 1720 on the poor laws makes this clear. The overseers of the parish for themselves, their successors and the rest of the inhabitants undertake 'in consideration of the sum of £10' to maintain the child and to free the reputed father from all taxes, charges and payments[5] – that is, from the weekly payment, usually 2s. 6d., demanded under an affiliation order.

These lump sums were often treated as a perquisite by the parish officers and were the occasion of a parish feast known as 'saddling the spit'. It was assumed that the child's life would not be long, and therefore the money might as well be spent on jollification. Defoe says that in some parishes the overseers were always ready for a feast and a sum of money to take charge of an illegitimate child.[6]

As to saddling the spit, as the parish feast used to be called, [said Hanway in 1766] it will not give a day of life to the infant: on the contrary, the custom of giving small sums seems to have induced an opinion that a parish child's life is worth no more than eight or ten months' purchase, and that there is a chance of its being but so many days, and consequently occasioning a speedy release from all expense, and the money may go in good cheer. Experience justifies this suspicion so far that the traffic of receiving money in some instances seems but a small remove from innocent blood.[7]

It was a vicious circle. The measures taken to enforce parental, responsibility for illegitimate children induced the father to pay a lump sum to rid himself of all claims, and this became a recognized way of providing for the children. The terrible mortality among infants entrusted to parish nurses encouraged parish officers to assume that the cost of maintenance would be small, and thus it followed that in many cases these had no wish for the survival of the children. To quote a Parliamentary Report of 1716:

A great many poor infants and exposed bastard children are inhumanly suffered to die by the barbarity of nurses, who are a sort of people void of commiseration or religion, hir'd by the churchwardens to take off a burthen from the parish at the cheapest and easiest rates they can, and these know the manner of doing it effectually.[8]

'I have been informed by a man now living,' said Burrington in 1757, 'that the officers of one parish in Westminster received money for more than five hundred bastards, and reared but one out of all that number.'[9] This is only a hearsay report, but at all events was not incredible at the time.

The activities of the parish officers – the 'parish impertinences' – on the birth of a child were said to be one cause of the exposure of infants in the streets. 'It is believed,' it was said in 1686, 'that one half of the children left to the parish in the streets are more to save credit and the trouble given by parish officers, than for want of three shillings per week to pay for them. . . .'[1] There were nurses or midwives who gave security to the parish to enable them to keep or dispose of children without molestation.[10] Such children, put out to nurse for a few years, if they survived, lived only, it was said, to swell the number of beggars and vagrants.[11]

The duty of the parish towards its children was to put them out to nurse and to apprentice them when they were old enough. Workhouses, which became general in London parishes (except in the City within the

Walls) after the Act of 1722, were intended, *inter alia*, to be both a substitute for the parish nurse and to provide a preliminary training in industry and virtue with a modicum of book learning. 'All the poor children now kept at parish nurses, instead of being starv'd or misus'd by them, as is so much complained of, will be duly taken care of, and be bred up to Labour and Industry, Virtue and Religion. . . .'[12] So said the parishes of St Giles and St James, pioneers in the building of parish workhouses. It was also hoped by enthusiasts that workhouses would

effectually cure a very bad practice in parish officers, who, to save expense, are apt to ruin children by putting them out as early as they can to any sorry master that will take them, without any concern for their education and welfare, on account of the little money that is given with them. However, there will be this one good effect from workhouses thus regulated, that the next generation of persons in town will be made better and the children of the poor, instead of being bred up in irreligion and vice to an idle vagabond life, will have the fear of God before their eyes, get habits of virtue, be inured to labour, and thus become useful to their country.[13]

The education aimed at was to teach the catechism, reading, and possibly writing and a little ciphering in the intervals of some industrial occupation. This ideal remained the same, whether in the parish workhouses after 1722, in the London Workhouse (established in 1698 under the Act of 1662), in the Foundling Hospital, especially in its early years, and in the infant poorhouses or nursery schools of the London parishes in the early nineteenth century. It was also the ideal of the London charity schools, but the fact that it was more difficult and more expensive to start an industrial occupation than a little rudimentary teaching, made the former an exception.[14] But the workhouse, like the spinning schools and like the workhouse set up by Firmin in Aldersgate in 1676, aimed at being a primitive kind of factory. The earlier workhouses aimed also at being self-supporting if not profitable, and therefore suffered from inevitable disappointments. In the later workhouses (after 1723) and in the charity schools, the object of the industrial work seems to have been to inure the children to labour and to help towards the expenses of the undertaking.[15]

A description of the London Workhouse in Bishopsgate Street in 1708 gives a picture of these methods and ideals in practice: thirty or forty children were put under the charge of one nurse in a ward, they lay two together in bunks arranged round the walls in two tiers, 'boarded and set one above the other . . . a flock bed, a pair of sheets, two blankets and a rugg to each'. Prayers and breakfast were from 6.30 to 7. At 7 the children were set to work, twenty under a mistress, 'to spin wool and flax, knit stockings, to make new their linnen, cloathes, shooes, mark, etc.'. This work went on till 6 p.m., with an interval from 12 to 1 for 'dinner and play'. Twenty children were called away at a time for an hour a day to be taught reading, some also writing. Some children, we are told, 'earn a halfpenny, some a penny, and some fourpence a day'. At twelve, thirteen or fourteen, they were apprenticed, being given, at the master's choice, either a 'good ordinary suit of cloaths or 20s. in money'.[16]

This is a description written in terms of praise, and the London Workhouse was handsomely endowed. In theory the children in parish workhouses were treated in much the same way. But the nurses were inmates of the house, generally dirty and decrepit, and London workhouses were apt to be terribly overcrowded. Hanway said he had known six or eight children crowded into one bed,[17] and in 1774 the parish of St Leonard's Shoreditch, petitioning for a Bill to buy ground for a new workhouse, said that they were obliged to put thirty-nine children into three beds, 'by which means they contract disorders from each other'.[18] The teaching in workhouses (a few parishes excepted) generally given by one of the inmates, was perfunctory to the last degree.

The dominant motive of London charities for children was to prevent vagrancy with its hideous results of disease and crime; all aimed at giving children a start in life by means of apprenticeship – the boys to be bound 'to the sea-service', or the more laborious trades, the girls as a rule to domestic service. Parish charities were closely inter-related with poor relief, other charities tended to provide for those who could not claim parish help. The methods in all cases were a preliminary training, followed by an outfit of clothes, the choice of a master and (usually) the payment of an apprenticeship fee. All were subject to the pressure of the demand that children brought up by the parish or by charity should not be placed on a level with those who were not so helped, far less given an advantage over them, and feeling sometimes ran high over the rivalry for industrial opportunity. The

idea of education for the children of working people except as a preliminary to some form of apprenticeship hardly existed till the end of the
century.

The charity-school movement in London belongs almost entirely to
the eighteenth century, dating from about 1696 or 1698, and being
superseded at the end of the century by the Lancasterian Schools, and
(a little later) by the National Schools on the methods of Lancaster and
Bell. The schools were intended only for the children of the actually
poor, not for those of the artisan who could afford to pay the few pence
a week[19] demanded by the many private-venture schools of the lowest
grade. At the end of the century it was estimated that about 6,000
children in London went to charity or parish schools, and Lancaster
estimates that 25,000 children of artisans went to low-grade schools at
a cost of about £1 a year to their parents.[20]

As the charity schools were an outcome of the movement for religious societies of the reigns of William III and Anne, some falling off
might be expected afterwards, but though the period of rapid expansion,
when schools were set up in most parishes, came to an end about 1714,
new schools continued to be founded throughout the century. Their
stability indeed was remarkable, as in many cases they depended on
annual subscriptions and the enduring interest of trustees and visitors.
There was a close connexion between charity schools and parish workhouses; both the schools and the workhouses were encouraged by the
Society for Promoting Christian Knowledge. The *Accounts* of both
institutions, published by the Society, suggest that the impulse to workhouses was in part due to some disillusionment with the results of day
schools in which domestic or industrial work was not possible. Indeed,
charity schools where the children were boarded and 'set on work'
were classed as workhouses.[21] The children from workhouses sometimes attended the local charity school, and at least one charity school
was situated in the workhouse.[22]

The object of the schools from the beginning was to preserve children from vagrancy and to fit them for some sort of regular work.
'Divers ministers or other sober parishioners observed abundance of
children in their parishes, destitute and neglected in their education
either by reason of the poverty of some parents or the carelessness of
others.' The system in general is defended as preparing children for

'services of the lowest kind', even such service being almost out of the question for those taken straight from

the dwellings of their beggarly parents. . . . Let such an one go to the habitations of such children before taken into a charity school, and he shall find them without shoes and stockings, perhaps half-naked, or in tattered raggs, cursing and swearing at one another almost before he can speak, or he shall find them with the like blackguard to themselves, rolling in the dirt and kennels, or pilfering on the wharfs and keys, or when grown to any bigness, crying of oysters, or the like employment, and wherever he finds them devoid of all breeding and good manners.

But after they have left school they are 'as much distinguished from what they were before as is a tamed from a wild beast'. It is with 'the ill-nurted cattal' [sic] who do nòt go to school 'that our prisons are daily filled and under the weight of which Tyburn does so often groan'.[23]

Such being the motives of the schools, the attitude of their supporters towards the teaching of reading, writing and ciphering, was apologetic; 'the utmost care' was taken 'not only to instruct the children in the knowledge of the Christian religion, but also to breed them up in such a manner that as they are descended from the laborious part of mankind, they may be bred up and inured to the meanest services'.[24] The rules were chiefly directed towards preventing the children from being little savages. Much stress is laid on the constant wearing of the school dress or badges, that their conduct in the street may be observed, and on their orderly and marshalled appearance in church twice every Sunday, as well as their massed appearance at anniversary sermons and at the annual service at St Paul's. They were to be publicly catechized from time to time, and the teachers were to take special care of their manners and behaviour, 'to suppress the beginnings of vice, such as lying, cursing, swearing, profaning the Lord's Day, obscene discourse, stealing, etc.' while the parents were to be 'put in mind to take particular care of sending their children clean wash'd and comb'd to the school lest otherwise they be offensive there'.[25]

Similar ideas underlay the educational methods of other charities, but as time went on, their directors, intent on doing the best for the children, and taught by experience, lost confidence in the advantages of the 'meanest services', and became less apologetic for teaching the three R's. The change is apparent in the Foundling Hospital, where it was at first intended that the education should be strictly limited: 'notwithstanding the innocence of the children, yet as they are exposed and abandoned by their parents they ought to submit to the lowest stations, and should not be educated in such a manner as to put them upon a level with the children of parents who have the humanity and virtue to preserve them, and industry to support them'.[26] The current theories were still more explicitly put in a charity sermon of 1760: the children at the Orphan Working School at Hoxton were to be taught 'not to be able scholars or fine penmen . . . but so much reading as every Christian who values his Bible would wish them to have, and no more writing than would be useful in the meanest situation. . . .'[27]

Education was thus regarded as occupational, a preliminary to apprenticeship and dependent on social status. Social status in an eighteenth-century parish depended largely on the poor laws, and especially on the law of settlement. A hard and fast distinction was drawn between the 'housekeeper' and the lodger, even if the former occupied only a single room in the tenement he rented.[28] In a typical metropolitan parish there were those who paid to church and poor, and therefore had an undoubted settlement or right to maintenance should misfortune come upon them, and, it was held, a moral claim to specially favourable treatment as 'decayed housekeepers', one of the usual categories of those receiving poor relief. Then there were the 'settled poor' receiving relief either in the workhouse or as parish pensioners. Besides these there were numbers of lodgers, labourers or artisans, who if they applied for relief were classed as 'casual poor', in the parish on sufferance, most of them with known settlements somewhere, possibly with certificates from their own parish. These probably avoided applying for relief lest they should be sent back to their place of settlement. Last of all there were the numbers of deserted children and vagrants whose settlements were often unknown and who were virtual outlaws, outside the pale of the parochial organization of society. The responsibility for these lay legally with the parish where they were found wandering, provided no other place of settlement could be discovered, but (except under local Acts after 1750) this obligation appears to have been generally ignored except in the case of foundling children. They are thus described by the Philanthropic Society, founded in 1788 to provide for such of them as had criminal associations:

they are a class which belongs to no rank of the civil community, they are excommunicates in police, extra-social, extra-civil, extra-legal; they are links which have fallen off the chain of society, and which going to decay, inure and obstruct the movements of the whole machine.[29]

A settlement was therefore regarded as a birthright, and an indisputable and desirable settlement became an object of ambition with the less prosperous classes. Towards the end of the century, it was said that a desire to establish a right to a settlement kept in being the practice of formal apprenticeship.[30] It was also the object of the parish officers to rid the parish of a burden by apprenticing poor children in some other parish. Thus the law of settlement, the practice of apprenticeship and theories on social status were inextricably interwoven, though all of them underwent modifications in the course of the century.

The apprenticeship of parish children was regulated by the famous Act of 1601, which enjoined that they should be bound by the parish officers with the consent of two justices, boys till they were twenty-four, girls till twenty-one or marriage. Under this Act the occupation was at first either farm labour or domestic service, and the children were compulsorily billeted upon one of the ratepayers of their parish. When the Act of 1691 added to the other ways of gaining a settlement that of having served an apprenticeship of at least forty days in a parish it became the general custom in many places to apprentice parish children in another parish. In this case the master could not be obliged to take the child, and a fee was given as an inducement (it was sometimes also given under the old system), thus putting the parish child on a level, financially, with those who benefited from endowments for apprenticing poor children, or with those whose parents could afford a small fee.

There were thus two kinds of parish apprenticeship. In one compulsion was applied to the master, to the parents (if there were any) and to the child; in the other, only to the parents and the child. The latter method is the one described by Dr Burn as being general – he gives it as one of the objects of the overseer 'to bind out poor children apprentices, no matter to whom or to what trade, but to take especial care that the master live in another parish'.[31] It was that used in the London district and therefore the only one with which we are directly concerned. The earlier system was still surviving locally at the time of the Poor Law Commission of 1832. It was then general in the south-west, where it was popular among farmers, and in the district round Leeds.

Parish apprenticeship, then (a form of poor relief), differed legally from ordinary apprenticeship in the longer term of servitude and the compulsory binding by the overseers with the consent of two justices. Moreover, in the indentures the master or mistress undertook 'to save the parish and the parishioners harmless' from any charge for the child's maintenance. Till the latter part of the eighteenth century the apprenticeship of parish children was the most generally approved part of the poor laws. It was a form of 'setting the poor on work', and while there were many complaints against compulsory rates – the law of maintenance, as Arthur Young calls it, and against the settlement laws, there was none in principle against the compulsory apprenticeship of poor children, though it was generally agreed that in practice the methods of the overseers left much to be desired.

The children to be apprenticed by the parish included, besides the foundlings and the illegitimate children, any children in the workhouse and also the children of those receiving parish doles. In the second half of the century, when many London parishes gathered into their workhouses vagrant children out of the streets, and when, thanks to Hanway and others, a larger number of children survived the dangers of the parish nurse and the workhouse, the number to be apprenticed greatly increased.

Apprenticeship, in one of its many forms, was still in the eighteenth century the most general way of giving a child a start in life. In practice apprenticeship had so many different and even contradictory aspects that the subject is intricate. In general, it was a means of getting into a skilled trade and escaping the risk of a prosecution under the Elizabethan Statute of Apprentices for working in it without having served a seven years' apprenticeship. In corporate towns it was a means of obtaining the freedom of the place, usually a necessary condition of setting up a trade there or even working as a journeyman. In some trades apprenticeship was used to prevent the over-stocking of the industry and so keeping up wages, but in others apprentices were used as cheap labour at the expense of journeymen. When not a necessary preliminary to exercising a trade it was often the cheapest and most convenient way of learning it. Again, apprenticeship was often the legal sanction of child labour, a binding by indenture for a term of years to some occupation in which it was not pretended that any industrial training was given or any future livelihood secured. This was blind-alley employment at its worst.

According to eighteenth-century practice in London, parish apprenticeship might conceivably fall into any one of these industrial classes, though the poor boy, whether bound by his parents or the parish, was unlikely to get into any but the less skilled and the badly-paid branches of trade. The object was to provide an immediate maintenance for the child in return for its labour and the available occupations were those where the fee was low because the master was poor or because child labour was profitable. In London the City companies were comparatively little concerned with industrial apprenticeship in general and with that of poor children in particular. Industry progressively left the City for the out-parishes, and the freedom of the City was chiefly sought by those who wished to open shops there. Therefore, though industrial apprenticeship was general, in a majority of cases it was not entered upon through the medium of a City company. Unless in exceptional circumstances indeed the parish child could not be bound according to the custom of London, as his apprenticeship usually began before the age of fourteen, and lasted till twenty-four. Any person, master or journeyman, man or woman, housekeeper or lodger, who would undertake to provide food, lodging and instruction, sometimes also clothes, medicines and washing, could take an apprentice, all the earnings of the apprentice, whether for the master or a third person, being the property of the master.

The treatment of the child, whether bound by his parents or the parish, the food, lodging, work, the kind of instruction and the 'reasonableness' of the correction that might be inflicted, all varied according to the fee that had been paid and the age of the apprentice – the very early binding being the special disadvantage of the poor child.[32] There was an infinite gradation from the child bound simply as a domestic drudge to the boy bound to an 'eminent master' in a highly-skilled handicraft or the young man bound to a mercantile business.

Though one category merges into the other, a dividing line can be drawn between 'apprenticeship for labour' and apprenticeship for education (not that one excluded the other). In one case the master expected the child's work to be profitable to him and the child expected to be maintained in return for his labour. In the other, a comparatively large fee was paid for the boy's maintenance and instruction and admission into an exclusive trade. Trades were graded according to the terms upon which a child could be apprenticed and the amount of capital required for setting up in them. The fee of £5 or so paid by the parish and by poor parents to the poorer sort of master, and the 'meaner' trades to ensure the complete maintenance of the child in return for its labour for a long period of years was a temptation to the needy to take apprentices whom they could not provide for. The better-paid trades protected themselves by high fees, which were of course waived in the case of sons bound to their fathers.

Both classes of apprenticeship had dangers of their own. We are here concerned with the various kinds of apprenticeship for labour, the start in life of the majority of children.* Though the apprenticing of poor children was regarded as one of the chief duties of parish officers and the best way to prevent the breeding of a race of beggars, complaints of the way in which the duty was carried out are many. This was written in 1700:

Apprentices put out by a parish are frequently placed with poor, ill-natur'd or unskilful masters, who either force them from them by a bad maintenance and severity, before their times are out, or when they are out, send them from them but bunglers in their trade, or masters of such a one as will turn to no account....[33]

A most unhappy practice prevails in most places [said a writer on the Poor Laws in 1738], to apprentice poor children, no matter to what master, provided he lives out of the parish, if the child serves the first forty days we are rid of him for ever. The master may be a tiger in cruelty, he may beat, abuse, strip naked, starve or do what he will to the poor innocent lad, few people take much notice, and the officers who put him out the least of anybody. For they rest satisfied with the merit of having shifted him off to a neighbouring parish for three or four pounds and the duty they owe to every poor child in

* Apprenticeship as to general training for life and work is considered in Chapter 6.

the parish is no further laid to heart. The greatest part of those who now take poor apprentices are the most indigent and dishonest, in a word, the very dregs of the poor of England, by whom it is the fate of many a poor child, not only to be half-starved and sometimes bred up in no trade, but to be forced to thieve and steal for his master, and so is brought up for the gallows into the bargain. . . . I know a poor old weaver . . . who . . . took a poor apprentice from another parish; he covenanted, as is usual, to teach him his trade, to provide and allow him meat, drink, apparel, etc., to save harmless and indemnify the parish whence he took him, and to give him two good new suits of wearing apparel at the end of his apprenticeship. This master had himself been several times convicted of theft and had then actually left off his trade through weakness and old age, and as soon as the money he had with the boy was spent, threw himself and family, apprentice and all, upon his parish.[34]

The literal truth of such indictments is clear from the many instances of hardship, cruelty and misfortune recorded in the appeals to Quarter Sessions for the discharge of apprentices from their indentures. The reports of the Old Bailey also tell a melancholy tale. Many were hung or transported as a result of the miseries or temptations of their term of servitude, so they say, or so the Ordinary of Newgate says. In a number of murder, manslaughter and rape trials the victim was a wretched apprentice. The details of these trials, and of many others where the facts are less grisly, throw a flood of light on social conditions in London.

It is impossible to read them without coming to the conclusion that, generally speaking, the relationship between master and apprentice was an unsatisfactory one. In the first place, even in favourable conditions, there was this fundamental difficulty. In the early stages of his apprenticeship the boy was probably a nuisance and an expense, he needed supervision and he spoiled work; before the end of his term he was conscious that he could earn a living for himself, but was forced to work for his master without pay. To the parish apprentice, bound till he was twenty-four, the grievance was still greater. The relationship needed a habit of self-restraint and a power of looking forward and back, rare at all times.

Then the position of the artisan, or even of the master in a large way, was not sufficiently stable to justify indentures of seven years or longer, binding upon the master, his heirs, executors and assigns. Among the most usual grounds for appeals to the Sessions for the discharge of an apprentice were that the master had absconded from his creditors, or was beyond seas, or a shelterer in the Mint or the Verge, or in one or other of the debtors' prisons (where it may be added the apprentice often accompanied the master). It was also often stated that the master had no work on which to employ the apprentice, or had given up his trade and kept a public-house where he made the apprentice work as a pot-boy. To these grounds of appeal were frequently added complaints of starvation, verminous beds and brutal treatment, while in many cases it appeared that the apprentice had been turned out of doors to beg or starve. In 1686, for instance, Thomas Browne was relieved from his apprenticeship to John Leake, a glover of St Margaret's Westminster, as his master had absconded, leaving him almost starved, naked, 'eaten up' with vermin, and 'cripled by beatings'.[35] In 1710 the Middlesex Sessions discharged Daniel Lee from Robert St John, a barber and peruke-maker of St Martin's in the Fields. The master had barbarously and immoderately beaten and misused his apprentice, had not allowed him sufficient diet and had not instructed him in his trade. 'The said Robert, by reason of his bad circumstances had for three months absconded . . . and gone into the Mint in Southwark for shelter, leaving his said apprentice in a starving condition, almost naked and wholly unprovided for.' St John's wife, being unable to provide for him, had advised him 'to pilfer and steal for his livelihood'.[36]

It often happened that a master who was on the verge of insolvency would take an apprentice for the sake of the fee, and in the case of poor parents this must have represented great sacrifices, made to ensure the child's complete maintenance for seven years or longer, and then his future livelihood. Having secured the fee, it was often to the master's interest to get rid of the child. This he did by ill-treating him so that he ran away or by tempting him to the kind of misconduct that would justify the cancellation of the indentures without an order from the magistrates for the return of any part of the fee. In the later stages of an apprenticeship it was the apprentice who was often anxious to be free from his servitude and would run away or behave outrageously to force his master to have his indentures cancelled.[37] There were frequent complaints that the master, instead of teaching a boy his trade, would keep him employed on some labourer's routine work or as a household drudge. There were often times when the small master or the journey-man taking job-work had no work to do and either hired out the apprentice to someone else or allowed him to roam about the streets to pick up a living as best he could.

The obligation to feed, clothe and house, in sickness or in health, for seven years or more often proved an intolerable burden, and, apart from designs on the fee, the master was sometimes tempted to take out-rageous steps to get rid of an unwanted apprentice. Sometimes he would contrive to get him taken by a press-gang;[38] in the days when the kidnapping of children for the plantations was general, he would dispose of him to the master of a ship to be sold in the colonies. Several cases of this kind were tried at the Middlesex Sessions,[39] and for one that was discovered where the boy had friends who could prosecute, there must have been many which never came to light – the disappear-ance of an apprentice was too common a thing to provoke suspicion.

Apprentices were traditionally idle. Adam Smith's condemnation of apprenticeship is borne out in the details of many cases: 'An apprentice is likely to be idle, and almost always is so, because he has no immediate interest to be otherwise.... The boys who are put out apprentices from public charities are usually bound for more than the usual number of years, and they generally turn out very idle and worthless. ...' To counteract the idleness of apprentices it was in many trades the custom to task them to a certain amount of work, the apprentice being paid for anything done over the 'stint', but this was contrary to the strict interpretation of the usual indentures and to an Act of Common Coun-cil of the City of London. It must also have led in many cases to seriously overtaxing the strength of the apprentice.[40]

The poorer, younger, and more friendless the child, the greater of course were the dangers and miseries of apprenticeship. At the bottom of the scale was the workhouse child, bound by the parish to be the drudge or domestic slave of a poor family, or the little boy sold by his parents to a chimney-sweep. In the former case, though the indentures might specify the teaching of some trade or 'the art of housewifery', there was no pretence of teaching anything. The boy might be a pot-boy at an alehouse or be employed at a livery stable, the girl the domestic servant of a family living in one room, or employed by her mistress to carry milk or hawk goods about the streets. The child from the streets or the workhouse was seldom a desirable inmate of a respectable household, and the fee given by the parish was an attraction to the very poor, and many who took apprentices were quite incapable of maintaining them. Hanway said in 1766: 'it is certain the apprenticeship of some parish children is as great a scene of inhumanity as the suffering others to die in infancy.'[41]

In two notorious cases of brutality towards apprentices the mistresses were by no means of the lowest social grade. There was the case of Mrs Sarah Meteyard and her daughter, both executed for the murder of a little girl of thirteen who had been starved and beaten. She kept a haberdasher's shop in Bruton Street and took parish apprentices to make nets and mittens. Four girls had been shut up in a little close room, 'a little slip about two yards wide at one end and comes off like a pennyworth of cheese', said one witness.[42] The case of Mrs Brownrigg is notorious. Of four apprentice girls treated with horrible brutality, one died, one apprenticed by the Governors of the Foundling Hospital ran away and went back to the Foundling and was discharged. The other two had been bound by the overseers of the precinct of Whitefriars. These poor children were taken as domestic drudges. At first sight the household compares favourably with those to which parish children were often consigned; Mrs Brownrigg was a successful midwife, her husband was a painter and plasterer, they had a house in Fetter Lane and 'lived in credit'.[43]

These two cases in the sixties roused public horror; earlier in the century cases of equal cruelty went unpunished and seem to have attracted little attention. In 1748 Elizabeth Dickens murdered her apprentice girl by beating and ill-treating her. The parish had given her the large fee of £6 because the child's habits were dirty. Evidence was given that the woman had sworn to kill the child but she was acquitted.[44] In 1736 James Durant, a ribbon-weaver, was tried for the murder of his apprentice, 'a very little boy' of thirteen or fourteen whom he had brutally beaten with a mop-stick. He was acquitted.[45] Fishermen's and watermen's apprentices were notoriously ill-treated. In 1733, John Bennett, a fisherman of Hammersmith, killed his apprentice, a boy of eleven. The child had been beaten with a rope and a tiller, and the medical evidence was that he had 'died of wounds and want of looking after and hunger and cold together'. The man was found guilty of manslaughter only.[46] Sometimes it was the apprentice who appeared in the dock. In 1735 Mary Wotton, a little girl of nine, who had been apprenticed fourteen months before by the parish to the wife of a certain John Easton, broke open her mistress's drawers, took twenty-seven guineas, ran away and was found in Rag Fair. She was sentenced to death.[47]

These are not isolated cases and there can be no doubt that those which came into court represent an infinitesimal proportion of the little apprentices who were beaten, starved and neglected, still less of those who ran away to become beggars and vagrants. Little girls especially were liable to be horribly ill-used. Sir John Fielding in his *Plan* for the Orphan Asylum which he founded in 1758, proposed also to receive girls apprenticed out of workhouses, 'as they are generally placed in the worst of families and seldom escape destruction'. The sort of place found for the workhouse girl is illustrated by the case of Ann Barnard, a child of twelve, bound to a woman who went about the streets crying old clothes, while her husband worked at a pot-house in Lambeth. The family lived in a garret in Bell Yard, Westminster, a place which the woman described as 'a very bad neighbourhood, there are robberies committed often on nights . . . nothing but wickedness in the place'. The little girl was left alone in the garret to look after the baby, and was assaulted by an inmate of the house, at whose trial these facts came to light.[48]

The retailing of milk in London was carried on by a low-grade of street seller, often the wife of an Irish labourer. Nicholas Larkin and his wife decamped in 1762 from their lodging and were supposed to have gone to Ireland; they had had a parish apprentice girl for five years. Before they left she was sent on an errand, to find on her return that the couple had disappeared. Before the parish could find another master for the unfortunate girl, they had to obtain a formal discharge from the Sessions.[49] To bind a child to a milk-seller till she was twenty-one was to consign her to a period of literal slavery. There could be no pretence of learning a trade or even 'the art of housewifery', though this was probably specified in the indentures. So long as apprentices were to be had from the parish, their services given away as it were together with a fee of £5 or so, it is not to be supposed that at the end of her servitude the girl would find a milk-seller who would agree to pay wages. The better class of milk-seller who dealt with the quality probably employed the fresh-looking country girls, who are sometimes described as carrying pails and crying milk through the streets of London.

The slavery implied by this kind of apprenticeship appears in the practice followed by some masters of hiring the child out to others. There was a dispute in 1735 between two parishes over the settlement of Alice Wheeler, a parish girl, bound to one George Wheeler, of St George's Hanover Square, who afterwards 'let her out for hire to a person in Marybone'.[50] Settlement cases discuss nice points as to whether apprentices have been assigned, hired or lent, and it is clear that the practice of hiring was fairly general. It was customary among chimney-sweepers, and we find that one John Jones, a cordwainer, before absconding, had 'lent' his apprentice to a chimney-sweeper who, it was said in 1726, 'beats and abuses him in the most barbarous and cruel manner'.[51]

Thus many parish children were apprenticed simply as drudges – girls to the lowest conceivable grades of domestic service, boys as helpers at stables or pot-boys. Others were apprenticed to trades, many to bakers and weavers, but the commonest trades for boys seem to have been tailoring and shoe-making, both trades whose lower grades at least were badly over-stocked in London. Both shoe-makers and tailors often worked at stalls in the street: these were generally botching tailors and cobblers. Journeymen shoe-makers took apprentices whom they employed on piecework given out by the master who was a shop-keeper. The lowest branch of the trade was translating. The translator bought old shoes collected by beggars or bunters (rag-pickers), re-soled them and patched them up to look watertight enough to sell.

There were also trades so unprofitable or disagreeable that only parish children or the children of the very poor were apprenticed to them. Besides chimney-sweeping, there was catgut spinning, 'a very mean, nasty and stinking trade'.[52] Button-mould-making is described as 'a very poor business, and requires so little to set up, that I imagine there are few or no journeymen. Their apprentices are generally the children of or apprentices of the lowest poor, and they therefore have nothing, or only what the parish gives them'.[53]

Poor boys were taken as apprentices by watermen and there were many abuses connected with this occupation. It was alleged that in time of war the watermen got their boys pressed into the Navy, in which case all their wages (and even their prize-money) were legally the property of the masters.[54] It was also said that such watermen

... as have no settled place of abode and areidle and profligate persons ... for the sake of small sums of money ... take great numbers of apprentices, who instead of being brought up to their proper calling ... are suffered to idle about, which brings them to pilfer for their sustenance, and for the generality, they become vagrants, and not seldom come to a fatal end.[55]

Apprenticeship to watermen, lightermen and fishermen was regarded as apprenticeship to the sea-service, because in time of war the king could claim the services of all apprentices who were over the age of eighteen, and was therefore regarded as the most desirable form of apprenticeship for poor boys.

Girls were also apprenticed by the parish to trades. It is not always clear whether they were intended to learn the trade or to work in the house – probably they were intended to make themselves generally useful. One Mary Carpenter was bound from Lambeth workhouse to a breeches-maker 'to learn the business and also household work'.[56] The indentures of a girl bound to a carpenter in 1741 specified that she was to be taught the art and mystery of a carpenter.[57] In some cases girls were bound to married women who carried on a trade separately from the husband, or to learn housewifery. In others the girl was bound to a man who covenanted that his wife should teach her housewifery. Parish children, both boys and girls, were bound to Bethnal Green weavers, but in the case of girls it is difficult to know whether they were taught weaving, though many women in London did weave. One parish child was turned over by her original master to a weaver who lived with a Billingsgate fishwoman. She sometimes wound quills for the man, but always went to market with the woman, and was also sent out alone to cry periwinkles and crabs, and, at night, radishes.[58]

On the other hand, there were cases when the parish seems to have been generous. In 1759 we hear of a poor girl of the parish of Chelsea bound to a mantua-maker in Westminster for £10. Fees of seven guineas seem to have been not unusual with parish boys. In 1749 the parish of Teddington bound a boy to a brushmaker of Goodman's Fields till the usual age of twenty-four and the master promised the churchwardens under a penalty of forty shillings to bind the boy to himself as a freeman of London when he should reach the age of four-teen. It is true that he did not keep the promise and perhaps never intended to, for presumably he would then have lost the three last years of the boy's term of servitude, the most profitable ones to the master, as the apprentice would have become free of the City at the age of twenty-one.[59]

Perhaps these apprentices with whom comparatively large fees were given were children of 'decayed housekeepers', and older, better grown and better educated than the usual workhouse child. On the other hand, large fees were sometimes paid as an inducement to take an unsatis-factory child. Masters were often ready to take boys who could do them some good at low fees, and indeed a master turning over an apprentice often demanded a payment for the loss of the boy's work during the unexpired term of servitude. Francis Place describes how his master, a breeches-maker, took a parish boy as a turn-over. But leather breeches-making was then a trade which was declining to the point of extinction.

He was a good lad [says Place], by no means so disreputable as I and my companions were, he was the son of a labouring man and had been appren-ticed by the parish of Barking. It is true he could not have kept company with us, as he had no money, but if he had had ever so much, he would have been, as he was, excluded from our society.

It was an age when social distinctions were rigidly marked. Place ex-plains that he and his friends when apprentices would not keep company with journeymen except in the workshop, nor with other lads whose fathers were not housekeepers.[60] A distinction was drawn between the apprentice for labour, who would be a journeyman when out of his time, and the apprentice with a good fee, who expected to set up for himself.

The children of the poorer sort, when they were not apprenticed to their own parents, were in most cases bound to masters who took them at the best in the expectation, often unduly sanguine, that the value of their work would be greater than the cost of their board and lodging. In very many cases they were taken for the sake of the fee, when their prospects were still worse. The position of the master who took such apprentices was apt to be precarious. He often had no work on which to teach and employ the boy, and with the best will in the world, could not feed and house an apprentice decently; as for clothing him, there are frequent complaints, not only that the master has failed to provide clothes, but that he has pawned those belonging to the apprentice.* When one remembers the general want of education, the drinking habits, the bad housing conditions, and the habitual resort to violence characteristic of the period, it is fairly clear that to entrust a boy or girl to the sole care of a struggling artisan, who hoped to make a profit out of the child's work, was not a satisfactory way of providing for a child. The surprising thing is, not that it often turned out badly, but that it sometimes turned out well.

It is of course true that the records of Quarter Sessions and of the Old Bailey show only the failures of the system. But on the other hand they show only a very small proportion of the failures. Innumerable apprentices ran away.[61] Innumerable complaints, both from masters and apprentices were made to the justices and to the rotation offices and (after 1792) to the police offices without coming before Quarter Sessions. There must have been an immense number of cases where the child was too poor, ignorant and friendless to be able to appeal against his master. There are, for instance, noticeably few chimney-sweeps' cases in the Sessions records.

Industrially, the apprenticeship of poor boys led to the over-stocking of trades. When a Bill was introduced in 1779 to throw open the bakers' and butchers' trades by making apprenticeship unnecessary, the Bakers' Company of London petitioned against it on the ground that 'the bakers' trade being principally carried on with the assistance of poor apprentices . . . the . . . bill would be extremely prejudicial to the bakers'.[62]

As early as 1710 the excessive number of apprentices taken by the framework-knitters, ten or more to one journeyman, gave rise to machine breaking in London. Many parish apprentices were taken by the Nottingham stocking-weavers, especially after 1728, when it was decided that they were outside the authority of the London Company. The fee of £5 given by the parish was an additional inducement to take them. One man had always twenty-five apprentices, more or less, and had not employed a journeyman for years. As a result, between 1740 and 1750

* See Appendix IV.

... the wages for making the common kind of worsted hose were reduced very low and many of the parish apprentices, ill-managed, ill-kept, ill-taught and little cared for, were reduced almost to starvation. Idle and dissipated habits were the consequence and became the precursors of general depreciation in the clothing and dwellings of the country framework-knitters.[63]

William Hutton, who was apprenticed in 1738 by his parents to the better-paid branch of silk-stocking-weaving, found at the end of his term that it was a starving trade by which it was impossible to live.[64]

The excessive number of apprentices taken by the journeymen weavers of Spitalfields had long been complained of. The Spitalfields Act in 1773 which provided for the fixing of wages by Quarter Sessions, forbade weavers to take more than two apprentices, to prevent, as Hanway said, 'the scene of misery which they had brought upon themselves'. Apprenticeship however, was by no means rigidly enforced among the London weavers, and in any case their wives and children often wove, whether apprenticed or not. The restriction nevertheless was beneficial. The way in which it worked was explained by William Hale, the Spitalfields manufacturer. Journeymen, he said, frequently suffered from taking even two apprentices, 'they take them because they can get work for them for a year or two, and then in a state of depression of trade they suffer from having them to maintain'. Except for the Act they would take many apprentices in times of temporary good trade in the hope of making a profit from their labour.[65]

In the course of the century the apprenticeship system was modified by the growing custom of out-door apprenticeship, and by the substitution for the legal seven years' indentures of contracts or arrangements by which a learner undertook to work for an employer (often a journeyman) for a low rate of wages or for some proportion of the wages which he actually earned in return for instruction in the trade. This was called clubbing, and was often arranged for a period of three years.[66]

These spontaneous modifications of an ancient system did not directly affect parish apprenticeship; for this the traditional contract was essential – namely, that the master was entirely responsible for the maintenance and morals of his apprentice in return for all the profits of his labour. Measures were taken however, to protect the poor apprentice, and especially the parish apprentice, from the dangers due to the (in practice) almost unlimited control given to the master by the apprenticeship system.

The grounds on which an appeal could be made by an apprentice for discharge from his master were that he had been given 'immoderate' or 'unreasonable' correction, had not been provided with sufficient meat, drink and necessaries, had been turned away by his master, or had not been instructed in his trade.[67] The master could apply for the discharge or correction (by a committal to Bridewell or to the County House of Correction) of his apprentice for behaving otherwise than as a good and dutiful servant and by breaking the covenants of the indentures by absenting himself, leaving his service, spoiling his goods, refusing to work or frequenting bad company. The first step towards getting a discharge was to apply to a justice, who could settle or compound the matter if he could get the parties to agree, or could send the apprentice to a Bridewell or House of Correction. If they failed to agree, an appeal had to be made to Quarter Sessions. A formal petition, probably drawn up by some justice's clerk or hedge lawyer, was made, setting forth the alleged grievances and praying relief. Both sides were heard, it is often said that they were represented by counsel, and witnesses were sometimes examined. The case was usually heard at the next Sessions after that to which the petition had been made, but was sometimes adjourned from Sessions to Sessions, so that relief was by no means immediate. Cases frequently went by default, the master having absconded, or, when the facts were very black, refusing to appear.

When indentures were cancelled, more especially when this was through the fault of the master, or when only a short part of the term had expired, the Sessions often ordered the return of a part of the binding fee, but such orders were of little use when, as often happened, the master was an absconding debtor.

In the case of apprentices bound according to the custom of London to a freeman of the City the appeal was in the first instance to the City Chamberlain, who could reprimand, admonish or commit to Bridewell. The place of Quarter Sessions was taken by the Lord Mayor's Court, where the facts were tried by a jury and the Recorder decided the points of law.[67]

The appeal to Quarter Sessions was a fair protection for the apprentice with friends who could afford the inevitable expense. In 1747 the special difficulties of the poor apprentice were first recognized by the law in an Act providing that any parish apprentice, or any other apprentice with whom a binding fee of not more than £5 had been paid, could complain to any two justices 'concerning any misusage, refusal of necessary provision, cruelty or ill-treatment'. The justices might summon the master or mistress to appear, and on proof of the complaint by oath might discharge the apprentice by warrant for which no fee was to be paid. In a similar way the apprentice might be discharged for misconduct.[68]

This was not a serious check to ill-treatment; it only gave the poor apprentice a readier and cheaper means of escape than that of a petition to the Sessions. In 1792 an Act was passed which probably gave a real measure of protection. It had been realized that as both masters and apprentices often had their own reasons for wishing to escape the obligations of the indentures, the Act of 1747 was sometimes an actual incentive to ill-treatment on one side or misconduct on the other. 'Whereas instances of such ill-treatment frequently occur,' runs the Act after reciting the Act of 1747, 'and it is fit that such discharge should not operate as an inducement to ... such ill-treatment....' It was therefore enacted that the justices might order any master or mistress to pay to the parish officers not more than £10 towards putting the apprentice out to someone else and to pay £5 for refusing to deliver up the apprentice's clothes. They might also compel the parish officers to enter into recognizances to prosecute masters for the ill-treatment of their apprentices.[69]

This was followed up a year later by an Act empowering two justices to impose fines on masters who were convicted of ill-treating apprentices with whom a fee of not more than £10 had been paid.[70]

But before this, chiefly owing to Jonas Hanway and to Saunders Welch, a very active Middlesex magistrate, an Act had been passed in favour of parish apprentices. About 1766 Hanway began a campaign against the binding of parish boys till they were twenty-four. This he calls an 'absurd tyrannical custom'.

Let us consider [he writes], that times are altered from Queen Elizabeth's days; such young persons as these are not supposed to be placed out in employments of great trust, or great ingenuity. Such occupations may repay the servitude till twenty-four – and such apprenticeships do frequently not commence till the age of seventeen, but this in question is a species of slavery....[71]

The clause in the Act of 1601 enjoining the binding of poor boys till the age of twenty-four may have been incorporated from the similar clauses in the earlier Acts against vagrancy.[72] It may have been intended to compensate the master upon whom the child was compulsorily billeted for the cost of his maintenance during the earlier part of the servitude, possibly it was designed to delay marriage at a time when there was a fear of over-population relatively to the producing power of the country. Probably the prevailing fear of 'masterless men' had something to do with it. At all events it was legal slavery and had become more than ever harsh and unjustifiable when the master took apprentices voluntarily for the sake of their labour, though compulsion was still applied to the child and the parents. And it obviously defeated its own ends by inducing apprentices to run away, or to behave badly in order to be discharged. The runaway apprentice was a sort of out-law, anyone who employed or harboured him could be prosecuted by his master, and till the indentures were cancelled, all the earnings of the apprentice were legally his master's property.[73] To quote Hanway:

If ... to save a few pounds in the fee the child is placed out to a taylor, a perukemaker, a baker, a butcher, from ten or twelve to the age of twenty-four, we must not be surprised at the mischiefs which generally attend such apprenticeships. That they are a fruitful source of contention and calamity to parish children and no less to their masters, many who administer justice in these cities can tell. The master, as aiming at too much service defeats his own ends. . . . Nor has a young man so good a chance of coming into the world with his master on his own account, if the master may dispose of him as his property till he is twenty-four.[74]

Hanway carried his point. He got a clause inserted in the Act of 1767 for 'the better regulation of the Parish Poor Children . . . within the Bills of Mortality'* enacting that parish boys were to be apprenticed to the age of twenty-one not twenty-four. This applied only to London, but the next year an Act was passed altering the age for the whole country. The Act of 1767 provided also that a minimum fee paid in two instalments should be given with parish apprentices. 'Whereas the sums of 20s. to 40s. now usually given . . . by the parishes are by no means adequate to the procuring such masters and mistresses as are in general fit and proper, and whereas there is a general neglect in the

* See above, p. 59.

moral and religious instruction of apprentices . . .' it was ordered that no parish child was to be bound for less than £4 2s. od., 42s. of which was to be paid at the end of three years. As a matter of fact many London parishes paid more than this and it was an open question whether a high fee did not do more harm than good by tempting the needy to apply for apprentices.[75] Withholding a part of the fee was a good arrangement, but whether this clause was observed by parishes in general may be doubted. It was afterwards however, as we shall see, included among the standing orders of St Andrew's Holborn (Hanway's parish), and was a rule of the parish of St James.

In 1802 came Sir Robert Peel's Act[76] for protecting parish apprentices in cotton mills, who were for the most part children from the London workhouses.[77] This is almost the last of the series of Acts for the protection of parish children (beginning with the Act of 1747), and is also the first tentative step towards the factory Acts of the nineteenth century. In spite of its innovating character it follows the line of tradition in providing for the daily instruction of the children in time taken from their daily work, just as the children in the London Workhouse a hundred years earlier had been called away in batches from their spinning and knitting. Other provisions link it with the new era. No child was to work more than twelve hours a day and night work was forbidden. Local inspectors, one a clergyman, the other a magistrate, were to be nominated by the justices. Unfortunately, while there were model employers, prepared to accept the principles of the Act and sometimes to go beyond them – Peel himself, Strutt, Ashton, Dale and (later) his son-in-law Robert Owen – there was no adequate machinery for enforcing it, and there were mills in which the existence of the Act was ignored.

In 1816, after an inquiry into 'the state of parish apprentices bound into the country from the parishes within the Bills of Mortality',* an important Act was passed to regulate the binding of parish apprentices,[77] which so hedged about with conditions obviously irksome to the master such apprentices as had come from distant parishes that it probably went far to discourage the employment of apprentice labour at all, a consequence which had been foreseen when Peel's Bill was under discussion.[78] The chief source of supply, moreover, had been

* See Appendix V.

London, and the Act forbade the sending of children of parishes within forty miles of London, a greater distance than forty miles which put Lancashire out of the question. There were also provisions to force the justices to give a real consideration to the suitability of the proposed master in all cases and the apprenticeship of parish children under the age of nine was forbidden. This Act was probably effective as it laid money penalties on overseers who infringed it – and still more important – laid down that unless its provisions were observed, the apprentice should gain no settlement, but remain a potential burden on his original parish.

So much for legislation concerning apprentices in general. There was one particularly forlorn set of children – the little climbing-boys or chimney-sweepers. The beginning of a movement for their protection seems to have been a letter to the *Public Advertiser* in 1760 (probably by Hanway) addressed to the magistrates of London and Westminster, urging them to instruct the 'proper officers' to summon the master of any boy found 'without covering for his nakedness'. Here and there a constable might perhaps have been found to carry out such an order but its effect must have been of the slightest. In 1767 when Hanway was protesting against the apprenticing of very young children by the parishes his attention naturally turned to the climbing-boys:

Among those who have placed out children so young as seven years of age, there are several parishes who apprentice them to chimney-sweepers. Chimney-sweepers ought to breed their own children to the business, then perhaps they will wash, clothe and feed them. As it is, they do neither, and these poor black urchins have no protectors and are treated worse than a humane person would treat a dog. . . . They often beg in the streets, and seem to be in much more real need than common beggars.[79]

Besides the miseries of neglect and ill-treatment, of being forced up chimneys at the risk of being burnt or suffocated, there were other hardships arising from the customs of the trade and the poverty and ignorance of the masters. As the boys were always black and usually in rags they were social outcasts, and were considered to belong to the class of beggars and thieves. They were made to beg by their masters and it is pretty clear that they were sometimes encouraged to steal. One master would take far more apprentices than he could employ – sometimes as many as twenty-four. In the winter he would hire them out at sixpence a day, and in the summer allow or compel them to subsist by begging. They were sometimes forced to bring their masters the money or clothes they were given.

In 1773 the Marine Society undertook an investigation into the condition of climbing-boys in London. They collected nineteen boys, clothed them and washed them, and encouraged them to talk. Each gave an account of himself 'without the least reserve or seeming exaggeration. ...' (Such boys had a great deal of a kind of independence as well as much ill-treatment. They roamed about the streets to get work – this was known as 'calling the streets', and they sometimes offered 'to sweep for the soot, oh!'.)[80] It was found that of the nineteen three only had been parish apprentices; there were parents who were 'ready to dispose of their children under the influence of a glass of gin'.[81] In 1785 Hanway found

... of late years not more than one parish within the Bills of Mortality where parochial officers place out their children to chimney-sweepers. ... Orphans who are in a vagabond state, or the illegitimate children of the poorest kind of people are said to be sold, that is, their service for seven years is disposed of for twenty or thirty shillings ... but it is presumed that the children of poor parents, who cannot find bread for a numerous family, make up by much the greater part of the climbing-boys.[82]

Hanway died before a Bill could be brought in to remedy these abuses. His work was taken up by David Porter, a master-chimney-sweeper, and a most remarkable man, who had long been in communication with Hanway.[83] Porter, supported by 'a committee of gentlemen' petitioned Parliament in 1788 for an Act for the protection of apprentices. He and another master in the trade gave evidence to the committee on the Bill. They told of the excessive number of boys, of their hiring-out at sixpence a day, of boys being bound as young as four years old, of the generally fatal disease of 'sooty warts' or chimney-sweepers' cancer, caused by the boys being habitually covered with soot and seldom washed; Porter knew of many boys who had served for four or five years without being washed at all. It was a common practice, he said, 'for parents to carry about their children to the master-chimney-sweepers and dispose of them to the best bidder, as they cannot put them apprentice to any other master at so early an age'.[84]

A Bill was brought in which was mutilated in the House of Lords and in its final form was very inadequate. No boy was to be bound under eight, and his servitude was to expire at the age of sixteen. No master was to take more than six apprentices or to let them out for hire. The streets were not to be called after midday, or before five in summer and seven in winter. Every boy was to wear a brass plate on the front of a leather cap with his master's name on it and any breach of the provisions of the Act was to be punishable by a fine of from £5 to £10 on a summary conviction before a single justice of peace. It was stated in the Act that parish children might be bound to chimney-sweepers, but only with the consent of their parents. A prescribed form of indenture was appended to the Act containing, besides the usual clauses, certain additional provisions: the apprentice was not to be assigned to another master without the consent of two justices. The master was to provide, at least once a year 'a compleat suit of cloathing with suitable linen, stockings, hat and shoes', besides the climbing suit. At least once a week he was to cause the apprentice to 'be thoroughly washed and cleansed from soot and dirt', and he was to require the boy to 'attend the public worship of God on the Sabbath day and permit him to receive the benefit of any other religious instruction'. He was not to force the apprentice to go up any chimney actually on fire[85] (extinguishing burning chimneys was the most profitable part of a sweep's business), and was in all things 'to treat his (or her) said apprentice with as much humanity as the employment of a chimney-sweeper will admit of '.[86]

This obviously did not go very far, and the Act, such as it was, was evaded. Still it was better than nothing. The provisions in the indentures gave specific grounds of appeal for discharge.[87] The Society for bettering the Conditions of the Poor took the matter up in 1797 and 1798 and supported the proposals of Porter, who had already written and distributed a forcible pamphlet. The interest and compassion of a part of the public had been roused, and judging from the appeals to Quarter Sessions there were many convictions under the Act. Colquhoun, the police magistrate, was formally thanked in 1803 by Angerstein for the committee of the Society for Improving the condition of the Infant Chimney-sweepers.[88] In 1802 a society was formed to promote the use of the machine to supersede the use of climbing-boys.[89]

But, as Porter pointed out, the root of the evil was the poverty of the trade. If, he said,

the practice of crying the streets was discontinued and the boys properly inspected and protected, masters would then take no more apprentices than they had employment for, the boys would not live upon the charity of spectators in the streets, the practice of letting them out would no longer prevail, and the masters would become respectable and comfortable and take a regular and stationary place in society. The difficulty with regard to their getting apprentices would be removed. Half of the climbing-boys are now [1798] purchased from needy and illiterate parents.

He estimated that out of about two hundred master-chimney-sweepers in London, there were not more than twenty who made a decent living.[90]

The beginning of public compassion for climbing-boys thus dates apparently from about 1760, although these poor children had been at the opposite extreme from 'golden lads and girls' probably since the use of chimneys became general. But chimney-sweepers, like link-boys and 'japanners' or shoe-blacks or vagrants (the Black Guard) had been regarded as villains ripening for the gallows rather than as objects of compassion. 'I think this branch' (chimney-sweeping), says a guide to London trades in 1747, 'is chiefly occupied by unhappy parish children, and may, for ought I know, be the greatest nursery for Tyburn of any trade in England.'[91] In 1718 the friends of Richard Meredith, aged five and a half, complained to the Westminster Sessions that he had been 'clandestinely and imprudently' bound by the parish officers of St Margaret's to a chimney-sweeper in St Giles till he should be twenty-four. The court discharged the child as he was 'of very tender years and too young to be put out an apprentice', and a relative had offered to take charge of him.[92] What was exceptional in the case was not the nature of the apprenticeship, but that the child should have had friends ready and able to appeal to the Sessions and offer to provide for him.

This legislation on behalf of poor apprentices, which covers the period from 1747 to 1816 (after which Parliament begins to be concerned with child labour in general), was probably largely inspired by the magistrates who had in many cases anticipated it by their recommendations. The friend of the ill-used apprentice was the better sort of magistrate, and it is clear that both individual justices and the Sessions did afford a measure of protection. Apprentices complaining of ill-treatment went to Bow Street, to a rotation office, or (after 1792) to one of the new police offices. John Fielding and Saunders Welch (who presided at Litchfield Street, the office which Dr Johnson attended for a whole winter in order to enlarge his knowledge of human nature) were particularly resorted to. It is interesting to remember that Welch is said to have begun life in the workhouse of Aylesbury and had been apprenticed to a London trunk-maker,[93] perhaps by his parish. It was he who represented to the Committee of 1766–7 the disastrous consequences of binding parish boys till the age of twenty-four.

John Fielding urged in 1766 that parish children should not be apprenticed to masters at a distance, nor bound before the age of fourteen, that they should be better clothed and a larger fee given with them and that they should be bound to housekeepers only, not to lodgers. He also urged the magistrates to use their authority to prevent the choice of unsuitable masters:

Parish children are to be bound out by the consent of two justices, and it often happens that their indentures are sent by the beadle to two different magistrates to get them signed, without producing before them either master, mistress, apprentice or parish officers, by which means poor children are frequently put out to improper persons, and surely it was intended by the legislature that all the parties should appear before the justices when they sign the indentures.[94]

Some of these recommendations were in process of time embodied in Orders of the Sessions and in Acts of Parliament. Minimum binding fees were laid down in the Act of 1767 for the better regulation of parish poor children within the Bills. An Order of Sessions of 1800 embodies the experience of a later generation of magistrates and enjoins the supervision of the justices in parish bindings urged many years before by John Fielding:

It being represented to this Court that several poor children bound out by different parishes to persons who carry on the business of tambour working and other trades in and about this metropolis, more especially those of a sedentary nature, are kept and employed ... in a manner extremely prejudicial to their health and that frequently the necessaries of life given to them by their masters and mistresses were not sufficient for their support, and it being stated that several cases of this sort come before the magistrates at the public offices and that complaints had been frequently made of the improper conduct and behaviour in other respects of masters and mistresses towards such poor apprentices. It is Ordered and . . . earnestly recommended that in every case where the assent of two justices is necessary to the binding out any child . . . that the two magistrates be present and acting together as by law intended at the time of such binding and that they require the attendance of the master and apprentice before them at the same time, and that the magistrates do make a strict inquiry . . . into the situation in life and circumstances of the person proposing to take such apprentice and that they satisfy themselves by proper inquiries of the fitness of such person to provide for and maintain such apprentices with sufficient and proper meat, drink and clothing, and to teach and instruct such apprentice in his business and that such person is in all other respects fit and proper to be entrusted with the care and instruction of such apprentice.[95]

This shows that the magistrates of the police offices or public offices were alive to the evils to be guarded against. Unfortunately, irresponsible justices could usually be found to sign indentures without investigation, as is shown by the report of the Committee of 1815 on London parish apprentices sent to the manufacturing districts.[96] The Act of 1816 was intended to remedy this, and probably did remedy it.

The increase in knowledge and in compassion which had resulted in legislation had also brought about administrative reforms. Experience had taught that much care was necessary in the choice of a master for poor children. The Quakers had long given special care to the selection of masters and mistresses, some responsible member of the Monthly Meeting being deputed to inquire into the suitability of each applicant for an apprentice.[97] In the latter part of the century it was usual in the better-managed London parishes for the standing orders made under local Acts to make special regulations for the apprenticing of parish children. Whatever shortcomings there may have been in practice, it was no longer the admitted policy to make the cheapest bargain for the parish regardless of the child. Such an order as that of the St Pancras open vestry in 1722 was out of date: 'Ordered that Mr Batt, Upper Churchwarden, should bind out William Lucas apprentice to what person or business he shall think most proper, and to make as cheap a bargain for putting him out as he can.'[98] Several parishes by their local Acts had taken the work of finding masters for the children out of the hands of the churchwardens and overseers and given it to the Governors and Directors of the Poor. This was done, for instance, by Marylebone with the excellent provision that no parish apprentice was to be turned over by his master to another master without their consent.[99] St James Westminster, in 1781, established a parish school of industry to prevent the children who had been brought up by cottagers on Wimbledon Common from returning to the very mixed society of the workhouse. The children were taught reading, writing and ciphering, the girls housework and needlework, the boys shoe-making, tailoring and pin-heading, and were apprenticed between the ages of twelve and a half and fourteen. Would-be masters and mistresses had to make a personal application to the Board of Governors and Directors, after which the 'proper officer' made an inquiry into the position and character of applicants and then made a written report to the Board. The child went 'upon liking' for a month, at the end of which both master and child were examined separately by the Committee. If the child's account was satisfactory indentures were made, a fee of £2 and a double outfit of clothing were given, with a warrant for a further sum of two guineas at the end of three years if the master had taken proper care of the child. Between 1782 and 1796, 738 children were thus apprenticed.[100]

The parishes of St Giles and St George Bloomsbury, and of St Andrew's Holborn and St George the Martyr had rules for the inspection of apprentices whose masters lived within the Bills, and the two latter parishes had the same regulations for apprentices' fees as St James Westminster (both observing the Act of 1767).[101] The Foundling Hospital paid great attention at the end of the century to the apprenticing of girls to domestic service. They were bound to 'housekeepers' only – not to lodgers, and only after strict inquiry, and only to families where some domestic servant was kept, and, as a rule, to no family which let lodgings. During the term of apprenticeship boys were visited by the schoolmaster, girls by the matron.[102]

These changes, legislative and administrative, were the result of much melancholy experience, and of that growth of social compunction which characterizes the latter part of the eighteenth century. There had also been a change in opinion, closely inter-related with the growth of knowledge of social conditions. An early training in industrial work was no longer the ideal of the social reformer. The movement for industrial education characteristic of the late seventeenth and early eighteenth centuries had subsided. There was a new movement for general education, which began with the Sunday schools (that of Raikes at Gloucester in 1781 is generally said to be the first, though it had forerunners), was carried on by the Lancasterian Schools, and then by the so-called National Schools. The Governors of the Foundling Hospital found by experience that a superior kind of education (relatively speaking) secured a better start in life for a boy than an early training in some industrial occupation, though they were careful to limit this conclusion to the special case of London.

Different occupations and manufactures for the boys have been at times introduced into the Hospital [wrote Sir Thomas Bernard in 1798]. The last that has been tried with much effect and continuance has been the spinning of worsted yarn. It was however attended with this inconvenience, that the boys who had been so employed were not so much in request as apprentices, and were not placed out so speedily or so well as those whose writing, reading and accounts had been more attended to and who had been occasionally employed about the house and garden. . . . The situation in which boys are very frequently placed is with London shopkeepers, to whom their being able to read, write, and keep accounts is of considerable importance. . . . No profit being in general to be made from the labours of children before twelve or thirteen years of age which can compensate for their being less adapted at that period and during their future life for useful and active employment . . . the idea of manufactures for the occupation of boys has been, after some experience and consideration, given up at the Foundling Hospital.[102]

Such a point of view could hardly have been expressed in an appeal to the public on behalf of a charity in the early eighteenth century. The charity schools had to encounter not only the sort of criticism of which Mandeville is the best-known exponent, but the fear of the ratepaying artisan or petty trader that charity children would compete with their own in the skilled trades and in clerkships. In 1728 Dr Watts (who was in advance of his time in his views on education) states, and then answers, the stock objections to them.

But if these children of the poor . . . be trained up in reading, writing, and arithmetick, will not this render them qualified for clerkship or book-keeping, or any better sort of place or employment. . . ? And then they become competitors for such places with others of equal talents who have yet far better pretensions to them. The sons of tradesmen and mechanicks who have paid publick taxes and even may have given bread and clothes to the poor, their sons have a right to be employed in all these stations . . . wherein there is a prospect of advancement in life. . . .

Answer, . . . there are none of these poor who are, or ought to be, bred up to such an accomplished skill in writing and accompts as to be qualified for any of these posts, except here and there a single lad whose bright genius . . . and constant application . . . have outrun all his fellows.

The writer makes the usual defence for the education of the poor: they learn to read the Bible, and a little writing and ciphering in a servant is useful to his master and even serviceable to a day labourer.

Why then, [it is objected] are they not all made servants either to gentlemen, to farmers or to housekeepers, why are they not bred up all to the plough in the country, or to be mere labourers in the city, or confined to household services or menial offices of life? Why must any of them be placed out in a way of apprenticeship to trades and manufactures? Even this is a discouragement to those persons of a little higher rank. . . .

The writer says that this is done in many cases but defends 'some small provision' in London and great towns for binding boys 'to the poorer trades such as shoe-makers, taylors, watermen, gardeners, workmen in timber, iron, etc.', as being more laborious and more useful than domestic service.

The master workmen address themselves frequently to the managers of these schools. . . . Let it be observed that the children of every common tradesman are aspiring to better business: the working shops and stalls of these meanest mechanick artificers want more hands and seek for artificers. . . .[103]

It was agreed at the end of the century that opinion had changed, the opinion, that is, of the social reformer. (Needless to say there were many who were as much opposed as ever to the idea of the education of the poor.) To quote Sir Thomas Bernard:

The absurd prejudices that *have* existed against extending the common and general benefits of education to the poor, and the extraordinary supposition that an uneducated and neglected boy will produce a mature age of industry and virtue, are now in a great measure exploded. Switzerland and Scotland and the northern counties of England, where the education and occupation of youth are particularly attended to, afford very gratifying evidence of the contrary position. . . .[104]

General education and apprenticeship were regarded as alternatives. Playfair interpolated into the annotated edition of the *Wealth of Nations* – which he published in 1805 – an essay by himself in defence of apprenticeship.

To free youth from the shackles of apprenticeship and to subject infancy to the authority of schoolmasters [he writes] is the present bent of political economists, and the public leans to the same opinion. . . . Reading and writing make no essential part of education in the lower classes. . . . To follow industry and learn to live on their income and be attentive to their duty, constitute the principal part of education in all the inferior ranks.

But experience had shown that apprenticeship did not necessarily impart such an 'education'. The apprenticing of boys and girls to 'arts masters' (working craftsmen) in Bridewell Hospital was an Elizabethan device for the industrial training of poor children. It was supported by private bequests for setting up as masters the young men who had been apprenticed there. During the latter part of the eighteenth century the establishment was generally condemned. In 1765 a committee was appointed on account of the 'enormous misbehaviour of the boys'. Throughout the century the court books and minute books were 'crowded with bitter complaints against either the arts masters or the apprentices. The former were dissolute, negligent, disorderly and irregular, the latter were . . . riotous, turbulent and very rarely good citizens'. A committee in 1792 concluded its investigation into the careers of the boys bound in the last twenty-six years by saying:

. . . nothing can be more objectionable than the present very defective and expensive mode of educating a few boys, chiefly from the country, to inferior trades for no good purpose whatsoever, except it be praiseworthy to see those very boys become beadles or fire-porters or follow some mean occupation . . . soon after the usual gifts have been received.[105]

An attack was also made on the principle of apprenticing poor girls from charity schools to domestic service by Mrs Cappe, an active social reformer. About 1785 she began to take an interest in the management of the girls' charity school in York, known as the Gray Coat School, where the regulations were that on leaving the girls were to be bound for four years to domestic service. She found this 'a most ruinous practice', and in 1786 the ladies of the school committee made a formal protest:

The ladies hope it will not be proposed that the girls shall as heretofore be bound apprentices for their labour. The obedience of a young person in that situation is little better than the obedience of a slave, and whatever plea, in some parish instances, may be drawn from necessity, it is generally found to be a compact really hurtful to the disposition of both parties, and terminates not infrequently in the ruin of the child so bound. If a charity school merely keeps a girl a few years, and then places her out apprentice, it exactly does what the parish would have been obliged to do, and no good whatever results to the child from the institution.

As compared with the ideas that had governed the foundation of the early charity schools, this was a revolutionary point of view and the gentlemen of the committee disagreed. But Mrs Cappe's facts and her logic were convincing. The children of the school were found to be 'generally diseased both in body and mind, their appearance sickly and dejected, their ignorance extreme', and according to the new master and mistress, 'their depravity truly deplorable'. She found the children's faults 'all of that class which are the result of scanty fare and harsh treatment', and argued that persons applying for such girls would be in necessitous circumstances themselves. Investigations showed that these anticipations were more than justified.

It appeared that some of these poor girls had been seduced by their masters, that some had run away . . . (in either of which cases, forlorn and unprotected, they generally became the victims of prostitution) and that the health of the others, not good when they left the school, had been completely ruined by ill-usage. . . .

All these dangers were likely to be even worse for the London workhouse girl, bound till she was twenty-one. Internal reforms were instituted, and the girls when they left were found places for wages, instead of being apprenticed for their food and clothing. The plan was a great success.[106] 'It is well known,' wrote Mrs Cappe, 'that an apprentice for labour of either sex, seldom turns out well, whether bound by the parish or a charity school.'

The fact was notorious. Hogarth makes Tom Nero, in *The Four Stages of Cruelty*, a St Giles in the Fields charity-school boy. In 1800 Mrs Cappe published an account of her experiences in York as a protest against the apprenticeship of poor children. In the next year a terrible case which had occurred gave her a further opportunity. One

Jouveaux, a tambour-worker, employed seventeen parish apprentice girls, and had so cruelly ill-treated and starved them that five had died 'in a decline'. The girls worked at embroidery on muslin from four or five in the morning till eleven or twelve at night, sometimes till two in the morning, and sometimes all night. Their food was usually bread and water, sometimes a few potatoes, sometimes rice boiled in water without salt. It was brought to them to eat at their embroidery frames. The seventeen slept in a garret in three beds. When there was no work they had Sundays to themselves, otherwise they worked on Sunday. Jouveaux moved his establishment from Hackney to Stepney Green at four o'clock one morning, because the neighbours had called out 'shame'. The girls' shrieks had been heard, and they had been seen seeking in the hog-trough for food.[107]

Mrs Cappe pointed out that the cause of such treatment

... was in the very nature of the contract itself. ... Children bound for their labour, and more especially girls, whether by a charity school, by the Foundling Hospital or by their respective parishes, are always liable to be, and in fact generally are, in some respect or other unkindly if not cruelly treated. ... How much soever, by the adoption of wise and humane regulations, their situation may be ameliorated, ... while human nature and the state of society remain what it is at present, children so bound will be less likely to conduct themselves well, and must always be exposed to improper and unkind, if not very cruel treatment.[108]

Yet, just at the time when social reformers, governors and directors of the poor, and even vestries had become aware of the dangers of apprenticeship, when the better-managed parishes were giving special care to the binding out of poor children, the greatest scandal in the history of poor-law apprenticeship arose, the wholesale carting of children from the London workhouses to the cotton mills of the north. What is the explanation of this?

Child labour in manufacturing processes was not new. Defoe in 1726 found with admiration in Halifax (as in Norfolk) 'hardly anything above four years but its hands [were] sufficient to itself'.[109] In 1712 (and probably long before) parish children were employed to turn the wheels in the sheds of the gold and silver thread-spinners of Cripplegate.[110] In 1764, in a petition for a Bill to incorporate a manufactory of cambrics and lawns at Winchelsea, it was stated

... that from the number of children they intend to take as apprentices from the Foundling Hospital, workhouses and other places where they can be got, they shall be able in three or four years to afford this manufacture at so low a rate that it will not be worth while for the French to smuggle in their cambricks.[111]

Children had long been employed, not only in their own homes but in the cloth mills of the south-west[112] and in the silk mills of Derby and Macclesfield and elsewhere.[113] But these children had for the most part lived in the district. When cotton mills were built far from towns for the sake of water-power, the wretched children were brought from a distance wholesale, and housed by their employers. At the same time, owing to the lessened death-rate among London parish children, and to the measures taken by the parishes to prevent vagrancy by housing deserted children in the workhouse, there were numbers of children to be provided for. This was a new problem: Hanway had complained in the fifties and sixties that few parish infants lived to be apprenticed.

However, though we might have expected to find children from the crowded workhouses of East London parishes, and from the poorhouses at Hoxton and Mile End where the little City parishes farmed out their poor, sent to the north, it is a shock to find St George's Hanover Square and St James Westminster, which undoubtedly gave real consideration to the fate of their children, among the London parishes sending apprentices to cotton mills. The explanation probably is that they thus disposed of the children for whom they found it impossible to get individual masters. The Directors and Governors of the Poor of these parishes would never have accepted the hawkers and milk-sellers, far less the chimney-sweepers, to whom some parish children were apprenticed. Respectable masters could apparently be found for the children who had been brought up, first on Wimbledon Common, and then at the St James' School of Industry in King Street. But there were also children in the parish workhouse, the vagrant children from the streets, and the children of those who spent recurrent periods in the workhouse, and went out in the summer for fruit-picking or tramping. Many children must have been sickly and ill-grown. For those for whom suitable masters or mistresses could not be found, the alternative presented itself of sending them wholesale to the manufacturing districts.

There is more than presumptive evidence for this. The Orphan

Asylum apprenticed girls to trades who from 'bodily infirmity' were unfit for domestic service.[114] The Quakers' School and Workhouse at Clerkenwell had similar rules.[115] The Foundling Hospital sent to a cotton mill the girls who were unsuccessful as domestic servants.

When any of our girls from the Hospital fail in their duties during their apprenticeships, we apprentice them to Mr Oldbarrow, a cotton-spinner at Mellor . . . and in upwards of fifty cases, Mr Oldbarrow has succeeded in making them useful members of society, in fact, he has never failed.[116]

In the ten years from 1802 to 1811, 5,815 children had been apprenticed by parishes within the Bills of Mortality. Of these, 2,026 (1,018 boys and 1,008 girls) had been bound to masters at a distance from London, chiefly to textile manufacturers. Of the remainder (2,428 boys and 1,361 girls), 428 had been bound 'to the sea-service', a term which included bindings to watermen, lightermen and fishermen, 528 to 'household employments' and 1,772 to 'various trades and professions'. There was a greater proportion of younger than of older children as well as of girls than of boys among those sent to the north, than among those bound in the neighbourhood of London. Among the former, children had 'not infrequently been taken back to their parents . . . and in several instances after the children have been taken into the country, they have been returned to their parish in consequence of the surgeon having pronounced them unfit'.[117] Many of the apprentices in the cotton trade, according to a protest of mill-owners against Peel's Act, 'being procured from poorhouses in London', were 'composed of the children of beggars, chimney-sweepers and others accustomed to live in total idleness and not infrequently addicted to stealing, swearing and other vices'.[118]

There were parishes within the Bills which in 1811 had not sent children to the manufacturing districts. These were Newington, Shadwell, Islington and 'some others'.[117] The reason probably was that there were industrial openings in those neighbourhoods. In Southwark, only the parish of St George had sent any considerable number, perhaps because there was a stocking-weaving establishment in Lambeth where (in 1795) sixty or seventy boy apprentices, chiefly from the Surrey workhouses, were employed.[119]

The fact that it was on the whole the weaker and younger children who were sent to the factories only makes their fate the harder, but the lot of these victims of poverty and bad nurture would probably have been at least equally wretched if they had been bound to individual masters or mistresses within the Bills. Wholesale parish apprenticeship to cotton mills was perhaps almost as much due to the anxiety of the parish officers to dispose of children as to that of the manufacturers to employ them. In 1811 when a Bill was brought in to forbid the binding of parish apprentices more than a certain distance from their parents, it was opposed by some of the London parishes as 'taking from them the means of disposing of the children of the poor belonging to them in the manner in which they had been accustomed to do'.[117] In 1817 the vestry-clerk of St George's Hanover Square gave evidence that the parish had formerly sent children to the factories, but that this had ceased since the Act [1816]: 'We cannot dispose of our children now, there will be more of them kept in the workhouse and brought up in the workhouse to be men and women.'[120] And it had been realized that the workhouse could not be that school of all the virtues which the early enthusiasts had expected. 'When they become the receptacles of youth,' said Sir Thomas Bernard in 1805, 'they destroy the hope of the succeeding generation. . . .'[121]

A public outcry arose against the practice of sending batches of parish children wholesale to the manufacturing districts because the new philanthropy found it intolerable and disgraceful. The old philanthropy was of a harsher kind, dominated by fears of starvation and vagrancy. Its ideal was the child who was self-supporting and inured to labour at the earliest possible age. It would probably have found the sight of hundreds of little creatures tying threads in a mill an edifying spectacle, and have seen in them objects preserved from the moral dangers of the London streets and from the iniquities of the Black Guard. The change in point of view is as remarkable as in the case of the slave trade. The old philanthropy, inherited by the early eighteenth century from the seventeenth, was the outcome of the social conditions of the time and of the generally accepted fact that the earnings of the labouring man and his wife were not enough to support a number of young children.[122]

The attack on sending children to the factories was largely based on the supposition that they were injured by being sent to a distance from

their parents. Earlier in the century it had been assumed even by philanthropists that parish children in general had been thrown irrevocably on
the parish, that they were orphans, or illegitimate children or foundlings
handed over to the parish, or deserted children, or that in any case
parental responsibility was at an end. In the middle of the century it
had been proposed to provide for all the 'infant poor' as foundlings by
sending them to the Foundling Hospital. It appears that the Foundling
Hospital itself in its early days aimed at sending the girls to be employed
in textile industries in the provinces. The intention seems to have been
to give the children some industrial occupation before they were old
enough to be apprenticed.

It will be extremely proper [says the regulation] to send out little colonies
of them, the boys to be employed in the manner before mentioned, in making
nets, thread, and small cordage under proper masters, at or near Yarmouth,
Lynn, Liverpool, Hull, etc., and the girls to Manchester, Nottingham, Brain-
tree, Devizes, etc., by which means the good effects of the charity will be more
visible, the money collected for their support more diffused, and the masters
and mistresses will be more readily and easily supplied with children than
they would be if they were to send to London.[123]

Nothing seems to have come of this plan, but in 1791 the united
parishes of St Andrew's Holborn and St George (Hanway's own parish
and a well-managed one) were paying 2s. a week each for fifty children
at silk mills.[101] Hanway said in 1767: 'I would keep no parish children
in great cities, they are wanted only for domestic service but become
less capable of laborious offices and less useful through their whole
lives.'[124] And in 1775 he urged the systematic transportation of parish
children to the country as a relief to overcrowded London:

The towns and villages of England send at least six thousand persons
annually to London. . . . We receive these supplies without making any
returns in kind, when it would be easy to transplant at least fifteen hundred
to two thousand parish pauper children yearly. If proper encouragement were
given to the capacities of our farmers, cottagers, manufacturers, and rural
mechanics to take charge of the overflowings of these monstrous cities we
need not send people abroad wantonly as if the labouring poor were of no
use at home.[125]

If we go back earlier still, we find the City of London disposing of
one hundred unwanted boys and girls by sending them as indentured

servants to Virginia. Though the step was more drastic, the motives were much the same as in the case of the children sent to cotton mills: to get rid of a burden, to supply the planters with the labour they needed – the Corporation being directly interested in the prosperity of the Virginia Company – and to 'discipline' the children. 'Some of the ill-disposed children,' they say in an appeal to the Privy Council, 'who under severe masters in Virginia, may be brought to goodness, and of whom the City is especially desirous of being disburdened, declare their unwillingness to go.'[126] This difficulty was overcome, and the City was able to deliver the children to the Virginia Company to be transported against their will.

The case of the cotton manufacturers, specious and self-condemned, as it seemed even in 1805, would have been generally approved fifty years earlier:

To children left upon parishes in general, and to the immense number with which the poorhouses in London are crowded, who from their vicious habits are unfit to be placed in private families, cotton mills and factories under proper regulations open a most desirable asylum, as the children are not only taught a trade by which they can at all times earn a livelihood, but under humane masters, they receive a considerable portion of religious and other education.

They urged the repeal of the Act of 1802 as

... necessary to the future success of a great number of persons embarked upon the manufacturing and spinning of cotton, who have not only contributed largely to the public revenue, but have at a heavy expense trained them up in the habits of industry and religion and rendered them (before a load upon society) now some of its most useful members.[118]

No one could read through the records of the Middlesex Sessions and of the Old Bailey in the eighteenth century and feel that the fate of the children in cotton mills, hard as it was, was worse than that of innumerable apprentices bound by parishes, by charities, by their parents, and sometimes by themselves. William Hutton saw in the newer mills an improvement on the state of things in the Derby silk mill of his youth. He describes how he was apprenticed to the mill by his parents in 1730 at the age of seven: 'Out of three hundred persons employed, I was by far the least and the youngest. . . . The confinement and labour were no burden, but the severity was intolerable, the marks of which . . . I shall carry to the grave.'[127] But, he explains in 1791, this account of his ill-treatment does not refer to the last fifty years: 'the erection of other mills has given a choice of place, and humanity has introduced a kinder treatment'.[128] Peel denied in the House of Commons that abuses were at their worst in large establishments, where, he said, 'it was to the interest of the masters to derive benefit from the labours of the apprentices, rather than to destroy them, as they had received them without a premium' – another member having said that the murder of apprentices by their masters was not infrequent, and instanced a case in 1787 of a baker who had shut a girl up in a heated oven.[129]

There were many evils in the apprenticeship system; the lot of the poor child apprenticed for his labour was often peculiarly unfortunate, and among poor children in general, the parish child had special disadvantages. His long term of servitude (before 1767) had deplorable results, and, with the best will in the world it was difficult to find a satisfactory master for the child from the workhouse or the London streets. As time went on however, his relative disadvantages grew less. Well-managed parishes and charitable institutions, such as the Foundling Hospital, whose children were by law apprenticed under the same regulations as parish children, or the Orphan Asylum, by giving a comparatively superior education, and paying special attention to the choice of a master, visiting the apprentice from time to time, and withholding part of the fee as an inducement to good treatment, had improved the lot of a certain number of poor children.

The repeal in 1814 of the Statute of Apprentices (1563), making seven years' apprenticeship compulsory, did not affect apprenticeship under the poor law, which lingered on till 1844. Indeed it was in a great measure parish apprenticeship which kept the old indoor apprenticeship system (in its least satisfactory form) crystallized in a modern environment. In spite of statutory safeguards the dangers due to barbarous and autocratic masters and mistresses could not be eliminated. One of the late degenerate descendants of the old London ballads, bought by Francis Place as a curiosity, purports to be the last dying speech (with embellishments) of Esther Hilmer, a tambour worker, executed in 1829 for the murder of a parish apprentice girl aged ten, whom she had starved and beaten. Out of seven parish girls bound to this woman, three had died:

> Since Mother Brownrigg's ancient doom,
>   Now sixty years and more,
> Such treatment to poor infants
>   Was never heard before[130]

it ran, untruthfully.

About two hundred years before, the ballad 'The cryes of the Dead', had related 'the late murther in South-warke, committed by one Richard Price, Weaver, who most unhumanly tormented to death a boy of thirteene yeares old, with two others before, which he brought to untimely ends. . . .'

> Many poore Prentisses
>   to himselfe did he bind,
> Sweete gentle children all
>   of a most willing mind:
> Seruing him carefully
>   in this his weauing art
> Whome he requited still
>   with a most cruel heart.[131]

Some of the evils of parish apprenticeship were inherent in the apprenticeship system, others were due to the law of settlement and the shortcomings of the overseer. Before 1815, temporary periods of depression apart, the evils had been to some extent mitigated by the demand for labour which modified the effects of the competition of the apprentice with the artisan or labourer. The depression of trade after the peace of 1815 added new evils. It became difficult to get employment for boys either as apprentices or for wages; parishes competed for masters and offered higher and higher fees in the attempt to get boys off their hands; independent workmen found it difficult to compete, and this was a great inducement to them to get their children into the workhouse, that they might be apprenticed by the parish.[132] However, there was some lessening of the old hardships. The custom of sending children to distant factories had been checked by the refusal of magistrates to sign indentures, as well as by the shifting of factories to towns with the change from water-power to steam. This shows that the supervision of magistrates had become effective, and one may suppose that apprenticeship to grossly unsuitable people, such as street sellers, had been stopped – as indeed one would conclude from the difficulty of finding masters and mistresses.

The Poor Law Commissioners of 1832 found that the evidence collected for them relating to apprenticeship was insufficient to justify 'the abolition of a mode of relief expressly pointed out by the 43rd of Elizabeth, and so much interwoven with the habits of the people in many districts'. The evidence, however, revealed the old evils, modified by the readiness of magistrates to listen to complaints on the part of apprentices, and by a refusal of some of them to sanction indentures to which masters, parents, and child, were not willing parties. 'The premium which is given with children . . . holds out a temptation to the needy to take them only to starve and neglect them.'

The immediate interest of the parish is to relieve themselves of their charge . . . they care little therefore for their prospects in after life and, which is of great importance, they are indifferent to the general consequences of bringing them up to trades already overstocked.[133]

Though the Commissioners of 1832 considered the evidence inconclusive, the Commissioners under the new poor law were explicit. They condemned the old compulsory billeting-out system, they condemned the more general premium system as

. . . having chiefly formed an inducement to persons of narrow means to whom the premium itself was exceedingly desirable as a means of escape from some temporary pressure and who took the children without having any great need of their services, or without the parish having any great regard to the means which these persons enjoyed of promoting the welfare of the children by carefully training them in a trade . . . so that a very large proportion of the children became dependent upon the parish to which they were apprenticed. One of the most prominent evils of the system, and which led to a large amount of chicanery in practice, was that this dependence upon the parish to which they had belonged, ceased by their obtaining a new settlement.[134]

The phraseology has changed in a hundred years, but the results of the system are much the same.

From an educational standpoint the Commissioners also condemned it. 'I conceive,' said Dr Kay, 'that the necessity for adopting the system of apprenticeship which led to so many pernicious consequences arose out of the absence of a proper place of industrial training in the work-

houses of the old corporations, and in the parochial workhouses.'[135]
The apprenticeship of parish children is, of course, much older than the
general establishment of workhouses. In its origin it was an Elizabethan
device by which the poor man's son was to be maintained, controlled,
and employed (without payment), in labouring or menial work till the
age of twenty-four, by one of the ratepayers of his parish. It was the
device of a poor community in which the traditions of villeinage were
not extinct, and it dates from a time when industrial and commercial
apprenticeship was the privilege of those of a superior status. It survived
(except for the age-limit) almost in its primitive form till nearly the
middle of the nineteenth century in districts where farmers found it a
convenient way of getting cheap labour. But in many places, and especially in the neighbourhood of London, some industrial occupation
soon became almost a necessity, and under the influence of the law of
settlement, parish apprenticeship approximated more and more to the
ordinary industrial apprenticeship of the poorest sort of child.

'Apprenticeship for labour' lent itself to all the ills that are connected with child labour and with sweating in an extreme form, with
this added evil that the apprentice was dependent on his master for all
the necessities of life, and was, in an immense number of cases, starved,
ill-clad, and ill-treated. And in proportion as the apprentice was
younger, feebler, less useful, and generally less desirable as the inmate
of a household, the worse master or mistress was he likely to get, while,
the fee once secured, he was apt to be regarded as an intolerable nuisance. On the other hand, some parish children were undoubtedly bound
to trades at which they were afterwards able to earn a living and do well,
and, in proportion as parishes and charities learnt the necessity of care
in the choice of a master or mistress, and of some supervision during the
term of servitude, the number must have increased.

One of the worst results of apprenticeship in general was that it threw
upon the world many runaway apprentices, and many apprentices
whose masters had disappeared or gone under. The poor children bound
to cotton-spinners were sometimes turned adrift in hundreds on the
bankruptcy of their masters. Children bound in London (as elsewhere)
ran away, or were left derelict in numbers. Apprentices who were sent
to a house of correction for being 'idle and disorderly' were almost
inevitably ruined by being thrown into the society of prostitutes and

vagabonds. Many apprentices wronged by their masters had not the conscious rectitude to support a formal complaint or appeal, and indeed those who appealed to a justice were often barbarously used for having dared to complain; the path of least resistance was to run away, and runaway apprentices were one of the chief sources of recruitment for vagrants and juvenile offenders. In a classification of 'juvenile delinquents' in London made in 1822, the seventh and worst class consists of 'boys who live with prostitutes, and subsist by housebreaking, etc.'. These were found to be 'mostly parish apprentices' with some 'respectably connected and refractory apprentices'.[136] There can be little doubt that this was at least equally true in the eighteenth century.

The movement for the protection of poor apprentices from ill-treatment was one of the earliest manifestations of the growing spirit of humanity. Acts of Parliament, individual magistrates and directors of the poor, an increasing dislike of harshness to children, undoubtedly did a great deal for some of the poor apprentices of London, but, as Mrs Cappe pointed out, the system inevitably encouraged ill-treatment. From the Middlesex Sessions records between 1700 and 1815, it is clear that the treatment complained of tended to become less violently brutal. There was a change in the attitude towards physical punishment of great importance to the apprentice complaining of 'immoderate correction', which in the earlier part of the century seems to mean manifest danger to life or limb.[137]

The movement of protest against the apprenticeship of children in cotton mills is significant of a further stage in the development of the sense of social responsibility, and is something more than an attempt to protect individuals from ill-treatment. It seems to date from the resolution of the Manchester justices in 1784, to refuse to sanction indentures of parish apprentices 'whereby they are bound to owners of cotton mills, and other works in which children are obliged to work in the night, or more than ten hours in the day'.[117] The evils complained of were not new, any more than the horrors of the slave trade were new when Clarkson began his campaign. Many generations of children had suffered hardships in silk mills which to Hutton seemed far worse than those endured in the newer and (in his opinion) more humanely regulated mills. The movement gathered force from many directions, and is significant of social changes. In London, the protest was against sending children out of reach of their parents, or of the inspection of parish officers, a point of view which in the sixties was outside the range of even the tender-hearted Hanway, though it was anticipated by Sir John Fielding; this shows how much times had changed since the wholesale abandonment of infants by desertion, exposure, and 'saddling the spit' was a dominant fact in the economy of London parishes. Moreover, 'the public mind', as Playfair complained, was turning towards a general education as the best introduction to life, rather than to the 'inuring to labour' of very young children which had been the ideal of an earlier generation. The country had become richer and labour more productive, toiling children no longer seemed the best safeguard against poverty and vagrancy. On the other hand, by the use of machinery these little apprentices had become so obviously profitable to the mill-owners that the children were seen as victims of industrial greed. Thus the movement for the protection of parish apprentices gradually merged into a protest against the employment of young children at all.

In all probability the evils of factory apprenticeship did not equal – they certainly could not have surpassed – the evils of apprenticeship to scattered masters and mistresses in the London district. The children who were sent to the north were those who would inevitably have gone to the worst surroundings nearer home. In the factories, however, the misery was concentrated and brought to light, remedies were seen to be possible, and a new phase in the history of the protection of children began, a phase which belongs to the nineteenth, not to the eighteenth century.

CHAPTER 6

THE UNCERTAINTIES OF LIFE
AND TRADE

Here malice, rapine, accident, conspire,
And now a rabble rages, now a fire;
Their ambush here relentless ruffians lay,
And here the fell attorney prowls for prey;
Here falling houses thunder on your head,
And here a female atheist talks you dead.

Johnson, *London* (1738)

THE dominating impression of life in eighteenth-century London, from the standpoint of the individual, is one of uncertainty and insecurity. It was a time when trade was expanding more rapidly than population, yet the Londoner was threatened with casualties of various kinds. During the hundred and twenty years between 1695 and 1815 England was at war for sixty-three years, at peace for fifty-seven, and she repeatedly underwent dislocating transitions from peace to war, and war to peace. On the whole (subject to much occasional distress), trade boomed in time of war and peace brought a corresponding depression and much misery – the jails and debtors' prisons were soon filled to overflowing. Walpole writes in January 1750: 'You will hear little news from England but of robberies, the numbers of disbanded soldiers and sailors have taken to the road, or rather to the street.'[1]

We have already seen how irregular was the work of the Spitalfields weaver. This was an extreme case, but irregularity was the rule in many London trades. Almost all were seasonal. Shipping, before the days of steam, besides its seasonal variations, was liable to sudden interruptions from contrary winds, sometimes the river was crowded, sometimes comparatively empty, and an enormous amount of labour, skilled and unskilled, was connected with shipping and the riverside. Even among customs officers, the lower grades were casual workers, 'glutmen' being taken on, to deal with sudden rushes of work.[2] This irregularity gave rise to much distress and much of what was then called depravity. A discouraging account of prospects in the house-painting trade in 1747 illustrates this:

There are a vast number of hands that follow this branch, as it may be learnt in a month, as well as in seven years: plaisterers, whitewashers, and everybody that can handle a brush now set up for house-painters. . . . There is not bread for one-third of them; and at all times in the City of London and suburbs, they are idle at least four or five months in the year. Their work begins in April or May, and continues till the return of the company to town in winter, when many of them are out of business. When they are employed they have in the longest days, half a crown, and some good hands three shillings, and in the shortest, two shillings a day, which, considering the time they are idle, is but a poor and precarious bread. . . . The journeymen of this branch are the dirtiest, laziest, and most debauched set of fellows in and about London.[3]

There were few trades which did not depend directly or indirectly on shipping or export, on building, or on the demands of the quality. The dead season was a serious thing when the world of fashion deserted London for four or five months at least, and the middle-class demand was comparatively undeveloped. The tailors for instance, in 1747, were said to be 'as numerous as locusts, out of business three or four months of the year, and generally as poor as rats'.[4] In 1834, Francis Place accounts for the fact that the wages of the London artisan had hardly fallen from the highest level reached during the war, by the seasonal character of London trades. 'In every London trade' – he has deleted the qualifying 'almost' – 'there is at least one period of the year when it is brisk, and another when it is slack; fluctuations at these times in the demand for labour are very great.'[5]

The reactions of these fluctuations in employment upon the little shopkeepers of London can be imagined. Under their influence even schoolmastering in its lower grades became a seasonal – and very un-certain – occupation. In many private-venture schools in London assistants were taken on to deal with a sudden influx of children (who paid perhaps threepence a week), and were dismissed as the pupils fell off, owing to the unemployment of their parents.[6]

It was a result of this state of things that earnings in London were often high, but nearly always uncertain, and this irregularity led to many other evils. The generally accepted point of view was that high wages were a direct cause of drunkenness and irregularity of work. 'Mr Fielding, and many others after him,' said Place,

... attributed the vices of the working people to the introduction of luxuries among them, but in this they were greatly mistaken. He saw that in very many cases the working people got drunk and were more dissolute in proportion to the ... wages they were able to earn. Hence he became an advocate for low wages. . . . It is, however, true that higher wages would have been very mischievous in the then state of society, in the state of ignorance in which the people were, a love of distinction can scarcely be said to have had any existence among them, and the more money they got, the more dissolute they would have been.[7]

And again he wrote in 1834, 'forty years ago the working people, with very few exceptions, were to a great extent drunken, dirty, immoral, and ignorant. He who was the best paid was the most dissolute. This is not so now, the case with few exceptions is reversed, the exceptions are happily on the other side'.[8]

High wages are rather to be regarded as a means than a cause of idleness and drunkenness, and even in 'the then state of society' they contributed to the general and increasing prosperity of trade which helps to explain the progressive diminution of social evils. Defoe was in advance of his time in seeing the advantages of high wages. The high price of labour he calls

... the vast hinge on which the wealth of the nation turns, and ... it cannot be the interest of England to reduce it. First ... the poor are enabled to live in a posture equal to the middling tradesmen in other countries; that many of them do not, is owing to the luxury and extravagance of our people. ... To reduce these wages just sufficient for life would be a diminishing the publick wealth to a degree inexpressible, and robbing England of the peculiar, which is her honour, that her poor live better than in any other part of the world.[9]

That was written in 1705; twenty-one years later, he says,

... the working manufacturing people of England ... make better wages of their work, and spend more of the money upon their backs and bellies, than in any other country. This expense of the poor ... causes a prodigious consumption both of the provisions and of the manufactures ... of our country at home and this creates what we call inland trade.[10]

'Luxury and extravagance,' manifested chiefly in excessive drinking and a passion for gambling, were common to all classes; there is no need to explain them by high wages; temptations to drink and gamble were interwoven with the fabric of society to an astonishing extent, and they did undoubtedly combine with the uncertainties of life and trade to produce that sense of instability, of liability to sudden ruin, which runs through so much eighteenth-century literature. The 'decayed housekeeper' meets one at every turn in the poor-law records; the debtors' prison and the sponging-house play a large part both in fiction and biography. Francis Place had little sympathy with the tavern-haunting, club-going, gambling London tradesman of the eighteenth century. His own early experience, both as an apprentice and in his own family, was unfortunate, but he repeatedly asserts that ruin through idleness and extravagance was the rule rather than the exception in the London of his youth. He describes old Joe France, the breeches-maker to whom he was apprenticed, as a typical London tradesman. 'He had done what is called a good business and might have saved money, but to do so was then the exception with common tradesmen.' His daughters were disreputable, his sons were thieves, the eldest 'a first-rate genteel pick-pocket' working at his trade as a blind. He lived in Bell Yard, Temple Bar,

... as perfect a sample of second-rate tradesmen's families as any place could be. ... It was inhabited by many men whose businesses were such as would have enabled them to bring up their families respectably and to put them out in the world with fair chances of success, yet scarce anyone did half as much as he might have done, and nearly all did the contrary. ... The same may be said of Fleet Street, and the Strand, and indeed of every part of the metropolis. In my time most of the youths were loose characters. Some families in the neighbourhood were even more disreputable than that of old Joe France. ... It must not be concluded ... that many families were not highly respectable in every sense of the word, but the number ... was small indeed in comparison with families now living in the same places, and in similar circumstances.[11]

Place gives a melancholy list of men with good businesses who became destitute through dissipation and gambling, especially in the State Lottery. In fact a large part of his early acquaintances seem to have ended their days in the workhouse or as street beggars. After describing some outstanding cases, he goes on,

I have a list of twenty-seven more, all of whom frequented my father's house [the King's Arms]. Every one ... might have lived genteelly and brought up their families respectably and placed them out in the world comfortably, but it was not the custom of the time to do so, and the result was inevitable ruin.[11]

He is speaking of things within his memory – that is of the London of the eighties and later, when conditions and manners had already improved. What were the customs that brought disaster to so many families?

London life centred round the tavern, the alehouse, and the club. Place says:

It was the custom at this time, as it had long been, for almost every man who had the means to spend his evening at some public-house or tavern or other place of public entertainment. Almost every public-house had a parlour . . . for the better class of customer.

In these rooms clubs had their meeting-places. His father when a Marshalsea Court officer and sponging-house keeper belonged to the 'House of Lords', held at the Three Herrings in Bell Yard, and frequented 'by the more dissolute sort of barristers, attorneys, and tradesmen of what were then called the better sort, but no one who wore a decent coat was excluded'. Place's father afterwards kept a public-house, and in this several clubs met. A punch club of about thirty members met every Monday evening at eight, and 'terminated when all the members were drunk', which usually happened between 12 and 2 a.m. There were about thirty members who paid a shilling a night whether present or absent. Two lottery clubs also met there weekly, each member paying a weekly sum towards buying lottery tickets, and sixpence for drink. A cutter club of lads who had a boat on the river was also held there.[11]

Such clubs differed only by the difference in the character of the members from The (Literary) Club and the other clubs beloved by Johnson. All classes frequented clubs in tavern parlours or in alehouses, according to their social status. The bond of union was as varied as the interests of their members. It might be mutual assistance or a common occupation, as in box clubs and trade clubs, or an interest in science or medicine, or in bull-baiting, or mere conviviality. There were spouting clubs where apprentices and others met to indulge a taste for public speaking.[12] There were cock and hen clubs where youths and prostitutes met to drink and sing songs, and chair clubs, so called because one of the company took the chair, which were often very disorderly gatherings in disreputable alehouses.

These clubs reflect the easy-going conviviality of the age, and also the darker side of London life. Brasbridge, who set up as a silversmith in 1770, published an account of his life in 1824, under the title of *Fruits of Experience*, as a warning against the neglect of business for the club and the tavern.

I divided my time [he says] between the tavern club, the card-party, the hunt, the fight, and left my shop to be looked after by others, while I decided on the respective merits of Humphries and Mendoza, Johnson, and Big Ben. Every idle sight, in short, was sure to have me for a spectator.

Then he enumerates his clubs:

... the Highflyer Club held at the Turf coffee-house, and so called in compliment to Mr Tattersall of Highflyer Hall ... the card club at the Crown and Rolls in Chancery Lane. .... I also spent my evenings at the Globe Tavern in Fleet Street. .... I likewise belonged to a sixpenny card club at the Queen's Arms in St Paul's Churchyard. .... Another place which I used to frequent ocassionally was the Cider Cellar in Maiden Lane. It was famous for its political debates and arguments. .... The Free and Easy under the Rose was another Society to which I belonged. It was founded sixty years ago at the Queen's Arms in St Paul's Churchyard. .... It consisted of some thousand members, and I never heard of any of them that incurred any serious punishment.

Place comments on this, and contrasts with it the Spread Eagle in the Strand, a resort of young men after the theatre, whose landlord remarked that 'his was a very uncommon set of customers, for what with hangings, drownings, and sudden deaths, he had a change every six months'.[13] As a matter of fact, poor Brasbridge's clubs were by no means of the disreputable sort, and he owed his ruin to a trusting disposition, an untrustworthy apprentice, and an open-handed hospitality, as well as to neglect of business. To understand the value which the nineteenth century set on respectability, one should, like Place, have experienced the disastrous effects of the lack of it. Brasbridge quotes the remark of an old acquaintance: 'Ah, I knew him well, he went to the dogs, as did all the card-players and sitters-up.'

Place and Brasbridge describe the last phase of an old tradition. Chair clubs and cock and hen clubs survived into the nineteenth century, and something of the spirit of the eighteenth century lingered on in such places as the 'Coal Hole' (probably Thackeray's 'Cave of Harmony') and the Cider Cellars,[14] but lawyers and well-to-do tradesmen no longer habitually met in free-and-easies in tavern parlours. Place writes in 1824:

There are still cock and hen clubs . . . in the lowest and most disreputable neighbourhoods . . . attended mostly by young thieves. There are also some chair clubs attended almost wholly by labouring men. They are very different from those of former times: there is but little drunkenness, and the songs they sing do not go beyond an equivoque.[11]

To analyse the social causes which made going to the dogs or the workhouse so common a fate in the prosperous eighteenth century, we must go behind the drinking and gambling, and the vicious circle of insecurity which these produced. The obvious starting point is the early training of the young. Apprenticeship was an essential part of the fabric of society. Although it was breaking down in its more rigid interpretations, most London boys destined for industry or trade served a term of apprenticeship. Its social effects were all-important as it was the chief part of the education of a great part of the community.

At the beginning of the nineteenth century, when manners, morals, 'juvenile delinquency' and the causes of mendicity and crime in London first became the subject of serious inquiry and general attention, it was very generally agreed that the growing custom of taking out-door apprentices was one of the causes of a decay of discipline among young people. The chaplain of Bridewell said in 1815:

I should think there can be no doubt that the present system of taking apprentices and binding them out of doors where they are not under the eye of their master is very mischievous. I think a great proportion of the apprentices we receive are . . . out-door apprentices; it is a very common custom now.[15]

Evidence to the same effect was given to the Committee on Police in 1816 – out-door apprentices, a recent development, were very disorderly.[16] Mr Thomas Chapman in his evidence to the Police Committee of 1828 is more explicit in considering out-door apprenticeship a fruitful source of crime. About 1762 he served his apprenticeship to

Strachan, the King's printer; the house was well regulated, and there were twelve young persons besides himself.

About ten years after . . . a very fatal and unhappy practice has taken place in London and Westminster and which has been followed up in the country of taking what is called out-door apprentices; it is the most destructive demoralizing thing that ever was introduced into the land. I have known in printing offices myself from that unhappy practice five out of a dozen that have been either hanged or transported: the fact is this, that at seven o'clock the business of the office ceases; they have to go home to their friends, maybe a mile or two miles off; there are a dozen of them together; you may easily imagine the consequences of these young lads being left upon the town. If there are one or two mischievous ones they corrupt the rest. 'At the time when you were an apprentice, all the apprentices were maintained in the house?' Yes, and hardly a disorderly character among them; now, if there are any bad characters among them it is among these apprentices.[17]

Strachan's printing-house must have been a very exceptional place, or else Mr Chapman's memory played him false. The weak point in this theory is that the journeymen printers of the early nineteenth century, the product of this degenerate kind of apprenticeship, were admittedly much improved in manners and sobriety, while apprentices were formerly, Place writes in 1828, 'much more vicious and profligate than they are now'.[18] Moreover, vagrants and juvenile delinquents were largely recruited from runaway apprentices, and especially parish apprentices, who of necessity lived under their master's roof.[19] (Place, however, disapproved of out-door apprenticeship.)[18] If out-door apprentices were unruly, so were indoor ones. Out-door apprenticeship seems indeed to have been a contracting out of some of the drawbacks of apprenticeship – the perpetual disputes over food and beds, and Sunday work, for instance. The theory that masters in general exercised a wholesome discipline over apprentices seems to have been theory only.

Do we not know [said Hanway in 1775] that there is but a small number of masters in these days who can or will keep their apprentices within doors in the evening when their shops are shut. How they go abroad without money, and how they get money is the dark and mysterious part of the story.[20]

Want of discipline in the young is one of those things which each generation in its turn asserts to be a new and dangerous development.

It is in the nature of boys to be disorderly, but there were many things in the old apprenticeship system which made natural disorderliness take a more serious turn.

The dangers of apprenticeship to the poor boy who was taken for the sake of his labour have already been discussed. Provided the master had not taken him for the sake of the fee and was able to maintain and employ him, it was to his interest that the boy should learn his trade and serve out his term, as the labour of the last years was the most valuable. In mercantile apprenticeship, and perhaps also in highly paid and exclusive crafts, the position was different. The boy was taken rather as a pupil than as a source of cheap labour. The tradition of the craft-guild and the City company was exclusiveness. The apprentice was apt to be regarded as his master's future rival – the more dangerous in that he could learn his master's trade secrets. Grosley, who visited London in 1765, explains the effects of this among London merchants and bankers of the first grade. These, he says, continued to take apprentices only when they could not avoid it, and then only some rich man's son with a fee of about £1,000. The lad 'either applies diligently to business or neglects it'. In the former case, the master argues,

... he will acquire a compleat knowledge of the state of my affairs, and when he has served out his apprenticeship he will avail himself of that knowledge to his own emolument and my prejudice. In the latter, I shall have a useless person in my house who will only disturb those that mind my affairs; [but, says Grosley] the merchants prefer the second case to the first, and for this reason do not require the apprentice to do any business, so that to the great satisfaction of his master, he spends his whole time in taking his pleasure.[21]

Thus the young man acquired idle habits, and probably fell a victim to the temptations of the town.

The master in a less outstanding position also dreaded rivals, and in his case there was the further temptation of the apprenticeship fee. This was used as working capital in his business, and if the boy could be got rid of by reason of his own misconduct, the master could keep the fee, avoid the expense of the boy's maintenance, and the trouble of teaching him, and escape the competition of a future rival. He might then take another apprentice and go through the same process again with profit to himself. A pamphlet of 1687 addressed to the judges describes this abuse as comparatively recent, but 'very common and notorious'.

It is certain and generally known to most men acquainted with the occurrences in this City of London, that of those youths who are daily put apprentices here, a very great number do miscarry, and never come to exercise the trades to which they were put. And of those, though many do miscarry through their own fault, yet that very many do miscarry either through the carelessness and negligence or the harshness and unreasonableness (or which too often happens) through the ill-designs and practices of their masters. This is so common and notorious that there is no part of the nation which hath not many examples of such unhappy young men, who might have been very useful in their generation, but by these means are driven into ill-courses, or become either altogether useless to the public and a burden to their relations. . . . These abuses . . . have not certainly been of long time practised, or however, not so notoriously and commonly, but have by degrees grown more frequent and notorious as the rates which have been given with apprentices have been raised, which have now within these twenty years . . . (or little more) risen to that height that may well prove a temptation to men who are continually employ'd in business for gain. . . . The master hath the use and benefit of the money all the while, which in many trades where the maintenance is of the best, is very considerable, 80 or 100l. and in some 200, 300, 400, and 500l. (for to such high rates are some now come).[22]

Ill-designs apart, the temptations of London were many and the unruly turbulence of apprentices was traditional. At its best, apprenticeship was an excellent commercial or industrial training, but it needed an exceptional master if not an exceptional boy. The most favourable conditions were when the apprentice became his master's journeyman and eventually inherited his business, either by marrying his master's widow, which seems to have been not unusual, or, with more romance, his daughter, like Hogarth's *Industrious Apprentice*. Place, describing his own apprenticeship, says that of twenty-one Fleet Street apprentices with whom he associated, only one besides himself – a man who married his master's daughter, was converted to Methodism and became a street preacher – made his way in the world respectably. He and his friends belonged to a cutter club: 'Our club was no better than many others; most of the members either robbed their masters or other persons to supply means for their extravagance.' Cox and stroke were both printers, out-door apprentices. Some years afterwards cox was transported for a robbery and stroke hung for a murder he did not commit; he could not prove an alibi 'being at the time committing a burglary with some of his associates'.[11]

London apprentice boys seem to have had no legitimate outlet for amusement and exercise; the ideal of the time was that they should be kept indoors in the evening. The cutter club was looked askance at. Sayer, the Bow Street officer, considered these clubs

... a great source of crimes ... there are more young men fall victims from that thing, than any one thing I know ... For instance I am an apprentice, and it is customary for many apprentices to raise money enough to buy a cutter; with this cutter they go up the river to Richmond or Kew, and they spend their two shillings or their crown piece or perhaps half a guinea. Those who cannot buy a boat, they go to Godfrey's and hire. . . . 40 or 50 of these boats go up . . . of a Sunday. These young men cannot support this expense and from that they commence thieves. It is this that hangs a number of young men, and so far it is the same as bull-baiting; for if by chance there should be a bull-baiting, they are sure to go to it.[23]

What wonder that the apprentices made themselves a nuisance in the streets? Place and his friends used

... to go to Temple Bar in the evening, set up a shouting and clear the pave-ment between that and Fleet Market of all the persons there. The boys all knew boxing, and if anyone resisted one or two would fall upon him and thresh him on the spot, nobody interfered. . . . This was one of their tricks, they played all sorts of blackguard tricks.[24]

Before Place's time things were much worse. It was usual for the boys of St Anne's parish to fight those of St Giles armed with sticks for 'a week or two before the holidays'. This fact survives, because in 1722 the captain of the boys of St Giles, a chimney-sweep aged twenty-one, was killed by another boy aged sixteen.[25] Earlier still, 'prentice riots were serious and frequent disturbances to the peace of London.

There was a theory that apprenticeship was valuable for the discipline imposed by the master and the training in the habits of a sober and industrious household. This was the ideal aimed at, and it corresponds with the indentures:

Taverns and alehouses he shall not haunt, at cards, dice, tables, or any other unlawful game he shall not play, matrimony he shall not contract, nor from the service of his said master day nor night absent himself. . . .

It may be doubted whether this sobriety of behaviour was ever general in London. In 1814 certain 'master manufacturers and tradesmen of Westminster' met to protest against the pending repeal of the Statute of Apprenticeship. Among the other advantages of the system, they alleged that 'youth become accustomed to subordination, imbibe domestic habits, and become well disposed to the Government by which they are protected'.[26] There is singularly little evidence of this. Colquhoun estimated in 1806 that there were seldom fewer than 150,000 youths in London 'bound to mechanical employments' and that, owing to the bad example of their masters in frequenting public-houses, this was 'a bad and immoral education'.[27] Neither social customs nor housing conditions made for 'domestic habits' among masters or apprentices.

The treatment of apprentices by their masters was apt to err from either an excess or a lack of discipline. As the eighteenth century was a stage in that decay of 'the Grand Law of Subordination' which has been going on in England since villeinage began to crumble, perhaps the lack of discipline was increasing. But what the result of this trend of the age may have been is another matter; a rigid discipline is often tempered with explosive reactions, and general lawlessness had been declining together with subordination. Generally speaking, it was the apprentice to a manual trade who was most likely to suffer from the almost unlimited authority given to the master, but on the other hand such a master was often unable to provide either work or maintenance, and the boy was therefore allowed to roam the streets to pick up a livelihood. Defoe's moral dialogues in the *Family Instructor* (1715), a popular little book, illustrate the theories and practice of the day with regard to apprenticeship from the educational point of view. The virtuous youth has a master who neglects the morals of his apprentices and omits to read family prayers. He says to his reprobate friend (bound to an exemplary master),

... we may run about where we will ... Sabbath day or any day or night. He never takes any thought for us, if we are but in the counting-house next morning when he wants us. .... I think my father has put me in the Devil's mouth and I am going the strait road to Hell. ....

The master, when the boy's father suggests to him that it is his duty to look after the morals and conduct of an apprentice, 'instructing him,

reproving him, restraining him, and if need be correcting him . . .'
answers,

. . . those things are out of doors long ago; do you think I'll trouble myself
with my apprentices at that rate? No, no, not I. I never struck a servant in my
life and if I should, who do you think would stay with me? Apprentices now-
adays are not like what they were when you and I were apprentices; now we
get a hundred pounds or two or three hundred pounds apiece with them;
they are too high for reproof or correction.

To his wife he remarks, 'youth are come to that pass, they will be under
no government now'. Discipline meant 'correction', and correction
meant corporal punishment. Theories as to the limits and merits of
corporal punishment were much modified in the course of the century.
　Sixty years later Hanway complains that

. . . there is scarce an apprentice boy turned fifteen years of age who, contrary
to the practice of our forefathers, is not suffered to go abroad almost as soon
as the shop is shut. These boys and young men challenge it as a kind of right,
and if the master is as dissipated as his servant, which is often the case, he
takes no thought till he finds himself robbed, which I believe happens much
more often than he discovers . . . many keep bad company, the society of
each other is dangerous . . . vice is costly, money must be supplied from what
quarter it may.[28]

That this is a true description of London apprenticeship can hardly be
doubted. Place said in 1835, 'the conduct of apprentices . . . was such
as can scarcely be believed without good evidence'.[24] As an apprentice
he went to cock and hen clubs and made the acquaintance of the lowest
grades of prostitutes who lived in Wapping and St Katherine's: 'I went
frequently among these girls – that is – I went with other lads . . . and
at that time spent many evenings at the dirty public-houses frequented
by them'.[29]

We were all sons of master tradesmen, or of persons of some consideration,
not sons of the very meanest of the people, yet among us this bad conduct
was suffered to exist unchecked, uncontrolled.[11]

Place was exceptional in not being ruined by such temptations; on the
contrary, his early experiences gave him a passion for reform and for
the education of the working people.
　Whether such customs were a new development, owing to an in-

creasing failure of masters to control their apprentices, may be doubted. An association between the women of the town and the apprentices whom they tempted to rob their masters is a London tradition.[30] There were temptations inherent in the very nature of the relationship in its most rigid as in its most relaxed form. The harsh discipline, the irresponsibility of the young man under his master's tutelage, dependent on him for all the necessaries of life, often unable to earn money legitimately on his own account,[31] would be likely to engender a desire to outwit his master and obtain pleasure and relaxation at all costs. Apprentices of the Restoration seem to have behaved much as Place and his companions did. We even hear of London apprentices having a 'club or general rendezvous' at a tavern as early as 1669, and going to it 'commonly every other night', a place where they had 'good wine and better company, being attended by two or three suburbian females who are the doxies of our comerades'.[32]

But such manners did not begin with the Restoration. *Barnewell, the London Apprentice*, the ballad on which Lillo based his play of the same name, was written before 1624, and we cannot suppose that the London of Nash and Greene was a decorous place. Chaucer's London apprentice of the fourteenth century behaves in much the same way as the black sheep of the seventeenth and eighteenth. He lives riotously, plays at dice and robs his master,

> At every bridal wolde he synge and hoppe,
> He lovèd bet the taverne than the shoppe.

The master for some time accepted this, although 'oftentyme he foond his box ful bare', but at length, lest he should corrupt the other servants, 'bad him go him with sorwe and with meschance'. Even the theory of the decay of discipline in the eighteenth century seems open to considerable doubt, and that of the deterioration of manners and morals is still more questionable.

On the other hand in Manchester in the early eighteenth century a state of things is described rather like the elusive conditions regretted by Defoe and others as those of the good old times in London.* Dr Aikin relates how apprentices to Manchester merchants 'were obliged

* They were perhaps to be found in London among the Quakers. See above, p. 206.

to undergo a vast deal of laborious work, such as turning warping mills, carrying goods through the streets on their shoulders and the like'. He describes how the master, his children and the apprentices were obliged to be in the warehouse at six in the morning before breakfast at seven, when each

... with a wooden spoon in his hand ... dipped into the same dish of oatmeal and water and thence into the milk pan. .... In George I's reign many country gentlemen began to send their sons apprentices to the Manchester manufacturers; but though the little country gentry did not then live in the luxurious way they have done since, the young men found it so different from home that they could not brook this treatment, and either got away before their time, or ... for the most part entered the army or went to sea. The little attention paid to rendering the evenings of apprentices agreeable at home, where they were considered rather as servants than as pupils, drove many of them to taverns, where they acquired habits of drinking that frequently proved injurious in after life.[33]

To return to the London apprentice. As we have seen, he had an almost unlimited freedom to spend his hours of leisure as he pleased, and the custom was for the elder apprentices at least to spend them, like their masters, at the alehouse or the tavern. This exemplifies the much complained of lack of discipline. The other extreme, the excess of it, is naturally not one of the current grievances of the time, but the long hours of work demanded of some of these boys may well have been partly responsible for the way in which they spent their leisure. The complaint book of the Chamberlain's office is illuminating. Apprenticeship to a freeman of London had certain safeguards which were absent in Middlesex, and it was free from the peculiar dangers attaching to parish apprenticeship and that of the poorest and most friendless children. Nevertheless, the rulings of the Chamberlain, supposed to be the guardian of the apprentices of London, show that the master, even at the end of the century (the records before 1786 are unfortunately burnt),[34] might make almost unlimited demands on the time and strength of the apprentice. In 1788, John Abraham, a printer, charged his apprentice with refusing to work after the usual time in the evening, and with using saucy and insolent language. Mr Chamberlain reprimanded the lad and ordered him home to his duty. In the same year William Green complained against his master, a barber, for refusing to let him go out on Sunday after working till one or two o'clock. Mr Chamberlain informed the lad he had no right to go out but when his master thought proper to give him leave, admonished him of his duty, and ordered him home to his master. A calenderer in 1791 complained against two apprentices for refusing to work on a Sunday when there was urgent necessity. They were both committed to Bridewell for three days. William Tomkins complained against his master, a silversmith, for beating him immoderately and making him work on Sundays till 11 at night. The master said the lad had behaved in a very insolent saucy manner which had provoked him to chastize him. Both parties were admonished (1791).[35]

The clause in the indentures forbidding the apprentice to absent himself from the service of his master made it possible to regard truancy as a serious offence. For instance, Edward Nairne, optician, complained against a boy for staying out two and a half hours when leave had been given for half an hour only, and the Chamberlain committed the culprit to Bridewell for three days. On the other hand, Valentine Townsend, accused by his master, a chair-maker, of 'neglect of business and disobedience, repeatedly going out without leave and coming home drunk and not earning near as much as he could', was only reprimanded and ordered home to his duty. The results of sending boys (and girls too) to Bridewell or to the county House of Correction, where they were not till the last quarter of the century (if then) kept apart from the prostitutes and vagrants who filled these places, may be imagined. Apprentices sent there were sure to be ruined said Ilive in 1757 from his own experience of Clerkenwell. 'It is of no other use than to swell the profits of the keeper and to benefit the tap.'[36] When an apprentice ran away, his natural resort was to sleep in an empty house, a market, or a brickfield or (if he had money) in a night-cellar or a common lodging-house. He was certain to meet boys who would tempt him to come with them and steal, and would blackmail him if he afterwards tried to get away from them.[37] Great temptations were held out to apprentices to pilfer. Not only the old-iron shops, but the green shops, the chandlers, and other petty traders dealt in old clothes and miscellaneous goods of all kinds and encouraged servants and apprentices to bring them stolen property.[38]

It was generally agreed that gambling, the club, the tavern, and the alehouse were responsible for bad masters and bad apprentices, resulting in bankruptcies, absconding debtors, runaway apprentices, and deserted children, and leading by an inevitable sequence to paupers, vagrants, and thieves. There was therefore a long series of attempts to prevent the meaner sort from playing at unlawful games and tippling in alehouses. Bacon says (in connexion with the statutes against vagrancy in the reign of Henry VII),

... there are ever coupled the punishment of vagabonds and the forbidding of dice, cards, and unlawful games unto servants and mean people, and the putting down and suppressing of alehouses, as strings of one root together, and as if one were unprofitable without the other.[39]

In the eighteenth century places of amusement multiplied and competed recklessly for custom.

Besides those great scenes of rendezvous where the noblemen and his taylor, the lady of quality and her tire-woman meet together and form one common assembly, what an immense variety of places have this town and neighbourhood set apart for the amusement of the lowest order of the people, and where the master of the house may be said to angle only in the kennels, where baiting with the vilest materials he catches only the thoughtless and the tasteless rabble.[40]

Fielding is expressing an ancient maxim with characteristic irony when he says,

... the business of the politician is only to prevent the contagion from spreading to the useful part of mankind ... and this is the business of persons of fashion and quality too, in order that the labour and industry of the rest may administer to their pleasures and furnish them with the means of luxury. To the upper part of mankind, time is an enemy and (as they themselves often confess) their chief labour is to kill it; whereas with the other, time and money are almost synonymous.[41]

As a matter of fact, the laws against tippling, playing unlawful games, and the like, had little effect. A somewhat stricter licensing policy in the second half of the century did something, and a gradual change of taste and fashion did more. The eighteenth-century attitude towards popular amusements was almost exactly the opposite of the modern one. It was assumed that they were necessarily connected with drinking to excess, and that they led to breaches of the peace and many social evils. The puritanic attitude towards popular amusements did not begin with either the Reformation or the Evangelicals, though these did their best to put in practice old maxims and to enforce old laws. Indeed, the recognition of the social value (apart from the military usefulness) of recreation seems first to have been realized in the later eighteenth century. The Marine Society learnt the necessity of providing an outlet for the boys in their ship-school, and arranged that they should play cricket.[42] Southey in 1807 (writing as a Spanish visitor to England) gives early expression to the more modern point of view:

They reproach the Catholic religion with the number of its holidays, never considering how the want of holidays breaks down and brutalizes the labouring class, and that where they occur seldom they are uniformly abused. Christmas, Easter, and Whitsuntide, the only seasons of festival in England are always devoted by artificers and the peasantry to riot and intoxication.[43]

Place regarded with disapproval even a family visit to a wells or tea-garden on Sunday.

It was my father's custom [he says] as it was that of a vast many others who were housekeepers, well-doing persons, and persons in business who ought ... to save money, to go to some public garden on a Sunday afternoon to drink tea, smoke, and indulge themselves with liquor. My father's principal place of resort was Bagnigge Wells, then standing in the fields.[11]

Hence we find the magistrates doing their best to put down not only gaming-houses, bull-baitings, and cock-fighting, but fairs, interludes, public shows, and minor theatres, and looking askance at wells and tea-gardens (some of which were certainly most undesirable places), while grand juries present them as nuisances. The attitude towards the amusements of the people is well illustrated by the opposition to various attempts to establish theatres in East London. In 1729 Thomas Odell opened a playhouse in Great Alie Street, Goodman's Fields. There was a clamour of protest. As the district was inhabited chiefly by working people, the theatre, it was maintained, would have 'very uncomfortable effects' upon their health, industry, and frugality.

Gentlemen who have no employment may sleep whole days and riot whole nights. ... Compare the life of a careful honest man who is industrious all day at his trade ... spends the evening in innocent mirth with his family, or perhaps with his neighbours or brother tradesmen; sometimes sits an hour or two at an alehouse, and from thence goes to bed by ten and is at work by five or six; compare this I say, with your mechanick of pleasure who is to frequent the theatre. . . . He must be a fine gentleman, leave his work at five at the farthest . . . that he may be drest and at the playhouse by six, where he continues till ten and then adjourns to a publick house with fellows as idle as himself.[44]

The Royalty Theatre opened near by in Well Close Square in the Tower Royalty by Palmer in 1785 was suppressed owing to the determination of the two patent theatres to preserve their monopoly, but petitions that it should be licensed and reopened roused the old protest that it would be fatal to industry and commerce.[45] It appears that brothels grew up round the theatres of East London as they did round Covent Garden. To quote the *Unviersal Spectator* in 1735: 'Whereas the street in which the theatre is built used formerly to be inhabited by silk-throwsters, ribbon-weavers, and others . . . now there is a bunch of grapes hanging at every door besides an adjacent bagnio or two.'[46] There was another place of entertainment in Goodman's Fields which shared the responsibility for the character of the neighbourhood, the Goodman's Fields New Wells opened in 1703. This, like Sadler's Wells and other similar places, was at various times complained of as a nuisance. The justices in 1751 found that 'plays, interludes, and other disorders', were often acted, the place being 'open to all persons to enter gratis . . . wine, punch, ale, and spirituous liquors being constantly sold at exorbitant prices, and there freely drunk during the said plays, interludes, etc.'.[47] Many complaints had been made against the Turk's Head bagnio in Ayloffe Street, and other notorious places in the neighbourhood. It was found that

. . . to the said plays and interludes great numbers of mean, idle, and disorderly people do commonly resort, and after the performance is over from thence go to the bawdy houses before mentioned, or to other houses of ill-fame near the said Wells or Playhouse, which the said justices apprehend are chiefly supported by the concourse of such idle and unwary people as the said plays draw together, greatly to the corruption of the morals of his majesty's subjects and the breach of the peace.

There was nothing new in this dread of the effects of theatres. The City had always been anxious to exclude them from her territory and they had been relegated to Southwark, like the stews and the bear-gardens, or had found shelter in the liberties of Blackfriars or Dorset gardens.

While English social reformers of a certain type deplored the breaking of the Sabbath and did their best to enforce the laws against Sunday trading, most foreign visitors saw in the dullness of the English Sunday one great cause of the drunkenness which was general on that day.

The law prohibits [said Archenholtz] on the only day on which the labourer and the tradesman can enjoy the open air and divert himself, all musick and dancing; so that the public gardens, the taverns, the bagnios and all public places, swarm with people, who without dancing, run to every sort of excess, to which that ridiculous law could not extend.[48]

Until lately [wrote Place in 1829] all the amusements of the working people of the metropolis were immediately connected with drinking – chair clubs, chanting clubs, lottery clubs, and every variety of club, intended for amusement were always held at public-houses. In these clubs every possible excitement to produce excess was contrived. These are nearly extinct. Then as to games of chance or dexterity, skittles, dutch-pins, bumble-puppy, drafts, dominoes, etc., were all provided by the publicans, and as these were the *only* amusements within reach of the working people, drinking was encouraged and promoted to a great extent, the money staked being always spent on liquor, or rather in the language of these places, the stake was either a pot of beer or a quartern of gin. . . . Drunkenness . . . was a common habit some fifty or sixty years ago, when all ranks got drunk. . . .[49]

It was not necessary to go to the alehouse for beer or gin as pot-boys kept workshops and dwelling-places supplied with liquors, and it was an even more serious danger that drinking customs were not only connected with amusements but were interwoven with everday life and work to an astonishing extent. The Hand-loom Commissioners discovered this in 1838, and described customs which were undoubtedly a legacy from the eighteenth century, probably from an earlier period. Drinking to excess, they found,

. . . common to all trades, and some more than others, only from peculiar circumstances connected with the mode of getting employment. It is extraordinary the number of drinking usages among the working classes to which custom has given the force of an irresistible law. It is to these usages, more than the temptation of liquor, that the sober and industrious are led imperceptibly to form habits of intemperance. Among the chief of these is the usage of exacting entry money or footing when a new journeyman enters a factory, or when a new apprentice is bound to a trade. The money thus raised is, with a few solitary exceptions, always spent in drink. . . . Shipwrights' apprentices pay a footing of £2 2s. and the penalty for non-payment is flogging with a hand-saw. . . . And besides these footings, fines are exacted from one another on all imaginable occasions that may furnish a fair pretext for raising drink money. . . . For a single individual to oppose himself to these customs is only to subject himself to serious annoyances and sometimes to personal injury.[50]

Benjamin Franklin made the attempt. In 1725 he worked in a London printing-house – Watts', near Lincoln's Inn Fields, where nearly fifty men were employed, a large establishment for the time. He was that (in those days) very exceptional thing, a water drinker, and after having paid his contribution in the press-room where he first worked he moved to the composing-room. Here a further contribution of 5s. was demanded and after resisting payment for two or three weeks he had to give in. Nevertheless, he established an ascendancy over the other compositors, as he induced them to alter their Chapel rules (the name at least a tradition from the days of Caxton), and many of them, he says, in the end followed his example and gave up 'their muddling breakfast of beer, and bread, and cheese, finding they could with me be supplied from a neighbouring house with a large porringer of hot-water gruel sprinkled with pepper, crumbled with bread, and a bit of butter in it for the price of a pint of beer, viz., three halfpence'. Franklin calls the other workmen 'great guzzlers of beer'. He says,

. . . we had an alehouse boy who attended always in the house to supply the workmen. My companion at press drank every day a pint before breakfast, a pint at breakfast . . . a pint between breakfast and dinner, a pint in the afternoon about 6 o'clock, and another pint when he had done his day's work . . . it was necessary he supposed to drink strong beer that he might be strong to labour.

In spite of Franklin's exhortations, 'he drank on . . . and had 4s. or 5s. to pay out of his wages every Saturday night for that muddling liquor. . . . And thus these poor devils keep themselves always under'.[51] Franklin's attitude towards strong beer was exceptional; not only gin, but tea was disapproved of, as interfering with its consumption.

The traditional rules of the London hat-makers or felt-makers as they existed at the beginning of the nineteenth century, have been described by one of their number:

When a young man came up to London and got employment for the first time, the first claim made upon him by his shopmates in his own department was 10s. for a 'maiden garnish'. All the men who partook of this paid their joinings ... a contribution of 3d. a head. Of course a good deal would depend upon the number ... who would partake of 'maiden garnish'. If the number was small, the inebriety would be large. A person ignorant of the way in which working men can inflict wrongs upon each other, would conclude that a new shopmate would be relieved from all further bacchanalian taxes. ... The payment of that 10s. was only the commencement of a series of financial inflictions. ... From these and a variety of other circumstances which I have not noticed, it was not surprising that the old felt-hatters were pro-verbial in their intemperate habits.[52]

These customs however, were slowly dying out with the better education and greater sobriety of the early nineteenth century – or at all events the huge quantities consumed in the good old days were reduced. In the case of the London journeymen coopers, the movement towards suppressing fines was connected with the development of a trade society. The fines as they existed in 1780, and probably long before, were many. On coming out of his time a young man had to pay, first, his footing, three gallons of beer, price 3s. 6d., then another gallon for each piece of work done for the first time, and an extra gallon for each different sort of timber used. Fines amounting to 16s. 4d. (to be spent on beer) were demanded, possibly in the course of a single week, for work done for which the payment was only 15s. 9d., and this was over and above both the footing and the timber fines. In 1787 the coopers raised a society but continued the fines. Owing to a defaulting treasurer this was short-lived. Another society was started in 1795 for the relief of old men in the trade and the fines were reduced to two gallons of beer. In 1821 the coopers established a 'union society' and did away with fines altogether.[53]

Whether such an order was altogether effective may be doubted. The extraordinary persistence of these old drinking customs in trades which kept their organization almost unchanged from the eighteenth century is seen in the case of the hatters and the West End tailors. Though the hatters had a 'strong and imperious' trade union which had 'abolished' fines, these fines still survived at the end of the nineteenth century. Maiden garnish was still paid for, while any offence against shop law was punished by 1s. 4d. for a gallon of beer, and 'joiners' added their twopence a piece. Among the tailors 'footing' was paid for, half a gallon of beer being provided by the newcomer, with subscriptions from those who wished to drink, and similar fines were paid for births, birthdays, marriage anniversaries, and the like.[54]

Drinking customs were also the rule for the initiation of the well-to-do youth into a trade or business. For instance an apprentice bound in 1785 to Thomas Evans, a wholesale London bookseller, was obliged to give an entertainment to his fellow-apprentices on returning from Stationers' Hall. A grand supper was provided: 'two immense bowls ... of negus and punch graced the head and foot of the table. . . . It occurred to me that great caution, a strong resolution and saying little among my noisy companions would alone save me from intoxication'.[55]

This custom of celebrating initiation into any new state of life was widespread. It is to be found in the 'garnish' extorted in prisons from newcomers to be spent on drink by their companions, and in the 'colt money' which was paid by the justices when they first took their seats on the Middlesex Bench. Moreover, as among the artisans, contributions were demanded at various stages of the justice's career. In 1722 it was unanimously agreed in a full meeting in Sessions of the gentlemen in the Commission of the Peace for Westminster that any justice who should 'acquire any title of honour or dignity, or be married, be desired by the Chairman ... to pay him one guinea each person, which money is to be applied by the Chairman in the same manner as the money called colt money is to be applied'.[56] A little later certain justices are deputed to take an account of the colt money, honour money and sockett money.

Then, for a large number of trades, the public-house was the recognized employment agency. There were houses of call in London for hatters, smiths, carpenters, weavers, boot- and shoe-makers, metalworkers, bakers, tailors, plumbers, painters and glaziers, and bookbinders,[57] and others. They were probably often kept by members of the trade concerned, retired or otherwise. For instance, in 1732, William Glover, a hat-maker, says that he keeps a public-house 'where journeymen often resort to him in order to get work in the hat-making trade, he being one that helps journeymen to work in that

business. . . .'[58] The more irregular the employment, the more serious
of course were the demands of the house of call. Of the working tailors
we are told in 1747 that

... the house of call runs away with all their earnings and keeps them constantly in debt and want. The house of call is an alehouse where they generally
use, the landlord knows where to find them, and masters go there to inquire
when they want hands. Custom has established it into a kind of law that the
house of call gives them credit for victuals and drink when they are unemployed; this obliges the journeymen on the other hand to spend all the money
they earn at this house alone. The landlord when once he has got them into
his debt is sure to keep them so, and by that means binds the poor wretch to
his house, who slaves only to enrich the publican.[59]

The tailors' house of call at the beginning of the nineteenth century
is described by a journeyman tailor who came to London to seek work
in 1810 (when he was only seventeen). He found work at once, he says,
by the way

... most in favour with my fellow-craftsmen as being thought more respectable
and more profitable than that of waiting upon masters to ask for work. This
was by causing my name to be entered in the call book of a tailors' trade club,
which was held, as all such clubs then were, at a public-house, thence denominated a house of call. To these houses the masters applied when they wanted
workmen. They could here procure if needful a fresh supply of men three
times per day, viz. at six ... at nine o'clock, and again at one. . . . The master
has the power of discharging a workman at his pleasure after having given him
three hours work or wages.

This first engagement was for one day only, for a journeyman taking
'an occasional job of master work'. But though the link with his fellow-
workmen was so slight, footing had to be paid; 'here I was, in due
form, invested with all the shop-board rights and privileges of the craft,
paying what was technically called my "footing" ... by treating my
work-fellows to a fair allowance of porter. . . . At night I was discharged
and again repaired to the house of call'.[60]

In the case of the tailors the house of call was so organized as to be not
only an employment agency, but (by the beginning of the nineteenth
century) a trade club whose rules were rigorously enforced on the
members and on the masters, and it was also a benefit society, the

journeymen's society organization depending on the houses of call. The public-house as the employment agency was at its worst in the case of the coal-heavers, where the publican was also a middle-man acting as employer. The coal undertakers, as these publicans were called, acted in combination and also acted as agents for the coal-owners and the masters of the ships in disposing of their coals;[61] they were thus all-powerful, and were able to defy or evade the attempts made to check their activities by Statute. They seem first to have become a serious grievance to the coal-heavers about 1750,[62] and there were repeated petitions to Parliament against their exactions. In 1758, in order to frustrate a Bill for which the coal-heavers were applying, the undertakers made a corner in shovels, so that these could only be obtained from them for each job.[63] The Act of 1758 which aimed at eliminating the undertakers proved defective; they continued to make deductions from wages, exact gratuities, charge for shovels, force the coal-heavers to take part of their pay in drink and favour those who drank most. Colquhoun, from his experience at the Thames Police Office, had an intimate acquaintance with the coal-heavers, who indeed made an armed raid on the office and the magistrates. He calls them 'a very depraved but useful and frequently ill-used class of men'. Though they could earn a pound a day and, occasionally (about 1800), as much as 27s. in a day of fourteen hours, they did not on an average take home more than 15s. a week. The publicans who employed them charged each man 1s. 4d. a ship, sent on board twelve shillings' worth of gin and porter per head; anyone who refused to take it lost his chance of future work and the 5s. a week maintenance money advanced by the undertakers between job and job. Colquhoun calculated that each man worked forty-five ships in a year, so that £30 out of his yearly earnings went to the undertakers as a matter of course.

It would seem to be worthy of enquiry [he writes] under what authority a commission of 13s. 4d. each ship is wrested from these poor ignorant people, and how far publicans ought to prescribe rules by which men shall be compelled to besot themselves with an immoderate and unnecessary amount of strong liquor, while their wives and children at home are often in want of the necessaries of life.[64]

An attempt was made to deal with the matter in an Act of 1807,[65] probably suggested by Colquhoun. It was drastic, but it was successfully evaded by the undertakers. All coal undertakers were to be licensed by the Court of Aldermen. No publican was to act directly or indirectly as an undertaker, and no coal-heaver was to be paid in an alehouse. Truck was forbidden, and so were deductions for baskets, shovels, etc. The undertakers' commission was fixed in the Act and so was the rate of coal-heavers' wages – three shillings a chaldron each.

This Act, ineffectual as it proved, is interesting as a piece of social legislation quite counter to *laissez-faire* principles, and also as an early attempt to prevent by Statute the payment of wages in public-houses. In 1843 an Act was passed which at last rescued the poor coal-whippers from their 'thraldom to the publican'. How terrible the effects of the old system had been appears from the enthusiasm with which they spoke of the Act. Mayhew was told by one of their number that

... a most miraculous change and one unparalleled in history (the man was a scholar) has been produced by altering the old method of employing and paying the men. . . . The sons are no longer thieves and the daughters are no longer prostitutes. Formerly it was a competition who could drink the most . . . .

£27 a year spent on drink was considered 'a very low average', and the children had been 'almost reared in the tap-room'.[66]

All attempts to prevent workmen from 'tippling in alehouses' were naturally futile so long as it was the custom for wages to be paid on Saturday night in an alehouse. There were many protests in the eighteenth century against this disastrous system, especially from magistrates, and the practice was even alleged as the reason why London working people were more 'idle, profligate, and debauched' than those of other places.[67] But there is no reason to suppose the custom was confined to London.

The first condemnation of the practice which I have been able to discover is that of John Fielding in 1761, which sums up the situation:

... tradesmen paying their workmen at public-houses commonly called pay-tables are very injurious, as the men are too often kept out of their money till late on Saturday night, out of indulgence to the publican, by which means the mechanic goes home drunk and empty-handed to his family, where distress begets words then blows.[68]

The intimate knowledge of cause and effect which this reveals was one of the first-fruits of the professional metropolitan magistracy. Fielding's policy of social propaganda, combined with the advertisement of his police establishment by means of newspaper paragraphs from Bow Street, is well illustrated by the following report:

One Hughes a labourer appeared against his master for a balance of 4s. 10d. due in part of the earnings of the week, and the master was ordered to pay the money. A circumstance arose in the course of this seemingly trivial affair which demands the attention of the public at large and particularly calls for that of the legislature. . . . It appeared that Hughes's earnings (except the sum in question) had been paid at what they call a pay-table at a public house. It is customary to bricklayers, carpenters . . . etc., to pay their people on Saturday nights at an alehouse. Mark the consequences: the labourer (otherwise a sober man) waits at an alehouse from 6, 7, 8, 9, to perhaps 10 or 11 o'clock before the master or foreman comes to the pay-table; in course they drink deep, the poor wife and children wait impatiently at home for the few shillings the husband is to produce – the man goes home drunk at midnight and beats his wife – on Monday she swears the peace against him. Their domestic happiness is for ever invaded, if not totally destroyed, and all this owing to the accursed custom of paying those labourers at an alehouse whose little demands might be as easily adjusted in the compting house of their employers.[69]

The custom was the more disastrous from the very late hours at which the men were paid, doubtless by arrangement between the publican and the master or foreman. According to *Low Life* (1764), between midnight and 1 a.m. on Sunday morning there were to be seen 'victuallers carrying the scores of tradesmen such as coachmakers, carpenters, smiths, plaisterers, plumbers and others in the building branch of business, to the pay-tables in order to clear their last week's reckoning, and if possible to get a trifle paid off from an old score'. At the same time 'poor tradesmen's wives' were 'hanging about their husbands at little alehouses, to secure some money to support their families before it is all lost at whist, cribbage, putt, and all-fours'. That this is not exaggerated is proved by the reports of Old Bailey trials; the fuddled artisan on his way home with his week's earnings was a prey for the various prowlers of the night. For instance, Thomas Read, a journeyman carpenter, was robbed in 1775 of a silver watch. He says, 'I staid late at the pay-table . . . I did not get away till 3 or 4 in the morning; we always spend a quart of beer a-piece. I was not drunk, nor was I quite sober. . . .'[70] Dr Fothergill speaks of the absurd custom of paying workmen in public-houses on Sunday evening 'where a scene of drunkenness ensues which is seldom completely over till the Monday or perhaps the Tuesday following'.[71]

From John Fielding's time onwards attempts were made to check the practice. Mr Justice Buller said at the Old Bailey in 1785 that he always recommended magistrates to take away the licence from any public-house at which wages were paid.[72] Wilberforce's Proclamation Society took the matter up in 1789 and suggested to the Middlesex Sessions that the justices should require at the next Brewster Sessions that no pay-tables should be allowed. The letter describes the effects of the custom much as Fielding had done, but shows also the influence of the new Evangelical movement:

... the purchase of necessaries is deferred to Sunday morning. The father of the family lies in bed; the mother goes to market; the children are hungry, clamorous, and squalid; the day is passed in a kind of coarse and semi-brutal indulgence, while the humanizing and improving duties of the Sabbath are never thought of.

The justices were asked first to point out these evils to the masters, and request them to give up the practice. If this was not enough, the publicans should be reminded that allowing workmen to remain on their premises for several hours tippling, whether to receive wages or otherwise, was forbidden by law. The Sessions resolved unanimously that the complaint was well founded and that the steps suggested should be taken. One justice said he had already approached several masters in different trades who had given up the practice and that their men had already benefited.[73] It was one of the licensing principles laid down by Colquhoun to grant no licence to any public-house where pay-tables were kept,[74] and as he took a prominent part at Brewster Sessions after 1792 in the Tower Hamlets, and after 1800 in Westminster, it may be supposed that the practice gradually became less general. In 1825 Place said the custom had 'of late years to a considerable extent decreased', and might

... perhaps be wholly put an end to, if workmen would generally request their employers to pay them at the factory or workshop ... every person so paid at a public-house has a fine put upon him, sometimes a pint, sometimes a quart of ale or beer ... others remain influenced by a desire not to let the old sots drink at their cost. The evils thus produced are enormous. The loss of time and bad habits and gross manners it engenders ruin thousands, who might otherwise be respectable members of society.[75]

The practice was one sanctioned by long use and deeply rooted in the customs of all classes. There is a tradition that the builders employed on Westminster Abbey in Edward III's reign were paid at the Cock in Tothill Street.[76] Vestries often met in public-houses. Coffee-houses, taverns and inns were used as places of call and places for transacting business by lawyers, physicians and merchants, though the custom became less general as the century went on. Sir John Hawkins comments on the reduction in the number of taverns; 'it is worthy of remark,' he writes in 1787, '. . . how little these houses of entertainment are now frequented and what a diminution in their number has been experienced in London and Westminster in a period of about forty years backward'.[77]

The transport system of the country depended upon inns and ale-houses. The place of the modern railway station and receiving office was taken by the inn yard. Riverside alehouses were the starting places for the west country barges. The hundreds of coaches and wagons which plied between London and provincial towns had their head-quarters in inns. The carriers and carters who came to London from the home counties had some public-house to which they regularly resorted, and there the simple countryman was apt to get into bad company. The numerous inns and alehouses which did this sort of business collected a crowd of hangers-on and helpers whose reputation was of the worst, many of whom were connected with the gangs of thieves who specialized in depredations on passengers' luggage and other goods. In 1818, when things had undoubtedly improved, *The London Guide* says:

. . . most people come up to town by coaches and wagons, a few on foot, and fewer still by water, therefore the inns at which the former put up are places of special resort for thieves and cheats of a better sort. The little public-houses along shore are frequented by a very ordinary and more desperate set. . . .

Nevertheless, owing to improvements in police, inn yards were then 'nothing like so much infested as they were twenty years ago'.[78] In 1832 a great improvement in stage-coachmen is ascribed to the greater speed of coaches; 'a coachman drunk on his box is now a rarity – a coachman quite sober, was, even within our memory, still more so', says a writer in the *Quarterly*.[79] In 1768 it was said 'Our stage-coachmen are perpetually drinking, they no sooner descry a sign than they find themselves thirsty'.[80]

Prisons were notoriously places of drunkenness and riot, partly because drink was freely sold there. The clause in the Act of 1751 forbidding spirits to be sold in prisons was for a long time generally ignored: after the efforts of the prison reformers began to take effect the Act was nullified by the freedom with which they were smuggled in from outside.[81] The tap for the sale of beer was a recognized and legitimate source of profit to the keeper, who either managed it himself or farmed it out; there was thus a public-house in every prison. Smaller prisons were sometimes even situated in public-houses; there was the old White Lyon in Southwark, and towards the end of the eighteenth century Whitechapel prison was also a public-house to which outsiders resorted to play skittles and drink; if the prisoners did not join them it was because they had no money. The jail of the Tower Royalty (not the Tower Hamlets as Howard says) was in a public-house in Well Close Square.[82] It was the custom for the debtors in Newgate to send out invitations to club meetings and convivial gatherings in their rooms at which drink was sold. Cards were sent out to invite people (who were not prisoners) to 'Mr such a one's Public – Free and Easy Society at No. – Mrs So-and-so's Route. – A dance at No. ' These, Neild says, took place generally twice and sometimes three times a week, though by 1807 the practice had been checked by 'the bar newly made by which the quantity of liquor daily consumed is ascertained'.[83] In the King's Bench there were at one time no less than thirty gin-shops, and in 1776, 120 gallons of gin were sold weekly besides other spirits and eight butts of beer a week; in the Fleet, though there was much more order and decency than in the King's Bench, there were still 'few hours in the night without riots and drunkenness'.[84] The parish watch-house, or round-house where night-charges were confined till they could be brought before a justice in the morning, or till they squared the constable of the night, was a place where drink was sold and where the treatment of the prisoner depended upon his consumption of liquor.[85]

It was common in the eighteenth century, as it seems to have been in the seventeenth, for publicans to be constables. This bred a multitude of evils and the justices repeatedly attempted to stop it though with very doubtful success. Apart from the inherent difficulty of controlling the occupation of an unpaid annual officer who had a right at common law to appoint a deputy, the justices were hampered by the fact that they had no direct right to choose and appoint constables. It seems to have been regarded as a counsel of perfection, hard to observe, that no publican should be a constable. In 1753 a manual of parish law quotes Chief Justice Holt's dictum that no man that keeps a public-house ought to be a constable, with the comment, 'if this should be a rule 'twould be hard upon the inhabitants in many places'.[86] Quarter Sessions made repeated orders that no publicans should be sworn in as constables and exhorted the stewards of the courts leet to see that they were not chosen.[87] The authority of the Sessions and the magistrates over the parish constables tended to grow weaker as the century went on, and parochial watch committees extended their powers. In 1805 one of a long list of proposals for the improvement of the police submitted by Dr Forde the Ordinary of Newgate to the Secretary of State, was that 'no police officer, patrole, or parish constable, shall be permitted to keep a public-house or tavern'.[88] By the beginning of the nineteenth century however, the abuse must have been much restricted as it is not dwelt on in the reports of 1812–28 on the police of the metropolis.

Thus, at his work and in his amusements, at liberty and in prison, it was difficult for the Londoner to escape the ever-present temptation to drink. Even the box clubs and friendly societies which increased rapidly in the latter part of the century were sometimes of doubtful benefit to their members owing to the dominance of the publican. These clubs, like the purely convivial ones, were held in public-houses. Indeed, it is not always easy to say where the distinction between the two is to be drawn, though the principle of the one was saving, of the other spending. Benefit societies or box clubs often degenerated into sharing-out clubs, and sometimes invested their funds in lottery tickets.[89] Friendly societies are not a new development of the eighteenth century; apart from the friendly society functions of the early guilds, often continued in their later phase of city companies, box clubs and benefit societies are to be found in the seventeenth century, but as the eighteenth century went on they multiplied.[90]

Unfortunately, they were apt not only to be financially unsound, as they were not based on calculations of the duration of life, but they were often promoted by a publican, and therefore conducted in his interest, not in that of the contributors. When the box was full, the temptation of sharing out the money was often irresistible. In some clubs a third of the contributions was spent in drink; and as each member had to spend so much for the good of the house at the monthly or fortnightly club meetings, the industrious and abstemious, it was said, learned to drink. The funds were not seldom misappropriated by the holder of the box and they were sometimes lent to members with partiality and on defective security.[91]

One of the most deeply-rooted principles of the benefit society was that it should provide its members – and usually their wives – with a funeral. It was also the rule in most clubs, perhaps inherited from the ancient traditions of the guilds, that the members should attend the funeral of a fellow-member or pay a fine for absence. In many cases a levy was made to raise the sum payable by the rules on a death and to defray the expenses incurred in assembling at the public-house for the funeral. The elements in this practice were, the general desire for 'a decent funeral' and 'decent mourning' in days when funeral celebrations were elaborate and prolonged; the very ancient tradition that all the members of the fellowship should attend; and the calculated interests of the publican who held the box, and of the undertaker who usually contrived to be a member of the society.

Till the Act of 1793[92] which provided that the rules of friendly societies should be enrolled at Quarter Sessions, these rules had attracted little attention. After this they were generally discussed and condemned by social reformers and actuarial experts.[93] Colquhoun who studied the rules of the enrolled societies laid stress not only on the frequent 'shocking injustice' in excluding members and the large sums spent on drink, but on the administration of funeral benefit which shocked his frugal Scottish mind.

There is one general principle that runs through that society which I highly disapprove, and that is, the ambition of the most miserable of them to have what they call a Decent Funeral; an undertaker generally endeavours to get into the society, that he may bury all of them, and that funeral takes from the funds which ought to go to the widow and the fatherless, or to enable them to set up a little shop. . . . There is a disposition among all the lower classes of the people to have what is called a decent funeral and this frequently amounts to from ten to fifteen pounds.[94]

The methods of the eighteenth century survived, not in the great well-managed friendly societies, but in unregistered societies, such as The Order of Loyal United Friends, described by Charles Booth as peculiarly a London Society – the name typical of the later eighteenth century, when many London societies were 'loyal' or 'patriotic' and their members 'Friends', 'Brothers', or 'Sisters'. They survive still more completely in the numerous publicans' Dividing Societies or Slate Clubs, and in the many small local clubs for providing their members with clothing which are so common in London (not only among factory girls), though these are less liable to the calamities and disputes which seem to have been the rule rather than the exception in the eighteenth century.[89]

Thus the consumption of strong drink was connected with every phase of life from apprenticeship (indeed from birth and baptism) to death and burial. Many of the evils connected with these convivial customs were aggravated by, if not due to, the excessive number of public-houses in London. There were too many publicans to make a legitimate living and so they were impelled to offer every sort of inducement to customers to remain tippling in their houses. Clubs of many kinds ranging from the drinking and gambling club, through various forms of sharing-out club to the benefit society, were promoted to attract custom. Employers or foremen, it may be supposed, were given a *quid pro quo* for the establishment of pay-tables. At the bottom of the scale thieves and prostitutes were harboured and the publicans acted as receivers of stolen goods.

Both Sir John Fielding[95] and Colquhoun pointed out the effects of an excess of public-houses and both urged that the remedy was the refusal of licences. Colquhoun analysed the takings of London ale-houses and came to the conclusion that it was quite impossible for many of the smaller houses to make a legitimate profit, while, as a matter of fact, insolvency and ruin were frequent. He recommended a policy of refusing licences, not only to houses which were ill-conducted, but to those which were shown to be superfluous from the frequent failures or removals of their occupants.[96] There was considerable feeling against such a policy, first on the ground that it was unfair to hinder a man from trying to earn a living, and secondly, that the justices could not be trusted to act impartially. Smollett voices the opposition to the refusal of licences which followed upon the Act of 1752, making a magisterial licence necessary for places of amusement:

The suburbs of the metropolis abounded with an incredible number of publick houses which continually resounded with the noise of riot and intemperance; they were the haunts of idleness, fraud, and rapine, and the seminaries of drunkenness, debauchery, and extravagance, and every vice incident to human nature; yet the suppression of these receptacles of infamy was an inconvenience which in some cases arose even to a degree of oppression. ... Many of the justices ... were men of profligate lives, needy, mean, ignorant, and rapacious, and often acted from the most scandalous principles of selfish avarice.[97]

As a matter of fact it would appear from the cases recorded in the Middlesex Sessions records that the trading justices abused their position, not by refusing licences, but by procuring them for those who had (very properly) been refused them at a licensing sessions, or by obstructing local attempts to put down notorious places. After the police Act of 1792 the unpaid metropolitan magistrates, cut off from judicial business, could still engage in licensing work and the trading justices are said to have turned their attention to the profits to be made from it. It is clear that licensing abuses abounded, especially in the eastern parishes. In the police report of 1817 much stress was laid on the refusal of licences in Shadwell and elsewhere, while infamous dancing places for sailors had been tolerated;[98] Bethnal Green suffered from the corrupt manœuvres of the boss Merceron,[99] and the longshore parishes from bad magistrates and a theory that the riverside population with its offscourings of the port of London made it useless to attempt to suppress disreputable alehouses.

Nevertheless the licensing policy had undoubtedly become stricter, the number of public-houses had decreased in spite of the growth of London. The Disorderly Houses Act of 1752 (25 Geo. II. c. 36), probably due to Henry Fielding, by which places of entertainment and music were required to have a justices' licence, reinforced the Act of

1751 against the gin-shop. One of the most useful activities of Wilber-force's Proclamation Society (from 1787) was its propaganda for using the licensing powers of the justices to combat social evils[100] – as for instance the payment of wages in public-houses. After 1792 disorderly brothels could no longer defy the magistrates by obtaining wine-licences from the Stamp Office.[101] In the nineties notorious tea-gardens and places of amusement were suppressed – places which it was said in 1816 'the better morals of the present day would hardly tolerate'. Those mentioned were the Blue Lion, (known as the Blue Cat) in Gray's Inn Lane, The Bull and Pound in Spa Fields, The Shepherd and Shepherdess, the Apollo Gardens, The Temple of Flora, and the Dog and Duck – the last three in St George's Fields. The two last, according to William Fielding, Henry's son, were

. . . certainly the most dreadful places in or about the metropolis . . . the resorts of women, not only of the lower species of prostitution, but even of the middle classes; they were the resorts as well of apprentices as of every sort of abandoned young men.

Since these two 'infernal places of meeting' had been closed, highway-men, he said, had been less heard of.[102] Place says that in his youth he had seen people waiting to see the highwaymen mount their horses at the Dog and Duck,[103] and had 'seen the flashy women come out to take leave of the thieves at dusk and wish them success'.[104] At the Blue Lion he had seen the landlord come openly into the long room with a lump of silver which he had melted for the thieves and pay them for it.

Place may be quoted again on the amusements at the ducking-ponds and places of resort round London:

There were scarcely any houses on the eastern side of Tottenham Court Road; there and in the Long Fields were several large ponds; the amusements here were duck-hunting and badger-baiting; they would throw a cat into the water and set dogs at her; great cruelty was constantly practised and the most abominable scenes used to take place. It is almost impossible for any person to believe the atrocities of low life at that time, which were not as now [1835] confined to the worst paid and the most ignorant of the populace.[104]

Something of a social revolution on a small scale was due to the introduction of a new kind of coffee-house about 1809 or 1810. This was both a cause and a result of the growing sobriety among London artisans. The tax on coffee was reduced in 1808 and coffee became a favourite breakfast for working men, taking the place of the old porter or purl and gin. These coffee-houses were open from 5 or 6 in the morning till 9 or 10 at night. They became popular and customers returned for other meals. One of their chief merits was that they provided newspapers and reviews. A journeyman tailor has described his satisfaction on discovering a coffee-shop near his place of work.

These shops [he writes] were but just then [1815] becoming general. They greatly pleased me, as I could *now* get suitable and timely refreshment in the morning and that too in a warm and otherwise comfortable room with the very pleasant accompaniment of a daily newspaper.

The next year a change of work brought him to a different coffee-shop.

Here I found the additional accommodation of magazines and review for reading the current numbers of which the proprietor made an extra charge of sixpence per month. This charge I was glad to pay for the sake of reading the *Edinburgh* and *Monthly Reviews,* together with the *Edinburgh*, the *European* and the *Monthly Magazines*. These however I read in the evening, while I took my coffee-supper, for I learned to drink coffee at that meal as well as at breakfast-time.

He used to retail the news to his fellow-workmen. Before he found the coffee-shop, his breakfast had been a pot of porter and a penny roll at a public-house, with an extra halfpenny for eating it out of the tap-room so as to read the newspaper and avoid tobacco smoke.[105] These coffee-shops were, Place says, 'the means of great improvement to the working people'.[104]

Terrible as were the effects of drink in the early nineteenth century, there had been a progressive improvement in the last fifty years of the eighteenth century. Another closely connected cause of misery and ruin was imprisonment for debt. The abuses connected with this remained so glaring, and the sufferings of individuals so grievous, that the great restriction in its scope has been given little attention. ''Tis reckoned there are about 60,000 miserable debtors perishing in the prisons of England and Wales,' wrote a critic of the system in 1716.[106] One naturally assumes that this is a wild exaggeration, but conceivably (and allowing for those dependent on the prisoners) it was not so very far from the truth. In 1714 it was said 'the Marshalsea alone generally contains seven or eight hundred prisoners . . . two or three commonly perishing in one day in this miserable and wasting condition'.[107] A Parliamentary Committee reported in 1719 that three hundred persons had died in the Marshalsea in less than three months.[108] Oglethorpe's committee in 1729 found the prisoners on the common side in the Marshalsea, then 'upwards of 350', literally dying of starvation. They took steps to feed them, but before this, the committee report, 'a day seldom passed without a death, and upon the advancing of spring not less than eight or ten usually died every twenty-four hours'.[109] Yet by 1729 the Act of 1725 had reduced the number of prisoners for small debts.

In 1779 the total number of prisoners for debt in England and Wales, according to Howard, was 2,076, ninety-two of whom were in the Marshalsea. In 1791 the total number was approximately 1,957, but the returns were not quite complete.[110] In the Marshalsea in 1811 there were sixty-seven prisoners,[111] in 1815, sixty-four, of whom only four were on the common side.[112]

Whitechapel prison, the franchise prison of the manors of Stepney and Hackney and the prison of a court which dealt only with debts under £5, at the beginning of the century had been a crowded pest-house. In 1712 the Middlesex Sessions had to make special arrangements for keeping order among the very numerous prisoners from White-chapel who were to be brought into court (in batches of ten) to be discharged under an Act for the relief of insolvent debtors.[113] The prison was capable of holding about a hundred people,[114] and one may suppose it actually at times contained very many more. Howard found that from 1774 to 1777 the number of prisoners had varied from twenty-seven to twenty, and in 1779 dropped to five. Between 1785 and 1792 there had never been more than three,[110] and in 1800 Neild found the prison clean and healthy, but empty.[115] By an Act of 1781 no one could be imprisoned there for more than forty days.

These two prisons, the Marshalsea and Whitechapel, were concerned with persons arrested for small sums, and the legislation of the century had aimed chiefly at their relief. It had restricted holding to special bail (or arrest on mesne process) in inferior courts first (in 1725) to sums of 40s. and upwards and then (in 1779) to sums of £10. Before 1725 it is said that the Whitechapel and Marshalsea Courts arrested for debts of a few pence, usually for 'vexation and revenge'.[106] This second Act took away from the Whitechapel Court the power of arrest on mesne process (already much restricted in 1725), and virtually did the same for the Marshalsea, as suits above £5 could be removed by the defendant to a higher court. 'Thus was the business of the Marshalsea Court destroyed, and more particularly that part of it which related to bailiffs.'[11] This is the testimony of Place, whose father, a Marshalsea Court officer with a lucrative sponging-house, found his business ruined by the Act and was forced to sell his office for what it would fetch. An intolerable power of oppression was thus taken away from the crowd of bailiffs and bailiffs' officers who had bought places under the Marshalsea and Whitechapel Courts, and had preyed upon the industrial population.[116]

At the beginning of the century tallymen had battened on the system, and imprisonment for debt made the wiles of these creatures terribly disastrous. In 1681 Firmin described tallymen as those who 'trust poor persons with 20s. worth of goods, or rather with twelve or fourteen shillings worth instead of twenty, to pay them by 6d. or 12d. a week, wherein if they fail to pay, they hurry them into prison, with great charge for arrests and proceedings at law, which many times exceed the said debt'.[117] A later writer says,

. . . every tallyman generally keeps a rogue of a servant who he makes a bailiff, and for every arrest, if the debt is not eighteen-pence, exacts ten shillings besides other fees. Whitechapel Court is cramb'd full of these miserable creatures, at the suit of tallymen, and 'tis these rogues that chiefly support that court as well as the Marshalsea, and for the better encouragement of villainy . . . the plaintiff, right or wrong, very rarely misses of getting the day; so that the whole number of insects, dependent on these wicked and barbarous courts, is on the bread, or rather the blood, of the poor. . . .[118]

In 1729 it was alleged that the Whitechapel officers and their followers were upwards of 500, and those of the Marshalsea 1,800, the total for the metropolis 'upwards of 3,000, a hopeful parcel to live upon the spoils of industry'.[119]

A petition to Parliament against imprisonment for debt runs:

. . . it is hardly possible to represent . . . the many grievances we are under upon the account of the Marshal's and Whitechapel Courts, and how many families are brought upon the charge of our parishes, and how many persons are ruined by being arrested and held to bail upon trivial actions and for little inconsiderable sums.[120]

Sometimes indeed persons were arrested for debts falsely sworn. When Amy, the servant of Defoe's *Roxana*, is anxious to get rid of her mistress's troublesome daughter, she swears a debt against her and has her shut up in Whitechapel prison. This is an alternative to murder and was expected to be equally effective.

There were other stages in the alleviation of these miseries which cannot be gone into here. They include the establishments of Courts of Conscience from 1749 onwards for small debts and the subsequent limiting of the term for which debtors under such courts might be imprisoned, as well as the founding of the Society for the Relief of Persons imprisoned for small Sums in 1772.[121] It was only a part of the work of the Society that in the first twenty years of its existence it had discharged an average of 700 prisoners a year, chiefly 'of the description of manufacturers, labourers, and seamen'. Moreover, owing to the efforts of the prison reformers, prisons had become less lethal and pestilential, while barbarous and deliberate ill-treatment does not seem to have survived Oglethorpe's inquiry of 1729, and the trial of Bambridge for murder.

The consequences of imprisonment for debt were so devastating that the reduction in the number of prisoners is of the greatest importance. Many families were left destitute because the wage-earner was either in prison or had fled from home to escape arrest; many apprentices were thrown on the world because their masters were in the Mint (before 1724) or in the Verge, beyond seas, or in a debtors' prison with no hope of release. A vindictive spirit and ruinous litigation were encouraged by the hordes of attorneys and bailiffs who had bought their offices and lived at the expense of the community. Children were brought up in the Fleet and the King's Bench with disastrous results. The Deputy Warden of the Fleet said in 1814 that he believed the Fleet to be the biggest brothel in the metropolis.[122] Debtors associated with felons. The utter despair of those arrested for debt, especially in the early part of the century, is seen by the violence with which arrest was resisted, and by the war waged on bailiffs by the shelterers in the Alsatias of the Mint, and the New Mint. 'Of how many murders, slaughters, and violent deaths, have dread of arrests and imprisonment been the cause?' asks a pamphleteer of 1714, 'if any man see another coming to lay violent hands upon him, to attach his person and haul his body to prison, nature teaches him to take the assailor for his capital enemy and to act the best he may in his own defence.'[123] In Henry Fielding's little band of thieftakers was one who had been accustomed 'to arrest common debtors who are usually of the desperate kind'.[124]

All this misery and cruelty had no effect at all in doing what it was supposed to do – secure the rights of property and the sanctity of contract. It had exactly the opposite effect. 'These miserable oppressions put men upon a kind of fatal necessity to turn knaves and wrack their wit to evade it all ... which by the help of lawyers, if they have money they may do. But where accrues the benefit of all this unchristian severity?' it is asked in 1716, 'to none but the very worst of rogues that tread on the face of the earth, viz. pettifoggers, jailers, keepers of spunging-houses, bailiffs, and their followers.' There were two main types of prisoners for debt: the man thrown into prison for a sum he could not pay which rapidly increased by the fees of lawyers and jailers. With them may be classed those against whom debts were falsely sworn, who were then arrested on mesne process. The other type was represented by the man who preferred to live an idle and riotous – or sometimes a penurious – life in prison on his creditors' money rather than pay his debts. A variant of this was the person who knew how to get committed to prison at the right moment and take advantage of an impending Act for the relief of insolvent debtors; another was the person committed (like Sam Weller) under a 'friendly action'. Dr William Smith, a real benefactor to the prisoners in London, and respected by them, estimated in 1778 that five-sixths of the prisoners for debt in England were fraudulent debtors:

When they can carry on their trade no longer, and some of their frauds are likely to come to light, they run to jail not empty handed, where they live in luxury and riot and declare open war against every law of God and man, and ay aside every law of decency and good order.[125]

Imprisonment for debt had thus a large share in the uncertainty of life and trade which was characteristic of the time. Drinking, gambling, and debt were links in a chain of misfortune which it was difficult to escape; their general connexion is obvious, but they had a direct connexion peculiar to the circumstances of the time. There was a practice known as 'buying carcasses' which is thus described:

> ... when a tradesman has not money to pay, the publican inquires what kind of workman he is; if he is informed that he is a very ingenious man, he then encourages him to drink till he gets considerably in debt for which he passes his note of hand, which the publican sells to some other person in the same trade with the debtor, who is obliged to work for his creditor or go to jail. By this means workmen are enticed to drink and inveigled from their masters.[126]

The same system was followed by the crimps who furnished food, liquor, and clothes at exorbitant rates to seamen and managed to make them get into their debt. They were then arrested and compelled to secure their release by giving a 'will and power' to receive their wages, prize-money, and all their possessions if they died. The crimps then procured another ship for their victims and received the crimpage money from the captain. 'Nothing can exceed the oppression which these poor people suffer,' said Colquhoun, 'while the crimps make large sums of money and live very extravagantly and profusely.'[127] At Bristol the slave ships were recruited in a similar way; seamen who boarded at certain public-houses were encouraged to spend more than they could afford and then offered the alternative of a slave ship or imprisonment for debt.[128] It may be presumed that the same device was used for getting men for those undertakings in general in which they entered unwillingly – the Navy, the Army, the East India Company's service, and indentured emigration to the colonies.

The general uncertainty of life appears vividly in the life history of the Place family. Francis Place deplored the absence of authenticated domestic annals of the working people as materials of social history. The changes of the early nineteenth century were so great that by the twenties and thirties the eighteenth century had to a great extent already been forgotten. He was exasperated by the social reformers and others who for the first time began to investigate social conditions, discovered a multitude of evils and assumed that they were new. It was as a contribution to social history that he recorded the vicissitudes of his own family, not because they were exceptional, but because they were typical. His father, born about 1717, had been apprenticed (probably by his parish) to a baker at Bury in Hertfordshire, who ill-treated him. He attacked his master with a hatchet and ran away to London where at first he managed to get work at some stables and kennels, and after two years became a journeyman baker. He married, lived (as was usual among bakers) on his master's premises, going home to his wife (who supported herself by needlework), on Saturday nights. He soon became a master-baker in the Borough and had a flourishing business, but was ruined by drink and gambling. At a single sitting he lost everything, including the furniture of his house and the goodwill of his business, leaving his wife to be turned into the street. She again earned a living by needlework and heard nothing of her husband for some months. However, he returned, again managed to take a baker's shop, and saved £800. Again he was ruined by gambling, and had to sell the lease and goodwill of his business, this time leaving his wife with a child and some furniture. After a year he came back, 'just as if he had returned from a walk', but penniless.

Place believes there was a third occasion of ruin by gambling in this period. During Francis Place's childhood, his father bought an office under the Marshalsea Court, and kept a sponging-house. This business, as we have seen, was destroyed by the Act of 1779, and he took the King's Arms public-house in Arundel Street. Here his final ruin was begun by a woman who went to the overseers of his parish and claimed to have been married to him by a Fleet marriage forty years before. He was advised to pay her a small weekly sum, but he refused, saying she had never been his wife. An action was brought against him in the Ecclesiastical Court which lasted three years, cost him about £1,000, and ended in his excommunication, an event which he celebrated with a supper party. Misfortunes followed. He failed to get a renewal of his lease from the Duke of Norfolk, who preferred a Catholic tenant, and he retired to the Fleet prison under a friendly action. Owing to the skill of Francis Place, then under seventeen, in disposing of the fixtures, etc., he saved about £250 from the wreck, with which his wife was anxious to set up a shop, confident that she could support the family. He lost the whole of it however, by gambling in the State Lottery. By this time he was an old man, entirely broken, lodging at a public-house within the Rules of the Fleet; his wife, though she was fifty-seven, supported the family by taking in washing.

Place's maternal grandfather was a sawyer who had taken a public-house at Hyde Park Corner; he was attacked by robbers when returning from Chelsea and died of his wounds. One of Place's sisters married a butcher, one of a miscreant family of thieves, fences, and prostitutes. He was sentenced to death for highway robbery in 1799, and was transported for life owing to Francis Place, who frustrated an attempt of his associates to secure a pardon, as he knew that this would only result in his being hanged eventually. His other sister and his brother had careers which were more or less discreditable and unfortunate. His own apprenticeship followed lines which were common: the ruin of his master's business, a night flitting of the family, known as shooting the moon, from Bell Yard to Lambeth, followed by his master's imprisonment in the King's Bench (and eventually by his retirement to the workhouse). It was less usual that the two apprentices should have managed to support the family for a time, but this was due to Place's exceptional energy and skill. As the result of a quarrel his indentures were given up about three years before the end of his term. He was by that time however (1789), though only seventeen, a more than usually competent breeches-maker, and although as a journeyman he had much experience of poverty and unemployment, he was completely successful as a master-tailor.[11]

The conclusion to be drawn from life-histories of this kind seems to be how fatally easy and how common it was to be ruined, the causes of ruin being more often social than economic, and how comparatively easy it was to recover from disaster. Place remarks that his father's repeated ruin, repeatedly followed by recovery, 'appears to us sober people of the present day almost incredible. But such men . . . were by no means uncommon in his time'. The further implication is that sobriety and steadiness must have had a scarcity value, and could hardly fail to raise a journeyman to the position at least of a foreman or manager, probably of an employer. Place indeed says as much. He wrote in 1829:

. . . there has at all times been a small number, now much increased in every class, of workmen who were . . . more sober and more industrious than the generality of their fellows; these were almost always good workmen . . . men who were paid higher wages than the general price paid in the trade or earning more wages at the common rate by the greater quantity of work they did.

These men saved money, obtained character and became masters, and by far the greatest part of the tradesmen and manufacturers in London and some other large towns were such men, or are the sons of such men.[11]

To go back to the career of Place's father. Fleet marriages and the State Lottery brought ruin to many people. Before the Marriage Act of 1753, though against the canons, marriage was valid without banns or licence, at any hour, in any building, and without a clergyman. In 1686 and 1712 fines were imposed on such marriages, and they became a civil offence, but fines, like ecclesiastical penalties, were useless against those who had neither money, liberty nor credit to lose. Prisons and their precincts being sheltering places for illicit traffic of all kinds, these marriages flourished especially in the Rules of the Fleet prison; they were also performed in the Rules of the King's Bench, and in the Mint in Southwark, and by certain clergymen who chose to consider themselves outside episcopal authority. A trade sprang up in the tenements and alehouses in the Rules of the Fleet, and pliers or touts competed for custom. Pennant describes Fleet Street as it was before 1753:

... in walking along the street in my youth ... I have often been tempted by the question, 'Sir, will you be pleased to walk in and be married?' Along this most lawless space was hung up the frequent sign of a male and female hand conjoined with 'Marriages performed within' written beneath. A dirty fellow invited you in. The parson was seen walking before his shop, a squalid profligate fellow clad in a tattered plaid night-gown, with a fiery face and ready to couple you for a dram of gin or a roll of tobacco. Our great Chancellor Hardwicke put these daemons to flight and saved thousands from the misery and disgrace which would be entailed by these extemporary thoughtless unions.

There were endless ramifications in the evil consequences of these marriages. Entries in the Fleet registers could always, for a consideration, be forged, antedated, or expunged. The practice was a direct incitement to bigamy, fictitious marriage for purposes of seduction, or marriage as the result of a drunken frolic. By persuasion, force, or fraud, women were taken to the purlieus of the Fleet, and there married, to be stripped of their fortune and deserted. Heirs (of either sex) were entrapped by fortune hunters. Women married insolvent debtors in order to rid themselves of their debts. There were men in the Fleet who made a trade of going through a form of marriage for the purpose, one

Welsh, a cordwainer, 'marrying' four women in fourteen months. In short, the system encouraged all the abuses of the age connected with marriage, yet another being the marriages arranged by parish overseers in order to throw the burden of maintaining a pauper and her children on some other parish.

On Saturday last, [says *The Post Boy*, in 1741] the churchwardens from a certain parish in the City, in order to remove a load from their shoulders, gave forty shillings and paid the expenses of a Fleet marriage to a miserable blind youth . . . who plays on the violin in Moorfields, in order to make a settlement on [of?] the wife and future family on Shoreditch parish. . . . Invited and uninvited were a number of poor wretches in order to spend the bride's future fortune.[129]

In spite of protests in the name of justice, liberty, democracy and morality, the practice was effectually stopped by Lord Hardwicke's Marriage Act which is a landmark in social history. It not only ended a sordid and demoralizing traffic, but a practice which cut at the root of security in family life.

The State Lotteries were a cause of widespread ruin and misery. About 1778 they became a regular method of raising money, previously they had been frequent financial expedients. While the lottery was being drawn – in 1802 the period was reduced from forty days to eight – there was great falling off in the takings of all tradesmen dealing with the poorer classes except pawnbrokers, who took in many more pledges, though there was a great reduction in redemptions. There was a mania among all classes for lottery insurances, by which any person could insure any number for any amount against coming up blank. These were illegal and often fraudulent, but they could not be stopped; the profits to the principals who remained in the background were enormous, they employed touts called 'morocco men' from the pocket-books they used, who went round the public-houses collecting money. Milkmen, barbers, greengrocers, keepers of chandlers' shops, the shoe-makers who lived in the cellars of Monmouth Street, women who could write, used to collect money for insurances. When these people were detected (and this was comparatively seldom), and imprisoned as vagabonds (after 1787), their employers would allow them two guineas a week, with which they lived in comfort in prison. The wit-nesses against them almost always appeared to have sold or pawned everything and to be reduced to the most abject poverty. Those who had been defrauded by the touts one year would undertake the touting business themselves the next and thus the poison went on spreading. The experience of poor-law officers was that workmen's wives were the chief insurers;

... the wife will tell her story that her husband has left her; if we investigate the case we frequently find that she has, unknown to her husband, kept back the money she ought to have applied to the necessaries of life, and on Sunday when he expects to find a clean shirt, all is at the pawnbrokers.

'We frequently have females come to us when the head of the family has lived in credit and reputation and all of a sudden they are in ruin, the husband gone, the children in rags.'[130] Besides the State Lottery there were illegal private lotteries, called Little Goes, which were grossly fraudulent, the drawings being manipulated, and their proprietors well-known bad characters. At these too 'the wives of many industrious mechanics' were defrauded and forced to pawn beds, wedding-rings, and everything they possessed.[131]

It is not surprising [writes Eden in 1801] that the lower classes in this metropolis should be much addicted to gambling, particularly in the lottery. The wheels at Guildhall are the only bankers of the poor. A maid-servant who has saved a guinea is sensible that if she attempts to be her own banker it will melt away piecemeal. Upon principles of prudence she purchases the sixteenth of a ticket, and concludes that her honesty and frugality will find their reward in a fortunate number.[132]

The journeyman who found himself suddenly forced to pawn even his tools or threatened with imprisonment for debt, only followed a general custom when he left his family and disappeared. The worst result of this very usual tragedy was in the number of deserted children in the streets of London, due to the fact that such people, if they were immigrants to London, probably had no parochial settlement there.

Mechanics, handicraftsmen, and labourers [wrote Sir John Fielding] ... daily come to London, whither they are soon followed by their families; where many of them have lived industriously, maintaining their wives and children till the latter have been almost old enough to go into the world. But about this critical period, their fathers either dying or absconding, the mothers are left to support the families, who often sink under the burthen, and the children, incapable of inquiring into or enforcing, their settlement, are turned into the streets. . . .[133]

In London in the eighteenth century we see a society which still clung to the old safeguards and prejudices, to the restriction of workers to their place of settlement, to rigid demarcations between class and class, to the exclusiveness of trades and corporations, to a fierce hatred of foreigners. But in spite of – sometimes even because of – these restrictions there was a ceaseless movement to and fro between the metropolis, Great Britain, Ireland, and the Continent, as well as upwards and downwards in the social scale. Leslie Stephen has pointed out that the eighteenth century is conspicuous for the number of men who rose from the humblest positions to distinction in science, art, and literature. And in the anonymous strata of labourers, artisans, clerks, shopkeepers and men of business, many rose from the bottom of the ladder to established positions. The corollary to the thousands of decayed housekeepers who filled the workhouses and debtors' prisons were the thousands of people of lowly beginnings who took their places, and as the middle classes were increasing,[134] there was more room for movement upwards than downwards.

At the same time the status of the poorer sort was improving. The average working man was becoming better educated, more self-respecting, and more respected. He is no longer supposed to belong to 'the vile and brutish part of mankind'. The change was noticed by Simond, who visited England during 1810 and 1811 after living for twenty years in the United States.

There is an ambition in parents [he writes] to give a better education to their children than they have received themselves, more apparent here than perhaps anywhere else; the desire and the hope of ameliorating their situation are general; and such is the proper sense every individual entertains of his rank as a man, that there is not one so low as to suffer the treatment he would have borne in former times. The usual language of masters to servants, and of superiors to inferiors, is infinitely more guarded and considerate than it used to be; blows and abusive epithets are only known in old novels and on the stage – the pictures of obsolete manners. The poor are become less ignorant and less abject. . . .[135]

Hence the complaints of the decline of subordination.

Place repeatedly insists on the change which had taken place within his memory, and it can be traced in many threads of the social history of the eighteenth century, obscured by the cry of degeneration that these changes provoked, and by the fact that legislation lagged behind opinion and practice; while from the very fact of the change, distress was more keenly felt. The change can be seen for instance in the history of charities and of parish apprenticeship; at the end of the eighteenth century it was no longer thought outrageous that a boy from the Foundling Hospital should be given an education which fitted him to be employed by a London shopkeeper. The rigidity of class distinctions was breaking down, as the idea of humanity began to gain upon the conception of a community made up of classes and sections.

A significant change had taken place in the character of plans for poor relief. For the later seventeenth and earlier eighteenth century the favourite scheme of social salvation was the large incorporated work-house or the labour colony into which not only derelicts but working people were to be collected to stop idleness, wandering and begging and to make their work profitable; only so, it was supposed, could 'the poor' be 'set on work'.[136] These were counsels of despair. In 1722, for instance, a scheme was brought forward for providing for the poor of the rich parishes of St Martin's (which then included the district after-wards formed into the parish of St George's Hanover Square), St James and St Anne Westminster, by means of a corporation to set the poor on work in a labour colony. It was based on the assumption that these parishes contained about a fifteenth of the population within the Bills, and that the total number of settled poor within the chosen dis-trict was 10,000. Of these it was estimated that 1,000 were incapable of work, the other 9,000 being 'chargeable and criminal poor', able, but not willing, to work, who lived by 'begging, stealing . . . or other vicious practices'. These 10,000 unprofitable persons, with a leaven of 1,500 industrious mechanics, husbandmen, and gardeners, were to be settled on 10,000 acres of land, where it was supposed they would not only be self-supporting, but, by division of labour and a steadiness of work unknown to the independent artisan or labourer, would make a profit for the corporation of £20,000 a year.[137] The significance of this absurd scheme lies in the assumption that in a labour colony only could 'the able poor' be induced to work. Similar ideas underlay the establishment of the Clerkenwell workhouse in 1665 for the Middlesex parishes within the Bills, in which 600 able poor and 100 infirm poor were to be maintained by the work of the former.[138]

The change of conditions in the latter part of the century is reflected in the new direction given to schemes for providing for the poor. There was a series of proposals for poor relief on the lines of friendly societies[139] – the result of their spontaneous multiplication – which shows a less pessimistic attitude, a disposition to regard the poorer sort as reasonable and responsible people in marked contrast with the earlier schemes – a change which reflects both the improving status and manners of the humbler folk and greater knowledge and administrative capacity among the governing classes. In London more particularly, it is significant that the plans for providing for the poor by hospitals and so superseding poor relief on account of its abuses, gradually gave way to schemes for supplementing parish relief by societies (such as the Strangers' Friend Society 1784) for those outside the scope of the poor laws. These later societies appeal for support, not on account of the notorious shortcomings of parish officers, but on the ground that they provide for hard cases.[140]

The great development of friendly societies[141] (in spite of the convivial and speculative character of many of them) shows that there was a growing spirit of providence and independence. That improvidence and passion for gambling which are sometimes regarded as peculiarly modern portents existed in an extreme form in eighteenth-century London, and even then, are perhaps rather to be considered as survivals than as new developments. The dependence on the pawnbroker and the loan-monger had long been a marked feature of London life; these people, like the tallymen, multiplied in the poorer quarters of the town, and throve upon the power of arresting for debt. They were, it was complained in 1678, 'the Nimrods, the private hunters, in this vast forest of chimneys, that draw the poor into their nets, and pick them to the very bone', while their bandogs were the bailiff and his setting cur, who usually died a violent death, 'and as they lived, hated, died, unpitied'.[142]

It was no small change that the people were becoming healthier, longer-lived, less subject to the calamities of imprisonment for debt, and to temptations to excessive drunkenness. The change in the attitude towards social questions which was the outcome of the new spirit of humanity, the new command of material resources, and the new belief in environment rather than Providence as the cause of many human ills was at least paralleled by a progressive revolution in manners after about 1760. Place writes in his Autobiography:

... the circumstances ... I have mentioned relative to the ignorance, the immorality, the grossness, the obscenity, the drunkenness, the dirtiness, and the depravity of the middling and even of a large portion of the better sort of tradesmen, the artisans, the journeymen tradesmen of London in the days of my youth may excite a suspicion that the picture ... is a caricature.

He anticipates, and tries to answer, the objection that it is necessary to give some reasons for such an improvement, and it is curious and suggestive to find that among his reasons are some of the changes to which both contemporary and modern writers ascribe a supposed deterioration:

Some of the good producing causes are a better regulated police, and a better description of police magistrates. The extension of the cotton manufacture which has done all but wonders in respect to the cleanliness and healthiness of women. The rapid increase of wealth and its more general diffusion subsequent to the revolutionary wars with the North American Colonies, and their wonderful and increasing prosperity. The French Revolution which broke up many old absurd notions and tended to dissipate the pernicious reverence for men of title and estate without regard to personal knowledge or personal worth. The stimulus it gave to serious thoughts on Government and the desire for information in every possible direction. The promotion of Political Societies which gave rise to reading clubs, the independent notions these encouraged and the consequent reformation of manners. The introduction of Sunday Schools, and the invaluable method of teaching employed by Joseph Lancaster. ... Schools, on the plan of Dr Bell and the miscalled National Schools, little as they teach. The desire which the general movement produced in all below the very rich to give their children a better education than they had themselves received and the consequent elevation all these matters have produced on the manners and morals of the whole community.[143]

An analysis of the causes of improvement still leaves the modern student marvelling that so much was achieved. The attitude of contemporaries was different. Colquhoun, for instance, who was responsible for much of the more pessimistic opinion of his day, saw in the poor relief, the hospitals, the charities of London, the absolute high-water mark of provision for misfortune. With all this, he asks, how is it possible that so much vice and misery should still exist?[144] Today the problem seems akin to that of the Army and Navy – how could men, recruited as were the British land and sea forces, not to speak of the corruption and bad administration which was rife, achieve such results? Part of the answer is probably the same in both cases. There had been a number of obscure reforms, whose cumulative effect was very great, which for the most part have been lost sight of in the more fundamental changes which took place later, and obscured by an increasing realization of evils and a growing intolerance of hardships. One can hardly suppose, for instance, that the grievances which led to the Mutiny of the Nore were worse than those endured by the unfortunate seamen in the expedition to Carthagena, so vividly described by Smollett in *Roderick Random*. The improvements in medicine and sanitation had bettered conditions both in London and at sea. The expansion of trade and the many opportunities of rising in the world had their counterpart in the prize-money, of which all sailors had a chance. The advance still remains surprising and we are reminded of the strange way in which human nature often manages to be so much better than the world has any right to expect. We can but admire the people who responded so quickly to the beginnings of an improvement in their environment. Then, in spite of restrictions, in spite even of the press-gang and the crimp, the eighteenth-century Londoner had an intense sense of personal freedom, and of his share in the heritage of British liberty. And freedom being primarily a state of mind, we must recognize, in spite of Rousseau and Disraeli and other scoffers, the undoubted fact that this sense of personal liberty had a real importance in the social life of the time.

Notes to the Introduction

Cross-references to notes sometimes refer also to the corresponding text

(1) In this book 'London' is used for the whole metropolis, or as the topographers say, for 'the Cities and liberties of London and Westminster, the Borough of Southwark and parts adjacent'. By the eighteenth century the term was already used in this sense. See *London and its Records*, by Miss Jeffries Davis, *History*, October 1921.

(2) This change was commented on so early as 1749: 'The decrease . . . of the trade of London in some particular branches is no proof of the decline of its trade in general; which is certainly much increased in other branches, and especially in the most safe, easy and gainful branches of agency, factorage, brokerage, negotiation and insurance for the other parts of the kingdom. And I believe . . . by these and other most profitable branches of trade and business now carried on in London, more and greater estates are daily made there, than have been elsewhere made by business in any trade or country.

'And hence it appears that the decline of trade so much complained of in the capital is . . . rather a variation and change of trade from one kind to another; a laying down of less lucrative and more hazardous employments in order to pursue others that turn to better accounts. Such, when compared with those of the merchant exporter, are those of agents, factors, brokers, insurers, bankers, negotiators, discounters, subscribers, contractors, remitters, ticket-mongers, stock-jobbers, and of a great variety of other dealers in money, the names of whose employments were wholly unknown to our forefathers. As also are those of governors, directors, commissioners, and of a vast train of secretaries, clerks, book-keepers and others, their attendants and dependents, most of which employs are peculiar to London, and are more lucrative than that of merchant exporter, and the profits of many of them must be vastly increased by the late great increase of the national debt.' (*An Essay on the Increase and Decline of Trade* . . . 1749, p. 34.) See also note 6, Chapter 1.

(3) A. L. Bowley, *The Change in the Distribution of the National Income*, 1880–1913, Oxford, 1920, p. 26.

(4) 'It is now grown into a kind of custom, even within the liberties of the City, for merchants to refuse taking up their freedom, lest they should be burdened with the usual inconveniences attending it.' (J. Tucker, *The Elements of Commerce and Theory of Taxes*, 1755, p. 88.)

(5) *A Journey from London to Genoa*, 1770, i, p. 43.

(6) *A Brief Description . . . of London*, p. xxiii.

(7) Add. MSS. 35143, fo. 149, Autob. ii.

(8) Add. MSS. 27828, fo. 60. Place's experience was chiefly of London, but in his opinion improvement was not confined to Londoners. In 1835 he was asked if he had 'seen the work of Dr Kay on the statistics of Manchester as to the state of the operatives of that town'. He answered, 'Yes, I know Dr Kay, and I believe what he says is correct; but he gives the matter as it now stands, knowing nothing of former times; his picture is a very deplorable one. I am assured that my view of it is correct by many Manchester operatives whom I have seen; they inform me that his narration relates almost wholly to the state of the Irish, but that the condition of a vast number of the people was as bad some years ago, as he described the worst portion of them to be now. Any writer or inquirer will be misled unless he has the means of comparing the present with former times.' (*Report on Education*, 1835, p. 838.)

Place's opinion is certainly borne out by the remarkable improvement in the health of Manchester in a period during which the population had quadrupled. In 1757 the death-rate was estimated at 1 in 25·7, in 1770 at 1 in 28, in 1811 at 1 in 74 and in 1821 it had still further improved. This great advance was ascribed to the efforts of Dr Percival and Dr Ferriar. F. Bisset Hawkins, *Elements of Medical Statistics*, 1829, p. 19. Blane, *Medical Dissertations*.

(9) It was a maxim of Dr Harrison (in *Amelia*) 'that no man can descend below himself in doing any act which may contribute to protect an innocent person or to bring a rogue to the gallows'.

(10) *Causes of the late Increase of Robbers*, 1751, p. xiv. See also *The Case of Bosavern Penlez*, p. 47 and *passim*.

(11) op. cit. 25 February 1752. Fielding's methods and point of view are well illustrated by his comments on this case: 'By the law of England as it now stands, if a larceny be absolutely committed, however slight the suspicion be against the accused, the justice . . . is obliged in strictness to commit the party, especially if he have not sureties for his appearance. . . . Nor will the trifling value of the thing stolen, nor any circumstance of mitigation justify his discharging the prisoner. Nay, Mr Dalton says, that when the felony is proved to have been done, should the party appear to demonstration innocent, the justice . . . must commit or bail. And however absurd this opinion may appear, my Lord Hale hath thought fit to embrace and transcribe it in his *Pleas of the Crown*. Thus, for a theft of twopence or threepence value, a poor wretch may lie starving and confined in jail near two months in this town, and in the country above half a year, before he is brought to his trial. The consequences of which are, first, that he is even thus punished infinitely above the degree of his guilt. Secondly, that he is absolutely undone, his business lost and his reputation gone for ever. Thirdly, that he is totally contaminated and corrupted by the conversation of notorious thieves. . . . In a word, he hath lost all restraints and acquired every incitement to villainy, and every qualification for it. . . .' He urges summary process before a magistrate instead of committal to the Sessions.

(12) See J. Fielding, *An Account of the Origin and Effects of a Plan of Police . . . and . . . a Plan for preserving those deserted Girls who become Prostitutes from Necessity*. '. . . On a search night when the constables have taken up near forty prostitutes, it has appeared upon their examination, that the major part of them have been of this kind, under the age of eighteen, many not more than twelve, and those, though so young, half eat up with the foul distemper. Who can say that one of these poor children had been prostitutes through viciousness? No, they are young, unprotected and of the female sex, therefore become the prey of the baud and debauchee.'

(13) Middlesex *Order Book*, 14 April and 19 May 1763. Fifty-seven justices presented a memorandum to the Sessions which runs: 'We are of opinion the opening of several public offices . . . for two magistrates to sit daily by rotation . . . for the administration of justice will not only add honour to the Commission, but be productive of several good purposes.'

(14) A guide-book to London gives the following list of rotation offices where 'two or more magistrates sit daily . . . from ten to three to hear complaints . . . the expenses of hearing at these offices is seldom above a few shillings. . . .

'For Westminster and the County of Middlesex –
     Bow Street, Covent Garden.
     Litchfield Street.
     Hyde Street, Bloomsbury.
     St Martin's Street, Leicester Fields.

For the City –
    Guidhall.
    The Mansion House.
For the Tower District and below Tower Hill –
    Worship Street, Shoreditch.
For Southwark –
    Union Hall, Union Street, Borough.'

Trusler, *The London Adviser and Guide*, 1786, p. 139.

(Bow Street was not a rotation office. The two last-mentioned survived as the new public offices under the Act of 1792.)

(15) The first conception seems to have been due to Harriott, an Essex magistrate, who put the plan without success first before the Lord Mayor, as conservator of the river, then before the Home Secretary, but it would, he says, 'have died in embryo' without Colquhoun's 'superior knowledge and insight into the management of obtaining attention to affairs of this kind'. (*Struggles through Life . . .*, 2nd ed. 1803, ii, p. 321.)

Colquhoun improved upon the plan, suggested fire-engines for the police barges, obtained the support of the West India merchants and then of the Government. The office checked the wholesale plundering of ships and warehouses which had threatened 'to overthrow the commerce of the port of London'. Before this, it was well known, says Colquhoun, 'that every public wharf and quay . . . was filled with criminal people . . . who prowl about under the pretence of seeking employment as porters and labourers. . . . It rarely happens that a magistrate in investigating the history of an idle or suspicious character . . . does not find that they have worked at the waterside. . . .' (*River Police*, 1800)

(16) They include the poor laws, Hanway's Act for the preservation of the Infant Poor, the Acts for protecting poor apprentices and that for climbing-boys, for regulating pawnbrokers, friendly societies and the employment of coal-heavers, and the Spitalfields Acts. See Index.

(17) The first of this series of local Acts was the Watch Act of St James Westminster and St George's Hanover Square in 1735 (8 Geo. II. c. 15), passed in spite of the opposition of the Dean and Chapter to the encroachment on their rights as lords of the franchise of Westminster, and soon imitated by other parishes. Parochial legislation for the poor began with St Martin's in 1750. The two next Acts for the poor, those of St Margaret and St John (25 Geo. II. c. 23) and St George Hanover Square (26 Geo. II. c. 97) laid down the general principles subsequently followed by London parishes. The two innovations of a paid rate collector and the power to receive deserted children into the workhouse regardless of their settlement, roused opposition: 'We apprehend,' runs a petition against the Bill for St George's, 'there can be no reason for increasing the parish expense by constituting a salaried officer hitherto unknown to our laws. . . .' It protests against 'a clause for taking care of all the poor children who shall happen to stray into this parish, which by the way, is little less than desiring a law to subject this opulent parish to the maintenance and support of all the vagabounds in the kingdom'. (*Reasons humbly offered . . . against the Bill for the better Relief and Employment of the Poor of the said Parish.*)

As they were drafted by the people who were to administer them they were enforceable, unlike earlier Acts for the metropolis. They were technically public statutes but were obtained on petition, as private Bills, a method by which changes were made of an experimental kind which would have roused much opposition in a public Bill of general application.

(18) Colquhoun, *Police of the Metropolis*, 2nd ed. 1797, p. 214.

(19) *Office of a Constable*, 1791, p. v.

(20) cf. S. and B. Webb, *Manor and Borough*, ii, p. 737: 'The medieval conception of public office was a freehold possession tenable for life, involving not obedience to orders, but the performances only of definitely customary duties, not remunerated by a salary, but entitling to the exaction of customary fees. The municipal corporations had lagged behind the parish vestries in the evolution which separates entirely the governing council from the executive officials and places them definitely in the position of salaried servants, amenable to orders and dismissible on due notice.'

(21) *Parliamentary History*, xi, p. 1,011.

(22) Feltham, *Picture of London*, 1802, p. 276.

(23) Hitchin, *A true Discovery of the Conduct of Receivers and Thief Takers in and about the City of London . . .*, 1718, p. 8.

(24) *First Report of the Society . . .* p. ii.

(25) Fielding, *Proposal for making an effectual Provision for the Poor . . .*, 1753, p. 9.

(26) Lettsom, *On the Improvement of Medicine in London*, 1775, pp. 21–2.

(27) Tyerman, *Life and Times of John Wesley*, 1870, ii, p. 160.

(28) W. Playfair, chapter on 'Education' interpolated into his annotated edition of Adam Smith's *Wealth of Nations*, 1805, iii, pp. 251–2. See p. 248, Chap. 5.

(29) Evidence to the Committee on Education, 1835, *Report*, p. 841. Place says: 'I . . . was a member of the Borough-road school at a time of its greatest difficulty. I worked hard with it. I saw the children of the most dissolute people on the face of the earth brought into order and taught as much as the school professed to teach them. At one time there were punishments for disobedient or neglectful behaviour; it was a system of humiliation which it was found useful to dispense with and it was dropped. . . . Mr Lancaster had a notion if he could allow boys to make a noise they would never consider it drudgery to be taught. I believe he was correct; there is in the school a perpetual noise; strangers find it confusion, but it is perfect order; the boys get the power of abstraction so as to go on with ease notwithstanding there is noise from the process going on.' (ibid.)

See also H. B. Binns, *A Century of Education, 1808–1908*, 1908.

(30) Add. MSS. 27826, fo. 192–3.

(31) *Narrative of the Rev. W. Wilson . . .*, 1739. (Quoted by Place, Add. MSS. 27828, fo. 51.)

(32) This was not an exceptional point of view. In 1744 the Ordinary of Newgate, in his published comments on the execution of boys belonging to the Black Boy Alley gang who had been terrorizing the town, calls England 'a place famous for good and wholesome laws, but, sorry I am to say it, infamous for not putting them into execution.' (London *Sessions Papers*). See also G. Olliffe, M.A., *An Essay humbly offered for an Act . . . to prevent capital Crimes and . . . promote a desirable Improvement and Blessing to the Nation*, 1731, which recommends breaking on the wheel, etc. etc., able-bodied vagrants to be sold for slaves in the Plantations or made galley slaves.

(33) J. B. Nichols, *Anecdotes of William Hogarth*, 1833, pp. 64–5.

(34) The method was by advertisement and by orders (and special payments) to the constables: e.g. 'This day, being Shrove Tuesday, the Peace officers . . . have been directed and are requested to use their utmost endeavours to prevent the no less barbarous than shameful custom of throwing at cocks; and as the press warrants for recruiting the Army are by this time delivered to most of the officers, it is to be hoped that some of these heroes will soon have their strength and courage employed more to their own honour and more to the advantage of their country.' (*Public Advertiser*, 7 February 1758.)

'Yesterday the constables of Holborn Division, Westminster, etc., went round their several divisions about Tothil Fields, Mill Bank, Tottenham Court and the Long Fields and other places contiguous to apprehend any dissolute fellows that might be found throwing at cocks, but the coasts were all clear, so that it is hoped this barbarous custom of the rabble is now entirely left off'. (ibid. 17 February 1768. cf. note 113, Chapter 2.)

(35) See notes 22, 164, 165, Chapter 3 and 5, Chapter 6.

(36) cf. the evidence of the Secretary of the Mendicity Society in 1826 on the use of the workhouse as a test of destitution: 'If the officers offer to take a family into the workhouse and employ the man . . . the magistrates have no power to enforce further relief, and a great many persons refuse to avail themselves of this offer . . . and in fact they support themselves.' Place remarks, 'this is the more remarkable since in many parts of this kingdom there is in whole parishes not a single labourer who is not a pauper. It proves very decidedly that the desire of independence is not destroyed in London as it is in the country. It proves also the advantages that still remain where no part of a man's wages is paid by the parish', (Evidence to the Committee on Emigration (14 October 1826) transcribed and annotated by Place, Add. MSS. 27825 (1), fo. 260). London seems to have been protected against an influx of labour from the country by the over-population of villages under the old poor law; the people preferred the certainty of maintenance to the uncertainty of work elsewhere, combined with the possible loss of their original settlement. 'Thousands of instances may be given where the labourers will not stir for fear of losing their parishes. I think the law of settlement is the great means of keeping the English labourers confined to their parishes; it appears to them to be running away from their heirlooms or freeholds.' (Poor Law Report, 1834, p. 157.) On the other hand there was a terrible influx of Irish labour to London (see note 54, Chapter 3). cf. the evidence of the Vestry Clerk of Bermondsey to the Poor Law Commissioners: 'there are great numbers of Irishmen employed in our parish; but they are only employed because English labourers cannot be got to do the same work for the same wages'. 'And what sort of wages are those?' 'Not less than from 10s. to 15s. a week. An English labourer might live upon this. But English labourers would have more because they are worth more. An English labourer does not require so much superintendence.' (ibid.)

(37) The transition is well illustrated by two pronouncements of Colquhoun, one in 1806:

'In a country where almost every year adds one or more millions to the value of manufactures exported to foreign countries and where the increase of the sale of labour abroad has more than kept pace with the increase of the population; where new manufactures are yearly springing up, and adding to the existing resources for the employment of the poor, and where the incalculable advantages these nations enjoy over every other, arising from their insular situation and the skill and capital everywhere diffused, must ensure the decided preference they have obtained over every country in Europe, there can be little danger of full employment even to an extended population.' (Treatise on Indigence, 1806, p. 146. For evidence as to war prosperity in London see note 96, Chap. 1.)

The title of the tract of 1818 tells its own melancholy tale: Considerations on the Means of affording profitable Employment to the redundant Population of Great Britain and Ireland.

(38) For instance, Rush, the Minister of the United States, describes an expedition to London east of Temple Bar in January 1818: In the crowded streets 'a large proportion were of the working classes, yet all were whole in their clothing; you could hardly see exceptions. All looked healthy, the more to be remarked in parts of the City where they live in perpetual crowds by day and sleep in confined places.' (R. Rush, Residence at the Court of London, 3rd ed. 1872, p. 51.)

(39) O. Williams, Life and Letters of John Rickman, 1912, p. 182.

Notes to Chapter 1

(1) Heberden, 'On the mortality of London', Medical *Transactions of the College of Physicians*, iv, p. 103. For the history of the Bills of Mortality and discussions as to their defects and omissions see C. H. Hull, *The Economic Writings of Sir William Petty*, 1899, i, pp. lxxx–xci; Maitland, *Hist. of London*, 1756, ii, p. 740 ff.; Ogle, 'Inquiry into the Trustworthiness of the Old Bills of Mortality', *Journal of the Statistical Society*, LV. p. 437 ff.; Christie, *Some Account of the Company of Parish Clerks*, 1893. For the actual variations between the Bills and the parish registers see Appendix I, *B*. Whether the Bills (and also the registers) became more or less defective as time went on is a matter of controversy; Price wrote in 1780, the Bills 'are indeed defective, but in consequence of a great decrease of dissenters, they are less so than they used to be'. *Essay on Population*, p. 60. Lysons found in 1795 that an excess of baptisms over burials at Bethnal Green was 'to be attributed to some private burial-grounds where the fees are somewhat lower than in that belonging to the parish'. *Environs . . .*, ii, p. 37. Malcolm attributed a decrease in burials in Whitechapel after 1783 to 'a number of cheap burying-grounds'; Jews certainly increased in the eastern parishes. *Londinium Redivivum*, iii, p. 230, etc.

(2) 'Sir J. Nickolls' (Dangeul), *Remarks on the Advantages and Disadvantages of France and Great Britain in regard to Commerce . . .* , 1754, p. 188.

(3) C. Morris, *Observations on the past Growth and present State of London*, 1751, p. 106.

(4) Price, *Observations on . . . the Population . . .* (Appendix to Morgan's *Assurances*, p. 274). This curious interpretation of luxury is illustrated by his account of the population of Birmingham:

'A.D. 1700   15,042 inhabitants,   6   to a house.
        1750   23,688   „ $5\frac{7}{16}$ „
        1770   30,804   „ $5\frac{1}{9}$ „

'In this account we see the gradual progress of luxury at Birmingham, the houses having increased so much faster than the people.' (ibid.)

In 1783 Price estimated that the populations of England and Wales had decreased by a million and a half since the Revolution, 'the inhabitants of the cottages thrown down in the country fly to London, there to be corrupted and perish.' (*Observations on Reversionary Payments*, ed. of 1783, Supplement II, p. 256.) 'In London those who used to live plain must now live high, those who used to walk must now be carried. This is the reason of the increase of consumption in London and not an increase of the inhabitants, for the number of inhabitants is certainly (if any regard is due to the Bills) less now than it was thirty years ago.' (ibid. p. 257 n.) His arguments were based partly on the burials in the Bills, partly on the returns of houses for the window tax (see note 42, Chapter 2) and inhabited house duty. See *Essay on the Population of England and Wales*, 1780.

(5) The returns for 1631 in the following table are from a report by the Lord Mayor to the Privy Council who had asked for an estimate of the number of mouths, fearing a scarcity, printed in Schedule C of the Report of the City Day Census, 1881. See *Notes and Queries*, 11th Series, i, p. 426, 1910.

Those of 1695 are Gregory King's estimate taken from the books of the Hearth Office and the returns of Chimney Money, plus an allowance of 10 per cent for omissions and of

	1631	1695	POPULATION RETURNS			
			1700	1750	1801	1811
1. City within the Walls	71,029	80,190	139,300	87,000	78,000	57,700
2. City without the Walls	40,579	164,450 (including the Borough)	69,000	57,000	56,300	68,000
3. The Borough (the five parishes of old Southwark)	18,660	..	100,000	94,700	98,700	75,000
4. Westminster	..	113,520	130,000	152,000	165,000	168,000
5. The out-parishes of Middlesex and Surrey	..	169,400	226,900	258,900	379,000	518,700
6. The five parishes not included in the Bills.	..	..	9,150	22,350	123,000	162,000
Total for the Metropolis	..	527,560	674,350	676,250	900,000	1,050,000
Population of England and Wales	..	..	5,475,000	6,467,000	9,168,000	10,488,000

2,440 souls for London's share of an estimated 80,000 uncounted travellers and vagrants. G. Chalmers, *Natural and Political Observations and Conclusions upon the State . . . of England by G. King, Esq.*, 1804. King allowed above five heads to a house, almost certainly too little.

The returns of 1700 and 1750 are based on the baptisms in the Parish Registers (see p. 42); those of 1801 and 1811 are those of the actual enumerations plus an allowance for the non-resident population of one-twenty-fifth for London, and one-thirtieth for the country at large.

The *London Summary* in the 1801 Census included (as did King) the Borough in the City without the Walls. There had been a long-standing dispute between the Corporation and the Surrey authorities as to the limits of their respective jurisdictions and the 1811 *Summary* reverses this retrospectively, and deducts the five parishes from the City Without adding them to the out-parishes. The discrepancy therefore between the two summaries gives the population ascribed to the Borough and this is the authority for the Borough totals in the above table for 1700, 1750 and 1801.

It is a bewildering fact however that the actual enumeration by parishes for the county of Surrey gives Southwark a total of only 67,448 in 1801 and 72,119 in 1811, so that the addition of a twenty-fifth fails to make the return of 1801 tally with the *London Summary*. Moreover, the smaller total includes the parish of Christchurch, which had been formed out of the liberty of Paris Garden Manor and had never been under the City as part of the Borough.

(6) This appears from the parish registers and Bills of Mortality (see Appendix I, *A* and *B*); it was also deduced in 1719 from the increased consumption of coal:

1695	315,427 chaldrons.	1709	344,645 chaldrons.
1702	323,583 „	1716	375,452 „

The writer (rather speciously) says, 'nor can it be fairly urged . . . that glass-houses, printing and damasking of stuffs and cloths consume large quantities, since those very manufactures entirely depend on the growth and improvement of the City. . . . The increase both of buildings and people is too evident to be deny'd, it were rather to be wished, it could be said, that an increase of trade contributed to the other increase; but there seems to be much stronger reason for believing that it is chiefly owing to other causes, whereof the Union of England and Scotland may be reckoned one and another (altogether as considerable) may be the Publick Funds, which have occasion'd the erecting of several new offices and societies . . . and have brought great numbers of other people to live in and about London; some upon the increase of their fortunes placed in the Exchequer, Bank, etc., to great advantage, and others to deal in stocks and funds, which being of that largeness and extent, have furnish'd new and shining equipages which have increased great variety of town traffick and employment. . . .' (*A Computation of the Increase of London* . . . 1719)

(7) Heberden, *Observations on the Increase and Decrease of different Diseases*, 1801, p. 32.

(8) Correspondence between Rickman and Sir F. d'Ivernois, 1827, printed in *Minutes of Evidence of the Population Bill Committee*, 1830. Rickman thought that neither the registered burials nor the deaths had increased in the last 120 years.

Average of registered burials in London:

1700–1780	24,657	
1781–1790	23,080	
1791–1800	24,470	
1801–1810	22,164	
1811–1820	23,331	(ibid.)

(9) *Population Returns* for 1811, Appendix, p. 20; *Returns* for 1821, p. 160. If the ratio of registered baptisms to the total population was not constant, but was lower at the height of the gin-drinking period, as there seems reason to suppose, the population of London in 1750 would be greater than Rickman's estimate, and the death-rate correspondingly less high.

(10) Proportions of baptisms to burials in London according to the Bills:

	Baptisms		Burials
1680–1700	681	to	1,000
1700–1720	721	to	1,000
1720–1740	649	to	1,000
1740–1760	638	to	1,000
(four years) 1761–1765	644	to	1,000

(C. Smith, *Tracts on the Corn Trade*, Supplement, p. 23.)

(11) 'The present fever (1741) on its first appearance seldom fixed itself on any but the poor people, and especially on such as lived in large towns, workhouses or prisons. Country people and farmers seemed for the most part exempt from it.' It was ascribed to millers and bakers using flour composed of horse-beans, peas, coarse unsound barley, etc., 'in the late scarcity and dearness of provisions'. (Maitland, *History of London*, 1756, i, p. 621.)

(12) Chalmers, *Domestic Œconomy*, 1812, p. 261.

(13) cf. Defoe on the increase of London between 1725 and 1727: 'Since our last volume [1725] we have to add . . . a large variety both of publick and private buildings; as a new

East India House building in the City and a South Sea Company House finished, both lofty and magnificent. Mr Guy's Hospital in Southwark . . . the additions to Bethlehem Hospital and several new steeples and churches. . . . Then there is a little city of buildings, streets and squares added to those mentioned before at the West side of Hanover and Cavendish Squares, with the repair of two terrible fires at Wapping and Ratcliffe.' (*Tour through the whole Island of Great Britain*, iii, p. 10.)

(14) Tooke, *History of Prices*, 1838, i, pp. 41–3.

(15) 'We have of late years greatly increased in the breeding of live-stock of all kinds, and the great supply from the northern parts of England and Wales have glutted the London markets. . . . This great increase has of late supplied the London markets with meat far beyond its consumption, and therefore lowered the price, so that the best or middling pieces have been sold cheap enough to be within the reach of the common people, therefore common pieces have not had so ready a vent as usual.' (*A proper Reply to the scandalous Libel . . . The Trial of the Spirits*, 1736.) (This had maintained that meat was cheap because spirit-drinkers did not eat meat and therefore the inferior pieces had to be buried.)

(16) Short, *New Observations on City, Town and Country Bills of Mortality*, 1750, p. 241. See also Appendix I, *D* and *E*.

(17) Another explanation sometimes given is that it was due to the collapse of the South Sea Bubble, e.g. Maitland, *History of London*, 1756, ii, p. 740. This interrupted the building of Cavendish Square, but it seems unlikely that it seriously affected the population of London between 1720 and 1750.

(18) op. cit., p. 115.

(19) *Considerations upon the Effects of spirituous Liquors . . .*, 1751.

(20) *Parliamentary History*, xii, p. 1,433.

(21) *Review*, 9 May 1713.

(22) 2 Wm. and Mary, Sess. 2 c. 3.

(23) 12 Anne Stat. 2 c. 3.

(24) Defoe, *Complete English Tradesman*, 1727, ii, Part II, p. 80.

(25) J. Collyer, *The Parent's and Guardian's Directory and the Youth's Guide in the Choice of a Profession or Trade*, 1761, pp. 122–3. See also *A general Description of all Trades*, 1747, pp. 78–80.

(26) Davenant, *Essay upon Ways and Means*, ed. of 1701, p. 134.

(27) *Order Book*, Westminster Sessions. April 1721. (*Cal.*)

(28) ibid. October 1721.

(29) Sir D. Dolins, *Charge to the Grand Jury of Middlesex*, 7 October 1725.

(30) *Order Book*, Middlesex Sessions, January 1725–6. (*Cal.*)

(31) Munk, *Roll of the College of Physicians*, ii, p. 55.

(32) Maitland, *Hist. of London*, 1756, i, p. 544.

(33) *C.J.* 9 and 12 March 1732–3.

(34) By another Act of 1729 (2 Geo. II. c. 28, s. 10 and 11) retailers of spirits had been required to take out a justice's licence as common alehouse-keepers.

(35) *Order Book*, Middlesex Sessions, January 1735–6. (*Cal.*) (Printed in an appendix to *Distilled Spirituous Liquours the Bane of the Nation*, 1730.)

(36) *Parliamentary History*, ix, p. 1,039.

(37) The magistrates and especially Colonel de Veil attempted at first to enforce the Act at some personal risk. 'It is beyond question, that the motives upon which the law was made, were in themselves right, and the intention of the legislature very just and reasonable; but the mischiefs that this law was intended to remedy had taken such deep

root, and the practice of drinking was become so general among the common people, that it certainly required great skill and caution to have eradicated it, which this Act was so far from doing, that it really heightened the evil by the addition of many others, as dangerous and detestable; for on the one hand, it let loose a crew of desperate and wicked people who turn'd informers merely for bread; and on the other it exposed numbers of unhappy people, who before the selling of spirituous liquors by retail became a crime, had got a livelihood thereby, to be distressed, beggared and sent to prison. So . . . the law . . . proved an encouragement to perjury, and gave an opening to a kind of legal oppression which quickly filled the Bridewells so full, and brought such numbers upon the parishes, that it was at last found necessary to soften the severity of this Act . . . by becoming relax in the execution of it. Before things took this turn, Colonel de Veil . . . ran a great hazard of being made a victim to that spirit of fury and resentment with which the mob were filled, even against such as were obliged by their offices to receive informations and to punish offenders upon conviction.' (*Biography of Sir Thomas de Veil*, pp. 38–40.)

Between September 1736 and July 1738 it was estimated that 12,000 informations had been laid against spirit retailers within the Bills of Mortality. There were 4,896 convictions and 4,000 claims for the reward of £5 allowed to the informer out of the penalty of £100. Three thousand people paid £10 to escape being sent to Bridewell. Malcolm, *Anecdotes of the Manners and Customs of London* . . . , 1808, p. 275.

(38) *Parliamentary History*, xii, p. 1,322. (Lord Bathurst, or rather Samuel Johnson, this being one of the debates written by him for the *Gentleman's Magazine*; see W. P. Courtney, *A Bibliography of Samuel Johnson*, 1915, p. 14.)

(39) cf. for instance the petition of the Ministers, Churchwardens, Vestrymen and Inhabitants of St Martin's in the Fields: 'that by the frequent and excessive use of spirituous liquors religion is scandalously prophaned, the health of the people destroyed, their strength and substance wasted, their lives shortened and the human species lessened and decreased; and that idleness and disorder take the place of industry and morality amongst the labouring and common people; and that numberless robberies in the streets and elsewhere, and even murders are committed by the common use of low-priced spirituous liquors; and that if an immediate restraint is not put to this pernicious vice, it will not only increase the above-mentioned evils, but also tend to the destruction of the trade and power of the kingdom. . . .' (*C.J.* 1 March 1750–51.)

(40) e.g. 'The extreme misery of the lowest description of Londoners received some amelioration about 1750, thro' the commendable inquiries and remedies made and applied by the Legislation relating to their monstrous excesses in drinking ardent spirits. . . .' (Malcolm, *Anecdotes* . . . , 1808, pp. 95–6.)

'In the early part of my life (I remember almost the time which Hogarth has pictured), when every house in St Giles, whatever else they sold, sold gin, every chandler's shop sold gin, the situation of the people was terrible.' (Evidence of T. Collins, a Middlesex magistrate, *Report on the Police of the Metropolis*, 1817, p. 203.)

(41) 24 Geo. II. c. 40. Other provisions were that spirit licences were only to be granted to such publicans as paid to Church and Poor, and (in London) rented a tenement of at least £10 a year. Brewers, inn-keepers, distillers, and dealers in spirits were not to act as justices in matters relative to distillers. Debts under 20s. for spirits were made irrecoverable. Penalties were laid on retailing spirits in prisons or workhouses. Assembling to rescue offenders under the Act was made a felony, punishable with seven years' transportation.

The opposition to this Act illustrates the tendency to denounce all police measures, and especially licensing restrictions, as attacks on British liberty. cf. the engraving *A Modern*

Contrast (1752): On one side is a distiller's, the sign of the Distillers' Arms, on the other a public-house, the sign of the Bear and Lamb inscribed, 'Spirituous Liquors sold here'. The distiller is being served with a writ, his wife and children are leaving the house, his casks are being staved. At the rival publican's drams are being drunk and the fat landlord and landlady shout 'We go according to law.' 'Ay, ay, we have a licence.' Justice with her sword and scales lies drunk on the ground and among the passers-by is a Frenchman who says, 'If dis be Angleterre me go to France.'

(42) R. Campbell, *London Tradesman*, 1747, p. 280.

As soon as spirit-retailers were required to take out a magisterial licence (see note 34) Quarter Sessions had recommended the justices not to grant licences to chandlers, 'inasmuch as a great many servants, apprentices and other persons are drawn in and inveigled by the keepers of such chandlers' shops to drink these strong-waters. . . . Whereby they . . . become intoxicated and uncapable of performing the business with which they are entrusted.' (Middlesex *Order Book*, October 1729.) (*Cal.*)

(43) cf. J. Tucker, *An Enquiry concerning the use of low-priced spirituous Liquors*, 1751.

(44) *A Brief Description . . . of London*, 1776, p. xxiii.

(45) *S. P. Dom.* Geo. III. 5 February 1773.

(46) R. Willan, *Reports on the Diseases in London*, 1801, p. 394.

(47) Burrington, *An Answer to Dr William Brakenridge's Letter*, 1757, p. 37.

Hanway wrote in 1759: 'The custom of the common people drinking great quantities of the most inflammatory and poisonous liquor, certainly created an incredible devastation amongst the children of the poor till the hand of Providence interposed by the instrumentality of His Majesty's ministers, to arrest the dreadful progress of it; and the people themselves seem at length to have discovered, that health and pleasure, food and raiment, are better than sickness and pain, want and wretchedness.' (*A Candid historical Account of the Hospital for . . . exposed and deserted Young Children*, 1759, p. 10.)

(48) From Spitalfields, Colchester and Norwich, *C.J.* 21 November, 4 and 5 December 1759.

(49) An attempt was made to satisfy the two conflicting interests by combining a drawback and bounty on export with the higher duty. The Corporation of London and other London merchants and employers foresaw the danger that relanding would lead to renewed cheap retailing, and petitioned against the drawback, which though passed was repealed the following year, having been found to be 'attended with many inconveniences.' (*C.J.* 24 January, 4 February, 17 and 21 March 1760.)

(50) *C.J.* 12 December 1783.

(51) Colquhoun, *Police of the Metropolis*, ed. of 1806, pp. 328–9.

(52) Silliman, *A Journal of Travels . . .*, iii, p. 89. This is confirmed by Simond (who had lived for twenty years in the United States): 'I am pleased to find that ardent spirits have not superseded malt liquors among the labouring class to the degree I had been led to expect. . . . Working people are not saturated with alcohol. . . . It is not uncommon in America for labourers to use in the course of the day a pint of rum, and many of them a quart; a dose which would kill outright any person not accustomed to it by degrees. This daily dose of poison costs the American labourer from one to two shillings a day, that is at least a fourth part of his earnings, and equalizes things between him and the European.' (*Journal . . .*, i, pp. 306–7.)

(53) Colquhoun, *Observations and Facts relative to Public Houses*, 1794. In the vastly greater London of 1830 the number of licensed houses is said to have been from 4,000 to 5,000. *Select Committee on the Sale of Beer*, p. 113.

(54) Quoted by Malcolm in *Anecdotes relating to London*, 1808, p. 96.

(55) *Sessions Papers*, February 1734.

(56) Hanway, *An Earnest Appeal for Mercy to the Children of the Poor*, 1766, p. 42.

(57) Fielding, *An Enquiry into the Reasons of the late Increase of Robbers*, 1751, p. 19.

(58) Sir T. Mildmay, *The Police of France*, 1763, p. 127 or 71.

(59) Hanway, *Letters on the Importance of the Rising Generation*, 1768, ii, p. 136.

(60) *An Account of the general Nursery or Colledg of Infants . . .* 1686.

(61) Coram said he had been a witness to the shocking spectacle of innocent children who had been murdered and thrown on dunghills. Perhaps some of these children had died a natural (or quasi-natural) death and the bodies had been so disposed of to save the expense of burial. There were cases of this a hundred years later. (Chadwick, *Supplementary Report on Intramural Interments*, 1843.) But see the *Old Bailey Sessions Papers passim* for trials of women for killing their illegitimate infants.

(62) Hanway, *A Candid historical Account of the Hospital for . . . exposed and deserted young children*, 1759, p. 23.

(63) ibid., pp. 24–5.

(64) ibid., p. 85. By this plan hospitals would be erected in all parts of the kingdom 'to be supported by the public purse or some peculiar tax.' (ibid. p. 9.) While in England dissatisfaction with the administration of the poor laws led to proposals for maintaining the poor in public hospitals for the young, the sick and the aged, in France where the poor were so provided for, proposals were made for parochial relief on the English method. In Paris (as in Dublin) the deaths among Foundling children were enormous.

In Paris in the middle of the century about one-fifth of all the children born were sent to the Foundling Hospital and about one-third of those dying died in hospitals. The figures are:

	Christenings	Sent to the Foundling Hospital
1751	19,231	3,783
1752	20,227	4,127
1753	19,729	4,329
	Burials	Deaths in hospitals
1751	16,673	5,517
1752	17,762	5,829
1753	21,716	7,167

The foundlings, who were sent within a day or two of their birth to be nursed in the villages round Paris, returned at the age of five or six, the boys to St Antoine, the girls to the Salpétrière, where poor Paris girls recommended by the curés were also received. The girls were housed in the court known as Notre Dame de Pitié and taught to read, sew and embroider.

Sir William Mildmay, who made investigations in Paris, calculated that out of the average of about 4,000 foundlings annually sent to be nursed, if two-thirds died under the age of five, and one-fifth of the survivors between the ages of five and twelve – which he calls an extreme supposition – there would be an average 'resting stock' of 7,465 children maintained in Paris. There were however in fact, only about 640 boys and 600 girls. The explanation given to him for this extraordinary diminution was that many children were reclaimed by their parents while at nurse in the country, 'the hospital being used as a public nursery for poor people's children'. He adds, 'the further difference is suspected to be owing to the insufficient nourishment they receive, as this particular charity as well as the general hospital adopts the preposterous system of taking in an unlimited number, whilst there is only a limited income'.

In Notre Dame de Pitié there were generally about 800 girls. Mildmay describes them as 'ranged together in two long apartments, working indeed at their needles, but covered with the itch, a distemper so universally spread amongst them, that so sure as a child is brought in, so surely it catches it. Whether this is owing to contagion or to low nourishment and want of exercise, they have not yet found any means of eradicating it. . . . A circumstance which cannot be mentioned without pity or detestation.' (*The Police of France . . .* , 1763, pp. 71–86 and 127–8.)

(65) The grants ceased in 1771, their total from 1756 exceeded £570,000. Pugh, *Life of Hanway*, 1787, p. 165. The number of children on the establishment at the end of each year (excluding children paid for by the parishes after 1767) was:

1752	559	1766	4,304	1780	532
1753	587	1767	3,794	1781	577
1754	600	1768	2,638	1782	623
1755	611	1769	1,141	1783	609
1756	1,764	1770	595	1784	610
1757	3,947	1771	498	1785	616
1758	4,568	1772	429	1786	603
1759	6,002	1773	410	1787	549
1760	6,068	1774	385	1788	509
1761	5,615	1775	377	1789	450
1762	5,360	1776	425	1790	407
1763	5,171	1777	448	1791	364
1764	5,031	1778	482	1792	344
1765	4,619	1779	497	1793	332
				1794	318

Account of the Foundling Hospital, 1796 (by the Treasurer).

(66) The above account is taken from: *An Account of the Hospital for the maintenance and education of deserted young children*, 1749; J. Hanway, op. cit.; *Some Objections to the Foundling Hospital considered*, 1761; Pugh, op. cit.; *Account of the Foundling Hospital*, 1796 (by the Treasurer); T. Bernard, *Account of the Foundling Hospital*, 2nd ed. 1799; *Report of the Society for Bettering the Condition of the Poor*, IV, Appendix No. VI, pp. 53 ff.; *Report of the Charity Commissioners*, 32, VI. p. 791 ff.; J. Brownlow, *Chronicles of the Foundling Hospital*, 1847 and *History of the Foundling Hospital*, 1858.

(67) *Fourth Report of the Society for Bettering the Condition of the Poor*, Appendix VI, p. 53.

(68) Hanway, *Letters on the Importance of the Rising Generation*, 1768, ii, p. 136.

(69) Pugh, op. cit. pp. 191–2.

(70) *Sketch of the State of the Children of the Poor . . . St. James Westminster*, 1792. cf. a vestry minute of the parish of St. Margaret's Westminster, as early as 1750: 'Discovered that out of 106 infants under twenty months old, 16 had been discharged with their parents and 83 had died, leaving only seven in the workhouse alive.' The report of a committee attributed this to the neglect and bad management of the nurses and advised the discharge of the nurses who were 'most of them capable of providing for themselves', and the removal of the surviving children with such others as might be admitted to country nurses, not to exceed 2s. 6d. per week for children that feed and 3s. for sucking children, the parish to provide proper clothing, till the infants reached two years. The vestry adopted the suggestions but gave the mothers the option of nursing their own children at the above rates of pay. *Annual Report*, 1889, p. 103.

(71) Howlett, *Examination of Dr Price's Essay . . .*, 1781, p. 91.

(72) Sir R. Manningham, M.D., F.R.S., *An Abstract of Midwifery for the use of the Lying-in Infirmary*, 1744. Men paid twenty guineas for instruction, women ten.

(73) J. Glaister, M.D., *Dr William Smellie and his Contemporaries*, 1894, passim.

(74) Lettsom, *Medical Memoirs*, 1774, p. 189.

(75) ibid. p. 187. The number of women delivered in the year 1774–5 was 5,428, nearly a third of the registered baptisms in the Bills of Mortality. The annual average was between 4,000 and 5,000 odd. *Account of the Lying-in Charity*, 1820.

(76)

	Proportions of deaths (fractions omitted)	
	Women	Children
23 November 1749–58 (31 December).	1 in 42	1 in 15
1759–68	1 „ 50	1 „ 20
1769–78	1 „ 53	1 „ 42
1779–88	1 „ 60	1 „ 44
1789–98	1 „ 288	1 „ 77
1799–1800	1 „ 914	1 „ 115

'This table . . . shows to what extent the lives of children may be preserved by proper attention and management.' (Willan, *Diseases in London*, pp. 323–4.)

(77) Heberden, 'On the Mortality of London', (*Medical Transactions of the College of Physicians*, iv, p. 105). cf. the Starkey paper in Hone's *Everyday Book*.

(78) In 1801 the Newcastle Infirmary was found to have 'all the faults of the older hospitals'. 'Some of the wards are too large, and all of them are too much crowded. . . . The ventilation is completely obstructed, while an ill-contrived necessary placed in each [gallery] contaminates the air. . . . All the bedsteads are made of wood and have flock mattresses.' The committee decided to have iron bedsteads as wooden ones were 'prolific sources for the propagation of vermin'. *An Account of a Plan for the . . . Improvement of the Infirmary at Newcastle*. St Thomas's Hospital had introduced iron beds before 1783 (see note 81 below).

(79) Percival, *Essay on the Internal Regulations of Hospitals, Works*, iv, p. 170.

(80) *London and its Environs Described*, 1761, i. p. 258 (account of St Bartholomew's); Howard, *Lazarettos . . .*, 1789, pp. 131–8.

(81) F. Bisset Hawkins, *Elements of Medical Statistics*, 1829, p. 78 ff.; Sir G. Blane, *Medical Dissertations*, i, p. 185 ff. See also note 92 below.

(82) These dispensaries had nothing to do with three earlier dispensaries set up by the College of Physicians (and praised by Garth in *The Dispensary*, 1699) the first in 1696, for selling medicines to the poor at cost price, which gave rise to an acrimonious dispute with the apothecaries, and had long been given up. See *A Vindication of the College of Physicians from the Reflections made upon them by the Apothecaries in Parliament*. [1712?]

(83) *The Midwifery Reports of the Westminster General Dispensary* read by Dr Bland to the Royal Society in 1781 illustrate the knowledge of social conditions gained by dispensary doctors as well as the general ignorance concerning them. He had investigated and recorded the cases of 1,389 women and discovered 'how exceedingly fertile the women of the poorer classes in this country are, and at the same time how unable to rear any considerable number of children'. He found the cause to be 'not any natural imbecility of constitution vitiated from the birth, many of those victims being born with all the appearance of health and vigour; but . . . rather the poverty of the parents'. He suggests that 'whether this great check to the population is in its nature irremediable' is a suitable subject for experiment by an abatement in the parents' rates and taxes, and concludes that

'it would be useful to learn the proportion of deaths in more opulent families,' (*Philosophical Transactions*, lxxxi, p. 355 ff.).

(84) In the first eight years 20,962 children were treated, of whom 699 were known to have died. *General Account of the Dispensary for the Relief of the Infant Poor*, 1787, p. 197. The credit for the first dispensary is ascribed to Wesley by his biographer; in 1746 he began distributing medicines and advice at the Foundry. Tyerman, *Life and Times of Wesley*, 1870, i, pp. 525–7.

(85) Lettsom, *On the Improvement of Medicine in London*, 1775, p. 51.

(86) The dispensary movement:

1769, Dispensary for the . . . Infant Poor, Red Lion Square, afterwards Soho Square.

1770, General Dispensary, Aldersgate Street.

1774, Westminster General Dispensary (especial attention to Midwifery, see note 82 above).

1777, The London Dispensary, Primrose Street, Bishopsgate Street (for the districts of Whitechapel, Shoreditch, Moorfields and Wapping).

1777, The Surrey Dispensary, Union Street, Borough.

*1779, Metropolitan Dispensary and Charitable Fund, Fore Street, Cripplegate.

1780, The Finsbury Dispensary, Union Street, Borough.

1782, The Eastern Dispensary, Alie Street, Whitechapel.

1783 The Public Dispensary, Carey Street.

1785, The St Marylebone Dispensary, General, Well Street, Oxford Street.

1786, The New Finsbury and Central Dispensary, West Smithfield.

1789, The City Dispensary, Bevis Marks.

*1792, The Universal Medical Institution. Old Gravel Lane, Ratcliffe Highway.

*1793, London Electrical Dispensary, City Road.

*1801, Bloomsbury Dispensary, 62 Great Russell Street.

*1805, London Dispensary for curing Diseases of the Eye and Ear.

Date? Middlesex Dispensary, Great Ailiff Street.

    „   Royal Universal Dispensary, Featherston Buildings, Holborn.

    „   St James Dispensary, Berwick Street, Soho.

    „   Ossulston Dispensary, Bow Street, Bloomsbury.

    „   Western Dispensary, Charles Street, Westminster.

The list is probably incomplete. It is compiled from Colquhoun's *Police of the Metropolis*, 1797, p. 380; Highmore's *Pietas Londinensis*, 1810, p. 332 ff.; J. J. Baddeley's *Account of . . . St Giles Cripplegate*, p. 213, and reports issued by the dispensaries. Those marked * are not mentioned by Colquhoun.

'From the eastern extremity of Limehouse to the western of Millbank; on the north from Islington and Somers Town to the south as far as Lambeth, and, by means of the Greenwich dispensary, to Newington and Peckham . . . a district of nearly fifty square miles, a system of medical relief is extended to the poor, unknown to any other part of the globe. About 50,000 poor persons are thus supplied with medicine and advice gratis, one-third of whom at least are attended at their own habitations.' (Feltham, *Picture of London*, 1802, p. 167.) See also note 101 below.

(87) Pictet, *Voyage . . . en Angleterre*, p. 333.

(88) London did not lead the way in the isolation of typhus cases as she had in the establishment of dispensaries. Chester, through Dr Haygarth, was the first, and was imitated by Liverpool, Manchester, Norwich, Hull, Dublin, Cork and Waterford, before London. Stanger, *Remarks on the Necessity and Means of suppressing Contagious Fever in the Metropolis*, 1802, p. 32.

(89) ibid., p. 19.

(90) Creighton, *History of Epidemics*, ii, p. 138. See note 92 below.

(91) The antiseptic properties of quicklime slacked in boiling water were a discovery of Howard made on his cottages in Bedfordshire and applied by him to prisons. *Lazarettos*, p. 118.

(92) cf. 'There are but few of the sick . . . that find their way into the great hospitals of London, which probably is to be imputed to there being but one day a week allotted for the admission of patients. Before a recommendation can be procured and the stated day come round, the sick person is either better or so much worse that he cannot be moved, or is perhaps dead. They are carried, however, in great numbers to parish workhouses, in which it frequently happens that during the cold months that the fever becomes as violent, and proves as fatal, as in the most crowded jails, hospitals or transports.' (Dr J. Hunter, 'Observations on Jail and Hospital Fever', *Medical Transactions of the College of Physicians*, 1779.)

(93) *History of the London House of Recovery*, 1817.

(94) *State of the Institution for the Cure and Prevention of Contagious Fever*, 1803.

(95) *Report of the Select Committee on Contagious Fever in London*, 1818, p. 14. It was one of the standing orders of the parishes of St Andrew's Holborn and St George the Martyr that all persons infected with fever who applied for relief or had developed fever in the workhouse should be sent to the House of Recovery and that a payment of two guineas a week should be made by the parish. *Standing Orders under the Act of . . . 1799 of the united parishes of St Andrew . . . and St George . . . n. d.*

(96) Bateman, recording in 1816 the cases of the Carey Street Dispensary wrote, 'the extraordinary disappearance of contagious fever from every part of this crowded metropolis cannot fail to have attracted the attention of the reader'. He concluded not without reason that the immunity of London from fever was due 'to the high degree of well-being among the poorer classes in years of plenty'. Creighton, op. cit., ii, pp, 103–4.

(97) *History of the London House of Recovery*, 1817. See also Dr Bateman's evidence to the Committee on Contagious Fever (*Report*, 1818) which gives the proportion of deaths from 1803 to 1818.

(98) In 1810 Dr Lettsom wrote to Dr Dixon of Whitehaven: 'the frequency of typhus fever with you is a fearful proof of the poverty, bad ventilation and crowded state of many of your inhabitants. When I was a young physician it was also frequent in London, but it is now almost extinct. There is a fever-house here purposely for the reception of infectious diseases; but during the last year seldom more than two or three have been within its walls at any one time. The improvements in London in opening streets, etc., have no doubt had considerable effect in this respect, joined with medical aid.' (Pettigrew, *Memoirs of Lettsom*, 1817.)

(99) Stanger, *Remarks on the Necessity and Means of Suppressing Contagious Fever in the Metropolis*, 1802, pp. 25–6. Bateman, *Reports on the Diseases of London*, 1819.

(100) Highmore, *Pietas Londinensis*, p. 111. (Dr Rowley is coupled with Dr Haygarth (see note 88) as a pioneer.) W. Rowley, M.D., *The Causes of the great Number of Deaths amongst Adults and Children in putrid scarlet fevers and ulcerated sore-throats explained, with the more successful modes of treating these alarming disorders as practised at the St Mary-le-bone Infirmary*, 1793. Dedicated 'to the Right Honorable and Honorable the Noblemen and Gentlemen, Directors and Guardians of the Poor in the Parish of St Mary-le-bone' (who were then having a new infirmary built in consequence of the success of the fever treatment). (ibid., p. 7 n.) See also Rowley, *A Treatise on Putrid Malignant Fevers*, 1804. Rowley was regarded with disfavour by the medical profession, his writings

were unscientific and boastful, and he was an anti-vaccinator (see Munk, *Roll of the College of Physicians*, ii, p. 340) but in the light of our present knowledge of typhus it is easy to see that his system may well have worked wonders, especially by comparison with the old methods of bleeding and purging.

(101) Account of the Samaritan Society by Dr Glasse (suggesting that other hospitals should imitate the London) in the *Second Report of the Society for bettering the Condition of the Poor*, 1798, pp. 93 ff. The principle of the after-care of patients seems to have been first adopted by the Lock Hospital in 1787 when it established the Lock Asylum for women and girls, who, on leaving the Hospital would be destitute and forced to return to their old profession; they did needlework and were trained for domestic service. This however was a rescue home rather than a medical charity. The Charity for Convalescents of St George's Hospital (1809) on a plan submitted by Dr Heberden was on the lines of the Samaritan; it also provided patients with surgical appliances. Other medical charities which deserve mention are the Society for the Relief of Sick and Maimed Seamen in the Merchant Service (1747), the National Truss Society (1786), Dr Turnbull having drawn attention to the great prevalence of hernia among the labouring poor. This was followed by the Rupture Society in 1796 and the City Truss Society in 1807. In 1793 the Sea Bathing Infirmary for the Poor of London was founded at Margate (opened 1796). The London Dispensary for curing diseases of the Eye and Ear opened in 1805 became the London Infirmary for the Eye in 1808, and the Royal Infirmary for the Eye (1805) was the outcome of the previous gratuitous treatment of the poor by Phipps.

When vaccination was introduced institutions for free vaccination multiplied in London, but from the beginning violent controversy raged round the whole question, and also between rival societies which seceded from one another in a bewildering way. The first vaccine dispensary was the Vaccine Pock Institution founded by Dr G. Pearson in December 1799. The Royal Jennerian Society was short-lived; it opened twelve stations in and near London for the free vaccination of the poor. The London Vaccine Institution was a secession from the Jennerian and had about fifteen stations. On the suspension of the Jennerian, the National Vaccine Institution under the patronage of the Government and the supervision of the Royal College of Physicians succeeded it. Yet another was the London Vaccine Institution (1806) for the inoculation of all applicants gratis, and for the free supply of vaccine to all practitioners who applied for it. Two dispensaries at least which had previously inoculated adopted vaccination – the Universal Medical and the Western (see note 80), while at the Bloomsbury Jenner himself superintended vaccination.

Highmore, *Piétas Londinensis*, 1810, p. 332 ff. Colquhoun, *Police of the Metropolis*, 1797 (see above, n. 86), the reports issued by many of the societies mentioned (catalogued under London in the B.M. Catalogue) and Pettigrew, *Memoirs of Lettsom*. For the vaccination controversy see *Report from the Committee on Dr Jenner's Petition respecting ... Vaccine Inoculation*, 6th May 1802.

(102) See, for instance, Wales, *Inquiry into the Present State of the Population of England and Wales*, 1781; W. Black, *Observations on the Small-pox*, 1781; W. Heberden, op. cit. and 'Some Observations on the Scurvy', *Medical Transactions ... IV*; F. Bateman, *Reports on the Diseases of London*, 1819; Gilbert Blane, *Select Dissertations*, 1833.

(103) 'Tea is an article universally grateful to the British population and has to a certain extent supplanted intoxicating liquors in all ranks, to the great advantage of society. . . . The modern use of tea has probably contributed to the extended longevity of the inhabitants of this country.' Blane, op. cit., i, p. 55.

See also Rickman's correspondence with d'Ivernois in 1827: 'It is not for Mr Rickman to assign causes of the decrease of mortality; if he might venture further than in the

Preliminary Observations to the Census of 1811 and 1821 . . . he would ascribe it to the general use of tea and sugar, and to the increased operation of the Poor Relief Laws, which ensure wholesome food and medical attendance to all. But these arguments would encounter contradiction in England. . . .' (*Minutes of Evidence, Population Bill Committee*, 1830.)

Hanway couples tea with gin as a destroyer of the race: 'The drinking gin, the use of tea among the poor and the infamous conduct of some nurses, concurred to render an hospital devoted to the care of infants more necessary in 1739 than it might be in 1708.' (*A Candid Historical Account* . . . 1759, p. 16.) It was his attitude towards tea which provoked the contempt of Dr Johnson.

(104) Blane, *On the Comparative Mortality of different Diseases in London*, in *Medical Dissertations*.

(105) W. Black, *Observations on the Small-pox*, 1781, p. 170.

(106) Burrington, *An Answer to Dr William Brackenridge's Letter* . . . 1757, p. 23.

(107) Heberden, *Observations on the Increase and Decrease of certain Diseases*, 1801, p. 37.

(108) Black, *Observations on the Small-pox*, p. 170.

(109) Howlett says that in villages and provincial towns inoculation had the opposite effect: 'When an epidemic appears inoculation takes place at once. . . . Where two or three hundred used to be buried in a few months, now perhaps not more than twenty or thirty.' *Examination of Dr Price's Essay* . . . 1781, p. 94.

(110) *English Local Government: Statutory Authorities for Special Purposes*, 1922, pp. 503–5.

(111) *Some Observations on the Scurvy*.

(112) *Report* . . . *on the Validity of the Doctrine of Contagion in the Plague*, 1819, p. 83. cf. also: 'Notwithstanding the plague, the remittent fever, the dysentery and the scurvy have so decreased, that their very name is almost unknown in London; yet there has, I know not how, arisen a prejudice concerning putrid diseases, which seems to have made people more and more apprehensive of them, as the danger has been growing less. It must in a great measure be attributed to this, that the consumption of Peruvian bark in this country has, within the last fifty years increased from about 14,000 to above 100,000 pounds annually.' (Heberden, 'On the influence of Cold upon the Health of the Inhabitants of London', *Philosophical Transactions*, 1796, pp. 282–3.)

(113) Add. MSS. 27827, f. 48.

(114) Add. MSS. 27828, fo. 120 ff.

(115) *Principles of Population*, 1822, pp. 252–3. Accounts of hospitals and workhouses show that the introduction of iron bedsteads in place of the old vermin-infested wooden ones with testers, had an effect comparable with the general use of cotton. See above.

Notes to Chapter 2

(1) Besides the evidence of Stow and of the early maps, returns of foreigners in London made owing to the Queen's fear of foreign conspiracies give valuable indications of the growth of the new industrial population growing up round the City. As the foreigners are particularized by name there was no room for exaggeration of numbers, though there may well have been omissions. Out of a total of 7,143 in December 1571, 4,287 were returned as in the City and its liberties, including 698 in Southwark or Bridge Ward Without and probably the Middlesex part of the parishes of Aldgate and Bishopsgate. From the 4,287, however, 210 and 33 should be deducted for the precinct of St Katherine's and part of the Liberty of East Smithfield counted twice over. Foreigners in Middlesex were distributed as follows:

Finsbury, Golden Lane, White Crosse Street and Grub Street 86.
Shoreditch 32.
St Leonards Shoreditch [another list] 226.
St Giles in the Fields 7.
Hamlet of Limehouse 11.
Liberty of the Minories [two pages missing] 92?
Hamlet of Poplar 18.
Hamlet of Ratcliffe 20.
Hamlet of Blackwall 15.
Libertie of the Tower 16.
Whitechapel 169.
Lordship of East Smithfield 284.
Precinct of St Katherine's by the Tower 210. (See note 17 below.)

The City returns include 217 in St Katherine's (among whom there is a special list of brewers' servants) and 33 in East Smithfield by the Tower.

Foreigners in Southwark were:

St Thomas's Hospital 67		St George's 58
St Saviour's	87	St Olave's 486

These were chiefly artisans. The occupations are not specified in the Middlesex returns. Many in the City were also artisans, but many were merchants, especially in the more central wards. There were many silk-weavers in Bishopsgate.

S. P. Dom. Eliz. LXXXIV. cf. also *S. P. Dom. Eliz.* LXXXII, a less complete return dated November 1571.

(2) 27 Eliz. c. 17. (Preamble.)
(3) Norden, *Speculi Brittanniae*, p. 47.
(4) W. Petty, *Taxes and Contributions*.
(5) Miss Jeffries Davis, 'The Great Fire of London', *History*, April 1923.
(6) This tendency was noticed as early as 1695 by Cary, the Bristol merchant: 'Another way to provide for those who are true objects of charity is by taking care that the Poor's

rates be made with more equality in cities and trading towns . . . especially the former, where the greatest number of poor usually residing together in the suburbs or out-parishes are very serviceable by their labours to the rich in carrying on their trades, yet when age or sickness or a numerous family makes them desire relief, their chief dependence must be on people but one step above their own conditions, by which means those out-parishes are more burthened in their parishes than the in-parishes are, tho' much richer, and is one reason why they are so ill-inhabited, no one caring to come to a certain charge; and this is attended with another ill-consequence, the want of better inhabitants makes way for those disorders which easily grow among the poor.' (*An Essay on Trade* . . . , 1695, pp. 167–8.)

The enormously heavy burden of poor rates in the eastern parishes attracted the attention of Colquhoun, who became a police magistrate for the Tower Hamlets in 1792 (a time of great distress in the silk trade), where he pointed out that 'the lower classes . . . are compelled to contribute largely to the fund for supporting the poor from the daily pittance which arises from labour . . . while in almost every other part of the metropolis, as the rich form a considerable proportion of the inhabitants . . . the burden does not attach. And thus it happens that in Spitalfields and Mile End New Town from five shillings in the pound are paid . . . and after all extremely inadequate to the wants of the poor, while St George's Hanover Square and St Marylebone paying only two shillings to two and sixpence in the pound, and the poor are abundantly fed, while the labouring people in that part of the town are eased of a heavy burden.' (*An Account of a Meat and Soup Charity established in the Metropolis in* . . . , 1797, p. 4 n.)

In 1743 it was urged in favour of making the hamlet of Bethnal Green into a parish, that many of the better sort had departed to the impoverishment of the place because 'dissoluteness of morals and a disregard for religion have greatly increased, too apparent in great numbers of the younger and poorer sort of inhabitants.' (*C. J.* 10 and 12 January 1742–3.) See below, notes 11 and 12.

(7) *Customs and Privileges of the Manors of Stepney and Hackney* . . . 1736. (Confirmed 21 Jas. I.)

These manors had long been held by the bishops of London. In 1550 Bishop Ridley surrendered them to Edward VI, who granted them to Lord Wentworth, the Lord Chamberlain. They were sequestered during the Protectorate, but after the Restoration the Wentworth family regained the manor of Stepney but not that of Hackney, which became the property of the Tyssen family (afterwards Tyssen-Amherst). H. G. C. Allgood, *A History of Bethnal Green*, 1894.

(8) *Middlesex Records*, 6 September 1784 (typescript Calendar). Their factiousness lay in their having 'sixteen large public conventicles as big as most churches' and persisting in holding private meetings when the conventicles had been suppressed. (This statement of the Justices was printed.)

(9) Archenholtz, *Picture of England*, p. 119.

(10) Crace Collection in British Museum, Maps, surveys of the parish of Stepney (including the hamlets) and separate surveys of Bethnal Green and Limehouse, by Joel Gascoyne in 1703.

The streets, courts and yards of Bethnal Green which are so closely packed that they have to be indicated (on a scale of 150 yards to the inch) by numbers and a key are:

Cock Lane,	King's Head Court
Sunn Court	Crown Court
Holland's Rents	

Anchor Street,
 Anchor Court
 Three Compasses Court
 Richardson's Rents

Brick Lane,
 Carter's Rents

George Street,
 Fine Court
 Puckridge's Rents

George Court
 Beaumond's Rents
 Collet's Rents

Fleete Street,
 Lowder's Rents
 Agnes Rents
 Blackbird Alley
 Herbert's Rents
 Ram Alley
 Cock Alley
 Scatchell Rents (or Noah's Arke)

Similar lists are given for other hamlets.

(11) The following estimates and enumerations of houses, etc., in Spitalfields bears out the evidence of maps, allowing for exaggeration in the estimates of 1710 and 1729 (made to support a claim to share in the money allotted to the building of new churches) and probably of 1750:

1710, 3,570 families, 21,420 persons. (*C.J.* 10 March 1710–11.)

1729, 2,500 houses, with 'a numerous poor'. (*C.J.* 14 February 1728–9.)

1732, 2,190 houses (about). (Parish Clerks' returns.)

1750, 2,400 houses, 1,000 of which are not rated to the poor, 'being inhabited by journeymen weavers and other artificers and labourers who cannot support themselves and their families without credit for small sums'. (*C.J.* 16 January 1749–50.)

1778, 2,022 houses. (*C.J.* 12 March 1778.)

1801, 2,021 houses, 145 being uninhabited, 15,091 persons. (*Census.*)
Similar returns for Bethnal Green are:

1710, 1,416 families, 8,496 persons.

1738, 800 houses, each with 'seven, eight or ten families' [? persons]. (*C.J.* 12 April 1738.)

1743, above 1,800 houses, more than 15,000 souls. (10 and 12 January 1742–3.)

1763, near 1,800 houses. (*C.J.* 9 February 1763.)

1801, 3,820 houses, 234 being uninhabited, 22,310 persons.
Compare Appendix III, *B.*

(12) In 1737 the parish officers petitioned that the hamlet being very poor could not afford to keep in repair their share of the highway to Shoreditch Church, the thoroughfare from Essex to Smithfield, which was 'extremely pocked and ruined', the greatest part of the inhabitants being journeymen weavers. (*C.J.* 4 March 1736–7. See also *C.J.* 12 April 1738; note 6 above and notes 51 and 52 below.)

(13) R. Seymour's edition of Stow's *Survey*, ii, 1735, p. 711.

(14) Lysons, *Environs of London*, iii, p. 445. The parish registers were especially defective as a test of the growth of population in this district, where Jews and dissenters were numerous.

(15) The growth of uniformity in the first half of the nineteenth century is thus described: 'Fifty years ago this metropolis . . . did not contain above one million of inhabitants. The extent . . . was commensurately small; and yet the inhabitants of the different districts were less acquainted with each other and more distinct in their manners, habits and characteristics, than they are in these days. The inhabitants of the extreme east of London knew nothing of the western localities but from hearsay and report and vice versa. . . . There was little communication or sympathy between the respective classes by

which the two ends of London were occupied. They differed in external appearance, in the fashion of their clothes, in their pleasures and in their wits. The cause of this mutual ignorance arose from the almost total want of communication which existed. . . .

'Each district was comparatively isolated, the state of isolation produced peculiarities and the peculiarities corroborated the isolation, and thus the householders of Westminster, whether noblemen, gentlemen, tradesmen . . . or of any other grade of society, were as distinct from the householders of every sort of Bishopsgate Without, Shoreditch and all those localities . . . as in these days they are from the inhabitants of Holland or Belgium. The precincts and purlieus of Westminster Abbey were unknown to those who inhabited within half a mile of them! The ramifications of the Seven Dials and that division of the town which may be called St Giles proper, was to the timid and respectable very properly a perfect *terra incognita*.' (J. Richardson, *Recollections . . . of the last Half-century*, 1856, pp. 3–4.)

(16) Strype's edition of Stow's *Survey*, 1720, ii, p. 34.

(17) Stow describes it as being 'now of late years inclosed about or pestered with small tenements and homely cottages, having inhabitants, English and strangers, more in number than in some city in England'. Maitland quotes a return of 1572 according to which the foreigners in the precinct were 425, many being shoe-makers:

> 328 Dutch
> 69 French (most hat-makers)
> 8 Danes
> 5 Polanders
> 2 Spaniards
> 1 Italian
> 12 Scots
> ───
> 425   (*History of London*, 1756, ii, p. 1,082.)

(18) The proclamations against new buildings, divided houses and inmates of 1580, 1602, 1607, 1608, 1615, 1618, 1620, 1625, and 1630 are in the British Museum collections.

(19) *Arguments concerning the New Buildings* [1678].

(20) Garrard, *Strafford Letters*, i, p. 263.

(21) See especially the Proclamation of 16 July 1615.

(22) Proclamation of 25 July 1608.

(23) *S. P. Dom. Car. I.* CCCLIX, a volume of returns made to the Council or the Lord Mayor of houses built by poor persons in the various parishes and liberties within the past seven years as well as of divided tenements and inmates. In 1608 the City complained that a servant of the Countess-Dowager of Derby had divided a house into twenty-one tenements, to the danger of infection, and refused to reduce them to four. Overall, *Remembrancia*, 1888, p. 45.

(24) Lysons, *Environs of London*, iii, p. 446; H. G. C. Allgood, *A History of Bethnal Green . . .* 1894, pp. 180–81.

(25) *Parliamentary History*, iv, p. 659.

(26) ibid., p. 946. A return of new buildings since 1656 was made by the church-wardens in connexion with this proposal, the total being 'about 10,000'. This return tallied with calculations from the Bills of Mortality and disproved some exaggerated estimates which were current, namely that 20,000, some said 30,000, houses had been built since 1656, St Martin's parish alone being supposed by 'wild conjecture' to have 3,500 new houses. It was estimated that there were two burials a year for every five houses built. A

Particular of the New-buildings within the Bills of Mortality and without the City of London, [i.e. within the walls] *from . . . 1656 to 1677. . . .* See Appendix III, *A.* cf. *An Apology for the Builder or a Discourse showing the Causes and Effects of the Increase of Building,* 1685, p. 2: 'The citizens are afraid that the building of new houses will lessen the rent and trade of the old ones. The country gentleman is troubled at the new buildings for fear they should depopulate the country and they want tenants for their land. And both agree that the increase of building is prejudicial to the Government and use for argument a simile from those who have the rickets, fancying the City to be the head of the nation and that it will grow too big for the body.'

(27) The petitions are of topographical interest:

i. The lessees of Rugby School petition that their lands in St Andrew's Holborn are for the most part built on and the remainder contracted for; should the Bill pass they will be prevented from making the best advantage for the said charity.

ii. Sir T. Skipwith Bart. and three others have bought freehold land lying contiguous to the buildings upon the west and north-north-east of Gray's Inn and Gray's Inn Lane in prospect of building thereon. They pray for a saving clause.

iii. Peter Foster, Salter of London, is seised in fee of property in the parish of St Botolph without Aldgate; a ninety-nine years' building lease will expire in 1713, the messuages thereon must be pulled down and rebuilt, but not on the old foundations. He prays relief.

iv. John Henderson and Thomas Steers have taken leases in Rotherhithe of Madam Howland [widow of the builder of the Howland Dock?] and are obliged by their contract to build.

v. Edward Nelthorpe Esq. and others, lessees for fifty-five years of Conduit Mead belonging to the Corporation of London intend to build a large commodious street from Albemarle Street, through the said Mead into a new street called Marlborough Street to his Majesty's Palace through the said Mead.

(*C.J.* 21 and 27 February, 4 and 11 March 1709–10.)

(28) Bardwell, *Westminster Improvements . . .* 1839, p. 29. It was then many years since there had been 'pleasant gardens of Tothill'. Francis Place writes in 1834: 'There is not a street in all London more improved than . . . Tothill Street. It is in no one respect like what it was – even the common soldiers and their women are improved. There is not as there used to be the same filth and rags and misery and open defiance of all decency – nor anything approximating to these things.' (Add. MSS. 27830, fo. 221.)

(29) Holinshed, *Chronicle,* iii, p. 1271.

When an Act (17 Geo. III. c. 60) was obtained to enable the inhabitants to enclose Hoxton Square, that is, to put a fence round the open space, there was a clause to extinguish any rights of common there might be in the land.

(30) See note 49, Chapter 4.

(31) C. Hitchin, *A true Discovery of the Conduct of Receivers and Thieftakers in and about the City of London . . .* , 1718, p. 15.

(32) 2 June 1764. See also issue for 13 August 1774: 'The builders and the work of their hands seem to have exerted their utmost to rival each other whether the builder or the building should first tumble to decay and ruin; the first frequently failing before the walls are half up and the latter falling before it was finished.'

cf. 'The rage or at least hurry of building is so great at present that the bricks are often brought to the bricklayers before they are cold enough to be handled, so that some time ago the floor of a cart loaded with bricks took fire in Golden Lane, Old Street, and was consumed before the bricks could be unloaded.' *Ann. Reg.* 1765, p. 113.

(33) 12 Geo. I. c. 35 amended by 3 Geo. II. c. 22.

(34) It was agreed that bricks had deteriorated when made by the methods prescribed by the Act and that 'no persons using the trade of a brickmaker, bricklayer or tilemaker are proper persons for this employment, in regard to the ill use they may be tempted to make of their power in screening themselves . . . and oppressing others in order to engross the making and sale of the unparliamentary bricks and tiles . . . as was notoriously practised under the first Brick Act'. (*Middlesex Records*, January 1729–30, Cal.) See also *C.J.* 16, 21, 26 February, and 9 March 1727–8, 29 April 1728, 6, 10, 12, and 20 February 1728–9, 1 April 1730, and *The Case of the Brickmakers and Tilemakers within the City of London and fifteen miles thereof.* . . .

(35) Noorthouck, *History of London*, 1773, p. 373.

(36) *Concise History of the City of London*, 1752, pp. 130–31 and D.N.B. (Killegrew).

(37) *Memoirs of Tate Wilkinson*, 1790, p. 81. See also Noorthouck, op. cit. p. 738, who says (1773) 'the claim of the Crown is reviving'. Light is thrown on the sanitary state of the liberty in Ritson's *Digest of the Proceedings of the Court Leet of the Manor and Liberty of the Savoy* . . . 1789.

(38) Concanen, *History of Southwark*, 1795, p. 275.

(39) By another Act of Elizabeth such leases in towns might be for forty years, dwelling-houses excepted. See *Report of the Select Committee on Church Lands*, 1839, VIII.

(40) *C.J.* 11 January 1797.

In the old houses in the City different floors in the same house were sometimes the freehold property of different people. In connexion with the City improvement scheme of 1760 evidence was given in the House of Commons 'that there are many houses within the said City and liberties wherein the several floors or rooms are the property or freehold of different persons, whereby disputes are frequently occasioned between them, touching the pulling down or rebuilding of the premises or the party walls thereof, and such rebuilding is thereby often prevented'. Several instances were given 'and particularly . . . four houses in the parish of Queenhithe which belong to the City except one chamber up one pair of stairs, which is private property and which the said City is desirous of purchasing, but the person who treated with them, not being able to make a legal title thereto, the said houses remain in a ruinous condition and cannot be rebuilt'. (*C. J.* 15 February 1760.)

(41) Dowell, *History of Taxation and Taxes* . . . 1888, iii, pp. 154 and 168–77.

(42) G. Chalmers, *Domestic Œconomy of Great Britain and Ireland*, 1812, p. 361 (quoting a return to the Treasury of 1754).

(43) Sir F. M. Eden, *Estimate of the Number of the Inhabitants of Great Britain*, 1800, p. 70.

(44) Among the 'small and base tenements' in Shoreditch Stow instances Russell's Row built on the site of some decayed almshouses sold to Russell a draper 'who new builded them and let them out for rent enough, taking also large fines of the tenants, neare as much as the houses cost him to purchase and building: for hee made his bargaines so hardly with all men that both carpenters, bricklayers and playsterers were by that worke undone. And yet in honour of his name it is now called Russell's Row.' *Survey*, ed. by Kingsford, II, pp. 74–5.

cf. also *Acts of the Privy Council*, 7 May 1598: 'Complaint hath been made unto us by divers inhabitants both in the Burroughe of Southwark and other the suburbs about London that certaine persons of wealthe thorough the covetous disposicion of certaine persons have of late yeres not onlie converted faire and large dwelling-houses into tenements with raysing of great rent of the same, but where manie of them being of good habillytie did inhabit those houses, and did paie all duties besides and other chardges with the rest of the paryshioners, now in their roomes are placed many poore people that have releefe from the parish, where the landlord reapeth great rents for small cottages and are subject to no chardg with the parish. . . .' (A letter to the judges praying them to devise a way by which the burden may be put upon the offenders against the proclamation and the parishes relieved of it.)

(45) Like many ambitious building schemes in London in the eighteenth century, that of building on the site of Clarendon House was not profitable to the first builders. Strype writes in 1720, Clarendon House and gardens 'being sold by the said Duke, was by the undertakers laid out into streets, who not being in a condition to finish so great a work, made mortgages and so entangled the title, that it is not to this day finished, and God knows when it will; so that it lieth like the ruins of Troy, some having the foundations begun, others carried up to the roofs and others covered, but none of the inside work done; yet those houses that are finished towards *Pickadilly* meet with tenants. In this building, which takes the general name of Albemarle Buildings, are these streets, *viz*. Bond Street . . . Albemarle Street . . . Dover Street, the best of all for large buildings . . . Stafford Street. . . .' (*Survey*, Book vi, p. 78.)

(46) *Autobiography of Roger North*, ed. by Jessopp, 1887, pp. 53–7; Seymour's edition of Stow, ii, p. 773; B. Chancellor, *Annals of Fleet Street*, pp. 86–7. G. Clinch, *Soho*, 1895, p. 162.

(47) Lysons, *Environs of London*, iii, p. 256.

(48) Press cutting dated 1810 in the Place Collection, Add. MSS. 27826, fo. 91.

(49) 'The present war has been a great check to the enterprising spirit of builders, consequently the improvements have been nearly confined to the northern side of the metropolis, and have chiefly been in the hands of one eminent builder, Mr Burton. The grounds are those belonging to the Foundling Hospital and the Duke of Bedford' (Malcolm, *Londinium Redivivum*, i, 1802, p. 5).

(50) op. et loc. cit. and a letter by Malcolm in the *Gentleman's Magazine*, November 1813, pp. 427–9.

(51) *C.J.* 3 March 1742–3.

(52) *C.J.* 2 February 1763.

(53) For instance, it is reported in the returns of 1637 (cf. n. 10) from St Alphage that Richard Rogers, joiner, had taken one of the chiefest house in the parish and divided it into three tenements for poor tradesmen; that 'Mr Chersley, a bricklayer dwellinge in Bread Street Hill hath within this five or six yeares at furthest built three tenements and also a shedd which is now made into a tenement'.

In 1778 one Hartley charged with burglary was alleged to have a room in a house for which he paid four guineas a year, the landlord being a bricklayer who 'built a place backwards and let the fore part of the house out'. (*Sessions Papers*, December 1778.)

Perhaps because working bricklayers so often undertook work on their own account, the work was quickly done. The usual number of bricks laid in a day by a bricklayer and his labourer was a thousand. For instance the *Builders' Dictionary* (1734) says, 'a bricklayer and his labourer (all their materials being ready) will lay in a day about a thousand bricks in whole work on a solid plan, and some dexterous bricklayers will lay twelve and some fifteen hundred'.

A specimen bricklayer's bill is interesting:

'Mr William Blakeway's Bill of Materials had and of Work done by Thomas Halling, Bricklayer, 5 June 1732.

	£	s.	d.
For 8,000 of bricks at 12s. per M.	4	16	0
„ 4,000 of tiles at 20.	4	0	0
„ 15 hundred of lime at 12s. 6d. per hundred	9	7	6
„ 14 load of sand at 2s. 6d. per load	1	15	0
„ 500 nine-inch paving tiles at 11s. per hundred	2	15	0
„ 30 ridge tiles at 1½d. per piece	0	4	4½
„ 3 weeks and 2 days work for myself at 3s. per diem	3	0	0
„ 25 days work and a half for my man at 2s. 6d. per diem	3	3	9
„ a labourer, 25 days work and a half at 1s. 8d. per diem	1	18	0
Their sum total is	30	12	5½ '

Alternative methods are given to that of the bricklayer working by the day, namely 'by the great' (by contract), or by measure, finding all materials at so much by the rod square or yard. See article *Bricks*.

(54) *Poor Law Report*, 1834, XXIX, Appendix, p. 428. The development of building estates in the poorer parts of London did not need much capital. The profits largely depended on securing a licence for one of the houses, after a stricter licensing policy had given these a scarcity value: 'Take a clerk from an Annuitant office, and enable him to purchase a lease of two or three acres of land for the purpose of parcelling it out for buildings, and after he has run up half a dozen shells of houses which *he* leaves to the purchasers to finish, grant him a licence to open one for a public-house, and the business is done. The house will fetch him £500 or £1,000.' This was a defence of the magistrates of the Tower Hamlets (by one of them) against the allegations of a Mr Beaumont, a building speculator who was aggrieved at the licensing policy of the justices in brewster Sessions. See note 98, Chapter 6. Rev. T. Thirlwall, *A Vindication of the Magistrates ... for the Tower Division from the charges ... in the Report of the Committee on the State of the Police in the Metropolis* ... 1817, p. 171.

(55) Brayley, *History of Surrey;* Wroth, *London Pleasure Gardens*, 1896.

(56) Fielding, *Inquiry into the Cause of the Late Increase of Robbers*, 1751, p. 76.

(57) Hanway, *Citizen's Monitor*, 1780, p. xvi. (A communication from Wm. Blizard afterwards printed in the latter's *Desultory Reflections on Police*, 1785.)

(58) J. C. Jeaffreson, *Middlesex Records*, ii, pp. xliii and 171.

(59) The Ordinary of Newgate in a plea for vigorous magistrates, urges that if the laws were put in execution London would become safe and 'the back of Great Queen Street and Long Acre, the lanes, holes and alleys about St Giles, etc. etc. etc., would become the residences of honest industrious people....' (Introduction to *Account of the Malefactors executed*, July 1745. In *Sessions Papers*.)

(60) *Middlesex Records* (Orders of Court, Westminster, June 1730). Sir John Fielding in 1766 ascribed the great number of brothels in Covent Garden partly to ruinous houses: 'One of the principal causes of the number of bawdy-houses being collected together in or near that parish, is there having been several estates in the courts and contiguous streets where the leases of the houses were so near expiring that it was not worth while to repair them till they were out, by which means they were let for almost nothing to the lowest of wretches, who hired three or four of them and filled them with common prostitutes. This made Exeter Street, Change Court, Eagle Court and Little Catherine Street so infamous that it was dangerous for persons to pass and repass.' (*Penal Laws*, p. 67.) A reason for these places being able to defy the magistrates was that (till 1792) they could obtain a

wine-licence from the Stamp Office which was a substitute for a magisterial licence. See note 101 to Chapter 6.

(61) *An Account of the Endeavours that have been used to suppress Gaming Houses* ... 1722, p. 20.

(62) In Butcher Row and the Back of St Clements were (in 1790) some of the oldest houses in London, built for the pioneers of the migration of the nobility from the City westwards. Two houses five storeys high were decorated with the fleur-de-lis and tradition ascribed this to the fact that Sully had lodged there. Malcolm scouts the legend and assigns the houses to the period of the latter part of the Hundred Years' War – the decoration a compliment to Henry V or VI. Their demolition was due to Alderman Pickett who carried through a scheme for improving the approach to the City and getting rid of what had become a nuisance. Shortly after the rebuilding was begun, war broke out and the promoters were involved in heavy losses. Malcolm writes: 'A stranger who had visited London in 1790 would on his return in 1804 be astonished to find a spacious area (with the church nearly in its centre) on the site of Butcher Row and some other passages undeserving of the name of streets which were composed of those wretched fabricks overhanging their foundations, the receptacles of dirt in every corner of their projecting stories, the bane of ancient London, where the plague with all its attendant horrors poured destruction on the miserable inhabitants. ... I never passed through the filth of these places without fancying the dreadful cross on the doors, where it undoubtedly had often really appeared. He that now passes St Clements area and is not grateful to the men who planned and the Parliament who permitted, the removal of such streets and habitations, deserves to live in a lazaretto'. (*Londinium Redivivum*, III, p. 397.)

Pickett Street was built on the site and was itself demolished for the building of the Law Courts.

St Clements had long contained crowded alleys; in 1637 'In Lyndes Alley soe many inmates and poore people pestered together that wee cannot find them out nor the charges.' (cf. above, n. 23.)

(63) In 1756 it was urged as a reason for building Blackfriars Bridge that the district would be cleared out and rebuilt; it was then described as filled with 'laystalls and bawdy houses, obscure pawnbrokers, gin-shops and alehouses; the haunts of strolling prostitutes, thieves and beggars, who nestling thus in the heart of the City, become a nuisance which it is worth all the money the bridge will cost to remove'. Part of this character it owed to its nearness to the prisons of the Fleet, Ludgate and Newgate and the House of Correction at Bridewell, and, till the Fleet was built over (1747), to that terrible open sewer, the Fleet ditch.

John Howes gives an interesting account of the reasons for which Edward VI gave Bridewell to the City, which throws light on the state of this district in the sixteenth century:

'Yt was lately buylded, and not without an infynite chardge, but the scytuation thereof ys suche that all the cost was caste awaie, there was no coming to yt but throughe stinckinge lanes and over a fylthy ditche which did so continually annoye the house that the kinge had no pleasure in it. And therefore the kinge being requyred by the Cyttizens to converte yt to so good a use, God moved his harte to bestowe yt to that use rather then to be at any charge in keping of yt or to suffer yt to falle downe and not be profitable to any. This I am suer was the reason that moved the king, for at that tyme it stood voyde and was daily spoylde by the kepers.' (*A Brief Note of the Order and Manner of the Proceedings in the first erection of the three Royal Hospitals* ... 1582, ed. by W. Lemprière, 1904.)

(64) Entick describes the improvements in his appendix to Maitland's *History of London* ed. of 1775, II, Appendix, p. 147.

'As you enter the eastern part of London, the passenger needs only pass down the Great Minories and the new buildings which fill all the west side from Aldgate High Street to Tower Hill, including George Street and John Street that open each a spacious passage into Poor Jewry Lane and Crutched Friars, and Hammett Street finished at the west extremity with an elegant half-circle of first-rate houses, instead of those wooden hovels, paltry erections and waste ground, which heretofore were the receptacle of whores and thieves under the City Wall from Aldgate to the Postern on Tower Hill, and he will meet with objects of wonder and amazement considering the shortness of the time in which these improvements and the new pavements after the first City re-paving Act in 1768 have been completed.' This part of London, St Botolph's Aldgate (Portsoken Ward) was crowded with poor in 1637. The parish returned a long list of divided houses and of no less than 925 'poore'. cf. above, n. 23.

(65) See notes 45, 46, 47 and 101 to Chapter 6.

(66) 'These filthy places receive all the sinks, necessary houses and drains from dye houses, wash houses, fell mongers, slaughter houses and all kinds of offensive trades; they are continually full of carrion and the most odious of all offensive stench proceeds from them; also the other part of the said ditches westward as far as Lambeth, many of which lye a great depth in mud. . . . The like of these are to be seen below Bridge from Horseley-down to Battle Bridge and all along the Back of Rotherhithe . . . and are justly the terror even of the inhabitants themselves. . . . Such notorious fountains of stench, enough to corrupt the very air and make the people sick and faint as they pass by.' (*Due Preservation from the Plague as well for Soul as Body*, 1722, pp. 29–30. Defoe?)

(67) *Report on Contagious Fever in London*, 1818.

(68) Maitland, *History of London*, 1756, ii, p. 1,315. See also below, note 114.

(69) Willan, *Diseases in London*, 1801, p. 255.

(70) T. A. Murray, *Remarks on the Situation of the Poor in the Metropolis*, 1801, pp. 5–6.

(71) Grose, *The Olio*, 1795, p. 75.

(72) *Middlesex Records, Orders of Court*, Cal., p. 153. Something verging on the common lodging-house seems to be implied in a Council letter of 1598: 'Wee are informed by the humble complaint of the inhabitants of Shoreditch, St Giles without Creplegate, Clarkenwell and of other the like places in the suburbs neere unto the Cyttie of London, that there are divers persons that are owners of small tenements and moste of them erected within these few yeres that doe lett the same out by the weeke and some for lesse tyme unto base people and to lewd persons that doe kepe evell rule and harbour theefes, rogues and vagabonds. . . .' (*Acts of the Privy Council*, xxviii, p. 427.)

(73) Welch, *A Proposal to render effective a Plan to remove . . . Prostitutes . . .* pp. 52–3. (Quoting a letter from himself to the Duke of Newcastle in 1753.)

(74) J. C. Jeaffreson, *Middlesex County Records*, iv, pp. liii–iv.

(75) There were many indictments at Quarter Sessions for leaving cellar doors open, e.g. at Westminster Sessions, 26 Charles II, there were fifty-three. (ibid.)

(76) This account is based on many incidental references to the milk business in the *Sessions Papers*. cf. T. Baird, *General View of the Agriculture of Middlesex*, 1794: Milk was (in 1794) sold by the cow-keepers to the retailers (who generally provided the milker) at $2\frac{3}{4}$d. a quart, retailed at $4\frac{1}{2}$d. greatly diluted with water, usually by a pump in the cow-keeper's milk-room, otherwise 'the retailers are not even careful to use clean water. Some of them have even been seen to dip their pails in a common horse trough'. 'It is a common

practice with the retailers . . . to carry the milk first home to their own houses where it is set up for half a day when the cream is taken from it . . . it is then sold for new milk. By which means what is delivered in the morning is no other than the milk of the preceding afternoon deprived of the cream it throws up by standing that time. . . . A cow-keeper informed me that retail milk dealers are for the most part the refuse of other employments, possessing neither character, decency, manners nor cleanliness. No delicate person could possibly drink the milk were they fully acquainted with the filthy habits of these dealers in it.' cf. Appendix VI, and the case of a parish child apprenticed to a milk-seller, note 49, Chapter 5.

Cows were sometimes driven through the streets and milked at the customer's door.

(77) For the 'Lactarium' cf. an advertisement of 1773:

'Lactaria, the Inventress of the Lactarium in St George's Fields presents her best respects to the Public in general, thanks them for past favours and lives in hope that her milk and syllabubs will be recommended to persons in the country. Boarding-school ladies and gentlemen that may come to town for the holidays, ladies and gentlemen going to the Magdalen or the Asylum are welcome to leave anything in her care. The room is kept warm with a good fire. There is a conductor to render it a safe place in case of lightning and a garde-robe for ladies. She will accommodate no disorderly people. The well-behaved who come to serve her, she is much obliged to, and begs such ladies as are fond of rural elegance will plead for Lactaria.' (*Public Advertiser*, 18 December 1773.)

(78) *Sessions Papers*, February 1786.

(79) ibid. September 1790. The occupant had been robbed of seventeen pairs of stockings which she had taken to mend.

(80) *Public Advertiser*, 7 January 1768.

(81) *Sessions Papers*, January 1794.

(82) ibid. January 1787.

(83) ibid. April 1760.

(84) ibid. July 1787.

(85) Misson, who visited England in 1697, says, 'it is not the custom for travellers to lodge in houses where the coaches, carriers, and other public vehicles set up. . . . At London they hardly so much as know what an *auberge* is. . . . The way of lodging if you are not entertained at a friend's house is to take a room ready furnished at so much a head.' (*Memoirs and Observations on his Travels over England . . .* 1719, p. 144.)

(86) *C.J.* 25 February and 2 March 1772.

(87) *Considerations on the Expediency of raising at this Time of Dearth the Wages of Servants that are not domestic, particularly Clerks in Public Offices*, 1767, pp. 6–7.

(88) *Observations on Public Houses*, 1794, p. 26. He makes the unjustifiable assumption that this was due to a recent deterioration of manners.

(89) *Sessions Papers*, 1795. The would-be tenant went out, returned in a quarter of an hour with another man ostensibly to share the lodging, and managed to steal a watch.

(90) *Autobiography*. Add. MSS. 35142.

(91) Colquhoun, *A Treatise on Indigence*, 1806, p. 283.

(92) See Appendix IV, Case 32.

(93) *Sessions Papers*, June 1785.

(94) Colquhoun, *Police of the Metropolis*, 1797, p. 33.

(95) cf. the articles of inquiry of the Westminster Annoyance Jury, 1734–5 (number xiv): 'You shall present all such persons as shall keep or lodge any inmates in their houses that are or shall be likely to be chargeable to any of the parishes within the said City and

Liberty.' (*Instructions and Orders by the Deputy Steward to the Annoyance Jury. . . .*) For the housekeeper, see note 28, Chap. 5.

(96) Arthur Young calls Camden House, the school where his daughter Bobbin was till her death in 1797 'that region of constraint and death'. 'The rules for health are detestable, no air but in a measured formal walk, and all running and quick motion prohibited, preposterous! She slept with a girl who could hear only with one ear, and so ever laid on the one side, and my dear child could do no otherwise afterwards without pain, because the vile beds are so small they must both lie the same way. . . . She never had a bellyful at breakfast. Detestable this at the expense of £80 a year.' (*Autobiography*, ed. by M. Betham Edwards, 1898, pp. 263–5.)

(97) *The Cabinet Makers London Book of Prices and Designs . . .* 2nd ed. 1793. (Library of the Victoria and Albert Museum.)

(98) See for instance note 4, Chapter 1.

(99) The defence against an indictment for a nuisance made by a man who kept from three to five hundred hogs off Tottenham Court Road which could be smelt from Great Russell Street was that 'this was the prosperest place for a hogstye when so many laystalls and cow lays were admitted in the outskirts of the town', while there were 'very nauseous smells before this hogstye was erected and since'. The hogstye it was said 'takes off a great many things in ye town y^t would otherwise be very offensive'. Moreover the leet jury had found it to be no nuisance. On the other hand it was a nuisance at common law to keep hogs in or near a great city. It was also pointed out that the hogs were at least a quarter of a mile from where the nightmen made their pits. Harris, *Life of Lord Chancellor Hardwicke*, i, p. 266.

(100) *Proposals for establishing a Charitable Fund in the City of London*, 1706, p. 19.

(101) C. Morris, *Observations on the late Growth and present State of London*, 1751.

(102) See note 104, Chapter 6.

(103) J. Richardson, *Recollections . . .* 1856, i, p. 7.

(104) Evidence was given to the Committee on Police of 1816 that bull-baiting was no longer practised in London, only bull-hanking, or chasing a bullock through the streets on market days; this was especially a sport of Bethnal Green. Another witness however said that bulls were baited in Tothill Fields. See also notes 116 and 117, Chapter 4, for bull-hanking.

(105) C. Jenner, *London Eclogues*, 2nd ed. 1773.

(106) W. Breighton, *History of Epidemics*, 1894, ii, p. 764.

(107) On Sunday afternoons in the summer 'some hundreds of people, mostly women and children', were to be seen, 'walking backward and forward on Westminster Bridge for the benefit of the air, looking at the boats going up and down the river, and sitting on the resting benches . . .' (*Low-life*, 1764, p. 72.)

(108) Vol. iii, p. 289. Dr Ferriar's experience was chiefly in Manchester and it is of the dangers of the Manchester fields that he is actually writing.

(109) *Fourth Report of the Commissioners under the Poor Law Amendment Act*, 1838, Appendix A, pp. 210 ff.

(110) Proclamation of 16 July 1615.

(111) *Critical Review . . .* 1734, pp. 27–8. Lincoln's Inn Fields in particular had long been an annoyance and even a danger. The Act of 1735 for its enclosure runs: 'Whereas the great square now called Lincoln's Inn Fields . . . hath for some years past lain waste and in great disorder, whereby the same has become a receptacle for rubbish, dirt and nastiness of all sorts brought hither . . . not only by the inhabitants . . . but by many others . . . also for want of proper fences to enclose the same great mischiefs have hap-

pened to many of his majesty's subjects . . . several of whom have been killed and others maimed by horses . . . many wicked and disorderly persons have frequently met together therein, using unlawful sports and games and drawing in . . . young persons into gaming and idleness and other vicious ways and courses and vagabonds, common beggars and other persons resort therein, whereby many robberies, assaults, outrages and enormities have been and continually are committed.' (8 Geo. II. c. 26.)

cf. Gay, *Trivia.*

(112) The result of this individual responsibility is described by a projector who wished to form a company for the paving of London: 'If everyone pave only before his own door, there never can be a true level or regular current observed, each one paving at several times, according to his own private interest or fancy, higher or lower, to accommodate some cellar door, cross kennel or some irregular ascent or fall, he hath no mind to alter, without any regard to the publick; so that it is by this means impossible for a common line to be observed. . . . Many, when they pave, have so little time in their houses, that they purposely do it slightly to last their own time only, and some out of covetousness, will either not pave at all, or so very little, that the streets are nothing the better. Where the paviours are allowed a sufficient price to do their work well . . . it . . . is their interest to have the work rather often doing than well done. . . . And also by raising every new pavement higher than their neighbours as is their constant practice the adjoining pavement is quickly spoiled.' (*Considerations humbly offered to . . . Parliament shewing the Necessity and Benefit of an Act to incorporate a certain select Number of Persons for the more beautiful and useful paving and cleansing the Streets . . . within the weekly Bills . . .* n.d.) See also *C.J.* 19 February 1728–9.

(113) The Paving Commissioners progressively extended their scope to deal with street nuisances in general. cf. a report to the House of Commons by Luke Ideson, the very active vestry clerk of St James Westminster, who was also clerk to the parish Paving Committee. 'That it is necessary that further regulations should be made with regard to the companies who furnish the inhabitants with water and that provision should be made for preventing the sweeping . . . any dirt or mud into the sewers or within a limited distance of the grates; that persons not belonging to . . . the scavengers frequently obtain by fraud the ashes from houses . . . and that some explanation is necessary with respect to the placing of signs; that the placing of goods, wares and merchandises, carriages, casks, packages, timber, wheels, materials for building and other things in the streets to the annoyance thereof ought to be prevented; that the keeping of open holes or funnels for the purpose of letting down coals and other things, and the manner in which brewers servants draw up barrels out of cellars or vaults wants regulating, and that it is necessary the foot-crossings should be ascertained, and provision made to prevent their being stopped by carriages or otherwise; and that the digging holes to make vaults and leaving them as well as areas open without fencing or placing any lights thereto is very dangerous and ought to be prevented, that the driving of cattle, carriages, casks and other things on the foot-pavement is a very great annoyance, as is also the standing of horses at farriers shops and the throwing of bricks, tiles and other things from the tops of houses; that it would be a great convenience if the power given to Commissioners to regulate the streets paved by them was extended to streets not new-paved; that the erecting bulks and stalls and sinking dung-holes and saw-pits within the jurisdiction of the Commissioners are very great nuisances, as is the custom of throwing at oranges and other things, or at cocks, pigeons and other fowls; and the making of bonfires and letting off gunpowder in the streets; that notices ought to be sent to the Commissioners of Sewers when any contracts are made for new paving, that the sewers may be previously emptied or repaired; that it

would be convenient to have the houses and lamps numbered. . . .' (*C.J.* 13 March 1776.)

(114) In the City the Commissioners of Sewers managed the paving operations, in other districts friction sometimes arose between the two sets of commissioners. Some Acts made specific provision for sewer-making, e.g. that for St Sepulchre's (12 Geo. III. c. 68) provided for making sewers in St John's Street and Cow Cross, a particularly unsavoury neighbourhood.

One Totton claimed to have invented the deep barrelled sewers used by the City in the works carried out in connexion with re-paving. His account of the state of London before the draining improvements that accompanied the new paving is interesting:

'Before 1766 your petitioner well remembers every person in Spital Square in the Liberty of Norton Falgate greatly inconvenienced by the springs in the liberty, insomuch that in his late father's house there the water . . . used to be three or four feet deep in the cellars; and the servants used to punt themselves along in a washing tub from the cellar-stairs to the beer-barrels to draw beer daily. . . .

'That this was the method which the chief of the inhabitants in the liberty also pursued to get at anything in their cellars, at the same time living in the stench of bilge-water, which rendered their situation . . . very prejudicial to their healths.

'And this was also the case with many of the inhabitants of Bishopsgate Street, and . . . with many inhabitants throughout the City . . . from himself being on his occasional returns to his house early and late, nearly suffocated with the stench of water, pumping or pailing up, in almost every street, from the cellars therein.' He claims that his object in proposing a new form of sewer had been 'the consideration of the distresses and inconveniences of the inhabitants of those places and also of Long Alley, where I was an eye witness to the water being up to the bedsteads on which they lay, many of them with their children in sickness, want and the utmost misery. . . .' (Steven Totton, *A Humble Representation . . .*, 1795.)

(115) Pugh, *Life of Hanway*, p. 139.

(116) W. Wales, *Inquiry into the present State of the Population . . .* 1781, p. 18.

(117) cf. a presentment of the Grand Jury of the City of London to the Sessions of October 1721 (when the plague was raging at Marseilles) '. . . that this Court would enjoyne the constables and watchmen, who must needs be sensible of the great quantities of soil cast into the streets in the night time when the inhabitants shut up their houses, to detect such persons and bring them to justice. And also all such who sweep the soil and dirt of their shops and houses into the streets, lanes and passages . . . leaving it there, whereby the passengers are much annoyed in their affairs.' (*Sessions Papers*)

It is significant of rising standards that Marylebone in 1755 obtained a local Act in which there was a clause forbidding night-soil to be thrown in or near the streets; in 1770 this was changed to 'within half a mile of the streets', a very usual clause in Paving Acts.

(118) Letter to the Duke of Newcastle, 18 February 1754. *S. P. Dom. Geo. II.* Bundle 153.

(119) *Middlesex Records, Sessions Book*, October 1745.

(120) As in Middlesex, lighting responsibility was divided between contributors to public lights and those who hung out lights themselves, but in the City the 'contractors were annually obliged to pay the City . . . £600 for the liberty of lighting the same. . . . Besides the contractors were only to receive six shillings per annum of every householder who paid to the poor, of such whose houses exceeded the rent of £10 per annum, and of those who put out no lights. . . .' (Maitland, *History of London*, 1756, I, pp. 521 and 565.)

(121) Archenholtz, op. cit., p. 131.

(122) J. Richardson, *Recollections*, 1856, i, p. 31.

(123) Ralph, *Critical Review* . . . ed. of 1783, p. 3.

(124) The terrible state of London graveyards attracted general attention in the nineteenth century (see G. A. Walker, *Gatherings from Grave Yards*, 1839); it seems probable that they were even worse in the eighteenth. Parishes from time to time obtained Acts enabling them to buy land for a new graveyard, but only under the pressure of an appalling state of things. For instance the two churchyards of St Andrew's Holborn (both together supposed less than an acre) were 'so offensive' in 1720 that they were shut up by order of the king and Council. Nevertheless, the fear of plague being over, they remained the only burying-grounds for the parish till the year 1747, when a Bill was applied for to enable the parish to buy land for a burial-ground. It was said that the inhabitants had nearly doubled in the past twenty years, and some ghastly evidence was given in support of the Bill. *C.J.* 5 February 1746-7.

The Poor's holes were a scandal throughout the century:

'It is well known that several out-parishes . . . are very much straitened for room to bury their dead; and that to remedy in part that inconvenience, they dig in their churchyards or other annexed burial-grounds, large holes or pits in which they put many of the bodies of those whose friends are not able to pay for better graves, and then those pits or holes (called the poor's holes) once opened are not cover'd till fill'd with dead bodies: Thus it is in St Martin's, St James's and St Giles in the Fields and other places. . . . How noisome the stench is that arises from these holes so stow'd with dead bodies, especially in sultry seasons and after rain, one may appeal to all who approach them. . . .' (*Some Customs consider'd whether prejudicial to the Health of this City* . . . 1721, pp. 7-10.)

In 1774 when the jails were attracting attention as dangerous to the health of the surrounding districts, a correspondent of the *Public Advertiser* (21 April) pointed out the necessity of attending also to churchyards and vaults: 'The greatest evil is what is called parish or poor's graves: these are pits capable of holding three or four coffins abreast and about seven in depth; are always kept open till they are full, then the tops are covered over with earth; and another pit about the same size is dug on the side of it, leaving the sides of the former coffins always open. . . . This is the common practice in a churchyard near the centre of this metropolis, and . . . the general practice is pretty similar from the best inquiries I have been able to make.' (Reprinted as an address to Parliament.)

Some steps appear to have been taken to stop this, as Pennant writes of St Giles in the Fields: 'in the churchyard I have observed with horror a great square pit . . . [etc. *ut supra*.] Notwithstanding a compliment paid me in one of the public papers of my having occasioned the abolition of this horrible practice, it still remains uncorrected in this great parish. The reform ought to have begun in the place first stigmatized.' (*London*, 1790, p. 180.)

(125) Add. MSS. 35147, fo. 286.

cf. also an entry made in September 1824 after a tour of inspection in East London, from the Tower to the farther end of Limehouse by the water-side, returning by Ratcliffe Highway and Rosemary Lane: 'Great as is the mass of poverty and misery of places along shore from the Tower to the Isle of Dogs, still, except in the very worst of these places and among the most wretched of the wretched, there is also considerable improvement. On the leading streets, such as Wapping, Wapping Dock, Wapping Wall, Lower Shadwell, Queen Street, Broad Street, Ratcliffe Highway, East Smithfield Street, Rosemary Lane, Cable Street and Knock Fargus, Back Lane and Brook Street, which run nearly parallel east and west in three lines, the improvement in all respects great. The old wooden houses in most of these places have either been pulled down or burnt down, and others of brick built in their places at different times commencing about forty years ago. The

London Docks have also been the cause of a large number of miserable houses being pulled down and of the streets being widened. One of these fires, the most extensive of them all happened on the 13 July 1794, it consumed upwards of 600 houses and cleared a large space which was soon afterwards built upon in a much better manner than before, as well in respect of the houses being of bricks, as of the widening of the streets &c. causing a great improvement in that neighbourhood. . . .

'No place has perhaps undergone a more complete change than Wapping. . . . From dirt and filth and rubbish and old miserable houses and noise and tumult and riot, drunkenness and obscenity to the state which has been mentioned. . . . Rosemary Lane and its continuation are the least improved, but still there are very considerable improvements. In these leading streets I carefully observed the children and can safely say they are equal, and in many respects superior, to the children of tradesmen in much more wealthy neighbourhoods west of Cornhill within my memory.' (Add. MSS. 27828, fo. 120.) See also note 134, Chapter 6.

(126) Add. MSS. 27827, fol. 52.

(127) [Chadwick] 'Life Assurances, Diminution of Sickness and Mortality', *Westminster Review*, Ap. 1728, p. 388. Reprinted with notes in 1837.

(128) 'Report on the State of the Inhabitants and their dwellings in Church Lane, St Giles', *Journal of the Statistical Society*, March 1848.

(129) Add. MSS. 35147, fo. 230 (1826).

Notes to Chapter 3

(1) *Parliamentary History*, iv, p. 679. See note 25, Chapter 2.

(2) '. . . for if they cannot get such employment as they expected or chuse to follow, many of them will not go home again to be laughed at . . . but enlist for soldiers, go to the plantations &c. if they are well enclined; otherwise they probably commence thieves or pickpockets. . . .' (J. Massie, *A Plan for the Establishment of Charity Houses for exposed or deserted Women and Girls . . .* 1758, p. 16.)

(3) 'In London, the compting houses are much supplied with country lads from Cumberland and Westmoreland, who exchange the plow and the flail for the pen and prove as expert with the one as the other.' (Housman, 'Tour', *Monthly Magazine*, February 1798, p. 108.)

(4) Quoted by Malcolm, *Anecdotes of the Manners and Customs of London . . .* 1808, p. 160.

(5) Burrington, *An Answer to Dr William Brakenridge's Letter*, 1757, p. 37.

(6) *Report on Education in the Metropolis*, 1816, p. 79.

(7) 'Midwifery Reports of the Westminster General Dispensary', *Philosophical Transactions*, LXXI, 1781, p. 355 ff.

Mr Martin ('Mendicity Martin') who started a plan for relieving London beggars and checking mendicancy found in 1796–7 that about 5,097 persons, including children, said they belonged to – that is, had settlements in – home parishes, distant parishes, Ireland, Scotland and foreign countries in the following proportions:

1. Home parishes (within ten miles of the metropolis)	about	2,231	persons including		1,384	children
2. Distant parishes	„	868	„	„	489	„
3. Ireland	„	1,770	„	„	1,091	„
4. Scotland	„	168	„	„	103	„
5. Foreign Countries	„	59	„	„	29	„

(*Mendicity Report*, 1814–15, Appendix 4.)

These figures do not give a basis of comparison with those of Dr Bland, who records place of birth, not place of settlement.

(8) *Some Account of the Life and Death of Matthew Lee executed at Tyburn . . . 1752 in the twentieth year of his Age*, 1752, 2nd ed. (A tract.)

(9) *Police of the Metropolis*, ed. of 1800, p. 634 n. (Probably an exaggeration; he overestimates the population of London.)

(10) Letter in the *London Chronicle*, 6 April 1758 (written 1753).

(11) *Brief Description of London and Westminster*, p. xxvii.

(12) 'It is generally allowed that country wenches make the best servants, and therefore most families are fond of having such; hence arises the custom of sending to inns to chuse out of the numbers that are weekly brought up.' (Letter in *London Chronicle*, 2 February 1758.)

(13) *Mendicity Report*, pp. 268–9. Evidence of Wm. Gurney, Rector of St Clement Danes: 'Many come for the early hay-time of the metropolis, but they always bring a large

suite with them, they mow their way back again. . . . They generally come too soon and the streets are filled with these poor people . . . stating they came up to get a job of work but the market is overstocked, there are so many Irish people here. The children are immediately set to begging in the street. They get a dreadful habit . . . in London of idleness and drinking.' See also the evidence of Sir Nathaniel Conant (the Bow Street magistrate) and of Montague Burgoyne.

(14) *Report on Irish and Scotch Vagrants*, 1828, p. 209 ff. Allowing for the increase in immigration after 1815, the account applies to earlier periods.

(15) The following description of the Rookery in 1850 when New Oxford Street had been built, but George Street and Church Lane had been left, 'the still standing plague spots of that colony', probably gives some idea of what the place was like a hundred years before, though we must remember that by 1816 St Giles was already said to have improved and that in 1750 it had contained 'eighty two-penny houses of the greatest infamy', while every fourth house at least had been a gin-shop (see Chapter 1).

'Rows of crumbling houses flanked by courts and alleys, culs de sac, etc., in the very densest part of which the wretchedness of London takes shelter. . . . Squalid children, haggard men, with long uncombed hair, in rags, with a short pipe in their mouths, many speaking Irish, women without shoes or stockings – a babe perhaps at the breast with a single garment, confined to the waist by a bit of string; wolfish-looking dogs; decayed vegetables strewing the pavement, low public-houses; linen hanging across the street to dry. . . .

'In one house a hundred persons have been known to sleep on a given night. . . . In these rooms are piled the wares by which *some* of the inhabitants gain their precarious living – oranges, herrings, water-cresses, onions, seemed to be the most marketable articles; and there were sweepers, cadgers or beggars, stray luggage porters, &c. lounging about. . . .

'But nine-tenths of the inhabitants are Irish; do we then set down to Irish nurture this account of wretchedness and immorality? God forbid! We believe that female profligacy is more rare in Ireland than in England, though poverty is more excessive. . . . But the Irish coming to London seem to regard it as a heathen city and to give themselves up at once to a course of recklessness and crime. . . . The misery, filth and crowded condition of the Irish cabin is realized in St Giles. The purity of the female character which is the boast of Irish historians here at least is a fable.' (Montague Gore, *On the Dwellings of the Poor*, 2nd ed. 1851, pp. vii and xii–xiv.)

(16) *Report on Education*, 1816, p. 53. The Roman Catholic clergy estimated that there were then 14,000 Irish in 'the Shadwell parishes'.

(17) ibid., pp. 220–21.

(18) *Passages from a working life*, ed. of 1873, i, p. 119.

(19) Marylebone Vestry Minutes, quoted by S. and B. Webb, *Parish and County*, p. 399.

(20) *Report on Education* . . . 1816, p. 261.

(21) The court was described in detail in the *Supplementary Report on Intramural Interments* of 1843, p. 661 n. The pigs seem to have disappeared but the inhabitants, according to the census of 1841, had increased to 944 and there were said to be twenty-six houses instead of twenty-four. The court was about twenty-two feet broad, the houses were three-storied buildings of ten rooms each rented at from about £20–£30 a year. The drainage was by means of a channel running down the centre of the court. (Structurally this was an improvement on the earlier courts, passages and 'dark entries', some of which were only three, four or five feet wide.)

(22) See *A Proclamation for suppressing the multitude of idle vagabonds and avoyding of*

certaine mischievous dangerous persons from her Majestie's Court, 21 February 1583.

(23) *A Proclamation for the speedy sending away of Irish Beggars out of this Kingdom.* . . .

One result of the Plantation of Ulster was an influx of Irish to London. cf. a letter from the Privy Council (30 April 1606) to Chichester, Lord Deputy of Ireland and the Irish Council: 'You shall understand that these parts about London and elsewhere are exceedingly pestered with a great multitude of beggars of that country . . . most of them peasants with wives and children, the disorder whereof must needs proceed by the negligence of the officers of ports and the owners of barks, for which we pray you to take better order and severely to punish all offenders; considering how great a dishonour it is that strangers should behold them in our highways and streets, and a great eyesore it is to his majesy's poor subjects in this kingdom.' (Printed in Lodge's *Desiderata Curiosa Hibernica*, i, p. 481.)

(24) Dekker, *Westward Hoe.*

(25) *Parliamentary History*, xiv, pp. 146 and 1302.

In 1774 there were pitched battles between English and Irish haymakers round Kingsbury, Edgware and Hendon. The English were the aggressors and eleven of the ringleaders were taken to Bow Street, where it appeared that they had resolved to put an end to the employment of the Irish. *London Chronicle*, 12–14 and 16–19 July 1774.

(26) F. A. Ebblewhite, *The Tin Plate Workers Company*, 1896, p. 26.

(27) Letter from Sir Robert Walpole to Horace Walpole, quoted from Coxe's *Memoirs* in *Parl. Hist.*, ix, p. 128 ff.

(28) *Spittlefields and Shorditch in an uproar or the Devil to pay with the English and the Irish. Being a full and particular Account of the sharp and bloody Battles that was fought* . . . (Broadsheet); *General Williamson's Diary*, Camden Society, 1912. (Under date 28 July 1736.) *Old Bailey Sessions Papers*, October 1736. *Gent. Mag.* 1736, pp. 285 and 422. Malcolm, *Anecdotes* . . . p. 275.

(29) Press cutting in B.M. Collection called *Alsatian Curiosities.*

(30) Malcolm, *Anecdotes* . . . 1808, p. 266.

(31) For instance, there was a fight in King Street, Westminster, between an Irish labourer, one Owen Crane, who 'carries bricks or rubbish' and also 'goes out to sell milk', and an Englishman who touched a basket Crane was carrying. Crane's opponent, who 'had more skill in boxing . . . flung him down a very hard fall' and then said he was not for fighting him 'by reason there were so many Irishmen belonging to Crane'. However, later on Crane struck the other man's wife and was mobbed. A free fight then seems to have taken place in which 'the [Irish] labourers were very mischievous with their shovels'. Four were arrested by a constable. Crane said 'no English booger should take him.' (*Sessions Papers*, September 1755.)

(32) Defoe, *The Behaviour of Servants*, p. 20.

(33) *Sessions Papers*, 28 June 1780.

(34) *A Proposal to render effectual a Plan to remove the Nuisance of Common Prostitutes* . . . 1758 (quoting a letter from himself to the Duke of Newcastle in 1753).

Other writers ascribed robberies with violence to Irish haymakers who preferred to remain in London rather than return to Ireland at the end of the season, or to 'pretended haymakers'. e.g. 'When this stranger has spent his gains, and, as out of season is out of employment, he generally sinks into want, becomes desperate, and supports himself by violent means; and I do not remember that before this practice of summer visits was so common with us, cruelties were so common among rogues. . . .' (*Publick Nusance considered* . . *by a Gentleman of the Temple*, n.d. [c. 1750?] p. 30.)

'. . . the abuses committed by some of these pretended haymakers are too flagrant not to excuse me at the hands of the worthy gentlemen of that race for wishing some stop were put to that importation, and that none should be permitted to land without a regular pass.' (*The Vices of the Cities of London traced from their Original . . . Dublin*, 1751, p. 20.)

The cases tried at the Old Bailey about the middle of the century seem to confirm the distinction Welch draws between the 'industrious Irish' and the professional ruffian. cf. below, n. 37.

(35) Sir Thomas Bernard states this on the authority of Hannah More and as an example of the effects of education: 'Mrs Hannah Moore mentioned to me that during the number of years that the late Mr Henry Fielding presided at Bow Street, only six Scotchmen . . . came before him. Mr Fielding used to say that of the persons committed, the greater part were of a sister island, where the natural dispositions of the people were quite as good, but the system of education neither so strict nor so generally adopted as in Scotland.' (*Third Report of the Society for Bettering the Conditions of the Poor*, p. 32 n.)

(36) See below, n. 60.

(37) cf. the career of Lot Cavenagh, a London foot-pad executed in 1743, aged 27. He was a Protestant, born in Dublin and apprenticed to an apothecary; he robbed his master and was turned out of doors. He went to France, he said that he was trapanned with six other lads for the French service and having, 'no notion of a soldier's life' stole some money, escaped to Calais and thence to England. A number of other Irish foot-pads about this time had come to England from France. Others came from Ireland, cf. the deposition of William Kelley *alias* Johnson, taken at the Poultry Compter, 3 June 1745:

'. . . William Kelley . . . saith that he came over to Chester and thence to London upwards of two months agoe in company with Thomas St Leger *alias* Montgomery and went to lodge at a shoemaker's in Gray's Inn Lane untill St Leger went with him to Patrick Cave *alias* Cavenagh in an alley opposite to St Andrew's Church, Holborn, to drink a dram, Cave's wife selling drams and punch. When . . . he and Cave agreed to lodge together there and having no money they took a walk out with Cave their landlord, and St Leger began to make his complaint to Cave that if he could be provided he would goe on the highway, but Cave persuaded St Leger and this examinant not to goe on the highway but to rob in town and he would provide them with pistols and other accoutrements. . . .' Kelley and St Leger then robbed a man in Lincoln's Inn, Kelley 'presenting a pistol to his breast while St Leger stood with his hanger drawn and the man readily delivered his money which was 18s. and so let him go about his business'. A long list of robberies follows. The goods were given to Cave, whose wife pawned them. The three men went on 23 May about twelve at night to the Strand, 'where they saw a gentleman with laced cloathes and Cave said "there's a good fowl".' They defrauded Cave of a share of the money. 'Cave used to lend Kelley a surtout livery coat and a laced hat to go out of [*sic*] these expeditions.' Kelley ends a long list of robberies (many in Lincoln's Inn Fields), 'this is all the robberies that I can recollect at present.' (Original MS. deposition, *Sessions Papers*, Guildhall.)

(38) Fielding, *An Enquiry into the late Encrease of Robbers*, 1751, pp. 92–4. To the words 'many thousands', a note is added, 'most of these are Irish'.

(39) Bell, *A Description of the Condition and Manners . . . of the Peasantry of Ireland such as they were between . . . 1780 and 1790 when Ireland was supposed to have arrived at its highest degree of Prosperity and Happiness*, 1804, p. 3.

(40) A. Young, *Tour in Ireland* [1776–9], ed. of 1892, ii, p. 40.

(41) *Report on the Police of the Metropolis*, 1817, p. 151.

(42) This was evidently the so-called Catholic Free School of St Giles, opened in 1813

to children nominated by subscribers. Its usefulness must have been much lessened by the fact that the scholars were taught to read in the Bible, thus alarming the Roman Catholic clergy, who were not reassured by a proviso that no creed, confession of faith or catechism should be introduced, when this rule was given as a reason for refusing to allow a priest to attend once a week to give religious instruction to the children. See *Annual Reports* of the School, 1814–16.

(43) Add. MSS. 27827, fo. 132.

(44) *Mendicity Report*, p. 284.

(45) *Report on the Poor Laws*, 1817, p. 122.

(46) The rapid increase of relief to the Irish, out of all proportion to the general rise in poor rates appears from a remark of Colquhoun: 'The expense of the casual poor who have no settlement in any part of the Metropolis, amounts to a large sum annually. In the united parishes of St Giles in the Fields and St George Bloomsbury to . . . £2,000 in 1796. It arose from the support of about twelve hundred poor natives of Ireland, who but for this aid must have become vagrants.' (*State of Indigence*, 1799, p. 14.) St Giles is said to have had a reputation in Ireland as a generous parish. *Report on Education*, 1816, p. 254.

(47) ibid., pp. 252–4. The Irish quarter was defined as lying between High Street and Broad St Giles on the south, Great Russell Street on the north, Tottenham Court Road and Charlotte Street Bloomsbury on the east. This was the Rookery, and in this small space there was said to be in 1816 a fluctuating Irish population of about 6,000 adults and from 3,000 to 4,000 children. (ibid. cf. note 15.)

(48) In May 1837 Mr Rawson of the Statistical Society read a paper on the state of the inhabitants of Calmel Buildings. (Montague Gore, *On the Dwellings of the Poor*, 2nd ed. 1851, p. 4.)

The custom of subletting rooms was rare among the English, but this characteristic of the Irish in the eighteenth–nineteenth centuries seems to have its parallel among the English in the seventeenth century. cf. an account of a crowded tenement house in Silver Street, in the parish of St Alban's, Wood Street, in 1637, where 'ten families dwell in so many single rooms, divers of which have also lodgers, all which dwellers are either pensioners of the parish or receive alms of the parish in money, bread or coals.' (*S. P. Dom. Charles I*, 359, XII, i.) See note 23, Chapter 2.

(49) *Report on the Police of the Metropolis*, 1817, pp. 350–51. The typhus epidemic of 1816–17 first appeared in a dirty court off Saffron Hill. Possibly the fever ascribed to the Sullivan wake may have been the beginning of the outbreak.

(50) *Supplementary Report on Intramural Interments*, 1843.

(51) cf. the evidence of the Inspector of the House of Recovery (see notes 88, 93 and 94, Chap. 1) to the Select Committee on Contagious Fever in London in 1818: Difficulties in the whitewashing of infected rooms arose, he said, from 'the number of Irish people living together, and we have a number of patients of that description, though . . . a refusal to have the apartment whitewashed seldom occurs'. 'Do you find the Irish people live together more promiscuously and in larger assemblies than the English?' 'Certainly.' 'In what part of the town do they principally inhabit?' 'In the neighbourhood of Saffron Hill, Gray's Inn Lane, Dyott Street, St Giles and also there are numbers of them at the east end of the town, at Whitechapel.' 'Are those quarters almost always affected by contagious diseases in the autumn?' 'Certainly more than other quarters.' (*Report*, pp. 22–3.)

(52) *Mendicity Report*, p. 240.

(53) *Report on the Police of the Metropolis*, 1828, p. 61.

(54) Till 59 Geo. III. c. 12, the Irish were not removed unless they committed an act of

vagrancy. After 1819, as children born of Catholic marriages were considered illegitimate and therefore entitled to a settlement in the parish in which they were born, and as the mother of such a child was irremovable during its infancy, many Irish were able to escape removal. It was said in 1834 that 'the parents knowing the dilemma in which parishes are thus placed, make use of the circumstances as a means of extorting relief, threatening to desert their children if their applications are unattended to.' (*Poor Law Report*, 1834, XXXVI, p. 184, k.) (Whitechapel.)

(55) Evidence of Mr Bodkin to the Committee on Emigration, 1826, as recorded by Place. Add. MSS. 27825, fo. 260. In the *Report* (p. 214) the wording is condensed.

(56) 'The Irish street-folk are, generally speaking, a far more provident body of people than the English street-sellers. To save, the Irish will often sacrifice what many Englishmen consider a necessary, and undergo many a hardship. . . . They will treasure up halfpenny after halfpenny, and continue to do so for years, in order to send money to enable their wives and children, and even their brothers and sisters, when in the depth of distress in Ireland, to take shipping for England. . . . But they will not save to preserve either themselves or their children from the degradation of a workhouse; indeed they often, with the means of independence secreted on their persons, apply for poor relief, and that principally to save the expenditure of their own money. . . . Not one of them but has a positive genius for begging – both the taste and the faculty for alms-seeking developed to an extraordinary extent.' (Mayhew, *London Labour and the London Poor*, i, 1851, p. 115.)

The custom of combining begging with street-selling was one of the reasons for the London costermongers' dislike of the Irish; Mayhew quotes the remark of one of the former, 'they'll beg themselves into a meal and work us out of one', p. 116.

(57) A. M. Hyamson, *A History of the Jews in England*, 1908, pp. 236 ff.; C. Booth *Life and Labour of the People in London Poverty*, iii, p. 174.

(58) Smollett, *History of England*, ed. of 1790, iii, p. 347. See also *Parliamentary History*, xiv, pp. 1390 ff.

(59) *Sessions Papers*, January 1743–4.

(60) Letter from Sir J. Fielding to the Earl of Suffolk, *S. P. Dom. Geo. III* parcel 8. It appears from the letter that there were three kinds of passes granted by the agents of the packets at Brill for the reception of passengers: whole, 13s., half, 6s., and 'poor' or gratis. cf. Cordosa's use of free passes.

(61) Lacombe, *Tableau de Londres*, 1784, p. 38.

(62) G. B. Hertz, *British Imperialism in the Eighteenth Century*, 1908, Chapter III.

(63) Colquhoun, *Police of the Metropolis*, 1800, p. 120.

(64) Some London Jews however were employed in industries. Diamond cutting was a Jewish industry (in Holland); it was also a London trade and in 1734 Moses Levi was a diamond cutter in London (*Sessions Papers*, December 1734). Pencil-making seems to have been a Jewish industry as early as the thirties (see the account of Joseph Isaacs in the text). Isaac Solomon was a maker of improved lead pencils in 1771 and a man of some standing (J. T. Smith, *A Book for a Rainy Day*, ed. of 1905, p. 177). In 1870, Samuel Solomons of Whitechapel, pencil-maker, was tried as a Gordon rioter. In a list of the six principal London embroiderers in 1763 there are two Jewish names (T. Mortimer, *Universal Director*). In 1767 Michael Jacobs was apprenticed to Mordecai Levy of Whitechapel, a glass-engraver (*Middlesex Sessions Book*, September 1771). Jewish working jewellers and watchmakers seem to have been not uncommon, though Jews were more often dealers in jewellery and watches. Poor Jewish girls are frequently described in the *Sessions Papers* as necklace makers.

(65) C. Russell and H. S. Lewis, *The Jew in London . . .* 1900, pp. 13–14.

(66) Archenholtz, op. cit., p. 177.

Blizard relates a discussion with 'a worthy and respectable Jew gentleman' on the possibility of a 'plan for the regulation of the lower order of Jews. . . .' His Jewish friend said that 'he was certain that the respectable part of the body would do all in their power and be happy to advance such a good design, but that the undertaking would be far more arduous than what I might imagine, for he believed there was hardly a robbery to any considerable amount in which many of these persons were not directly or indirectly concerned. That some of them had crucibles and furnaces always ready for melting down gold and silver; others were constantly employed in different parts of the kingdom in disposing of stolen property, while yet others were sent to Holland and various foreign parts to get rid of articles which cannot be safely or advantageously exposed in this country.' (Desultory Reflections on Police, 1785, pp. 43–4.)

(67) J. Picciotto, Sketches of Anglo-Jewish History, 1875, pp. 259–63.

(68) Report on Handloom Weavers, 1840, XXIII. p. 114.

(69) Add. MSS. 27287, fo. 145–6.

(70) Lacombe, op. cit., pp. 171–2.

(71) 'The sugar refiners employ for the most part Hamburgers.' G. Burrington, An Answer to Dr William Brackenridge's Letter, 1757, p. 37. It appears from the Sessions Papers that labourers in sugar houses were German, Dutch or Irish.

(72) De Fauconpret, who had no lenient eye for London failings, remarks in 1816: 'On a imprimé bien des fois que les étrangers ne peuvent faire un pas à Londres sans y être insultés par le peuple. L'impartialité dont je fais profession me porte a saisir cette occasion pour déclarer que ce reproche est de toute injustice. Vous n'avez pas à craindre plus d'insultes en cette ville qu'à Paris, et mon expérience me porte à croire que ceux qui se plaignent d'en avoir essuyés se les étaient attirées par quelque imprudence.' (Six Mois à Londres en 1816, Paris, 1817, p. 109)

(73) The strong feeling against French immigrants and French goods is illustrated by the engraving by Boitard (himself a Frenchman) called The Imports of Great Britain from France (1757), a view of passengers landing at the Custom House or Billingsgate quay from the French packet. The 'Explanation' runs, 'Four tackle porters staggering under a mighty chest of birthnight cloathes, behind, several emaciated high liv'd epicures, familiarly receiving a French cook, acquainting him that without his assistance they must have perish'd with hunger. A lady of distinction offering the tuition of her son and daughter to a cringing French Abbé, disregarding the corruption of their religion, so they do but obtain the true French accent; her Frenchified, well-bred spouse readily complying. The English chaplain regretting his lost labours; another woman of quality in raptures, caressing a French female dancer, assuring her, that her arrival is to the honour and delight of England. On the front ground, a cask overset; the contents, French cheeses from Normandy, bien raffinie, a blackguard boy stopping his nostrils, greatly offended at the haut-goût; a chest well cramm'd with tippets, muffs, ribands, flowers for the hair, and other such material bagatelles, underneath, conceal'd cambricks and gloves; another chest, containing choice beauty washes, pomatums, l'eau d'Hongrie, l'eau de Luce, l'eau de Carme, &c. &c. &c., near French wines and brandies. At a distance landing, swarms of milliners, taylors, mantua makers, frisers, tutoresses for boarding schools, disguis'd Jesuits, quacks, valet de chambres, &c. &c. &c,' (British Museum Collection, No. 3653).

cf. also the print called The Dreadful Consequences of a General Naturalization to the Natives of Great Britain and Ireland (1751) in which Britannia enthroned holds a cornucopia which attracts the longing looks of a crowd of foreigners, – a French boy in sabots, a Bohemian woman with three children, a Dutchman, an Italian, a Turk, an African, etc.

English master manufacturers, crowded out by foreigners, are going towards a ship in which their workmen have already embarked. (ibid., No. 3124.)

(74) Archenholtz, *Picture of England*, pp. 54–6. Malcolm, *Anecdotes*, 1808, pp. 39–43.

(75) Howell, *State Trials*, xx. p. 72. This case reversed a declaration of Yorke and Talbot in 1729 that masters had property in their slaves even while in England. See Clarkson, *History of the Abolition of the Slave Trade*, 1839.

(76) J. Fielding, *Penal Laws*, ed. of 1768, pp. 144–5.

(77) This uncertainty appears clearly in Blackstone's *dicta* on slavery and British liberty: 'The spirit of liberty is so deeply implanted in our constitution and rooted even in our very soil, that a slave or negro, the moment he lands in England, falls under the protection of the law and so far becomes a freeman, though the master's right to his service may possibly still continue.' (*Commentaries*, I, 1765, p. 127.)

'And now it is laid down that a slave or negro, the instant he lands in England, becomes a freeman, that is, the law will protect him in the enjoyment of his person and his property. Yet with respect to any right the master may have lawfully acquired to the perpetual service of John or Thomas, this will remain exactly in the same state of subjection for life, which every apprentice submits to for a space of seven years and sometimes for a longer term. . . .

'The slave is entitled to the same protection in England before as after baptism; and whatever service the heathen negro owed of right to his American master, by general, not by local law, the same (whatever it be) is he bound to render when brought to England and made a Christian.' (ibid., p. 423. See also Clarkson, op. cit.)

(78) W. J. Hardy, *Middlesex Records*, p. 6.

(79) *Middlesex Records* (*Cal.*) September and October 1717.

(80) ibid., June 1725.

(81) P. Hoare, *Memoirs of Granville Sharpe*, 1828, ii, p. 4.

(82) C. B. Wadstrom, *An Essay on Colonisation . . .*, 1794. Pugh, *Life of Hanway*, pp. 210–11; McPherson, *Annals of Commerce*, 1805, iv, p. 36. C. P. Lucas, *Historical Geography of the British Colonies*, iii, *W. Africa*, 1913, pp. 284–7.

(83) *Report on Lascars . . . 1814–15.*

(84) *A Letter to Archibald Macdonald Esq., on the intended Plan for Reform in what is called the Police of Westminster*, 1784, p. 17.

(85) *Life of William Wilberforce*, 1838, iv, p. 154.

(86) *Lascars and Chinese, a short Address to Young Men . . . 1814.* It was alleged by a magistrate in 1817 as an excuse for licensing scandals in the Tower Hamlets that 'little good can be done by taking away the licenses of houses in Shadwell for this reason, that the population consisting entirely [an obvious exaggeration] of foreign sailors, lascars, Chinese, Greeks, and other filthy dirty people of that description. . . .' (*Report on the Police of the Metropolis*, 1817, p. 195.)

(87) *Lascars and Chinese. . . .* The lascars themselves said that in the six months before February 1814 from 120 to 130 had died (ibid.), but the Parliamentary Committee (see below) said that in spite of overcrowding, the mortality seemed small.

(88) 54 Geo. III. c. 134.

(89) *Mendicity Report*, p. 316.

(90) Burt in 1730 compares the women washing clothes in the river at Inverness with the London codders, 'as people pass by they divert themselves by talking very freely to them, like our codders and other women employed in the fields and market gardens round London.' (*Letters from a Gentleman in the North of Scotland . . . 1818, i, p. 48.)

(91) T. Baird, *Report on the Agriculture of Middlesex*, 1793, p. 21. P. Foot, *idem*, 1794,

p. 29. Middleton, *idem*, 1798(?) p. 382. Lysons, *Environs of London*, i, p. 27. Eden, *State of the Poor*, 1797, ii, p. 419. J. T. Smith, *Mendicant Wanderers through the Streets of London.*

Sir R. Phillips gives a highly coloured picture of these fruit carriers, less convincing than the more sober accounts: 'The high vegetable season in summer as well as peculiar crops at other times call for exertions of labour, or rather slavery, scarcely paralleled by any other class of people. Thus in the strawberry season, hundreds of women are employed to carry that delicate fruit to the market on their heads. . . . They consist for the most part of Shropshire and Welsh girls, who walk to London in droves at this season to perform this drudgery. . . . I learnt that these women carry upon their heads baskets . . . weighing from 40 to 50 pounds and make two turns in the day from Isleworth to market, thirteen miles each way; three turns from Brentford . . . nine miles [Eden says, sometimes two from Brentford, the pay being sixpence a journey], and four turns from Hammersmith . . . six miles. For the most part they find some conveyance back. . . . Their remuneration for this unparalleled slavery is 8s. to 9s. per day, each turn from the distance of Isleworth being 4s. or 4s. 6d. and from Hammersmith 2s. or 2s. 3d. Their diet is coarse and simple, their drink tea and small beer costing not above 1s. or 1s. 6d. and their back conveyance about 2s. or 2s. 6d. so that their net gains are about 5s. per day, which in the strawberry season of forty days amounts to £10. After this period the same women find employment at lower wages for sixty other days, netting about £5 more. With this pittance they return to their native country. For beauty, symmetry and complexion they are not inferior to the nymphs of Arcadia. . . . Their morals too are exemplary – they live hard, they sleep on straw in hovels and barns, and they often burst an artery or drop down dead from the effect of heat and over-exertion . . . .' (*A Morning's Walk from London to Kew*, 1817, p. 225.)

(92) 'There is a class of occasional paupers who at certain seasons of the year gain a support by hay-making and hop-picking, who are either improvident or unable through ignorance or want of industry and cleanliness in external appearance to make any further provision for themselves.' (Hanway, *Citizen's Monitor*, 1780, p. 104.)

(93) Thornton, *History of London*, 1784, p. 380.

The Middlesex and Westminster Justices did this by issuing 'general privy search warrants' for a certain night. As the result of a search-night in November 1776, 39 or 40 persons were sent to the Navy from the Finsbury division, thirteen from St Giles and St George, Bloomsbury, 56 from parishes in the Tower division; the Lords of the Admiralty were asked to pay 5s. to the constable or other person 'who shall apprehend any able-bodied landsman within the Bills of Mortality upon such able-bodied landsman being received into His Majesty's service.' (Middlesex *Order Book*, November 1776.)

(94) J. Hanway, *An Account of the Marine Society . . .*, 1759, p. 159.

(95) See advertisements in the *Public Advertiser*, 9 February 1769 (and subsequently).

(96) The obvious shortcomings of a scheme which sent boys straight to sea from the London streets gave rise to various plans for giving a preliminary training. In 1786 a training-ship was decided upon. A ship of from 300 to 400 tons capable of holding 150 to 200 boys was put under the command of a carefully chosen naval officer, with a boatswain, boatswain's mate, carpenter, cook, and schoolmaster, and was moored off Greenwich. *Bye-laws . . . of the Marine Society*, 1792.

(97) cf. the following affidavit against spiriters in 1671: against William Haviland 'generally called a spirit', and of W. Haviland against John Steward for spiriting persons to Barbadoes, Virginia and other places for twelve years, 'five hundred in a year, as he has confessed'. Also against William Thiene, 'who in one year spirited away 840; Robert Bayley, an old spirit, who had no other way of livelihood'.

Cal. of State Papers Colonial, Addenda, 1574–1674, p. 521.

In 1668 Ashley Cooper was petitioned to move a law to make the punishment for spiriting death, there were then three ships in the river on which children had been embarked and 'though the parents see their children in the ships, without money they will not let them have them.' (*idem*, 1661–8, p. 555.)

(98) J. C. Jeaffreson, *Middlesex County Records*, iv, p. li.

(99) *The London Spy.*

(100) Ilive relates an instance of such an invitation witnessed by himself while a prisoner in Clerkenwell Gaol, but frustrated by the turnkey's wife, an excellent woman. Both the keepers of bagnios and trading captains, he says, were in the habit of procuring the release of these girls by paying their fees. He adds, 'this artifice of our trading captains in inveigling away great numbers of the young men and women, selling them, &c., is a great drain on the inhabitants of this island . . . ,' (*Reasons . . . for the Reformation of the House of Correction in Clerkenwell*, 1757, p. 26.)

(101) cf. the estimate of the old penal system by a parliamentary committee on transportation in 1785.

'That the old system of transporting to America answered every good purpose that could be expected from it. That it tended directly to reclaim the objects on which it was inflicted, and to render them good citizens. . . . That it was not attended with much expense to the public, the convicts being carried out in vessels employ'd in the Jamaica or tobacco trade, that for many years Government paid £5 a man and afterwards no premium at all, the contractor being indemnified . . . by the price at which he sold their labour. [This change may well have been a satisfactory one for the convicts.]

'That the convicts . . . were usually removed into the back country and finding none of the temptations . . . which occasioned their offences at home, it does not appear that the police or peace of the colonies suffered in any considerable degree. . . .' (*C. J.* 28 July 1785.)

(102) In Pennsylvania the wages of white hired labour were considered too high, a negro was too great an initial outlay. Kalm says that the wages of a free servant were £16–20 a year in Pennsylvania currency, of a maid-servant £8–10. A·passage cost from £6–8 sterling, and the usual price paid for a man's service for four years was £14. *Travels in North America* (1748–51), Pinkerton's *Travels*, xiii, p. 500. In Virginia and Maryland a large supply of cheap labour was wanted for the tobacco plantations and in Maryland white bound servants were always preferred to slaves. E. I. MacCormac, *White Servitude in Maryland*, 1904, pp. 33–4.

(103) W. Eddis, *Letters from America* . . . 1769 to 1777 . . . 1792, pp. 67–8.

(104) E. I. MacCormac, op. cit. p. 74.

(105) By the Act of 1717, which put penal transportation on a statutory basis, there was a provision by which those under twenty-one (but over fifteen) who could not legally make contracts, might enter into indentures for a passage to the plantations for a term not exceeding eight years, provided they were made before a justice of the peace of the City of London or two justices elsewhere. This was because, 'there are many idle persons . . . under the age of one-and-twenty . . . lurking about in London and elsewhere, who want employment, and may be tempted to become thieves if not provided for'.

The original record of such an indenture, the words in italics being written in the blanks of a printed form, runs as follows:

London the *30th* day of *May*
One thousand eight hundred and *thirty-nine.*
Be it remember'd that *Thomas Heath of the parish of St Leonards Shoreditch, weaver, his*

father and mother being dead did by indenture bearing like date herewith agree to serve *Nathaniel Wilson of London, Chapman*, or his assigns *four* years in *Maryland*

and did thereby declare himself to be of the age of *twenty* years, a single person, no apprentice, nor covenanted or contracted servant to any other person or persons. And the said Master did thereby covenant at his own cost, to send his said servant to the said Plantation; and at the like cost to find him in all necessary clothes, meat, drink, washing, and lodging, as other servants in such cases are usually provided for and allowed,

Thomas Heath

Allowed by me at Guildhall
London this 30th day of March
1739.   (Sessions Papers, Guildhall)

(106) MacCormac, op. cit., p. 101.

(107) *Treasury Papers* 47–9, 10, 11. (Public Record Office.)

(108) In a year of fifty-four weeks from 11 December 1773 to 26 December 1774. In 1775 up to 17 July (after which, though perfunctory returns continue to be made till 7 April 1776, there are no more bound servants), the totals are: Maryland, 894; Virginia, 88; Philadelphia, 43, New York, 29.

(109) *Sessions Papers*, April 1776. (Case of Quirforth, John and Jane Dennison. Dennison was sentenced to one month's imprisonment, and to find security for good behaviour for one year, Mrs Dennison and Quirforth to three months and to find security for two years.)

(110) MacCormac, op. cit., and J. C. Ballagh, *White Servitude in Virginia.*

(111) According to Colquhoun, convicts were preferred because 'they generally were more adroit and had better abilities than those who voluntarily engaged themselves to go to America.' (*Police of the Metropolis*, 5th ed. 1797, pp. 299–300 n.) Priest says (1796): 'The laws respecting the redemptioners are very severe, they were formed for the English convicts before the Revolution.' (*Travels in the United States of America*, 1802, p. 144.) cf. J. C. Hurd, *The Law of Freedom and Bondage in the United States*, 1858, i, p. 220. 'The legal condition of indented servants was essentially different from that of chattel slaves in its origin and duration. . . . But notwithstanding this difference and the fact that laws were enacted for their special protection recognizing them as legal persons, yet their general condition and disabilities, during its continuance, seem in many respects to have been the same, and much of the colonial legislation . . . in reference to servants applied both to such persons and to negro and Indian slaves.'

Some of the laws may be quoted:

New Hampshire, 1718. An act for restraining the violence of Masters towards their Christian servants: '. . . if any man smite out the eye or the tooth of his man-servant or maid-servant or otherwise maim or disfigure them much, unless it be mere casualty, he shall let him or her go free from his service, and shall allow such further recompense as the Court of Quarter Sessions shall adjudge them'. Pennsylvania, 1700. An Act for the better regulation of servants: 'A servant is not to be sold out of this government without his consent, nor assigned over except before a justice. For every day's absence from his service he is to serve five days longer term.' (This clause might well be an unfortunate one for the servant. In the notorious Annesley case arising out of the kidnapping of the supposed heir by his uncle's orders in Dublin in 1728, it appears that the boy, aged about twelve, was sold in Pennsylvania for seven years, and as a penalty for running away did not get free till thirteen years later. According to the *Daily Post* (12 February 1741), he attempted to escape 'but was retaken, and by a law of the country oblig'd for his elopement to serve seven years more'. See *State Trials*, xvii, p. 1139 ff.; *Memoirs of an Unfortunate Young Nobleman*, 1743; and Andrew Lang, *The Annesley Case*, 1913 (*Notable English Trials*). Smollett interpolates a version of the story into *Peregrine Pickle*.)

Delaware, 1739. An Act for the better regulation of servants and slaves: 'No indented servant to be sold into another Government without the approbation of at least one justice.'

North Carolina, 1742. An Act concerning servants and slaves mentions (section 19): 'a peculiar class of servants imported being tradesmen or workmen in some art receiving wages yet bound.' (ibid., pp. 239, 287, 292, 295.)

(112) According to the census of Maryland in 1752, free inhabitants numbered 98,557; servants 6,870; convicts 1,981, so that the ratio of bound servants was about one in eleven as it had been in 1660. MacCormac, op. cit., p. 29.

(113) J. Boucher, *A View of the Causes . . . of the American Revolution in thirteen Discourses preached in North America . . .* 1763–5, 1797, p. 183.

(114) J. C. Ballagh, op. cit., p. 83 n.

(115) W. Priest, *Travels* [1793–7] *in the United States . . .* 1802, p. 144.

(116) In 1820 many ships were engaged in bringing German peasants from European ports as redemptioners, laws having been passed in America for their protection. Neither English nor Irish were considered in Pennsylvania to make good servants, but the Welsh, who resembled the simple German peasants, were approved of, and 'cargoes of Welsh redemptioners frequently enter the Delaware'. Frances Wright, *View of Society and Manners in America . . .* 1822.

(117) *New and Accurate Account of the Provinces of South Carolina and Georgia*, 1731, p. 30. (By Oglethorpe, see R. Wright, *Memoir of General James Oglethorpe*, 1867.)

(118) *An Account shewing the Progress of the Colony of Georgia . . .* 1741, p. 18. (Force Collection, i.)

(119) *Anglo-Jewish Encyclopædia*, S. V. Georgia.

(120) Oglethorpe, op. cit., p. 34.

(121) *A State of the Province of Georgia attested upon oath in the Court of Savannak . . . 1740.* London 1742. (Force Coll., i), p. 12.

(122) J. Massie, *A Plan for the Establishment of Charity Homes*, 1758, p. 99.

(123) Crabbe's description in *The Village* is borne out by many other accounts. cf. J. M. Good, *Dissertation on the Diseases of Prisons and Poor-houses*, 1795, p. 49, 'In many villages in this kingdom the parish houses for the reception of the poor are nothing but clay huts, with a clay floor below and an apartment above formed entirely by the striding of the thatched roof. This roof, excepting where, fortunately . . . it is broken through by time and tempests . . . is generally covered with cobwebs. But if the roof be entire, the whole room is commonly as dark as a Siberian hovel. There may perhaps be traces left of the place where formerly there was a window . . . but the glass being in general destroyed, its place is supplied by old ballads and other papers. . . . Of such abodes in this kingdom, I could give a hundred instances were they not too common to need instancing.'

(124) 'It is a common practice to send paupers whc have committed no act of vagrancy by passes, instead of orders, to save expense to the parish removing. . . . Some get travelling passes signed by a magistrate generally of some corporate town, under which they beg or rather extort money from parish officers, who are induced to give it them for fear of worse consequences, upon their promise to quit that place immediately. Others procure themselves to be sent by passes to places where they have no settlement, for reasons best known to themselves, and the money given for apprehending them too often facilitates this means of imposition upon the public, by rewarding some accomplice in the fraud.' (T. Gilbert,

Observations upon the Resolutions of the House of Commons with respect to the Poor . . . 1775, p. 40.) The practice was forbidden by an Act of 1792, but this was powerless to stop it. Colquhoun said in 1815: 'Of late it is inconceivable the number that have received passes from the magistrates to go to their different parishes; which we give now, though directly in opposition to the Act of 1792. . . . That Act has been found impracticable. It arose from the Lord Mayor and the magistrates giving innumerable passes, of which I am afraid many make the very worst use, but we are very glad to get them out of the town that they may be subsisted in the quarter to which they belong, as where they have friends, in that way we are relieved of a very considerable number who must otherwise beg in the streets . . . .' (*Mendicity Report*, p. 280.) See also *Report on the Vagrant Law*, 1821, p. 129. 'The system of conveyance by pass has been found to be of great inefficiency, cozenage, and fraud; it is in complete consonance with the wandering habits of vagrants: it is made a matter of trade.'

(126) Middlesex *Order Book*, under dates, 14 July 1757 and 1 March 1759.

(127) *Mendicity Report* (evidence of Thomas Davis), p. 289.

(128) 'So notorious is the practice of turning these pests of society adrift on their entrance into a new jurisdiction, that a very small number of those who are passed ever reach the final place of their destination, excepting however one very numerous tribe which consists of Irishmen, who come over to work at hay and harvest, and having sent home what they can save of their earnings by one or two trusty associates, throw themselves on the county and are conveyed as vagrants, but generally without punishment, in such numbers as become a serious charge to the kingdom in general, and an intolerable grievance to the western counties.' (Note on Locke's Report to the Board of Trade of 1697 [1792], p. 129.)

(128) *The Farmer's Letters to the People of England*, 2nd ed., 1771, pp. 353-4.

Notes to Chapter 4

(1) Angeloni [Shebbeare], *Letters on the English Nation*, 2nd ed., 1756, p. 6.

(2) *A Journey from London to Genoa*, 1770, i, p. 42.

(3) Wendeborn, *A View of England*, p. 267.

(4) T. Mortimer, *Elements of Commerce*, 1773, p. 45 n.

(5) Grosley, *A Tour to London*, 1772, p. 84.

(6) *Review*, 14 April 1705.

(7) Quoted by W. Cunningham, *Growth of English Industry and Commerce*, 3rd ed. 1896, p. 559.

(8) The trades of London, wages, earnings, hours, apprenticeship fees, and capital necessary for setting up in business, together with much information on methods and organization, are set forth in: (1) *A General Description of all Trades* . . . 1747 (copies in the Guildhall Library and the Goldsmith's Library but not in the British Museum); (2) R. Campbell, *The London Tradesmen* . . . 1747; (3) J. Collyer, *The Parents' and Guardians' Directory and the Youths Guide in the Choice of a Profession or Trade*, 1761. (1) Deals mainly with trades from the City standpoint; (2) and (3) with that of Middlesex, Westminster and the out-parishes: generally deprecate a seven years' apprenticeship for mere shopkeeping, etc. (3) is evidently based on (2), while neither appears to have any connexion with (1). Kearsley's *Table of Trades*, 1786, is admittedly based on (3) but gives earnings, etc., in a tabular form without explanatory text. Several entries suggest that advances of wages since 1761 have not been fully incorporated. *The Book of Trades* (six editions between 1804 and 1815) is more popular and less complete than its predecessors. A comparison of these five books gives much information on London wages, etc. Wages in the building trades are given in Tooke, *History of Prices*, i, p. 98. (Greenwich Hospital Accounts), in Jupp and Pocock, *History of the Carpenters Company* (Somerset House Accounts). They are also to be found in *The Builders' Dictionary* (1734), *The Builders' London Price-Book*, and other similar publications. The London *Sessions Papers* give much incidental information on wages and methods: the question of a man's usual earnings was often raised as presumptive evidence of his innocence. Place collected information on London wages, some of which he published in *The Gorgon* (1818). Tailors' wages after 1720 were regulated by Act of Parliament, but more than the statutory rate was often paid.

(9) Mrs Charke, who was a strolling player for some years, came to the conclusion that 'it would be more reputable to earn a groat a day in cindersifting at Tottenham Court than to be concerned with them' – that is with the generality of strolling players, the 'rights' of those bred to the profession being 'horribly invaded by barbers, 'prentices, taylors, and journeymen weavers . . . .' (*A Narrative of the Life of Mrs Charlotte Charke written by herself*, 2nd ed., 1755, p. 188.)

(10) Mrs Charke's *Life* throws much light on the vicissitudes of performers at fairs, etc.

(11) R. Campbell, op. cit., p. 165.

(12) In 1747 the journeyman could earn from 30s. to £2 a week, and was 'never out of work'; Place's brother-in-law, a journeyman chair-carver, could earn about 1788 'full £4 a week all the year round', chairs and other small pieces of furniture being sent to his workshop and he always had much more than he could do. Though 'a good workman and

remarkably swift', he was 'an ignorant besotted fellow who would work hard and drink hard, he had never saved a single shilling'. *Autobiography*, i, fo. 172–3.

(13) Gwynne, *London . . . Improved*, 1766, p. 58 n.

(14) Larwood and Hotten, *History of Signboards*, 1866, p. 37.

(15) Le Blanc, *Letters d'un François*, 1745 (written 1737–44), i. p. 65. cf. also, '*Dans les sciences fondées sur le calcul, de même que dans les arts qui dépendent de la règle et le compas, les Anglois sont devenus les maîtres des autres nations: Le même différence qui est entre les géometres ordinaire et Newton, se trouve entre nos ouvriers françois et un artiste tel que Graham . . . qui a imaginé ce bel instrument, qui entre les mains de nos Académiciens, vient de nous révéler la véritable figure de! a terre,*' (ibid., p. 59). Graham (an optical-instrument maker who had been apprenticed to a London watchmaker) supplied the French Academy with the apparatus used for the measurement of a degree of the meridian. (D.N.B.) He was the first distinctly to make known the diurnal and horary variations of the magnetic needle. *Philosophical Transactions*, 1724–5, xxxiii, p. 332.

(16) *C. J.*, 19 April 1758.

(17) *A General Description of all Trades . . .* 1747, p. 92.

(18) Mayhew, *London Labour and the London Poor*, ii.

(19) See the annual accounts of the charity, published in the *London Evening Post* (e.g., 7 April 1743).

(20) *A General Description of all Trades . . .* 1747, pp. 50–51. There was perhaps not much loss in giving up the calendering business as wages were only from 10s. to 12s., and hours were uncertain, though 'commonly said to be from 5 to 9'. Campbell (ibid.) says that labourers were employed, wages 9s. to 12s. (cf. note 8.)

(21) cf. *London Chronicle*, 12 December 1761: '. . . a number of bills of indictment were preferred and found before the Grand Inquest against the rebellious journeymen cabinet-makers, who have lately combined together to raise their wages and lessen their hours of working, etc. The combination among journeymen peruke-makers, shoe-makers, taylors, etc., cabinet-makers, etc., is a growing evil and wants to be remedied, but there is a much greater amongst their masters who agree together what price they will have for everything they make or sell, and this is universal with most tradesmen. Don't the butchers sell their mutton at 3½d. a pound, their beef at 4d. . . . , when they buy the best mutton in the carcass at seven farthings a pound, and the best ox will not fetch above 2d. a pound in Smithfield Market! If the butchers would be content with a reasonable profit, the journeymen and labourers might be content with less wages; but when they pay so dear for all the necessaries of life, it cannot be so well expected.'

(22) Place writes: 'I have before me now tables of the weekly wages of journeymen tradesmen in London, who, in their different trades, may amount to about 100,000 men, all of whom had separate trade-clubs for many years, and, in spite of the Combination Laws, did, from time to time, raise their wages by means of strikes. In these trades the ordinary wages in 1777 was from 18s. to 22s. a week.

'From 1777 to 1794 there were few strikes and very little advance in wages. During this period the price of food rose somewhat, but the price of most other necessaries fell. . . . Soon after the commencement of the war . . . prices rose enormously, and in one of these trades, a very numerous trade [tailors, see *Gorgon*], a strike took place in 1795 when the wages were raised from 22s. to 25s. In 1802 another strike raised the wages to 27s. In 1807 another . . . to 30s. In 1810 another . . . to 33s. and in 1813 another strike raised the wages to 36s. at which sum they have remained ever since.

'The journeymen in the other trades raised their wages in a similar proportion, though not precisely at the same periods. . . . Every trade had not a regular club, and in these trades wages did not rise in the same manner and to the same extent as they did in better organized trades. In some very few trades in which there were no associations there was no rise at all [typefounders, see *Gorgon*].' (*Trade Clubs, Strikes, Wages*, 1834. (MS. of a tract for working men.) Add. MSS. 27834, fo. 107.)

(23) Evidence to the Committee on Artisans and Machinery, 1824, *Report*, p. 137, etc.

(24) *Trade Unions Condemned, Trade Clubs Justified* [MS.]. Add. MSS. 27834, fo. 63.

(25) *C.J.*, 29 December 1775.

(26) Middlesex *Sessions Book*, April 1777.

(27) *Humble Petition to the Journeymen Saddlers and Harnessmakers* . . . (printed). Add. MSS. 27799, fo. 114. The extreme genteelness of this trade is illustrated by the fact that the petitioners estimate their expense for clothing during the seven years apprenticeship at from £110 to £150.

(28) *Gorgon*, 28 November 1818. Add. MSS. 27799, ff. 89–91.

(29) Evidence to Committee on Artisans and Machinery, 1824, *Report*, p. 55.

(30) According to Campbell; the *General Description* . . . gives them as from 10s. to 30s. and upwards, 'medium' from 16s. to a guinea.

(31) Chamberlain's *Complaint Book*, Guildhall, under date 6 October 1791.

(32) *C.J.*, 28 February 1745–6.

(33) Middlesex *Sessions Books*, 8 April 1771.

(34) Campbell, op.cit., but the *General Description* says: 'They take an apprentice often with £5 who must hold his work from 6 to 9, which is clean, neat, and easy. When out of his time he may earn from 10s. to 20s. a week, and if he can purchase three or four frames which cost about £8 or £10 a-piece, and have 40 or 50l, then he may turn out for a master, for they have the materials, as woolsted, thread, cotton, or silk, sent them in to work up for the shopkeepers.' Collyer (1761) gives the cost of a frame as £15. cf. notes 63 and 64, Chapter 5.

(35) *C.J.*, 25 February 1778. Evidence of Mr Richard Marsh, Hosier, Temple Bar.

(36) Adam Smith, *Wealth of Nations*, 1776.

Hanway says: 'We are told of instances of one man's earning 20s. or more money, in one long summer's day, by unloading coals from a lighter, and of his drinking out 15s. or 16s. in beer. These adventures do not happen every day.' (*Letters on the Importance of the Rising Generation*, 1768, ii, p. 189.) See also note 64, Chapter 6.

(37) *Report on the Poor Laws*, 1817, pp. 57–8 and p. 66.

(38) *Considerations of the Expediency of raising at this Time of Dearth the Wages of Servants that are . . . not domestic, particularly Clerks in Public Offices*, 1767, pp. 7–9. See note 87, Chapter 2.

His expenditure on clothes, etc., was:

	£	s.	d.
A suit of cloaths, second cloth at 14s. per yard	4	10	0
A beaver great coat	1	5	0
A hat	0	12	0
A wig	0	18	0
Four day shirts, 3 ells each, at 3s. 1½d. per ell	1	17	6
Making ditto	0	10	0
Two coarser shirts, to lie in, that the day shirts may be kept the cleaner, at 1s. 6d. per ell	0	9	0
Making ditto	0	4	0
Four pocket handkerchiefs	0	6	0
Four huckaback towels	0	3	0

	£	s.	d.
Four round stocks	0	4	0
Making handkerchiefs, towels and stocks	0	1	0
Two pair of yarn stockings for winter	0	4	0
Two pair of twisted ditto for summer	0	7	0
A wollen night-cap	0	1	0
Four pair of shoes	1	0	0
Soling and heelpiecing ditto twice at 1s. 8d. each	0	3	4
Mending shirts, stockings, and cloaths	1	0	0

(39) *The Case of the Journeymen Taylors . . . residing within the weekly Bills of Mortality*, 1752. (Quoted by F. W. Galton, *Select Documents illustrating the History of the Tailoring Trade*, p. 49.)

(40) Defoe has much to say on the importance of a wife's having a knowledge of her husband's business in order to be able to carry it on after his death. It appears that the complete aloofness of the wife customary in the big goldsmiths' and booksellers' businesses in London was imitated from vanity in smaller concerns. *Compleat English Tradesman*, 1727, p. 287 ff. But the evidence of the *Sessions Papers* in a vast number of trials for shoplifting, etc., is that the wife frequently served in the shop, and had an expert knowledge of the goods, private marks, and so on. The smaller the business, the more general of course was the practice. See Appendix VI.

(41) Muralt, *Letters describing the character and customs of the English and French Nations*, 1726, p. 11.

(42) C. de Saussure, *A Foreign View of England . . .* 1902, p. 206.

(43) R. Reuss, *Londres et l'Angleterre en 1700 . . .* 1905.

(44) *Modern London*, 1804. (Description of plate.)

(45) *Sessions Papers*, June 1737. Case of Ann Mudd, who was burnt at the stake for stabbing her husband.

(46) J. Churton Collins, *Voltaire, Montesquieu and Rousseau in England*, 1808, pp. 9 and 12.

(47) They were so frequently robbed of them that a watch must have been a very usual possession and one suspects they were an eighteenth-century substitute for a savings bank account. A London journeyman printer working in 1826 in Paris on pirated editions of English books is described by a fellow-workman as 'a cockney of the very first water . . . born and bred among the worshippers of Saint Monday'. 'His notions of economy and foresight were on a par with his ideas of sobriety. He considered himself fully provided against every emergency by the possession of a capital silver watch upon which he could raise £2 whenever he wanted it . . . .' (*The Working Man's Way in the World*, p. 67.)

(48) *Sessions Papers*, December 1767. In 1797 a labourer to a lath-render and dealer in coals was robbed of a gold watch, value £3, two guineas, and other things. (ibid., February 1797.)

Defoe in 1709 puts the standard of living of the artisan above that of the farmer. He divides the population into seven classes:

1. The great, who live profusely.
2. The rich, who live very plentifully.
3. The middle sort who live well.
4. The working trades who labour hard, but feel no want.
5. The country people, farmers, &c., who fare indifferently.
6. The poor, that fare hard.
7. The miserable, that really pinch and suffer want.

Take the fourth sort for a medium . . . suppose a carpenter, a smith, a weaver, or any such workman . . . that is industrious, works hard and feels no want, let him live in the country or city, north or south, where you will. . . . If the gentlemen eat more puddings, this man eats more bread, if the rich man drinks more wine, this drinks more ale or strong beer for it is the support of his vigour and strength. If the rich man eats more veal and lamb, fowl, and fish, this man eats more beef and bacon, and add to it has a better stomach. . . . As to the milk, if the rich man eats more butter, more cream, more white meats . . . our workman eats more hard cheese and salt butter than all the others put together. (*Review*, 25 June 1709.)

(49) Malcolm, *Anecdotes* . . . i, pp. 58–63. *London Magazine*, 1763, pp. 616 and 674.

(50) cf. note 133, Chapter 6.

(51) *The Form of a Petition submitted to . . . those Noblemen and Gentlemen who desire to subscribe what sums shall be necessary for relieving, reforming, and employing the Poor . . .* 1722.

(52) *Considerations of the East India Trade, wherein all the Objections to that Trade are fully answered . . .* 1701.

(53) Derham, *The Artificial Clock and Watch Maker*, 1696, Introduction.

(54) *C.J.*, 27 February 1798. See also Atkins and Overall, *The Clockmakers Company*.

(55) Campbell, op. cit., pp. 251–2.

(56) Collyer, op. cit., pp. 288–9. He says: 'As both the masters who keep shop and the journeymen they employ, take apprentices, very different sums are given with boys in this business.'

(57) The trade, however, was badly distressed in 1813 and 1817. In 1818 it was said that it had never recovered its former state of 1796; there had been some improvement to 1808 and then a further decline. Many causes for the depression were alleged, but these seem to have been rather results than causes. *Report on the Laws relating to Watchmakers*, 1818. See also Atkins and Overall, op. cit.

(58) J. Travers, *An Essay to the Restoring of our decayed Trade . . .* 1675, p. 36.

(59) *Review*, 20 March 1705. Defoe is writing of the riots against the engine-loom, which were in 1675 not 'in and about 1679 and 80' as he supposed.

(60) Massie, *Reasons humbly offered against laying any further British Duties on wrought Silks of the Manufacture of Italy, the Kingdom of Naples, Sicily, or Holland*, 1768, p. 3. (Goldsmiths' Library)

(61) *C.J.*, 4 March 1675. Evidence of Mr Nathaniel Paterson, a London throwster: the Act 'encouraged many people, and him in particular, to set up silk mills in imitation of Sir Thomas Lombe's manufacture . . . for organzining silk for warp and throwing it [for] trams'.

(62) For example: 'S. Cole and Co., Weavers, at the Peacock corner of Bedford Street and Maiden Lane beg leave to inform the Public they have now on sale of their own manufacture a large and elegant assortment of silks consisting of Brocades, Tissues, Peruvians, Sattins, stripped and corded Tabbies, Tobines, and enamelled Mantuas, Armozians, Ducapes, Lustrings, &c. &c., with great variety of black silks fabricated on the Italian principle, which they propose to sell retail on the same terms as to wholesale dealers.

'A quantity of flowered and striped silks of last year's pattern will be sold extremely low.

'The lowest price at a word and no pattern cut.'

(*Public Advertiser*, 18 February 1769.)

(63) This account is taken from Campbell and Collyer (see note 8), and from the

reports in *C.J.*, 4 March 1765 and 14 April 1766, supplemented by incidental information from the *Sessions Papers*. See also the model cash-book of a London mercer for January 1725 in Defoe's *Complete English Tradesman*, 1728, supplement, pp. 46–67. The mercer buys lengths of silk from various weavers, and occasionally from macklers, who, it may be noted are women. He also buys a bale of thrown silk. See also notes 65 and 83 below.

(64) 1695: 'A weaver with £20 may set a loom at work which will employ his family, and the piece being made may be ready money with which, and the increase of the prime stock, he may employ more looms.' (*The Weavers Answer to the Objections made by the Lustrings Company.*)

1761: 'Some of the masters only keep a loom or two at work and such a master may set up with £50 or £100. But there are others who are great dealers and employ from £500 to £5,000 in trade. These last require from £20 to £100 with an apprentice who will be chiefly employed in the counting-house.' (Collyer, op. cit., p. 250.)

(65) *Sessions Papers*, February 1733. (Case of Harry Fowl.)

(66) *C.J.*, 14 February 1739–40 and 16 January 1749–50.

(67) *Proposals for establishing a Charitable Fund for the City of London . . .* 1706, p. 13.

(68) *A Brief State of the Question between the Printed and Painted Calicoes and the Woollen and Silk Manufacture . . .* 1719, p. 41. cf. the position of the domestic weaver in 1826; 'the employer of these domestic weavers has no occasion for fixed capital, and credit being too often a cheap commodity, he can furnish the material for weaving with little or no circulating capital, and when a glut arises in the market, such employers and employed are immediately involved in one common mass of misery.' (*Morning Chronicle*, 1 May 1826.)

(69) W. Hale, *A Letter to Samuel Whitbread, Esq., M.P.*, 1806.

(70) Mr John Peregol, a master-weaver working for the be-spoke trade, that is working to order for the mercers, gave evidence that 'good workmen may earn from 15s. to 18s. per week'. (*C.J.*, 4 March 1769.) Campbell (1747), says a journeyman weaver may earn a guinea or 18s. if constantly employed. But these earnings would be subject to heavy deductions. 'T.S.,' a weaver in London, instances the lowness of the wages of weavers and other textile workers throughout the country to controvert the cry that 'if we want a trade we must work cheaper'. He adds: 'take our silk-weavers, and do they get more than 10s. or 12s. per week and pay two boys out of it, unless they make rich works which take a month or six weeks before they get a penny'.

Reasons Humbly offered for passing the Bill for the Hindring the Home Consumption of East India Silks . . . [1697?]

Weaving wages were low at least from the seventeenth century, cf. Heaton, 'The Assessment of Wages in the West Riding of Yorkshire in the seventeenth and eighteenth centuries.' *Economic Journal*, xxiii, p. 545 ff. and the basic reason seems to have been that given by the Norwich weavers to the Hand-loom Commissioners: 'If weavers are wanted . . . they may be struck into existence in a month; some branches may be done by boys and girls, and what can be done by a boy can never reach above a boy's wages.' (This did not apply to certain branches of silk-weaving, but even these were influenced by the ease with which other branches were learned.) *Report of the Hand-Loom Commissioners*, 1840, xxiii, p. 156.

(71) *A Further Examination of the Weavers' Pretences . . .* 1719, p. 13.

(72) *Report . . .* 1840, XXIV, p. 716. Evidence of W. Bresson of Daniel Street, Orange Street, Spitalfields, examined by Mr Hickson, 1838.

(73) *The Case of the Linen Drapers and other Dealers in printed Calicoes and Linens*, 1720.

(74) *The Case of the Printers of Calicoes and Linens*, 1720.

(75) *The Just Complaints of the poor Weavers* . . . 1719, pp. 28–30.

(76) 18 February 1769. cf. *A further Examination of the Weavers Pretences, being a particular answer to the Just Complaints etc.*: 'He plainly owns . . . the great increase of their numbers in late years and the weavers themselves know very well that if there was but a regulation made amongst them so as to restrain the unqualified journeymen and to limit the taking of 'prentices they could not have any occasion to complain for want of work.'

(77) *A List of Prices in those Branches of the Weaving Manufactory called the Black Branch, and the Fancy Branch, together with the Persians, Sarsnets, Drugget Modes, Fringed and Italian Handkerchiefs, Cyprus and Draught Gauzes and Plain and Laced Nets.* 'Printed in the year 1769 at the expense of those manufacturers' journeymen who were subscribers for carrying on the work.' (Goldsmiths' Library)

(78) J. Anstie, *Observations on the Importance and Necessity of introducing improved Machinery into the Woollen Manufacture*, 1803, p. 79 n.

(79) Lords Sessional Papers, 1823, *Minutes of Evidence relative to the Wages of the Silk Manufacturers.* (Evidence of W. Hale.)

(80) *Sessions Papers*, July 1760.

(81) ibid., July 1784.

(82) ibid., July 1777.

(83) One Jane Collins, who 'keeps looms in the weaving way for the master weavers and employs poor people', had an apprentice girl aged ten who used to wind quills for the weavers in her house. The child was brutally treated by her son, a carpenter, but he was acquitted of causing her death. (ibid., December 1766.)

(84) *Minutes of Evidence* . . . 1823 (as in n. 79).

(85) *C.J.*, 7 February 1765. cf. *An Answer to a Paper of Reflexions on the Project of laying a Duty on English Wrought Silk*: 'The throwsters . . . will employ several hundred persons more than they did before as winders, doublers, and others belonging to the throwing trade, who for the greatest part are poor seamen and soldiers wives, and thereby take off a burthen that now lies on several parishes . . . for their support. . . .'

(86) *Chambers's Encyclopædia*, edition of 1752 and 1782 (s.v. *Silk, Mill*, and *Milling of Silk*); Campbell and Collyer, op. cit.; cf. also, a later description of the process in *The Operative Mechanic*, by J. Nicholson, 2nd ed., 1825, p. 392 ff.

(87) *Sessions Papers*, February 1755.

(88) *Account of Several Workhouses*, 2nd ed., 1732, *passim*.

(89) *C.J.*, 4 March 1765.

(90) See J. H. Clapham, 'The Spitalfields Acts, 1773–1824', *Economic Journal*, xxvi, pp. 380 ff.

(91) 'During the late war, when by our glorious successes we cleared the seas in all parts of the world of the French Marine, we almost entirely ruined their foreign trade, in which is to be included their manufactured silks. This occasioned a brisk trade in those articles here, and, by a natural consequence a greater number of hands to be employed in and bred to the silk weaving. Now, when affairs are returned to their old channels and the French have no interruption in carrying their silks to foreign markets, it must of course be felt in Spitalfields very severely, although the trade may be in no worse condition than . . . before the war.' (*Letter to the London Chronicle*, 18 May 1765.)

Similar evidence was given in the House of Commons: 'during the late war the silk trade was very brisk, and since the peace it has declined very much'. *C.J.*, 14 April 1766.

(92) *The Case of great Numbers of Weavers now working to the Royal Lutestring Company*, n.d., 1695? cf. J. Travers, op. cit., note 58, p. 16: 'Ribbon weavers and silk weavers and other such like artificers, in and about London, and within other parts of the kingdom ... are so miserably impoverished that they are ready to perish for want of necessary food to keep life and soul together.' This is ascribed to 'the importation of foreign prohibited commodities'.

(93) *C.J.*, 3 March 1742–3. See also note 12, Chapter 1.

(94) *C.J.*, 9 February 1763.

(95) *C.J.*, 14 April 1785.

(96) 'Memoirs of William Hawes, M.D.', *European Magazine*, June 1802.

(97) *General Account of the Agriculture of Middlesex*, ed. of 1798, p. 438; ed. of 1807, p. 576.

(98) *Second Report of the Committee on Lotteries*, 1808, p. 205.

(99) *Report on the Poor Laws*, 1817, p. 40.

(100) *Edinburgh Review*, xliii, 1825–6, pp. 78–9.

(101) See note 65, Chapter 5.

(102) *Report of the Select Committee on the Silk Trade*, 1831–2, p. 731.

(103) ibid., pp. 796–7.

(104) G. Townsend Warner in *Social England*, iv, 1896, p. 128. These engine-looms were found in use at Leeds in 1724 by Stukeley (*Itinerarium Curiosum*). According to Campbell ten or a dozen pieces could be made at once, but 'not so good as those made by hand'. (op. cit., p. 258.)

(105) Hale, *Pleas of the Crown*, 1736, p. 143. In 1675 there was great distress among silk-weavers, see note 92.

(106) Jeaffreson, *Middlesex County Records*, iv, 1892, pp. xxvii–ix and 61–3. These sentences were severe: the pillory on three successive days, a fine of 500 marks and imprisonment till the fine was paid – equivalent, presumably, to a life-sentence, failing a pardon. (It had, however, been discussed by the justices whether the riots did not constitute treason – levying war against the king – as had been decided in the case of London apprentices' riots in 1601. Hale, op. et loc. cit.)
The value of the destroyed looms varied from £6 to £12.

(107) *Public Advertiser*, 8 January 1768.

(108) *Report on Hand-loom Weavers*, 1840, XXIII, p. 23.

(109) ibid., p. 89.

(110) *Report on Education*, 1835, p. 777.

(111) *Report on Hand-loom Weavers*, p. 77.

(112) *C.J.*, 14 April 1766. cf. *A Further Examination of the Weavers, Pretences* ... 1719, 'the weavers themselves know very well that if there were but a regulation made amongst them so as to restrain the unqualified journeymen and to limit the taking of apprentices they could not have any occasion to complain for want of work'.

(113) *Sessions Papers*, October 1744. (Account by the Ordinary of Newgate.)

(114) ibid., March 1740–41.

(115) Applications to the Sessions for changes in the list of prices were made at different times by different branches of the trade and the subject is extremely complicated. Lists of prices were given to the Committee on the Silk Trade of 1832 from which the following items have been taken as representative. Other branches were raised at different dates.

	1769*	1795†	1806†	1825‡	1832‡
For a double sarsnet	6½d.	7½d.	8d.	—	4½d.
A thousand 8 thread	10d.	12d.	14½d.	14½d.	10d.
A thousand 10 thread	14d.	15d.	17d.	17d.	12d.
A thousand 12 thread	16d.	18d.	21d.	21d.	16d.

(Although some prices are lower in 1832 than in 1769, the flying-shuttle had recently been introduced into silk-weaving and it by no means follows that earnings were less.) *Report on the Silk Trade*, 1832, p. 722.

(116) *Report on the Police of the Metropolis*, 1816, p. 151.

(117) *Report of the Select Committee on Education*, 1835, p. 784.

(118) op. cit., p. 689. A witness calls this market a fair held every Monday and Tuesday morning. Children came to be hired for the week at a wage of 1s. 2d., 2s. 2d., or 3s. 2d., the odd twopence being for the child, the rest for the parents. ibid., p. 74. From Hickson's account, it appears that comparatively well-to-do people sent their children to be hired in this way.

(119) *Report on Contagious Fever* . . . 1818, p. 22.

(120) *Report on the Poor Laws*, 1834, XXXVI.

(121) C. Rey, *The Weavers True Case*, 1719, p. 27.

(122) *Report on Hand-loom Weavers*, 1840, XXIII, p. 81.

(123) Evidence to the Committee on Education, 1835, *Report* . . . p. 852.

(124) Letter to Hume, 9 February 1824. Add. MSS.

(125) *Memoirs of the late Thomas Holcroft*, edited by W. Hazlitt, 1816.

(126) *C.J.*, 3 May 1738.

(127) Campbell, op. cit. A merchant-exporter of leather gave evidence in 1738 that he had been bound to a leather-cutter in 1686 when there were about eight or ten of the trade in London, but that they had much increased of late and the leather trade was much improved.

(128) 'A practice hath lately prevailed of working in the country, manufactures for sale in London, which formerly employed great numbers of journeymen in this city. This is visible in the articles of shoes, in which there are fewer by many hundreds retained at work than were twenty years ago . . . and this method will probably be followed in many other branches of consumption – especially as the carriage from the country to London, by the improvement of the roads, becomes easier.' (C. Morris, *Observations on the past Growth and Present State of . . . London*, p. 110.)

(129) *Low-Life* . . . .

(130) *Report on Hand-loom Weavers*, 1840, XXIII, p. 121.

(131) Evidence to the Committee on Artisans and Machinery, 1824, *Report*, pp. 137–8, 144–5.

(132) Marginal note by Place on his copy of the *Report on Artisans and Machinery*. Add. MSS. 27800, ff. 165–7.

(133) *A Pepysian Garland*, ed. by H. E. Rollins, 1922, p. 445.

(134) Mayhew, *London Labour and the London Poor*, ii, p. 312.

(135) C. Lamb, *Album Verses*, 1830, p. 57.

(136) Winks, *Lives of Illustrious Shoemakers*, 1883, p. 232.

* Before the Spitalfields Act and according to the printed list of 1769 (see note 77), when the journeymen 'did not propose to make advancements, only to establish what we had . . .' that is to stop the price-cutting which had been taking place since 1763.

† Under the Spitalfields Acts.   ‡ After the repeal of the Acts in 1824.

(137) Housman, 'Tour of England', *Monthly Magazine*, 1797, p. 202.

(138) *Report of the National Truss Society*, 1842. For institutions for the supply of trusses, see note 101, Chapter 1.

(139) The statements in the text as to unhealthy trades are taken from the books numbered (1), (2), and (3), in note 8, except where another reference is given.

(140) Chamberlain's *Complaint Book* (MS.).

(141) *Report on Hand-loom Weavers*, 1840, XXIII, p. 119.

(142) Sir George Baker had a wide reputation for his studies in lead poisoning and read a succession of papers on it to the College of Physicians between 1767 and 1785; for instance in 1767: 'Almost every day's experience furnisheth physicians with examples of painters and plumbers and the other numerous artificers employed either in manufacturing the several preparations of lead, or in applying them to their respective uses; who after having suffered the most extreme torment from the collic of Poitou, are restored to health and remain free from that disease, so long at least as they quit their usual business or pursue it with greater caution.' (*Medical Tracts . . . 1767–85*, 1818, pp. 124–5.)

(143) See note 86, Chapter 1.

(144) Ramazzini, *Diseases of Tradesmen*, 2nd ed. (1750), of the English translation by Dr James, who writes in the introduction that the book had been translated into all European languages, eagerly bought up at almost any price and 'justly become what we commonly call a standard-book'.

Espriella (Southey) says in 1807 of Birmingham: 'Some I have seen with red eyes and green hair, the eyes affected by the fires to which they are exposed, and the hair turned green by brass-works.' (*Letters from England*, ed. of 1808, i, p. 192.) According to Simond (*Journal*) the green hair allegation was resented in Birmingham.

(145) *Monthly Magazine*, 1800, p. 64.

(146) Willan, *Diseases in London*, 1800, p. 300.

(147) Dr George Fordyce (practised in London c. 1760–1802), quoted in Middleton's *Agriculture of Middlesex*, 1798, p. 13.

(148) For the combinations among the London tailors, see F. W. Galton, *Select Documents illustrating the History of the Tailoring Trade*, 1896.

(149) Middlesex *Sessions Books*, 19 January and 1 May 1764.

(150) The master tailors of Westminster petitioned the Secretary of State in July 1764 against the combinations of the journeymen, asking for a letter to the justices to remove doubts as to their powers under the Act and to 'strike a terror into the delinquent journeymen and be a means of putting a stop to the combination'. The account they gave of the award of the Sessions ignores that of the previous May as to hours and lays stress on that of January: 'Notwithstanding this order is in favour of the journeymen taylors, they still continue their combinations, and on Monday last, when they ought to have continued at work from 6 in the morning till 8 in the evening, according to the said order, all or the greatest part of them to the number of several thousands, refused to work according to the said order and quitted their services and are now in idleness about the town.' (S. P. Dom. Geo. III, iii, 76–84 b.)

(151) J. T. Dunning, *Some Account of the London Consolidated Society of Book-binders* in the Social Science Association's *Report on Trade Societies*, 1860, p. 23 n.

(152) *Sessions Papers*.

(153) *Life of Robert Owen by Himself*, 1857, p. 19.

(154) F. M. Thomas, *A Record of a Hundred Years*, 1900, p. 99.

(155) *Report on Education in the Metropolis*, 1816, pp. 50 and 65. They also made

N

trousers at 5d. a pair, finding the thread. (A description of the Covent Garden district in 1813; soldiers' wives were making army clothing.)

(156) *Sessions Papers*, May 1753.

(157) ibid., 1765.

(158) *The Cries of London*, 1839, p. 81.

(159) *Autobiography.*

(160) *Reminiscences*, ed. of 1904, i. p. 367. 'Several years ago, though it could scarcely be supposed now [1830] such is the better taste of society generally, an execution at Tyburn was considered by various classes as a public holiday.' (ibid., p. 372.)

(161) Lacombe, *Tableau de Londres*, 1784, p. 180. For the general attitude towards the amusements of working people see notes 39 to 45, Chapter 6.

(162) *Improvement of the Working People*, 1834 (written 1829), p. 15. (Quoted by Graham Wallas, *Life of Place*, p. 163.)

(163) The Court Book of the Founders Company records under date 9 November 1767: 'An apprentice having applied for his freedom, his master objected that he had not served him faithfully, having refused to work longer than from 6 in the morning until . . . 8 in the evening; whereas he ought to have worked until 9 o'clock. The Court were of opinion that the usual hours were from 6 to 8 . . . and admitted him to his freedom.' (Williams, *History of the Founders Company*, p. 154.) See notes 34 and 35, Chapter 6.

(164) *Trade Unions Condemned, Trade Clubs Justified*, 1834, MS. of a tract for working-men in Add. MSS. 27834, p. 51.

(165) ibid., p. 63. 'In brisk times there are not hands enough to do the whole business in the usual way in which hands are employed, and it frequently happens that masters will voluntarily give a temporary advance of wages to their men to prevent their going to other masters, and as inducements to other men to leave their masters and come to them. In some cases they agree that the number of hours worked in a day shall be increased, sometimes both increasing the number of hands and the pay per hour. In trades where men are paid by the day and a certain quantity of work is considered a day's work, the rule is suspended and each man is paid according to the quantity of work he can do, working as many hours as he pleases. I myself as a master-tailor have paid at times from 6s. to 20s. a week each, additional wages.'

(166) ibid., p. 45.

(167) *Memoirs of a Working Man*, pp. 123–4.

(168) Add. MSS. 27828, fo. 129.

(169) *A Discourse of Trade*, 2nd ed. 1694, p. 81. (Written 'long before' 1669.)

(170) Malcolm, *Anecdotes*, i, p. 43.

(171) *Mendicity Report*, 1814–15, p. 268 ff.

(172) Add. MSS. 35145, fo. 71.

A French visitor writes, 'public beggars are less common in London and even in Great Britain than in most of the other countries of Europe. There is poverty, as elsewhere, but the great number of charities and the tax for the poor seem to have authorized the Government to forbid begging in the streets.' (Nougaret, *Londres* . . . 1816, ii, p. 304.)

Notes to Chapter 5

(1) *An Account of the General Nursery or College of Infants set up by the Justices of the Peace for the County of Middlesex . . .* 1686.

(2) Hanway in 1766 singles out St Clement Danes for special condemnation. Its first workhouse was not opened till 1772 or 1773 so that it continued the old custom of putting out children to nurse. In nine months the parish officers had entrusted twenty-three children to Mrs nurse Poole; two of these had been discharged, three were still alive, 'departed out of this transitory life after breathing the vital air about one month, eighteen . . . .' For 'this piece of service to the parish' she had been paid two shillings a week for each child. *An earnest Appeal for Mercy to the Children of the Poor*, p. 139. See also Chapter 1 and Appendix II.

(3) cf. the arrangements made by Moll Flanders for lying-in at Bath; she passed as the wife of an absent Sir Walter Cleave. *Moll Flanders*, 1721.

(4) In 1699 one of the overseers of St James, Westminster, was ordered by the Sessions to return to 'Mrs Jane Northgood and Mrs Margaret Tressilian £10 in money and a velvet scarf, unjustly exacted by him as security to the parish respecting a child since dead whom he unjustly alleged to be a bastard'. (W. J. Hardy, *Middlesex County Records*, p. 200.)

(5) *Laws concerning the Poor*, 4th ed. 1720, p. 82.

(6) 'Some vestries indeed are more barefaced and even make a trade of a parish. I mean those churchwardens and vestries who lump it with harlots and whoremongers and take bastards off their hands at so much per head for which they get a good treat from two guineas to five according to the circumstances of their chap, which they call sadling the spit, besides a good sum with the bantling, which 'tis to be feared is entirely sunk, all being done by connivance.' (*Parochial Tyranny*, 1727, p. 19.)

(7) Hanway, *An earnest Appeal for Mercy to the Children of the Poor*, 1766, p. 29.

(8) *C.J.*, 8 March 1715–16.

(9) Burrington, *An Answer to Dr William Brakenridge's Letter . . .* 1757, p. 23.

(10) The 'governess' of Moll Flanders was a London midwife who had a lying-in establishment, 'the sign of the cradle' and had given security to the parish for children born in her house.

(11) cf. the Ladies' Memorial praying for a charter for the Foundling Hospital (1739): 'No expedient has yet been found out for preventing the frequent murders of poor miserable infants at their birth, or for suppressing the inhuman custom of exposing newly-born infants to perish in the streets, or the putting out such unhappy foundlings to wicked and barbarous nurses who undertake to bring them up for a small and trifling sum of money, do often suffer them to starve . . . or if permitted to live, either turn them into the streets to beg or steal or hire them out to loose persons by whom they are trained up in that infamous way of living and sometimes are blinded maimed or distorted in their limbs in order to move pity and compassion and thereby become fitter instruments of gain to those vile merciless wretches.'

(12) *The Case of the Parish of St Giles in the Fields.* . . . See also *The Case of the Parish of St James, Westminster, as to their Poor and a Workhouse designed to be built for them.*

(13) *Account of Several Workhouses*, 2nd ed. 1732, p. ix. This enthusiastic description

of workhouses was written for the Society for Promoting Christian Knowledge 'in order to recommend and forward throughout the kingdom the execution of the same scheme, wherein a particular regard ought always to be had to such an education of poor children as may by bringing them up in the faith, knowledge, and obedience of the gospel, prove . . . the most effectual means to their becoming useful members of the community'. (*Account of the Society for Promoting Christian Knowledge*, 1807, p. 8.)

(14) cf. *An Account of several Charity Schools lately erected*, 1710. After describing how work had been provided for the charity school of St Margaret's, Westminster (spinning wool, mending and making shoes, sewing and knitting), the writer adds: 'But after all . . . notwithstanding the number of the schools . . . , there are at present (and will be till the poor shall be reformed by a better education) more poor children in divers parishes than the richer sort . . . are able to educate, and much less able to set to work, which requires some considerable stock.'

(15) In some districts 'working schools' sprang up which were in effect little factories run for the profit of the mistress who disposed of the children's work to dealers and commission agents, the children earning a small sum for their parents. There were spinning schools, straw-plait schools, and lace schools. Lace schools still survived in 1872, see Mrs Bury Palliser, *History of Lace*. Flax spinning schools were established in Ireland in 1708 by the Irish Linen Board, see R. Stephenson, *Report to the Irish Linen Board*, 1755, p. 44.

(16) Hatton, *New View of London*, 1708, p. 151, and pp. 750–51.

(17) Hanway, *Defects of Police*, 1780, p. 126.

(18) *C.J.*, 21 January 1774.

(19) The journeymen saddlers in 1777 say that schooling, if any could be afforded, would cost threepence a week. See note 26, Chapter 4.

(20) Lancaster in 1803 describes the schools at which the 'children of mechanics were generally educated. First the dame school', which he calls the Initiatory School, but generally known as the horn-book school, then 'the second class of schools. . . . The masters of these are often the refuse of superior schools and too often of society at large. The pay and number of scholars are alike low and fluctuating; of course there is little encouragement for steady men either to engage or continue in this line; it being impossible to keep school, defray expenses, and do the poor children regular justice without a regular income. Eventually many schools, respectable in better times, are abandoned to men . . . who use as much chicane to fill their pockets as the most despicable pettifogger. . . . These schools are chiefly attended by the children of artificers, etc., whose pay fluctuates with their employment, and it is too often withheld by bad principle. Debts are often contracted that do not exceed a shilling, then the parents remove their children . . . and never pay it . . . In these schools the number of children increases so much in the summer that it is impossible for the master to do them justice; therefore an assistant becomes necessary, but he cannot retain one for long, for as the scholars decrease in the winter his income of course shrinks . . . and perhaps poverty and misery stare him in the face'. (*Improvements in Education*, 1803, pp. 11 and 19.) To turn schoolmaster was the resource of the ruined and discredited artisan or shopkeeper. See Appendix IV, case 22.

(21) For instance, the Gray Coat Hospital or School of St Margaret's, Westminster, was in 1701 allowed, rent free, a house belonging to the parish, and received parish children at the same weekly rate as had previously been paid to parish nurses. This, like the Burlington Charity School was classed with workhouses. *Account of Several Workhouses*, 1725 and 1732.

(22) This was the case in 1732 in several of the City workhouses. In St Dunstan's in the East, twelve charity children belonging to the Tower Ward School were maintained in

the workhouse. In Mile End Old Town the charity school for twenty-one boys and ten girls was in the workhouse building. (ibid., 1732.)

(23) *A Memorial concerning . . . an Orphanotrophy or Hospital for the Reception of Poor Cast-off Children or Foundlings in order to the saving the lives of many poor Innocents yearly and to the rendering of all useful to the Public instead of hurtful Members thereof; as those who survive, by being brought to begging, generally prove.* [c. 1728.] By a Rector of one of the Parish Churches without the City Walls. pp. 17–19.

(24) *Weekly Miscellany*, 19 May 1733. Quoted by Malcolm, *Anecdotes*, i, p. 31.

(25) *Account of Several Charity Schools . . .* See also *A Short Account of the Several Kinds of Societies set up of late Years for the promoting of God's Worship, for the Reformation of Manners and for the Propagation of Christian Knowledge,* n.d. pp. 3–4.

(26) Maitland, *History of London*, 1756, ii, p. 1299.

(27) A sermon by E. Pickard, p. 23, 1760, for the benefit of the Orphan Working School of Hoxton, erected the same year. (Twenty boys had then been admitted and the Governors had decided to admit twenty girls.)

(28) The distinction between the housekeeper and the lodger, taken for granted by Londoners, surprised the foreigner. Archenholtz thus describes it: 'The poorer people, provided they are not absolute beggars, do their utmost to obtain a house for themselves and to become according to the English expression a *housekeeper;* for besides the convenience attending it, there are also certain privileges attached to the condition. Accordingly the most wretched tenement hired under their own name is preferred to the first floor of another house. . . . It often happens that in such a house the whole furniture consists of a bed, a table, and a few chairs and yet the quality of housekeeper gives the proprietor a certain degree of credit, and people make no difficulty in lending him money or goods.' (Archenholtz, op. cit., p. 265.)

(29) *First Report of the Philanthropic Society . . .* p. 16.

(30) Lord Mansfield in 1784 in deciding a settlement case which turned on whether a certain written engagement constituted apprenticeship, said: 'If these agreements were allowed to give settlements, there would be an end of indentures of apprenticeship, and also of the revenues derived from them.' The arrangement was that one, John Wylde, had agreed with a weaver at Great Bolton to teach him to weave counterpanes in return for half his earnings for two and a half or three years. After a year and a half he married and paid the weaver a pound to be free from the agreement but continued to work for him as a journeyman. Burn, *Justice of the Peace*, ed. of 1793, iii, p. 434.

(31) Burn, *History of the Poor Laws*, 1764, p. 212.

(32) Poor parents often bound their children apprentices when they were very young, as for instance to chimney-sweeps (see note 84). cf. the petition of Samuel Austin to be discharged from his master: 'That petitioner was under the age of nine years and not being a parish child was bound as apprentice to George Norfolk of Turnmill Street . . . dealer in fish and garden stuff and that £5 was given with him to the said George Norfolk. And the petitioner is informed and believes that the duty for the said £5 was never paid to the Stamp Office. The petitioner begs leave humbly to shew further that the petitioner being now above the age of fourteen years dislikes both his master and his employment and is desirous to be bound apprentice to a trade. Therefore humble prays that this Court would be pleased to take his case into consideration (and for these reasons that he was bound at an age when he could not legally enter into covenant and for that his indenture was never enrolled and the duty paid).'

Both parties were summoned to appear. Petitioner's master refused to come, saying to the deliverer of the summons that he 'might take . . . Samuel Austin with him for that he would not trouble himself or lose a day's work'. The apprentice was therefore discharged. Samuel Austin was evidently a remarkable boy. Middlesex Records, *Sessions Book*, January 1752.

In 1728 John Rooksbee of St Giles in the Fields, aged nine, was discharged from William Newbee of Wapping, shoe-maker, to whom he had been bound for ten years. His mother had paid Newbee £7 but his master had treated him with great brutality, not only compelling him to drink water, but beating his head and body with a great leathern strap and afterwards with a broomstick so that he had been disabled in his left hand ever since. His master tied him to a bedpost, so that he was in danger of losing his left eye. The Court declared the indenture void. *Middlesex Records*, Calendar, October 1728.

Instances of such bindings are comparatively rare in the Sessions records, because, one may presume, it was seldom that their victims were able to appeal. Many of course must have come before individual justices after the Act of 1747. (See note 68.)

(33) *Some Thoughts concerning the Maintenance of the Poor*, 1700, p. 12.

(34) *Enquiry into the Causes of the Increase of the Poor*, 1738, p. 43.

(35) *Middlesex Records*, January 1683–6. (Calendar.)

(36) ibid., October 1710.

(37 In 1754 an Islington wood-carver was charged with stealing planks and plants from the next-door house. It was adjudged that this was a malicious prosecution on the part of his apprentice who was anxious to be discharged. Evidence was given that the apprentice used to break his work and then lay a stick in his master's way 'in order that his master might beat him and that he might get his indentures sued out by his uncle'. He said, 'he had a scheme to sue out his indentures and then he could work for himself and earn a great deal of money'. (*Sessions Papers*, February 1754.)

The following case was tried at Bow Street (before Sir John Fielding) on 15 January 1772:

'Robert Perryman appeared against his apprentice, John Burch, for absenting himself from his service and staying out for a number of nights. The lad, having nothing to offer in his defence, was ordered to Bridewell for a month, to be kept to hard labour, on which he said he would go for a year if the justices would discharge him from his master.' Press cutting, B. M. Collection, *Alsatian Curiosities*.

(38) See Appendix IV, cases 1 and 27.

(39) Jeaffreson, *Middlesex Records*, IV, p. 87. (He instances a case tried 30 Charles II.)

(40) Hutton, apprenticed to his uncle a silk-stocking weaver of Nottingham, says it was more usual for apprentices to be under than over the stint, in which case they were in debt to their master. Owing to his father's carelessness in executing the indentures he himself had to pay for his clothes during his servitude out of the money thus hardly earned, a condition which he found intolerable. *Life of William Hutton by himself* . . . ed. of 1841, p. 9.

Francis Place apprenticed in 1787 to a leather breeches-maker, was paid half a man's wages (and afterwards at a higher rate) for anything that he earned above the stint, and thus made about 6s. a week. *Autobiography*, Add. MSS. 35142, fo. 134.

(41) *An Earnest Appeal for Mercy to the Children of the Poor* . . . 1766, p. 105.

(42) Villette, *Annals of Newgate*, iv, p. 167.

(43) *Gentleman's Magazine*, 1767, p. 433 ff.

(44) *Sessions Papers*, February 1748.

(45) ibid., June 1736.

(46) ibid., January 1733.

(47) ibid., July 1735.

(48) ibid., February 1784 (Rape Trial).

(49) Middlesex, *Sessions Book*, 1762.

(50) Strange, *Reports*, p. 1001.

(51) *Middlesex Records*, Calendar, July 1726.

(52) J. Collyer, *The Parents and Guardians Directory*, 1761, p. 99.

(53) ibid., p. 85.

(54) cf. a case quoted by Burn illustrating the legal doctrine that a master is entitled to the earnings of an apprentice who leaves his service. cf. *Hill* v. *Allen*, in Chancery 3 February 1747, 'the bill was by an apprentice who, against his master's consent quitted his service of a shipwright . . . and went on board a privateer, which took a very considerable prize, whose share thereof, being £1,200, the master claimed. By Lord Hardwicke: "in general, the master is entitled to all that the boy shall earn, consequently if he runs away . . . the master is entitled at law to all his earnings; and in this case, there is nothing in equity to relieve." But he said he would send the case to be tried at law unless they would agree to compound the matter, which he recommended to them, and thought, as the boy's share was so very large, the balance ought to be in his favour. And the master agreed to accept £450. *Vezey*, 83.' (*Justice of the Peace*, 1793, i, p. 90.)

(55) *Reasons for passing the Bill for better regulating the Company of Watermen Lightermen, and Wherrymen of the River Thames*, n.d. [?1729]. Several apprentices gave evidence on behalf of the Bill to show that they were not employed by their masters who, however, refused to turn them over to active watermen, e.g., 'William Green said he . . . has served about a year and three-quarters . . . and is now about sixteen . . . but his master has no boat, nor ever had since he was bound. That he hired a boat as long as he could be trusted. That his master gets his livelihood by helping his father-in-law to carry out small beer . . . and that he himself earns now and then sixpence a day by riding a spare horse to a brewhouse. And he further said that his master is not able to support him, and that he is almost starved . . . .' (*C.J.*, 27 February 1728–9.)

(56) She was tried for the murder of her master and confessed that she had put poison in his food. As there was some evidence that the death was not due to the poison she was acquitted. *Sessions Papers*, May 1752.

(57) MS. indenture of Rebecca Clark, a poor child of the parish of St Giles, Cripplegate, annexed to the following petition to the Lord Mayor and the other justices of the Sessions of the City of London: 'That your petitioner had only served upwards of half a year . . . that her master had £5 consideration money of the parish, 40s. of which to be laid out in clothes, £3 for his use. . . . That your petitioner hath been beat and abused by her said master that her right arm was so much bruised that your petitioner might have lost the use of it but for your Lordship's great goodness and clemency in getting her into St Bartholomew's Hospital. . . . Her master hath kept her so low in clothes and other necessaries that in the hard winter of January last . . . she was obliged to wear shoes without soles, and for want of necessary apparel (her clothes being in a tattered condition) was almost perished with cold. She prays for discharge, and that her master may be ordered to refund the consideration money.' The petition is signed with her mark and endorsed 'Discharged by consent of the Master'. (*Sessions Papers*, Guildhall Records, 1742.)

(58) *Sessions Papers*, May 1774. (Case of J. Amenet, her master, tried for rape.)

(59) *Middlesex Sessions Book*, April 1754.

(60) Place, *Autobiography*.

(61) Advertisements for run-away apprentices were numerous. Two of 1730 are as follows:

'Whereas John Tyler, a man child five foot and a half or better, who is apprenticed to

Mary Hart, widow, a baker in BlackFryers, absented himself from his said mistresses service on Thursday last. He is of a sandy complexion and pretty fat: He had no waiscoat on, only a light fustian frock with flat mettle buttons, a pair of drugget breeches of an olive colour and a pair of gray stockings.

'Whoever entertains or harbours him, if it be but one hour, I will show no more favour than the law directs; and whoever will bring him back to his said mistress, shall have a half-peck loaf reward.'

'Whereas Richard Dodd, son of Joel Dodd, Post-master of Highworth in Wiltshire, being apprentice to William Saul, Citizen and Joyner of London, has absconded from his said master's service on Sunday, 31 July 1730. He is being cry'd down in London; his master is informed he is being harboured about Marlborough or Highworth. . . . He is a tall thin youth, about five foot eight or nine inches high with a cast in his right eye; Whosoever brings the said Richard Dodd to his aforesaid master shall have a handful of sawdust for their pains: Whosoever harbours, entertains, or detains, the said Richard Dodd must expect the severity of the law.' (Press-Cuttings.) *Alsatian Curiosities*.

According to *Low-Life* (1764), London apprentices chose the time between one and two a.m. on Sunday morning for running away: 'Apprentices who intend to run away from their masters are packing up their cloaths that they may make off by the help of the trap-door on the top of the house, while all the family are fast asleep.'

(62) *C.J.*, 17 March 1779.

(63) Felkin, *History of the Machine-wrought Hosiery and Lace Manufacturers*, 1867, pp. 72 ff. and 82.

(64) *Life of William Hutton* . . . p. 18.

(65) *Report on the Petitions of the Ribbon Weavers* . . . 1818, p. 48.

(66) For instance in 1785 a bricklayer's labourer aged eighteen 'clubbed' with John Rolfe, a bricklayer at Cottishall, Norfolk, for three years to learn bricklaying. He was to work for Rolfe at 5s. a week for the first year, 7s. for the second, 8s. for the third. Durnford and East, *Reports*, V, pp. 193–4.

Francis Place when he left his apprenticeship to a breeches-maker, could not at once get work as a journeyman, it was therefore proposed that he should work for his brother-in-law a journeyman chair-carver for three years on similar terms, but they could not agree as to the rate of wages for the three years. *Autobiography*. See note 17, Chapter 6.

(67) In the case of apprentices bound to a freeman of London there were further grounds for discharge:

That the apprentice was under fourteen when he was bound.

That the master neglected to enrol him in the Chamberlain's Office during the first year of servitude.

That the master had moved outside the liberties of the City of London.

(Emerson, *A concise Treatise on the Courts of Law of the City of London*, 1794, p. 66.)

(68) 20 Geo. II. c. 19, s. 3.

(69) 32 Geo. III. c. 57.

(70) 33 Geo. III. c. 55.–

(71) Hanway, *An Earnest Appeal for Mercy to the Children of the Poor*, 1766, p. 109.

(72) Some of the harshest statutes against vagrancy contained provisions for the compulsory apprenticing of the children of vagrants till the age of twenty-four. By 1 Ed. VI. c. 3, the sturdy beggar might be made a slave for two years, and if he ran away, for life, and the sons of vagrants might be apprenticed till they were twenty-four, the daughters till they were twenty. See also 27 Henry VIII. c. 25, and 3 and 4 Ed. VI. c. 16.

(73) See note 54 above. The master of an apprentice who was 'seduced from his service' to work for someone else might waive his action for tort and bring one for payment for work and labour against the person who tortuously employed him. See *Bright* v. *Lucas* (37 Geo. III.), *Peake's Cases*, 1829, pp. 121–2.

(74) Hanway, op. cit., p. 107.

(75) The Committee of the Foundling Hospital in 1766 thought it better to give no fee at all. They sometimes however gave from £5 to £7 in 'nurse money' to induce a master to take a child of from eight to ten. Hanway says that some well-regulated parishes gave from £5 to £10 while others 'place children frequently in bad hands for £3 only'. op. cit., pp. 111–14.

(76) 42 Geo. III., c. 73.

(77) 56 Geo. III. c. 139. 'In the populous districts of England, the same causes which produce population, provide support for the inhabitants of all ages, by various occupations adapted to their means. Thus in manufacturing districts the children are early taught to gain their subsistence by the different branches of those manufactures. In districts where collieries or other mines abound, they are accustomed almost from their infancy to employments under ground, which tend to train and inure them to the occupation of their ancestors. But in London the lower class of the population is not of that nature, but is composed of many different descriptions, consisting of servants in and out of place, tradesmen, artisans, labourers, widows, and beggars, who being frequently destitute of the means of providing for themselves, are dependent on their parishes for relief, which is seldom given without the parish claiming the exclusive right of disposing at their pleasure of all the children of the person receiving relief. The system of apprenticeship is therefore resorted to of necessity, and with a view of getting rid of the burthen of supporting so many individuals and . . . it is probably carried to a greater extent there than anywhere else . . . .' (*Report on Parish Apprentices bound into the Country from the Bills of Mortality*, 1815.)

The children employed at a mill at Backbarrow in 1814–15 were all parish apprentices, chiefly from London (aged 7–11), with a few from Liverpool workhouse (aged 8 or 10 to 15). *Report on the State of Children in Factories*, 1816, p. 178.

(78) The Attorney General, arguing in 1802 that the Bill ought to include all children, not only parish apprentices, said, 'Was not the direct tendency of the present Bill to destroy apprenticeship altogether? Would not the manufacturers employ children as free labourers in place of apprentices to evade the law?' *Parl. Register*, LXXX, p. 458.

(79) 'Letters to the Guardians of the Infant Poor', quoted in *London Chronicle*, 28–30 July 1767. The beginning of the movement in behalf of climbing-boys seems to have been a letter in the *Public Advertiser*, August 1760, signed Ambulator [? by Hanway], quoted in Hanway's *Sentimental History of Chimney-Sweepers* . . . 1785, p. xx.

(80) By 1804 this had been given up. *Modern London* . . . 1804. (Description of plate of a chimney-sweeper.)

(81) Hanway, *The State of young Chimney-Sweepers' Apprentices*, 1773. (Goldsmiths' Library.)

(82) *Sentimental History*, p. 25. See also J. P. Andrews, *An Appeal to the Humane on behalf of the most deplorable class of Society, the Climbing Boys* . . . 1788, p. 8: 'few parishes if any, now bind their poor to chimney-sweeps'.

(83) Walpole writes in 1784: 'I have been these two years wishing to promote my excellent friend Mr Porter's plan for alleviating the woes of chimney-sweeps, but never could make impression on three people; on the contrary, have generally caused a smile.' (*Letters*, ed. by Toynbee, xiii, p. 220.)

In 1789 he wrote to Dr Lort asking for a letter of recommendation for Porter's son who was about to enter Trinity College, Cambridge: 'The father is one of the best and most respectable men upon earth and one whom I esteem, after Mr Howard and Mr Hanway, as one of the apostles of humanity. He has long been labouring to alleviate the horrid sufferings and consequential miseries of those poor victims, chimney-sweepers, and was the author of the mitigations obtained for them from Parliament last year – a plan he is still pursuing further. He has a good fortune and very good sense and is one of the humblest of men. With Mr Hanway and Mr Tyrwhit he was very intimate. He is a master chimney-sweeper himself; every Sunday he has his apprentices washed and cleaned, carries them to church and then gives them a good dinner of beef and pudding.' (ibid., Supplementary Volume, p. 30.)

(84) *C.J.*, 1 May, 1788.

(85) A chimney-sweeper of Knightsbridge gave evidence in 1788 that when he was about ten years old he was sent up a chimney that had been on fire for forty-eight hours, and that his master came and found fault with him 'in so angry a manner as to occasion a fright, by which means he fell down into the fire and was much burnt and crippled by it for life'. (ibid.) Extinguishing burning chimneys was the most profitable part of a chimney-sweeper's business.

(86) 28 Geo. III. c. 48.

(87) Porter gave evidence in 1788 that about 1776 he applied to Sir John Fielding for redress in the case of a boy who had been ill-treated by a person to whom he had been let out on hire, and that upon consideration Fielding was of opinion that the law did not authorize him to afford redress.

(88) Iatros, *A Biographical Sketch of Patrick Colquhoun*, 1818, p. 40. Farington records the conversation at a dinner at Angerstein's house in 1803: 'Mr A. gave me an account of the proceedings of those who have united for the relief of chimney-sweepers. Their object is (if it must be carried on without doing it by machinery) to have inspectors appointed under an Act of Parliament to examine into the conduct of all those who have apprentices for the purpose – and that all persons shall act under licences revocable on bad behaviour being reported. Boys employed on the *present* footing obtain for their masters from £40 to £50 a year each. The value of the soot collected in London and sold for manure is averaged at £50,000 a year. Another regulation proposed is not to allow the boys to cry their trade in the streets by which they would be saved from a sad exposure in bad weather and from very early hours.' (*The Farington Diary*, ed. by J. Greig, ii, 1923, p. 91.)

(89) The society for promoting the use of the machine for sweeping chimneys formed in 1802 circulated a list of the chimney-sweepers who used the machine, Highmore, *Pietas Londinensis*.

(90) *Second Report of the Society for Bettering the Conditions of the Poor*, p. 153. (Information supplied by Porter.)

(91) R. Campbell, *London Tradesman*, 1747, p. 328.

(92) *Middlesex Records*, Calendar, 1718.

(93) J. T. Smith, *Nollekens and his Times*, 1920, p. 100.

(94) J. Fielding, *Penal Laws* . . . 1768, pp. 414–15.

(95) Middlesex Records, *Order Book*, May 1800.

(96) 'The magistrates of the West Riding . . . and of Lancashire . . . may in vain pass humane resolutions . . . if these wholesome regulations can be entirely done away with by the act of two magistrates for Middlesex or Surrey who can . . . defeat these humane objects by binding scores or hundreds of children to manufacturers in a distant country. . . .

Indeed, in so slovenly and careless a manner is this duty frequently performed ... that in frequent instances the magistrates have put their signatures to indentures not executed by the parties.' (*Report on Parish Apprentices* ... 1815.) (cf. Appendix V.)

(97) Minute Books preserved at Devonshire House, E.C.

(98) W. E. Brown, *St Pancras Poor*, 1905, p. 7.

(99) 15 Geo. III. c. 21.

(100) *Sketch of the State of the Children of the Poor* ... *St James, Westminster*, 1796.

(101) *Hints and Cautions for the* ... *Churchwardens of the* ... *parishes of St Giles and St George* ... *made by the Vestry* ... *printed 1781, reprinted 1791; Rules* ... *for the Government of the Workhouse of St Andrew Holborn and St George the Martyr made by the Governors and Directors of the Poor, April 1791; Standing Orders under the Act of* ... *1799 of the united parishes of St Andrew Holborn and St George the Martyr.* ...

(102) Sir T. Bernard, *Account of the Foundling Hospital*, 2nd ed. 1799, pp. 66–7.

(103) I. Watts, *An Essay towards the Encouragement of Charity Schools*, 1728, p. 37.

(104) *Report of the Society for Bettering the Conditions of the Poor*, 1799, p. 277.

(105) W. Waddington, *Considerations on the Origin and proper Objects of the Royal Hospital of Bridewell*, 1798.

(106) Mrs Cappe, *An Account of two Charity Schools* ... 1800. Mrs Cappe's methods had been anticipated in a remarkable way at the beginning of the century by the ladies who set on foot and managed the Greenwich Charity School for girls. It was founded in 1700 for thirty girls, enlarged to forty in 1716, and is the subject of an enthusiastic report in the *Account of Several Workhouses* (1725 and 1732). The girls were four years in the school, were taught to spin the flax and wool of which their clothes were made, and were governed 'with as little severity as possible'. They were trained in domestic service, and the trustees (ladies) 'purposely avoid binding any of the children out apprentices, choosing rather to place them out to a year's service for 25s. to 30s. wages'. For a second year they were paid 40s. and for a third 50s. At the end of six months, if they did well, they were given a striped gown and petticoat and 20s. Any girls out of place owing to the death or removal of a master or mistress were allowed to live in the school till another place was found. 'The ladies' says the report, '... seem to have carry'd it to the utmost perfection, so as to enable the children to shift honestly by their own industry, if it should be their lot to be cast into any part of the kingdom where they might be friendless.' The second edition of the *Account* adds, 'they are never permitted to serve in public-houses, and if they do the cloaths and money usually given ... are not allowed'.

(107) *The Times* (Law Report), 23 May 1801.

(108) Letter to *Monthly Magazine*, 1801.

(109) Defoe, *A Tour thro' the whole Island of Great Britain* ... iii, p. 107.

(110) *The Case of the Parish of St Giles, Cripplegate.*

(111) *C.J.*, 3 February 1764.

(112) For instance in 1748 there was a dispute as to the settlement of Ann Stokes. As a child she had worked for a cloth manufacturer at Chew Magna, Somerset. She worked for a year and a half at weekly wages of 1s. 6d. in the summer and 2s. in the winter, living with her aunt. She then agreed to work for the same master for a year, living in his house. Mr Justice Denison said: 'This is a little girl hired to burl cloth; probably twenty children were so hired. The hiring was for a week. She lay at home and was at home on Sundays. ... I know this cloth-making business and am therefore afraid of the consequences of extending these settlements too far. These cloth-workers hire perhaps a hundred children in different parts of the work ... ' (Burrow, *Settlement Cases*, I, p. 282.)

(113) In 1757 another settlement case turned on the early life of 'a bastard child who ...

was hired with the consent and direction of this mother (he being then about eight years of age), to work at a silk-mill there for the term of three years at sixpence a week for the first year, ninepence a week for the second year, and thirteen pence . . . for the third. The master was not to find diet or lodging and the service was to be only eleven hours in the six working days. . . . He frequently absented himself for which deductions were made from his wages. He lodged the whole three years with his mother at Macclesfield who received his wages, which not being sufficient to maintain him . . . the overseers . . . of his birthplace allowed sixpence a week.' (Burn, *Justice of the Peace*, 1793, iii, p. 438.)

William Hutton, who worked at the Derby silk mill from the age of seven, lived at home and was paid weekly wages but he was an indentured apprentice, bound for seven years in 1730. See below, notes 127 and 128.

(114) *Account of the Asylum . . . for Orphan Girls within the Bills of Mortality* . . . 1773.

(115) *Rules and Orders for the Government of the Friends School and Workhouse at Clerkenwell*, 1780. (They were to be 'bound apprentices to such business or employments as shall appear suitable'.)

(116) *Report on Education in the Metropolis*, 1816, p. 433. (Evidence of the Secretary of the Foundling Hospital.)

(117) Report of the Committee . . . on the Number and State of Parish Apprentices bound into the Country from the Bills of Mortality . . . 1815. See Appendix V.

(118) 'Observations on an Act . . . respecting Apprentices employed in Cotton and other Factories.' Printed (with adverse comments) in *Report of the Society for Bettering the Condition of the Poor*, IV, 1805, Appendix, p. 12.

(119) An apprentice at this establishment was brought by his friends to Bow Street, 'to shew one of the modes of punishment adopted by the master, when one of the boys committed any fault. It consisted of an iron collar, fastened round the neck with a padlock. The lad said he had worn it above a month, and that he understood it was his master's intention that he should wear it till he was out of his time'. (*The Times*, August 1795, quoted by Ashton, *Old Times*, p. 268.)

(120) *Report on the Poor Laws*, 1817, p. 66.

(121) *Report of the Society for Bettering the Condition of the Poor*, IV.

(122) cf. *The Report to the Board of Trade in 1697*, by Locke:

'The children of labouring people are an ordinary burthen to the parish, and are usually maintained in idleness, so that their labour also is generally lost to the public, till they are twelve or fourteen years old. The most effectual remedy for this that we are able to conceive, and which we therefore humbly propose, is, that working schools be set up in each parish, to which the children of all such as demand relief of the parish, above three and under fourteen years, whilst they live at home with their parents and are not otherwise employed for their livelihood, by the allowance of the overseer of the poor, shall be obliged to come. By this means the mother will be eased of a great part of her trouble in looking after and providing for them at home and so be at more liberty to work; and the children will be kept in much better order, be provided for, and from their infancy be inured to work, which is of no small consequence for the making of them sober and industrious all their lives after; and the parish will be either relieved of this burthen, or at least of the misuse in the general management of it; for a great number of children giving a poor man a title to an allowance from the parish, this allowance is given once a week or once a month, to the father in money, which he, not seldom, spends on himself at the alehouse, whilst his children (for whose sake he had it) are left to suffer, or perish, from the want of necessaries unless the charity of neighbours relieve them. We humbly conceive that a man and his wife, in health, may be able to maintain themselves and two children;

more than two children at one time under the age of three years will seldom happen in one family; if therefore, all the children above three years old be taken off their hands, those who have never so many, whilst they remain themselves in health, will not need any allowance for them. We do not suppose that children of three years old will be able, at that age, to get their livelihood at the working school, but we are sure, that what is necessary for their relief will more effectually have that use, if it be distributed to them in bread at that school, than if it be given to their fathers in money. What they have at home from their parents is seldom more than bread and water, and that, many of them, very scantily too. If therefore, care be taken, that they have each of them their bellyful of bread daily at school, they will be in no danger of famishing, but on the contrary they will be healthier and stronger than those bred otherwise. . . . And to this may be added also, without any trouble, in cold weather, if it be thought needful, a little warm water gruel, for the same fire that warms the room, may be made use of to boil a pot of it. . . .

'Another advantage also of bringing poor children thus to a working school, is, that by this means they may be obliged to come constantly to church every Sunday along with their schoolmasters or dames, whereby they may be brought into some sense of religion, whereas ordinarily now, in their loose and idle way of bringing up, they are as utter strangers both to religion and morality as they are to industry. In order therefore to the more effectually carrying on this work to the advantage of this kingdom, we further humbly propose that these schools be generally for spinning or knitting, or some other part of the woollen manufacture, unless in countries where the place shall furnish some other materials for the employment of such poor children.'

Reprinted in *Report on the Poor Laws*, 1817, p. 14.

(123) Maitland, *History of London*, 1756, ii, pp. 1299–1300.
(124) Hanway, *Letters on the Importance of the Rising Generation*, 1767, ii, p. 128.
(125) *Citizen's Monitor*, 1780, pp. 195–6.
(126) *Cal. of State Papers Colonial*, 28 January 1620.
(127) *Life of William Hutton* . . . 1841, p. 7.
(128) Hutton, *History of Derby* (1791), ed. of 1817, pp. 159–60.
(129) Hansard, *Parliamentary Debates*, xx, p. 518.
(130) Add. MSS. 27828, fo. 113. (A broadside printed by Catnach and sold in the streets on the day of the woman's execution.)
(131) *A Pepysian Garland*, ed. by H. E. Rollins, 1922, p. 223 ff.
(132) *Poor Law Report*, 1834, Appendix II, Whitechapel parish: 'During the War there was much less difficulty and considerably less expense. We have about twenty-five young persons fit to go out, but by all the exertions of the overseers they cannot find means to get rid of them. . . . During the last six years we have got several off to fishermen at Greenwich and Barking, but that source now fails us. . . . We have constant complaints from private individuals stating that as the parishes give high premiums, they as private individuals have not the means of getting their children off, which brings them again to find means to get them into a workhouse to effect that purpose.'
(133) *Report*, 1834, XXVIII, Appendix A, pp. 431–3.
(134) *Report on the Poor Law Amendment Act*, 1838, XVIII, (1) p. 470 (Dr Kay).
(135) ibid., p. 469.
(136) Add. MSS. 27826, fo. 201. (Transcript of letter from Mr Henry Wilson to Peel, 26 July 1822.) cf. note 37, Chapter 6.
(137) See, for instance, Appendix IV, case 18.

Notes to Chapter 6

(1) cf. S. T. Janssen's note to the table of death sentences from 1749 to 1771 which he published in 1771: 'It is worth observing that as a great many idle men and lads are taken into the sea- and land-services during a war, so we then find the gangs of robbers soon broken . . . nor are one half the number of criminals condemned. . . . It is further observable that at the conclusion of a war, through very bad policy, when we turn adrift so many thousand men, great numbers fall heedlessly to thieving so soon as their pockets are empty and are at once brought to the gallows. The wise ones survive a while by 'listing with experienced associates, by which means in a few years those numerous and desperate gangs of murderers, house-breakers, and robbers, have been formed which have of late struck such a terror within the Metropolis.' See also note 95, Chapter 3.

(2) Colquhoun, *Commerce and Police of the River Thames*, 1800, pp. 173–4.

(3) R. Campbell, *The London Tradesman*, 1747, pp. 103–4.

(4) ibid., p. 193.

(5) *Trades Unions Condemned, Trades Clubs Justified*, 1834, Add. MSS. fo. 63. See note 165, Chapter 4.

(6) See note 20, Chapter 5.

(7) Add. MSS. 27827, fo. 55.

(8) *Trade Clubs, Strikes, Wages*. (Printed copy in Add. MSS. 27834, fo. 75 ff.)

(9) *Review*, 14 April 1705.

(10) *The Complete English Tradesman*, 1726, p. 317. Defoe, however, was by no means consistent on the subject. See *The Behaviour of Servants, passim*, for a protest against high wages.

(11) *Autobiography*, Add. MSS. 35142.

(12) cf. T. Murphy, *The Apprentice*, 1756, p. 8: 'What's a spouting club?' 'A meeting of 'prentices, clerks, and giddy young men, intoxicated with plays, and so they meet in public-houses to act speeches; there they all neglect their business, despise the advice of their friends and think of nothing but to become actors.'

(13) Add. MSS. 27828, fo. 33.

(14) cf. S. M. Ellis, *A Mid-Victorian Pepys*, 1923, pp. 156–7.

(15) *Mendicity Report*, p. 275.

(16) *Report on the Police of the Metropolis*, 1816, p. 262.

(17) *Report on the Police of the Metropolis*, 1828, p. 115. Out-door apprenticeship was probably general in the country before it became so in London, where the custom of the City was generally followed in the out-parishes. It was 'not a civic thing or very little so' the Upper City Marshal said in 1816. (ibid.) (See below, note 31.) Complaints made to the City Chamberlain of failure to pay the agreed allowance to an apprentice were apt to be dismissed as 'not coming under the cognizance of the Chamberlain' (e.g., complaint of John Luker against his master, a founder, 8 September 1790). In 1720 the Westminster magistrates decided that the indentures of a day apprentice bound for four years only were void in law. To assimilate out-door apprenticeship to the rigid interpretation of apprenticeship it seems to have been usual to execute indentures in the old manner with an additional deed specifying payments by the master for board and lodging which the

apprentice or his friends undertook to provide for himself. (See Middlesex *Sessions Books.*) In the clothing districts in the country out-door apprenticeship seems to have been frequent and its terms openly recorded in the indenture. A Gloucestershire indenture of 1714 provides for a form of out-door apprenticeship which was very usual at the end of the eighteenth century as is shown by disputes concerning settlement under the poor law. Francis Haskins was bound to Edward Wyal, Weaver, for 4½ years to find himself in food, drink, washing, lodging, and apparel. He might go home every Saturday to Monday and was to be paid 2½d. out of every shilling made by his master in the first, 3d. the second and third years, 4d. in the fourth. *Victoria County History of Gloucester,* ii, p. 161. cf. the indenture at Corsley, Wilts., of 1700, quoted by O. J. Dunlop, *English Apprenticeship and Child Labour,* pp. 352–3. The apprenticeship of children at the early silk mills seem to have been out-door apprenticeship. See *Life of William Hutton.*

(18) A London printer, in business for about 20 years gave evidence before the Committee on Artisans and Machinery, in 1824, that printers had much improved, 'a printing-office was like a public-house on a Monday when I was an apprentice, and now we have no drinking at all'. (*Report,* p. 55.)

Hone comments on the improvement in press-men 'who are becoming as respectable and as intelligent a class of operatives as they were within recollection, degraded and sottish'. (*Every-day Book,* 5 August 1825.) Place confirms this by saying: 'I can recollect the time when to every press there was a rum bottle, when . . . as Mr Hone says . . . they were as drunken, as dirty, and as ragged as any sort of workmen whatever, they are not so now, and this is attributed, I believe truly, to the practice which has for many years existed of taking out-of-doors apprentices. These, until lately, were in very large numbers and as most of them were sad blackguards, so they are now, as journeymen less improved than their fellows.' (Add. MSS. 27827 or 6.)

(19) Out-door apprenticeship was strongly opposed by the London journeymen printers in the early nineteenth century as converting the apprentice into a kind of indentured journeyman. The real point at issue seems to have been the desire to restrict the number of apprentices, but they claimed that out-door apprentices being often taken with little or no premium would be the children of indigent parents, insufficiently educated to make good printers, would inevitably succumb to the temptations of the town and would drive away the respectable journeymen by their depraved manners, 'when the apprentices have got above the controul of the journeymen with manners and language contracted at public-houses, night-houses, and brothels, at those hours when they would, if they had been indoor apprentices, have been under their master's roof, and emboldened by their numbers, encouraging each other in their insolent and offensive behaviour to the men . . . .' (Printed sheet *To the Booksellers of London and Westminster,* in Add. MSS. 27799, fo. 97, Place Collection.)

(20) Hanway, *Citizen's Monitor,* 1780, p. 57.

(21) Grosley, *A Tour to London,* 1772, i., p. 112.

(22) *Relief of Apprentices wronged by their Masters, how by our Law it may effectually be given and obtained without any special new Act of Parliament for that Purpose,* 1687.

(23) *Report on the Police of the Metropolis,* 1816, p. 213. cf. above, p. 279.

(24) *Report of the Select Committee on Education,* 1835. Evidence of F. Place, p. 834.

(25) *London Sessions Papers,* May 1722. (Case of Elias Dyer, indicted for murder, found guilty of manslaughter.)

(26) *Resolutions of the Master Manufacturers and Tradesmen of the Cities of London and Westminster . . . on the Statute of 5 Elizabeth c. 4.* Freemason's Tavern, 14 July 1814.

(27) *Police of the Metropolis,* ed. of 1806, p. 315.

(28) *Citizen's Monitor*, 1780, p. 241.

The way in which each generation in its turn helps to build up the legend of the good old times is illustrated by a speech in support of the bill for prohibiting the sale of intoxicants to young persons: 'Mrs Wintringham . . . "under the old apprentice indenture system, which was now out of date, apprentices were bound not to frequent public-houses or alehouses, and this Bill would be a substitute for that old system".' (*The Times*, 10 March 1923.)

(29) Add. MSS. 27828, fo. 119.

(30) cf. *The Poor Whore's Complaint to the Apprentices of London*, printed in *Bagford Ballads*, 1877, i, p. 491:

> But goldsmiths' men who cash have in their hands
> Enough to buy a stately house and lands,
> Shall be most welcome. We will say no more
> But when such come be sure to ope the dore.
> The mercers men out of their masters' goods,
> May most of us supply with scarfs and hoods,
> And linnen drapers with a piece or two,
> Of lawn or Holland may be useful too.
>
> Something we know may now and then be made,
> By over-work or sleight of hand in trade,
> How e'er you get it, so't be silver, we
> Without all niceness will contented be.
> But such of you who careless masters have,
> May most securely for expenses save.
>
> Yet when you see a seasonable time,
> What e'er you do, you must not judge a crime:
> But reason thus: Who helps to get it? I.
> Then part is mine. But this is by the by.

(31) The question of the payment of apprentices is closely bound up with that of out-door apprenticeship. (See notes 17 and 19.) By an Act of Common Council of Henry VIII, if a citizen gives his apprentice wages or permits him to take part in his own getting or gains, suffers him to go at large or serve a foreigner, or agrees for money or otherwise for his services and afterwards procures such apprentice to be made free by servitude, both the master and the apprentice may be disfranchised. Emerson, *A concise Treatise on the Courts of Law of the City of London*, 1794, p. 69. Whether this was ever strictly observed may be doubted. Mrs Elianor James who wrote early in the eighteenth century that she had been in the element of printing above forty years protests against paying apprentices: 'I would not have you give him any encouragement as money, but that he should serve the term of his indentures as an apprentice without, for giving him money makes him a journeyman before his time.' (Nichols, *Literary Anecdotes*, i, p. 307, quoting Mrs James's *Advice to all Printers in general*.)

In 1745 the Court of the Pewterers Company consulted the Chamberlain on the point, who answered 'that a master by his oath [as a freeman of London] could not give his apprentice wages and the apprentice forfeits thereby his freedom'. (Welch, *History of the Pewterers Company*, 1902, i, p. 191.)

Besides out-door apprenticeship, there was a legitimate way of escaping the rigour of the prohibition of wages. The apprentice could be made free by redemption on the payment of a fine as was done in the case of those who married during their term of servitude, or for some other reason had not served out their term. Many instances of this are recorded in the *Repertories*. For instance, in 1761 Thomas Bird, bound in 1754 to Joseph Turner, a locksmith and member of the Company of Needlemakers, prayed to be admitted to the freedom of the City on payment of a small fine. In 1760 his master had allowed him wages and remitted the final year of his term of servitude. The Court ordered that he should be admitted to the freedom in the Company of Needlemakers on paying £1 3s. 4d. to Mr Chamberlain for the City's use. *Repertories* (MSS.), vol. 166. (Guildhall Records.)

(32) Meriton Latroon, *The English Rogue*, 1668–9, ii. p. 163. The description of the behaviour of the apprentices is interesting. 'My master was not only a taylor but kept a broker's shop, wherein he sold all sorts of clothes new and old. He lived in one of the principallest streets in the City, and was in good esteem with his neighbours, who were all persons of some quality, not of the meaner sort, but substantial tradesmen, as goldsmiths, grocers, drugsters, scriveners, stationers, &c., and I (being now well fitted with clothes and having my pockets pretty well lined with money which I had still kept by me) was a fit and welcome companion to the best sort of apprentices, in whose society I did soon insinuate myself, and having money to spend equal with the best, I came acquainted with a whole gang of such blades that all was nothing in comparison to what I soon experimented from them, for their masters being of the wealthiest sort of citizens and keeping country houses at Newington, Hackney, Stepney, &c., they often had opportunity in their absence to meet and keep their club or general rendezvous which was commonly every other night at one of the taverns near adjoining: and my master who did well understand that I was frequently abroad, and in what company I spent my time, did not in the least oppose or contradict me therein, for I soon found that these young blades, tho' apprentices, were yet my master's best customers, for there was none of them but had a sute or two of clothes à la mode which commonly lay at our house, which they put on when they had any frolick out of town, either at Christmas, Easter, or Whitsuntide, or at any other time, when, pretending some urgent occasion, they would give their masters the slip.'

(33) J. Aikin, M.D., *A Description of the Country from thirty to forty Miles round Manchester*, 1795, pp. 182–3.

(34) The following cases are all taken from the earliest surviving *Complaint Book* (1786 to 1791, nearly six years). During this time Wilkes was Chamberlain and it appears from Dibdin's *Memoirs* that he heard complaints in person. See note 35.

(35) This judgment may be compared with one in the case of Thomas Dibdin, bound to Rawlins, a rich upholsterer, he and the other lads being termed 'articled young gentlemen', 'apprentice' being considered derogatory in the establishment. Dibdin scorned the shop and was absorbed in a model theatre which he made in the evenings. His master found him employed on it in working hours, smashed it in pieces and threw it on the fire and struck Dibdin on the cheek. Dibdin thereupon went to the Guildhall and poured out his grievances to the Chamberlain, Wilkes. The master was summoned, Dibdin was ordered to attend to his business and the master was 'admonished not in future to degrade his dependents by *coups de bâton*, which spoiled the spirit of London apprentices, whose legal guardian he was'. This illustrates the different treatment considered suitable for the well-to-do apprentice and 'the apprentice for labour'. Compare with this Wilkes' decisions in two other cases at about the same time:

Richard Morris complained against his master a cabinet-maker for 'not teaching him his business and repeatedly beating him cruelly and turning him out of his service and not having sufficient necessarys which several evidences in Court confirmed. Mr Chamberlain admonished both parties of their respective duties and dismissed them.' (29 November 1787.) Richard Packer complained against his master, a cabinet-maker 'for repeatedly striking him. The master in answer said the lad had aggravated him to strike him by his insolent behaviour. Mr Chamberlain dismissed the Complaint as frivolous.' (17 May 1786.)

'The bias of the Chamberlain's Court would appear to have been on the side of the master (which is in contrast with the general tenor of the decisions of Quarter Sessions or of court justices in Middlesex) though doubtless it was some protection against gross ill-usage. In 1854 the Commission on the Corporation of London elicited the fact that complaints of masters against apprentices were in the proportion of ten to one and the Chamberlain, Sir John Kay, said that the jurisdiction of the Chamberlain operated rather for the protection of the master than of the apprentice.' (*Report on the Corporation of London*, 1854, pp. 596 and 594.)

(36) *Reasons offered for the Reformation of the House of Correction at Clerkenwell* . . . 1757, p. 33.

(37) cf. the deposition of a boy, Edward Vaughan, before a City Magistrate (Sir John Barnard), at Guildhall, 19 September 1746: 'who on his oath saith that about six weeks agoe he became acquainted with Thomas Bishop . . . about . . . eighteen years, and John Travelly . . . aged about thirteen . . . who inquired whether this examinant was out of work . . . thereupon they asked him if he would go out with them a-thieving, which this Examinant was then averse to, but being told by the two said boys there was no danger and they would secure him from harm, he was prevailed upon to go along with them and they kept company together about three days before they went a-thieving, when on the third day they followed a cole cart . . . into Red Lyon Street, Holborne, and then . . . when the coles was delivered, Bishop went in and brought out a silver spoon which they rann away with and Bishop broke it and defaced the mark, one part of which he offered to sell to a brasier in the New Market at Fleet Ditch who bought it. The other he sold, but for what this examinant knows not, and gave him 2s. and part thereof in order to buy some clothes and victualls. So this examinant, being under great concern for what he had done, left him and quitted their company for the space of seven or eight days, when by the information of one Betty Smallman who keeps a bawdy house in Wild Street, near Drury Lane, the said two boys found him out where he had gott into work and there they threatened to transport him unless he would goe along with them, so for fear he left the place he was at work and went along with them to Somersett House where Travalley stole from out of the stables there a pair of stockings and a shirt which they carried to the said Betty Smallman and sold to her for 5s. of which he had 16d. for his share, after which he runn away from them . . . and got into work at a wharfe in Whytefriars where they in about a fortnight found him out and threatened to charge him with a constable and pelted him with stones across the lighters, whereby he was obliged to goe along with them again, and the day after they all of them . . . followed a cart into Grosvenor Square and Bishop and Travelly under pretences of trimming the coles went into the gentleman's house and brought from thence two silver spoons which they together runn away with to the said Betty Smallman and told her how they came by them and she bought them for 12s., but the money was shared between the said Bishop and Travelly, this examinant refusing to have any part thereof for fear of the ill-consequences and thereupon he left them again and got into work without being found out by them, but on Wednesday last as he was washing himself in the kennell in Cheapside they picked him up again and threatened to prosecute him if he would not goe along with them, that thereupon being very much afraid, he went along with them and laid with them that night and the next day about seven o'clock they

came into the Poultry to a lynnen draper's shop and Bishop and this examinant went in to buy a handkerchief and while they were trafficking for the said handkerchief Travelley stole a parcel of handkerchiefs and runn away with them. Then Bishop slipt out and runn away likewise, but this examinant was kept by the master of the said shop and further this examinant saith not.' (*Sessions Papers* (MS.), Guildhall.)

(38) cf. the case of Robert Payworth a boy of twelve who worked for a barber on Fish Street Hill and was to have been his apprentice. He took a shoe to a cobbler to be mended; the cobbler's wife asked him if he had anything to sell, he answered, 'an old whitish handkerchief'. She then said, 'get whatever you can, I'll buy it for I buy anything'. The result was that the boy was induced to steal his master's property. He was convicted of theft, branded with a cold iron and then admitted to give evidence. *London Sessions Papers*, May 1752. In 1816 the Upper Marshal of the City gave evidence on the temptations to pilfering: 'there is scarcely what is called a chandler's shop in any part of the metropolis ... but buys old bottles and linen or anything that a servant-girl when she goes there to purchase things can take with her. The green-stalls will purchase things of them and they find a facility in raising money by the encouragement women keeping these shops give them.' (*Report on Police*, 1816, p. 262.)

(39) *Works*, ed. by Spedding, vi, p. 224.

(40) Fielding, *Increase of Robberies*, 1751, p. 9.

(41) ibid., p. 11.

(42) See note 97, Chapter 3.

(43) Alvarez Espriella, *Letters from England*, 1808, ii, p. 169.

(44) *A Letter to the Right Hon. Sir R. Brocas, Lord Mayor of London, by a Citizen* (R. P. Hare), 1730.

(45) *C.J.*, 9 April 1794. Later, The Rev. T. Thirlwall, a magistrate for the Tower Division, wrote an indignant pamphlet against the opening of the theatre: 'The Royalty Theatre has been the rendezvous of bawds and prostitutes, who as soon as it is opened make it their constant resort.... The consequence is that the streets are infested with these unhappy wretches, attended by gangs of thieves and prostitutes whom they engage for their bullies.' (*A Solemn Protest against the Revival of Scenic Exhibitions and Interludes at the Royalty Theatre ... by ... a Member of the Society for the Supression of Vice ...* 2nd ed. 1803, p. 8.) This tract shows a member of Wilberforce's Society (at first known as the Society for enforcing his Majesty's Proclamation against Vice (1787) or the Proclamation Society) repeating the arguments that had been used in 1730 (see note 44) and long before. Indeed the puritanic attitude towards sports and amusements from the middle ages to the early nineteenth century cannot be understood without a knowledge of the very real social evils which seemed to be inevitably connected with them. See notes 60 and 61, Chapter 2, for the character of the district round the Covent Garden theatres.

(46) Quoted in *The Gentleman's Magazine*, April 1735, pp. 191-2.

cf. Sir J. Hawkins, *Life of Johnson*, 1787, pp. 75-6: 'although of plays it is said that they teach morality, and of the stage that it is the mirror of human life, these assertions are mere declamation ... on the contrary, a play-house and the regions about it, are the very hot-beds of vice: how else comes it to pass that no sooner is a play-house opened in any part of the kingdom, than it at once becomes surrounded by a halo of brothels? Of this truth the neighbourhood of ... Goodman's Fields has had experience; one parish alone, adjacent thereto, having to my knowledge expended the sum of £1,300 in prosecutions for the purpose of removing those inhabitants, whom, for instruction in human life, the play-house had drawn thither.' See also note 98 below.

(47) *Middlesex Records, Order Book*, 28 February 1750-51. These disorders were largely

due to one of the justices, Sir Samuel Gower, who had procured licences for the brothels and disorderly houses when the other justices at licensing sessions had refused them. Moreover he was himself the landlord of the scandalous New Wells to which he gave 'all countenance and encouragement . . . by being present with his wife and family . . . commending and otherwise encouraging the actors'. Though he had promised amendment at the previous October Sessions, complaints were renewed in January and 'he continues to behave as aforesaid'. (ibid.) In the following September the justices were still discussing how to 'make good the said charges against him'.

(48) Archenholtz, *Picture of London*, pp. 166–7.

(49) Place, *Improvement of the Working People*, 1834 (written 1829), pp. 19–20.

(50) *Report on Hand-Loom Weavers*, 1840, XXIV, p. 696.

(51) B. Franklin, *Autobiography*, ed. of 1905, pp. 54–5.

(52) *A Glimpse at the social conditions of the Working Classes during the early part of the present Century*, J. D. Burn, p. 39.

(53) *Fines and Forfeits imposed by journeymen coopers on a young man coming out of his time in the year 1780* (written 1825). Add. MSS. 27803, fo. 213.

(54) Booth, *Life and Labour*, Series I, vol. iv, pp. 143–4; ibid., vol. vii, pp. 27–8, 1896.

(55) *Fifty Years Recollections of an Old Bookseller*, 1837, p. 47.

(56) The justices in 1684 ordered that the guinea given by every justice of the peace as colt money should be laid out on a piece of plate and not be spent 'in wine or treatment as formerly' (Middlesex, *Sessions Book, Cal.* January 1783–4), but whether this was strictly observed seems open to doubt. By the beginning of the nineteenth century the term colt money had been replaced by the more decorous 'spoon-money'. In 1806 the Westminster Sessions order 'that every gentleman who shall qualify himself to act as a justice of the peace for the city and liberty do in future pay the sum of five guineas for spoon-money and that on the first day that such gentlemen shall appear at the dinner-table the housekeeper do present the spoon-book to him for his signature and payment of the above sum'. (Westminster *Sessions Book*, Ap. 1806.)

(57) G. Wallas, *Life of Place*, p. 211. (Letter from Place to Hume describing his canvassing of the various trades at their houses of call against the Combination Laws.)

(58) *C.J.*, 29 February 1731–2.

(59) R. Campbell, *The London Tradesman*, 1747, pp. 192–3.

(60) *Memoirs of a Working Man*, 1845, p. 122. Place in *The Gorgon* says that the hours of call for the Flints, who worked by the day only, not like the Dungs by the day or piece, were at nine in the morning, at one and at nine in the evening. No man was allowed to ask for employment, each went, with some exceptions, in the order in which his name stood in the books of the house of call, and no man might refuse to go, under a heavy fine rigorously exacted, 1818, pp. 157–8. For the London tailors their trade organization and combinations see F. W. Galton, *Select Documents illustrating the History of the Tailoring Trade*.

(61) *C.J.*, 9 and 12 May 1729.

(62) *Case of Mr Reynolds*. . . . About 1751 the undertakers were said to stop 8s. in every 20s. earned by the coal-heavers and to sell them small beer for the price of strong, bad brandy and other strong liquors in short measure and at the best prices without their daring to complain. (ibid.)

(63) *C.J.*, 2 June 1758.

(64) Colquhoun, *River Police*, 1800, pp. 144–6.

(65) 47 Geo. III. c. 68.

(66) Mayhew, *Life and Labour*, 1861, iii, pp. 235–6 and 247.

(67) T. Mortimer, *Elements of Commerce*, 1773, p. 452 n.

(68) J. Fielding, *Observations on Penal Laws*, 2nd ed. 1768, p. 107 (1st ed. 1761).

(69) *Public Advertiser*, 9 September 1772. Not only out-door trades but tailors and weavers paid wages in public-houses, e.g. one, Grant, gives evidence, 'I am a taylor, I was at a public-house paying my men from 8 o'clock.' *London Sessions Papers*, June 1780. Benjamin Wright, a weaver, states 'I was drinking at the Cock with my master who there paid me 13s. 6d. at 10 o'clock.' (ibid. February 1724-5.) (Case of Robert Grayer, etc.)

(70) ibid., October 1775.

(71) Fothergill, *Essay on the Abuse of Spirituous Liquors*, 1796, p. 14.

(72) *London Sessions Papers*, February 1785. (Case of William Bull.)

(73) *Middlesex Order Book*, July 1789. (Proceedings on the letter from the Secretary of the Committee of the Society for carrying into effect His Majesty's Proclamation against Vice and Immorality, enclosing copy of a report from the committee dated 3 March.)

(74) *Observations on Public-Houses*, 1794, p. 7. Iatros, *Life of Colquhoun*, pp. 21 and 43.

(75) Add. MSS. 28801, fo. 57. (A newspaper article by Place.)

(76) Walcott, *Westminster*, 1849, p. 281.

(77) Hawkins, *Life of Dr Johnson*, 1787, pp. 87-8.

(78) *The London Guide* . . . 1818, pp. 1-2.

(79) *Quarterly Review*, 1832, xlviii, p. 361. (Article by 'Nimrod'.)

(80) Hanway, *Letters on the Importance of the rising Generation*, 1768, ii, p. 189.

(81) Dr Forde, the Ordinary of Newgate, remarked in a letter to Bentham in 1783 that it was difficult for the keeper to prevent spirits being smuggled in, 'women who are chiefly the conveyors of them secrete them in such ways that it would be termed the grossest insult to search for them'. (Published by Basil Montague.)

(82) Howard, *The State of Prisons in England and Wales*, 1784, pp. 238-9.

'As the debtors are generally very poor I was surprised to see once ten or twelve noisy men at skittles. . . . I found they were admitted here as at another public-house. No prisoners were at play with them.'

(83) Neild, *State of Prisons*, 1812, p. 452.

(84) Dr William Smith, *The State of the Gaols in London, Westminster, and the Borough of Southwark*, 1776, p. 43.

(85) 'In February 1694-5 Quarter Sessions made an order against alehouse-keepers serving as head boroughs or beadles. Complaint had been made that such officers had been in the habit of taking persons whom they apprehended to their own houses or to "places called round-houses" and keeping them there till they had spent great sums of money in eating and drinking and lodging, and then releasing them without bringing them to a justice; that the offenders had been taken to these alehouses and round-houses after they had been committed to the New Prison and Bridewell; and that seamen and others liable to be pressed for the fleet, took shelter in these houses . . . .' (W. J. Hardy, *Middlesex County Records*, p. 129.)

It was one of the resolutions of the Committee of 1770 on the burglaries recently committed in London and Westminster 'that larger and more convenient round-houses should be provided in the City and Liberty of Westminster . . . and that no liquor should be sold in them'. (*C.J.* 10 April 1770.)

(86) Shaw, *Parish Law* (a book concerned primarily with London), 8th ed. 1753, p. 341.

(87) In 1695 (see note 85); in 1712, on a complaint that alehouse-keepers applied to the stewards of courts leet to be sworn in as constables '. . . with intent to favour and connive at several offenders who keep houses of bawdy, musick-houses, and other disorderly houses, and by that means encourage such offenders and refuse to present them to this or

any other court of justice'. *Midd. Records*, Cal., April 1712. In 1762 a committee of justices recommended to the Sessions that no victualler should be sworn in as constable 'if any other fit person can be found . . . many instances of partiality having been found by such victuallers'. (Middlesex *Order Book*, 15 July 1762.) In 1785 the Sessions ordered that a circular letter should be sent to all the justices and the stewards of the courts leet recommending that care should be taken that no alehouse-keeper should be sworn in and that beadles who kept alehouses should be suppressed according to the order of 1694. (ibid., 25 February 1785.)

In 1736 the report on the excessive use of spirituous liquors (see note 35, Chapter 1), stated that nearly half the constables were victuallers and dealers in spirituous liquors . . . 'as every other trade makes interest to be excused . . . *they* are the only persons who covet it, which your committee apprehend must arise from some profit . . . to themselves and they are therefore of opinion the laws against drunkenness, lewdness, and profaneness are not likely to be put in execution while alehouse-keepers and retailers of strong liquor are most commonly the persons appointed to execute such the said laws. . . .'

(88) Forde, *Hints for the Improvement of the Police* (published by Basil Montague).

(89) *Monthly Magazine*, September 1797, pp. 200–1. A return of the numbers belonging to Friendly Societies was made in the Poor Law Returns of 1803, but members of clubs for supplying articles of clothing, hats, shoes, and the like were included. These were numerous in London but nearly always came to grief, as those who drew the first shares failed to continue their payments, and the other members lost their money. They were promoted by tradesmen supplying the articles in question. Place got up two breeches clubs to provide himself with work while he was unemployed, but on both occasions this happened. *Autobiography*.

(90) An interesting but perhaps rose-coloured account of box-clubs is given in *A new and compleat Survey of London*, 1742, ii, pp. 1141–2.

'There are in this city and suburbs another sort of societies, both of men and women (which are very numerous) denominated *box-clubs*, for the relief and mutual support of the poorest sort of artisans during sickness or other incapacity, whereby they are render'd incapable of getting their bread. These clubs . . . are supported by an amicable contribution of two, three, or six pence a week by each member; who weekly meet at a certain alehouse, where they spend twopence each, and wherein they have orders for their better regulation, and a strong box, or chest with divers locks for the conservation of their books, cash, papers, &c. Tho' these societies consist of the meanest and rudest of the citizens, yet by their admirable regulations and constitutions (of their own making) they are kept in best order and decorum. . . . Those of these societies which are of a long standing and have amassed a considerable sum of money for a fund, oblige every member at his admission into the club, to pay five shillings entrance-money, and in some ten shillings. However they are not entitled to receive any benefit from the Box till twelve months after such admission. The advantages arising to the several members . . . are that every member, when sick, or lame, whereby he is render'd incapable of working, during his . . . incapacity receives seven shillings and sixpence a week, provided his indisposition does not come from a venereal cause. . . . And when any of the members die, they are not only buried in a very decent manner by the society, at the expense of three pounds and attended to the grave by the whole club, but likewise, the widow, or nominee of such deceased member, receives from the society the sum of five pounds. And for preventing all frauds . . . upon any of the said societies, all persons that are detected in working during the time of their being supported by the Box are immediately upon conviction expelled by the Club.

'These great and numerous societies which consist of many thousands of members are a very great ease to the several parishes. . . . Divers of these societies are in so flourishing a condition at present, that they have thought of reducing their subscription to one-half, notwithstanding several thereof expend above ninety pounds a year. The talk of such reductions has occasion'd some of the said clubs to raise their entrance-money from five to twenty shillings.'

(91) J. T. Becher, *The Constitution of Friendly Societies*, 1824, p. 51, Sir F. M. Eden, *Observations on Friendly Societies*, 1801, p. 23. cf. the evidence of Morgan to the Select Committee on the Poor Laws of 1817, 'in general these clubs have been so badly conducted that they have been obliged to break up, and I advise them continually to do so', [that is, to break up the stock and begin again on Dr Price's system, based on calculations of the duration of life].

(92) 33 Geo. III. c. 54.

(93) E.g., 'They are formed from the crude suggestions of the most ignorant, who, in order to procure a sufficient number of subscriptions often propose the most extravagant terms, so that it soon becomes a matter of very little consequence to the greater part of the subscribers, whether they are robbed by their treasurer or ruined by the multitude of their claimants.' (Preface by Morgan to the 6th ed. of Price's *Observations on Reversionary Payments*, 1803.)

'I have said these societies are impositions on the public proceeding from ignorance and supported by credulity and folly. But this is too gentle a censure. There is reason to believe that worse principles have contributed to their rise and support. The older members believe they will last out their time.' (ibid., 7th ed., i, p. 145.)

Thus the mathematicians. The social reformers were generally less scathing, saw the good intentions, but were sometimes led to think a savings bank would be a safer alternative. See G. Rose, *Observations on Banks for Saving*, 1816; Eden, *State of the Poor*, 1797, and *Observations on Friendly Societies* 1801; Communications to the *Monthly Magazine*, 1797 (see note 88); and Colquhoun, *Treatise on Indigence*, 1806, pp. 111–17, who writes: 'The generally well-intentioned promoters of these friendly societies are unskilled in algebraical calculations . . . their little stock is not seldom annihilated before they are aware of it and the box is shut up against all relief, by which old members who have contributed for a series of years are frequently disappointed and deceived with respect to that assistance during sickness and infirmity to which they had looked forwards. . . .'

(94) Evidence to the Committee on Mendicity, 1815, *Report*, p. 286.

There were also burial societies. Eden quotes the advertisement of a London society: 'A favourable opportunity now offers to anyone, of either sex, who would wish to be buried in a genteel manner, by paying a shilling entrance and twopence a week for the benefit of the stock. Members to enter above fourteen and under sixty years of age, if approved of, and to be free in six months from the day of entrance. The deceased to be furnished with the following articles; a strong elm coffin covered with superfine black and furnished with two rows all round, close drove, with best black japanned nails and adorned with rich ornamental drops, a handsome plate of inscription, angel above the plate, flower beneath, and four pair of handsome handles, with wrought gripes; the coffin to be well-pitched, lined, and ruffled with crape, a handsome crape shroud, cap, and pillow. For use, a handsome velvet pall, three gentlemen's cloaks, three crape hatbands, three hoods and scarves, and six pair of gloves, two porters equipped to attend the funeral, a man to attend the same with hat and gloves; also the burial fees paid if not exceeding one guinea. The members that have already entered are 337 up to 1 September 1800.' (Observations on Friendly Societies, 1801, p. 15.)

cf. the account of benefit societies promoted by undertakers in Chadwick's Supplementary Report to the *Report on the Sanitary Conditions of the Labouring Population*, 1843.

(95) J. Fielding, *Penal Laws relating to the Metropolis*, 1768, p. 414.

(96) Colquhoun, *Observations and Facts relative to Public-Houses*, 1794.

(97) Smollett, *History of England*, 1790, iii, pp. 330–31. (cf. above, note 41 to Chapter 1.)

(98) These allegations were however denied by the Rev. T. Thirlwall (see above, note 45), himself a licensing magistrate for the division, who throws considerable doubt on the accuracy and disinterestedness of a building speculator who had been chiefly responsible for them. In spite of the astonishingly rapid increase of population since 1801, new houses, he says, 'have been licensed with the most sparing hand'. He thinks however, that the 950 public-houses in the Mile End district should be reduced by about one-third. *A Vindication of the Magistrates . . . for the Tower Division from the Charges . . . in . . . the Report . . . on the State of the Police . . . 1817*. (A book for which he was called to the bar of the House of Commons.)

(99) See S. and B. Webb, *Parish and County*, p. 79 ff. and 563 ff.

(100) See S. and B. Webb, *History of Liquor Licensing . . .* p. 49 ff.

(101) John Fielding repeatedly protested against the issuing of wine-licences by the Stamp Office (without inquiry on payment of the fee) which enabled disorderly houses to dispense with a justice's licence. See *Penal Laws*, 1768, pp. 65–6, and his evidence to the Committee of 1770 on burglaries in London and Westminster: 'brothels and irregular taverns . . . without licence from the magistrate are another great cause of robberies, burglaries, and other disorders. . . . The principal of these houses are situate in Covent Garden, about thirty in St Mary le Strand, about twelve in St Martin's in the vicinity of Covent Garden, about twelve in St Clements, five or six in Charing Cross, and in Hedge Lane about twenty. . . . There are many more dispersed in different parts of Westminster, in Goodman's Fields, and Whitechapel, many of which are remarkably infamous and are the causes of disorders of every kind, shelters for bullies to protect prostitutes, and for thieves; are a terror to the watchmen and peace officers of the night, a nuisance to the inhabitants of the neighbourhood and difficult to be suppressed by prosecution for want of evidence, in short, pregnant with every other mischief to society.' (*C.J.*, 10 April 1770.)

(102) *Report on the Police of the Metropolis*, 1816, p. 129. See also Wroth, *The London Pleasure Gardens of the Eighteenth Century*, 1896.

(103) Add. MSS. 27826, fo. 189.

(104) *Report on Education*, 1835. Evidence of Place, pp. 836–7.

(105) *Memoirs of a Working Man*, pp. 186 and 187. See also *Report on the Police of the Metropolis*, 1817, p. 486.

(106) T. Baston, Esq., *Thoughts on Trade and a Public Spirit*, 1716.

(107) *Piercing Cryes of the poor and miserable Prisoners for Debt . . .* 1714, p. 5.

(108) *C.J.*, 21 January 1718–19.

(109) *C.J.*, 14 May 1729.

(110) *C.J.*, 2 April 1792. (*Report of the Committee appointed to inquire into the Practice and Effects of Imprisonment for Debt.*)

(111) Neild, *State of Prisons*, 1812.

(112) *Report of the Committee on the King's Bench, Fleet and Marshalsea Prisons* 1814–15, iv, p. 553.

(113) *Middlesex Sessions Book*, July 1712. In the following September the following time-table was made for discharging debtors: on 16 September, the prisoners from Newgate

from 8 a.m., prisoners from St Katherine's (the franchise prison of St Katherine's by the Tower) from 2 p.m. 17 September, from 8 a.m. prisoners from Whitechapel. All were to be brought in in batches of not more than twenty-five at a time. (ibid. September 1712.) These arrangements afterwards disappear from the *Sessions Books*.

(114) A survey made by the Board of Works in 1780 after the Gordon Riots with a view to housing prisoners, Newgate and the King's Bench having been burnt. *S. P. Dom. Geo. III*, XXI.

(115) Neild, *Account of persons imprisoned for Debt in England and Wales*, 1800, pp. 47–8.

(116) The business of the Marshalsea Court shortly before the Act of 1779 is thus described by Dr William Smith: 'There is a constant fluctuation in the Marshalsea; most of the prisoners are confined for small sums and seldom remain long. More useful manufacturers and ingenious artists and their families are distressed and even ruined by litigious suits, frequent arrests and imprisonment from the Marshalsea Court than from any other court in the kingdom. Ten thousand writs are supposed to be yearly issued out of its office in Clifford's Inn, and above one thousand persons are supposed to enter a year into that old ruinous prison,' (*State of the Gaols in London* . . . 1777, p. 28). The jurisdiction of the Marshalsea extended over a radius of twelve miles from the king's court, but its activities had already been much reduced by the Act of 1725, and by the establishment of Courts of Conscience for the Metropolis after 1749 for which the Marshalsea officers had been given compensation. Though the Courts of Westminster did not hold to special bail for less than £10 the Marshalsea and other 'inferior courts' did, and before the Act of 1725 it was said that it arrested and held to bail for any sum from twopence to a thousand pounds. *The State of the Marshal's Court*, n.d.

(117) Firmin, *Proposals for the Employment of the Poor*, 1682, p. 41.

(118) T. Baston, Esq., *Thoughts on Trade and a Publick Spirit*, 1716, p. 127.

(119) *The Committee's Memorial* . . . [against Bambridge, 1729], and *Reasons against confining Persons in Prisons for Debt*, n.d.

(120) *A Petition for the Erecting of Courts of Conscience*, n.d. [1689?].

(121) This society did much to relieve the miseries of poor prisoners. They found that by far the greater number of prisoners for small sums were 'of the description of manufacturers, labourers, and seamen'. In its first twenty years it discharged about 700 prisoners a year at an average cost of 45s. each, usually a composition with their creditors, 'who at length accepted of such small compositions in satisfaction of debts for which whole families had been for years in a state of extreme distress'. They also found an average of 150 persons a year who, under the Lords Act of 1759 were entitled to an allowance of 4d. a day from their creditors (known as the groats) but were too poor to sue for it. For these they obtained their groats. In 1785 the Society published an account of the anomalies in the practice of Courts of Conscience, that of the City of London, the oldest court, was to imprison for an unlimited period, that of Middlesex established in 1750 was restricted by law to a term of three months in Newgate which extinguished the debt, while it was the custom of the courts of Westminster and the Tower Hamlets, whose prisoners were committed to Tothillfields Bridewell and the Clerkenwell House of Correction respectively to imprison for forty days only. In 1781 the patentee of the Whitechapel Court obtained an Act reducing fees and limiting the term of imprisonment to one week for every pound of the total debt and costs (which were limited to 15s.). As a result of the Society's publication an Act was passed in the same year limiting the term of imprisonment for debtors committed by Courts of Conscience in London, Middlesex, and Surrey, and abolishing fees paid by them to jailers. In 1786 these provisions were made general. No one committed by a Court of Conscience in England and Wales could be imprisoned for more than twenty

days for a debt of twenty shillings, or forty days for one of forty shillings, with an extension to thirty and sixty days for debtors found guilty of fraudulently concealing their effects. No jailer was to demand fees on a penalty of £5. As these courts and their prisoners were numerous, the relief to small debtors was very great. See evidence of the Society to the Committee of 1792 (see note 110), and Neild, *State of Prisons*, 1812, p. 61.

(122) *Report of the Committee on the King's Bench, Fleet and Marshalsea* . . . p. 20.

(123) *Piercing Cryes* . . . p. 20. cf. the case of Reason and Tranter, two officers of the Sheriff of Middlesex, tried for murder in the Court of King's Bench in 1722, for having shot in the most barbarous manner a Mr Lutterell whom they had arrested for £10. Lutterell had fetched a pair of pistols, but had laid them on the table and moved to the other end of the room, 'declaring that he did not design to hurt the defendants, but he would not be abused'. They were found guilty of manslaughter only. *State Trials*, xvi, p. 1 ff.

(124) J. Fielding, *A Plan for preventing Robberies . . . with an Account of the Rise and Establishment of the real Thieftakers*, 1755.

(125) W. Smith, *Mild Punishments sound Policy*, 1778, p. 64.

(126) ibid., p. 42.

(127) Colquhoun, *A Treatise on the Commerce and Police of the River Thames*, 1800.

(128) Clarkson, *History of the Abolition of the Slave Trade*, i, p. 294.

(129) This account is chiefly taken from Burn, *History of Fleet Marriages*. See also, G. E. Howard, *A History of Matrimonial Institutions*, and J. C. Jeaffreson, *Brides and Bridals*, The London *Sessions Papers* also throw much light on the subject, especially on bigamous marriages and false entries in the so-called Fleet Registers.

(130) *Second Report of the Committee on Lotteries*, 1808.

(131) Ashton, *History of Gambling in England*, p. 237.

(132) Eden, *Observations on Friendly Societies*, 1801, p. 29.

(133) *An Account of the Receipts and Disbursements relating to Sir John Fielding's Plan for the Preserving of distressed Boys by sending them to Sea as Apprentices in the Merchant Services* . . . 1769.

(134) This was certainly true of London; it was also said to be true of the country as a whole: 'the middle classes are receiving recruits from the lower in much greater number than the latter do from the former. This state of things is clearly proved by the vast number of neat houses of the smaller class arising in every part of England, in exchange for the crowded and filthy dwellings formerly inhabited by the artisans which are as rapidly in every county disappearing, this view is further strengthened by referring to the great increase in the consumption of all those articles which form the comforts of those a few steps above the indigent class. Thus, within the last twelve years, the increased use of soap, candles, leather, sugar, and other articles is evidence to shew that the augmentation of our inhabitants is chiefly in that class of society who are not compelled to live on the lowest description of food. . . . The increase in the . . . capitals accumulated in the various savings banks in a few years from two to fourteen millions sterling afford other grounds for taking a favourable view of the situation of those one or two steps above the condition of mere day labourers . . . .' (W. Jacob in *Second Report on Agriculture and Corn in Europe*, 1828, xviii, p. 149.)

(135) Simond, *Journal of a Tour and Residence in Great Britain* . . . 2nd ed. 1817, ii, p. 180. cf. his estimate of England: 'If I was asked at this moment, [September 1811], for a summary opinion of what I have seen in England, I might probably say its political institutions present a detail of corrupt practices – of profusion – and of personal ambition, under the mark of public spirit, very carelessly put on, more disgusting than I should have

expected. . . . On the other hand, I should admit very readily, that I have found the great mass of the people richer, happier, and more respectable than any other with which I am acquainted. I have seen prevailing, among all ranks of people, that emulation of industry and independence, which characterize a state of advancing civilization, properly directed. The manners, and the whole deportment of superiors to inferiors, are marked with that just regard and circumspection, which announce the presence of laws equal for all. By such signs I know this to be the best government that ever existed. I sincerely admire it in its results, but I cannot say I particularly like its means.' (ibid., ii, p. 387.)

(136) cf. the tracts and proposals summarized by Eden, *State of the Poor*, i, and Fielding's *Proposal for making an effectual provision for the Poor, for amending their Morals and for rendering them useful Members of Society*, 1753.

(137) *The Form of a Petition submitted to . . . those Noblemen and Gentlemen who desire to subscribe what sums shall be necessary for relieving, reforming, and employing the Poor . . .* 1722.

(138) J. C. Jeaffreson, *Middlesex County Records*, iii, 1888, p. 337. The workhouse was enjoined by the famous Act of 1662. See also W. J. Hardy, *Middlesex County Records*, 1905, p. 296.

(139) In 1769 the gentlemen of Devon petitioned for a Bill 'for the more effectual relief of the poor of Devon' by a regulation of the voluntary friendly societies which had sprung up there. *C.J.*, 23 January 1769. (Such a scheme for the Devonshire agricultural labourer was not likely to be financially possible and the Act was repealed, the justices of the peace for Devon petitioning that a clause might be added to the Bill for repeal enabling the parish officers to make good out of the rates the deficiencies in the funds of the societies caused by the experiment. *C.J.*, 29 January 1773.)

The general schemes were:

1772, that of Baron Maseres for selling parish annuities on a basis of 3 per cent. A bill to this effect passed the Commons, but was thrown out by the Lords in 1774.

1786, Mr Acland proposed a general club or friendly society to which everyone might, and some should be compelled to, subscribe.

1786, Mr Haweis proposed a general compulsory system of friendly societies, the employer of every poor man was to pay one thirty-sixth or one twenty-fourth part of his employee's earnings, to which a shilling in the pound was to be added from a fund to be contributed to by every occupier in lieu of the poor-rate.

1787, Mr Townsend, in *Dissertations on the Poor Laws*, proposed to make contributions to a society while in health a condition of relief, and to ensure the means to contribute there were to be parish workshops with certain employment. See *Report . . . for Bettering the Condition of the Poor*, IV, App. xv, and V, p. 11.

(140) cf. *Address . . . from the Philanthropic Society*, 1791, p. 9 n. 'To those who may conceive that this society is in any degree anticipated by the liberal provision which is made throughout the kingdom for the poor, or that any part of this plan might be adopted in our workhouses, the reply is obvious. The overseers . . . do their duty if they receive every applicant for relief: our business is with those chiefly who do not apply. It is the part of the Society to inspect the abodes of profligacy and dishonesty to find out the proper objects, and to allure them from their evil habits and connexions by peculiar advantages and peculiarly good treatment.'

(141) Colquhoun estimates that there were 1,600 friendly societies in and near London of which about 800 had registered themselves under the Act of 1793 (33 Geo. III. c. 54): 'composed of mechanics and labouring people who distribute to sick members and for funerals sums . . . amounting on an average to . . . 20s. a year, and consisting of about 80,000 members . . . .' (*Police of the Metropolis*, 1797, p. 381.)

(142) *Four for a Penny, or Poor Robin's Character of an unconscionable Pawnbroker and ear-mark of an Oppressing Tallyman* ... Harleian Misc., IV, p. 148.

(143) Add. MSS. 35142, fo. 38.

(144) *Police* ... p. 381. It is true that Colquhoun ascribed the cause of the supposed deterioration to defects in police: 'It must be evident as the miseries of the poor do not appear to be alleviated and their morals grow worse, that there must be some cause to produce effects so opposite to what might have been expected from such unparalleled philanthropy; the cause indeed may easily be traced in the general system of police....' This is lost sight of by many who have used the assertion of deterioration to support a variety of theses. The assertion, however, is not borne out by the facts of social history. Place remarks: 'Mr Colquhoun ... did not perceive that a material change for the better was going on among the people, and that getting drunk and quarrelling were gradually declining. He did not observe that among clerks to merchants and bankers and other persons, drinking and fighting had no place, and he did not see that by means of the better education workmen in London were approximating to the class mentioned, and that in proportion ... their grossness of conduct would leave them. That this has been the case is apparent to everyone of fifty years of age to whose remembrance I have called the period of their youth. That a huge mass of vice and misery exists is but too true, that in the metropolis there is an increase of vicious and miserable, *ceteris paribus*, in respect of the population, then and now, I deny, on the contrary I assert that the proportion of crimes has greatly diminished.' After describing the decline of drunkenness, the greater cleanliness and decency of manners, he goes on: 'Could this change in manners have taken place without a corresponding change in morals? The answer must be, it could not and it has not ... I really know no one thing in which any *class* or description of persons from the richest tradesman to the meanest person living has retrograded.... If this be so, how has this change been brought about? ... The general answer is the gradual advance of school education, breaking down the absurd reverence for their betters as they used to be called. ... These people have learned to lay out their money in a better way, to spend less in drinking and more in useful ways, to ensure less in the lottery, now indeed happily put an end to ....' (Add. MSS. 27827, ff. 48–52 (1824).)

1. VITAL STATISTICS

A. Baptisms and Burials according to the Parish Registers. *Population Returns,* 1801, ii, pp. 44-18.

Year	City within the Walls (1)		City without the Walls (2)		Out Parishes (3)		Westminster (4)		Parishes outside the Bills (5)		Total	
	Baptisms	Burials	Baptisms	Burials	Baptisms	Burials	Baptisms	Burials	Baptisms	Burials	Baptisms	Burials
1700	2,287	2,645	4,888	5,887	5,761	7,337	3,445	4,429	204	289	16,585	20,587
1710	2,169	2,835	4,470	6,983	5,198	8,275	3,433	4,975	194	443	15,464	23,701
1720	2,193	2,711	5,984	7,441	6,185	9,362	4,328	5,936	216	526	18,906	25,976
1730	1,861	2,455	5,851	7,180	6,559	10,124	4,202	5,550	407	890	18,880	26,199
1740	1,515	2,538	4,398	7,534	6,815	13,067	4,672	6,565	379	1,381	17,779	31,085
1750	1,429	2,031	4,508	5,758	6,606	11,098	4,039	5,312	498	1,364	17,080	25,563
1760	1,507	1,724	4,375	4,747	6,802	9,433	3,949	4,833	523	1,264	17,156	22,001
1770	1,596	1,683	4,824	5,211	7,880	10,078	4,289	6,017	1,200	1,959	19,789	24,948
1780	1,437	1,655	4,499	4,598	7,638	9,654	4,075	5,604	1,599	2,340	19,248	23,851
1790	1,468	1,269	4,948	3,634	9,344	9,701	4,786	4,755	2,320	2,146	22,866	21,505
1800	1,247	1,546	4,134	4,717	9,645	12,817	4,151	6,490	2,599	3,691	21,776	29,361

It must be remembered that 1710, 1740 and 1800 were years of dearth and disease, and that 1790 was an exceptionally healthy year according to the Bills of Mortality.

By a misprint in the *Population Returns* the total Burials for 1720 are given as 23,976 instead of 25,976.

(1) 98 parishes.

(2) 17 parishes, including the Borough of Southwark as in Appendix III, *B*, and omitting the precinct of Whitefriars.

(3) 22 parishes: St Anne Limehouse, Christchurch Middlesex, Christchurch Surrey, St Dunstan Stepney (in separate hamlets), St George Bloomsbury, St George's in the East, St George Queen Square, St Giles-in-the-Fields, St James Clerkenwell, St John Hackney, St John Wapping, St Katherine Tower, St Leonard Shoreditch, St Luke Old Street, St Mary Islington, St Mary Lambeth, St Mary Magdalen Bermondsey, St Mary Newington, St Mary Rotherhithe, St Mary Whitechapel, St Matthew Bethnal Green, St Paul Shadwell.

(4) As in Appendix III, *B*, omitting the Verge of the Court and adding the precinct of the Savoy.

(5) Kensington, Chelsea, St Marylebone, Paddington, St Pancras.

B. Variation between the Parish Registers and the Bills of Mortality. *Population Returns*, 1811, ii, p. 200, and 1821, ii, p. 160.

Year	Baptisms		Burials		Year	Baptisms		Burials	
	P.R.	B.M.	P.R.	B.M.		P.R.	B.M.	P.R.	B.M.
1700	16,381	15,616	20,298	20,471	1794	19,784	18,689	20,537	19,241
1710	15,270	14,928	23,258	24,620	1795	19,567	18,361	22,704	21,179
1720	18,690	17,479	25,450	25,454	1796	20,187	18,826	20,661	19,288
1730	18,473	17,118	25,309	26,761	1797	20,466	18,645	18,058	17,014
1740	17,400	15,231	29,704	30,811	1798	19,598	17,927	20,755	18,155
1750	16,582	15,548	24,199	23,727	1799	19,581	18,970	20,376	18,134
1760	16,633	14,951	20,737	19,830	1800	19,177	19,176	25,670	23,068
1770	18,589	17,109	22,989	22,434	1801	18,275	17,814	19,434	19,374
1780	17,649	16,634	21,511	20,517	1802	20,411	19,918	20,260	19,379
1781	18,834	17,026	22,860	20,709	1803	21,308	20,983	19,803	19,582
1782	18,547	17,101	19,271	17,918	1804	21,769	21,543	16,829	17,038
1783	18,186	17,091	21,249	19,029	1805	21,067	20,295	17,862	17,565
1784	19,467	17,179	20,005	17,828	1806	21,655	20,380	17,130	17,937
1785	20,173	17,919	20,841	18,919	1807	21,277	19,416	19,319	18,334
1786	19,904	18,119	21,645	20,454	1808	21,376	19,906	20,068	19,954
1787	19,743	17,508	21,514	19,349	1809	22,108	19,612	17,313	16,680
1788	20,054	19,559	19,816	19,697	1810	21,298	19,930	20,951	19,893
1789	19,315	18,163	22,131	20,749	1811	22,732	20,645	17,327	17,043
1790	20,546	18,980	19,359	18,038	1812	22,526	20,404	19,080	18,295
1791	20,212	18,496	21,074	18,760	1813	23,014	20,528	17,840	17,322
1792	20,862	19,348	21,325	20,213	1814	22,852	20,170	21,271	19,783
1793	20,106	19,108	23,153	21,749	1815	25,271	23,414	19,821	19,560

The burials in the parish registers for 1720 are given in the returns as 23,450, a misprint for 25,450, see *A* above, parish summary.

C. Baptisms and Burials under five years of age according to the London Bills
of Mortality for 100 years in five periods of twenty years each and two
periods of fifty years. T. R. Edmonds, 'On the Mortality of Infants in
England', *Lancet*, 1835–6, i, p. 692.

Ages	1730–49	1750–69	1770–89	1770–1809	1810–29	1730–79	1780–1829
0–2	190,200	153,886	140,810	117,070	112,135	421,259	292,842
2–5	44,887	39,808	39,248	42,501	39,659	105,714	100,389
5–10	18,488	15,760	15,349	15,537	16,471	42,262	39,343
10–20	16,006	14,629	15,221	12,187	14,213	38,541	33,715
20–30	40,666	34,972	31,222	26,244	27,768	91,913	68,959
30–40	49,679	41,188	37,158	35,638	35,579	110,042	89,200
40–50	51,178	42,903	40,057	38,660	39,385	114,289	97,894
50–60	41,123	34,875	33,791	33,961	36,598	93,168	87,180
60–70	32,080	30,221	28,453	28,368	33,935	76,436	76,601
70–80	23,288	21,285	20,724	20,533	27,248	55,215	57,863
80–90	11,735	9,327	8,394	8,639	12,693	25,231	25,557
90–100	1,955	1,379	1,176	1,273	2,155	3,929	4,009
100	182	94	118	72	71	327	210
Total burials	521,467	440,327	411,721	380,683	397,910	1,178,346	973,762
Total baptisms	315,456	307,395	349,477	386,393	477,910	796,029	1,040,602
Dying p.c. under five years	74·5	63·0	51·5	41·3	31·8	66·2	37·8

D. The mean annual number of deaths in London produced by twenty classes of disease out of 100,000 living, according to the Bills of Mortality. J. R. M'Culloch, *Account of the British Empire*, 4th ed., 1854, ii, p. 613. (Contributed by Farr.)

	1629–35	1660–79	1728–57	1771–80	1801–10	1831–35
1. Chrisomes, overlaid, convulsions, worms, teething, mold-shot head, dropsy on the head, inflammation of brain, rickets, liver-grown, canker, thrush, croup, whooping-cough	1,681	1,591	1,827	1,682	789	625
2. Small-pox	189	417	426	502	204	83
3. Measles	16	47	37	48	94	86
4. Scarlet-fever	..	..	..	..	..	53
5. Fever	636	785	785	621	264	111
6. „ , spotted	45	90	..	..	..	..
7. Plague	125	1,225	..	..	..	..
8. Dysentery	221	894	50	17	1	1
9. Surfeit or cholera	63	148	1	..	..	135
10. Inflammation	..	..	10	31	101	307
11. Pleurisy	14	6	10	5	4	39
12. Asthma and tisick	..	..	112	85	89	136
13. Consumption	1,021	1,255	905	1,121	716	567
14. King's evil, scrofula	14	19	5	5	..	3
15. Dropsy	146	349	218	225	131	133
16. Apoplexy and suddenly	47	30	48	55	49	59
17. Palsy and lethargy	14	17	12	18	19	28
18. Old age and bed-ridden	370	388	415	324	241	357
19. Casualties	65	76	85	70	40	57
20. Child-bed and miscarriage	80	100	43	47	32	43
21. Unknown causes	..	..	..	..	..	88
22. Other diseases	253	565	211	144	146	289
Deaths in 100,000 living .	5,000	8,000	5,200	5,000	2,920	3,200

E. Number of annual deaths from certain diseases according to the London Bills of Mortality out of 100,000 living in the ten years ending with 1780 and with 1810 respectively. J. Milne, *A Treatise on the Valuation of Annuities and Assurances*, 1815, p. 472.

	1780	1810		1780	1810
Apoplexy	55	49	Fevers	621	264
Asthma	85	89	Gout	15	13
Child-bed and			Measles	48	94
miscarriage	47	32	Palsy	17	19
Consumption	1,120	716	Small-pox	502	204
Dropsy	225	131	Old age	324	241
				3,059	1,852

II. INFANT MORTALITY AMONG LONDON PARISH CHILDREN

A. 1750–5. (Ages not specified.) Figures collected by Hanway from the Parish Officers. J. Hanway, *Letters on the Importance of the Rising Generation*, 1768, ii, pp. 80–1.

	Born and received	Discharged	Dead	Remain alive in 1755
St George, Hanover Square	288	115	137	36
St Luke, Middlesex	53	..	53	..
St Giles-in-the-Fields and St George, Bloomsbury	415	228	169	18
St Andrew above Bars and St George the Martyr	284	57	222	5
St Anne, Westminster	66	30	28	8
St Saviour, Southwark	156	91	56	9
St Paul, Shadwell	32	11	12	9
St Martin-in-the-Fields	312	147	158	7
St Margaret and St John, Westminster	128	32	68	29
Lambeth	76	53	23	..
Christ Church, Surrey	39	19	18	2
St Giles without Cripplegate	209	131	62	16
St Botolph without Aldgate	119	57	33	29
St James, Westminster	161	103	58	..
	2,239	1,074	1,077	168

B. 1763 carried on to 1765. (Children under four.) Selected by Hanway as examples of the best and worst parishes from the Register of the Parish Infant Poor according to 2 Geo. III. c. 22. ibid., ii, p. 123.

	Born and received in 1763, exclusive of those delivered to mothers in the year	Of whom were illegitimate	Delivered in 1764 and 1765	Remain	Of whom are dead by the end of 1765
St Sepulchre	9	3	..	9	9
St Clement Danes*	7	6	..	7	7
St John and St Margaret, Westminster	32	18	4	28	24
St Andrews above Bars and St George the Martyr	59	53	..	59	57
St George, Hanover Sq.	41	19	2	39	34
St James, Westminster	12	8	2	10	10
St George, Middlesex	4	1	..	4	4
St Martin's-in-the-Fields	31	9	2	29	27
St Luke, Middlesex	19	9	1	18	18†
St George, Southwark	9	4	3	6	6
St James, Clerkenwell	18	9	1	17	17
St Giles and St George, Bloomsbury	50‡	9	1	49	43
	291	..	16	275	256

* No workhouse.   † No account of 11, presumed dead.   ‡ Mostly casual

C. 1765. (Ages under four.) Selections by Hanway from the Register of the Parish Infant Poor. J. Hanway, *An earnest Appeal for Mercy to the Children of the Poor . . .* 1766, p. 135.

	Born and received	Discharged	Remaining	Of whom from 1 to 4 years old	Of whom dead	Under 12 months old	Of whom dead	Dead per cent from 1 to 4 years old	Dead per cent under 12 months
Parishes without the Walls									
St Andrew, Holborn	58	13	45	22	8	23	15	35	69
St Bartholomew the Great	3	..	3	..	..	..	..	..	..
St Bride*	10	2	8	6	..	2	1	..	50
St Botolph, Aldersgate	11	..	11	6	1	5	3	16	60
St Botolph, Aldgate	28	6	22	12	3	10	8	25	80
St Botolph, Bishopsgate	29	9	20	10	3	10	8	30	80
St Dunstan in the West	5	..	5	1	..	4	..	..	..
St George, Southwark	24	12	12	3	2	9	5	66	55
St Giles, Cripplegate	39	22	17	9	5	8	6	55	75
St John, Southwark	28	12	16	8	3	8	6	37	75
St Olave, Southwark	25	12	13	9	2	4	4	22	100
St Saviour, Southwark	48	12	36	19	10	17	8	[sic] 5	48
St Sepulchre, Newgate	49	13	36	17	11	19	15	64	79
Parishes in Middlesex and Surrey									
St Anne, Middlesex	12	1	11	6	..	5	2	..	40
Christ Church, Southwark	16	5	11	10	5	1	1	50	100
Christ Church, Middlesex	34	17	17	3	2	14	7	66	50
St Dunstan, Stepney	16	4	12	8	1	4	1	12	25
St George, Middlesex	19	1	18	12	8	6	4	66	66
St Andrew above Bars and St George the Martyr	141	17	124	34	20	90	64	60	71
St George, Bloomsbury and St Giles-in-the-Fields	178	62	116	67	22	49	39	33	80
St James and St John, Clerkenwell	78	33	45	31	14	14	11	46	80
St John, Hackney.	19	9	10	8	1	2	1	12	50
St John, Wapping	35	8	27	20	2	7	3	10	43
St Katherine, Tower	4	2	2	..	..	2	1	..	50
St Leonard, Shoreditch	65	7	58	36	8	22	6	22	27
St Luke, Middlesex	41	2	39	16	5	23	15	31	65
St Mary, Islington	14	5	9	6	1	3	1	16	33
St Mary, Lambeth	39	11	28	19	2	9	6	10	66
St Mary Magdalen, Bermondsey	24	8	16	10	7	6	4	70	66
St Mary, Whitechapel	19	1	18	12	1	6	..	8	..
St Mary, Newington	10	..	10	3	..	7	1	..	14
St Mary, Rotherhithe	20	..	20	11	4	8	5	36	55
St Matthew, Bethnal Green	16	..	16	16	5	..	..	41	..
St Paul, Shadwell	21	9	12	9	2	3	3	22	..

* No workhouse.

C. 1765. (Ages under four.) – *continued*

	Born and received	Discharged	Remaining	Of whom from 1 to 4 years old	Of whom dead	Under 12 months old	Of whom dead	Dead per cent from 1 to 4 years old	Dead per cent under 12 months
Parishes in Westminster									
St Anne*	24	9	15	5	1	10	5	20	50
St Clement Danes*	31	6	25	6	4	19	17	66	90
St George, Hanover Square	142	32	110	47	10	63	44	21	70
St James, Westminster	71	38	33	12	6	21	14	50	66
St John and St Margaret	108	20	88	60	17	28	18	28	64
St Martin-in-the-Fields	101	37	64	34	12	30	20	35	66
St Mary, Strand	3	1	2	1	..	1	1	50	100
St Paul, Covent Garden*	15	4	11	6	3	5	2	50	40

* No workhouse.

D. 1768–78. (Ages under six.) Returns from the Register of Parish Infant Poor kept according to 7 Geo. III. c. 39 made to a Committee of the House of Commons appointed to inquire into the state of the infant poor and the working of the Act. *C.J.,* 1 May 1778.

	Received under six	Died	Returned to their parents	Apprenticed	[Died p.c.]
St Giles-in-the-Fields and St George, Bloomsbury	1,479	177	956	319	11·9
St Margaret's and St John's, Westminster	1,109	181	766	172	16·3
St Ann's, Westminster	324	100	152	76	30·8
St James, Westminster	861	215	250	243	24·9
St Clement Danes	257	113	84	89	43·9
St Andrew's above Bars and St George the Martyr	756	137	308	207	18·1
Saffron Hill	231	30	82	95	12·9
St James, Clerkenwell	701	104	456	116	14·8
St Mary, Whitechapel	449	69	102	286	15·3
St Saviour's, Southwark	539	105	205	187	19·4
St Leonard, Shoreditch	586	99	178	185	16·5
St John, Southwark	154	48	65	127	31·1
St Botolph, Aldgate	421	103	103	234	24·4
St Martin's-in-the-Fields	1,512	463	736	321	30·6
St Paul, Covent Garden	51	8	27	36	15·1
	9,727	2,042	4,600	2,794	

E. The Parish Clerks' Summary of the state of Parish Infants in 1773, made according to the Act 1767. J. Hanway, *The Defects of Police,* 1775, p. 102.

Total Number	6,885 *
Transferred from 1772	3,515
Received into workhouses, etc., in 1773	3,370
Ages, above four and not exceeding fourteen	4,623
Under four years	2,252
Of the total number:	
Foundlings, or children found in the streets	104
Illegitimate	797
Casual poor infants	255
Number placed out apprentice in 1773	425
Infants that died in the country at nurse	116
Remained in the country at nurse	1,226

* The children in the City Parishes within the Walls were not included. 1772–3 were years of distress and bad trade.

III. THE GROWTH OF LONDON

A. The Formation of New Parishes

1660. St Paul, Covent Garden, from   St Martin-in-the-Fields
                                                        By 12 Car. II. c. 37. The precinct had already been declared parochial by patent of 7 January 1645.

1670. St Paul, Shadwell, from   Stepney
                                                        By 22 Car. II. c. 14 (private).

1671. Christ Church, Surrey, from   St Saviour's, Southwark
                                                        By 22 & 23 Car. II. c. 28 (private).

1678 or 1686. St Anne, Soho, from   St Martin-in-the-Fields
                                                        By 30 Car. II. c. 7 (private) and 1 Jac. II. c. 20. Consecrated March 1685–6.

1685. St James, Westminster, from   St Martin-in-the-Fields
                                                        By 1 Jac. II. c. 22.

1694. St John, Wapping, from   Whitechapel
                                                        By 5 & 6 Wm. and Mary.*

c. 1720. St Mary, Stratford Bow,† from   Stepney
                                                        Ancient Chapel of ease consecrated as the parish church, 26 March 1719.

1723. St George the Martyr,‡ from   St Andrew's, Holborn.
                                                        Consecrated 1723.**

---

* According to Hatton, *New View of London*, 1708, but the statute is not discoverable among either the public or private acts in the *Statutes at Large*.

† Not included in the Bills of Mortality. Since the first institution of parish registers the district had kept its own records of baptisms and burials and these had never been included in the Stepney Registers or in the London Bills. Lysons, *Environs of London*, iii, p. 446 n.

‡ These parishes remained united with their mother parish for purposes of poor relief and local government.

** By 10 Anne c. 11 (an extension of 9 Anne c. 22) for building fifty new churches in and about London and Westminster, the Commissioners under the Act might describe the new parish by a deed enrolled in Chancery, and after enrolment and the consecration of the church, the district should become a parish.

1724. St George, Hanover Square, from	St Martin-in-the-Fields Consecrated 1724.
1728. St John, Westminster,* from	St Margaret's, Westminster By 1 Geo. II, statute 2 c. 15.
1729. Christ Church, Spitalfields, from	Stepney By 2 Geo. II. c. 10.
1729. St George's in the East (formerly the hamlet of Wapping-Stepney), from	Stepney By 2 Geo. II. c. 30.
1730. St Anne, Limehouse, from	Stepney By 3 Geo. II. c. 17.
1731. St George, Bloomsbury,* from	St Giles-in-the-Fields By 3 Geo. II. c. 19.
1733. St John, Southwark (Horselydown), from	St Olave. By 6 Geo. II. c. 11.
1733. St Luke, Old Street, from	St Giles without Cripplegate. By 6 Geo. III. c. 28.
1743. St Matthew, Bethnal Green, from	Stepney. By 16 Geo. II. c. 28.

* These parishes remained united with their mother parish for purposes of poor relief and local government.

B. Houses and Population

	New houses built[1]		Number of houses				Population		Mean number in a house, 1801
	1620–56	1656–77	1708[2]	1732[3]	c. 1737[4]	1801[5]	1710–11[6]	1801[5]	
CITY WITHOUT THE WALLS									
St Andrew's Holborn	..	550*	700	..	737	636+16	..	5,511	8·8
St Bartholomew the Great	47	11	c. 300	324	324	324+13	..	2,645	8·1
St Bartholomew the Less	..	..	134[7]	143	141	68+0	..	471	6·9
St Botolph without Aldersgate	30*	102*	c. 700*[8]	c. 700*	546	557+24	6,000*	4,161	7·4
St Botolph without Aldgate	520*	50*	1,300	1,300	1,239	1,171+31	24,600*	8,689	7·4
St Botolph without Bishopsgate[9]	265	208	1,676	c. 1,800	1,709	1,285+48	10,056	10,314	8·0
St Bride	146	126	c. 1,400	c. 1,400	1,052	830+51	..	7,078	8·5
Bridewell Precinct	..	..	..	91	91	61+2	..	453	7·2
St Dunstan in the West	..	72	c. 458	858	471	405+7	..	3,021	7·4
St Giles without Cripplegate	517*	..	c. 4,000*	1,800	1,895	1,509+28	42,600*	11,446	7·5
St Sepulchre	127*	35*	c. 1,400	..	1,226	856+36	15,000*	8,092	9·4
Precinct of Whitefriars	..	..	213	..	213	88+1	..	783	8·8
Minories	6	16	120	123	129	93+5	..	644	6·9
MIDDLESEX									
FINSBURY DIVISION									
Old Artillery Ground (Liberty)	..	..	..	..	202	185+5	..	1,428	7·7
Glass House Yard (Liberty)[8]	..	..	..	..	160	152+2	..	1,221	8·0
St James, Clerkenwell	..	199	1,146	1,900	1,889	3,320+107	9,000	23,396	7·2
St Luke, Old Street	..	..	..	3,010	3,035	3,776+61	..	26,881	7·1
St Mary, Islington	..	25	325	c. 937	502	1,665+80	..	10,212	6·1
St Mary, Stoke Newington	..	..	..	..	..	208+13	..	1,462	7·0
St Sepulchre's	..	..	359	..	676	531+6	..	3,768	7·0

* No distinction between the City and Middlesex parts of the parish.

B. Houses and Population – continued

HOLBORN DIVISION	New houses built[1]		Number of houses				Population		Mean number in a house, 1801
	1620–56	1656–77	1708[2]	1732[3]	c. 1737[4]	1801[5]	1710–11[6]	1801[5]	
St Andrew's, Holborn	..	..	c. 2,100	..	1,863	1,858 + 51	30,000[10]	15,932	8·5
St George the Martyr	..	..	..	666	782	721 + 15	..	6,273	8·7
St Clement Danes	..	..	..	..	..	660 + 21	..	4,144	6·2
Duchy of Lancaster (Liberty)	..	..	..	..	..	71 + 4	..	474	6·2
St Giles-in-the-Fields	141	889	c. 3,000	above 2,000	2,010	2,792 + 137	34,800	28,764	10·3
St George, Bloomsbury	..	..	..	c. 900	954	916 + 16	..	7,738	8·4
St John, Hampstead	..	..	..	..	..	691 + 47	..	4,343	6·4
St Marylebone	..	..	..	..	577	7,209 + 555	..	63,982	8·8
Paddington	..	..	..	..	..	324 + 33	..	1,881	5·8
St Pancras	..	..	..	..	122"	4,173 + 253	..	31,779	7·6
Rolls Liberty	..	..	c. 188	220	291	330 + 14	..	2,409	7·0
Savoy Liberty	..	..	..	76	..	38 + 2	..	320	8·4
Saffron Hill, Hatton Garden and Ely Rents (Liberties)	..	..	819	..	791	900 + 39	..	7,500	8·3
TOWER DIVISION									
St Anne, Limehouse	..	..	..	c. 1,000	1,262	755 + 11	7,020	4,678	6·1
St Botolph, Aldgate	..	..	c. 1,000	c. 1,200	..	1,097 + 25	..	6,153	5·6
St Dunstan's, Stepney[12]	1,625	2,137	c. 8,000[12]	5–6,000[12]	4,338[12]	..	..	..	..
Christchurch, Spitalfields[13]	..	..	..	c. 2,190	2,244	1,876 + 145	21,420	15,091	8·0
St George-in-the-East	..	..	..	above 2,000	1,946	4,029 + 119	19,020	21,170	5·2
St John, Hackney	..	51	..	above 600	722	2,050 + 84	..	12,730	6·2
St John, Wapping	..	..	1,292	c. 1,600	1,342	998 + 38	7,500	5,889	5·9
St Leonards, Shoreditch	348	144	c. 2,000	c. 2,500	2,266	5,732 + 381	13,200	34,766	6·0

B. Houses and Population – continued

	New houses built[1]		Number of houses				Population		Mean number in a house, 1801
	1620–56	1656–77	1708[2]	1732[3]	c. 1737[4]	1801[5]	1710–11[5]	1801[6]	
TOWER DIVISION – Continued									
St Mary, Whitechapel	291	423	c. 1,876	3–4,000	2,792	3,497 + 192	18,000	23,666	6·7
St Mary, Stratford Bow	..	..	..	..	..	340 + 10	..	2,101	6·1
St Matthew, Bethnal Green[13]	..	..	..	..	1,659	3,586 + 234	8,496	23,310	6·5
Mile End, New Town (hamlet)	..	..	..	..	393	610 + 26	6,462	5,253	8·6
Mile End, Old Town (hamlet)	..	..	..	..	406	1,627 + 38	2,820	9,848	6·0
Norton Falgate (Liberty)	..	..	..	..	261	252 + 8	..	1,752	6·9
St Paul, Shadwell	..	289	1,626[14]	1,800	1,696	1,550 + 48	13,002	8,828	5·6
Poplar and Blackwall (hamlets)	..	..	..	c. 200	497	756 + 30	5,136	4,493	5·9
Ratcliffe (hamlet)	..	..	..	..	1,383	925 + 16	21,360	5,666	6·7
St Katherine's, Tower (Liberty)	51	24	850	c. 867	..	505 + 18	..	2,652	5·2
Liberty of the Tower Without	..	..	..	..	..	82 + 2	..	563	6·8
WESTMINSTER									
St Anne	..	..	c. 1,500	c. 1,500	337	1,294 + 88	12,000	11,637	8·9
St Clement Danes	183	253	1,729	1,750	1,691	961 + 37[15]	11,004	8,717[15]	9·0
St George, Hanover Square	..	..	..	c. 1,432	1,909	4,344 + 91	..	38,440	8·8
St James	..	..	c. 3,000	c. 4,300	3,517	3,430 + 169	30,000	34,462	10·0
St Margaret	..	490	3,039	above 2,350	3,282	2,357 + 97	28,000	17,508	7·3
St John	..	..	..	c. 1,660	..	1,268 + 121	..	8,375	6·6
St Martin-in-the-Fields	..	1,780	3,773	c. 5,000	3,089	2,791 + 112	40,000	25,752	9·2
St Mary le Strand	..	37[16]	c. 300[17]	266	326	166 + 9	..	1,704	10·2
St Paul, Covent Garden	342	59	above 500	600	631	598 + 22	4,950	4,992	8·3
The Verge of the Palaces of Whitehall and St James	..	..	..	..	..	241 + 11	..	1,685	6·9

B. Houses and Population – continued

	New houses built[1]		Number of houses				Population		Mean number in a house, 1801
	1620–56	1656–77	1708[2]	1732[3]	c. 1737[4]	1801[5]	1710–11[6]	1801[5]	
THE BOROUGH OF SOUTHWARK (BRIDGE WARD WITHOUT)									
St George	144	231	740	above 740	1,503	3,811+153	7,500	22,293	5·8
St John	..	..	..	..	1,255	1,531+ 25	..	8,892	5·8
St Olave	147	385	c. 200[18]	3,000	2,012	1,336+ 38	17,400	7,481	5·5
St Saviour's	339	..	c. 2,500	..	2,554	2,547+114	14,004	15,596	6·1
St Thomas	160	..	c. 300	c. 130	229	178+ 2	..	2,078[19]	11·6
SURREY									
Christchurch[20]	..	100	c. 800	c. 1,000	1,011	1,530+ 56	3,102	9,933	6·4
Bermondsey	528	349	c. 1,500	1,900	1,111	3,137+ 66	12,000	17,169	5·4
Lambeth	383	185	c. 1,350	..	1,625	4,789+220	..	27,939	5·8
Newington	247	107	620	700	751	2,865+ 75	..	14,847	5·1
Rotherhithe	59	219	1,145	1,500	1,320	1,780+ 16	5,502	10,296	5·7

Notes to Appendix III *B.*

1. A. *Particular of new Buildings within the Bills of Mortality and without the City* within the Walls *now taken by the Churchwardens of the several parishes and the . . . Account of new Houses from 1620 to 1656.* The returns for 1620–56 were those made in connexion with Cromwell's levy in 1656 on houses built since 1620; it was supposed that the numbers fell short of the houses built and the returns for 'some parishes' were missing. ibid. The returns of 1656–77 were made in connexion with the Bill to tax houses built since 1656, see Chapter 2.

2. Hatton, *New View of London,* 1708.

3. *New Remarks of London by the Company of Parish Clerks,* 1732.

4. Maitland, *History of London,* editions of 1739 and 1756. There is no indication of the precise date of the returns, which, except in the case of Bethnal Green are the same in both editions. In the later edition the statute for making the hamlet into a parish is quoted in full, this estimates the houses at 'about 1,800', population at 'over 15,000' but the usual returns of houses, parish officers, etc., are omitted; in the earlier edition they are included, Middleton in his *Agriculture of Middlesex,* 1798, speaks of Maitland's returns as made for 1737.

5. *Population Returns,* 1801. In the 'houses' column the second figure stands for unoccupied houses.

6. An estimate of the population in those parishes 'where additional churches are deemed to be most needed', returned by Convocation to Parliament. The figures are obtained by multiplying the supposed number of 'families' by six, in two cases (St Martin's and St James, Westminster) by ten, and in one (St Margaret's, Westminster) by seven. *C. J.,* 10 March 1710–11. Many of the totals are clearly exaggerated.

7. Not including the Hospital.

8. The Middlesex part of this parish was the Liberty of Glasshouse Yard. Maitland writes, 'till of late (1739) there was but one government in this parish, but the poor of this liberty having increased considerably of late, occasioned the City liberty to separate from them and each to maintain its own poor'. *History . . . 1756,* ii, p. 1351.

9. In the Census returns the positions of St Botolph, Bishopsgate and St Botolph, Billingsgate are reversed, the latter appearing (incorrectly) in the City without the Walls.

10. Would include the Liberty of Saffron Hill, etc., as well as the future parish of St George the Martyr, Queen Square.

11. Such houses as are 'contiguous to the suburbs of London'.

12. Stepney was little more than a geographical expression after its hamlets were recognized as separate units for poor relief, rating, etc. See *Survey of Stepney,* 1703, by Joel Gascoyne in the Crace Collection which shows the parish divided between the hamlets. The numbers for Stepney purport to be the number of houses in the hamlets which had not become parishes.

13. See note 11, Chapter 2.   14. 'Besides the rooms for 228 Alms people.'

15. See under Middlesex, Holborn Division.

16. Returned as the Savoy, whose chapel was used as the parish church of St Mary le Strand until the latter was rebuilt (consecrated January 1723–4) births and deaths being recorded in the Savoy Registers and Bills of Mortality.

17. Includes the houses in the Savoy (see Holborn Division) but does not include 76 shops in the New Exchange.

18. A misprint for 2,000?   19. Not including St Thomas's Hospital, population 429.

20. See note 5, Chapter 1.

C. Changes in the Rateable Value of London Parishes

There is no basis for an exact comparison of the rateable value of Middlesex parishes at different periods of the eighteenth century, because till 1797 the county rate was a definite sum levied in a fixed proportion on the different parishes and liberties. It was stereotyped by an Act of 1739 (12 Geo. II. c. 29) for the consolidation of various county payments which ordered that the rate was to be assessed on the different parishes in the proportion which had been customary and was to be paid out of the poor rate. The amount of the county rate was fixed from time to time and additional money was also raised by multiplying the number of rates. County expenditure increased rapidly, especially after 1757; it was chiefly for prisons, bridges, the passing of vagrants to their place of settlement, and (after 1757) the allowance made to the families of men serving with the militia. In 1704 a county rate was £400, after 1739 it was £1,200, in October 1757 it was raised to £1,600 and by 1796 it had become £11,000.

As the effect of the Act of 1739 had been to fix the proportions paid by the parishes at those which had been customary in 1709, when Covent Garden had been a fashionable district and Marylebone a country village, the incidence of the rate became grossly unfair. In 1779 the parish officers of Covent Garden appealed to Quarter Sessions against the rate. Their parish was charged with a sum of £69.5, its rental value as assessed to the poor rate being under £30,000, while Marylebone, whose assessed rental value was about £140,000, paid only £7.5. The Sessions decided that they had no power to alter the assessment. In 1797, on petitions from many of the Middlesex parishes, an Act (37 Geo. III. c. 65) was passed ordering the county rates to be levied on the same basis as the poor's rate, each parish to make a return of the rental assessed to the poor and to specify the relation between the assessment and the actual value. Protests however were made by the parishes of Marylebone and St Pancras against 'this equalizing system of property, founded on the visionary basis of equity in opposition to the existing and the genuine principles of the Constitution'*.

	Assessment of a county rate of £1,200 on the hundred of Ossulston, according to the Act of 1739. (c. 1750) (From Middlesex *Order Books*)			Incidence of a rate of ¾d. in the pound, January 1800. ibid.		
	£	s.	d.	£	s.	d.
Westminster Division						
St Margaret	65	2	6	215	11	3
St Martin-in-the-Fields	91	2	4½	405	17	9
St George, Hanover Square	45	11	3	1,150	5	0
St James	90	19	6	508	10	3
St Clement Danes	35	0	3	99	1	9

* For the number and value of County rates see the Middlesex *Order Books, passim.* For the appeal of 1779 see Middlesex *Sessions Books* under dates 8 July 1779 and 21 May 1791. For the petitions for and against the Bill of 1797 see *C. J.* 24 February, 6 and 24 April 1797. (The petition quoted is that of St Pancras.)

	Assessment of a county rate of £1,200 on the hundred of Ossulston, according to the Act of 1739. (c. 1750) (From Middlesex *Order Books*)			Incidence of a rate of ¾d. in the pound, Jan. 1800. (ibid.)		
	£	s.	d.	£	s.	d.
Westmister Division – continued						
St Mary le Strand	8	15	0	13	11	6
St Anne	41	11	4½	184	5	6
St Paul, Covent Garden	30	8	1½	106	15	6
	408	10	4½			
Holborn Division						
St Giles-in-the-Fields	80	0	0	416	12	0
St Andrew, Holborn	91	2	4½	281	2	0
Liberty of Saffron Hill, Hatton Garden and Ely Rents	17	11	4½	55	15	6
The Rolls	10	10	9	28	6	0
St Pancras	11	7	6	352	6	9
Hampstead	7	5	6	56	18	0
St Marylebone	4	7	9	1,116	15	6
Paddington	2	19	0	14	7	9
St Clement Danes, Duchy Liberty	29	15	3	78	9	9
St Mary le Strand	8	10	1½	21	9	9
Precinct of the Savoy	4	5	1½	7	16	3
	234	12	0			
Finsbury Division						
St Luke	24	18	6½	240	17	0
Liberty of Glass House Yard	3	11	2½	7	5	6
St Sepulchre	10	12	3	32	16	3
St James, Clerkenwell	18	5	6	175	6	0
St Mary, Islington	16	18	9	136	16	6
Stoke Newington	3	6	6	20	4	9
Hornsey	8	7	3	32	16	3
Friern Barnet	2	10	9	7	9	8
Finchley	5	5	6	21	8	0
	93	11	3			
The Tower Division						
St Mary, Whitechapel	30	5	6	127	18	9
Christchurch	20	16	6	80	11	0
St Leonard, Shoreditch	17	19	3	188	5	6
Norton Falgate	4	9	3	12	12	9
St John, Hackney	17	16	9	141	3	9
Bethnal Green	10	4	3	87	0	0
Mile End, Old Town	7	13	9	55	1	6
Mile End, New Town	2	16	0	19	5	3

The Tower Division—continued

	£	s	d	£	s	d
St Mary at Stratford Bow	3	18	4½	15	15	0
St Leonard, Bromley	4	6	7½	12	15	3
Poplar and Blackwall	8	8	3	33	17	6
St Anne, Limehouse	7	9	6	23	10	6
Ratcliff	12	19	7½	30	9	6
St Paul, Shadwell	16	12	6	40	5	6
St George	19	8	1½	94	18	9
St John, Wapping	17	3	3	46	8	0
Liberty of East Smithfield	14	4	9	46	8	6
Precinct of St Katherine	8	2	10½	18	13	6
	224	5	1½			

The Liberty of the Tower

	£	s	d		
The Liberty of the Tower within	11	12	0	..	
The Liberty of the Tower without	1	12	0	..	
The Liberty of the Old Artillery Ground	4	0	10½	..	
Parish of Trinity Minories	2	11	0*	..	
	8	8	1½*		

Kensington Division

	£	s	d	£	s	d
Kensington	11	12	0	105	17	9
Chelsea	7	16	3	133	9	0

* Never collected, and assessment eventually given up, the Tower Liberty being a royalty, no part administratively of the County of Middlesex.

IV. APPRENTICESHIP CASES FROM THE MIDDLESEX SESSIONS RECORDS

* Denotes a parish apprentice   † An apprentice bound by a charity

1. Benjamin Edge was in 1710 discharged from his apprenticeship with Thomas Jackson of Goodman's Fields, tallyman, upon proof that the said Jackson had caused him to be impressed into His Majesty's service from his said master's house, and the said apprentice is very apprehensive his master will convey or cause him to be conveyed away into some place of danger. (January 1709–10, Calendar.)

2. Joseph Vincent discharged from Peter Bingham of Shoreditch, baker, who by his severity hath so affrighted and terrified the said apprentice that when he apprehended his master's anger he would sometime abscond and hide himself from his rage and violence. His master had not allowed him sufficient clothing, and being barefoot, gave him sixpence to buy a pair of shoes. Not being able to buy a pair for sixpence he durst not go home for fear of his master's furious passion

till about eight o'clock of the night, when his master refused to admit him in and the next day caused him to be sent to the House of Correction where he has remained ever since at hard labour. The master was ordered to deliver to the boy's mother a piece of cloth belonging to the apprentice, to enable her to clothe her son. (April 1711, Cal.)

3. Sarah Gibson discharged from her apprenticeship to Joanna Worthington of St Andrew's Holborn widow, mantua-maker, upon proof that the said Sarah, instead of learning the trade of a mantua-maker had been employed in common household work, cleansing and washing lodgers' rooms and had been immoderately beaten and not allowed sufficient food. (July 1715, Cal.)

4. Richard Morgan released from apprenticeship to Michael Beadle of St Giles, shoemaker. He was first apprenticed to Thomas Barker of the same parish and trade but as his master evilly treated him he was released from his indentures and bound to Beadle, who also ill-used him and in May last was arrested for debt and carried to Wood Street Compter, where he still remains unable to provide for his apprentice. (July 1717, Cal.)

5. John Besswick apprenticed in 1715 to Peter Steel of St James Westminster, bricklayer, petitioned that the said Steel caused him to make bricks and burn them in his cellar, that he is unable to learn the trade in consequence and that his said master has given him immoderate chastisement. Now, upon information that the said Steel has caused his apprentice to do other business than that of a bricklayer, and has beaten him, kicked him on the groin, struck him with the iron part of a trowel and with the edge of a plumb rule, the said apprentice is to be discharged. (April 1719, Cal.)

6. Mary Neale discharged from Elizabeth Prendergast, mantua-maker, who had set up a victualling house and obliged her said apprentice to draw drink and carry it abroad to customers, fetch in pots and scour them and to wait upon nine African recruits whom the said Elizabeth had taken into her house to bed and board. (May 1721, Cal.)

7. Samuel Wood discharged from James Heley, goldsmith. He had not been instructed in the art of a goldsmith or in the business of a buckle maker, which Heley mostly followed, but was wholly employed in drawing potts of drink and carrying the same out to his customers. About three months ago Heley broke and went into the Mint. He had not only beaten him in a most inhuman manner, but had not provided him with common necessaries. (April 1722, Cal.)

8. John Perry was discharged from James Edgerton of St Martin's in the Fields, cordwainer, who had very much beat and abused him and had sometime since conveyed the petitioner on ship for Ireland, but being driven back by stress of weather, left him in Liverpool in Lancashire without anything to subsist upon. His master went from thence to Ireland and hath not been heard of since. (October 1724, Cal.)

9. Edward Carr was discharged from George Beall of St Martin's in the Fields, house carver. His master had neglected his business, set up a dog chaise, compelling Carr to run before the said chaise as his footman for the space of a year; he

lost all his business, ran himself into debt and absconded leaving his apprentice in a miserable and starving condition. The court ordered £6 of the apprentice fee to be refunded to Carr to enable him to put himself to another master. (June 1728, Cal.)

10. Henry Hurst discharged from John Merchant of Poland Street, barber and perriwig maker, who had not allowed him sufficient meat, drink, washing and lodging, and had absented himself from his house for fear of being arrested for debt, whereby petitioner could not be sufficiently instructed in his trade, had several times pawned the petitioner's clothes without his consent and entered himself a soldier in the Guards. (January 1728–9, Cal.)

11. Nicholas Scotcher was discharged from John Turner, of St James Westminster, blacksmith, who had given him such cruel usage that 'he is bursten'; he took no care to have him cured and even refused to let a surgeon (sent by petitioner's mother) look after him. (October 1729, Cal.)

12. Sarah Wise was discharged from Samuel Elwick of St James Clerkenwell. She had been put to him to learn the art and mystery of a hair-twist for the term of ten years and had served nearly five, during which he had only given her one stuff gown and one bays petticoat, and had not provided her with enough to eat and drink so that she has had to beg bread from her neighbours. Her 'bed is a very small flock bed and six of them lays therein, some at the foot and some at the head' Her master has been in Newgate jail for six months so that she is left destitute and 'turned out into the wide world'. (February 1729–30.)

13. William Adams was discharged from Joseph Bidwell of the parish of St Giles in the Fields, carpenter, upon complaint that his master did not instruct him in his trade, but employed him 'in driving a chair with boys and girls in it for halfe-pence a piece drawn by two or three dogs and is sent for this purpose to most of the little fairs about this town'. Petitioner's parents and others had reproved Bidwell who said he would employ the petitioner to black shoes about the streets the remaining part of his time, and had refused to find clothes according to the indentures. Petitioner's master and mistress had pawned the clothes provided by his parents. (August 1732, Cal.)

* 14. William Martin, a parish child, discharged from Henry Price, tailor in St Botolph without Aldgate, on the application of the officers of the said parish. Jack Carter gave evidence that he had been to Prices' house and found that he had gone to Boston in New England. (August 1733, Cal.)

15. John Plummer was released from John Gilbert of Stepney, framework knitter, who being involved in debt had made himself a prisoner in the Rules of the King's Bench prison (which is far distant from the apprentice's mother and friends) had whipped him with a horsewhip and bruised his arms shoulders and back with the butt end thereof so that it must have mortified had not great care been taken in due time. His master had not allowed him sufficient clothing, his shoes have great holes through the soles thereof whereby his health is much endangered. (May 1736, Cal.)

16. Richard Jones discharged from Thomas Dudfield of Wapping, sail-maker.

He was bound in 1734 but his master left off his trade and kept an alehouse and obliged the apprentice to draw and carry out beer, which he has complied with for fear of being evilly treated. Fourteen months ago Dudfield failed and has since absconded. (September 1737, Cal.)

17. Philip Foster was discharged from Henry Basting of Crown Court, St Anne's parish, Westminster, bricklayer, who far from performing the covenants then agreed on (five years before) when Foster was bound to him, namely, instructing him in his business and finding him food and raiment, has often, through 'an extravagant and vile way of living' deserted his apprentice, 'in such a manner that he has not only become an object of charity, but even of the world's censure.' (June 1738, Cal.)

18. John Sharp petitioned to be discharged from Mr James Willis writing master of St Anne's Limehouse. He had served upwards of five years. . . . For a year past had not had sufficient meat and drink nor had his master found him in washing. He was often beaten with a cane and was seldom without bruises in the face having had black eyes for a month together. He was struck a violent blow on the head with a ruler and was obliged to have the assistance of a surgeon and his master turned him out of the house, swearing he would break his neck downstairs. The Court found there was not sufficient reason to discharge the apprentice but Willis stated he was ready to part with Sharp on his mother paying him forty shillings. (February 1740–41, Cal.)

† 19. James Clarke was discharged from Peter Wigley of Chancery Lane, peruke-maker who became a bankrupt in August 1739 and ever since has been no settled housekeeper. Wigley has frequently beaten him with a truncheon by which means he was so bruised that he was hardly able to dress himself. The Court finds that the Corporation of the Sons of the Clergy paid £15 to Wigley, Clarke being the son of a clergyman. Wigley was ordered to refund £5. (October 1740, Cal.)

20. Esau Smith was discharged from William Smith of St Sepulchre's, Middlesex‡ (the master failing to appear in court). His master soon after the binding, being much in debt, went to Birmingham so that he was forced 'to apply to his parents for maintenance, which out of charity they indulged him in for fourteen days'. His master's wife 'with specious and fair promises . . .' prevailed on petitioner to go to Birmingham, where she said his master had a very good business. He found him a journeyman only, and 'during petitioner's stay in Birmingham he was used in a very cruel and barbarous manner by his said master who horsewhipped him and obliged him to work night and day and at the same time deprived him of the necessaries of life'. (Middlesex Records, *Sessions Book* (MS.), 13 January 1746.)

* 21. Francis Blandy, a parish apprentice was discharged from Robert Lane, leather dresser of St James Westminster, to whom he was bound by the parish of St Andrew Holborn in 1742, to serve till the age of twenty-four. About eighteen months ago Lane 'failed and went away by night . . . and took the petitioner with him as far as Newcastle, where he left him without any person to take care of him.'

‡ Trade not stated.

Petitioner was almost starved before he could get back to town to his mother with whom he has been ever since. He cannot learn where his master is gone but believes Scotland. 'There being no probability of his return, petitioner will be inevitably ruined unless discharged. . . .' (ibid., 16 December 1747.)

22. Davis Pritchard was discharged from William Bowler of Aldgate, Middlesex, barber and peruke maker. Bowler took no care to instruct the petitioner, 'being frequently drunk and almost continually absent from his shop. . . . Being arrested for a large sum [he] caused himself to be removed to the Rules of the Fleet Prison and conveyed off all his goods . . . and shut up his shop, and sent petitioner home to his friends, so that in case they had not relieved him . . . he must have perished in the street. . . . The petitioner and his friends have several times applyd to the said William Bowler requesting him to provide for the petitioner but . . . he . . . only said petitioner might come and live with him which is in a garrett at an alehouse in the Rules aforesaid, where the said Bowler has no manner of business and intends as the petitioner is informed to turn schoolmaster.' (ibid., 22 April 1748.)

23. Charles Cuplinn discharged from Walter Simmons of St Anne's Westminster, bricklayer, who has neglected to instruct the petitioner, has not sufficient business to employ him, has 'frequently given him stinking and unwholesome foods, and upon complaint thereof hath beaten him and threatened to kill him. In September last he left his house in Drury lane where he left petitioner and where he carries on his trade and took an alehouse in the parish of Stepney where he principally resides so that petitioner is obliged to go almost every night to . . . Stepney whereby he is under great apprehensions of being some time or other in his passage over the fields in that parish murdered or stript by reason those fields are now and for sometime past have been greatly infested by thieves and robbers. . . .' (ibid., 18 January 1750–51.)

* 24. Sarah Bennett was discharged, on the petition of the overseers of Chelsea, from George Good, victualler, to whom she had been bound by the parish in August 1749 at the age of eleven, till the age of twenty-one or marriage. Her mistress beat and abused her barbarously so the girl came to the parish officers and complained that 'she was afraid of being killed, her mistress was so extreme passionate'. Mistress and apprentice were taken before a justice and the mistress 'promised to be more favourable to the girl for the future, but the very same day beat and abused the girl most violently without any the least provocation only because the girl had been with the parish officers to complain'. The girl ran back to the parish officers and had been kept in the workhouse ever since. The overseers pray for her discharge that she may be bound to someone else and that the forty shillings paid by the parish may be refunded. The Court ordered twenty shillings to be refunded and all the clothes of the apprentice to be delivered up. (ibid., 19 January 1750–51.)‡

‡ An exceptional case in two ways: first, because the parish had not followed the usual practice of apprenticing to a master in some other parish; secondly, because this is a case that could have been decided by two justices without coming before the Sessions.

25. John Edlestone discharged from John Tudway, tinplate worker of St Giles in the Fields, by consent of his master, to whom he had been bound for £15. He was treated very cruelly 'by horsewhipping, knocking him down with his fist and striking him with other blunt weapons that first came to hand.' He applied to a justice for a warrant against his master, who was discharged on promising better behaviour. He declared to petitioner that 'he had done the worst day's work he had ever done in his life and that if he could not punish . . . him one way he would the other by letting him go like a blackguard in raggs before he should have any better. . . . The hours of working in the petitioner's trade are from six in the morning to nine at night. After nine, having served almost four years [he] some-times went to see his friends. . . . And when he came home about ten o'clock, his master ordered his family not to let him into his house . . . so that petitioner hath been obliged to walk the streets all night for which reason . . . [he] was on com-plaint of his master committed to the House of Correction . . . and that . . . being tired out with ill-treatment, did in . . . June last enter himself on one of His Majesty's ships of war, where after he had been some time his friends prevailed on him to return to his said master . . . [who] . . . absolutely refused . . . to let . . . him come into his house to work at his trade, nor will he either consent to turn the petitioner over to another master or to give him up his indenture to be cancelled, so that the petitioner must unavoidably have been a vagrant about the streets for six months past . . . unless he had been received and supported by his friends.' (ibid., 23 February 1753.)

* 26. Robert Hawkes, apprenticed by the parish of Low Layton, Essex about eleven years ago to John Dumbleton pump-maker who keeps a public-house in Whitechapel to learn the art and mystery of a pump-maker, and still has four years to serve, petitions for discharge. 'For the whole eleven years . . . instead of being learnt his trade of a pump-maker he hath been almost constantly employed in drawing of beer, both Sundays and working days and has never been suffered to go to Church once. . . . And the petitioner hath undergone violent severities and ill usage . . . during the whole term . . . by being beat with sticks and whips and by flinging petitioner in a horse pond on a cold frosty morning without the least provocation. And on the 14th day of March last the petitioner's master knockt him down with a hand saw and beat and bruised the petitioner so violently that he was not able to see out of his eyes for some days.' He was discharged. (ibid., 10 April 1755.)

27. The father of William Newton prays for his son's discharge from James Noakes, watch-movement-maker of Charter House Square. In August last the boy 'not only with the consent but even at the instigation of his said master, as the petitioner is credibly informed . . . went on board His Majesty's ship The Flamborough's Prize'. He has received no complaints of his son who 'would have made him a faithful and diligent apprentice so far as depended on him and the petitioner has been informed . . . that he had been of late many times beaten . . . for not being able to accomplish a branch of the business about which he had not been employed a reasonable time . . . [for] . . . any proficiency therein, and the

petitioner really thinks his said master took this harsh and cruel method to weary out the said William Newton and . . . make him desirous to quit his service.' (ibid., 16 September 1757.)

28. William Dimon, bound April 1764, prays for discharge from Thomas Beare, chaser and engraver (apprentice fee £20). For about six months Beare 'kept a house in Southampton Buildings, Holborn and had a journeyman and himself both working . . . but soon afterwards the said Thomas took a profligate course of life and thereby lost very near the whole of his business and got greatly into debt and for some months past has been obliged to abscond and screen himself in the Verge of the Court . . . for many months past . . . the petitioner had not anything to do or anyone to instruct him, his master keeping very disorderly hours. . . . His said master and his wife insist on the petitioner's employing his time in making their fires and doing other household work and also looking after their young child of about eight months old. . . . The petitioner's master (when he can safely gett there) resorted to a house in the Savoy . . . which had a balcony projecting over the water where many lighters laden with coals lie . . . his said master had several times obliged the petitioner to go on board such lighters in the night time and fill pails which his master hauled up . . . for his own use.' He was discharged, no one appearing for the petitioner. (ibid., 18 January 1766.)

29. Francis le Strange bound 1774 to George Freeland, stationer, of the Liberty of the Rolls for £21 prays discharge. He is not allowed enough food 'and that often unwholesome and not fit for any Christian and that the tea . . . is always so bad and nauscious that he is obliged to throw the greatest part of it away'. When there were three apprentices 'all three lay together in one bed in a small cock loft. . . . The petitioner's master being . . . very much addicted to drinking he often staying out till twelve, one, two, three, and four o'clock in the morning when the petitioner's said mistress used always to send him and the other apprentices . . . when so out (which has sometimes been six or seven nights together) to all the public-houses in Holborn and the Strand and all round the neighbourhood and it is very seldom they can find him and when the public-houses are shut up he then goes to the watch-house where they are sure of finding him, and it is often impossible to get him home and are always obliged to sit up till he does come home notwithstanding which they are often obliged to be up at four, five and six . . . in the morning to their writing'. In the following Sessions the petitioner and other apprentice aged twelve who had been beaten and turned out of doors were discharged, the master being ordered to repay the £21 received from the father of the younger boy. (ibid., February and March 1778.)

† 30. William Gogney, son of William Gogney, citizen and farrier deceased prayed for discharge from Richard Meach [watchmaker?] of Clerkenwell to whom he had been bound by the Governors of Christ's Hospital for £10. His master has neglected to teach him and 'has lately . . . sold off his tools and implements and declined his business and without the consent of the petitioner or his friends

intends to make a property of him . . . and assign him over to another person in a different branch for a consideration of £30 which the said person refusing to pay, the petitioner is like to be harassed and hawked about from one person to another (untill his said master has made his bargain of him) and thereby lose all his further time of instruction. . . . Notwithstanding the petitioner has but one year and seven months to serve of his time, yet he is not so proficient . . . as he ought to be by reason of his said master's neglecting to teach . . . him, and is not capable when out of his time of earning more than ten or twelve shillings instead of thirty shillings or more per week as he ought to have done in case he had been properly instructed'. He is discharged. (ibid., 13 January 1780.)

31. William Stephenson the son of a coachmaster deceased, of St Giles in the Fields, who in 1789 being aged fourteen, put himself apprentice to Andrew Gilchrist of 92 Wardour Street, upholder and cabinet-maker for fifteen guineas, prays discharge. . . . 'He had not been very long with the said Andrew Gilchrist when he found that [he] lett lodgings to kept women and some of them boarded with him and he became very much reduced in his circumstances and about two years ago was arrested and went to Newgate . . . he . . . obtained a letter of licence for one year . . . but for debts contracted since and not performing his engagements in the said letter, in November last . . .' was arrested, went to the King's Bench, thence to the Fleet, and 'is in very insolvent circumstances'. A great part of his furniture had been conveyed away secretly, his landlord made a distress for rent. All or most of his customers are women of the town 'and a great part of petitioner's time was employed in going after them for money, some of them paying in instalments at a guinea and half a guinea per week and was frequently obliged to go on the Lord's day. . . . The petitioner is very deficient in his business . . . he has been taught nothing of the cabinet or upholstery business . . . only put to making deal tables'. His master has refused to discharge him or turn him over, but 'insisted the petitioner should bring his chest of tools which he had purchased with his own money to the Fleet prison to work there . . . he said they would serve them both to work with, he not having any tools of his own. . . . He has been advised not to do so, the said Andrew Gilchrist not having any business to do and as the petitioner conceived, a very improper place for him to work or be in'. He was discharged. (ibid., April 1793.)

32. John Jefferd was discharged from John Hall of Cross Lane Long Acre, coach carver to whom he had been bound in 1797 for £20. 'About twelve months ago the said John Hall took a public-house in Parker's Lane, St Giles where he lodged the petitioner in a garrett with four beds and where any person who came for a night's lodging might and did sleep, in consequence of which the petitioner found vermin upon his body and linen . . . [He] had frequently beat petitioner in a very severe and cruel manner . . . [and] . . . had not sufficient business to keep petitioner in employment. . . .' (ibid., 24 April 1799.)

† 33. Richard Pack prayed for the discharge of his son from William Taylor, boot- and shoe-maker of Homer Street, Paddington to whom he had been bound in December 1813 by the Asylum for Deaf and Dumb Children for a fee of £5

paid by the Society and £15 paid by the petitioner. The apprentice had been chiefly employed in cleaning old boots and shoes, he had latterly been kept very short of food. About a fortnight since the master quitted his residence, locked up his house and had not since returned. The boy went home to the petitioner, who also asked for an order for the fee paid to be refunded. The apprentice was discharged but no order was made for repayment of any part of the fee. (ibid., September 1814.)

Though not so numerous as apprentices' petitions, there are also many petitions from masters for the discharge of an apprentice who spoils work repeatedly or is an impossible inmate of the household, for instance:

34. Elijah Peck petitioned for the discharge of his apprentice, bound for a fee of £10 about fourteen months before. After the first three months of his term the boy 'absented himself at eight sundry times both by night and day . . . even for a fortnight together, sometimes for about a week, and at other times has likewise disposed of his clothes and returned . . . sometimes by himself, at other times brought home by the watchman all in rags. . . . It was not safe to lodge and entertain the said apprentice any longer for that by his own confession at the times he so absented himself he . . . did with loose idle and disorderly boys that went about picking of pockets co-habit and of their felonious gain did receive and partake'. (ibid., 22 February 1770.) The majority of such boys it may be supposed simply ran away.

V. DISPOSAL OF APPRENTICES BY THE PARISHES WITHIN THE BILLS OF MORTALITY (those of the City within the Walls excepted), during the ten years 1802–11, according to the *Report . . . on the number . . . and . . . state of parish apprentices bound into the country . . . 1815.*

Total number, 3,446 males
              2,369 females

              5,815

Of these   2,428 males
              1,361 females

              3,789 were bound to trades, the sea-service or household employments in or near London

The ages of these 3,789 were as follows:
           15 under 8
        493 from 8–11
        483 „ 11–12
      1,656 „ 12–14
      1,102 „ 14–18

Their employments:

        484 to the sea-service, etc. (includes apprentices to watermen, lighter-men and fishermen)

        528 to household employments

   2,772 to various trades and professions

   1,018 males

   1,008 females

   2,026 were bound to persons in the country

Their ages:

        58 under 8

   1,008 from 8–11

     316 „ 11–12

     435 „ 12–14

     207 „ 14–18

       2 ages not given

   2,026

Their employments:

Silk throwsters	118	
„ manufacturers	26	144
Flax dressers	21	
„ spinners	58	
„ manufacturers	88	175
Sail-cloth manufacturers	8	
Woollen manufacturers	4	
Worsted spinners	2	
„ manufacturers	146	174
Carpet weavers	2	
Frame-work knitters		9
Earthenware manufacturers		3
Cotton spinners	355	
„ weavers	67	
„ manufacturers	771	
„ twist manufacturers	7	1,493
Calico weavers	198	
Fustian manufacturers	71	
Cotton candlewick manufacturers	24	
Manufacturers (supposed to be cotton)		28
		2,026

Information as to the above children in answer to precepts addressed to the masters:

Now serving under indentures	644
Served their time and now in the same employ	108
Served and settled elsewhere	99
Dead	80
Enlisted in the Army or Navy	86

Quitted their service, chiefly run away   166
Not bound to the persons mentioned in the return kept by the Company of
    Parish Clerks   58
Sent back to their friends   52
Transferred to tradesmen in different parts of the Kingdom   246
Incapable of service   18
Not accounted for or mentioned   5
Not satisfactorily or intelligibly accounted for by the persons to whom they
    were bound, or by the overseers where the masters have become bankrupts   435

————
2,026

VI. WOMEN'S WORK – OCCUPATIONS OF MARRIED COUPLES

(Taken from the *Sessions Papers*. The occupations are those of the witnesses, prosecutors and prisoners appearing at the Old Bailey.)

	Man	Wife
1. Sept. 1737.	Sells milk	hawks fruit
2. July 1783.	'A lame man who cannot earn his bread', lets lodgings (Shehan)	keeps a green shop
3. Oct. 1797.	'A worker at the water-side' (dishonest)	keeps a broker's shop
4. Sept. 1788.	Saloop seller (helps wife)	saloop seller in Moorfields
5. Sept. 1728.	Watchman	sells cakes and gingerbread
6. Sept. 1789.	Watchman	quilter
7. Dec. 1744.	Chairman	sells milk
8. Dec. 1766.	Chairman	keeps 'a house of lodgers' and sells pease porridge and sheeps heads in her shop
9. Feb. 1780.	Coal heaver	keeps a house for lodgers (apparently disreputable)
10. May 1748.	Sailor (alleged)	shoplifter, says she 'works at her needle'
11. Jan. 1794.	Foremastman on man-of-war	does slop-work
12. Dec. 1735.	Soldier in the Guards	keeps a milk-cellar, 'the sign of the Cow'
13. Jan. 1759.	Recruiting sergeant in the Guards	sells old clothes (fence), used to keep a public-house
14. Sept. 1798.	Soldier (made prisoner at Ostend)	keeps the Feathers public-house Broadway, Westminster
15. April 1745.	Driver to a hackney coachman	takes in washing

Man	Wife
16. Sept. 1767. Sugar baker [labourer]	takes in washing
17. Sept. 1789. Labourer	makes up children's frocks and bed-gowns
18. Feb. 1797. Labourer (Irish)	barrow-woman, sells fruit, says she keeps a house in Gray's Inn Lane
19. June 1738. Lath-binder, porter or match-cutter	stay-maker (daughter sells matches)
20. Sept. 1794. Porter	takes in washing, formerly had a milk-walk
21. Sept. 1785. Brickmaker	'I work at tayloring, I have nothing but what I work for'
22. Dec. 1766. Lighterman	market-woman
23. Sept. 1798. Waterman	says her husband maintains her (but occasionally hawks old clothes)
24. 1731–2. Waterman (employed two wherries) (murdered his wife)	kept a public-house
25. May 1768. Seller of poultry [hawker?]	Billingsgate woman
26. June 1791. Useful man in warehouse of wholesale haberdashers	makes up scarlet cardinals and hats for the firm
27. Feb. 1798. 'Belongs to the East India Company' [works in warehouse?]	keeps a lodging house for seafaring men. (Ratcliffe Highway)
28. May 1746. Sack weaver	sack weaver
29. May 1768. Ribbon weaver (alleged cutter)	weaver
30. May 1774. Weaver	Billingsgate woman
31. Sept. 1784. Weaver	keeps a green shop
32. Oct. 1784. Weaver	engine-windster
33. Oct. 1757. Shoe-maker	sewer of books
34. Oct. 1759. Shoe-maker	deals in old iron and rags 'keeps a broker's shop' (fence)
35. April 1760. Shoe-maker	binds upper leathers of shoes
36. Oct. 18. 1763. Shoe-maker (killed his wife by throwing milk pail at her, acquitted)	milkwoman
37. Jan. 1765. Shoe-maker	dealer in old clothes, hardware, etc.
38. Feb. 1767. Shoe-maker	milliner
39. Jan. 1786. Cobbler	keeps a green stall
40. April 1794. Shoe-maker	'I deal in the street'
41. Sept. 1735. Tailor (works at a stall in St Martin's Court)	works with her husband
42. May 1757. Tailor	takes in plain work

	Man	Wife
43. Dec. 1759.	Tailor (Jew at Houndsditch)	necklace-maker
44. July 1774.	Tailor	weaver
45. April 1781.	Tailor	mantua-maker, takes in lodgers
46. Mar. 1759.	Bricklayer	travelled with a puppet show, also knitted gloves (thief)
47. 1741.	Man-servant (John Hall – murdered his master)	stocking and haberdashery shop, Princes Street, Leicester Fields, stock appraised at £195
48. Jan. 1791.	Man-servant	keeps a haberdashers and hosier's shop, Bury Street, St James
49. Feb. 1792.	Man-servant	keeps a milk-cellar, takes in washing
50. Oct. 1778.	Both 'keep the fairs and statutes'	makes hats and bonnets to sell at fairs
51. July 1777.	Wire-drawer	charwoman
52. Dec. 1750.	Shagreen case-maker	goes out washing and charing
53. June 1767.	Smith	'I carry out work [pokers, etc.] which he makes to sell among the brokers'
54. June 1794.	Blacksmith (keeps a house in George's Alley, Field Lane)	goes out milking (perhaps a milk carrier)
55. July 1800.	Blacksmith	keeps a chandler's shop
56. Sept. 1798.	Letter founder	keeps a green stall
57. Feb. 1780.	Pocket-book-maker ('a bad fellow')	works for a stay-maker (alleged able to earn 10s. or 12s. a week and to support her husband). Shop lifter
58. Jan. 1783.	Tin plate worker	lacquers lanterns, etc., made by her husband
59. June 1758.	Ivory cutter	binds shoes
60. Feb. 1798.	Cooper (Lower Shadwell)	'I follow a little weaving when I can'
61. Feb. 1780.	Journeyman shipwright	sells fish
62. July 1779.	Basket-maker	keeps a public-house
63. Sept. 1783.	Watch-motion-maker and lock and spring-maker (executed for coining)	keeps a school for children (also a coiner)
64. June 1753.	Perriwig-maker	quilter of petticoats
65. Jan. 1777.	Peruke-maker and hairdresser	milliner
66. Mar. 1753.	Butcher in St James Market	keeps a butcher's shop in Oxford Market

Man	Wife
67. Sept. 1782. Confectioner (Jew)	'butcheress' in Petticoat Lane
68. April 1784. Carpenter	hawks stoneware
69. Dec. 1751. Carpenter	makes cloaks
70. Oct. 1757. Carpenter (Wapping)	has a shop for linens, checks and stockings
71. Oct. 1757. Journeyman carpenter (Shadwell)	keeps a shop
72. Sept. 1783. Surveyor and carpenter	haberdasher
73. Sept. 1784. Journeyman carpenter	landlady of the Man in Compass (resort of thieves)
74. Feb. 1780. Joiner and case-maker	keeps a toy shop
75. Dec. 1746. Cabinet-maker	keeps a grocer's [chandler's?] shop
76. Jan. 1749. Inlayer of tortoiseshell (was apprenticed in a merchantman and had been schoolmaster in a man-of-war)	keeps a herb shop
77. Feb. 1796. Upholsterer	works at husband's business
78. April 1777. Sadler	milliner
79. Jan. 1779. Silversmith (working)	keeps milliner's shop
80. Feb. 1794. 'Officer of the police'	sells coals and keeps a broker's shop
81. Jan. 1798. Butter salesman in Newgate Market	poultry dealer (sells to the trade)
82. April 1758. Tallow chandler	plumber (separate house)
83. Dec. 1755. Surgeon	keeps a poulterer's shop in Turtle Street
84. Jan. 1774. Attorney (almost 50 years in Kensington)	keeps the Kensington Coffee House
85. Feb. 1794. 'I am in the law'	keeps a milliner's shop
86. Sept. 1800. Attorney	worker of muslin shawls at Hoxton (employs workwomen)

BIBLIOGRAPHY

Including the more general sources only, authorities on special points will be found in the notes. General political and economic histories of the period are omitted, and so, for want of space, are parish histories and accounts of City Companies.

Contemporary fiction, plays, poems, and the classical biographies and collections of letters, although essential authorities of the greatest value, are not included as they are fully dealt with in the bibliographies of the *Cambridge History of Literature.*

I. BIBLIOGRAPHIES

1. *London* in British Museum Catalogue. Useful for reports issued by London societies and charities.

2. The card index of the Guildhall Library. Especially for parish histories and the accounts of City Companies.

3. Miss E. Jeffries Davies, 'London and its Records,' *History*, October 1921 and January 1922. (Indispensable.)

4. C. Welch, *Notes on London Municipal Literature*, 1895. (Slight.)

5. W. S. Sonnenschein, *The Best Books, Part II*, 1912, E. § 17, pp. 860–70. (London: history, topography, etc.)

6. *Catalogue of Prints and Drawings in the British Museum Division I. Political and Personal Satires*, vols. i–iv (1689–c. 1770) by F. G. Stephens and E. Hawkins, 1873–83. (A valuable guide to the social history of the period with many references to contemporary books and newspapers.)

7. Bibliographies in G. Unwin's *Gilds and Companies of London*, 1908, and *Industrial Organisation in the Sixteenth and Seventeenth Centuries*, 1904. (Though they deal with an earlier period they throw much light on eighteenth-century developments.)

8. S. and B. Webb, *Local Government* (see section X below); valuable bibliographical notes.

9. *The Times Handlist of English and Welsh Newspapers*, 1620–1920.

MAPS

10. *London* in British Museum Catalogue of Maps.

11. *Catalogues of Maps, Plans, and Views of London* ... *collected by F. Crace, edited by F. G. Crace*, 1878.

12. Sir L. Gomme, 'The Story of London Maps', *Geographical Journal*, xxxi, May and June, 1908. (Illustrated by a map showing the growth of London from 1560 to 1887.)

II. MANUSCRIPT SOURCES

PUBLIC RECORD OFFICE

1. *State Papers Domestic* (S. P. Dom.) to 1783.

2. *Treasury Papers*, T. 47–9, 10, 11. (Records of Emigration, 1773–5.)

GUILDHALL

3. Guildhall Sessions Papers. (Miscellaneous documents arising from the petty sessions held at the Guildhall by the aldermen as justices of the peace for the City – petitions, depositions, duplicates of removal orders and vagrant passes, etc.)

4. Complaint Book of the Chamberlain's Office.

WESTMINSTER GUILDHALL

5. Middlesex Sessions Records (*Sessions Books and Orders of Court*). See also below, Section III. 4.

BRITISH MUSEUM

6. The Place Collections. (Especially Add. MSS. 27798–27807; 27823; 27825–27829; 27834; 35142–35147, *Autobiography.*)

III. PRINTED SOURCES

1. *Statutes at Large.* These give titles of, but do not include, the majority of local acts for London; original printed copies of these are bound up in volumes called *Public Acts* or *Road Acts* in the Newspaper Room of the British Museum.

2. *Commons Journals.* (*C. J.*)

3. *Calendar of Home Office Papers.* State Papers Domestic *of the Reign of George III.* Four Vols. 1760–73. Edited by J. Redington and R. A. Roberts, 1878–99. (As the State Papers have been rearranged, the numbers in these calendars no longer correspond with the original documents.)

4. Middlesex Sessions Records

    (*a*) J. C. Jeaffreson, *Middlesex County Records.*

    (*b*) W. J. Hardy, *Middlesex County Records*, Calendar of the Sessions Books, 1689–1709, 1905.

    (*c*) Typescript Calendar of Sessions Books and Orders of Court, 1710–48. (Copies in British Museum, Public Record Office and Westminster Guildhall.)

5. *Bills of Mortality.* Records of the baptisms and causes of death and burials published by the Company of Parish Clerks issued to subscribers. There were both weekly bills and *General Bills* or yearly summaries from the weekly returns. See also '*A Collection of the Yearly Bills of Mortality from 1657 to 1758 inclusive. . . . To which are subjoined – I. Observations on the Bills of Mortality by Captain J. Graunt. II. Another Essay concerning the City of London . . . by Sir W. Petty. . . . III. Obervations on the past Growth and present State of the City of London by C. Morris. IV. A comparative View of the Diseases and Ages and Tables of the Probabilities of Life for the last thirty Years by J. P[ostlethwayte] Esq., F.R.S.,* 1759. (Edited by Dr W. Heberden not Dr T. Birch, see C. Hull, *Econ. Writings of Sir W. Petty,* ii, p. 641.)

6. The *Whole Proceedings upon the King s Commission of Oyer and Terminer and Gaol Delivery for the City of London and also the Gaol Delivery for the County of Middlesex,* known as *London Sessions Papers* or simply *Sessions Papers.* Till 1775 these appear to have been private-venture publications with a sensational appeal, but giving a complete account of the trials of the Old Bailey, sometimes *verbatim*, sometimes abridged, and coming out immediately after the Sessions. They were however used as a record of proceedings, and it was resolved at a Common Council of 17 November, 1775 'that the Proceedings . . . be regularly . . . published by the Recorder and authenticated with his name'. The succeeding Sessions Papers therefore appear 'revised and published by' the Recorder of London, but this imprint soon disappears from the title page.

They contain invaluable information as to industrial and social life, while the Ordinary's *Accounts* of the persons executed which are bound up with them are a mine of information on manners and contemporary opinion.

7. Parliamentary Papers.

(Many earlier Parliamentary Reports are printed in the Commons Journals or included in the collection of *Reports* (1715–1802) *from Committees of the House of Commons printed by order of the House and not inserted in the Journals.* Sixteen volumes, 1803–20.)

(a) Population:
    Population Returns, 1801, 1811, 1821, 1831.
    Comparative Account . . ., 1801–1831, 1831, XVIII.
    Minutes of Evidence before the Population Bill Committee . . ., 1830, IV.

(b) Police:
    Eighteenth Report of the Select Committee on Finance . . ., 1810, IV.
    Report on the State of the Nightly Watch of the Metropolis . . ., 1812, II.
    Report on the Police of the Metropolis . . ., 1816, V.
       „ „ „ „ „ „   „   „ 1817, VII.
       „ „ „ „ „ „   „   „ 1818, VIII.
       „ „ „ „ „ „   „   „ 1822, IV.
       „ „ „ „ „ „   „   „ 1828, VI.

(c) Social and Industrial Conditions:
    Report . . . on Lotteries, 1800, II.
    Report . . . on Local Acts . . . for the Poor since 1800, 1813–14, IV.
    Report . . . on several Petitions relating to the Apprenticeship Laws, 1812–13, IV.
    Report . . . on Parish Apprentices bound into the Country from the Bills of Mortality, 1814–15, V.
    Report . . . on the State of Mendicity in the Metropolis, 1814–15, III, and 1816, V.
    Report . . . on Lascars and other Asiatic Seamen, 1814–15, III.
    Report . . . on the State of Madhouses, 1814–15, IV.
    Report . . . on the State of Children . . . in Manufactories . . ., 1816, III.
    Report . . . on the Education of the Lower Orders in the Metropolis, 1816, IV.
    Report . . . on the Petitions of the Watchmakers of Coventry, etc., 1817, IV.
    Report . . . on Laws relating to Watchmakers, 1818, IX.
    Report . . . on the Poor Laws, 1817, IV.
    Report of the Lords Committee on the Poor Laws, 1817, 1818, V.
    Report . . . on the Employment of Boys in sweeping Chimneys, 1817, VI.
    Report . . . on Contagious Fever in London, 1818, VII.
    Report . . . on the Petitions of Ribbon Weavers . . ., 1818, IX.
    Report . . . on the Laws relating to Vagrants . . ., 1821, IV.
    Minutes of Evidence . . . on the Wages of the Silk Manufacturers. Lords Sessional Papers, 1823, XIII.
    Reports . . . on Artisans and Machinery, 1824, V.
    Report . . . on Emigration. . ., 1826, IV.
    Report . . . on Irish and Scotch Vagrants . . ., 1828, IV.
    Report . . . on the Silk Trade, 1831–2, XIX.
    Report . . . on the Poor Laws, 1834, XXVII, XXVIII, XXXV, XXXVI, XXXVII.
    Report . . . on Education, 1835, VII.
    Reports . . . on the Poor Law Amendment Act, 1838, XVIII, 1, 2, 3.

Fourth Report of the Poor Law Commissioners for 1838. Appendix A 1838, XXVII.

Reports . . . on the State of Handloom Weavers, 1840, XXIII, XXIV.

Report . . . on Intra-mural Interments, 1842, X.

Supplementary Report on the Results of a special Inquiry into the Practice of Interment in Towns by Edwin Chadwick, 1843, XII.

Report of the Commissioners on Inland Revenue, 1870, XX, ii. (Home consumption, etc., of British spirits since 1684.)

8. Parliamentary Debates.

Cobbett, *Parliamentary History* (to 1803).

Hansard, *Parliamentary Debates* (1803–).

The Parliamentary Register (1774–1813).

9. Law Reports.

These give much information on social history. Settlement cases in particular throw light on conditions of employment, apprenticeship, etc. Among many others the following may be noted:

Sir J. Burrow, *A series of the Decisions of the Court of King's Bench in Settlement Cases, 1732 to 1768,* 1768.

S. Douglas, *Reports of Cases . . . in the Court of King's Bench . . .* 2nd ed., 1786.

Durnford and East, *Reports of Cases . . . in the Court of King's Bench,* 1785–1800. 1787–1800.

Sir J. Strange, *Reports of adjudged Cases in the Courts of Chancery, King's Bench, Common Pleas and Exchequer . . .,* 1756.

For *causes célèbres* see T. B. Howell, *A complete Collection of State Trials.* 1816–26.

IV. ANNALS AND TOPOGRAPHY

Though these books belong to two main categories – histories and surveys – (with minor subdivisions), it is impossible to draw a dividing line between the two, as the histories nearly always include a contemporary survey, and even the strictest of surveys generally give historical notes as well as information on local government, charities, etc.

H. Chamberlain, *A compleat History and Survey of . . . London . . .,* 1770.

Concise History of the City of London, 1752.

J. Entick, *A New and accurate History and Survey of London . . .,* 1766.

J. Feltham, *The picture of London for 1802.* (Many later editions.)

W. Harrison, *A new and universal History, Description and Survey . . .,* 1775.

[E. Hatton], *New View of London,* 1708.

D. Hughson [E. Pugh], *London, being an accurate History and Description . . .,* 1806–9.

B. Lambert, *The History and Survey of London and its Environs . . .,* 1806.

London and its Environs described . . ., 1761. (Dodsley)

D. Lysons, *Environs of London . . .,* 1792–9.

W. Maitland, *The History and Survey of London. . . .* Editions of 1739 and 1756, also edition of 1772 with additions by Entick.

J. P. Malcolm, *Londinium Redivivum,* 1802–7.

A new and compleat Survey of London by a Citizen . . ., 1742.

The Microcosm of London, 1808–9 (Ackermann). Illustrations by Pugin and Rowlandson.

Modern London, 1804 (R. Phillips).

New Remarks of London . . . *by the Company of Parish Clerks,* 1732.

J. Noorthouck, *History of London* . . . 1773.

T. Pennant, *Account of London,* 1790, 2nd ed., 1791: *Some Account of London,* 5th ed., 1813.

J. Ralph, *A Critical Review of Public Buildings* . . . *in and about London* . . ., 1734. Reprinted with large additions, 1783.

T. Smart, *A short Account of the several Wards, Precincts, Parishes, etc., in London,* 1741. (The City only.)

J. Stow, *A Survey of London,* 1603, ed. by C. L. Kingsford, 1908.

Strype, *Stow's Survey* . . . *brought down from* . . . *1633* . . . *to the present Time,* 1720. Also the edition of 1754–5.

R. Seymour [J. Mottley] *Stow's Survey* . . . *the Whole being on Improvement of Mr Stow's and other Surveys,* 1734–5.

W. Thornton, *History of London,* 1784.

See also the surveys of Middlesex made for the Board of Agriculture called *General View of the Agriculture of Middlesex,* by T. Baird, 1793 (three editions); P. Foot, 1794; J. Middleton, 1798, 2nd ed., 1807.

V. ADMINISTRATION, POLICE, THE POOR, CHARITIES, ETC.

(Besides these, other books and tracts of a similar kind are referred to in the notes.)

Account of several Workhouses, 1725. Enlarged edition, 1732. (Written for the Society for Promoting Christian Knowledge.)

Account of several Charity Schools lately erected. (Published for the Society for Promoting Christian Knowledge annually from 1705 to 1713.)

Account of several Endeavours that have been used to suppress Gaming Houses and of the Discouragements that have been met with, 1722.

E. Bott, *Decisions of the Court of King's Bench upon the Laws relating to the Poor* . . . *revised by F. Const.,* 1793.

R. Burn, *Justice of the Peace and Parish Officer.* Many Editions from 1755.

W. Blizard, *Desultory Reflections on Police,* 1785.

S. Clapham, *Sessions Law,* 1818.

P. Colquhoun, *Observations on* . . . *Public Houses,* 1794.

 The State of Indigence and the Situation of the Casual Poor in the Metropolis explained, 1799.

 A Treatise on Indigence exhibiting a general View of the National Resources for Productive Labour, 1806.

 A Treatise on the Commerce and Police of the River Thames, 1800.

 A Treatise on the Police of the Metropolis, 1796, 7th ed. 1806.

D. Defoe, *Augusta Triumphans* . . ., 1729.

 Everybody's Business is No-body's Business . . . 2nd ed., 1725.

Sir W. M. Eden, *State of the Poor,* 1797.

H. Fielding, *Charge to the Grand Jury of Westminster,* 1749.

 Enquiry into the Causes of the late Increase of Robbers . . ., 1751.

 Journal of a Voyage to Lisbon, 1755. (Introduction.)

 A Proposal for making an effectual Provision for the Poor . . ., 1753.

 A true State of the Case of Bosavern Penlez, 1749.

John Fielding, *An Account of the Origin and Effects of a Plan of Police,* 1753.

 Penal Laws relating to the Metropolis, 2nd ed., 1768.

Jonas Hanway, *A candid historical Account of the Hospital for exposed and deserted young Children* . . . 1759.

   The Citizen's Monitor, 1780. (Reprint of *Defects of Police*, 1775.)
   An Earnest Appeal for Mercy to the Children of the Poor, 1766.
   Letters on the Importance of the Rising Generation of the labouring part of our fellow-subjects, 1768.

Highmore, *Pietas Londinensis, the History, Design and Present State of the various public Charities in and near London*, 1810.

J. Massie, *An Account of a Plan for Charity Houses* . . ., 1758.

R. Nelson, *An Address to Persons of Quality and Estate*, 1715.

M. Nolan, *A Treatise on the Laws for Relief and Settlement of the Poor*, 3rd ed., 1814.

J. Howard, *The State of the Prisons in England and Wales* . . ., 3rd ed., Warrington, 1784.

   An Account of the Principal Lazarettos in Europe . . ., Warrington, 1789.

Reports of the Society for Bettering the Condition and Increasing the Comforts of the Poor, 1798–1808.

J. Paul, *The Parish Officers Complete Guide*, 6th ed., 1793.

J. Ritson, *The Office of a Constable*, 1791.

J. Shaw, *Parish Law*, 8th ed., 1753.

Sir T. de Veil, *Observations on the Practice of a Justice of the Peace intended for such Gentlemen as design to act for Middlesex or Westminster*, 1747.

Saunders Welch, *Observations on the Office of a Constable, with Cautions for the more safe Execution of that Duty* . . ., 1754.

   Proposal to render effective a Plan to remove . . . Prostitutes from the Streets of this Metropolis . . ., 1758.

VI. TRAVELS, IMPRESSIONS OF FOREIGNERS AND PSEUDO-FOREIGNERS

Alvarez Espriella (Southey writing as a Spaniard), *Letters from England*, 1807. (See American edition, 1808, with notes by the American editor.)

Angeloni (Shebbeare writing as an Italian), *Letters on the English Nation*, 2nd ed., 1756.

Angiolini, *Lettere sopra l'Inghilterra, Scozia, e Olanda*, Firenze, 1790.

Archenholtz, *A Picture of England*, 1797. (Written *c.* 1780.)

Baert, *Tableau de la Grande Bretagne* . . . (1800.)

G. A. Crapelet, *Souvenirs de Londres en 1814 et 1816*, Paris, 1817.

S. Curwen, *Journal and Letters* . . . (1775–84), 1842, (American loyalist.)

D. Defoe, *A Tour thro' the whole Island of Great Britain* . . ., 1734–37. (See also the sections on London in the editions of 1742, 1753, 1769 and 1778.)

A. J. B. de Fauconpret, *Quinze Jours à Londres au fin de 1815*, 1816.

   Six Mois à Londres en 1816, 1817.

Faujas de Saint Fond, *A Journey through England and Scotland in . . . 1784*, ed. by Sir A. Geikie, 1907.

G. L. Ferri di San Costante, *Londres et les Anglais*, Paris, 1804.

M. Gonzalez, *Voyage to Great Britain*, 1730. Pinkerton's *Travels*, ii.

P. J. Grosley, *A Tour to London* (1765), trans. by T. Nugent, 1772.

W. Hutton, *A Journey to London* (1784), 2nd ed., 1818.

Pehr Kalm, *Visit to England* (1748), trans. from Swedish by J. Lucas, 1892.

Lacombe, *Tableau de Londres, un Précis de la Constitution de l'Angleterre et de sa décadence . . .*, 1794. (Reprint of *Observations sur Londres par un Athéronome de Berne*, 1777.)

J. B. Le Blanc, *Lettres d'un François*, 1745. (Written 1734–7.)

de Levis, *L'Angleterre au Commencement du dix-neuvième Siècle*, 1814.

I. Macky, *A Journey through England*, 1722–3.

Magalotti, *Travels of Cosmo III . . . through England* (1669), 1821.

J. H. Meister, *Letters written during a Residence in England*, 1791. (English Translation 1799.)

Misson, *Mémoires et Observations faites par un Voyageur en Angleterre avec une Description particulière de ce qu'il-y-a de plus curieux dans Londres*, 1698. (Engllish Translation by Ozell, 1719.)

C. Moritz, *Travels through various parts of England in 1782.* (Pinkerton's *Travels*, ii.)

Muralt, *Lettres sur les Anglois et sur les Voiages etc.*, 1725.

Narrative of the Journey of an Irish Gentleman through England in . . . 1752. Ed. by W. C. Hazlitt, 1869.

Nougaret, *Londres, la Cour et les Provinces d'Angleterre, d'Ecosse et d'Irlande*, Paris, 1816.

Pictet, *Voyage de trois Mois en Angleterre . . . en 1801*, Geneva, 1802.

Memoirs of Charles Lewis, Baron de Poellnitz, 3rd ed. 1745. (Vols. iii and v.)

R. Reuss, *Londres et l'Angleterre en 1700 décrites par un Commis-négociant Strasbourgeois* (J. Zetner), Strasbourg, 1905.

Mme. Roland, *A Trip to England* (1784), *Works*, 1800, p. 166 ff.

C. Saladin, *L'Angleterre en 1800*, Cologne, 1801.

C. de Saussure, *A Foreign View of England in the Reigns of George I and George II* (Letters), 1902.

J. B. Say, *De l'Angleterre et les Anglais*, 1815.

B. Silliman (of Yale University), *A Journal of Travels in England, Holland and Scotland in . . . 1805 and 1806.*

L. Simond, *Journal of a Tour and Residence in Great Britain . . . 1810 and 1811 . . .*, 1815.

Voltaire, *Lettres sur l'Angleterre*, 1726–9.

Wendeborn, *A View of England towards the Close of the Eighteenth Century*, 1791. (Author's translation from German.)

VII. BIOGRAPHY, REMINISCENCES, AND CONTEMPORARY DESCRIPTIONS OF SOCIAL LIFE

Chiefly books which throw light on 'low life' – in the eighteenth-century sense – philanthropy or administration. See also, besides the bibliographies in the *Cambridge History of Literature*, vols. ix, x, xi, the following bibliographies in the *Cambridge Modern History*: vol. vi, 1909. 'Memoirs, Correspondence and Papers', pp. 846–8, 'Biographical and Miscellaneous', p. 849, 'Wesleyan and Welsh Revivals', pp. 856–7; vol. viii, 1904. 'Biographies', pp. 845–6; also, for historical biography, political and social, W. S. Sonnenschein, *The Best Books, Part III*, 1923, F. §§ 24 and 25.

H. Angelo, *Reminiscences*, 1828–30.

S. Bamford, *Early Days*, 1849.

Fifty Years' Recollections of an Old Bookseller, 1837.

J. Brasbridge, *Fruits of Experience . . .*, 1824.

J. Britton, *Autobiography*, 1830.

[J. D. Burn], *A Glimpse at the Social Conditions of the Working Classes during the early part of the present Century*, n.d.

[T. Carter], *Memoirs of a Working Man*, 1845.

A Narrative of the Life of Charlotte Charke . . . by herself, 1755.

Iatros, [Yates], *A Narrative of the Life and Works of Patrick Colquhoun*, 1818.

B. Franklin, *Autobiography*, ed. by W. Macdonald, 1915.

J. Pugh, *Remarkable Occurrences in the Life of Jonas Hanway*, 1787.

E. Hardcastle [W. H. Pyne], *Wine and Walnuts*, 1823.

Sir J. Hawkins, *The Life of Dr Johnson*, 1787.

Memoirs of the late Thomas Holcroft edited by W. Hazlitt, 1816.

The Life of William Hutton. . . ., 1816.

Charles Knight, *Passages of a Working Life*, 1864–5.

Memoirs of Lackington . . . 13th ed., 1810.

T. J. Pettigrew, *Memoirs of . . . J. C. Lettsom*, 1817.

Roger North, *Lives of the Norths*, ed. by A. Jessopp, 1890.

Life of Robert Owen by himself, 1857.

G. Parket, *A View of Society in High and Low Life*, 1781.

Memoirs of Mrs Letitia Pilkington by herself, 1754–84.

J. Richardson, *Recollections of the last half century*, 1856.

Memoirs of the Life of Sir Samuel Romilly written by himself . . . 2nd ed., 1840.

P. Hoare, *Life of Granville Sharp*.

[C. M. Smith], *The Working Man's Way in the World, being the Autobiography of a Journeyman Printer*. 1853.

J. T. Smith, *Nollekens and his Times*, 1829. Reprinted 1920.

A Book for a Rainy Day, or, Recollections of the Events of the years 1766–1833, 1845. Reprinted 1905.

T. Somerville, *Memoirs of my own Life and Times, 1741–1814*, Edinburgh, 1861.

An Account of the Life and Dealings of God with Silas Told . . . written by himself, 1786.

Memoirs of the Life of the Rev. Dr Trusler . . . by himself, Bath, 1805.

Memoirs of J. H. Vaux written by himself, 1819. Edited by Baron Field.

The Life and Times of Sir Thomas de Veil, 1748.

The Journal of the Rev. John Wesley, Four Vols., 1906, Everyman's Library; edition edited by C. Curnock, eight vols. with additions from previously unprinted MS. 1909–16.

The Life of William Wilberforce by his Sons, R. I. W. and S. W., 1838.

Tate Wilkinson, *Memoirs . . .*, 1790.

General Williamson's Diary, Camden Society, 3rd Series, xxii, 1912. See also above, section II. 6.

VIII. MISCELLANEOUS

W. Hone, *The Every-day Book . . .*, 1826–7.

Low-life, or one Half the World knows not how the other Half lives . . ., 1752, 3rd. ed., 1764.

J. P. Malcolm, *Anecdotes of the Manners and Customs of London during the Eighteenth Century . . .*, 1808, 2nd ed., 1810. (A Compilation from contemporary books, newspapers and official documents.)

J. T. Smith, *The Cries of London*, 1839.

Vagabondiana or Mendicant Wanderers through the Streets of London, 1817.

E. Ward, *The London Spy*, 1699–1703.

IX. PERIODICALS AND NEWSPAPERS

The Annual Register, 1758–
The Edinburgh Review, 1803–
The Gentleman's Magazine, 1731–
The London Magazine, 1732–
The Monthly Magazine, 1796–
The Quarterly Review, 1809–
The Covent Garden Journal, 1752. (H. Fielding.)
The London Chronicle, 1757–
The London Evening Post, 1727–1808.
The Public Advertiser, 1753–
(Among many others.)

X. SOME LATER BOOKS

C. Booth, *Life and Labour of the People in London*, 1902–3. (For survivals, developments and comparisons.)

C. Creighton, *History of Epidemics*, ii, 1894.

A. Dobdon, *William Hogarth*, 1907.

O. J. Dunlop, *English Apprenticeship and Child Labour*, 1912.

B. Kirkman Gray, *History of English Philanthropy*, 1905.

J. L. and B. Hammond, *The Town Labourer, 1760–1832*, 1917.
The Skilled Labourer, 1760–1832. 1919.

E. Halévy, *La Formation du Radicalisme Philosophique*, Paris. 1901–3.

G. J. Holyoake, *Self-help a Hundred Years ago*, 1890. (Based on the *Reports of the Society for Bettering . . . the Condition of the Poor*. See section V above.)

G. Ives, *A History of Penal Methods*, 1914.

H. Mayhew, *London Labour and the London Poor*, 1851 and 1861.

London County Council, *Survey of Greater London*, (In progress.)

C. Phillipson, *Three Criminal Law Reformers*, 1923.

J. L. Pike, *History of Crime in England*, 1873–6.

G. V. Portus, *Caritas Anglicana, or an Historical Inquiry into those Religious etc. Societies that flourished in England, 1678–1740.*

W. E. Schultz, *Gay's Beggars' Opera, its Content, History and Influence*, Yale Univ. Press, 1923.

Leslie Stephen, *History of English Thought in the Eighteenth Century*, 1876.
The English Utilitarians, 1900. (Especially vol. i.)

F. H. Spencer, *Municipal Origins. An Account of Private Bill Legislation relating to Local Government, 1740–1835*, 1911.

Victoria County History, Middlesex, ii, 1911.
Surrey, ii.

S. and B. Webb, *History of Local Government* (indispensable):

    i. *Parish and County*, 1906.
    ii–iii. *Manor and Borough*, 1908.
    English Prisons under Local Government . . ., 1922.
    Statutory Authorities for Special Purposes, 1923.

History of Liquor Licensing . . ., 1903.
History of Trade Unionism, 1894.
G. Wallas, *The Life of Francis Place, 1771–1854,* 1898.
H. B. Wheatley and P. Cunningham, *London Past and Present,* 1891.

MAPS

London Topographical Society, reproductions of old maps. In progress.
G. E. Mitton, *Maps of Old London,* 1908.

Supplement to
The Bibliography, 1964

G. Armitage, *Bow Street Runners, 1729–1829*, 1932.

T. S. Ashton, *Economic Fluctuations in England, 1600–1800*, Oxford, 1959.

T. S. Ashton, *An Economic History of the Eighteenth Century*, 1955.

T. S. Ashton, *The Industrial Revolution*, Oxford, 1948.

R. Bayne Powell, *Eighteenth Century London Life*, 1937.

E. D. Bebb, *Nonconformity and Social and Economic Life, 1660–1800*, 1935.

J. B. Botsford, *English Society in the Eighteenth Century as influenced from Overseas*, New York, 1924.

Witt Bowden, *Economic Society in England towards the end of the Eighteenth Century*, 1926.

D. G. Browne, *The Rise of Scotland Yard: A History of the Metropolitan Police*, 1956.

M. C. Buer, *Health, Wealth and Population in the Early Days of the Industrial Revolution*, 1926.

J. H. Clapham, *An Economic History of Modern Britain*, i, 1926.

E. G. Dowdell, *A Hundred Years of Quarter Sessions: The Government of Middlesex from 1660 to 1760*, Cambridge, 1932.

J. C. Drummond and A. Wilbraham, *The Englishman's Food in Five Centuries*, 1939.

F. H. Dudden, *Fielding: his Life, Works and Times*, 2 vols., Oxford, 1952.

M. D. George, *England in Transition* [c. 1690–1815], 1931, Penguin Books, 1953, 1964.

E. W. Gilboy, *Wages in Eighteenth Century England*, Cambridge, Mass., 1934.

G. Talbot Griffith, *Population Problems of the Age of Malthus*, 1926.

Sir A. Heal, *London Tradesmen's Cards of the Eighteenth Century*, 1925.

J. J. Hecht, *The Domestic Servant Class in Eighteenth Century England*, 1956.

A. R. Humphreys, *The Augustan World*, 1954. Harper Torchbook edition, 1963.

J. H. Hutchins, *Jonas Hanway, 1712–1786*, 1940.

B. M. Jones, *Henry Fielding, Novelist and Magistrate*, 1938.

M. G. Jones, *Hannah More*, Cambridge, 1952.

M. G. Jones, *The Charity School Movement*, Cambridge, 1938.

W. S. Lewis, *Three Tours through London in the Years 1748, 1776, and 1797*, New Haven, 1941.

W. S. Lewis, and R. M. Williams *Private Charity in England, 1747–1757*, New Haven, 1938.

R. Leslie-Melville, *The Life and Work of Sir John Fielding*, 1934.

H. McLachlan, *English Education under the Test Acts*, 1931.

W. H. Manchée, *The Westminster City Fathers, 1585–1900*, 1924. Extracts from Minutes of the Burgess Court.

D. Marshall, *English People in the Eighteenth Century*, 1956. *Eighteenth-Century England*, 1962.

D. Marshall, *The English Poor in the Eighteenth Century*, 1926.

Sir J. F. Moylan, *Scotland Yard*, 1929, 1934.

R. H. Nichols and F. A. Wright, *The History of the Foundling Hospital*, 1935.

Ivy Pinchbeck, *Women Workers in the Industrial Revolution, 1650–1850*, 1930.
J. Quinlan, *Victorian Prelude: A History of English Manners, 1700–1830*, New York, 1941.
L. Radzinowicz, *A History of English Criminal Law from 1750*, i, 1948.
B. Rodgers, *Cloak of Charity: Studies in Eighteenth Century Philanthropy*, 1949.
A. Redford, *Labour Migration in England, 1800–1850*, 1926.
W. E. Schultz, *Gay's Beggars' Opera: its Content, History and Influence*, New Haven, 1923.
F. H. W. Sheppard, *Local Government in St Marylebone, 1688–1835*, 1958.
Sir H. L. Smith, *The History of East London from the Earliest Times to the End of the Eighteenth Century*, 1939.
K. Smith, *The Malthusian Controversy*, 1951.
A. S. Turberville, *English Men and Manners in the Eighteenth Century*, Oxford, 1926.
A. S. Turberville (ed.), *Johnson's England*, 2 vols., Oxford, 1933.
F. A. von Hayek (ed.), *Capitalism and the Historians*, Chicago, 1954.
W. J. Warner, *The Wesleyan Movement in the Industrial Revolution*, 1930.
J. B. Williams, *Guide to the Printed Materials in English Social and Economic History, 1750–1850*, 2 vols., New York, 1926.
Basil Willey, *The Eighteenth Century Background*, Penguin Books, 1960.

Foreign Impressions

Bibliographies: *A Reference Guide to the Literature of Travel*, vol. i, Seattle, 1935.
G. E. Russell, *The Exploration of England. A Select Bibliography of Travel and Topography: 1570–1815*, 1935.
J. G. A. Forster, *Ansiechten vom Niederrhein, England und Frankreich*, 1791.
E. G. Geijer, *Impressions of England 1809–1810*. Translated E. Sprigge and C. Napier, 1932.
Ethel Jones, *Les Voyageurs Francais en Angleterre, 1815–30*, Paris, 1930.
Lichtenberg's Visits to England as described in his Letters and Diaries. Translated and annotated by M. L. Mare and W. H. Quarrell, Oxford, 1956.
R. M. Pillet, *L'Angleterre vue à Londres et dans ses Provinces pendant un séjour de dix Années*, Paris, 1815. Tr. Eng., 1818, Boston.
Sophie von La Roche, *Tagebuch einer Reise durch Holland und England* [*1787*], Offenbach, 1791. Tr. Eng., 1938.
F. de La Rochefoucauld, *A Frenchman in England, 1784*. Tr. and notes by S. C. Roberts, 1933.
F. M. Wilson, *Strange Island, Britain through Foreign Eyes, 1395–1940*. With Bibliography, 1955.

Articles in Periodicals

A. W. Coats, 'Economic Thought and Poor Law Policy in the Eighteenth Century', *Econ. His. Rev.*, 2nd Series, xiii, pp. 39–51, 1960.
M. D. George, 'The London Coal Heavers', *Econ. Journal*, Hist. Supplement, 1927.
H. J. Habakkuk, 'English Population in the Eighteenth Century', *Econ. Hist. Rev.*, 2nd Series, vi, pp. 117–33, 1953.

B. Hamilton, 'The Medical Professions in the Eighteenth Century', *Econ. Hist. Rev.*, 2nd Series, iv, pp. 141–69, 1949.

R. M. Hartwell, 'The Rising Standard of Living in England, 1800–50', *Econ. Hist. Rev.*, 2nd Series, xiii, pp. 397–416, 1961.

D. Marshall, 'The Old Poor Law (1660–1795)', *Econ. Hist. Rev.*, viii, 1937.

W. J. P. Wright, 'Humanitarian London from 1688 to 1750', *Edinburgh Review*, ccxlvi, 1927.

And other articles in the *Economic History Review, Economic Journal, History Supplement* and the *American Journal of Economic History*.

There is much valuable material in the London County Council's *Survey of London*, now edited by F. H. W. Sheppard (last volume being 32, 1963), and in *London Topographical Record* (last volume 21, 1958), published by the London Topographical Society, both works in progress.

INDEX

Acts of Parliament: Tudor Statutes against vagrancy, 237, 278, 376; apprentices (1563), 256, 273; to regulate leases of church lands (1570, 1572), 85, 336; against new buildings (1593), 80, (1656), 81; Poor Law (1601), 221, 237, 258; Settlement (Poor Law, 1662), 116, 216, 395; for the lighting, etc., of the metropolis (1690), 109; for settlement by apprenticeship (1691), 221; distilling trade thrown open (1691 and 1713), 42–3; Civil List Act (1702), 85; for transportation of felons (1717), 356; for regulation of tailors' wages (1721), 206, 369; for parish workhouses ('for amending the laws relating to the settlement, relief and employment of the poor', 1722), 216; for relief of poor prisoners for debt (1725), 298, 299, 393; to regulate brickmaking (1726 and 1730), 84, 336; Licensing Act (1729), 46; spirit retailers required to have justices' licence (1729), 321; for the assessing of county rates (1739), 413; Licensing Act (1743), 48, 49; distillers permitted to retail (1747), 49; for poor apprentices (1747), 236; Licensing Act (1751), 49, 291, 296, 322–3; Disorderly Houses' Act (1752), 295; Marriage Act (1753), 305–6; Jewish Naturalisation Act (1753), 132; Lords' Act (for relief of prisoners for debt, 1759), 393; for registration of parish infants (1762), 58; for protection of coal-heavers (1758), 286; for the better regulation of parish poor children within the Bills of Mortality (1767), 59, 237, 245; for parish apprentices (1768), 237; Spitalfields Act (1773), 186, 188, 191, 195, 234; Building Acts (1667–1772 and 1774), 86; to prevent frivolous arrests (1779), 298, 303; to limit term of imprisonment under Courts of Conscience (1786), 393–4; for climbing-boys (1788), 241; Alien Act (1792), 134; for establishment of police offices ('for the more effectual administration of the office of a justice of the peace . . . in and near the metropolis', 1792), 21, 295, 315; for poor apprentices (1792), 236; on use of vagrant passes for removals (1792), 359; issue of wine licences by the Stamp Office forbidden (1792), 296, 338; Friendly Societies' Act (1693), 293, 395; for regulating the county rate of Middlesex (1797), 413; establishment of Thames Police Office (1800), 21, 315; for apprentices in cotton mills (Peel's Act, 1802), 238, 252, 377; for protection of coal-heavers (1807), 286–7; for protection of Asiatic seamen (1814), 144; for parish apprentices (1816), 238–9, 244, 253; for protection of coal-heavers (1843), 287

Acts of Parliament, Local: obtain by metropolitan vestries, 22–3, 316; for formation of new parishes, 406–7; for lighting and watching, 109–11; for paving, 22, 67, 107–9, 340; for administration of poor relief, 31, 100, 244–5, 315, 328; Whitechapel Prison, 298–9

Advertisements: for emigrants, 149; for runaway apprentices, 375–6; for runaway slaves, 141–2; shopkeeper's, 364

Aldgate, 75, 94, 340. See St Botolph

Alehouses, lodging in, 102. See publichouses

Amusements, 18, 207, 296–7; of apprentices, 272; of the people, attitude towards, 278–81, 387; places of, 278, 279, 281, 295, 296

Angerstein, J. J., and climbing-boys, 241, 378

Annesley Case, 357–8

Annoyance juries, presentments of, 102–3, 108, 341–2

Apprentices: as cheap labour, 182, 200–201, 223, 233–4, 365; earnings of, property of the master, 231, 375; hiring out of, 230;

Apprentices – *contd.*

hours of, 370: ill-treatment of, 224–30, 233, 239, 249–51, 256–7, 277, 374, 375, 415–23; Legislation for protection of, 236–41; manners of, 268–9, 271–5; in Manchester, 275–6; order of Sessions on behalf of, 243; payment of, 227, 374, 384–5. *See* parish apprentices

Apprenticeship: difficulties of, for Jews, 132, 135, 137; grounds for discharge from, 235, 376, 415–23; industrial consequences of, 233–4, 252; to journeymen, 160, 177, 182, 193, 197, 200–201, 202, 208, 364; not essential for tailors, 210; or for weavers, 188, 190; not used in certain trades, 160–61; out-door, 234, 268–9, 382–3, 384; social consequences of, 231, 268–78; of young children, 373–4, *see* chimney-sweepers. *See* child labour, indentures, parish apprenticeship

Apprenticeship Fees, amount of, 165, 166, 177, 270, 271, 274; chicanery concerning, 226; temptation of, 228, 232–3, 257, 258, 271

Armstrong, Dr, founds the first dispensary, 63

Artisans, 31, 159, 194; skill of, 164; labourers to, 161. *See* journeymen, F. Place

Bacon, on vagrancy and unlawful games, 278

Bailiffs and bailiffs officers, 299, 301, 394

Bakers, apprentices of, 233

Bakers' Company, 233; petitions against spirit drinking, 49

Ballads, quoted, 200, 257, 384

Bankers and merchants, apprenticeship to, 270

Baptisms, relation of, to burials, 38–9, 55, 320, 397, 398, 399

Barber, Francis, 142

Barbers sell spirits, 47

Barbone, Dr, as a speculative builder, 87–8

Baretti, G., on the London populace, 17, 138

Bateman, Dr, 66

Bedford Estate, 89, 337

Beds, concealed in furniture, 103; iron, effects of, 326, 330

Beer, merits of, 35, 50

Beggars, 211–12, 252, 370; Irish, 121, 123, 348, 349, 352; lascars as, 143–4, 145. *See* vagrants

Bell Yard, Temple Bar, 265, 266

Bentham, Jeremy, 21

Bermondsey, 94, 403, 411

Bernard, Sir T., on education, 247, 350; on industrial training at Foundling Hospital, 246; on scientific investigation of social problems, 25; on workhouses, 253

Bethnal Green, 76–7, 81, 89, 94, 106, 179, 295, 332, 333, 342, 403, 414; formation of the parish, 407; population returns for, 333, 410, 412; bull hanking in, 191–2

Bethnal Green Road, market for child labour in, 192, 368

Bills of Mortality, 35–6, 318; compared with parish registers, 398, 399; decrease of baptisms in, 37–8; of burials, 37; fluctuations in, 37–41; effect of Foundling Hospital on, 56–7; parishes in, 35, 397; variations of causes of death in, 67–8, 400

Birmingham, population and housing in, 318

Black Boy Alley, 91, 97

Blackfriars: Bridge, 75, 93, 107, 339; Precinct, 107, 281, 339

Blackstone, Sir W., on liberty, slavery and apprenticeship, 153, 354

Bland, Dr, records of cases, 118

Blane, Dr, on improvement in health, 67, 70; on tea-drinking, 329

Bookbinders, 206

Boswell, explores Wapping, 78. *See* Dr Johnson

Bowley, Professor, cited, 313

Box Clubs. *See* friendly societies

Boys, homeless, 146–7. *See* apprentices

Brewers, 160

Brick, building in, encouraged by James I, 80

Brick kilns, 105, 106

Bricks, defective, 83–4, 336; making of, 416; number laid in a day, 337

Bricklayers, etc., as building speculators, 90–91, 337; methods of, specimen bill, 337–8

Bricklayer's labourer, training of, as bricklayer, 376

Brickmakers' Company, powers to regulate brickmaking misused by, 84, 336

Bridewell, 339; apprentices committed to, 235, 277, 374; apprenticeship in, 248

Brownrigg Case, 228, 257

Budgets, family, 169; of a clerk, 100, 169–70, 362–3; of a journeyman tailor, 170

Builder, the speculative, 87–90, 337, 338

Building, attempts to prevent, 78–82; by encroachment, 79, 82; cost of, 338; developments, 73–5 (1725–7), 320–21; (1802–15), 89

Bull baiting, 18, 105, 208, 272, 342

Bull hanking, 191, 342

Burial grounds, 111, 114, 345

Burial Societies, 390

Butcher Row, 93, 339

Butchers: of Clare Market, 124; women as, 172

Cabinet-makers, 165

Cadogan, Dr, on the nursing of children, 61

Cadogan Estate, 88

Calmel Buildings, 122–3, 129, 348, 351

Camden Town, 88

Cappe, Mrs, on apprenticeship, 248–50

Carmen, 161

Carpenters: as speculative builders, 90; exhausting work of, 203; sell spirits, 47

Cary, on unequal incidence of poor rates, 331–2

Cellars: constructed owing to restrictions on building, 33, 79; occupied by the poor, 95, 96, 98, 113, 114; both dwelling places and shops, 98–9; Irish in, 113, 129; proposals to prohibit, 66; state of, 95, 344. See milk-cellar

Census of 1801 and 1811, 35; returns for London, 318–19, 408–11

Chadwick, B., on improvement in housing and manners, 112

Chair-carver, 163; earnings of, 360

Chairmen, 120, 125, 159

Chamber-master, 175, 176, 178, 197. See domestic system

Chamberlain's Court, 386. See city chamberlain

Chandlers, 161, 387; sale of spirits by, 45, 47, 49–50, 322, 323

Charcoal fires in industry, 202, 204

Charing Cross, 392

Charities, 20, 312; for 'black poor', 143; for children, 55–7, 63, 165, 216 ff., 248–9; emergency organization of (Palatines), 139; medical, 59–66, 327, 329; for watchmakers, 178. See Marine Society, Philanthropic Society, etc.

Charity schools, 26, 216–17, 218–20, 246–9, 372–3, 379

Chartist Movement, 31

Chaucer, Cook's Tale quoted, 275

Chelsea, 37, 133, 137, 231, 304, 415, 419

Child labour, 222–3; in cloth mills, 379; in cotton mills, etc., 250–53; in London silk trade, 183, 184–5, 192, 194, 195–6; in manufacturing processes, 250–56; in silk mills, 254, 380. See apprenticeship, London Workhouse, parish apprenticeship, schools (working)

Children, allowance from poor rate for, 380–81; boarding out of, 59, 215–16, 325, see nurses; in debtors' prisons, 300; deserted, 55–6, 213, 254, 308, 315; as felons, 229; illegitimate, 213, 214–15, 405; improvement in health and appearance of, 71; in nursing of, 61, 68; industrial training for, 216–17, 244–5, 246, 254, 372, 380–81. See apprentices, charities, education, infants, parish apprentices

Chimney-sweepers, 161, 252; apprentices to, 227, 239–42, 377–8; loan of apprentice to, 230

Chinese sailors, 145, 354

Christ's Hospital, 55, 421

Cinder-sifters, 161

City Chamberlain, apprenticeship complaints to, 235–6, 276–7, 382, 385–6

City Improvement Scheme, 93, 107, 339

Clare Market, 83, 93, 94, 124

Cleanliness, improvement in, 17, 23, 24, 69–70, 71–2, 110–13

Clergy, apprenticeship of their children, 165, 418

Clerkenwell, 74, 340, 402, 403, 405, 408, 414; watchmaking in, 175, 176, 178

Climbing-boys. See chimney-sweepers

Clink Liberty, state of, 85, 94

Clockmakers' Company, 176

Clothes, cost of, 71, 362–3; clubs for providing, 294, 390

Club, The, 266

Clubs: blasphemous, inquiry concerning, 44; burial, 391; convivial, 266–7, 274, 275, 281, 385; sporting, 382

Coach-carver, 163

Coach-painter, 163

Coal, consumption of (1695–1716), 319

Coal-heavers, 31, 120, 161; exploited by publicans, 286–7, 388; wages of, 168–9, 362

Cocks, throwing at, 30, 317, 343

Coffee-shops, introduction of, 296–7

Colour-makers, 160

Colquhoun, Patrick, and climbing boys, 241–2; founds Thames Police Office, 21, 315; licensing policy of, 289, 294–5; on apprenticeship, 273; on coal-heavers, 286; on convicts, 357; on crimps, 302; on effects of dear gin, 52; on employment and a redundant population, 317; on friendly societies and funerals, 293–4; on improvident customs, 102; on Jews, 134–5, 137; on national degeneration, 311–12, 396; on the police of London, 22, 23, 315, 396; on vagrant passes, 359; on unequal incidence of poor rates, 332

Colt money, paid by justices, 284, 388

Combinations, 166, 205, 361

Common lodging-houses, 54, 97–8, 340; Irish in, 97, 113, 126–7, 129

Communications, difficulties of, 103

Conant, Sir N., on beggars and poor relief, 211–12; on decrease of crime, 29

Conduit Mead, building lease of, 335

Constables, as publicans and spirit-sellers, 47, 292, 389–90

Coopers, drinking customs of, 283

Coram, Thomas, and the Foundling Hospital, 55–6

Cordwainers' Company, 196, 198

Corn, cheapness of, 40, 42; dearness of, 51

Corporate property, 84

Corporation of London, decline in importance of, 16–17; petitions against spirit-drinking, 49

Cotton manufacture, effect on cleanliness, 72; on silk trade, 188

Cotton manufacturers, case of, 255, 380

Cotton mills, etc., parish apprentices in, 250–56, 423–5

Country people, dangers to, in London, 119–20

Court leet, 17; constables chosen in, 292, 389–90. See annoyance juries

Courts of Conscience, 300, 393–4

Covent Garden, 74, 92, 93, 338, 392; carriers to, 145

Coventry, colt-apprentices at, 202

Cow Cross, 91, 92, 344

Craftsmanship, artistic, 162–4; scientific, 164, 177

Crime, change in character of, 17, 29, 126; effect of emigration on, 152; among Irish, 126, 350; among Jews, 134–5, 136, 353; and parish apprenticeship, 224–5, 226, 259–60; supposed increase of, 28–9, 396

Criminal law, ferocity of, 30, 119, 229

Crimps, 302

Cromwell, Oliver, building policy of, 81

Customs officers, as casual workers, 262

Cutter Clubs, 266, 272

Dangers of the streets, etc., 24, 92–3, 103, 108

Davenant, Sir W., on spirit-drinking, 44

Davis, Miss Jeffries, cited, 107, 313

Dearth, effects of, 39, 40

Death-rate: changes in, 38–40; decline of, 17, 32, 38–9, 70–72; among dispensary patients, 63; effect of spirit-drinking on 55; of infants, 39, 398–9; in the Foundling Hospital, 56–7, 58; in hospitals, 61–2, 63; in maternity cases, 61, 326; among parish children, 17, 68, 325, 401–5; possibly over-estimated, c. 1720–50, 320

Debt: imprisonment for, effects of, 152, 300–302; prisoners for, 153, 226, 297–301

Debtors: absconding, 278; apprentices of, 148, 225–6, 259, 415–23 *passim*

Defoe: on apprenticeship, 273–4; on child labour, 250; on the distilling trade, 42, 43; on drink, 50; on effects of high wages, 264; on growth of London, 320–21; on indentured emigration and transportation, 148; on numbers of ribbon weavers, 178; on overseers and parish children, 214, 371; on Popery, 125; on wages of artisans, 160; on work of married women, 363

[Defoe?], on sanitary nuisances, 94, 340

Dekker, quoted, 124

De Veil, Colonel, 19; and Irish rioters, 125; attempts to enforce the Gin Act, 321–2

Disease, industrial, 68, 202–5

Diseases, change in nature of, 68, 69–70; relative mortality from, 400

Dispensaries, 62–4, 327; for cheap medicines, 326

Disraeli, 209, 312

Distillers, 43, 51, 160; Company, 42, 43

Distilling trade: development of, 43; importance of, 41–2; privileges to, 43–4

Divided tenements, 334; prohibited, 78–81

Docks, London, building of, 75, 346

Dog and Duck, 90, 296

Dollond (optician), 177, 189

Domestic system, 15, 174–5, 202, 365. *See* shoemakers, silk trade, watch-makers, weavers

Dorset Gardens, liberty of, 281

Drinking: amusements connected with, 280–81; customs connected with, 282–95; decline of, 17, 291, 295–7; and high wages, 263–4. *See* distilling trade, gin, licensing policy, spirits

Drury Lane, 93, 94

Duke's Place, Jews in, 132, 133

Dyers sell spirits, 47

East India Company, and lascars, 143–5; and London, contrast with West London 75, 76; theatres in, 279–80, 387; and Smithfield, 93, 95, 331, 345

Education: advance in, 18, 26, 29, 246–7, 311, 396; ideals of, for poor children, 216–20

Edward VI and Bridewell, 339

Elizabeth, attempts to prevent building in London, 78–80

Emigration, indentured, 147–54, 355–8; to Georgia, 153; to Sierra Leone, 143; returns of, 150, 357

Employment, irregularity of, 32, 175, 204–5, 209–10, 211, 262–4, 382. *See* silk trade, shoemakers

Engels on the *Conditions of the Working Classes*, 209

Engine loom, 188–9, 367

Entrepôt trade, 162

Environs of London, amenities of, 106–7

Evangelicalism, 25, 279, 289

Evelyn, John, on the 'mad intemperance of building', 87

Fairs, 162, 279, 417

Fee Lane, 100

Ferriar, Dr: *Advice to the Poor*, 106; improvement in health of Manchester ascribed to, 314

Fever: change in character of, 70; deaths from, 400; epidemics of, 39, 40, 320; intermittent, 67. *See* typhus

Fever Hospital. *See* House of Recovery

Field Lane, 91, 94

Fielding, Henry: *Amelia*, 19, 314; as Bow Street magistrate, 19–20, 314; *Covent Garden Journal*, 20; on common lodging houses, 126–7; on dangerous districts, 91; and Disorderly Houses Act, 295; on ignorance concerning the poor, 25; on the Irish, 126, 350; *Jonathan Wild*, 18; on popular amusements, 278; on spirit-drinking, 49; thief-takers of, 301

Fielding, Sir John, and apprentices, 243, 378; as Bow Street magistrate, 20–21, 314; on deserted children, 307–8; on Irish immigration, 126; on Jewish immigration, 126, 133–4; on maidservants, 119; and Marine Society, 147; on Negro slaves, 140; on payment of wages in public-houses, 287–8; on the price of porter, 50; on public houses,

Fielding, Sir John — *contd.*
294; on wine licences from the Stamp Office, 392
Fielding, William, 296
Financial business, growth of, 16, 313
Fire of London, effects of, 74, 107
Fires, effects of, 40, 346; frequency of, 40, 43
Firmin, T., on tallymen, 299; workhouse of, 216
Fishermen, in Lambeth, 112; apprentices of, 164–5, 228, 231
Fishing trade, 164–5
Fleet Ditch, 94, 101
Fleet Market, 93; basket-women in, 173; built, 107
Fleet Prison, 291; children in, 300; rules of, 305
Fleet marriages, 305, 306
Flying shuttle, in silk trade, 368
Food, cheapness of, 40; dearness of, 52, 208, 361. *See* corn
Footing, or entry money, 281–2, 283, 284, 285
Fordyce, Dr, on health of industrial population, 205
Foreigners, ill-treatment of, 137, 138–9, 353–4
Founders' Company, 370
Foundling Hospital, 17, 55–8, 61, 216, 220, 254, 325, 371; apprenticeship by, 228, 245–6, 252, 377; building estate of, 88, 89, 337
Foundlings, 211, 213–14, 254, 405
Framework-knitters, apprentices of, 233–4, 374; earnings of, 168, 362
Franklin, B., and the drinking customs of printers, 282; rent paid by, 101
Freemasons, company of, 81
Free Willers. *See* redemptioners
French Revolution, effects of, 27, 311
Friendly societies, 292–4, 390–91, 395
Funerals, 293–4; among the Irish, 129–30
Furnished rooms, lodging in, 99–101, 102, 104; furniture in, 101

Garnish, among hatmakers, 283–4; in prisons, 284
Garret-master, 175; shoemaking by, 197. *See* domestic system
Garrets, 95, 100

Garth, *The Dispensary*, 326
Gay, *Beggars' Opera*, 18, 172; *Trivia* quoted, 93
Georgia, founding of, 153–4; indentured servants in, 154
Gilders, palsy among, 203
Gin-drinking, 41–55, 322; effect on death-rate and birth-rate, 41, 68, 323. *See* distilling trade, spirits
Gin-shops, returns of, 45, 46, 53–4
Girls, trades to which apprenticed, 172, 183, 231. *See* women, work of
Glaziers, palsy among, 203
Golden Lane, 92, 94, 95, 100, 125, 331
Goldsmid, Abraham, 137
Goldsmith, O.: *Citizen of the World* cited, 146; on luxury, 37
Goodman's Fields, 93; disorderly houses in, 392; theatres in, 279–80, 387
Gordon Riots, 125
Governors and Directors of the Poor, 244–5, 251
Graham (watchmaker), 177, 361
Gravel Pits, Irish in, 121
Graveyards. *See* burial grounds
Gray Coat Hospital, Westminster, 372
Gray Coat School, at York, 248–9
Gray's Inn Lane, 92, 106, 335; Irish in, 351
Great Queen Street, 92, 338
Great Russell Street, 74, 342, 351
Greek sailors, 354
Greenwich Charity School, 379
Greenwich Fair, 173
Grub Street, 100, 331

Hackney, 94. *See* Stepney and Hackney
Hanway, Jonas, and the 'black poor', 143; and climbing-boys, 239–40; on the death-rate among parish infants, 55, 57–8; on the dissipations of apprentices, 269, 274; on the environs of London, 106; on the Foundling Hospital, 56–9; on the necessity for statistical information, 25, 58; on parish apprentices, 228, 236–7; on parish children, 254; on parish infants, 214–15; on reduction in spirit-drinking, 323; on tea-drinking, 330; on weavers' apprentices, 234; on workhouses, 217

Hatmakers, drinking customs of, 282–4

Hawkins, Sir J., on play-houses, 387; on taverns, 290

Haymakers, Irish, 120, 347–8

Haymarket, 74, 92

Health, improvement in, 17, 68–72. *See* death-rate

Herberden, Dr William, Jn.: on the Bills of Mortality, 36, 38; on decrease of child mortality, 61; of putrid diseases, 330; on improvements in health of London, 69–70

Hernia, prevalence of, 203

Highways, state of, 105

Hogs, breeding of, 105, 342

Hogarth, 18, 30, 49, 50, 54, 100, 101, 120, 158

Holidays of journeymen and apprentices, 207; riot and intoxication on, 279

Homeless, sleeping places of the, 83, 102, 147, 173–4

Hospital fever. *See* Typhus

Hospitals, defects of, 61–2, 326, 328; death-rate in, 62, 63; establishment of, 61; lying-in, 60–61

Houndsditch, 93, 133; brokers in, 136

Hours in London trades, 205–8, 361; of apprentices, 276–7, 370

House of Call: for tailors, 210, 284–6, 388; trades using, 284, 388

House of recovery, 64–6, 328, 351

Housekeeper (householder), decayed, 220, 232; superior status of, 102–3, 104, 220, 373

House-painter, irregular employment of, 263

Houses, empty, as sleeping-places, 102, 173–4; new, collapse of, 83, 335; ruinous, 83

Housing, effect of custom on, 103; first state intervention in, 145; improvement in, 111–15; of the London Irish, 99, 121–2, 129, 193, 323, 356, 359; of the London poor, 86–7, 106–7, 359. *See* cellars, common lodging-houses, garrets, sheds, stalls

Huguenots, 117; and silk trade, 178, 179

Hunter, Dr John, on fever, 64, 328

Hutton, William, apprenticeship in silk mill, 255–6, 380; to stocking weaver, 374

Immigrants, proportion of, to native Londoners, 118

Improvement Acts, 102, 107; object of, 115. *See* Acts of Parliament, Local

Indentured emigration, 147–54

Indentured labour, and Negro slaves, 141–2

Indentured servant, legal status of, 149, 357–8; treatment of, 149–51

Indentures, of apprenticeship, common form of, 272, 384–5; of parish apprenticeship, 224; for servitude in colonies, form of, 356–7

Industrial organization, great variety of, 164. *See* domestic system

Industrial population, growth of, in sixteenth century, 75–6, 331

Industrial Revolution, 15

Infants, diseases of, 68. *See* children, death-rate, Foundling Hospital

Inmates or lodgers, prohibited, 78–80, 103, 341–2

Inns and Alehouses, headquarters of, transport system, 290. *See* public-houses

Inoculation for smallpox, 63, 68, 329

Insurance as substitute for or addition to poor relief, schemes for, 395

Irish, as emigrants to America, 149, 152

Irish Brigade, deserters from, 126, 350

Irish immigrants, 97, 103, 120–31, 145, 319; crime among, 125–7, 349, 350; disorders among, 124–5, 128, 130, 349; in Manchester, 313; occupations of, 120–21, 131; and poor relief, 131, 352; sanitary state of, 103, 113, 114, 348; and vagrancy laws, 156–7, 359; as weavers, in Spitalfields, 181–2. *See* housing, riots

Iron bedsteads, effects of, 326, 330

Jacob's Island, 94

James I, proclamations against building by, 80–81, 107

Jenner, Charles, *London Eclogues* quoted, 106

Jenner, E., and vaccination, 329

Jews: emigrate to Georgia, 154; immigration of, 131–7; brutality towards,

Jews – *contd.*
137–8; in East London, 76; occupations of, 352; poverty and crime among, 133–6
Johnson, Dr: *London*, quoted, 83, 262; on London, 116; and London lodgings, 103; on luxury, 37; Parliamentary debates by, quoted, 24, 41–2, 48; on printers' earnings, 167. *See* Boswell
Jonson, Ben, quoted, 136
Journeymen, manners of, 311; wages of, 166–9. *See* apprenticeship, artisans
Justices of Peace. *See* magistrates, trading justices
Juvenile delinquency, 25, 260; ascribed to outdoor apprenticeship, 268–70; caused by apprenticeship, 277

Kay, Dr (afterwards Sir J. Kay-Shuttleworth): on apprenticeship, 258–9; on the state of Manchester, 313
Kensington, 37, 53, 415
Kidnapping for plantations, 147–8, 150–51, 227
King, Gregory, estimates of population, 318
King's Bench Prison, 291; children in, 300; rules of, 305
Knock Fargus, 345

Labour: skilled and unskilled, gulf between, 31, 159, 160, 165; waterside, 315
Labourers, wages of, 166, 168–9, 362; sell spirits, 47
'Lactarium', 98, 341
Lamb, Charles, quoted, 201
Lambeth, 75, 94, 112, 340; stocking weaving in, 252, 380
Lancaster, Joseph: methods of, 26, 311, 316; on private schools, 372
Lancasterian Schools, 26, 218, 246, 311, 316
Landed interest, distilling trade essential to, 41–2, 51
Lascars, 143–5, 354
Latroon, M., *English Rogue*, quoted, 275, 385
Lead poisoning, 68, 203; institute for treatment of, 203; investigations into, 369
Leasehold system, 84–5
Lettsom, Dr: on decrease of typhus, 65,

328; on effects of dispensaries, 63; on ignorance concerning the poor, 25; on sanitary and medical improvements and decline of typhus, 328; his treatment of typhus, 106
Licensing policy, and speculative building, 338. *See* magistrates
Licensing scandals, 295, 392
Lighting of the metropolis, 109–10, 344
Lillo, G., *Barnwell*, 18, 275
Limehouse, 77, 94, 409, 415; formation of the parish, 406
Lincoln's Inn Fields, 106, 107, 342, 350
Local Acts. *See* Acts of Parliament, local
Lodgings, furnished, 100–101, 102, 341
London Workhouse, 216–17
Long Acre, 92, 338
Long Fields, 105, 296
Lord Mayor's Court, appeals to, for discharge of apprentices, 235–6
Lottery, State, 303, 305, 307–8
Luxury, complaints of, 27, 36–7, 103, 264
Lying-in charities, and hospitals, 60–61

Machinery, effect on silk-weaving slight, 188; in silk-throwing, 185–6
Magistrates: 17, 19, 20–21; attempt to restrict gin-drinking, 44, 45–8; and parish apprentices, 236, 238, 241–4, 257, 260, 378–9; and places of amusement, 279, 280; and recruitment for Navy, 146, 355. *See* De Veil, H. Fielding, Sir J. Fielding, police magistrates, Quarter Sessions, trading justices, S. Welch
Manchester, death-rate, decline of, 314; petitions against spirit-drinking, 49; state of, in 1835, 313
Manchester magistrates, and children in cotton mills, 260, 380
Manchester merchants, apprentices to, 275–6
Mandeville, B. [*Fable of the Bees*], 246
Manners, improvement of, 308. *See* F. Place
Manningham, Sir Richard, establishes a school of midwifery, 60
Marine Society, 21, 146–7, 355; and climbing-boys, 240; ship-school of, 279
Marseilles, plague at, 41, 97, 344

Marshalsea Court, 298–9, 393

Marshalsea Prison, 297–8

Martin, 'Mendicity', 347

Maryland, emigration to, and white servitude in, 148, 149, 150, 151–2, 356, 357, 358

Marylebone, 35, 38, 75, 121, 122, 332, 409, 413, 414; infirmary of, 66–7; local Acts, 245, 344

Masons, wages of, 166

Meat, cheapness of, 40, 321

Medicine, improvement of, 62, 66–7, 72

Mendicity Society, 131

Mendoza, Daniel, 138, 267

Meteyard Case, 228

Methodism, influence of, 26

Middle classes, increase of, 16, 308, 394

Middlesex Bench. See magistrates, Quarter Sessions

Midwifery, improvements in, 61

Midwives, and nurse children, 215; training of, 60

Mile End, building at, 83; public-houses in, 392

Mile End Green, 83

Mile End New Town, 77, 332, 410, 415; journeymen weavers in, 179, 193

Mile End Old Town, 77, 410, 415

Milk-sellers: 98, 131, 161, 340–41; apprentices of, 229–30

Mint, the (in Southwark): 94, 101, 416; irregular marriages in, 305; shelterers in, 226, 300

Murray, Dr, on the housing of the poor, 96

National deterioration, theories on, 28, 396

Negroes, 139–43. See slaves

New buildings, fear of, 78–9, 334–5; prohibition of, 78–82, 116; returns of, 334–5, 408–12

New Road, 75, 89

New River, 107

Newgate, debtors in, 291; spirits in, 389

Norden, John, quoted, 74

Nurses, parish, 372; enormities of, 17, 55, 68, 215, 216, 371

Occupations, changes in, 16

Offices, of burden, 23; of profit, 23

Oglethorpe, General, and Georgia, 153–4; and debtors' prisons, 298, 300

Orphan Asylum for Deserted Girls, founding of, 21

Owen, Robert, as London shop assistant, 206

Packet boats, travel by, 133, 134, 352

Paddington, 37, 121, 122, 409, 414

Painters, lead poisoning among, 203. See house-painters

Palatines, poor, 139

Paris, comparisons with, 55, 110, 123, 324–5

Parish apprenticeship, in cotton mills, etc., 250–54, 255, 423–5; evils of, 215–16, 220–21, 222, 224–5, 244–5, 253, 257–61, 366; fees paid by parish, 228, 229, 231, 233, 377; minimum fees fixed by law, 237–8; by standing orders of parish, 238, 245; and law of settlement, 220–21, 239, 256, 258; occupations under, 184, 210, 227–31, 237, 239, 243, 424; term of servitude under, 221; term reduced, 236–8; two kinds of, 221–2. See apprentices and apprenticeship

Parish officers, and apprenticeship, 216, 221, 224, 236, 243, 245, 253, 258; and the House of Recovery, 65; and infants, 56, 58, 213–15, 311. See vestrymen

Parish registers, baptisms and burials in, 397; compared with Bills of Mortality, 398–9; population and death-rate calculated from, by Rickman, 37, 39; specially inadequate as evidence of population in East London, 333

Parishes, formation of new, 35, 406–7; rateable value of, 413–15

Pauperism, fostered by parish apprenticeship, 258, 380–81

Paving, on the old model, 343

Paving Acts, effects of, 67, 107–8. See Improvements Acts, Local Acts

Paving Commissioners, 343

Peace (1815), effects of: 31–2, 131, 317; on parish apprenticeship, 257, 381

Peel, Sir Robert (the elder), 238, 256

Pennsylvania: emigration to and white servitude in, 149–52; wages in, 356

Percival, Dr: on defects of hospitals; 62,

Percival, Dr. — *contd.*
improvement in health of Manchester, ascribed to, 314
Petticoat Lane, 93, 95, 136, 210
Petty, Sir W., quoted, 74, 318
Pewterers' Company, 384
Philanthropic Society, 221
Physicians, College of, protest against spirit-drinking, 46; quarrel with Apothecaries Company, 326
Pickett, Alderman, 339
Piece-master, 175. *See* domestic system
Piece-work, earnings by, 167, 175. *See* wages
Place, Francis: family history of, 302–4; on amusements of the people, 279, 281, 290; on apprentices, 232, 269, 271, 272, 274; on beggars, 212; on charity schools, 26–7; on comparative freedom of London from pauperization, 316; on cheap cotton, 71–2, 311; on effects of excessive labour, 207–8; on the fall in the death-rate, 70–72; on housing, 111–12, 113; on improvement in manners, 17–18, 28, 31, 70–72, 112, 128, 137–8, 208, 210, 264, 297, 311–12, 335, 346, 396; on the Irish, 128; on journeymen, 164; on Lancasterian schools, 311, 316; on London tradesmen, 266; on the 'lower orders', 209; on payment of wages in public-houses, 289–90; on seasonal unemployment, 263; on shoemakers, 200; on Spitalfields weavers, 194–5; on state of Manchester, 314; on supposed increase of crime, 28–9, 31; on tailors' houses of call, 388; on trade clubs and strikes, 208; on treatment of Jews, 137–8; on wages, 166, 208–9, 361–2; on work of married women, 195–6, 200
Plumbers, 163, 203
Police: chaos of, leads to dangerous districts, 91; improvements in, 19, 20, 21, 24, 28, 311
Police magistrates, 19, 21, 311; apprenticeship appeals to, 242–3; and poor relief, 211. *See* Colquhoun, Conant
Poor, Directors, Governors and Guardians of, 22, 26, 31, 244–5, 250, 251
Poor, houses for, attempts to prevent building of, 78, 81

Poor-house, in villages, 358
Poor law, effect of Irish immigration on, 131; improvement of administration, 17, 31. *See* Acts of Parliament, local Acts, parish apprenticeship, pauperism, poor rates, poor relief, settlement, workhouses
Poor Commission (1832), 222, 258
Poor rates, on tenement houses, 86, 90, 100; unequal incidence of, 341–2
Poor relief, change in character of schemes for, 309–10, 395; effect on begging, 370; greater liability in, 211–12; improved health ascribed to, 330; to the Irish, 129, 351; provisions for children, 213–17
Poor's holes, 111, 345
Poplar, 77, 143, 331, 410, 415; Irish in, 122
Population of London, 15, 35, 37–40; statistics of, 318–20, 408–11; estimated proportion of immigrants, 118; of Jews, 134; of lascars, 144; of Negro slaves, 140
Porter, David, and climbing-boys, 240–42, 378
Porters, 159, 161
Press, use of, for charitable propaganda, 24, 139
Pressgang, apprentices taken by, 227, 231, 415; and landsmen, 146, 355
Price, Dr Richard, calculations of duration of life, 391; on luxury, degeneration and depopulation, 27, 36–7, 318
Prices, rise of, 52, 361
Printers, drinking among, 282, 383; earnings of, 167; improvement of, 383; outdoor apprentices to, 383
Prisoners for debt, reduction of, 17, 298–9
Prisons, apprentices in, 226; recruiting in for women emigrants, 148, 356; as moral and sanitary nuisances, 324, 339; sale of drink in, 291; spirits in, 389
Proclamation Society. *See* Wilberforce
Proclamations against Irish beggars, 123, 349; against new buildings, inmates and divided tenements, 79–81, 334
Publicans as constables, 47, 292, 389–90
Public-houses, clubs in, 266, 281; friendly societies in, 292; as employment agencies, 284–6; evils of redundant, 294–5; in prisons, 291; returns of, 54, 323; wages paid in, 287–90. *See* houses of call

Quaker, as apprentice, 206
Quakers, and apprenticeship of poor children, 244, 252
Quarter Sessions (City), apprenticeship, appeal to, 375
Quarter Sessions (Middlesex and Westminster): and apprentices, 243–4; apprenticeship, appeals to, 225–6, 235–6, 242, 373–4, 415–23; and common lodging houses, 97; and constables, 292, 389–90; licensing order (1729), 323; and payment of wages in public-houses, 289; and slaves, 141; and spirit-drinking, 44–7; and tailors' wages, 369; wages appeals to, 166, 168, 169
Quinine (Peruvian bark), increased use of, 330

Rag fair, 101, 210. See Rosemary Lane
Ramazzini, on industrial disease, 203–4, 369
Ratcliffe, 75, 77, 331, 410, 415
Ratcliffe Highway, 93, 345; Irish in, 128; lascars in, 144
Redemptioners, 149–51, 357, 358
Rents, paid by artisans, etc., 100, 101, 104, 111, 169, 170, 193
'Rents', 87, 332–3
Repertories cited, 385
Rickets, decrease of, 67–8, 71
Rickman, on decline of death-rate, 32, 329–30
Ring, Mr, vaccination by, 64
Riots, against Gin Act, 48, 322; against Irish labour, 124–5, 349; weavers', against wearers of printed calicoes, 182; due to price-cutting and unemployment, 183, 188; against the engine loom, 185, 188–9, 361. See Gordon Riots
Ritson, Joseph, on local Acts for the metropolis, 22–3
Romilly, Sir S., *Memoirs* of, 18; controverts supposed increase of crime, 29
Rookeries, 90, 92, 111
Rookery, the, 113, 348; Irish in, 121, 129, 348, 351
Rosemary Lane, 93, 95, 345. See Rag Fair
Rotation offices, 21, 314; apprenticeship appeals to, 243
Rotherhithe, 94, 96, 335, 340, 403, 411

Rowe, Sir Thomas, founds 'Colledge of Infants', 55
Rowley, Dr, treatment of fevers, 66, 328–9
Rugby School, building estate belonging to, 335

Saddlers, 166–7, 169, 362
Saddling the spit (parish feasts), 214
Saffron Hill, 92, 94, 121, 130, 351, 405, 409, 412
Sail-cloth weavers, 167–8
St Andrew Holborn, 245, 401, 402, 403, 406, 408, 413; board out children in silk mills, 254; burial grounds, 345
St Anne Soho, 309, 401, 402, 404, 405, 406, 410, 413
St Botolph Aldgate, 340, 403, 408; tenements in, 100
St Clement's, 65, 93, 94, 339, 392, 410, 413, 414; parish children in, 213–14, 371, 402, 404, 405
St George Bloomsbury, 245, 401, 402, 403, 405, 409; formation of the parish, 406
St George Hanover Square, 253, 309, 332, 401, 404, 410, 413; formation of the parish, 406
St George the Martyr, 245, 401, 402, 403, 405, 409; formation of the parish, 406
St George's Fields, 75, 88, 90, 94, 98, 341;
St George's in the East, 77, 408, 409, 417; formation of the parish, 406
St George's Southwark, 94, 402, 403, 411
St Giles in the Fields, 74, 92, 94, 95, 97, 99, 245, 331, 401, 402, 403, 405, 409, 413; burial ground, 345; common lodging-houses of, 54, 97, 126; gin-shops in, 54, 322; Irish in, 113, 120, 121, 128, 129, 351; lascars in, 143, 145; Negroes in, 142; workhouse of, 216
St Giles without Cripplegate, 340, 401, 403, 408
St James Square, 80
St James Westminster, 309, 401, 402, 404, 405, 410, 413; boards out parish children at Wimbledon, 59; burial ground, 345; establishes a lying-in infirmary, 60, 67; formation of the parish, 406; parish school of industry, 245; workhouse of, 216

St Katherine's by the Tower, Liberty or Precinct of, 75, 79, 94, 274, 331, 334, 403, 410, 415; prison of, 393

St Luke's Cripplegate (or Old Street), 401, 402, 403, 408; formation of the parish, 407; Irish in, 128; watchmaking in, 176

St Leonard's Shoreditch, 331, 403, 405, 409, 414; workhouse of, 217

St Margaret's Westminster, 410, 413; charity school of, 372; parish infants of, 325, 401, 402, 404, 405

St Martin's-in-the-Fields, 401, 402, 404, 405, 410, 413; burial ground, 345; parishes formed from, 406

St Mary le Strand, 392, 404, 410, 412, 413

Saint Monday, 200

St Pancras, 94, 409, 413, 414; vestry order of, 244

St Sepulchre's, 344, 402, 403, 408

Samaritan Society, 67

Sancho, Ignatius, 142

Sanitary nuisances, 77, 94, 105, 107, 109, 111, 113–15, 129, 130, 339, 340, 343–4, 345

Sanitation, improvements in, 61, 69–70, 108, 110–11, 343–4

Savoy, liberty of the, 84–5, 412, 414

Schoolmaster, low status of, 152, 372; seasonal unemployment of, 263, 372

Schools: boarding, 342; National, 311; private-venture, 218, 263, 372; Sunday, 26, 246, 311; working, spinning, etc., 216, 372, 380–81. See charity schools, Lancasterian Schools

Scurvy, decrease of, 67

Sea-service, apprenticeship to, 231, 252, 423, 424

Servants, domestic, 119–20, 171, 173, 217, 221, 227, 247, 248–9, 252

Settlement (poor law) and apprenticeship, 221–2, 230, 257, 373; effect of, on migration, 116, 155, 317; on social status, 220–21; and illegitimate children, 214, 371; in relation to Irish immigrants, 352

Sewers: open, 77; improvement of, 108, 110, 343–4

Shadwell, 77, 94, 121, 143, 345, 348, 354, 401, 403, 410, 415; formation of the parish, 406; licensing in, 295, 392

Sharpe, Granville, 142

Shed-dwellings, 80, 96, 99, 107

Shipwrights, 282

Shoemakers, 162, 196–202, 204; earnings of, 198, 200; irregularity of work, 200; manners of, 199–201; parish apprentices to, 201; ready-made and bespoke, 196, 197; sell spirits, 47; struggle between large and small masters, 196–7; surgical, 196

Shop assistants, hours of, 206

Shopkeepers, 159, 161, 171

Shoreditch, 76, 92, 93, 94, 97, 331, 340; weavers' riots in, 188

Sierra Leone, first settlement at, 143

Sign-painters, 163–4

Silk, importation of, 179–80; duties on, 179, 364; interruption of supply, 180, 188

Silk fabrics, importation prohibited, 180

Silk mills, children in, 251, 255, 380

Silk throwing, development of the industry, 185–6

Silk Trade (Spitalfields), 178–96; compared with clothing trade, 180–81; connexion between that of London and Dublin, 120; earnings and piece rates in, 181, 183, 191, 196, 365, 367–8; fluctuations in, 180–81; organization of, 179–80, 364–5; women and children in, 181, 183–5, 195–6, 365. See weavers

Simond, on social conditions in England, 211, 308, 394–5

Simpson (mathematician), 189

Skinners' Company, 89

Slaves, as domestic servants, 140–42; in plantations, compared with white indentured labour, 151, 357–8. See Negroes

Smallpox, 66, 68, 400

Smellie, Dr, and improvements in midwifery, 60

Smith, Adam, cited, 100, 155, 203

Smiths' trade, branches of, 163

Smithfield, 92, 94

Smollett, and licensing restrictions, 295

Soap-boilers, 160

Sobriety, increase of, 296–7, 396; scarcity value of, 304. See drinking

Social status, distinctions in, 96–7, 102, 159–60, 165, 220, 232

Society for Bettering the Condition of the Poor, 25, 241, 380
Society for Promoting Christian Knowledge, 218, 372
Society for Relief of Persons imprisoned for small Sums, 25, 300, 393
Somers Town, 88–9, 94
Somersett Case, 140, 141, 142
South Sea Bubble, 321, 369
Southey, on Birmingham, 369; on popular amusements, 279
Southwark, 92, 94, 122, 331, 336; population of, 319, 411; weavers' riots in, 188
Spirits, retailers of, 45, 46–7, 53–4; restrictions on retailing, 47–50, 321, 322–3; on distilling, 51. See gin, distilling trade
Spiriters (kidnappers), 355–6
Spital Square, 179, 344
Spitalfields, 76–7, 128, 186–8, 192–3, 210, 332, 333, 403, 414; building of church, 124; formation of parish, 406; infant in, 192; population, returns of, 333, 409; silk trade of, 178 ff.
Spitalfields Market, children hired in, 174; women hired in, 184
Spittle, the, 92
Sports, nature of, 105, 279. See amusements, bull-baiting, bull-hanking, cocks, cutter clubs
Stalls, as dwelling and working places, 96, 99
Standard of living, 173, 208, 264–5, 364
Stanger, Dr, proposes legislation for public health, 66
Star Chamber, used to enforce building policy, 80
Starvation, deaths from, 173–4
Stepney, 409, 412; hamlets of, 76–7; formations of parishes from, 406; weavers' riots in, 188
Stepney and Hackney, liberty of the manors of, 75, 79, 332. See Whitechapel Court. Prison of, see Whitechapel prison
Strachan (printer), apprentices of, 167, 269
Stow, John, on building and encroachments, 75–6
Stratford Bow, weavers' riots in, 188
Street nuisances, 343–4

Street-sellers, 161
Strikes, 166, 206, 361, 369, 375
Stuarts, building policy of, 80–81
Sugar refiners, 160, 204; employ foreigners, 138, 353
Sunday, drunkenness on, 281, 289
Sweating, 32, 176, 259. See apprenticeship
Synagogue, the, 132, 133, 134

Tailors, 162, 204; drinking customs, 284, 285; combinations for reduction of hours, 205–6, 369; not exclusive, 210; radical opinions of, 31; sell spirits, 47; seasonal unemployment of, 263; wages of, 361. See house of call
Tallow-chandlers, 161, 204
Tallymen, 299, 310, 415
Tambour workers, 243, 250, 256
Tea-drinking, 27, 67, 329
Tea-gardens, 18, 162, 279, 296
Textile trades, 210; low earnings in, 167, 168, 365
Thames Police Office, 21, 315
Theatres, 279–81
Tide ditches, filthy, 94, 340
Tilers' and Brickmakers' Company, 84, 336
Tin Plate Workers' Company, 124
Titles, defective, a cause of ruinous houses, 84, 336
Tobacconists, 160; sell spirits, 45, 47
Tompion (clockmaker), 176, 177
Tothill Street, 80, 82, 335; the Cock in, 290
Tottenham Court, cinder-sifting at, 161, 360
Tottenham Court Road, 296, 351
Tower Hamlets, character of population in 1684, 76, 332; licensing scandals in, 354; sail-cloth industry in, 167. See East London, Stepney, and individual hamlets
Tower Hill, 340
Tower liberty or royalty, 331, 415; prison of, 291
Trade Clubs, 283, 285
Trades of London, bibliographical note on, 360; dangerous and unhealthy, 202–4; general character of, 162; grading of, 165; migration of, from London, 16, 188, 195, 199, 368; nauseous, 94
Trading justices, 19, 28, 295

Translator (cobbler), 99

Transportation to America, 147–51, 356

Turnmill Street, 92, 95

Tyburn, executions at, 18, 20, 207

Typhus, deaths from, 65, 66, 70; districts where prevalent, 94, 130, 351; epidemics of, 40, 64, 70; fresh-air treatment of, 66, 106; ignorance concerning in 1741, 320; in hospitals, 62, 327; measures for treatment and prevention of, 64–6, 327–8

Unemployment, after 1815, 317; seasonal, 262–3, 380; See peace

United States, 24, 52, 211, 323; emigration to, 147, 152

Vaccination, 63–4; institutions for, 329

Vagrancy laws, effects of, 155–6, 358–9

Vagrants, 146–7, 211; deserted children as, 56, 213; Irish, 123; Jewish, 134; resort to London, 117; runaway apprentices as, 229, 231, 260. See beggars

Van Hoven, on position of Jews, 135–6

Verge of the court, shelterers in, 226, 421

Vestries, growth of powers of, 17, 22. See Acts, local

Vestrymen, 22, 23, 65, 244. See parish officers

Vinegar-makers, 160

Virginia, emigration to and white servitude in, 148–52; kidnapping for, 355

Virginia Company, transports children to Virginia, 255

Voltaire, impressions of working people, 173

Wages, 165–9; of artisans, 160, 361, 362; effects of high, 264–5; fall in, after 1815, 31, 317; of labourers, etc., 168–9, 317 (Irish), 131; regulation by statute (tailors), 205, 369; (coal-heavers), 286–7, (see also Spitalfields Act); rise in, after 1793, 208–9; of textile workers low, 365. See shoemakers, watchmaking, weavers

Walpole, Horace, and chimney-sweepers, 377–8; on street robberies, 262

Walter, John, complaint against apprentice by, 167

Walworth, 94, 111

Wapping, 143, 162, 345, 409, 415; form-

ation of parish, 406; Irish in, 121; public-houses in, 274

Wapping-Stepney, 77, 406

Ward, Ned, on indentured emigration, 147–8

Wars, effects of, 16, 27, 30, 31, 147, 317, 382; on building, 88, 337; on silk trade, 183, 184, 188, 366–7

Washerwomen, hours of, 207

Watch, as substitute for savings-bank account, 363

Watch gilding, dangerous, 202

Watch-houses, 291, 389

Watchmaking, 175–8; apprentices, 177–8; distress in, 178; division of labour in, 175–7; women employed in, 176

Water supply, 110–11

Watermen, apprentices of, 228, 230–31, 375

Watts, Dr, defence of charity schools, 246–7

Weavers (silk), distress among, 180–81, 186–8, 193–4, 333, 366–7; apprentices, excessive number of, 182, 234, 366; education and social condition of, 189, 192, 194–5; emigration of, 150; gin-drinking among, 46, 47, 52; grades among, 181, 189–91; Irish, 120, 124, 181–2, 188, 190; irregular payments to, 189, 365; irregular work of, 175; low earnings of, 167, 181; List of Prices (piece rates), 183, 366; recreations of, 189, 191–2; relative prosperity of, 188; unhealthiness of work, 194; women as, 183–5. See Bethnal Green, riots, silk trade

Webb, S. and B., on dirt and disease in eighteenth-century London, 69; quoted, 316

Welch, Saunders, 20; on common lodging-houses, 97; on Irish immigrants, 125–6; and parish apprentices, 236, 243

Well Close Square, prison in, 291; theatre in, 280

Wen, the great, 36, 73

Wesley, John, 26; first dispensary ascribed to, 327

West Indies, emigration to, 148, 150

West London, migration to, from City, 104

Westminster, 73–4, 92, 96. See Acts, local

Westminster Bridge, 75, 107, 113, 342

Westminster Sessions. *See* Quarter Sessions

Whitechapel, 75, 93, 94, 331, 403, 405; Irish in, 122; lead-works in, 203; weavers' riots in, 188

Whitechapel Prison, 291, 298–9

Whitechapel Court, 298–300; Act for, 393

Whitecross Street, 92, 95, 331

Wilberforce, and lascars, 144; Proclamation Society, 289, 296, 387

Wilkes, as City Chamberlain, 385

Willan, Dr, on deaths from spirit-drinking, 51; on the rooms of the poor, 95–6; on unhealthy trades, 204

Williams, Sir Charles Hanbury, quoted, 48–9

William III, called founder of silk trade, 178–9

Wimbledon Common, parish children boarded out on, 59, 245, 251

Window tax, effects of, 86

Wine Licences, granted by Stamp Office, 296, 338–9, 392

Women, hardships of, 174, 307; married, apprenticeship to, 231; effect of employment of, 195; occupations of, 145–6, 161–2, 167–8, 172, 175, 176, 177, 183–6, 197–8, 200, 202, 207, 355, 365, 366, 370, 425–8; work ill-paid and irregular, 174, 207, 370

Workhouse infirmary, as hospital, 66–7

Workhouses (London), chief source of supply of apprentices in cotton mills, 238, 377; children in, 215–17, 251, 252, 253, 315, 401–5; connexion with charity schools, 218–19, 372–3; deaths of infants in, 17, 25, 55, 58–9, 325; fever in, 66; gin in, 45–6; as lying-in infirmaries, 60; silk-winding in, 185; as test of destitution, 31, 317. *See* London Workhouse

Working People, improvement in status of, 308–9; manners of, 208; prosperity of, 32, 160, 173, 317. *See* F. Place, standard of living

Young, Arthur: on Irish cabins, 127–8; on migration to London, 157